Microsoft® Windows Server 2008™ Security Resource Kit

Jesper M. Johansson
with the Microsoft Security Team

PUBLISHED BY
Microsoft Press
A Division of Microsoft Corporation
One Microsoft Way
Redmond, Washington 98052-6399

Library of Congress Control Number: 2008920563

Printed and bound in the United States of America.

1 2 3 4 5 6 7 8 9   QWT   3 2 1 0 9 8

Distributed in Canada by H.B. Fenn and Company Ltd.

A CIP catalogue record for this book is available from the British Library.

Microsoft Press books are available through booksellers and distributors worldwide. For further information about international editions, contact your local Microsoft Corporation office or contact Microsoft Press International directly at fax (425) 936-7329. Visit our Web site at www.microsoft.com/mspress. Send comments to rkinput@microsoft.com.

Acquisitions Editor: Martin DelRe
Developmental Editor: Devon Musgrave
Project Editor: Maureen Zimmerman
Editorial Production: S4Carlisle Publishing Services
Technical Reviewer: Mitch Tulloch; Technical Review services provided by Content Master, a member of CM Group, Ltd.
Cover: Tom Draper Design

Body Part No. X14-14926

Contents at a Glance

Table of Contents

What do you think of this book? We want to hear from you!

Microsoft is interested in hearing your feedback so we can continually improve our books and learning
resources for you. To participate in a brief online survey, please visit:

www.microsoft.com/learning/booksurvey/

What do you think of this book? We want to hear from you!

Microsoft is interested in hearing your feedback so we can continually improve our books and learning resources for you. To participate in a brief online survey, please visit:

www.microsoft.com/learning/booksurvey/

Acknowledgements

In no particular order, the authors have a number of people to thank for helping produce this book. These people provided invaluable input during the development of the book and helped ensure that high quality standards were met.

Chase Carpenter, Aaron Margosis, Paul Young, Pablo F. Matute, Dana Epp, Charlie Russel, Wolfgang Schedlbauer, Nick Gillot, Steve Riley, John Michener, Greg Cottingham, Austin Wilson, Chris Black, Ed Wilson, Erin Bourke-Dunphy, Kirk Soluk, Lara Sosnosky, Lee Walker, Tal Sarid, Dan Harman, Richard B. Ward.

And, especially, Mitch Tulloch, our technical editor, who read everything in the book; Becka McKay, our copy editor, who was fantastic about taking the voices of 12 authors and making them sound like one; Devon Musgrave, who got us started and made sure we had some idea of what was expected; Maureen Zimmerman, who got us finished, and sort of on time; and, finally, Martin DelRe, who did more work than he deserved, dealing with 12 different authors.

Introduction

If you are like us, you are really excited right about now. No, not because we finished this book, but because the fact that we did means that there is a new operating system to explore! Even if you are not the type to get excited about such things, you hold in your hands *the* comprehensive technical security resource for Windows Server 2008.

Windows Server 2008 is an upgrade to Microsoft's flagship server operating system. A significant amount of effort has been devoted to making sure it is not only of high quality, but also has the appropriate security features to enable safe deployment. This book is meant as your companion and guide as you explore these features and investigate how you can use them to provide better services or make your life easier. Along the way, the book also documents features that have never before been documented for the intended audience: the IT professional.

This book contains all the technical details you have come to expect from a Resource Kit. It is put together by 12 world-class experts, each recognized as a leading authority on his or her particular topic. Among them they have written more than 20 books. However, first and foremost they are IT professionals.

Overview of the Book

The book has 16 chapters, plus a bonus chapter on the CD. The chapters are divided into the following three sections.

Part I: Windows Security Fundamentals

- **Chapter 1, "Subjects, Users, and Other Actors"**   This chapter discusses how users and other subjects are managed in Windows.

- **Chapter 2, "Authenticators and Authentication Protocols"**   After a subject is identified, it must authenticate the identification. This chapter covers how authentication works in Windows.

- **Chapter 3, "Objects: The Stuff You Want"**   Users access objects such as files, registry keys, and so on. That means the objects must be secured. This chapter discussed how that happens.

- **Chapter 4, "Understanding UAC"**   Microsoft introduced User Account Control (UAC) in Windows Vista. If you are primarily a server administrator, you mostly need to understand UAC to manage your servers properly. However, if you work in any kind of broader area of IT, you need to know how to use UAC to protect your network. This chapter tells you how.

- **Chapter 5, "Windows Firewall(s)"**   The primary firewall in Windows is the Windows Firewall with Advanced Security. This chapter covers how it works in Windows Server 2008.

- **Chapter 6, "Services"**   When a process must run regardless of whether a user is logged on, that process is installed as a service. Services, therefore, represent a significant attack surface on your computers and it is important that you understand their security implications.

- **Chapter 7, "Group Policy"**   When running Windows networks you are doing yourself a disservice if you do not use Group Policy. Most security modifications we make to systems are done using Group Policy.

- **Chapter 8, "Auditing"**   Security is not very useful unless you can use it to prove who did what. Auditing is a fundamental component of all security. This chapter covers in detail how auditing works in Windows.

Part II: Implementing Identity and Access (IDA) Control Using Active Directory

- **Chapter 9, "Designing Active Directory Domain Services for Security"**   Anyone can create an Active Directory deployment, but to actually create one that enhances the security of your network takes skill. This chapter shows you how.

- **Chapter 10, "Implementing Active Directory Certificate Services"**   Public Key Infrastructures (PKI) are seen by many as an unnecessary complication. Nothing could be further from the truth. For many (if not most) environments, they are a necessary complication. This chapter covers what is new in PKI in Windows Server 2008.

Part III: Common Security Scenarios

- **Chapter 11, "Securing Server Roles"**   One of the first things you will notice about Windows Server 2008 is that the old methods for installing applications have been removed. Instead you get Server Manager, which works on a roles-based metaphor. In this chapter you will learn how this impacts security, and how to use roles to protect servers.

- **Chapter 12. "Patch Management"**   Unfortunately, every server needs updated now and then. Software, being the most complex thing ever built by mankind, is not perfect. Patch management is not easy, but if you have the right tools and a good process you can significantly ease the burden.

- **Chapter 13, "Managing Security Dependencies to Secure Your Network"**   Every computer is dependent on something, or someone, for its security. Managing these dependencies well is probably the most important thing you can do to protect your network. In this chapter we discuss dependencies, show you how to do threat modeling on your network, and introduce you to one of the most valuable security concepts today: server isolation.

■ **Chapter 14, "Securing the Branch Office"**   One of the areas where Windows Server 2008 introduces significant new security features is in branch office scenarios. This chapter shows you how to take advantage of all of them.

■ **Chapter 15, "Small Business Considerations"**   Windows Server 2008 comes in more flavors than any other server operating system Microsoft has built. Two of those are designed specifically to meet the unique security needs of small and medium-sized businesses. If you run a network in a small business, this chapter is an invaluable resource.

■ **Chapter 16, "Securing Server Applications"**   The point of most servers is to provide some application support. While this book cannot possibly talk about every application that could run on a server, Microsoft ships the IIS 7.0 application platform with Windows Server 2008. This chapter shows you how to manage security in that component.

> **Find Additional Content Online**   As new or updated material becomes available that complements this book, it will be posted online on the Microsoft Press Online Windows Server and Client Web site. Based on the final build of Windows Server 2008, the type of material you might find includes updates to book content, articles, links to companion content, errata, sample chapters, and more. This Web site will be available soon at *http://www.microsoft.com/ learning/books/online/serverclient*, and will be updated periodically.

Document Conventions

The following conventions are used in this book to highlight special features or usage.

Reader Aids

The following table describes the reader aids used throughout this book to point out useful details.

Reader Aid	Meaning
Note	Underscores the importance of a specific concept or highlights a special case that might not apply to every situation.
Important	Calls attention to essential information that should not be disregarded.
Caution	Warns you that failure to take or avoid a specified action can cause serious problems for users, systems, data integrity, and so on.
On the CD	Calls attention to a related script, tool, template, or job aid on the companion CD that helps you perform a task described in the text.

Sidebars

The following table describes the sidebars used throughout this book to provide added insight, tips, and advice concerning different Windows Vista features.

Sidebar	Meaning
Direct from the Source/Field	Contributed by experts at Microsoft or Microsoft Most Valuable Professionals (MVP) to provide "from the source" and "from the field" insight into how Windows Vista works, best practices for managing security, and troubleshooting tips.
How It Works	Provides unique glimpses of Windows Server features and how they work.

Command-Line Examples

The following table describes style conventions used in documenting command-line examples throughout this book.

Style	Meaning
Bold font	Used to indicate user input (characters that you type exactly as shown).
Italic font	Used to indicate variables for which you need to supply a specific value (for example *file_name* can refer to any valid file name).
Monospace font	Used for code samples and command-line output.
%SystemRoot%	Used for environment variables.

Companion CD

In addition to the book itself, you also get a CD with some great tools on it. System requirements for running the CD are at the back of this book. Included on the CD are:

Elevation Tools

UAC has undoubtedly introduced an additional level of complexity in managing systems. Undoubtedly this was a long overdue change that implements absolutely necessary changes in how we run our computers. However, as administrators, we sometimes need to modify files that only administrators have access to, or need to quickly get to a folder with a command prompt. This set of tools add some new right-click functionality to Windows Explorer, shown in Figure I-1. Most notably, right-click any folder, select Elevate Explorer Here and answer the elevation prompt(s). This will launch a Windows Explorer window running with a full administrative token at whatever location you chose. You also get the elevate.exe tool, which elevates any application from a command prompt.

Passgen

Passgen is a tool that enables you to manage passwords on the built-in Administrator account and service accounts across a network. It is designed to help you ensure that you have unique passwords on the Administrator account, and can also set passwords on any accounts and configure services to start properly in those accounts.

Figure I-1   When you install the Elevation Tools you get a set of new right-click options on the context menu in Windows Explorer.

Management Scripts

A set of scripts to manage Windows is also included on the CD. Among them is a script to get configuration information on a computer, including installed software. These scripts all require Windows PowerShell. The following scripts are included on the CD:

CreateLocalUser.ps1

Creates a local user on a local or remote computer.

EvaluateServices.ps1

Counts services on a local or remote computer. It then produces a report that tells how many services are auto, how many are manual, and how many are disabled. It then counts how many accouts are used: localsystem, localservice, networkservice, and user defined accounts. Finally, it prints detailed information. An option allows you to display the report when it is finished.

FindAdmin.ps

Lists the members of the local admin group on a specific computer.

FindServiceAccounts.ps1

Identifies services and their startup accounts on a local computer or remote computer. This script can produce a complete list of the services and their accounts for one or more computers.

ListUserLastLogon.ps1

This script will list the last logon date of a specific user onto a local or remote domain. The script will allow multiple users to be supplied for the *-user* parameter.

LocateDisabledUsers.ps1

Locates disabled users in a local or remote domain.

LocateLockedOutUsers.ps1

Locates locked-out users in a local or remote domain.

LocateOldComputersNotLogon.ps1

Locates computer accounts in a local or remote domain that have not logged on for a specified number of days.

LocateOldUsersNotLogOn.ps1

Scans a local or remote domain for user accounts that have not logged on to the domain for an extended period of time.

LookUpUACEvents.ps1

Lists User Account Control events on a local or remote computer.

ScanForSpecificSoftware.ps1

Scans for the existence of a specific piece of software.

ScanForSpecificUpdate.ps1

Scans for a specific update or updates on a local or remote computer. The script will also produce a listing of all updates installed on the computer.

ScanConfig.ps1

The ScanConfig.ps1 script produces a listing of the following information: installed software updates, ActiveX objects, browser helper objects, network interfaces, proxy settings, auto run, services, unsigned drivers, and the firewall policy.

UnlockLockedOutUsers.ps1

Unlocks user accounts that are locked out.

WhoIs.ps1

Retrieves whois information from an Internet whois server.

eBook

If you would rather have a searchable electronic copy of the book, you can find one on the CD.

Bonus Chapters

An additional chapter, "Implementing Active Directory Rights Management Services" by Kurt Dillard, is on the CD. This chapter contains late-breaking information that did not make it in time to be included in the main book. To make sure you have the information, we put it on the CD.

Also on the CD are sample chapters from related Microsoft Press books.

Chapter-Related Materials

Some chapters have additional documentation or electronic tools; these are mentioned in the book text and located on the CD.

Links to Tools Discussed in the Book

Rather than give you versions of downloadable tools that become stale as soon as you buy the book, we provide the following links to downloadable tools that are discussed throughout the book, or that are just useful tools to have:

Windows PowerShell

Windows PowerShell is a new command-line shell and scripting language designed for system administration and automation. Built on the .NET Framework, PowerShell allows IT professionals and developers to control and automate the administration of Windows and applications. Windows PowerShell is available at *http://www.microsoft.com/downloads/ details.aspx?FamilyID=c6ef4735-c7de-46a2-997a-ea58fdfcba63&DisplayLang=en* (for Windows Vista x64 editions) and *http://www.microsoft.com/downloads/details.aspx?FamilyID=af37d87d-5de6-4af1-80f4-740f625cd084&DisplayLang=en* (for Windows Vista x64 editions).

Process Explorer

Many of the examples in the book show Process Explorer, which is an amazing tool that tells you more about what is going on on your computer than you ever dreamed possible. Process Explorer is available at *http://technet.microsoft.com/en-us/sysinternals/bb896653.aspx.*

Microsoft Network Monitor

The newest version of Microsoft Network Monitor is an immensely powerful and useful network management and troubleshooting tool. It lets you see all network traffic entering and exiting your computer. It is an indispensable part of any administrator's toolbox. Network monitor is available at *http://www.microsoft.com/downloads/info.aspx?na=22&p=2&SrcDisplayLang=en&SrcCategoryId=&SrcFamilyId=&u=%2fdownloads%2fdetails.aspx%3fFamilyID%3d18b1d59d-f4d8-4213-8d17-2f6dde7d7aac%26DisplayLang%3den.*

Privbar

Privbar is a toolbar for Windows Explorer and Internet Explorer that tells you whether you are an administrator or a standard user. As shown previously in Figure I-1, privbar is extraordinarily useful in combination with the Elevation Tools because it shows you at a glance whether the interface you are using is running as an administrator. Unfortunately, the version of privbar available at the time of this writing works in Windows Vista, but not in Windows Server 2008. Privbar is available at *http://blogs.msdn.com/aaron_margosis/archive/2004/07/24/195350.aspx.*

Digital Content for Digital Book Readers: If you bought a digital-only edition of this book, you can enjoy select content from the print edition's companion CD.
Visit **http://go.microsoft.com/fwlink/?LinkId=108240** to get your downloadable content. This content is always up-to-date and available to all readers.

Resource Kit Support Policy

Every effort has been made to ensure the accuracy of this book and the companion CD content. Microsoft Press provides corrections to this book through the Web at the following location:

http://www.microsoft.com/learning/support/search.asp

If you have comments, questions, or ideas regarding the book or Companion CD content, or if you have questions that are not answered by querying the Knowledge Base, please send them to Microsoft Press by using either of the following methods:

E-mail: rkinput@microsoft.com

Postal mail:

Microsoft Press

Attn: Microsoft Windows Server 2008 Security Resource Kit

One Microsoft Way

Redmond, WA 98052-6399

Please note that product support is not offered through the preceding mail addresses. For product support information, please visit the Microsoft Product Support Web site at the following address:

http://support.microsoft.com

Part I
Windows Security Fundamentals

In this part:

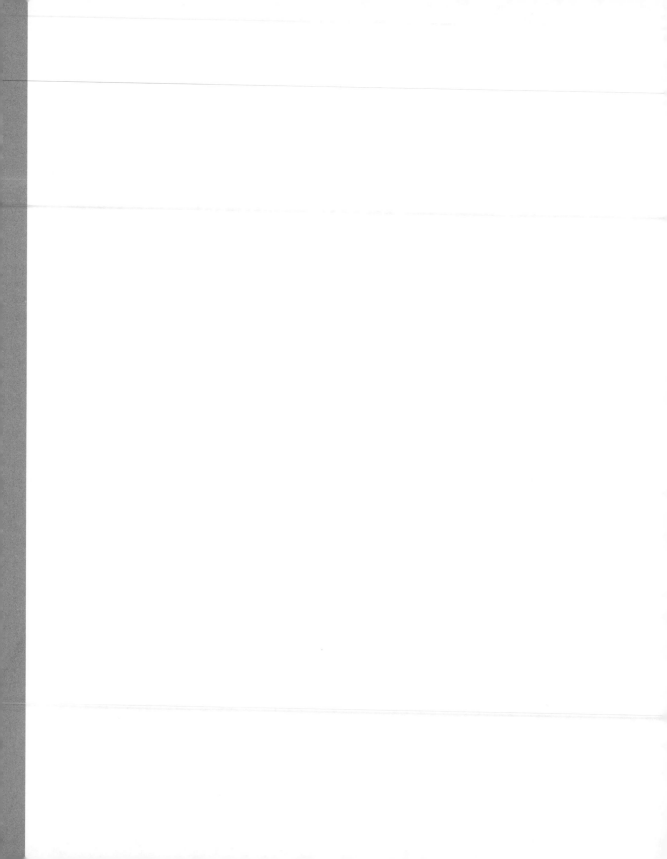

Chapter 1
Subjects, Users, and Other Actors

— Jesper M. Johansson

At the most basic level, everything in security boils down to *subjects* and *objects*. Objects are the things you protect, and subjects are the things you protect objects against. Subjects and objects are used in authentication (proving who you are), authorization (granting access to something), and auditing (tracking who accessed what). These concepts are fundamentally very simple. Subjects are users. Objects are files. Authentication, authorization, and auditing all have to do with how subjects and objects interact. That is the way it used to be, and in some simpler systems, that's the way it still is.

Windows, however, supports some immensely rich semantics when it comes to security and has greatly extended the definition of a subject and an object. A subject can be much more than just a user, and the representation is far more complex than just a basic user identifier. Windows also refers to them differently. You will very often come across the term *security principal*. In Windows parlance, a security principal encompasses not only the typical subject (what we would think of as a user) but also groups and computers. A security principal is anything that can be assigned a security identifier (SID) and that can be given permission to access something. In this chapter you will learn about the various things that can be security principals, and how they are identified in Windows operating systems in general, as well as what is new in Windows Server 2008. In Chapter 3, "Objects: The Stuff You Want," you will learn about the other side of security: objects.

The Subject/Object/Action-Tuple

Managing security very often comes down to the subject/object/action-tuple. The subject is the actor that is trying to take some action on an object. For example, a user may try to access a file, as shown in Figure 1-1.

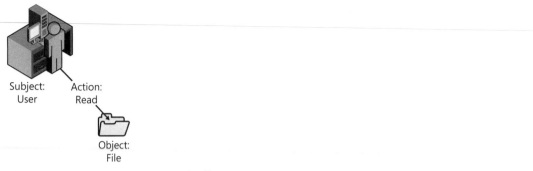

Figure 1-1   A user attempts to read a file.

When a user tries to read the file, the operating system checks whether permissions are set on the object—the file—that permit the subject—the user—to perform the action. If the permissions are there to grant the user those permissions, the access request succeeds. If the permissions do not grant the subject the requested permissions, the access request is denied. So far, this is all very simple.

In Chapter 3, you'll learn far more about how permissions and the actual access checks work. In this chapter we will focus on how the subject is defined. As mentioned earlier, various things can be considered subjects. In most situations, subjects are users, but that is not always the case. In the next section we will discuss the different types of subjects, and after that we will go over how Windows represents those subjects internally.

Types of Security Principals

Subjects—or as we shall henceforth refer to them, security principals—in a Windows-based system, and by extension a Windows-based network, can be much more than just plain users. However, the user is still the most basic concept.

Users

A user is just that: some distinct entity that logs on to a computer. Fundamentally, all the security principals are at least somewhat related to users.

In Windows, there can be two types of users: local and domain. A local user is defined in the local Security Accounts Manager (SAM) database on a computer. Every Windows-based computer has a local SAM, which contains all the users on that computer.

> **Note**   With one major exception, all Windows NT-based operating systems support the same basic security constructs, although the richness of the semantics has changed, notably starting with Windows 2000. The major exception is that Active Directory, available in server versions starting with Windows 2000, supports a very different feature set than the client versions and prior versions of Windows NT.

Note   From this point on, when the book refers to "Windows-based computer" or just "Windows" in the generic, we refer specifically to all computers in the Windows NT line of operating systems. This includes:

- Windows NT 3.1
- Windows NT 3.5
- Windows NT 3.51
- Windows NT 4.0
- Windows 2000
- Windows XP
- Windows Server 2003
- Windows Vista
- Windows Server 2008

It is commonly thought that domain controllers (DCs) do not have a local SAM and hence no local users. This is incorrect. Even a DC has a local SAM, but the accounts in its SAM can only be used in Directory Services Restore Mode. By default, two user accounts are always in the local SAM: the Administrator and the Guest. The Guest account is always disabled by default.

Note   When we spell "Administrator" or "Administrators" with a capital "A," we are referring to the user or the group, respectively. When we spell it in all lowercase—"administrator"—we are referring to some user account or person that has administrative privileges. The same holds for other entities, such as "Guest" and "guest."

On Windows Server 2008 the Administrator account is enabled by default (with the exception of Windows Server Code Name 'Cougar' (The small business server version of Windows Server 2008. As of this writing, the official product name had not been announced.)) and is the account you must use to log on to the computer the first time. On Windows Vista the Administrator account is disabled by default and can only be used under very restrictive circumstances. In either case, it is highly recommended that you create additional accounts for each person that will be administering a given computer. If you are subject to almost any kind of regulation, this is a requirement (Libenson, 2006). One account should be each person's own personal administrative account. If the administrators also need to use the computer for non-administrative tasks, they should also have personal non-administrative accounts.

The other type of account is a domain account. These are defined on the DC(s) for the domain and can be used on any computer in the domain. Domain accounts can have a considerably larger number of properties associated with them as compared to a local account. Compare Figures 1-2 and 1-3.

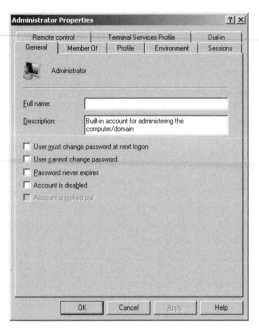

Figure 1-2   The Properties window for a local account.

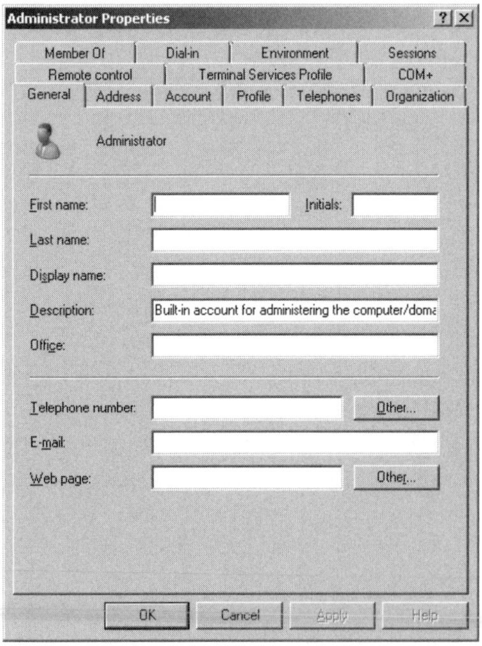

Figure 1-3   The Properties window for a domain account.

Domain accounts have a richer set of semantics, covering a variety of attributes in an organizational environment, such as telephone numbers, management relationships, e-mail accounts, and so on. Domain accounts are also far more useful in a network because they can be used and assigned permissions on computers across the network. Defining accounts in the domain also simplifies management. To learn more about Active Directory, see Chapter 9, "Designing Active Directory Domain Services for Security."

Computers

A computer is really just another type of user. In Active Directory this is particularly true and is borne out by the inheritance model in Active Directory. The inheritance structure leading to a computer is shown in Figure 1-4.

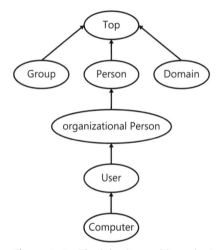

Figure 1-4   The inheritance hierarchy in Active Directory shows how users and computers are related.

You will notice several very interesting things in Figure 1-4. First, as you can see, all classes in Active Directory derive from a root class called *Top*. In fact, even *Top* is listed as a subclass of *Top*. Second, as you can see, the *User* class is derived from the *organizationalPerson* class. The *organizationalPerson* class is derived from *Top*. Third—and this is the most interesting part—the *Computer* class is derived from the *User* class. In other words, in object-oriented parlance, a *Computer* is a kind of user. This seeming anthropomorphizing of computers does actually make a lot of sense, though, because computers need to be treated as subjects as well, and have almost all the same attributes as users.

Groups

A subject, you will recall, is something that attempts to access an object. The operating system verifies this access attempt by checking the permissions of the object. Very early on, operating system designers realized that it would be very unwieldy to assign permissions to every single object to every single user that needed it. To solve that problem, they permitted users to be members of groups. This permits us to assign permissions to groups in addition to users. A *group* may not be a user, but a group is still a type of security principal because it can have an identifier, just like users and computers. In Windows a user can be a member of many groups and an object can have permissions assigned for many groups. Nested groups are also permitted, with some restrictions.

A non-domain controller has only two types of groups: built-in ones and local ones that the administrator has defined. In Active Directory, however, you will find six different kinds of security groups: built-in Domain Local, Global, and Universal groups; and user-defined Domain Local, Global, and Universal groups. Domain Local groups can only be assigned permissions to resources in the domain they are defined, but they may contain users, universal, and global groups from any trusted domain or forest, as well as Domain local groups from their own domain.

A Global group may only contain users and global groups from the domain it was defined in, but may be assigned permissions to resources in any domain in the forest the domain is part of, or any trusting forest.

A Universal group may contain users and Universal and Global groups from any domain. A Universal group may be assigned permissions to resources in any trusting domain or forest.

While a stand-alone server comes with only two groups by default—Administrators and Guests—a domain comes with a relatively large number, of all three types. Figure 1-5 shows the default groups in a domain. All are designated as Security Groups, which means they can

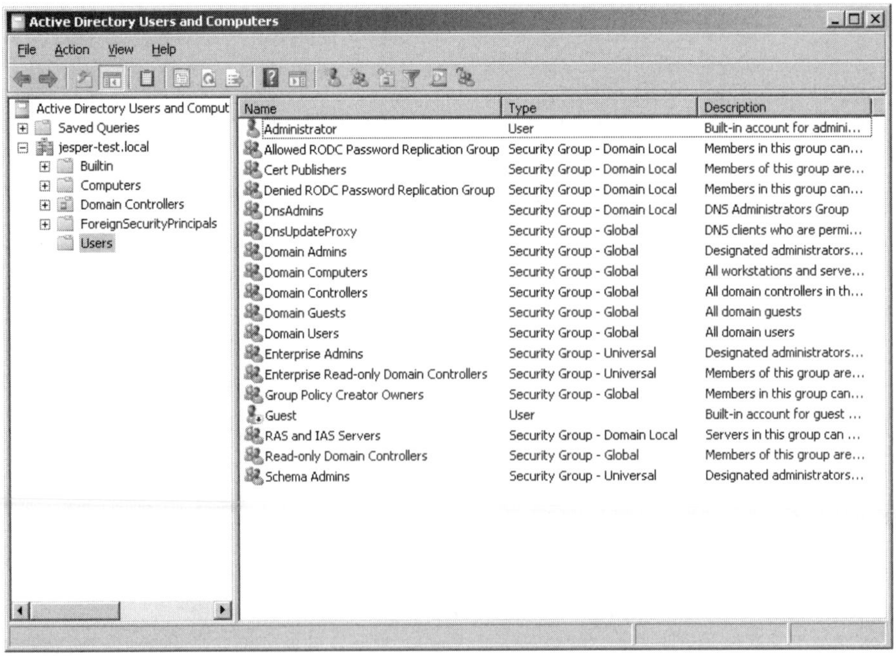

Figure 1-5   A substantial number of groups are defined in the Users container in Active Directory by default.

be assigned permissions. Security groups should not be confused with Distribution Groups, which are used by Microsoft Exchange Server to group users into groups so that you can send e-mail to a group of people at one time. Both are defined in Active Directory.

In addition to the groups defined in the domain, which exist only in domains, there are also built-in local groups. These are groups defined in a different hierarchy, by a different authority, than the domain groups. Built-in groups are not considered domain groups per se, but rather are built in on all or at least some Windows-based computers, regardless of whether they are domain controllers. They exist on all Windows-based computers, but are defined in AD on DCs. For example, the Administrators group is a built-in group that exists on all Windows-based computers, while Domain Admins is a domain group that exists only on domains. Figure 1-6 shows 21 built-in groups on a test computer.

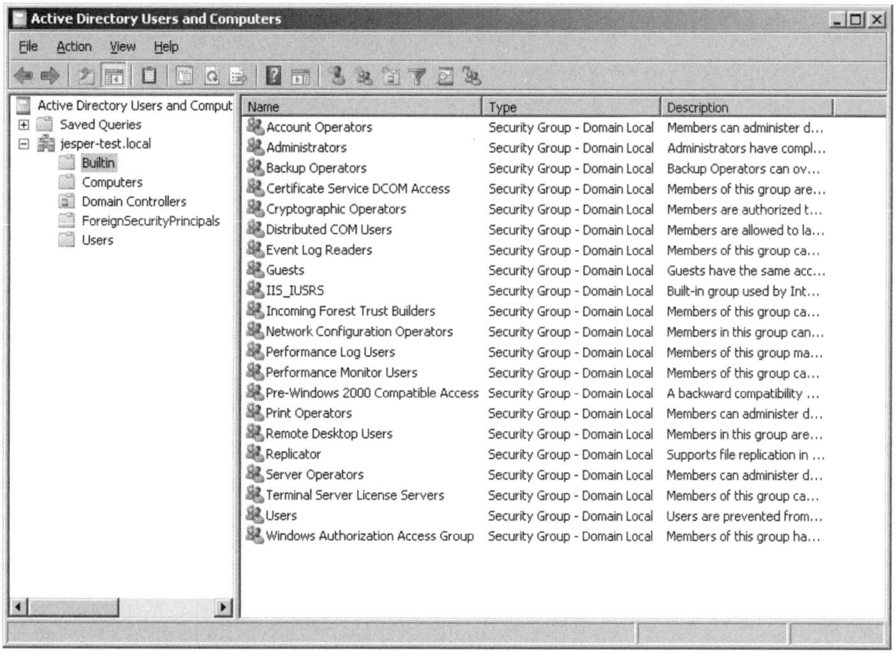

Figure 1-6   Additional groups are so-called "built-in groups."

However, if you were to attempt to assign permissions to an object you would find *still* more groups. In fact, on a basic DC, you would find no fewer than 63(!) groups and built-in security principals, as shown in Figure 1-7.

The additional 26 groups are abstract concepts representing a dynamic group of security principals. They are usually referred to as *special identities*.

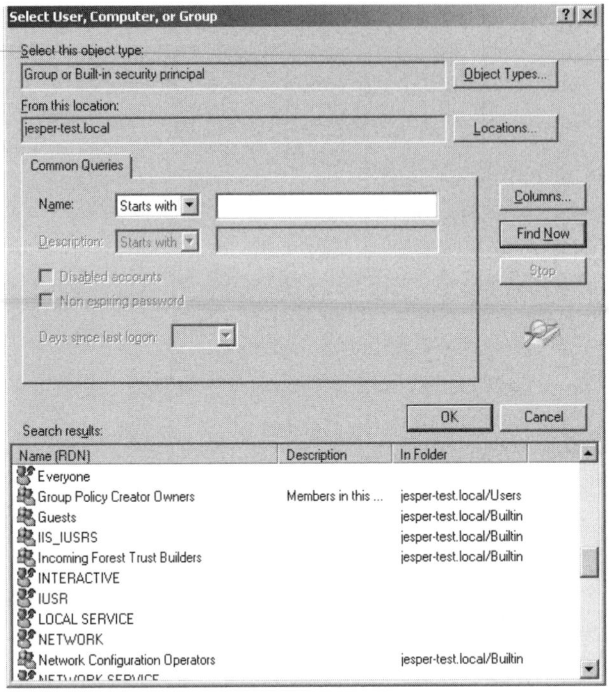

Figure 1-7   You will find no fewer than 63 groups and built-in security principals on a DC.

Abstract Concepts (Log-on Groups)

In addition to the somewhat tangible groups that you define on a computer, as you can see in Figure 1-7 there are also others. These are groups that represent some dynamic aspect of a security principal, such as how a user or other security principal has logged on. For example, the INTERACTIVE group shown in Figure 1-7 includes all users that logged on to the console of the computer and via Terminal Services. By contrast, the NETWORK group includes all users that logged on via the network. By definition, a user can only be a member of one of these groups at a time, and membership in them is assigned at log-on time. You can use them to grant permissions to all users logging on a certain way.

You will see other groups of this nature as well. Of particular note are the Everyone and Authenticated Users groups. The Everyone group includes, as the name implies, every user accessing this computer—except that starting with Windows XP completely anonymous users are not included. Guests are, however. The Authenticated Users group, while also populated dynamically, includes only those users that actually authenticated. That means that guests are not included in Authenticated Users. That is the only difference. Because the only guest account that exists on the operating system is disabled, however, there is *no functional difference between Authenticated Users and Everyone* unless you have taken manual steps to enable the Guest account. In spite of this, many administrators have lost many an hour of sleep over the fact that "everyone in the world has permissions on my server," and have taken very drastic steps to modify permissions to rectify this situation; typically these modifications have completely disastrous results. *You have no reason whatsoever to make these kinds of modifications.* Either you want guests to have permissions to your computer and you enable the guest account, or you do not, and you leave it disabled. If you do want guests to have permissions, you need the permissions for Everyone. If you do not, Everyone will not be any different from Authenticated Users. Some people argue that making these changes are "defense in depth" changes. That would be true if we were to define "defense in depth" as "changes we cannot justify any other way." The fact is that they provide very little security and carry a very large risk. Leave the defaults alone. If this is not persuasive enough, you should also refer to Microsoft Knowledge Base Article 885409, which states, in a nutshell, that whole-sale permissions replacement can void your support contract. When you do that, you basically build your own operating system, and Microsoft can no longer guarantee that it works.

It is also worth pointing out the difference between Users, which is a built-in group, and Authenticated Users. The difference is the rather obvious fact that Authenticated Users includes *every* user that has authenticated to the computer, including users in different domains, users that are members of local groups other than Users, and users that are not members of any groups at all (yes, such a thing is possible). In other words, the Users group is far, far more restrictive than Authenticated Users. In spite of this, this author has seen organizations that attempted to replace permissions for Users with permissions for Authenticated Users in an attempt to harden their systems. Needless to say, these attempts were largely unsuccessful, both with respect to security and, particularly, with respect to stability.

Services

A persistent debate about host-based firewalls has gone on for years. Many people, supported eagerly by the vendors selling the products, argue that host-based firewalls must filter outbound traffic to be worthwhile because doing so protects the remainder of the network from a compromised computer. More objective minds point out that if a computer is compromised, the malware is already present on it, and can bypass or disable the host-based firewall entirely.

Of course, if the malware got on the computer by compromising some application that actually ran with least privilege, this argument does not hold. In recent years Microsoft has spent a significant amount of time factoring services to run with lower privileges, but a service running as a particular user could still control any other service running as the same user, and could do anything that service could. Therefore, if ServiceA could send traffic through the firewall, but ServiceB could not, ServiceB could take over ServiceA and send traffic as long as they both run as the same user.

To address this problem Microsoft needed a way to apply permissions to a process, or more specifically, to a service. To do that, services became security principals in their own right starting with Windows Vista and Windows Server 2008. Each service now has an identifier that can be used to apply permissions against. By marking the permissions for that identifier as restricted—see Chapter 3 for more information on restricted access control list entries—we can even ensure that a particular security principal must be present when making a request, regardless of what other permissions are listed on the object. Suddenly it became meaningful to use outbound, host-based firewall filters in some situations, which is why the firewall in Windows Vista and Windows Server 2008 now supports them. By default, it blocks outbound traffic from services except on ports that are needed by those services. This is, frankly, as much security as you can ever expect from a host-based firewall.

Security Identifiers

Thus far we have been skirting the issue of identifiers. I mentioned earlier that a security principal is an entity that can have a security identifier (SID), but I never defined security identifier. Simply put, a SID is a (mostly) numeric representation of a security principal. The SID is actually what is used internally by the operating system. When you grant a user, a group, a service, or some other security principal permissions to an object, the operating system writes the SID and the permissions to the object's Access Control List (ACL).

SID Components

A SID is composed of several required elements. Figure 1-8 shows the different components of a SID.

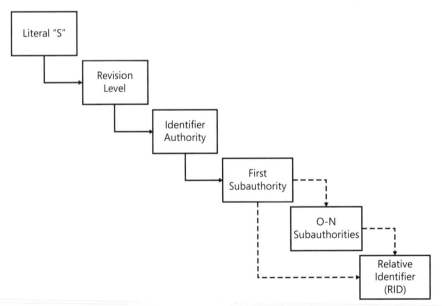

Figure 1-8   A SID has a defined structure with several required elements.

SIDs always start with the literal "S," which denotes them as a SID. They also always end with a relative identifier (RID). In between, they have 0 or more sub-authorities. The second value in a SID is always a revision level, which currently is always 1.

SID Authorities

After the S-1- prefix, the remainder of a SID can vary greatly, but it always begins with an identifier authority denoting what entity issued them. Table 1-1 shows the currently used identifier authorities.

Table 1-1   SID Identifier Authorities

Identifier Authority	Description
0	SECURITY_NULL_SID_AUTHORITY. Used for comparisons when the identifier authority is unknown.
1	SECURITY_WORLD_SID_AUTHORITY. Used to construct SIDs that represent all users. For example, the SID for the Everyone group is S-1-1-0, created by appending the WORLD RID (0) to this identifier authority, thereby selecting all users from that authority.
2	SECURITY_LOCAL_SID_AUTHORITY. Used to build SIDs representing users that log on to a local terminal.
3	SECURITY_CREATOR_SID_AUTHORITY. Used to construct SIDs that represent the creator or owner of an object. For example, the CREATOR OWNER SID is S-1-3-0, created by appending the creator owner RID (also 0) to this identifier authority. If S-1-3-0 is used in an inheritable ACL, it will be replaced by the owner's SID in child objects that inherit this ACL. S-1-3-1 is the CREATOR GROUP SID and has the same effect but will take on the SID for the creator's primary group instead.
5	SECURITY_NT_AUTHORITY. The operating system itself. SIDs starting with S-1-5 were issued by a computer or a domain. Most of the SIDs you will see start with S-1-5.

Direct from the Source: History of SIDs

The original concept of the SID called out each level of the hierarchy. Each layer included a new sub-authority, and an enterprise could lay out arbitrarily complicated hierarchies of issuing authorities. Each layer could, in turn, create additional authorities beneath it. In reality, this created a lot of overhead for setup and deployment, and made the management model group even more baroque. The notion of arbitrary depth identities did not survive the early stages of development, although the structure was already too deeply ingrained to be removed.

In practice, two SID patterns developed. For built-in, predefined identities, the hierarchy was compressed to a depth of two or three sub-authorities. For real identities of other principals, the identifier authority was set to five, and the set of sub-authorities was set to four.

Richard B. Ward, Architect
Windows Core

After the identifier authority the SID has some number of sub-authorities. The last of these is called the relative identifier and is the identifier of the unique security principal within the realm where the SID was defined. To make this idea a little more concrete, consider the following SID:

```
S-1-5-21-1534169462-1651380828-111620651-500
```

As you have seen, the SID starts with S-1-5, indicating that it was issued by Windows NT. The first sub-authority is 21 (0x15 in hexadecimal). The 21 defines this as a Windows NT SID that is not guaranteed to be universally unique. It will be unique within the domain of its issuance, but there may be other SIDs in the universe of computers that have the same exact value. The first of the sub-authorities is very often a well-known sub-authority. Table 1-2 lists the more commonly encountered well-known sub-authorities.

Our SID then has three additional sub-authorities: 1534169462, 1651380828, and 111620651. These do not in and of themselves have any implicit meaning, but together they denote the domain or computer that issued the SID. In fact, the SID for the domain is S-1-5-21-1534169462-1651380828-111620651, and all SIDs issued in that domain will start with that value and end with some unique RID for the user or computer they denote. In this case the SID ends with 500, which is a well-known RID denoting the built-in Administrator account. 501 is the well-known RID for the built-in Guest account and 502 is the well-known RID for the Kerberos Ticket Granting Ticket (krbtgt).

Table 1-2   Well-Known Sub-authorities

Sub-authority	Description
5	SIDs are issued to log-on sessions to enable permissions to be granted to any application running in a specific log-on session. These SIDs have the first sub-authority set to 5, and take the form S-1-5-5-x-y.
6	When a process logs on as a service it gets a special SID in its token to denote that. This SID has the sub-authority 6, and is always S-1-5-6.
21	SECURITY_NT_NON_UNIQUE. Denotes user and computer SIDs that are not guaranteed to be universally unique.
32	SECURITY_BUILTIN_DOMAIN_RID. Denotes built-in SIDs. For example, the well-known SID for the built-in Administrators group is S-1-5-32-544.
80	SECURITY_SERVICE_ID_BASE_RID. Denotes SIDs for services.

Service SIDs

As mentioned earlier, services also have SIDs in Windows Vista and Windows Server 2008. Service SIDs always start with S-1-5-80 and end with a number of sub-authorities that are deterministic based on the name of the service. This means that a given service has the same SID on all computers. It also means that you can retrieve the SID for an arbitrary service even if it does not exist. For example, to see what the SID would be for the "foo" service, run the **sc showsid** command, as follows:

```
C:\>sc showsid foo
NAME: foo
SERVICE SID: S-1-5-80-2639291829-767035215-3510963033-3734144485-3832470211
```

If you try this on one of your servers, you will come up with the same answer. If you would rather have the friendly name for the service, use NT SERVICE\foo.

Well-Known SIDs

When a developer writes a program for Windows, he often needs to know the SID of some security principal. Usually SIDs can be easily constructed if only the RID is known because it is just appended to the computer or domain SID, as in the case of the Administrator account. However, for convenience, it is often desirable to have a shorter and static form of some SIDs. To provide this, the security model used in Windows includes a significant number of *well-known SIDs*—SIDs that are always the same across all computers. A few universally well-known SIDs are the same on all operating systems using this security model. These are the SIDs that start with S-1-1, S-1-2, or S-1-3, including some that were discussed earlier in the chapter, such as the CREATOR OWNER SID: S-1-3-0.

In addition, Windows NT has a significant number of well-known SIDs. S-1-5-32 is the well-known SID for the built-in domain, for example. It can, in turn, be combined with a well-known RID to form a well-known SID for a particular account. For example, the SID for the built-in Administrators group, whether on a domain or on a stand-alone computer, is always S-1-5-32-544. Table 1-3 lists some of the more commonly used domain-relative RIDs. In the case of built-in groups the domain-relative RIDs can be combined with S-1-5-32 to form a SID that is valid on any computer where that user or group is relevant. Other accounts are appended to the domain to form the complete SID. This is the case with Domain Admins, for example, which takes the well-known RID 512 to create a SID such as S-1-5-21-1534169462-1651380828-111620651-512.

Table 1-3   **Well-Known Domain-Relative RIDs**

RID	Description
500	Administrator
501	Guest
502	Krbtgt
512	Domain Admins
513	Domain Users
514	Domain Guests
515	Domain Computers
516	Domain Controllers
544	Built-In Administrators
545	Built-In Users
546	Built-In Guests

SIDs may look very complicated, but once you understand the structure, they become quite simple to decipher. With a little practice, you will easily be able to tell whether a SID refers to a service, a well-known principal, or a user in a domain. In chapter 3, we will see how these SIDs are used to manage permissions.

Summary

Security principals and SIDs underlie so much of Windows security that as an administrator, you must have at least a basic understanding of how they work. SIDs are the fundamental building blocks of a token, which, in turn, is the basic entity used to check whether access is permitted. Understanding how these components function together and being able to assign permissions effectively using users, groups, domain groups, and the log-on types will enable you to be far more effective, and encounter far less surprises, as you delve deeper into Windows Security.

Additional Resources

- Libenson, E. "Controlling Privileged Accounts to Comply with SOX Section 404." *http://www.s-ox.com/Feature/detail.cfm?articleID=2178.*

- Microsoft Knowledge Base article "Security Configuration Guidance Support." *http://support.microsoft.com/kb/885409/en-us.*

Chapter 2
Authenticators and Authentication Protocols

— Jesper M. Johansson

Recall from Chapter 1, "Subjects, Users, and Other Actors" that the actors in a computer are called subjects or principals. Once you have a principal, that principal needs some way to prove that it really is who it claims to be. Consider the very real-world case in which you wish to purchase something with a credit card in a store where they actually understand security. You have your identity: you. However, the store's personnel do not know who you are so they require some proof—an authentication that you are who you say you are. To provide proof of identity you use an authenticator of some form, such as an identity card or a passport. You present this to the store clerk in a fairly routine fashion, as an authentication protocol.

The virtual world is no different, with the exception that the entity to which you have to authenticate understands that a signature on the back of a credit card is not an authenticator; that is, it provides absolutely no proof of identity. Therefore, you need a stronger form of authentication. In this chapter, we will discuss how Windows handles authenticators and which authenticators it supports.

Something You Know, Something You Have

Generally speaking, there are three types of authenticators:

- Something you know

- Something you have

- Something you are

17

Something You Know

A secret that you know, and in many cases share with the system you want to access, is the simplest and most pervasive form of authenticator. A password is a perfect example of something you know.

Something You Have

A token of some kind that you are in possession of is a different kind of authenticator. You authenticate as yourself by proving that you are in possession of this token. An example is a smart card (discussed later in the chapter) or a RSA SecurID one-time password device (*http://www.rsa.com/node.aspx?id=1156*). These types of tokens are almost always combined with something you know, and can greatly strengthen the quality of the authentication claims.

Something You Are

Some systems use something you are as an authenticator. These typically fall in the category of biometric authenticators: tokens that attempt to measure something about you. Examples include retina scans, fingerprints, blood samples, and voice recognition. Some people also consider typing cadence while typing a password a biometric authenticator. However, that is debatable; it really just measures more parameters about the "something you know" factor. As such, it can easily be captured and replayed by the same system that can capture and replay the original authenticator—without harming or inconveniencing the subject. Therefore, it fails to provide proper two-factor authentication.

Biometric systems are inherently imprecise. While DNA provides an exact match, most people would be reluctant to donate a blood sample to use a computer (although some computers I have used felt like they were squeezing blood out of me). Most biometric factors are not as precise. For example, fingerprints are considered to be unique. However, it is questionable that recording it multiple times results in exactly the same print, as well as whether a machine can produce the same analysis result of the same print twice. Therefore, biometric authentication systems typically operate on a range of acceptable values, and when you store your authenticator you must record it several times. Based on this, the system develops the acceptable range for your authenticator. To successfully authenticate, subsequent attempts must fall within that range.

Biometric systems suffer from many other shortcomings. First, with the exception of typing cadence, they require special-purpose hardware devices on every client, some of which can be quite intrusive. The same is true for some "something you have" systems, such as smart cards.

Second, as mentioned above, biometric methods are imprecise and a close match is all that is needed. With some methods this can be fatal. If, for some reason, your biometric authenticator has changed, you will fail the authentication. For instance, if you use voice recognition you may not get in if illness or fatigue affects your voice. Likewise, an ill-fated weekend of home improvement projects may result in losing the digit you need to log on come Monday morning.

Third, many people consider biometric authentication very intrusive. Having extremely personal details such as fingerprints stored on a computer system is not to many people's liking.

Fourth, many security experts consider biometrics oversold. The companies in the business of selling biometric systems often make impossible claims. For example, a company making a software solution that measures typing cadence claims to protect customers against keystroke loggers, making stolen passwords worthless. That is impossible. For example, the user must still type the password on the client, and a keystroke logger on the client could be easily augmented to capture all the same information that the biometric software is capturing. This information could be easily replayed to successfully authenticate. This solution, in fact, fails to mitigate a single problem with passwords, but aggravates the problem that users must remember their passwords because it breaks solutions that rely on secure client-side storage of randomly generated passwords, such as Password Safe (*http://passwordsafe.sourceforge.net/*).

Fifth, there is a common misperception that biometric systems are secure because they are inherently a part of the user and cannot be left lying around the way passwords written on a sticky note can. However, this ignores the fact that biometric authentication sequences can not only be captured, such as fingerprints on a glass, but the tokens themselves are also most definitely removable. There have already been recorded instances of thieves making off with biometric authenticators (Kent, 2005). Less intrusive methods of capturing authenticators have also been used. For example, the Chaos Computer Club in Germany published a training video a few years ago showing how to produce a synthetic fingerprint by lifting one off a bottle.

Finally, there are relatively few choices for biometric authenticators. For example, in a system using fingerprints you only have 10 choices. If one of them is compromised or lost you have nine left to choose from. This makes cycling your authenticators regularly difficult because you will run out relatively soon. Because capturing and replaying credentials is a real risk, the lack of choices of authenticators is a threat not to be discounted.

For all these reasons, Windows does not natively support biometric authentication. Third parties do produce add-on software and hardware for biometric authentication. Microsoft also sells a fingerprinting device, although this latter device is clearly labeled as a non-enterprise grade security device. However, for all the reasons stated previously, biometric authenticators in general are not enterprise-class authenticators and should not be used in enterprises or to protect sensitive personal or corporate information. For enterprise use, smart cards and passwords can be far more secure, flexible, and easily integrated into ordinary business practices. The remainder of this chapter will focus on those two technologies.

Understanding Authenticator Storage

Anytime you have an authenticator, you have to store some form of it so that it can be compared at run time to what the principal enters when authenticating. The storage method differs depending both on the type of authenticator and how the designer built the system.

In this section we will discuss various ways authenticators are stored in Windows, particularly focusing on passwords because they are more commonly used and subject to far more variation than smart cards.

Smart cards rely on certificates. (For more information about certificates, see Chapter 10, "Implementing Active Directory Certificate Services.") The smart card itself holds the secret portion of the certificate. The authentication system, in this case an Active Directory domain, holds the public portion. Therefore, when you use smart cards, no secrets related to the smart card need to be stored on the domain controllers (DCs). This makes smart cards simpler in some ways than passwords to manage.

Note   As a practical matter, most systems that use smart cards escrow the secret keys in a central location. Windows includes that functionality as well. By doing so you gain the ability to access any secrets protected with smart card credentials, for example, for forensic purposes. However, it also means that you now have sensitive secrets to protect on your network.

Passwords, in virtually every implementation available today, are shared secrets. The secret the user uses to log on with is the same as the one the authentication server uses to authenticate the user's access. This means that passwords are sensitive secrets and must be protected.

In early shared computer systems, passwords were simply stored in clear-text in a text file. The passwords in those systems were never really meant to keep people out because only a small group of people had access to the system in the first place. They were mostly used to control which environment you received. Eventually, however, the passwords in the password file were encrypted or hashed.

Encryption and Hashing

Encryption is based on the word *cryptography*, which, literally, means "hidden writing." Encryption is the process of using cryptography to hide writing, or to convert something from a readable form—typically called clear-text or *plaintext*—into an obscured form, typically referred to as the *ciphertext*. Decryption is the reverse operation—converting something from ciphertext to plaintext.

While encryption uses cryptography to convert something into unreadable but reversible form, *hashing* is a closely related function that converts plaintext into unreadable and irreversible form. A *hash* can, for example, be used as a checksum to compare two plaintexts. If they both generate the same hash, you have reasonably good assurance that the plaintexts are identical. A hash is also typically far smaller—proportional to the plaintext—than a ciphertext. Therefore, hashes are very well suited to uses like password storage.

Most Unix-based systems still use this exact form of password storage, with two slight modifications. First, the password file, typically stored in /etc/passwd, now contains no password hashes but just user names and IDs. The actual hashes are stored in the shadow password file—for example, in /etc/passwd.shadow. While the password file itself is world-readable, the shadow file is readable only by superusers.

Second, because password hashes were originally world-readable in the /etc/passwd file, they had to be protected against comparison attacks. Imagine a situation in which you and I both have user accounts on the same computer. My password is "pas$word!" and, by sheer coincidence, you choose the same password. With a straight hash, we would both have the same password hash stored in the /etc/passwd file. I could search the file for my hash, and then search for any other accounts with the same hash. If I found any, I would know that they had the same password I had. This is an unacceptable situation. The solution is to add a randomly generated salt to the password before hashing it. A *salt* is simply a random value that is added to the password before hashing it. The salt is stored in clear-text in the password database. This way, even if two passwords are identical, they will have different salts and therefore different hashes. The process is shown in Figure 2-1.

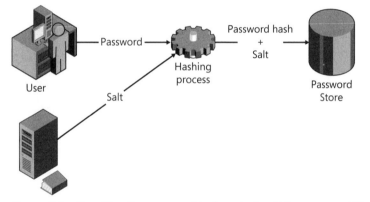

Figure 2-1   By salting the password before storing it the password file is protected against comparison attacks.

Windows uses variants on all these techniques to store passwords. In the following sections I will cover the five primary ways Windows stores passwords used to authenticate users to Windows itself.

LM Hash

The LM hash is not actually a hash at all, although it has some of the same properties. It is a one-way function, and is usually referred to internally as the LMOWF (LanManager One-Way Function). In Windows Vista and Windows Server 2008 the LM hash is not stored by default, nor is it used by default during a network authentication. However, on earlier versions of Windows the LM hash is typically both stored and transmitted by default. Therefore, knowing how the LM hash works is worthwhile. Note that both Windows Vista and Windows Server 2008 can be configured to store or authenticate with the LM hash, but this is not recommended because of weaknesses in the algorithms.

Direct from the Field: LM Hash History

The LM hash was first used by Microsoft in its LAN Manager network operating system, the last version of which was released in the early 1990s. LAN Manager ran on top of IBM's OS/2 operating system. When Windows NT was first released in 1993 it was imperative that the new operating system interoperate with LAN Manager so that organizations that had invested in LAN Manager did not suddenly find that their investments were useless. However, this also meant that even though Windows NT supported far better security structures than LAN Manager, Windows NT security still suffered from LAN Manager design decisions made in the mid-1980s. In 2006 Microsoft shipped the first operating system that disabled the LAN Manager password hashing mechanism by default, although it can still be enabled. It took 13 years to deprecate this feature.

Jesper M. Johansson
Windows Security MVP

The LM hash is created using a large number of relatively complicated steps, shown in Figure 2-2. The process starts when a user creates a new password. The password is immediately converted to all uppercase. In other words, passwords stored using the LM hash are case-insensitive.

After the password is converted to uppercase it is padded out to 14 characters. If the password is already longer than 14 characters, it could theoretically be truncated at this point, but in practice, the process just fails and no LM hash is generated if the password is longer than 14 characters. This is why you get a warning about compatibility with older operating systems when you set a password longer than 14 characters.

Next, the password is split into two 7-character chunks. This is because they will now be used as a key in a Data Encryption Standard (DES) encryption, and the Data Encryption Algorithm (DEA, the algorithm used in DES) operates on 56-bit chunks. These chunks are used as the key to encrypt a fixed value.

Finally, the results of the two DES operations are concatenated and the results are stored as the LM hash. The hash is stored either in the Security Accounts Manager database (if the password is for a local account on a stand-alone computer or a domain member) or in the DBCS-Pwd attribute of the user object in Active Directory.

This explains why an attacker is able to deduce how long a person's password is just by looking at the hash. If the second half of the LM hash is AAD3B435B51404EE, the second half of the password is blank and the password is no longer than seven characters. If both halves are AAD3B435B51404EE, the password is entirely blank.

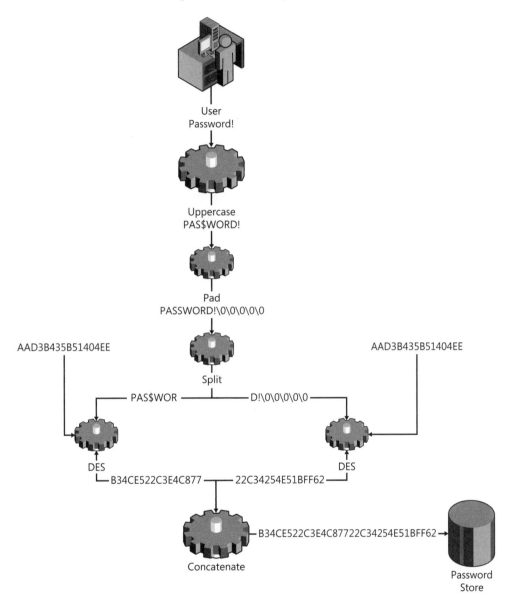

Figure 2-2 The LM hash is created using a series of complicated steps.

NT Hash

When Windows NT first came out in 1993 a new password storage method was introduced. This mechanism is far simpler than the LM hash, as shown in Figure 2-3.

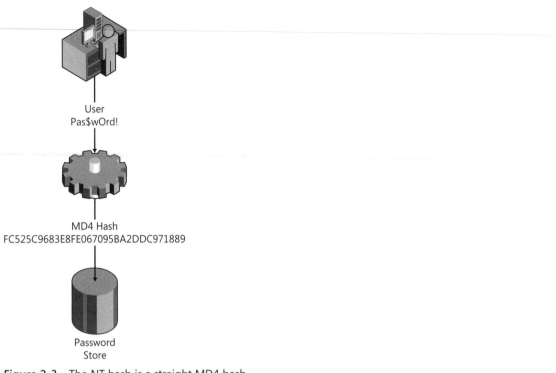

User
Pas$wOrd!

MD4 Hash
FC525C9683E8FE067095BA2DDC971889

Password
Store

Figure 2-3   The NT hash is a straight MD4 hash.

The NT hash, or NTOWF as it is referred to internally, is stored either in the SAM or in the Unicode-PWD attribute of an AD user.

Note that neither the NTOWF nor the LMOWF are salted. Windows has never salted passwords for the simple reason that the password databases were never readable to others, so the lookup issue was never particularly interesting as an attack vector. To read the databases you have to be an administrator in the first place, meaning you have already fully compromised the computer or domain. Furthermore, shared-secret authentication systems have a very interesting property that we shall discuss shortly and which bears on this issue.

Password Verifier

If you have worked in a Windows Active Directory environment, you probably noticed that you can carry a domain-joined laptop computer with you and authenticate to it using a domain account even though you are not connected to the domain. This particular bit of magic is thanks to something called the *password verifier*. The password verifier, often referred to outside of Microsoft as *cached credentials*, is a local copy of your domain password hash that you can use to log on locally. In operating system versions prior to Windows Vista, it was created using the process shown in Figure 2-4.

In recent years attackers have focused in on the password verifier and have started creating tools to crack it. While it is a salted hash of a hash, and therefore quite difficult to crack, cracking it is possible if the password is not very strong. To combat this, in Windows Vista and Windows Server 2008 the calculation for the password verifier was modified, as shown in Figure 2-5.

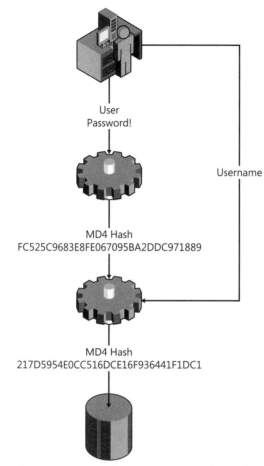

User
Password!

Username

MD4 Hash
FC525C9683E8FE067095BA2DDC971889

MD4 Hash
217D5954E0CC516DCE16F936441F1DC1

Figure 2-4   In earlier versions of Windows, the password verifier was simply a hash of a hash, salted with the user name.

While there is no way to protect weak passwords, the improved password verifier calculation makes for a much stronger verifier. By running the old verifier through a large number of PKCS #5 operations, a brute-force cracker would only be able to compute about 10 tests per second. This provides adequate protection against all but the very weakest passwords.

In Memory

When a user logs on interactively or using terminal services Windows caches the user's password hash (the NT hash and, if the computer is configured to store it, the LM hash). The hash is held in a memory location available only to the operating system, and of course, any process that can act as the operating system. When a user tries to access a network resource that requires authentication, the operating system uses this cached hash to authenticate with. This is what enables transparent authentication to network resources. As soon as the user logs off or locks the workstation, the memory location is automatically purged.

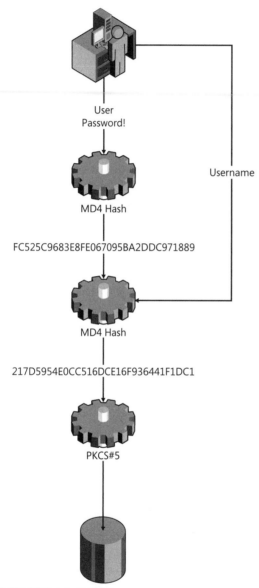

User
Password!

MD4 Hash

Username

FC525C9683E8FE067095BA2DDC971889

MD4 Hash

217D5954E0CC516DCE16F936441F1DC1

PKCS#5

Figure 2-5   The password verifier is far stronger in Windows Vista and Windows Server 2008 than in prior versions.

These hashes have been subject to a fair bit of debate after it was shown that if a domain administrator is logged on, any other user that is an administrator can read that domain administrator's password hash and use it to authenticate to a DC as a domain admin. This really should be obvious to any observer, however, and, quite frankly, is putting far too much effort into the attack. If an attacker has already compromised a workstation, it would be far easier to simply install a sub-authentication package, which gets the password in clear-text during the log-on process. These packages are supported to enable pass-through, single sign-on to non-Windows network devices, just like the NT hash is cached to support single sign-on to Windows devices. Although it would be possible to remove the cached password hashes, most users would rebel at having to type their passwords every time they accessed a network resource. If these cached password hashes were removed, the computer would no longer be able to authenticate transparently to non-domain network resources on behalf of the user.

The problem, therefore, is not really with how Windows caches the NT hash, nor with sub-authentication packages, but rather with operational practices. A domain administrator should never log on interactively to a workstation used by a user with local administrative privileges unless that user is as trusted as all the domain administrators. By following this simple principle, you can keep this legitimate functionality from becoming an attack vector. For more information on managing this, see Chapter 13, "Managing Security Dependencies to Secure Your Network."

Reversibly Encrypted

Finally, Windows has an option to store passwords reversibly encrypted. When a password is stored reversibly encrypted, it can be reversed to plaintext. Obviously, this means that no cracking is needed. Storing passwords reversibly encrypted is disabled by default, and is generally only needed in two circumstances. First, it is required if you need to use certain older authentication protocols for remote access, such as the CHAP or Digest protocols. Second, it is required if you wish to perform advanced analysis on your passwords after they are set. For instance, some organizations want to go through and analyze whether passwords contain certain words. Those organizations must store the passwords reversibly encrypted.

To enable reversible encryption, or check whether it is still disabled, use the Group Policy Editor, as shown in Figure 2-6.

The vast majority of organizations do not need reversible encryption, and as clients are upgraded to support more secure authentication protocols, there should be fewer and fewer reasons to do so. However, reversible encryption is another way Windows can store passwords, and it is important to know that it is there.

Important   Many people cringe when they hear that Windows can store passwords reversibly encrypted. After all everyone knows that storing passwords in plaintext is bad. However, this really misses the point. In every password-based system today, *passwords are plaintext-equivalent*! Password-based systems use shared secrets. In the authentication process, the only secret used is the one that is stored on the authentication server. If an attacker gets hold of the authentication server's password database, or the shared secret some other way, he has everything he needs to authenticate. The only thing he needs to do now is insert himself at the appropriate step in the authentication process so that he can send the shared secret instead of the password it is derived from. Currently several tools are freely available on the Internet that do this with Windows authentication across the network.

The fact that passwords are plaintext-equivalent, in and of itself, is not a security problem. It only becomes a problem when an attacker obtains a password hash. However, as you should realize by now, those are fairly well protected in Windows. If an attacker manages to obtain a password hash, he has already compromised the computer as much or more than he would be able to with that password hash! In other words, that password hash gives him no additional privileges on an already compromised computer.

If passwords are valid on other computers, however, it is possible that an attacker can further a compromise using the password hashes. Furthermore, because password hashes are cached in memory, an attacker may be able to obtain domain administrative credentials from a member computer if a domain administrator is logged on. This, however, is largely an operational problem related to how you run your network. If you follow the advice in Chapter 11, you will adequately protect yourself against that vector.

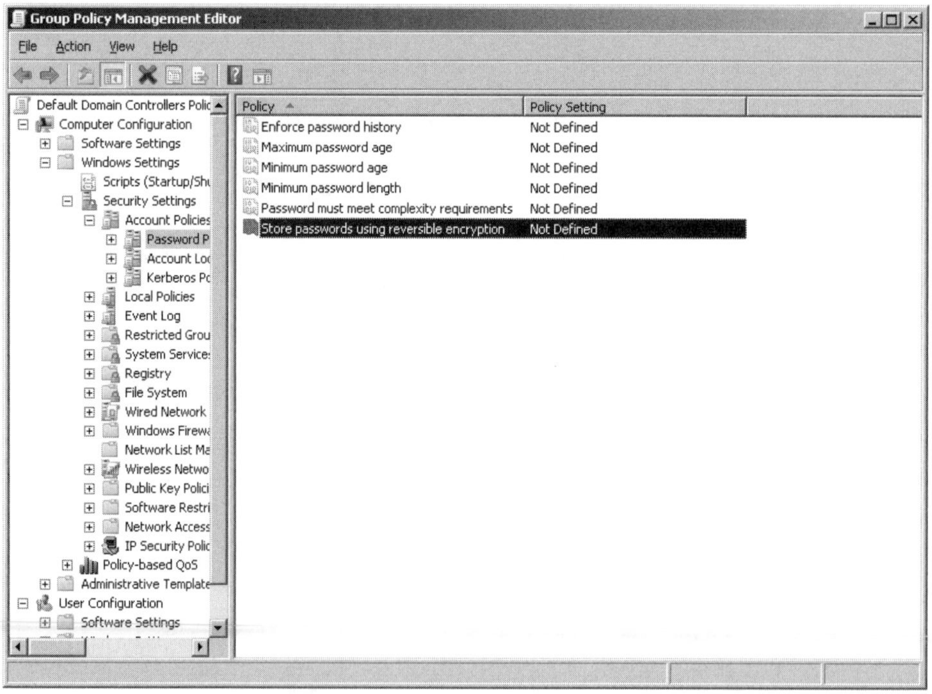

Figure 2-6   To configure a computer or a domain to store passwords reversibly encrypted use this Group Policy setting.

Authentication Protocols

So far, we have discussed how passwords are stored on Windows. Perhaps even more important is how they are used. Passwords are authenticators—they are used to authenticate a user to a computer. If the user is logging on interactively to a local account, the flow is quite simple:

1. User uses the Secure Attention Sequence (SAS, also known as the "three-finger salute," or just Ctrl+Alt+Delete) to bring up the log-on dialog box. This causes the Local Security Authority Sub-System (LSASS) to spawn a new session and load WinLogon in that session. WinLogon in turn loads the LogonUI.

2. User types in the user name and password.

3. The WinLogon process takes the password, hashes it to an NT hash, looks up the user name in the local SAM, and compares the NT hash to the one that is stored for the user. If the two match, the logon is successful.

4. If sub-authentication packages are installed on the computer, the log-on information is passed to those for additional processing. Otherwise, user32.exe is invoked and the user's environment is loaded.

This process is quite straightforward because there is a secure channel all the way from the LogonUI, which takes in the plaintext credentials the user types, to the comparison of the credentials. However, when authentication is taking place over the network it becomes a bit more complicated because you have to worry about how the authentication claims are transferred between the client where the user is sitting and the authentication server that hosts the accounts database. On Windows, this can take many forms, which I will discuss in the following sections.

Basic Authentication

Basic authentication is the simplest of all forms of authentication. It just transmits the raw log-on information across the network. In other words, the user name and password are sent across the network either as clear-text, or in a form that will transmit intact across the network, such as Base-64 encoded. In some implementations, this is referred to as the Password Authentication Protocol (PAP). Basic authentication is quite common in older network protocols such as Telnet, FTP, POP, IMAP, and even in HTTP. Today it may be used, for example, in the RPC/HTTPS connector mechanism used to connect a Microsoft Office Outlook client to an Exchange server across the Internet. In that case the credentials are traversing inside an encrypted channel to the Exchange Server or the ISA Server, whichever is terminating the connection. However, other than across an encrypted channel such as in the Outlook-Exchange example, Basic authentication should be avoided.

Challenge-Response Protocols

Challenge-response protocols are designed to obviate the need to transmit a password in clear-text across the network. They all essentially operate the same way, shown in Figure 2-7.

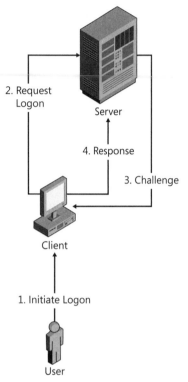

Figure 2-7   All challenge-response protocols are based on the same model.

The basic model for a challenge-response protocol is that a user initiates a logon, upon which the client makes a request to the server. The server creates a challenge, which often is just a random value, and sends this to the client. Meanwhile, the client has collected the user's credentials. The credentials are then combined with the challenge in a cryptographic operation. The result becomes the response. The actual implementation may differ, but the basic structure is always the same. Challenge response protocols supported by Windows include Digest authentication, the LM/NTLM family, and Kerberos.

Digest Authentication

Digest authentication is not a native protocol in Windows. It is used primarily with Internet Information Services (IIS) in accordance with RFC 2617 for Web-based authentication, and also with some third-party Lightweight Directory Access Protocol (LDAP) servers. Digest authentication is designed as a replacement to Basic authentication. It is considered relatively weak, and makes some security trade-offs on the authentication server.

The challenge-response sequence in Digest authentication is composed as follows:

1. The server generates a random nonce and sends it to the client. A *nonce* is simply a randomly generated number. It is commonly used in authentication protocols as a value that is permuted by an authenticator, as we shall see throughout this section.

2. The client computes an MD5 hash of the user name, authentication realm (domain in Windows), and password.

3. The client computes an MD5 hash of the method and the digest URI.

4. The client computes an MD5 hash of the result of operation 2, the server nonce, a request counter, a client nonce, a quality protection code, and the result from operation 3. This is the response value provided by the client.

5. The server computes all the same values.

The main concern with Digest authentication happens in step 2. As you can tell, the client response is computed with the actual password, not a hash of the password. This means that to validate the client's response the server must have access to the clear-text password in step 5. Hence, if you want to support Digest authentication, you must configure your domain to store passwords using reversible encryption.

LM and NTLM

Contrary to Digest authentication, both LM and NTLM are considered native protocols in Windows. They are very similar, differing mainly in the hash used to compute the response. LM was first used in the LanManager product mentioned earlier. NTLM was designed as a replacement for LM and was released with Windows NT 3.1 in 1993.

LM and NTLM are used in authentication in workgroups of Windows NT–based operating systems. They are also used in a domain environment if either the client or the server is not a domain member, or if the resource being accessed is specified using an IP address as opposed to a host name. Otherwise, Kerberos is used in Active Directory domains. The reason LM/NTLM must be used when accessing a resource using an IP address is that Kerberos is based on fully qualified domain names (FQDNs) and there is no way to resolve one of those from an IP address because each host can have multiple aliases.

The authentication flow in LM and NTLM typically occurs together. The same message includes both protocols, and no negotiation takes place regarding which protocol is to be used. This is one of the few instances where Windows does not negotiate protocols prior to a transaction. The aggregate flow is shown in Figure 2-8.

All Windows NT–based operating systems prior to Windows Server 2003 worked as shown in Figure 2-8, sending both the LM and NTLM responses by default. In Windows Server 2003 only the NTLM response was sent by default, while the LM response field was mostly unused. Both protocols were accepted inbound. Starting with Windows Vista and Windows Server 2008, this has changed, as I will explain next.

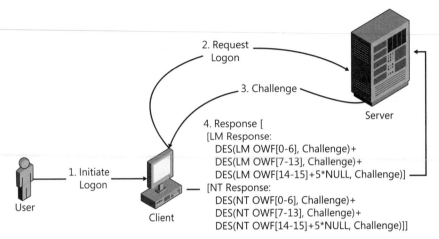

2. Request
Logon

3. Challenge

Server

4. Response [
[LM Response:
DES(LM OWF[0-6], Challenge)+
DES(LM OWF[7-13], Challenge)+
DES(LM OWF[14-15]+5*NULL, Challenge)]

1. Initiate
Logon

[NT Response:
DES(NT OWF[0-6], Challenge)+
DES(NT OWF[7-13], Challenge)+
DES(NT OWF[14-15]+5*NULL, Challenge)]]

User

Client

Figure 2-8   The LM and NTLM protocols are typically sent together.

NTLM v2

Starting with Windows Vista, and also with Windows Server 2008, both LM and NTLM are deprecated by default. NTLM is still supported for inbound authentication, but for outbound authentication a newer version of NTLM, called NTLMv2, is sent by default instead. Prior versions of Windows (back as far as Windows NT 4.0 Service Pack 4) could be configured to behave this way, but it was not the default. Technically speaking, the computer will accept LM for inbound authentication but by default neither Windows Vista nor Windows Server 2008 store the LM hash. Therefore, there is no way for them to authenticate an inbound LM response.

You can control the authentication behavior, starting with Windows NT 4.0 Service Pack 4, using the LMCompatibilityLevel registry setting, shown in Group Policy as Network Security: LAN Manager Authentication Level. (See Figure 2-9.)

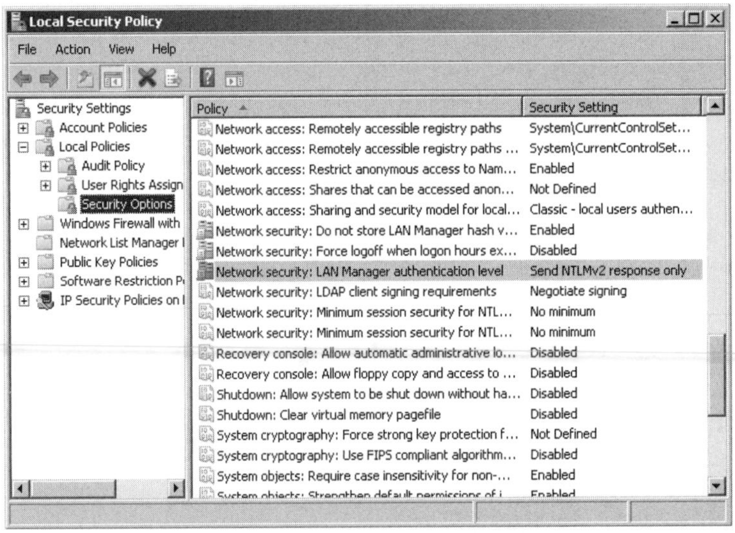

Figure 2-9   The LAN Manager Authentication Level setting governs the authentication behavior in non-domain authentication.

The default value for LMCompatibilityLevel in Windows Vista and Windows Server 2008 is 3, or Send NTLMv2 Response Only. Tables 2-1 and 2-2 show how the possible values affect a computer when acting as the client and authentication server, respectively. It is important to recognize that the settings in Table 2-2 only relate to the server that performs the authentication, which is the one that contains the user accounts database. Any intermediate servers simply pass on the request to that server. This means that for domain members, Table 2-2 is only relevant on DCs and domain members authenticating against their local accounts.

Table 2-1   Impact of LMCompatibilityLevel on Client Behavior

Level	Group Policy Name	Sends	Accepts	Prohibits Sending
0	Send LM and NTLM Responses	LM, NTLM, NTLMv2, Session Security is negotiated	LM, NTLM, NTLMv2	NTLMv2 Session Security (on Windows 2000 below SRP1, Windows NT 4.0, and Windows 9x)
1	Send LM and NTLM—use NTLMv2 session security if negotiated	LM, NTLM, NTLMv2, Session Security is negotiated	LM, NTLM, NTLMv2	NTLMv2
2	Send NTLM response only	NTLM, NTLMv2, Session Security is negotiated	LM, NTLM, NTLMv2	LM and NTLMv2
3	Send NTLMv2 response only	NTLMv2, Session Security is always used	LM, NTLM, NTLMv2	LM and NTLM

Table 2-2   Impact of LMCompatibilityLevel on Authentication Server Behavior

Level	Group Policy Name	Sends	Accepts Inbound	Prohibits Sending
4	Send NTLMv2 response only/refuse LM	NTLMv2, Session Security	NTLM, NTLMv2	LM
5	Send NTLMv2 response only/refuse LM and NTLM	NTLMv2, Session Security	NTLMv2	LM and NTLM

On all versions of Windows prior to Windows Server 2003 the default value was 0. On Windows Server 2003 the default value was 2. On Windows Vista and Windows Server 2008 the default value is 3.

NTLMv2 is a much improved version of NTLM. It also uses the NT hash. However, it also includes a client challenge in the computation. Figure 2-10 shows the authentication flow under NTLMv2.

As Figure 2-10 shows, the NTLMv2 protocol uses not only a client challenge, but also computes two HMAC-MD5 message authentication codes to create the response. It also includes a time stamp to mitigate replay attacks. Figure 2-10 also shows an LMv2 response, which is included in the response. The LMv2 response is a fixed-length response as opposed to the NTLMv2 response. It is included to provide the ability for pass-through authentication with earlier versions of Windows such as Windows 95. When NTLMv2 was first designed, those systems were prevalent.

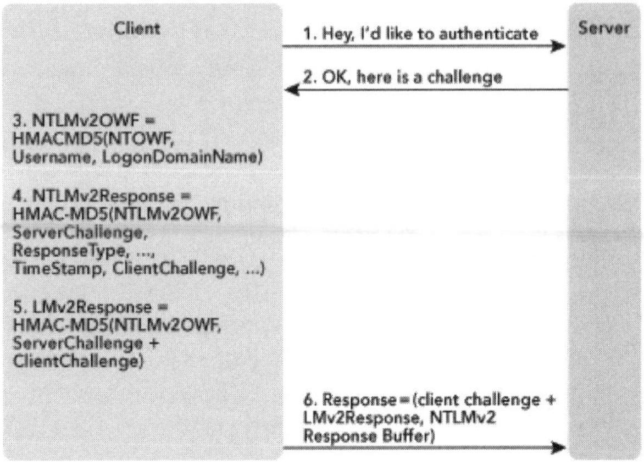

Figure 2-10   The NTLMv2 protocol uses HMAC-MD5 and a client challenge.

Windows 9x did not support NTLMv2 natively, but did pass through the LM response. However, it would strip pieces of the variable-length NTLMv2 response, breaking the authentication. To prevent this problem the LMv2 response was included in the LM response field. Because it has the same length as the LM response it passes through to the authentication server unharmed and can be used to complete the authentication. Today it is still passed when NTLMv2 is used. However, the authentication server always starts out the authentication process by seeing whether there is an NTLMv2 response that validates successfully. If there is, the authentication succeeds. Therefore, while the LMv2 response still exists, it is rarely used for authentication.

NTLM++

Around the Windows 2000 time frame Microsoft added another NTLM-family protocol to Windows. This one does not have an official name. In some places in the implementation it is referred to as NTLM2, to contrast with NTLM3, which is actually NTLMv2. In other places it is called NTLM++. It was never documented, but was discovered externally by several people, including Eric Glass, Christopher R. Hertel, and Hidenobu Seki, and is even picked up by the Ethereal network traffic analyzer, which refers to it as *NTLM2 Session Security*. This is because it was always observed in conjunction with LMCompatibilityLevel set to 1, which enabled NTLMv2 Session Security, which also was poorly understood. Microsoft added NTLM++ to make certain man-in-the-middle attacks more difficult while retaining the ability to pass through authentication when connecting to servers running earlier versions of Windows. In a sense then, NTLM++ is an intermediate step between NTLM and LMv2/NTLMv2.

When NTLM++ is used the LM response field is populated with a client challenge instead of the LM response, as shown in Figure 2-11.

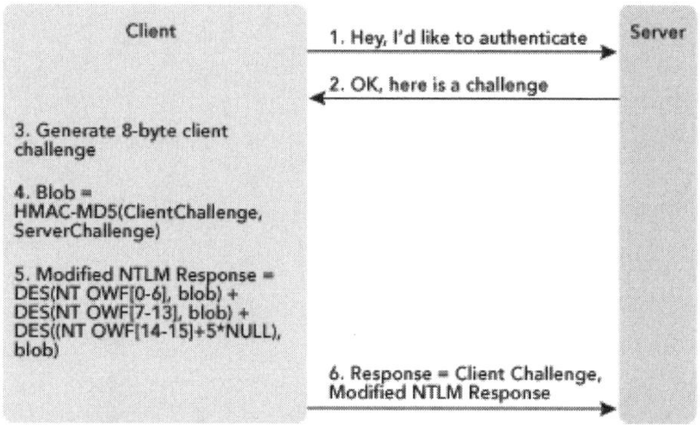

Figure 2-11   The NTLM++ protocol includes a modified NTLM response and a client challenge.

The NTLM response field contains a modified NTLM response calculated exactly the same way as the original NTLM response, but using an HMAC-MD5 of the client challenge and the server challenge as the challenge, instead of just the server challenge.

The computer uses NTLM++ whenever NTLMv2 Session Security is enabled. Starting with Windows 2000 Security Rollup Pack 1 (SRP 1), all computers will automatically send the NTLM++ response on the first attempt. This means that starting with that release, the effective LMCompatibilityLevel setting is actually 1 on all computers.

For reference, NTLMv2 Session Security actually refers to a stronger computation of session keys that are used by applications that request session security after the connection is set up. It is related to authentication protocols only in that it is managed with the same setting.

Kerberos

Kerberos is used in domain environments when host names (including fully qualified domain names) are used to connect. This is most of the time, unless the user specifically requests a connection to an IP address. Like the NTLM family, Windows implements Kerberos as a Security Support Provider (SSP) and Kerberos also uses the NT hash for authentication, but any similarities with the other protocols really end there.

Kerberos provides authentication both for the user who is trying to connect and between the client and the server. This is quite a departure from NTLM, which does not provide the user with any assurance that the server is the computer she thinks it is. Kerberos is also designed with the explicit assumption that the network is hostile; that some adversary is able to intercept all traffic; and that the adversary has the ability to read, modify, or delete any traffic sent across the network.

To accomplish all this, Kerberos relies on encryption as well as time synchronization. By default in Windows, the synchronization between client and server must be within five minutes of each other. You can modify this setting if you are in an environment with high potential skew. To do so, change the maximum Tolerance For Computer Clock Synchronization value in Computer

Configuration\Windows Settings\Security Settings\Account Policies\Kerberos Policies in a GPO that applies to the computers for which you want to change the time skew. Remember, however, that the effective maximum time skew will the lowest in the transaction. Either computer can reject the transaction if the time stamp is outside its permitted time skew.

To understand how Kerberos works, let us analyze the exchange shown in Figure 2-12, which shows how a user logs on to a workstation and then requests a file from a file server.

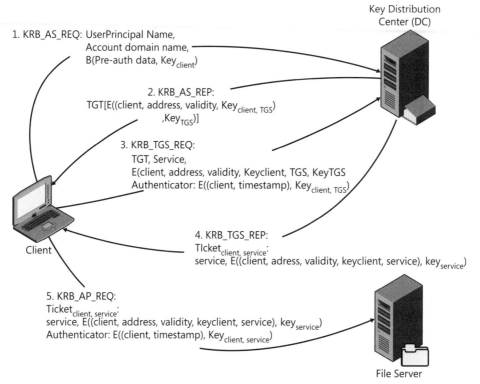

Key Distribution Center (DC)

1. KRB_AS_REQ: UserPrincipal Name,
                Account domain name,
                B(Pre-auth data, Key$_{client}$)

2. KRB_AS_REP:
TGT[E((client, address, validity, Key$_{client, TGS}$)
                ,Key$_{TGS}$)]

3. KRB_TGS_REQ:
     TGT, Service,
     E(client, address, validity, Keyclient, TGS, KeyTGS
     Authenticator: E((client, timestamp), Key$_{client, TGS}$)

4. KRB_TGS_REP:
     TIcket$_{client, service}$:
     service, E((client, adress, validity, keyclient, service), key$_{service}$)

Client

5. KRB_AP_REQ:
Ticket$_{client, service}$:
service, E((client, address, validity, keyclient, service), key$_{service}$)
Authenticator: E((client, timestamp), Key$_{client, service}$)

File Server

Figure 2-12   This exchange occurs when a computer starts and requests a file from a file server.

The exchange in Figure 2-12 consists of the following parts:

1. After the computer starts it creates some preauthentication data, consisting of, among other things, a time stamp. This preauthentication data is encrypted using a key derived from the computer's password. It is then packaged in a KRB_AS_REQ (Kerberos Authentication Service Request) packet and sent to the Authentication Service (AS) which resides on the Key Distribution Center (KDC), which, as it turns out, is the DC.

2. The AS constructs a Ticket Granting Ticket (TGT) and creates a session key that the client can use to communicate with the Ticket Granting Service (TGS), which also resides on the DC in Windows. This key is denoted with Key$_{client,TGS}$ in Figure 2-12. It is transmitted to the client encrypted with the client's own public key. This message is sent back as the KRB_AS_REP.

3. The client now sends a KRB_TGS_REQ message to the Ticket Granting Service (TGS) on the KDC to request a ticket for the file server. This request has the TGT in it, and also includes the service the client wants to access and information on the client encrypted with the TGS public key. The KRB_TGS_REQ includes an authenticator, which is essentially a time stamp encrypted with the session key the client shares with the TGS.

4. The TGS responds with a KRB_TGS_REP message that includes a ticket for the service the client requested. It contains the same information the client sent in the KRB_TGS_REQ, but this time is encrypted using the server's public key. In other words, the client cannot read this data. The TGS also creates a session key that the client can share with the server and encrypts it with the session key the client shares with the TGS.

5. Finally, the client sends its ticket for the service to the server, in a KRB_AP_REQ message. The client information, along with the client-server session key, is encrypted using the server's public key, and the message also includes the client's authenticator, which is encrypted using the shared session key.

When a user logs on to the client, the same process is repeated, but this time the messages include user information. The Kerberos client sends another KRB_AS_REQ, but encrypts the preauthentication data with a key derived from the client's password—or rather, the client's NT hash. The KDC validates the authentication based on that information. In the KRB_AS_REP the client receives a TGT that the user can use to contact the TGS. The TGT includes session keys for the KDC along with Security Identifiers (SIDs) for the user and all the groups the user is a member of. From then on, the client will use the user's TGT for requests made on behalf of the user.

Kerberos is clearly a rather complicated protocol, but it has proven remarkably robust in Windows. It also proves to be extensible in that the user's preauthentication data can just as easily be encrypted with some secret not derived from a password. This happens in smart card–based authentication, which I will discuss next.

Smart Card Authentication

A smart card is, in most cases, a credit card–sized device that contains a memory chip. These devices have many uses. For example, they are used to provision a phone's identity in the Global System for Mobile (GSM) communications cellular telephone system and its derivatives. Smart cards may also be used to authenticate to Windows. In that case they contain an X.509 certificate. (See Chapter 10 for more information about certificates.) The certificate contains a private key, and the corresponding public key is stored in the user object in Active Directory.

When the user authenticates using a smart card, WinLogon will ask for a PIN code instead of a password. It then contacts the smart card provider and provides it with the PIN code along with the preauthentication data. The smart card provider uses the PIN code to access the smart card, which will encrypt the preauthentication data that the Kerberos SSP will use in the KRB_AS_REQ message. From then on, most things happen the same way in a smart card logon as in a normal password-based logon, with one major difference: If the user logs on with a smart card, she never provided a password. This means that if the user tries to access any resources that cannot use the Kerberos system, the computer must prompt her for a password. To avoid that, Windows handles passwords a bit differently in smart card–based logons.

Smart Cards and Passwords

All accounts have a password hash stored on the DC. In fact, even if the user is required to log on with a smart card there is a password hash. When you configure an account to require smart card logon, the DC will actually create a random password, hash it, and store it in the user object.

When a user logs on with a smart card, the KDC actually provides the client with the user's password hash during the log-on process. These credentials are sent encrypted with the client's public key. The Kerberos SSP on the client will decrypt them and cache them in the same way it would cache them if the user had entered them at the log-on prompt. The computer then uses these credentials to log on seamlessly to computers that, for whatever reason, are unreachable using Kerberos. This means that even with smart card logon required, the hashes are still exposed on the client to any rogue software that happens to run as an administrator. Using smart cards does not protect the password-based credentials any more than password-based logons do. Therefore, all the same cautions apply against the attacks we shall discuss next.

Attacks on Passwords

At this particular juncture, it is worth taking a little detour into attacks, if for no other reason than that so many people are concerned about them. The primary concern with respect to passwords is obviously bad guys getting at them. Once they have them, or some representation thereof, the question is how they use them. Let's start by investigating how a potential attacker can obtain a password, or some form of it.

Obtaining Passwords

Attackers have several ways to get hold of your passwords. The following sections list them in order of ease of attack and prevalence (roughly speaking).

Ask for Them

An astonishing number of people, up to three-quarters in some studies, are willing to part with their passwords in trade for something they value more, like chocolate in one particular study (Wagner, 2004).

Capture the Passwords Themselves

Apart from just asking for them, the most fruitful, simplest, and possibly most common way to attack passwords today is to use a keystroke logger to capture them in plaintext as the user enters them. There are many different kinds of keystroke loggers. An innocuous option is using a hardware device that mounts between the keyboard and the computer and has onboard memory to hold all keystrokes. It can be surreptitiously installed or removed in a matter of seconds. Such a device will get access to everything that the computer sees, including all keystrokes, metadata such as typing cadence, and so on. A software program, commonly found in malware and spyware today, can also capture all keystrokes, and can typically capture metadata as well, not just passwords. Some of these include an automatic upload feature to a Web site or an Internet Relay Chat (IRC) channel. Others include a small Web server that the attacker can use to retrieve the goods.

However, the simplest and most direct route for an attacker to capture only passwords is to write a sub-authentication package. Windows, like any other industrial-strength operating system, includes functionality for third parties to extend its authentication subsystem to authenticate to other network devices. An attacker can, with just a few application programming interface (API) calls, write a sub-authentication package that will receive all passwords in plaintext when a user logs on. With some more effort, the attacker can augment the package with the same features as a more general keystroke logger, but generating far less noise because it is specialized to capture only passwords.

Both of the software options require administrative privileges to install, meaning that the attacker must first completely compromise the computer. Physical compromise would also be sufficient to install these types of tools; and it is quite telling that keystroke loggers are now found regularly on public access computers, especially at conferences.

Capture the Challenge-Response Sequence

It is rare that passwords are passed over the network in any form today, and even rarer to see new implementations of plaintext protocols such as FTP, POP, and Telnet. However, even with challenge-response protocols the attacker can often capture both the challenge and the response and attack the combination. It requires more calculations than attacking ordinary hashes, but can be very fruitful if the password is weak.

Capture the Hashes

This is the quintessential attack that everyone worries about. If an attacker has access to the password hashes, he can crack them or use them in some other way. There are several ways to crack them, as we shall see shortly. The most common way to capture the hashes is to compromise the authentication server that stores the passwords. As you will see in Chapter 13, "Securing the Network," the more dependencies you have in your network, the easier this attack is to perpetrate.

Another option—less common but equally valid—is to compromise a computer where someone is already logged on. When a user logs on, as I mentioned earlier, Windows caches that user's NT hash in memory. An attacker with complete control over the computer can retrieve that hash and use it in the same way as any other hash. Again, this is a problem largely related to your operational practices. As you will see in Chapter 13, if you do not expose sensitive hashes on computers that are less sensitive (and hence less secure), you will not have this problem. In addition, if a criminal manages to compromise a computer to this extent, she can easily capture the plaintext password as well, as we will see in the next section.

Guessing Passwords

Finally, the attacker can simply try to guess passwords. This is the easiest method to remedy, and also the least fruitful, or at least it should be. Anyone who has an Internet-connected Windows computer and actually looks at the log files will see attempts at this. Figure 2-13 shows a failed attempt on one of my computers on the day I was writing this chapter.

Most attackers use automated password "grinders" that attempt to log on using either Terminal Services or Windows Networking (Server Message Block, or SMB). The log-on attempt in Figure 2-13 is actually an Internet Information Services log-on attempt, which I know only because the host does not respond on either Terminal Services or SMB across the Internet.

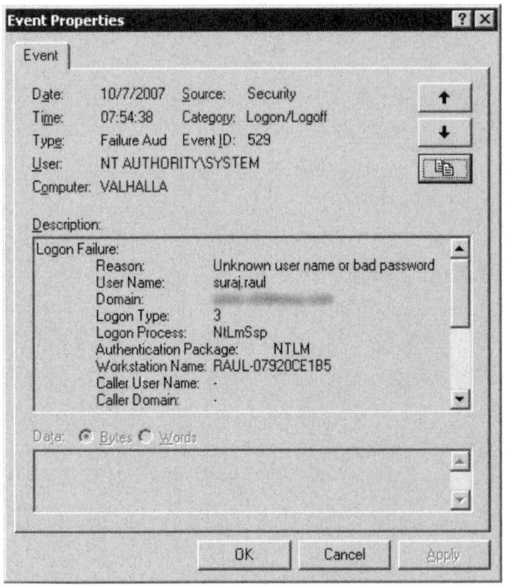

Figure 2-13   Anyone with an Internet-connected Windows computer will get failed log-on attempts in his or her event logs.

The automated password grinders will typically try common user names, such as Administrator, with a dictionary of passwords. Shockingly, they must be successful enough with that approach to make it worthwhile to continue. Many people argue that you should rename the Administrator account to fool attackers, and some even say to create a decoy account called Administrator. This has absolutely no effect whatsoever. The error message is the same whether an account does not exist with the name Administrator or whether the attacker gets the password wrong. Therefore, from the attacker's perspective, he cannot tell whether you have an account called Administrator. He can only tell that he did not get in. You can assure yourself that he will not get in simply by setting a reasonably strong password. For example, if the password is 15 characters long and seemingly random (meaning that it seems random from the attacker's point of view) the attacker will have to try 542,086,379,860,909,058,354,552,242,176, or so, times before he succeeds. More than likely he will move on before he succeeds in guessing that password.

You May Want to Leave Your Passwords Blank

As with all versions of Windows since Windows XP, user accounts with blank passwords cannot log on from the network in Windows Server 2008. This is actually a genius design, which can be used to great effect for the local Administrator account.

In a typical datacenter the servers are locked inside racks. In many cases, not everyone has access to every rack. Only those personnel who need to get into particular servers can get into those racks. The racks themselves are in locked rooms that require badge and PIN access. Datacenters have guards (often armed) in parking log booths and in the reception area. To get to the corridor by the server room you have to pass the surly looking, and very bored, guard at the reception and usually pass through a man-trap that weighs you both on the way in and the way out. (What happens if you weigh less when you leave, by the way?) To get to the reception you pass another guard, in a booth, probably with a gun, in the parking lot. In that situation, are your servers physically secure? More than likely you would say yes. If so, why not leave the password blank for the built-in Administrator account? The only people that can use it are the ones that get past the two guards, the mantrap, the badge scanner, have the PIN code to the right room, and the key to the right rack. More than likely, if someone has all of those, he belongs in there and needs to use that account—and has a way to get at the password should he need to. Obviously, he should not use it for daily use, but if everything breaks and he needs to log on as the built-in Administrator, he knows what the password is and can get in very easily.

Leaving the password blank solves one of the huge problems in network security: how do you keep the admin account from having the same password on every server in the network? It is very difficult to argue that leaving the password blank compromises security in any way at all—when you have adequate physical security. Unfortunately, it is probably going to be far more difficult to convince an ill-informed security auditor that leaving the password blank is more secure than setting the same eight-character password he requires on every single server. If you promise to try though, I'll do my part. Having a password that is only usable by someone inside the data center is far, far more secure than having one massive security dependency between thousands of servers, all using the auditors' ill-conceived, preferred solution.

Using the Captured Information

Assuming the attacker has captured something, how does he go about using it? If he has captured a plaintext password, the answer is relatively straightforward. He just needs to find somewhere to type it. However, if he has captured a challenge-response sequence, or a password hash, the problem is slightly more complicated.

Cracking Passwords

The most common attack is to crack the password. By "crack" in this case, we generally mean that the attacker creates a password hash or a challenge-response sequence based on some trial password and compares it to the hash or response that he captured. If the test succeeds, the trial password is the right password.

As you have seen earlier in this chapter, several additional computations are involved in computing a challenge-response sequence as opposed to computing a straight hash. It stands to reason, therefore, that cracking a captured challenge response sequence takes significantly longer than simply cracking a password hash. On commonly available hardware today you could compute anywhere from 3 million to 10 million hashes per second, while you could compute only a third as many challenge-response pairs. If the bad guy only has the password verifier, he will be able to compute only 10 per second, rendering them effectively uncrackable unless the password is exceptionally weak.

Several approaches to cracking passwords speed up the process. An attacker can try with a dictionary of common words, or common passwords (Burnett, 2005). The attacker can also try a brute-force attack using all possible passwords of some given character set. For performance reasons, the attacker may choose to greatly trim the character set. My own research has shown that users pick 80 percent of the characters used in passwords from a set of only 32 characters. Finally, the attacker can try a hybrid approach, basing the test password on some dictionary with characters permuted. For example, the attacker may try common substitutions, such as using "!" or "1" instead of "i", "@" instead of "a" or "at", "3" instead of "e" and so on. Finally, to really speed up the attack at run-time, the attacker can spend some time up-front generating a list of hashes and then use a pre-computed hash attack.

Precomputed Hash Attacks

Precomputed hash attacks are very simple in concept. The first common use of them was in Gerald Quakenbush's Password Appraiser tool from the late 1990s. The tool shipped with several CDs full of password hashes. Several years later, Cedric Tissieres and Philippe Oechslin developed Ophcrack, which cracked LM hashes using precomputed hashes, but used a time-memory trade-off to reduce the amount of storage space required to hold the hashes. Rather than storing all the hashes, they stored only a portion of them along with all the passwords that created that hash. At run time the cracker would simply look up which set of passwords possibly matched the hash it needed to crack, compute the hashes for all the options, and compare them to the hash. This was significantly slower than Password

Appraiser, but many orders of magnitude faster than brute-force cracking. Zhu Shuanglei implemented the same technique in the immensely popular Rainbow Crack tool, which can crack almost any hash format out there. Precomputed hash attacks are often referred to as Rainbow Cracks or Rainbow Table Attacks after that tool.

Precomputed hash attacks have created immense media buzz, and many, many people, and many self-styled security "experts" have opined about how bad they are and how they work only because Windows is flawed and how Microsoft needs to fix Windows to prevent them. Typically they accompany these claims with statements about how (of course) other operating systems had the foresight to protect against these attacks. These characterizations are gross simplifications that fail to account properly for either history or reality.

First, Windows is not flawed in that it does not take into account precomputed hash attacks in its design. It is true that use of a salt in the password-hashing mechanism would combat precomputed hash attacks. However, it simply was not (and still is not) an interesting threat to protect against. As I mentioned earlier, if an attacker has access to your hashes, *your computer or network is already in the worst state of health*—you have already been hacked at least as badly as what the attacker can do with those password hashes by cracking them.

Furthermore, do not be lured into thinking that the designers of competing operating systems had the foresight to protect against these attacks. Salts were added to protect against the fact that the password file was world-readable. Precomputed hash attacks were not relevant when those platforms were designed. Keeping hundreds of gigabytes, or even terabytes, of password hashes was not particularly feasible when the computer had 16KB of core memory and a tape drive.

Second, it makes no sense whatsoever to start salting Windows password hashes to protect against precomputed hash attacks. Consider how the authentication protocols work. If you change the hashing mechanisms, you must also introduce a new authentication protocol because the old ones rely on the old hashes. The last time a new authentication protocol was actually retired was in Windows Vista when LM was retired. That took 13 years from the introduction of its replacement. Changing the hashing mechanism to add a salt would certainly stop precomputed hash attacks. However, it would take 13 years or so before the old NT hashes were gone. And, because *password hashes* are *plaintext equivalent*, with or without a salt, it would not solve the real problem. Anyone who claims that merely salting passwords is a necessary change to Windows either has not thought the problem through, or fails to understand it.

Why Password Cracking Should Not Be Your Biggest Concern

It is important not to lose sight of the fact that in every case that involves compromise of actual hashes, the attacker has defeated all the security systems and has complete control over at least a system that will provide him with advanced access, and probably to a system that holds all the secrets—the DC. In other words, if an attacker has hashes to crack, you have already been severely hacked and bad guys with password hashes should be the least of your concerns. Regardless of whether the attacker manages to use the hashes directly or crack them, your network is beyond repair already. Your only solution is to rebuild any compromised computer—including the entire network if a domain or enterprise admin account could be compromised—from scratch or from a backup that is provably not compromised.

Pass-the-Hash Attacks

Password hashes are plaintext equivalent. You have seen that stated several times, and it should be eminently clear by now. The secret used by the server to verify the client's identity is the same secret the client uses to prove its identity. This is true of *all* shared secret authentication protocols, not just those used by Windows. If a criminal manages to capture that secret, he can simply use it to prove his identity, *without any knowledge of the password used to create that secret.*

This is a crucial point. If we can accept the fact that password hashes are plaintext equivalent the way we think about password security changes. First, we can immediately see why replacing the current NT hashes with salted ones is meaningless, because the salted ones are also plaintext equivalent. Protecting against stolen hashes with a salt is a bit like putting a band-aid on a severed limb; it is unlikely to have much impact on the actual problem. Second, we can also see that the core problem is not password hashes, but attackers with access to them. The only real, technical, solution is to move completely away from challenge-response protocols to public key protocols. However, this requires a substantial change to all platforms and is unlikely to happen anytime soon.

Therefore, the real solution is to stop attackers from getting at password hashes. To do that we need to minimize the exposure of password hashes and we need to ensure that we adequately protect our authentication servers. Chapter 13 discusses these topics in depth.

Protecting Your Passwords

You can mitigate every one of the attacks we have discussed so far by either using better passwords, or managing and operating your network more securely. Chapter 13 goes into depth about how to manage and operate the network more securely. Obviously, because password hashes are plaintext equivalent, using strong passwords will not mitigate all the attacks outlined so far. However, it will have a significant impact on many of them.

What constitutes a strong password? The answer is: a long password! No single factor is more important than length when it comes to password strength. Table 2-3 shows how long a password composed from *n* characters chosen randomly from a set of 32 characters resists both guessing and cracking attacks.

Table 2-3   Password Attack Resilience for 32-Character Character Sets

Length	Guessing Resilience in Days	Cracking Resilience In Days
6	10	0
7	331	0
8	10,605	1
9	339,355	27
10	10,859,374	869
11	347,499,971	27,800
12	11,119,999,080	889,600
13	355,839,970,558	28,467,198
14	11,386,879,057,845	910,950,325

As you can tell from Table 2-3, the strength of the password goes up dramatically the longer it gets. A 14-character password composed of randomly chosen symbols from a known 32-character character set resists guessing for more than 31 billion (!) years. Even an 8-character password would be impossible to guess in a reasonable time as long as the attacker cannot rely on heuristics. The 14-character password resists a cracking attack for 2.5 million years, but of course it is still plaintext equivalent, so resistance to cracking is really only relevant in the case of a captured challenge-response sequence.

The question, however, that many want answered is how important the character set is in password strength. Obviously, the larger the character set the attacker has to contend with, the stronger the password is. However, the effect is nowhere near as drastic as length. Table 2-4 shows the same data as Table 2-3, but for passwords composed using a character set consisting of 95 characters.

Table 2-4   Password Attack Resilience for 95-Character Character Sets

Length	Guessing Resilience in Days	Cracking Resilience In Days
6	7,090	1
7	673,551	54
8	63,987,310	5,119
9	6,078,794,461	486,304
10	577,485,473,802	46,198,838
11	54,861,120,011,233	4,388,889,601
12	5,211,806,401,067,100	416,944,512,085
13	495,121,608,101,375,000	39,609,728,648,110
14	47,036,552,769,630,600,000	3,762,924,221,570,450

As Table 2-4 shows, the passwords based on the set of 95 characters are certainly stronger than ones based only on 32. However, a 6-character password from the 95-character set is weaker than an 8-character password from the 32-character set. Realizing that difficulty dealing with complexity is often a human weakness, many people would probably have a simpler time remembering an 8-character password composed of a small set of commonly used characters than a 6-character password composed of characters they hardly ever use. You can use these numbers to develop an appropriate strategy for different people, depending on how they think. However, it is clear from this data that if we can simply get users to use longer passwords, we can solve a lot of password-related problems. Fundamentally, passwords are a perfectly acceptable, very convenient, comprehensible, and simple-to-implement authentication mechanism. The only flaw in the equation is that people are not good at remembering passwords. If we could only remove the people that use them from the system passwords are probably the best way to authenticate to a system. Fortunately, we can.

Note   The password resilience data presented in Tables 2-3 and 2-4 are based on a theoretical attacker than can guess 600 passwords per second or crack 7.5 million passwords per second. These numbers are significantly greater than what can be achieved today both with respect to password guessing and cracking captured challenge-response pairs, using a single machine.

Managing Passwords

Left to their own devices, people will not pick very good passwords. Yet we need them to pick longer ones to protect themselves. To reconcile that dilemma, we need to rethink some old concepts that many hold as truth.

Use Other Authenticators

First, a password that the user does not know is better than one the user does know. If you use smart cards and configure the system to require smart card logon, every account will still have a password, but it will be a long and random password. Its hash can still be stolen from any computer that the user logs on to, providing that malware running as the operating system is present on that computer, but the password, for all practical purposes, can never be guessed.

Record Passwords, Safely

Those of us who cannot require the use of smart cards on our networks must live with the fact that the user must know the password. To help them remember their passwords, the Chinese invented this marvelous technology in the second century CE. It is called "paper". That is correct. I just implied that users *should* write down their passwords. Currently most organizations have a password policy that requires minimum 8-character passwords, and they must have three different character sets in them. The result? Users pick passwords like "Seattle1", which, if you check it, complies with the policy. "Test1234" complies as well, as does "Password1", "Passw0rd", and "Pa$$word". If you were given the choice, wouldn't you rather have a user carry a little piece of paper in her wallet with the words "Get a skinny tall latte before work!" on it? If a bad guy got hold of that note, the user would know pretty quickly and could take appropriate steps to reset the password (assuming you have told her how to do that), and what exactly would the bad guy do with the note? Which system does the password belong to? Is it even a password, or is it a shopping list? A password the user can write down is far easier to manage than one she has to memorize after typing twice. Moreover, for all the other passwords we use every day, you can use an electronic password management tool, such as Password Safe (*http://passwordsafe.sourceforge.net*). Which is really worse: a weak password that the user can remember after typing it twice, or a very strong one that is securely recorded? What exact exposures are we worried about here?

Now imagine that you told your users that they could keep the password on a note until they remembered them, and after that they had to put the notes in the secret disposal bin, or eat them, whichever they preferred. If you do that, your users may even let you set the password policy to require 10 characters and live to tell the tale.

Stop Thinking About Words

Notice that in the preceding discussion the imaginary password was "Get a skinny tall latte before work!" That is not a password. It is a *passphrase*. Nothing says that passwords have to be words anymore. The very term—*password*—is wrong. Windows will happily accept up to 127 characters, chosen from the entire keyboard (including the space bar) in a password. Recall also that we concluded earlier in the chapter that the longer the password is the stronger it is. Using a passphrase is the perfect way to add length to your password. Passphrases are long and therefore strong. They are simpler to type and easier to remember than contorted strong passwords, such as hG%'3m.^. Simply put, passphrases just work the way people are used to working already. People are used to thinking about words. I have seen seven-year-old children use passphrases successfully. In addition, a phrase such as the latte one is far, far longer and many orders of magnitude stronger than the contorted strong password. If we assume a worst-case scenario, in which the attacker knows that we use passphrases, knows that this one is seven words long, and even knows the dictionary of words it was composed from, it could still take millions of years to guess—even if the attacker uses an attack tool that permutes words as opposed to characters. The set of possibilities is so many times larger than the set of characters on a keyboard. If you wanted to improve the strength a little, do one of the common substitutions somewhere. For example, replace an "a" with "@", or an "l" with a "1", or an "e" with a "3", or an "o" with a "0". In our eight-character password we'll be lucky to get one of those substitutions, merely doubling the possibilities. In the case of the passphrase, we get 12 possible substitutions just with those 4 substitution options, increasing the total search space 4,096 times! Passphrases are immensely powerful as an authenticator.

Set Password Policies

Finally, you should of course have password policies. You need both written organizational policies and technically enforced policies. The written policies are beyond the scope of this book, but should include policies that are realistic—in other words, *don't ban writing passwords down.* You should also have an implementation guideline that helps people understand how to pick passwords.

Technical policies should be enforced domain-wide, and also on member computers if you use local accounts on member computers. They should require complexity, long passwords (10 or more characters are highly preferable, accounting for the fact that it will take you some time to get people to pick good passwords) and should cycle the passwords regularly. However, tie the policies together logically. If you require 10-character passwords, it is almost certainly acceptable to keep them for 6 months or a year. With eight characters you should change them every 3–6 months. With anything fewer than eight characters, you should consider changing passwords monthly.

Policies can be managed with Group Policy (GP). Figure 2-14 shows where in GP the settings are.

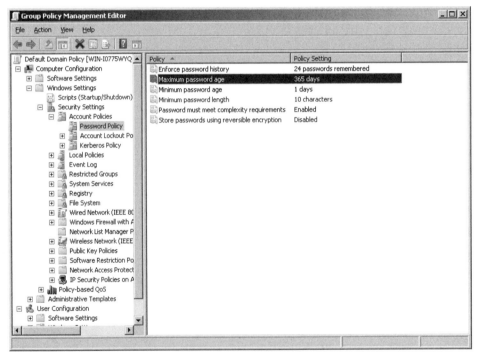

Figure 2-14   Password policies can be managed with Group Policy.

Password policies applied with domain scope apply to domain accounts. Password policies applied to an organizational unit scope apply to local accounts on all member computers in that OU.

Fine-Grained Password Policies

A persistent request from customers has been the ability to manage password policies so that different users in the domain have different password policies. In Windows Server 2008 this is finally possible, with *fine-grained password policies*. Fine-grained password policies are available in all editions of Windows Server 2008, but only if the domain functional level is set to Windows Server 2008. In other words, you must first upgrade all your domain controllers to Windows Server 2008 before you can use this feature.

The primary purpose of fine-grained password policies is to apply stricter settings to privileged accounts and less strict settings to the accounts belonging to normal users. In other cases you might want to apply a special password policy for accounts whose passwords are synchronized with other data sources.

Fine-grained password policies apply only to user objects, or *inetOrgPerson* objects if you use those instead of user objects, and global security groups. Fine-grained password policies are implemented using a password settings container (PSC) under the System container of the domain. (See Chapter 9, "Designing Active Directory Domain Services for Security," for more details on Active Directory.) The PSC stores one or more password settings objects (PSO) that hold the actual policies. Figure 2-15 shows a PSC with two PSOs.

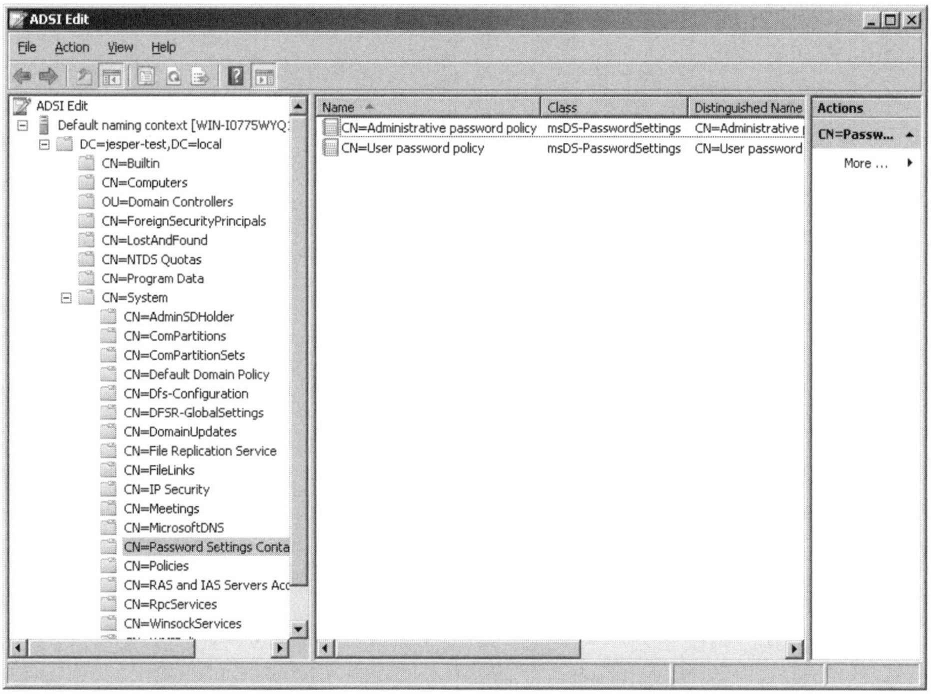

Figure 2-15   This domain uses one password policy for administrators and another for users.

Unfortunately, Microsoft did not provide a very good user experience for managing fine-grained password policies in Windows Server 2008. To configure a separate password policy for administrators, follow these steps:

1. Run the ADSI Edit tool by typing **adsiedit.msc**.

2. Connect to your domain by right-clicking the ADSI Edit node in the left-hand pane and selecting Connect To. Type in the name of the domain.

3. Expand the domain, expand the DC node, navigate down to CN=System, and select CN=Password Settings Container.

4. Right-click CN=Password Settings Container, select New, and then select Object.

5. Select the *msDS-Password Settings* object, as shown in Figure 2-16.

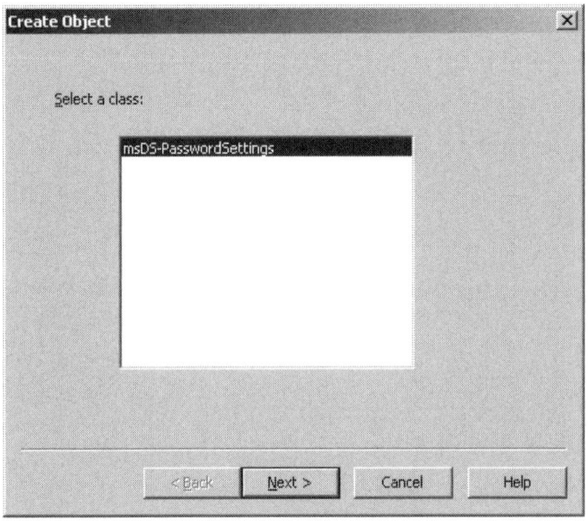

Figure 2-16   To create a fine-grained password policy, you need to create a new *msDS-PasswordSettings* object.

6. Name the new object something memorable, such as **Administrative password policy**.

7. Click Next, and set the precedence value for this object. This value governs which policy takes precedence if two policies apply to the same user. The lowest precedence wins.

8. Walk through the rest of the wizard and set values for all the items. The possible values are listed in Table 2-5.

9. After you configure the lockout duration you will see the screen shown in Figure 2-17. At this point you need to configure which users this PSO applies to. To start that process, click More Attributes.

10. From the Select A Property To View drop-down list, select *msDS-PSOAppliesTo*.

11. Type in the distinguished name (DN) of the user or the global security group you want this policy to apply to. For example, to apply it to the Domain Admins group, use the following syntax, replacing the DC attributes with your domain information:

CN=Domain Admins,CN=Users,DC=jesper-test,DC=local The net result is shown in Figure 2-18.

Table 2-5   Fine-Grained Password Policy Values

Attribute Name	Description	Acceptable Value Range
msDS-PasswordSettingsPrecedence	Defines which policy takes precedence if more than one policy applies to a given user. The policy with the lowest precedence wins.	Greater than 0
msDS-PasswordReversibleEncryptionEnabled	Whether passwords are stored with reversible encryption. False means they are not.	FALSE / TRUE
msDS-PasswordHistoryLength	How many passwords the system remembers for a user. Practically speaking, this means the user cannot reuse a password until he has chosen at least this many different ones.	0 through 1024
msDS-PasswordComplexityEnabled	False if password complexity is not required for these user accounts. True if password complexity is required.	FALSE / TRUE
msDS-MinimumPasswordLength	The minimum length for a password. Note that passwords can be up to 255 characters long, but older systems support entering only 127-character passwords.	0 through 255
msDS-MinimumPasswordAge	The minimum age that a password must be before it can be changed again. Setting this to some reasonable value, such as a day or two, ensures that a user cannot cycle through the password history automatically and change the password back to the one that she just had. This value (and all other time values), is entered in DAYS:HOURS:MINUTES:SECONDS format. Hence 02:00:00:00 is two days.	(None) 00:00:00:00 through msDS-Maximum PasswordAge value
msDS-MaximumPasswordAge	How old a password can be before it must be changed. To have passwords that never expire, use the value (Never). Otherwise, set a date in the standard time value format, such as 180:00:00:00.	(Never) msDS-Minimum PasswordAge value through (Never) msDS-Maximum PasswordAge cannot be set to zero

Table 2-5   Fine-Grained Password Policy Values

Attribute Name	Description	Acceptable Value Range
msDS-LockoutThreshold	How many tries a user gets at the password before it is locked out. To disable account lockout, set this to 0.	0 through 65535
msDS-LockoutObservationWindow	The time interval used to calculate the number of incorrect password tries. If this value is set to 00:00:30:00, for example, the user gets *msDS-LockoutThreshold* tries in 30 minutes and then the counter is reset.	(None) 00:00:00:01 through *msDS-LockoutDuration* value
msDS-LockoutDuration	How long the account remains locked out before it is automatically unlocked. To require administrative unlock set it to (*Never*).	(None) (Never) *msDS-Lockout ObservationWindow* value through (Never)

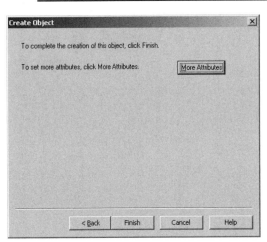

Figure 2-17   When you get to this screen, configure who the object applies to.

Tools to Manage Fine-Grained Password Policies

By now you have probably already figured out that Microsoft kind of ran out of time to build good tools to manage fine-grained password polices. Fortunately, there are some options out there. Joeware.net has a command-line tool available at: *http://www.joeware.net/freetools/tools/psomgr/index.htm*

A GUI tool is available for PowerGUI, based on the Windows PowerShell feature of Windows Server 2008:

http://powergui.org/entry.jspa?externalID=882&categoryID=46

Another free GUI tool is available from Special Operations Software:

http://www.specopssoft.com/wiki/index.php/SpecopsPasswordPolicybasic/
SpecopsPasswordPolicybasic/

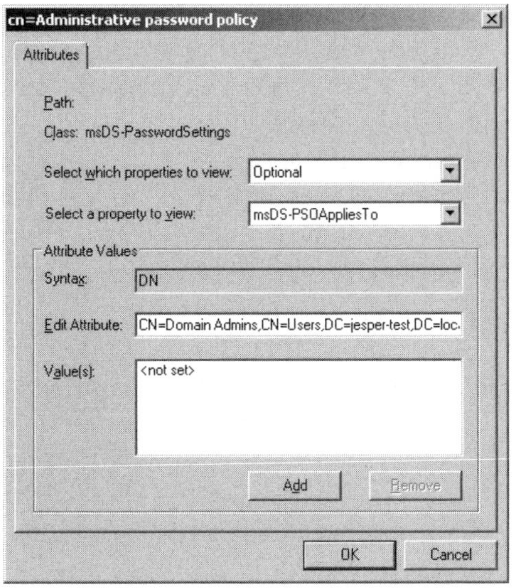

Figure 2-18   You use the *msDS-PSOAppliesTo* attribute to apply the policy to a group or a user.

Precedence and Fine-Grained Password Policies

I mentioned earlier that a precedence value is associated with fine-grained password policies. This value is for resolving conflicts when two PSOs apply to a single user. The DC does not merge policies, so there must be some way to resolve the conflict. The resolution works as follows:

1. If only one PSO is linked to the user object, that PSO is the resultant PSO. If more than one PSO is linked to the user object, a warning message is logged to the event log and the one with the lowest precedence value is the resultant PSO.

2. If no PSOs are linked to the user object, the system compares the precedence values of all the PSOs linked to groups the user is a member of. The PSO with the lowest precedence value is the resultant PSO.

3. If neither of these methods results in a PSO being the most preferred, the default domain policy applies.

Summary

Passwords and authentication is a complicated and very interesting area. It underlies so much of what we do in all other areas of security. While you do not have to be an expert on authentication to manage Windows servers, you must have enough of an understanding of the basic concepts to make intelligent decisions about authentication. If you have ever dealt with consultants or auditors you have probably run into one of the few, but far too many, who do not understand passwords and authentication, but yet make requirements regarding how they should be managed. More than one network has been either destroyed directly by these changes, or hacked afterward because the changes were ineffective against the relevant attacks. Only by understanding enough about how authentication works can you make reasoned decisions about how to protect the keys to the kingdom—the authenticators used to access your network.

Additional Resources

- Burnett, M. *Perfect Passwords: Selection, Protection, Authentication.* (Syngress, 2005).

- Johansson, J. M. *Protect Your Windows Network.* (Addison-Wesley, 2005).

- Johansson, J. M. "The Most Misunderstood Security Setting of All Time." *TechNet Magazine.*

- Kent, J. "Malaysia Car Thieves Steal Finger," at *http://news.bbc.co.uk/2/hi/asia-pacific/4396831.stm.*

- Microsoft Corporation. "Server Core Installation Option of Windows Server 2008 Step-by-Step Guide," at *http://technet2.microsoft.com/windowsserver2008/en/library/47a23a74-e13c-46de-8d30-ad0afb1eaffc1033.mspx?mfr=true.*

- Microsoft Corporation. "Step-by-Step Guide for Fine-Grained Password and Account Lockout Policy Configuration," at *http://go.microsoft.com/fwlink/?LinkID=91477.*

- Wagner, M. "The Password Is: Chocolate," at *http://informationweek.com/story/showArticle.jhtml?articleID=18902123.*

Chapter 3
Objects: The Stuff You Want

— Jesper M. Johansson

I know what you are thinking: We are two chapters into this book and all we have talked about so far is users! People! Who cares about them? Well, I have good news and bad news. The good news is that we are about to start delving into abstract and mysterious technical concepts such as security descriptors. The bad news is that this is all to better serve our people and provide them with secure data access.

Ignoring the people for a while, which I know we would all very much prefer to do, *objects* are what we call the things we want to protect from the users (or provide the user access to—if you have not worked in security as long as I have). In this chapter we will discuss the technologies used to control access to objects. This is one of the more technical chapters in the book. I believe it is important for an administrator to understand the core details of how these technologies work to be able to effectively manage Windows. We will discuss tools for managing objects and how access control has changed in Windows Server 2008—and a small section on Role-Based Access Control appears at the end. Before we get to those, however, I need to make sure the terminology is clear.

Access Control Terminology

If you have not worked with fundamental Windows security constructs before, you have a lot of alien terms to learn. Even if you have worked with security infrastructure in other operating systems, some unique terminology is used in Windows. This section will define the major concepts used in access control in Windows.

Securable Objects

The basic unit of security management in Windows is a *securable object*. A securable object is simply some type of object that can have permissions applied to it. The securable object you probably have worked with the most is a file. In the NTFS file system, files and directories both can have permissions associated with them. As a practical matter, the permissions are actually stored in the file system metadata, not with the file itself—but that is a technical detail that really does not matter to a system administrator. The different types of securable objects include:

- Files
- Directories
- Registry keys
- Active Directory objects
- Kernel objects (events, semaphores, mutexes)
- Services
- Threads
- Processes
- Firewall Ports (new with Windows Vista and Windows Server 2008)
- Window stations and desktops

Security Descriptors

All securable objects have one thing in common: they have a *security descriptor* (SD) associated with them. The SD is the construct that contains all the security information associated with the object. A security descriptor is not a particularly complicated construct. Figure 3-1 shows it in pictorial form.

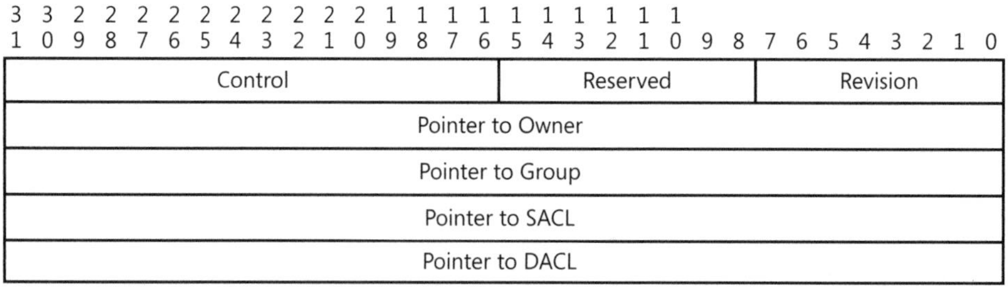

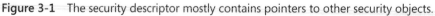

3 3 2 2 2 2 2 2 2 2 2 2 1 1 1 1 1 1 1 1 1 1		
1 0 9 8 7 6 5 4 3 2 1 0 9 8 7 6 5 4 3 2 1 0 9 8 7 6 5 4 3 2 1 0		
Control	Reserved	Revision
Pointer to Owner		
Pointer to Group		
Pointer to SACL		
Pointer to DACL		

Figure 3-1   The security descriptor mostly contains pointers to other security objects.

The security descriptor can be viewed as a table containing five rows of 32 bits each. The top row in Figure 3-1, as with subsequent figures, shows the bit position of each element. Notice that it seems to count backward. This stems from the endianness of the Intel processors that Windows runs on. For more information see the sidebar "Why Does Windows Count Backwards?"

Why Does Windows Count Backwards?

Figure 3-1 and subsequent pictures that show tabular bit structures have a row at the top with numbers that go in what appears to be reverse order. Those are the bit positions for the objects in structure. For example, the revision of an SD is 8 bits, contained in bits 0–7 of an SD. The pointer to the owner starts at bit position 32, and so on.

The columns appear to go backward because Windows is what is called a *little-endian* operating system. All memory structures are stored in such a way that the bits are counted from right to left. This is actually an artifact of the processor architecture and, in the case of Windows, the endianness is driven by the x86 architecture that was until recently the predominant architecture on Windows. The x64 architecture also uses little-endian.

Endianness has led to significant religious debates among those who like to debate such things. Both methods have advantages, and in reality you rarely need to deal with this issue unless you are a developer.

The final four rows in the SD are all pointers to something else. The second row in Figure 3-1 is a pointer to a Security Identifier (SID) representing the owner of the object. The third row is a pointer to a SID representing the primary group of the owner. The primary group concept is used only for POSIX compliance, not for native Windows operations. In POSIX, permissions are granted to only three entities: the owner, the owner's group, and world (Everyone). To have a group to grant permission to, Windows includes a concept of a primary group, and this is where it shows up in an SD. The final two rows have pointers to the system access control list (SACL) and discretionary access control list (DACL), respectively.

The first row contains a version number that currently is always 1, 8 reserved bits, and a control field. The control field contains a number of flags that describe the nature of the security descriptor. The field can take on a combination of different values, most of which are shown in Table 3-1, which also shows the Security Descriptor Definition Language (SDDL) flag for the value, if one is available. That flag's use will be explained in greater detail later in this chapter. For the moment, you may ignore it.

Table 3-1   Security Descriptor Control Flags

Flag Name	SDDL Flag	Flag Value	Description
SE_OWNER_DEFAULTED		0x0001	The Security identifier (SID) pointed to by the Owner field was provided by a defaulting mechanism.
SE_GROUP_DEFAULTED		0x0002	The SID pointed to by the Group field was provided by a defaulting mechanism.
SE_DACL_PRESENT		0x0004	This SD points to a DACL. If this flag is not set, this SD has a NULL DACL.

Table 3-1   **Security Descriptor Control Flags**

Flag Name	SDDL Flag	Flag Value	Description
SE_DACL_DEFAULTED		0x0008	The DACL was set by some defaulting mechanism as opposed to explicitly. This is common for system objects, but not for things like file system objects, registry keys, and so on.
SE_SACL_PRESENT		0x0010	This SD has a pointer to a SACL.
SE_SACL_DEFAULTED		0x0020	The SACL was set by some defaulting mechanism.
SE_DACL_AUTO_INHERIT_REQ	AR	0x0100	The DACL must be inherited by child objects. If this flag is set on a directory, for example, the DACL is inherited by subdirectories and files. This flag specifies an old inheritance mechanism used primarily in Windows NT 4.0 and earlier. The flag is ignored by most utilities today. Newer versions of Windows suppport inheritance of individual entries in the ACL.
SE_SACL_AUTO_INHERIT_REQ		0x0200	The SACL must be inherited by child objects. As with the equivalent DACL flag, this mechanism is no longer used.
SE_DACL_AUTO_INHERITED	AI	0x0400	The DACL was inherited from a parent object, such as a directory.
SE_SACL_AUTO_INHERITED		0x0800	The SACL was inherited from a parent object.
SE_DACL_PROTECTED	P	0x1000	The DACL is protected from inheritance. This means that a parent's DACL will not override the child's DACL.
SE_SACL_PROTECTED		0x2000	The SACL is protected.

Access Control List

The fourth pointer in the security descriptor points to a discretionary access control list (DACL). A DACL is one of three different types of access control lists (ACLs), of which Windows supports two.

The three types of ACLs are used for different purposes. An ACL is typically used to record permissions on an object. Discretionary and mandatory access control lists (MACLs) serve that purpose.

A DACL is what we normally mean when we discuss ACLs in Windows. A DACL is discretionary because it can be managed by the administrator or object owner. The administrator can, for example, grant some other user permission to write to an object, and the system enforcing the permissions will honor that request. When the administrator believes that the other user no longer needs access to the object, she can modify the permissions. The system's only responsibility is to enforce the permissions set by the administrator or the owner, or any other user with permission to change permissions. The permissions, meanwhile, are at the discretion of some user.

A MACL, on the other hand, is not managed by any given user. All data receives a label specifying its sensitivity. Based on that sensitivity, the system will enforce access control over the object. The big difference here is that the actual operations any given user is permitted to take on the object are *not* at the discretion of any user in the system. The permissions are entirely enforced by the system. This is what makes the ACL mandatory. If you have taken the CISSP exam, or studied theoretical security models, you will probably have heard about the Bell-LaPadula model of security. That model describes a mandatory access control (MAC) system. Windows does not support MACLs.

Finally, there are system ACLs (SACLs). SACLs are identical to DACLs in structure. However, where DACLs control who can do what with the object, SACLs control which access attempts get audited. For example, let us say we have an ACL that applies write access for Administrators. If that ACL is a DACL, it grants Administrators permission to write to the object. If that ACL is a SACL, it causes an audit event to be generated upon any attempt to write to the object by any member of Administrators. More information on SACLs and auditing is available in Chapter 8, "Auditing."

ACL Structure

Like a security descriptor, an ACL has a structure that can be visualized in tabular form, the header of which is shown in Figure 3-2. However, unlike a security descriptor, where the variable-sized contents—such as the DACL and SACL—are defined as pointers, giving the security descriptor itself a fixed size, this structure does not fit an ACL because it can be of almost arbitrary length.

3 3 2 2 2 2 2 2 2 2 2 2 1 1 1 1 1 1 1 1 1 1		
1 0 9 8 7 6 5 4 3 2 1 0 9 8 7 6 5 4 3 2 1 0 9 8 7 6 5 4 3 2 1 0		
ACL Size	Reserved 1	ACL Revision
Reserved 2	ACE Count	

Figure 3-2   The ACL header holds metadata of the ACL.

The first portion of an ACL, reading left to right as at least Westerners are used to, is a 16-bit value holding the size of the ACL in bytes. This means that an ACL can be up to 64 kilobytes (KB). Apart from the revision, the only other interesting aspect is the ACL Entry (ACE) count. The ACEs are attached to the ACL but are usually thought of as a separate structure.

Access Control List Entry

The ACE is essentially where the rubber meets the road in access control. The ACE defines the subject and what permissions that subject has to the object. The ACE structure is shown in Figure 3-3.

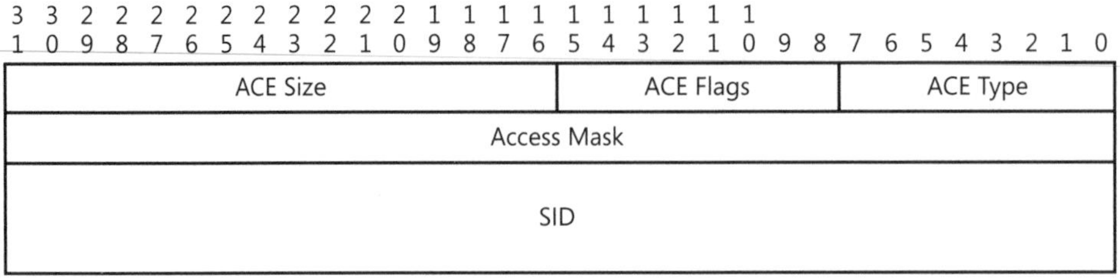

3 3 2 2 2 2 2 2 2 2 2 2 1 1 1 1 1 1 1 1 1 1		
1 0 9 8 7 6 5 4 3 2 1 0 9 8 7 6 5 4 3 2 1 0 9 8 7 6 5 4 3 2 1 0		
ACE Size	ACE Flags	ACE Type
Access Mask		
SID		

Figure 3-3   The ACE is variable-sized because it contains a SID, which is variable-sized.

The first part of an ACE is the size attribute. It also is a 16-bit value, but obviously an ACE cannot be that large because that would make it too large to hold in an ACL. However, the ACE is variable-sized because it contains a SID, which is variable-sized. The SID defines which subject the ACE applies to. The ACE also has a set of 8 flags, as well as 8 bits defining the ACE type. The flags define how the ACE was created or processed. Some of the more interesting flags are shown in Table 3-2, which also shows the Security Descriptor Definition Language (SDDL) shortcuts. These will be discussed in more detail in the section "Security Descriptor Definition Language" later in the chapter.

Table 3-2   Important ACE Flags

Flags	SDDL Shortcut	Interpretation
OBJECT_INHERIT_ACE	OI	This ACE should be inherited by children that are objects.
CONTAINER_INHERIT_ACE	CI	This ACE should be inherited by children that are containers.
NO_PROPAGATE_INHERIT_ACE	NP	This ACE will be inherited by children, but only one level deep. After the ACE is inherited, the system clears the OI and/or CI flags.
INHERIT_ONLY_ACE	IO	This ACE is only inherited. It does not control access to the object where the ACE was originally defined.
INHERITED_ACE	ID	This ACE was inherited from a parent.
SUCCESSFUL_ACCESS_ACE_FLAG	SA	This ACE belongs in a SACL and causes audit events on successful access attempts.
FAILED_ACCESS_ACE_FLAG	FA	This ACE belongs in a SACL and causes audit events on failed access attempts.

As you can tell from Table 3-2, the ACE flags are primarily used to govern the inheritance behavior of the ACE. However, they also are used to define the behavior of an ACE in a SACL.

As mentioned earlier, 8 bits are used for ACE types. Table 3-3 shows the more interesting of the ACE types.

Table 3-3   ACE Types

Type	SDDL Shortcut	Description
ACCESS_ALLOWED_ACE_TYPE	A	The permissions defined in this ACE define the access the subject specified in the SID has to the object. These types of ACEs are commonly referred to as *access allowed ACEs*.
ACCESS_DENIED_ACE_TYPE	D	This ACE is used to deny access to the object. The permissions defined in the ACE will be compared to the access attempt, and if it contains any of them, the access attempt is denied. These types of ACEs are commonly referred to as *access denied ACEs*.
SYSTEM_AUDIT_ACE_TYPE	AU	This ACE belongs in a SACL.
ACCESS_ALLOWED_OBJECT_ACE_TYPE	OA	This ACE type is identical to the A type above, but applies to an Active Directory object as opposed to a file system object.
ACCESS_DENIED_OBJECT_ACE_TYPE	OD	This ACE type is identical to the D type, but applies to an Active Directory object as opposed to a file system object.
SYSTEM_AUDIT_OBJECT_ACE_TYPE	OU	This is an audit ACE in a SACL on an Active Directory object.
SYSTEM_MANDATORY_LABEL_ACE_TYPE		This ACE is not used for either access control or auditing, but instead defines the integrity level of the object the ACE applies to. For more on integrity labels, see "Integrity Labels" later in the chapter.

These flags and types may seem esoteric at this point. However, by the time we get to discussing SDDL later in the chapter, it will become clear that it is important to know what all these types and flags mean to both interpret permissions and to create permissions.

The last part of the ACE that we have not discussed yet is the *access mask*. The access mask actually defines the permissions or audit settings on the object.

Access Masks

An access mask is simply a 32-bit structure. It is divided into three main sections, as shown in Figure 3-4.

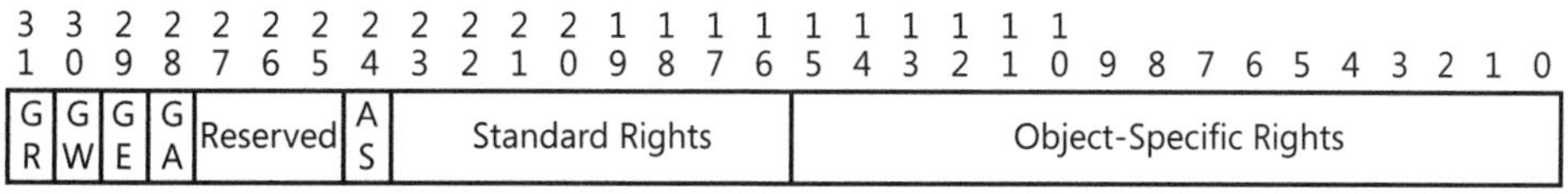

Figure 3-4   An access mask defines the actual permissions using a 32-bit structure.

Each of the bits in the access mask can be either on or off (1 or 0). If a bit is set to 1, the permission it represents is granted. If it is 0, the permission is not granted. If the access mask belongs in an access allowed ACE and permission is not explicitly granted, it is implicitly denied.

The four high-order bits in the access mask define what are known as *generic permissions*. They are essentially collections of permissions that match what you might find in operating systems with simpler access control models. GR means generic read and would, in an access allowed ACE, grant the subject read access to the object, regardless of the object type. This permission can also defined as FR for FILE_GENERIC_READ and KR for KEY_GENERIC_READ, applying generic read permissions to files or registry keys respectively. Likewise, GW is generic write and GX is generic execute. GA is a shortcut for a combination of all three of the others. The exact meaning of these settings differs depending on the object. For example, if you set GX permission on a directory, you just gave the subject the right to traverse through the directory to a subdirectory or file that the subject has access to.

This brings up a very important point about access masks. The actual shortcut name of the permission, such as GR and FR, is only important insofar as it defines which bit in the access mask is turned on. If an access mask is created using FR but applied to a registry key, the permission granted is KEY_GENERIC_READ because bit 31 will be set. This may not sound like a logical thing to do, but when you start investigating permissions in the form of SDDL strings you will very often find file generic permissions applied to registry keys, object permissions applied to files, and so on. It is important to remember that all those permissions define bitmasks. The actual meaning of that bitmask is analyzed according to the object type when the access check happens.

The 8 bits shown for standard rights in Figure 3-4 are used similarly, although only the low-order 5 bits are actually used. The standard rights are:

- DELETE – The ability to delete the object. This permission is defined as 0x10000, or bit 16 in Figure 3-4 set to 1.

- READ_CONTROL – The ability to read the object's security descriptor, excluding the SACL. This permission is defined as 0x20000, or bit 17 in Figure 3-4 set to 1.

- WRITE_DAC – The ability to change permissions on this object (write DACL). This permission is defined as 0x40000, or bit 18 in Figure 3-4 set to 1.

- WRITE_OWNER – The ability to change the owner of an object. This permission is defined as 0x80000, or bit 19 in Figure 3-4 set to 1.

- SYNCHRONIZE – The right to use the object for synchronization. For example, if a process needs to be informed when an object changes state it creates a synchronization handle on the object. It will then be notified when the object changes state. This permission is defined as 0x100000, or bit 20 in Figure 3-4 set to 1.

There are also combinations of the standard rights, but they are primarily of interest to programmers, and you will not see them unless you read developer documentation. Therefore, we will ignore those for the moment.

Finally, we have 16 bits of object-specific rights in the access mask. The object-specific rights allow you to configure permissions that are valid only on some objects. Table 3-4 lists and explains the object-specific rights for file system objects. Note that only 8 of the bits are actually used for file system objects. If you are interested in object-specific rights for other types of objects, please consult the developer documentation on *http://msdn.microsoft.com*. Search for object-specific rights and whatever object type you wish to learn more about.

Table 3-4   File System Object-Specific Rights

Definition	Value	Bit	Description
FILE_READ_DATA	0x1	0	On a directory this grants the right to list the contents of the directory.
FILE_LIST_DIRECTORY	0x1	0	Read permission. On a file this grants the right to read the file.
FILE_WRITE_DATA	0x2	1	File write permission. On a file this right grants permission to write to the file.
FILE_ADD_FILE	0x2	1	This right is used on a directory and permits a grantee to create a file in the directory.
FILE_APPEND_DATA	0x4	2	On a file this permits a user to append data to the file.
FILE_ADD_SUBDIRECTORY	0x4	2	On a directory this permits a grantee to create a new subdirectory.
FILE_READ_EA	0x8	3	On a file this grants permission to read the extended file attributes. Extended file attributes are not normally used on Windows today. They were originally included to provide compatibility with applications written for OS/2.
FILE_WRITE_EA	0x10	4	On a file this grants permission to write extended attributes.
FILE_EXECUTE	0x20	5	Execute permission. On a binary executable, this grants the right to execute the file.
FILE_TRAVERSE	0x20	5	Directory traversal permission. This permission allows the grantee to traverse through a directory that it does not have access to in order to get to a subdirectory that it is granted access to. However, all subjects on Windows have the Bypass Traverse Checking (SeChangeNotify) privilege, which will give them this right regardless of whether the permission is granted.

Table 3-4   File System Object-Specific Rights

Definition	Value	Bit	Description
FILE_DELETE_CHILD	0x40	6	On a directory this permits a grantee to delete the directory and everything it contains.
FILE_READ_ATTRIBUTES	0x80	7	On a file this grants the right to read the normal file attributes.
FILE_WRITE_ATTRIBUTES	0x100	8	On a file this grants the right to write file attributes.

By now you are probably wondering whether you really have to know about all these details to administer Windows. The answer is no, you do not. Many administrators do not know these details and manage to quite successfully make services available to their users. However, if you care to manage permissions you really ought to know how all these structures interrelate. And if you plan on managing permissions on Server Core installations, or interpreting permissions set on directories, you will almost certainly need to know these details. The same is true if you wish to delegate permissions management on any object to a user who is not supposed to be a full administrator.

The definitions in the tables are listed in a particular format—namely, the one used by developers and defined in the Software Development Kit (SDK). Rather than reinventing new definitions, it is reasonable to use those to refer to the various permissions throughout the remainder of this chapter and the rest of the book.

You can of course read the permissions in the graphical user interface ACL editor (known as ACL UI), and then you can see friendly versions of this data. However, that is a very inefficient way to do it, and it does not help you interpret security templates, for instance, nor troubleshoot a permissions dump in SDDL format. To do that, you need to understand how these permissions are formed. You may, for instance, come across a permission such as 0x1200a9. You can probably figure out by now that it represents some combination of the bits in the preceding tables. 0x1200a9 is equivalent to 100100000000010101001. If we paste that into Figure 3-4, we get something like Figure 3-5.

Figure 3-5 demonstrates the process we must use to analyze a permissions grant such as 0x1200a9. That grant consists of several of the bits from the access mask. To know what it means, we must convert that hexadecimal (base 16) value to binary, which you can do with the Windows Calculator if you set it to scientific mode. Then we map it against the access mask, as shown in Figure 3-5. The bits that are set correspond to permissions granted.

Lest you now think this is a contrived example of a DACL that does not exist, Figure 3-6 shows the ACL UI representation of the ACE in question.

As you can tell from Figure 3-6, 0x1200a9 is very much a real permission. It is, in fact, what gives standard users the ability to read files and list directories on an entire volume. In addition, you may notice that the ACL UI in Figure 3-6 is not entirely correct. It is missing the Synchronize permission. You cannot, in fact, grant that permission with the GUI.

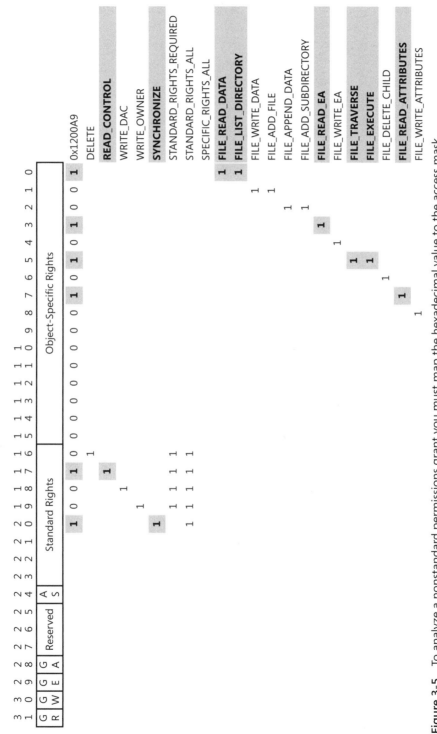

Figure 3-5   To analyze a nonstandard permissions grant you must map the hexadecimal value to the access mask.

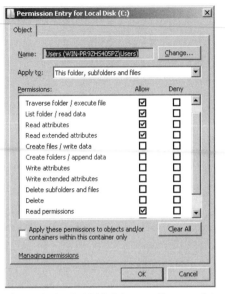

Figure 3-6   0x1200a9 is actually one of the
ACEs on the root of a drive.

Relationship Between Access Control Structures

Before we leave the various access control structures behind and move on with other
terminology in the world of object security, it may be useful to just revisit for a moment the
way the structures relate to each other. Figure 3-7 shows this relationship.

A security descriptor has two pointers to SIDs—the owner and group SIDs. In addition, it has
pointers to the two ACLs. In practice, it is not uncommon for one or more of these pointers to
be set to null (all zeros). In this case, the object is lacking one or more of the structures. We
shall discuss this in more detail later. It is most common with the SACL to have a null pointer
because many objects do not have a SACL. If one of the other pointers is null, some interesting
bugs can occur. For example, even built-in tools can fail spectacularly if the DACL pointer
is null.

Note also in Figure 3-7 that, while it only shows one ACE in each ACL, additional ACEs can be
attached and would just extend the length of the ACL.

Inheritance

ACLs can be inherited from parent objects to child objects. For example, a directory can
contain an ACL that applies to the directory, but also applies to files and subdirectories. These
days, however, it is more correct to say that it is the ACEs that get inherited, not the ACL.

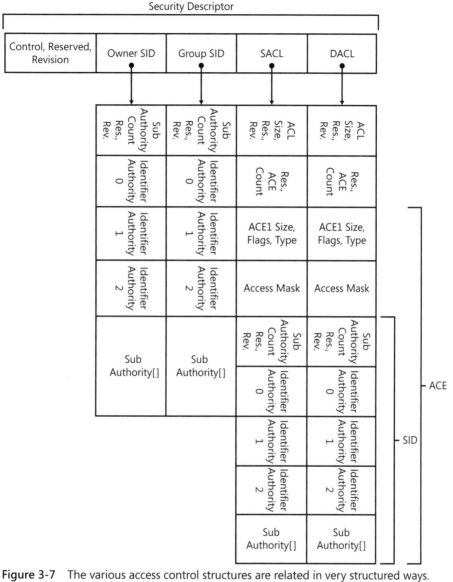

Figure 3-7 The various access control structures are related in very structured ways.

Prior to Windows 2000, it was actually the ACL that got inherited. The security descriptor control flags, such as SE_DACL_AUTO_INHERIT_REQ (often seen in an SDDL string as AR), are a leftover from that period. Since Windows 2000 however, the *AUTO_INHERIT_REQ flags are essentially ignored. Likewise, the AI flag (SE_DACL_AUTO_INHERITED) is essentially ignored. Rather, the inheritance flags are now set on individual ACEs, greatly increasing the expressive power of inheritance, but also complicating matters for the system administrator.

The inheritance flags were shown previously in Table 3-2. These are the flags you would need to know to parse an SDDL string, or if you write software that needs to do this. If you work only in the GUI, you would see them in the form of Figure 3-8 instead.

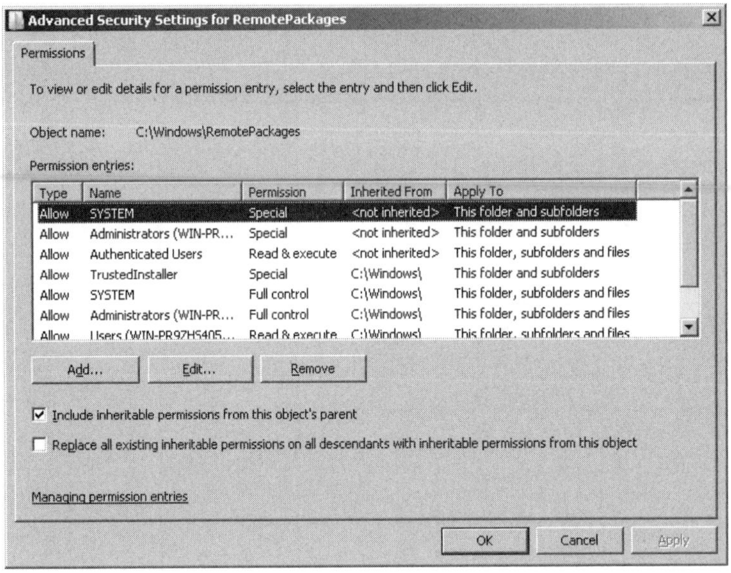

Figure 3-8   ACL UI surfaces the inheritance flags using several mechanisms.

In Figure 3-8 you can see a directory that has both inherited ACEs and noninherited ones. The Inherited From column shows where they came from. The Apply To column shows how they are propagated further. The first ACE, for SYSTEM, is apparently only for folders. There is a Full Control ACE for SYSTEM that is also inherited further. This apparent redundancy is quite common in ACLs.

In addition, you see two check boxes at the bottom of Figure 3-8. Those can be thought of as dynamic representations of ACL flags from Table 3-1. Include Inheritable Permissions From This Object's Parent causes all inheritable permissions to be propagated to this object. If this flag is not checked, it is equivalent to setting the P flag in the security descriptor. The second check box, Replace All Existing Inheritable Permissions, does not represent any flag. It simply causes permissions to be re-inherited. Some tools interpret use of the AI flag from Table 3-1 the same way, notably the Security Configuration Editor (SCE). Therefore, if you need to use Group Policy to trigger inheritance propagation on some object or container, you can use the AI flag, with no other ACEs specified in a security template.

Figure 3-9 shows another way ACL UI surfaces the inheritance behavior.

The inheritance behavior of the ACE is set at creation time. The drop-down menu for Apply To in Figure 3-9 represents combinations of the inheritance flags we have seen before, as shown in Table 3-5.

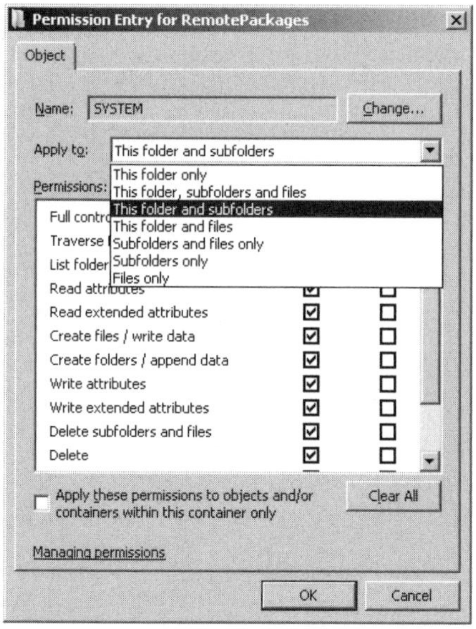

Figure 3-9   When you create or modify an ACE you get to pick its inheritance behavior.

Table 3-5   ACL UI Inheritance to Flag Mapping

ACL UI Term	Flags
This folder only	<none>
This folder, subfolders, and files	OI CI (object inherit, container inherit)
This folder and subfolders	CI
This folder and files	OI
Subfolder and files only	OI CI IO (inherit only)
Subfolders only	CI IO
Files only	OI IO
Apply these permissions to objects and/or containers within this container only	NP (no propagation inherit ACE)

Inheritance takes some getting used to, but once you understand the major concepts it becomes quite clear and the major complication is understanding how it impacts large hierarchies. You need to know the following main concepts:

- Container inheritance causes ACEs to be inherited by containers, while object inheritance causes ACEs to be inherited by objects. You also need to understand what the definition of a container and an object is for a particular object type.

- A protected ACL overrides all inheritance from its parents.

- An inherit-only ACE is not used to control access on the container where it is defined.

- A no-propagation ACE applies only to the container where it is defined.

Next, however, to truly appreciate inheritance, you need to understand how the actual ACEs are evaluated in an access check, so we now turn to that. To start out we need to understand the concept of a security token.

Security Tokens

When a user logs on to a Windows computer, the operating system creates a *token* for the user. This token contains a statement of who the user—the subject—is, what groups it is a member of, and what privileges it has. In some cases, under User Account Control (UAC), the operating system actually creates two tokens for the subject. You can read more about that in Chapter 4, "Understanding UAC."

You can view the tokens using Microsoft's Process Explorer tool, which is available at *http://www.microsoft.com/technet/sysinternals/ProcessesAndThreads/ProcessExplorer.mspx*. Figure 3-10 shows the filtered standard user token for an administrator under UAC. Figure 3-11 shows the full administrative token for the same user.

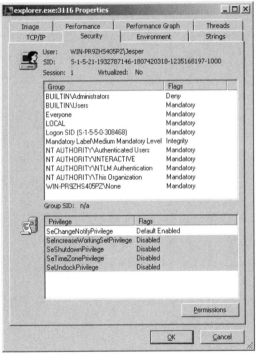

Figure 3-10   A filtered token has almost all the privileges removed and has the Administrators group set to Deny.

Figures 3-10 and 3-11 demonstrate several important points. First, notice that in the filtered token the Administrators SID is set to Deny. This means that it can only ever be used to deny access to something. In other words, if an ACL contains an allow ACE for Administrators, the filtered token would not match. Only if the ACE were a deny ACE would there be a match.

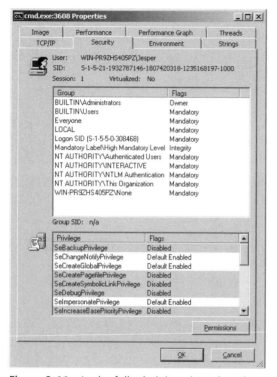

Figure 3-11 In the full administrative token the user's full complement of privileges is listed.

Second, notice that many of the privileges in both tokens are disabled. This does not mean the user cannot use those privileges. All it means is that a process that needs them needs to first enable them, which can be as simple as a single function call. Disabling the privileges serves to protect the user only from accidental privilege use. It provides no security benefit.

Third, notice the sheer number of SIDs in the token. Although you may only see two groups when you inspect the user's group membership (Users and Administrators in this case), a lot of other SIDs indicate how the user logged on, among other things. All subjects, except anonymous users, have the Everyone SID in their token by default. All subjects who authenticated—in other words, not anonymous users or guests—also have the Authenticated Users SID in their token. This means that because the Guest account is disabled by default, Everyone and Authenticated Users are functionally equivalent. This has been the case since Windows Server 2003 and Windows XP.

The tokens in Figures 3-10 and 3-11 also have several SIDs denoting the log-on type. First, there is the LOCAL SID, which means the user logged on to a terminal physically connected to the computer. We also see the Logon SID, which is an identifier for the log-on session assigned to this user. Most of the windows in a user's session are protected to the Logon SID. Then we have the INTERACTIVE SID, which states that this user is logged on interactively to the computer, as opposed to over the network. The difference between this SID and the LOCAL SID is that terminal server users have the INTERACTIVE SID but not the LOCAL SID.

There is also a SID, NTLM Authentication, which defines that the user logged on using NTLM, as opposed to Kerberos. We also have the This Organization SID, which means the user is defined in the same organization as the computer account. Obviously this SID will always be present on a stand-alone computer. Finally, we see the None SID. This is not actually a SID that is being used. Its Relative Identifier (RID) is 513, which makes it Domain Users. It shows up on non-domain-joined computers (as in this example) as a kind of place holder for the Domain Users SID.

Access Check Process

When a process attempts to access a securable object, the operating system compares the access token to first the DACL and then (if it is present) the SACL on the object. The comparison with the DACL focuses on three factors:

- The requested access (for example, read, write, execute, delete)
- The SIDs in the token
- The ACEs in the object's DACL

The comparison process starts by evaluating any SIDs set to Deny in the token. If any of those match a SID in a deny ACE, the operating system compares the requested access to the access mask in the ACE. If any bits show up as set to 1 in both, the access attempt is denied at that point with no further comparison.

If there are no matches on Deny SIDs, the process continues by evaluating each ACE in turn. Three possible stopping conditions will cause the evaluation to cease. First, the evaluation stops as soon as any ACE or combination of ACEs grants any combination of SIDs in the token all the requested access. If this happens, the access is granted.

Second, if any deny ACE is encountered that denies any SID in the token any of the requested access rights, the evaluation stops and the access attempt is denied.

Finally, if the end of the ACL is encountered, the evaluation stops. If it reaches this point without having all the requested access rights granted by some ACE, the access attempt is denied.

Regardless of how the access check turns out, the operating system then evaluates the SACL, if present, to see if an audit even should be generated.

As you can probably tell from what we just said about the access check, the order in which the ACEs are evaluated is critical. If you have a deny ACE that denies the user access to the object, but an ACE matching some SID in the user's token grants all the requested access rights is encountered first, the evaluation will stop and the access attempt is granted. For this reason ACEs should be stored in an ACL in a defined order:

1. Noninherited deny ACEs
2. Noninherited allow ACEs

3. Inherited deny ACEs

4. Inherited allow ACEs

Various tools, such as ACL UI, will correctly put the ACEs in this order. They will also fix an out-of-order ACL when they open it. In addition, the icacls.exe command-line tool contains a /verify option that you can use to verify that ACLs are in the right canonical form. However, the operating system contains no automatic enforcement of this order, and it is disturbingly common for developers to create ACLs that have ACEs in the wrong order. This can cause access attempts that should be denied to be granted.

You should also note that if explicitly defined allow ACEs grant a user access, those will take precedence over inherited deny ACEs. This has caused confusion among administrators in the past.

Restricted Tokens

The standard access check can be modified in a few ways. One is if the user has a privilege that permits overriding the access check. For example, a user with the right to back up files can bypass any ACL for read purposes, while a user with the right to restore files can bypass any ACL for write purposes. Another method, which is used quite a bit more in Windows Vista and Server 2008 than in the past, is using restricted tokens.

A *restricted token* is created using the CreateRestrictedToken application programming interface (API). If a process presents an access token that is restricted, the operating system performs two separate access checks. The first access check is the normal one and ensures that the ACL on the object grants all the access methods requested to some combination of the SIDs in the token. The second access check works exactly the same way, but checks the ACL only against the restricting SIDs. To understand how this works, assume an access token has Administrators as a regular SID, and Users as a restricted SID. Further, assume we have an object that grants Administrators: Full and Users: Read. If a process with such a token tries to open the object for Read and Execute, the access attempt will fail because the access check must pass against the restricting SID—the Users SID. In this case, Users only has Read, and the access attempt was for Read and Execute.

Restricted tokens include a special SID: S-1-5-12 if it is a normal restricted token and S-1-5-33 if it is a write-restricted token, as shown in Figure 3-12. Normal restricted tokens have been around for a long time. In Windows Vista and Windows Server 2008, a new variant called the *write-restricted token* was introduced. With a write-restricted access token, the second access check is performed only for write access checks. Let us assume that the token in our previous example was write-restricted, not just restricted. In that case the access would still pass, because the second access check would not be performed (the access attempt was not for a write operation). Now assume the access attempt was for Read and Write instead. In that case a write-restricted access token would cause the access attempt to fail because now the second access check fails because Users is write-restricted, and Users only have Read permission on the object.

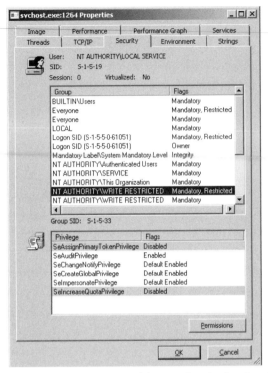

Figure 3-12   A process with a restricted token is subject to a modified access check.

Write-restricted tokens are primarily used with services, as well as when you select the Protect My Computer And Data From Unauthorized Program Activity check box when using Run As on earlier versions of Windows. In Windows Vista and Windows Server 2008, however, a few services, such as the Svchost.exe process that hosts the firewall-related services and the base filtering engine, have write-restricted tokens. Such a token will include the write-restricted SID, S-1-5-33 (NT AUTHORITY\WRITE RESTRICTED). The actual restricting SIDs are the service SID or SIDs (in the case of an Svchost.exe process where all service SIDs would be write-restricted), the log-on session SID, and the Everyone SID. In other words, a write-restricted service can only write to objects that Everyone can write to, or that were explicitly made available for it to write to.

Integrity Labels

You probably noticed the *integrity label* in Figures 3-10, 3-11, and 3-12. Every process now has a label that defines its integrity level. Integrity labeling is typically a component of mandatory access control. However, it defines the integrity associated with the process. A process at a particular integrity level can write to objects at its own integrity level or lower, and read objects at its own integrity level or higher.

Table 3-6 shows the integrity labels available in Windows Server 2008 (and Windows Vista). Most objects in the operating system are set to medium integrity by default. A standard user token is also set to medium integrity. Therefore, there is no difference in most functionality from prior versions of Windows. However, Internet Explorer in Protected mode runs with a low integrity label. This means that Internet Explorer cannot write to most parts of the operating system by default. *Note that this security benefit is lost if UAC is disabled!*

Table 3-6   Integrity Labels in Windows Server 2008

Integrity Level SID	Name
S-1-16-0	Untrusted process. Used for anonymous processes in some configurations.
S-1-16-4096	Mandatory Label\Low Mandatory Level. This level is used for Internet Explorer in Protected mode by default.
S-1-16-8192	Mandatory Label\Medium Mandatory Level. This is the default for standard users and the limited token for administrators in Admin Approval mode.
S-1-16-12288	Mandatory Label\High Mandatory Level. This is used for the full token for administrators in Admin Approval mode.
S-1-16-16384	Mandatory Label\System Mandatory Level. This is used for system processes and services.
S-1-16-20480	Protected process. Used for certain protected processes, such as Digital Rights Management processes.

The integrity labels are stored as an ACE for the SID shown in Table 3-6 in the SACL on the object. This means that to modify the labels the user has to have permission to modify the SACL. The owner and administrators can do this.

Empty and NULL DACLs

As mentioned earlier, if a process does not have a DACL, it is said to have a NULL DACL. A NULL DACL is a very important construct in that it means no access control has been defined on the object. Consequently, it is equivalent to allowing every subject full control over the object.

Typically, NULL DACLs are a result of programmer error. For example, the updater program for some Microsoft games was broken and would create files with a NULL DACL. NULL DACLs also were quite common on system objects in the Windows NT 4.0 time frame before the behavior was changed for those objects to apply a default DACL at create time.

An empty DACL is not the same as a NULL DACL. In the latter case, the object has no access control defined. In the former, with an empty DACL, it does have access control defined, but nobody has been granted access to the object. Consequently, it is equivalent to saying that nobody gets to access the object in any way. Fortunately, the owner of the object can typically override the permissions and change them.

Security Descriptor Definition Language

Earlier in the chapter we referred to SDDL, the security descriptor definition language. SDDL was originally conceived as a way for developers to create permissions in string format. It ended up also being used in many tools, notably command-line tools and the Security

Configuration Editor, which is used in Group Policy to set permissions. Therefore, it is reasonable to expect that a system administrator on Windows is familiar with the language.

SDDL maps very closely to the format of a security descriptor. It has the following format:

- Owner SID

- Group SID

- DACL flags and all DACL ACEs in string format

- SACL flags and all SACL ACEs in string format

It is also not uncommon to see a shortened version that does not include the owner and group SIDs. This is the case with the SDDL strings produced by the cacls and icacls command-line tools. To see the entire SDDL string you need a tool such as subinacl, which is available for download from *http://download.microsoft.com*. Figure 3-13 shows the SDDL string that defines the permissions on the root of the C: drive.

Figure 3-13   The complete SDDL string on any object can be displayed using the subinacl tool.

Figure 3-13 shows that the owner is a SID: S-1-5-80-956008885-3418522649-1831038044-1853292631-2271478464. This is the SID for the TrustedInstaller service, Windows Modules Installer. It owns all operating system–related objects in the file system. TrustedInstaller is also configured as the primary group on these objects.

You may also see the SDDL string in Figure 3-13, shown as O:TIG:TI. TI is a shortcut name for TrustedInstaller, the entity represented by the SID in Figure 3-13. Because that version is a little easier to read, we will analyze that. Notice that it contains two tokens: O:TI and G:TI. The parameters are concatenated without any spacing, making the SDDL string somewhat complicated to read. This is bound to cause confusion, so to parse these strings you need to remember that O: prefixes the owner and G: prefixes the group.

Also notice the start of the DACL in Figure 3-13, which begins with "D:PARAI". The "D:" is the prefix for DACL, even though it appears connected with the TI SID. "P" means the DACL is protected against inherited ACEs from parent objects (even though there are no parent objects here). "AR" is the old-style inheritance required flag, which is no longer used but very often present in a security descriptor. And "AI" means the DACL was inherited. Because it obviously was not, it must have been written programmatically to have these flags all set. You should never see all of those set, particularly not P in conjunction with AI, unless the ACL has been manually modified.

The remainder of the security descriptor is far easier to read if we reformat it. It may be instructive to go through and analyze it.

Interpreting an SDDL String

Broken out into its components, the DACL on the root of the C: drive is:

1. (A;OICI;FA;;;SY)
2. (A;OICI;FA;;;BA)
3. (A;OICI;0x1200a9;;;BU)
4. (A;CI;LC;;;BU)
5. (A;CIIO;DC;;;BU)
6. (A;OICIIO;GA;;;CO)

The first ACE applies to LocalSystem (SY). It is an object inherit and container inherit ACE granting full control (FA).

ACE number two is identical to the first but applies to the built-in Administrators group (BA).

ACE three is the first of three user ACEs. We analyzed that one earlier and concluded that it amounted to read and execute plus READ_CONTROL and SYNCHRONIZE.

ACE four is another user ACE. It is inherited by folders (CI) but uses an unknown permissions specification: LC. LC is actually a shortcut used on Active Directory that means List Children. This much we can tell from the ACE Strings explanation at *http://msdn2.microsoft.com/en-us/library/aa374928.aspx*. However, to understand what permissions are granted by it when used on a file we need to convert it to a bitmask. To do that we need to know what the constant ADS_RIGHT_ACTRL_DS_LIST that LC is a shortcut for represents. For that we turn to the ADS_RIGHTS_ENUM enumeration at *http://msdn2.microsoft.com/en-us/library/aa772285.aspx*. It tells us that ADS_RIGHT_ACTRL_DS_LIST means 0x4. 0x4 corresponds to bit 3 in Figure 3-5. That bit, when set on a directory as we have here, gives the subject the right to create a subdirectory.

SDDL shows directory-specific shortcuts when you view permissions on a file because the engine that generates the SDDL does not understand the object types. It simply reads the access mask and matches that as best as it can to an enumeration of permissions. The directory-specific permissions simply happen to show up first and therefore are what you see.

The same happened in ACE five. There we see DC, which is short for ADS_RIGHT_DS _DELETE_CHILD. It means 0x2, or bit 2 being set. On an Active Directory object, that would give you the right to delete a child object. On a directory, however, bit 2 gives you the right to create a file in the directory. Taken together, these two ACEs give users the right to create new subdirectories and to create files in subdirectories.

Finally, we have an ACE for the creator/owner (CO). This is another inherit-only ACE which applies to all child objects. It grants whoever creates a child-object full control (GA) of the child object.

Taken together, these ACEs have the visual definition shown in Figure 3-14.

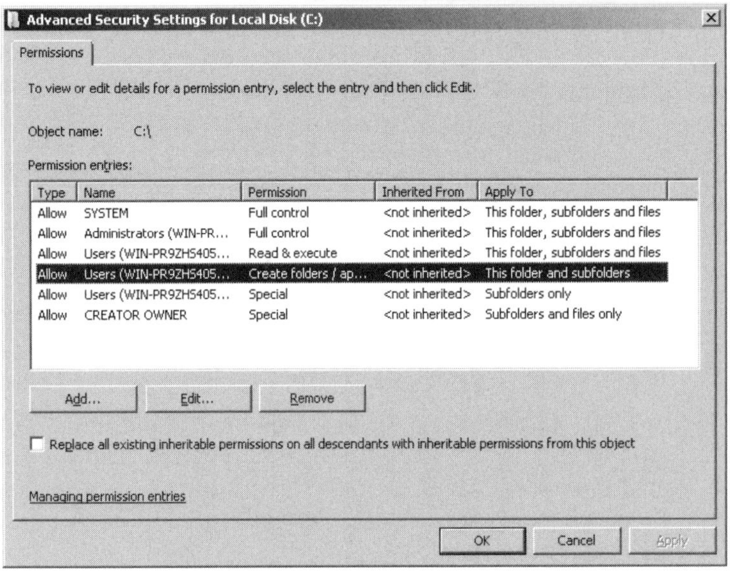

Figure 3-14   The ACL UI can be used to verify that you interpreted the SDDL string correctly while you are learning.

At this point you should have a better understanding than most of how access control works in Windows. You have even seen a number of tools used to manage permissions. In the next section we will provide a slightly deeper look, focusing on the tools.

Direct from the Source: Modifying ACLs Can Be Hazardous to Your Network Health, and Your Career

When you are trying to secure a computer, ACLs can be a friend or foe. I am part of the Solution Accelerator Team inside of Microsoft. Among other things, my team builds the security guides for many Microsoft products. ACLs are an aspect of security we always consider but rarely use on a large scale. Numerous third-party recommendations change the default ACLs on a system—some with small tweaks; others include large numbers of changes. A few years ago we released KB885409 to document the issues that can result from these changes.

One of the biggest challenges with changing ACLs for system files and utilities is the unknown (but often significant) impact on application compatibility. Several years ago we had a customer modify the ACLs on the root of the C:\ drive and propagate these changes to all subfolders. This configuration was then rolled out to all of their environments, resulting in thousands of unusable computers. Unknowingly, they had reduced the level of security and broken dozens of utilities and applications.

Changes to the ACLs of individual files may reduce this risk and often provide the desired results. The utilities that come with any operating system or product can provide huge benefits for administrators. Often an attacker can also use these utilities to enumerate details about the environment, perform nefarious deeds, or cover his own tracks. Limiting use of these resources should be carefully considered. While they may reduce additional system threats, they can also cause significant pain when managing the system or troubleshooting issues in the middle of the night.

Over the years, Microsoft has paid particular attention to this detail, and our team has seen a significant decrease in the need for changes to the default ACLs. That said, these changes are always a factor to consider as part of the risk analysis of a system, especially for areas and applications that contain critical data.

Chase Carpenter, Product Unit Manager
Solution Accelerators - Security and Compliance

Tools to Manage Permissions

There are three large classes of tools to manage permissions: built-in GUI tools such as ACL UI, built-in command-line interface (CLI) tools such as icacls, and other tools such as subinacl. In this section we will very briefly introduce the major ones. The ACL UI is relatively self-explanatory, and we have already discussed it earlier. Therefore, this section focuses on the other two categories.

cacls and icacls

Change ACLs (cacls) has been built into Windows for many years. It is a command-line tool that was not entirely updated in Windows 2000 when the inheritance model changed. Consequently, Microsoft introduced improved cacls (icacls) in Windows Vista and Windows Server 2008. Although a far more powerful tool than cacls, icacls suffers from some first-generation bugs, as well as from one notable shortcoming: it has no way to simply print an ACL as an SDDL string. Hopefully this will be resolved soon, because cacls is in the process of being deprecated and will likely disappear from the operating system at some point.

In addition to basic functionality, icacls includes some advanced features that were previously not available in built-in tools:

- Saving and restoring ACLs. Using the /save and /restore options, icacls can save an ACL. You can save the ACL to a file and even view that file. However, contrary to its appearance, the file is not a text file. It is, in fact, in a binary format that is identical to a Unicode text file except that it is missing a two-byte marking designating it as such at the beginning of the file. Consequently, if you open the file in Notepad, Notepad will insert that marking. This causes the file to be unusable to restore your ACLs from. You may want to append a .bin extension to your save files just to mark them as binary.

- Substituting SIDs. The ability to move permissions granted to one SID to another SID is a very useful feature in icacls. You do this with the /substitute option on the /restore command when you restore an ACL

- Changing owner. Using the /setowner switch, icacls can change the owner of an object.

- Find all permissions for a particular user. It is not uncommon to need to produce a list of all permissions for a particular user. You can easily do that using the /findsid option. This could be very useful in an audit situation.

- Resetting ACLs. If an ACL has been destroyed for some reason, you can reset it to the inherited ACL using the /reset option. Keep in mind, however, that this does *not* help you restore permissions to their defaults if you destroy the permissions on critical operating system files. Those normally do not use inherited permissions. *There is, in fact, no way to restore the default permissions.* This is why it is unsupported to change permissions on critical operating system files. See KB 885409 for more details.

- Grant/Deny/Remove. You can, of course, grant, deny, and remove permissions for any SID.

- Set integrity level. The functionality to manage the integrity level is also included in icacls. A few times I have seen users unable to delete objects because they were running with medium integrity (the default) and the object had a high label. The /setintegritylevel switch can fix that.

- View SDDL. As mentioned earlier, icacls does not have a way to view the SDDL string, but cacls does. Use **cacls <object>/s.**

- Remove inherited permissions. Nor does icacls have a way to remove inherited permissions. To do that you need to use cacls without the /E switch.

Warning   There is a bug in the underlying component used by cacls, icacls, and external tools such as subinacl that can cause serious confusion. To see the bug, open a command prompt at %systemroot%\system32\ and run **icacls c:**. Then run **icacls c:** and compare the results. They will be different. C: is not a valid directory. This causes the component that retrieves the ACL to fail and instead retrieves the ACL from the current directory. Do not forget that you always need to end all paths in all three of these command-line tools with a backslash (\).

SC

SC, the command-line service configuration utility, can show and manage ACLs on services. It only shows them in SDDL, however. To see this, run **sc sdshow <servicename>**. You can set the ACL on a service using **sc sdset <servicename> <SD in SDDL format>**.

subinacl

Earlier you saw subinacl used to show a security descriptor. More powerful than all the built-in CLI tools combined, subinacl is also correspondingly more complicated. However, it is the only tool that can manage permissions on all these objects:

- Services
- Files
- Cluster shares
- Printers
- Shares
- Registry keys
- SAM objects
- The IIS metabase (which is no longer used in IIS 7)
- Processes
- Kernel objects

Clearly, subinacl is primarily for very advanced administrators. However, it can be invaluable when you need to do some advanced ACL work.

Major Access Control Changes in Windows Server 2008

Windows Server 2008, and Windows Vista, introduce a few changes to access control over prior versions of Windows. A couple of these changes are quite subtle, but two will be very important to many administrators. Let us start by looking at the subtle ones.

TrustedInstaller Permissions

Many objects in Windows, as you saw earlier, are now owned by the TrustedInstaller service. This means that even administrators will find plenty of objects that they cannot modify without first changing the permissions on them. As an administrator, you are never quite completely locked out, of course, but you will almost certainly at some point run into a situation where you try to modify an object and get an access denied. This should be a trigger to question whether you really should be changing this object. The purpose of these restrictions is to maintain stability.

Network Location SIDs

As you saw in Figures 3-10 and 3-11, network location SIDs are present in security tokens. Including SIDs for INTERACTIVE, NETWORK, and so on in an ACL permits an administrator to control access to a particular object based on the access method. In Windows Server 2008 and Windows Vista, two new network location SIDs were added: DIALUP and INTERNET. The former applies to users connecting via a dial-up connection, while the latter applies to anyone connecting over a network connection that is not considered to be the local site.

File System Name Space Changes

It is hard not to notice that the Documents And Settings directory that we have known since Windows 2000 is now renamed to %systemdrive%\Users, with significant portions moving into %systemdrive%\ProgramData. Microsoft did this to simplify the file system namespace. However, many legacy applications use the full paths to the old directories instead of relying on environment variables. To avoid breaking such applications, Microsoft created junction points and symlinks from the old namespace to the new one. As a migration step, all those junctions and symlinks were outfitted with a Deny ACE to prevent listing the directory. In other words, you can specify a file in the old Documents And Settings directory, but you cannot open that directory in Windows Explorer. If you try to open it you will get an access denied error. Many people have grumbled about this since Windows Vista first came out. It is worth knowing how this happened.

Power User Permissions Removed

One of the more significant changes is that the permissions for Power Users have been all but stripped. A few remnants may still exist, but for all practical purposes, Power Users are no longer any more powerful than Standard Users. This is a transitional step toward the eventual deprecation of the Power Users group altogether. The original intent behind the Power Users group was for it to be a group that would be able to do some sensitive things, but would not be outright administrators. However, by the time all the various permissions were added to make the group meaningful, they were a hairsbreadth from being administrators. In reality, making a user a Power User was tantamount to making her an administrator. Because it provided no value and was potentially misleading, Microsoft embarked on disabling the group. UAC now fills the purpose that Power Users failed to fill.

OWNER_RIGHT and Owner Rights

The final change is perhaps the most interesting. Prior versions of Windows have always had the Creator/Owner SID. Creator/Owner is typically used in inheritable ACEs to grant permission to whoever creates a child object. It is replaced at create time with the SID for the actual creator.

In Windows Vista and Windows Server 2008 there is a new, related SID: OWNER_RIGHT. While Creator/Owner is replaced at object create time, OWNER_RIGHT is not. OWNER_RIGHT was created because there is now a change in permissions for owners.

In prior versions, the owner of an object always had implicit permission to change the DACL on an object. Many administrators requested the ability to change this behavior so that users could not change permissions on their own files. This functionality is provided in Windows Vista and Windows Server 2008 through the OWNER_RIGHTS SID. If the OWNER_RIGHTS SID is applied to the object, it will supersede the implicit rights of owners. Therefore, placing an OWNER_RIGHTS ACE for modify permissions on an object effectively means the owner cannot change the permissions on the object.

If the owner is replaced on the object, the OWNER_RIGHTS ACE is set to inherit-only, even if it is on a file. This effectively disables the ACE until the administrator can make sure that the permissions do not block everyone out.

User Rights and Privileges

We have alluded to one final aspect of access control several times, but never fully explained it: user rights and privileges. *User rights* and *privileges* are often used interchangeably. However, they are in fact very different constructs. User rights only govern the methods by which a user can log on. Privileges, however, determine what users can do after they have logged on. You saw privileges in a token in Figures 3-10 and 3-11. Privileges are managed in Group Policy under the User Rights Assignment node, shown in Figure 3-15.

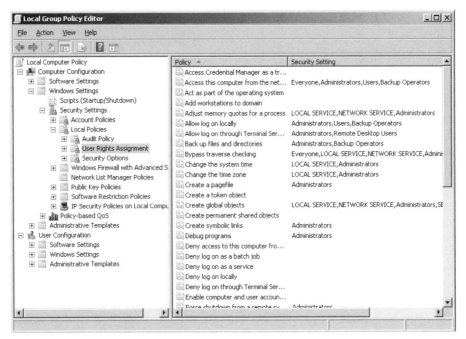

Figure 3-15   You can manage privileges in Group Policy.

In many tools—such as the tokens shown in Process Explorer—privileges show up in a different format than they do in Group Policy. Table 3-7 shows both strings for all privileges, along with an explanation of what the privilege means. Bolded privileges in Table 3-7 are extremely sensitive privileges that give the holder very advanced rights on the computer.

Table 3-7   Privileges in Windows Server 2008

Constant/value	Friendly Name	Description
SeAssignPrimaryTokenPrivilege	Replace a process level token	Permits the holder to assign a new token to any process. This privilege can be quite sensitive if held in conjunction with a privilege that permits the holder to obtain a process token.
SeAuditPrivilege	Generate security audits	Permits the holder to create arbitrary security event log events. An attacker can use this to insert arbitrary data into the event log.
SeBackupPrivilege	**Back up files and directories**	**Permits the holder to access all parts of any file or object, regardless of the ACL on the object. In other words, it grants read access to any object.**
SeChangeNotifyPrivilege	Bypass traverse checking	This privilege is enabled for all users. It causes the system to permit traversal through directory hierarchies that the user does not have access to. As the name implies, it also permits the user to receive notifications of changes to a securable object.
SeCreateGlobalPrivilege	Create global objects	Permits the holder to create objects such as symbolic links in an object manager namespace assigned to a different session.
SeCreatePagefilePrivilege	Create a pagefile	Grants the holder the right to create a pagefile.
SeCreatePermanentPrivilege	Create permanent shared objects	A permanent object is not deallocated when it is no longer needed by anyone. This privilege is somewhat sensitive in that it could permit a malicious user to consume resources on the computer, as well as pre-create objects on which more sensitive processes rely.
SeCreateSymbolicLinkPrivilege	Create symbolic links	The ability to create symbolic links has long been a source of vulnerabilities in Unix-based operating systems. A malicious user can create a symbolic link with the same name as an operating system binary, but that points to a malicious program. If an administrator executes the symbolic link the malicious code would run, not the intended operating system binary. To mitigate that risk Windows includes this privilege.

Table 3-7   Privileges in Windows Server 2008

Constant/value	Friendly Name	Description
SeCreateTokenPrivilege	**Create a token object**	**This is a highly sensitive privilege that permits the user to create security tokens for arbitrary users with arbitrary group membership. A subject holding this privilege can become any other user on the computer.**
SeDebugPrivilege	**Debug programs**	**This is one of the most sensitive privileges in the operating system. It permits the holder to debug any process, including those belonging to other users. Using this privilege the holder can inject code into another process and have it execute in the context of the subject that started that process. This is, for example, how all the programs that dump password hashes work.**
SeEnableDelegationPrivilege	**Enable computer and user accounts to be trusted for delegation**	**This is another very sensitive privilege, but only in a domain environment. It enables the holder to configure accounts that are trusted for delegation. Accounts that are trusted for delegation can create security tokens.**
SeImpersonatePrivilege	Impersonate a client after authentication	Permits the holder to create an impersonation token for a user. A few years ago a common attack was to set up a named pipe with a name similar to a common share. When a user is connected to the pipe the malicious program that created it could impersonate the user and take any action the user could. In Windows Server 2008 only a subject holding the *SeImpersonatePrivilege* can carry out the impersonation step.
SeIncreaseBasePriorityPrivilege	Increase scheduling priority	Permits the holder to change the priority for a process. A subject that holds this privilege could starve the system of resources by making a single process consume all processor cycles.
SeIncreaseQuotaPrivilege	Adjust memory quotas for a process	Permits the holder to change how much memory is allocated to a process.

Table 3-7   Privileges in Windows Server 2008

Constant/value	Friendly Name	Description
SeIncreaseWorkingSetPrivilege	Increase a process working set	This privilege is relatively new. Previously, this behavior was governed by the *SeIncreaseQuotaPrivilege*. *SeIncreaseWorkingSetPrivilege* permits a holder to change the working set for its own processes and is therefore less sensitive.
SeLoadDriverPrivilege	**Load and unload device drivers**	**Permits the holder to load a device driver. This is an extremely sensitive privilege because it permits the holder to load code that executes in the kernel, with no security restrictions whatsoever.**
SeLockMemoryPrivilege	Lock pages in memory	Permits the holder to lock pages in memory so they do not get paged to disk.
SeMachineAccountPrivilege	Add workstations to domain	Permits the holder to add computers in a domain. This privilege has no effect on a stand-alone computer.
SeManageVolumePrivilege	Perform volume maintenance tasks	Permits the holder to perform certain tasks directly on a disk volume, such as defragmenting the volume.
SeProfileSingleProcessPrivilege	Profile single process	Permits the holder to gather certain performance data related to file prefetching on a process.
SeRelabelPrivilege	Modify an object label	Permits a user to modify the label on any object, even ones the user cannot modify the SACL on.
SeRemoteShutdownPrivilege	Force shutdown from a remote system	As the name implies, this privilege permits the holder to shut down the computer remotely.
SeRestorePrivilege	**Restore files and directories**	**A very sensitive privilege that permits the holder to write to any file or registry key.**
SeSecurityPrivilege	Manage auditing and security log	Permits the holder to manage the security event log, such as changing the size, emptying the log, and viewing the events in it.
SeShutdownPrivilege	Shut down the system	Permits the holder to perform a graceful shutdown of the computer.
SeSyncAgentPrivilege	**Synchronize directory service data**	**Permits the holder to read all objects and properties in Active Directory.**

Table 3-7   Privileges in Windows Server 2008

Constant/value	Friendly Name	Description
SeSystemEnvironmentPrivilege	Modify firmware environment values	Some computers use nonvolatile RAM to store system configuration parameters. This privilege permits the holder to modify those parameters.
SeSystemProfilePrivilege	Profile system performance	Permits the holder to get performance data on the entire system.
SeSystemtimePrivilege	Change the system time	Permits the holder to modify the system clock. This is considered a sensitive operation because if a user can modify the system clock, he can make audit event appear out of order.
SeTakeOwnershipPrivilege	**Take ownership of files or other objects**	**Permits the holder to take ownership of any object, regardless of the DACL on the object.**
SeTcbPrivilege	**Act as part of the operating system**	**A holder of this privilege can perform some very sensitive operations, such a creating process tokens with arbitrary SIDs in them.**
SeTimeZonePrivilege	Change the time zone	New privilege in Windows Vista and Windows Server 2008. This privilege was added to permit standard users to change the time zone on the operating system without having to have permission to modify the system clock.
SeTrustedCredMan AccessPrivilege	**Access Credential Manager as a trusted caller**	**Permits the holder advanced access to the credential manager subsystem, primarily for the purpose of back up. It allows the holder to back up and restore all entries in the credential manager. This privilege is not normally granted to any user, although some processes, such as WinLogon and the local security authority subsystem (LSASS) have it by default.**
SeUndockPrivilege	Remove computer from docking station	Permits the holder to perform a graceful undocking of a laptop from a docking station. Note that lacking this privilege, the user can still simply push the eject button on the dock, or steal both the dock and the computer.

It is important to understand how the privileges in Table 3-7 function. Just as important is understanding the risk you run by modifying—particularly removing—privileges from groups that have them by default. Doing so can have a significantly adverse effect on the stability of your computer—and, as more than one administrator has discovered, on your longevity with your current employer. If you manage these privileges properly, you can improve the security of your computer by modifying the assignment of privileges. If you manage them improperly, you can render one or more computers unbootable at best, and a serious security hazard at worst.

RBAC/AZMAN

Before we leave the topic of access control behind and move on to other subjects, it is worth mentioning the Authorization Manager (AZMAN). AZMAN is not new in Windows Server 2008, but is not very well known. It is used to allow third-party developers to implement their own access control mechanisms, orthogonal to those provided by the operating system. Notably, developers can leverage AZMAN to implement a role-based access control (RBAC) system.

What we have described so far is identity-based access control. Instead of basing the access control on the identity of the subject, RBAC bases it on role membership. In and of itself this is not incompatible with identity-based access control, but the constructs used in RBAC are tied to a representation of the real world and roles. For example, a user may be part of the "expense report approvers" role, permitting the user to approve expense report.

This part of role-based access control can be implemented using the conventional access control mechanisms. However, RBAC also permits constraints to be placed on the roles a user can be a member of. A static constraint prevents a user from simultaneously being granted two roles. An example of a static constraint would be if a cashier supervisor must never be able to serve as a cashier. RBAC also supports dynamic constraints, which permit the user to be able to claim two roles, but not simultaneously. Continuing the previous example, a cashier may also be a cashier supervisor, but must not be allowed to act in both roles at the same time.

This is a very short introduction to RBAC, and Windows does not support it for managing Windows itself. However, if you manage or write line-of-business applications on Windows you may need to know more about RBAC. To learn more, see the white paper at *http://technet2.microsoft.com/windowsserver/en/library/72b55950-86cc-4c7f-8fbf-3063276cd0b61033.mspx?mfr=true*.

Summary

Access control is a topic that many administrators may not know as well as they should. The inheritance mechanisms in Windows, for example, are quite complex and very powerful. A lack of respect for the complexity, as well as misunderstanding how access control works, has led many administrators, often at the behest of auditors who understand far less about how Windows works, to perform wholesale DACL replacement. In the process, they have completely destroyed one or more computers. At one point I was involved in an incident where a customer had deployed a Group Policy object to replace Everyone with Authenticated Users, which, as I mentioned earlier, are functionally equivalent. The result was that the Administrator's profile was world-readable, the Recycle Bin did not work, and no users could log on. If the customer had only done this on a single computer it would have been bad enough, but the policy was deployed to more than 10,000 computers before it was disabled. Every single one of those computers needed to be reimaged to restore normal operations fully. Had the customer understood how DACLs really work, it may have been able to pull that change off—better still, it would have realized it was unnecessary.

Additional Resources

- Microsoft Knowledge Base Article 885409, "Security Configuration Guidance Support," at *http://support.microsoft.com/?kbid=885409*.

Chapter 4

Understanding User Account Control (UAC)

— Darren Canavor

With a shift in the way people use computers, such as performing banking transactions, making online purchases, and sharing and storing personal information, a new set of security threats emerged. Windows users were largely running with administrative privileges all the time. If the user accidentally installed malicious software (malware) onto such a computer, that malware—which had administrator access—could do anything. In Windows Vista and Windows Server 2008, the new User Account Control (UAC) feature is designed to apply the principle of "least privilege": Only give enough access to perform the task with as few disruptions as possible to the user experience. That includes all interactive users, with the exception of the built-in Administrator account. This may sound simple, but the challenge required a solution encompassing extensive changes to the core operating system, changes in industry perception of the standard user desktop and broad adoption of standard user best practices by the independent software vendor (ISV) community.

Note Although UAC is available in Windows Server 2008, it is primarily considered a client feature. To a systems administrator, the impact of UAC on Windows Server 2008 focuses on using Group Policy to manage Windows Vista client UAC policies.

What Is User Account Control?

UAC can help prevent unauthorized changes to a computer by allowing the user to verify actions before they happen. When a user designated with elevated privilege logs on to Windows Vista and Windows Server 2008, two access tokens are issued: a full access token and a filtered standard user access token. The filtering process removes the administrative privileges, and disables the Administrative group Security Identifiers (SIDs), resulting in a filtered standard user access token. The standard user token is then used to start the Windows desktop (explorer.exe) and all subsequent child processes. Consequently, all applications run with the standard user token by default, and only when granted permission by an administrator will the application run with a full access token. Note that because applications inherit the privilege level of the parent process, if the parent process is running with a full access token, the new child process will inherit and run without prompting the administrator for permission. For example, if you launch a command prompt as an administrator, any process you launch from within the command prompt will run as an administrator.

On the CD Elevating Explorer

By default Explorer.exe is designed not to be elevated. Consequently, if you right-click the binary and select Run As Administrator it will launch a new window, but in the same context as the original. On the companion CD, you will find a set of elevation tools, including a tool that puts an Elevate Explorer Here item on the right-click menu of any folder. Using that tool, you can launch an elevated Windows Explorer instance anywhere you wish.

How Token Filtering Works

When a user logs on to a Windows Vista or Windows Server 2008 computer, the operating system examines the Relative IDs (RIDs) and privileges of the user. The user will receive two tokens (filtered and full) if her account possesses any of the RIDs listed in Table 4-1 or any of the privileges listed in Table 4-2.

Table 4-1 UAC List of Restricted RIDs

Restricted RIDs	Description
DOMAIN_GROUP_RID_ADMINS	Administrative domain user account
DOMAIN_GROUP_RID_CONTROLLERS	Domain Controllers group
DOMAIN_GROUP_RID_CERT_ADMINS	Certificate Publishers group
DOMAIN_GROUP_RID_SCHEMA_ADMINS	Schema administrators group
DOMAIN_GROUP_RID_ENTERPRISE_ADMINS	Enterprise Administrators group
DOMAIN_GROUP_RID_POLICY_ADMINS	Policy Administrators group
DOMAIN_ALIAS_RID_ADMINS	Administrative local user account
DOMAIN_ALIAS_RID_POWER_USERS	Power Users group
DOMAIN_ALIAS_RID_ACCOUNT_OPS	Account Operators group, Server only

Table 4-1   UAC List of Restricted RIDs

Restricted RIDs	Description
DOMAIN_ALIAS_RID_SYSTEM_OPS	System Operators group, Server only
DOMAIN_ALIAS_RID_PRINT_OPS	Print Operators group, Server only
DOMAIN_ALIAS_RID_BACKUP_OPS	Backup Operators group
DOMAIN_ALIAS_RID_RAS_SERVERS	RAS and IAS servers group
DOMAIN_ALIAS_RID_PREW2KCOMPACCESS	Pre-Windows 2000 Compatibility Access group
DOMAIN_ALIAS_RID_NETWORK_CONFIGURATION_OPS	Network Configuration Operators group
DOMAIN_ALIAS_RID_CRYPTO_OPERATORS	Cryptographic Operators group

Table 4-2   UAC List of Restricted Windows Privileges

Restricted Windows Privileges	Description
SeCreateTokenPrivilege	Required to create a primary token
SeTcbPrivilege	Identifies holder as part of the trusted computing base
SeTakeOwnershipPrivilege	Take object ownership without being granted discretionary access
SeBackupPrivilege	Required to perform system-wide backup tasks
SeRestorePrivilege	Required to perform system-wide restore tasks
SeDebugPrivilege	Can debug the memory of a process owned by another account
SeImpersonatePrivilege	Required to impersonate a client after authentication
SeRelabelPrivilege	Required to modify an object's mandatory integrity level

The filtered standard user token will have all Windows privileges removed except the list of standard Windows privileges shown in Table 4-3.

Table 4-3   UAC List of Standard Windows Privileges

Standard Windows Privileges	Description
SeChangeNotifyPrivilege	Required to receive file or folder change notifications
SeShutdownPrivilege	Required to shut down a system remotely
SeUndockPrivilege	Required to undock a laptop
SeReserveProcessorPrivilege	Required to modify user processor privilege
SeTimeZonePrivilege	Required to adjust the computer's time zone

The filtered access token has all the RIDs from Table 4-1, if present, marked as USE_FOR_DENY_ONLY. It also has the privileges listed in Table 4-2 removed. The unmodified full administrator access token is linked to the filtered access token and is used when requests are made to launch applications with a full administrator access token.

You can find more information on RIDs in Chapter 1, "Subjects, Users, and Other Actors." You can find more information on Windows privileges in Chapter 3, "Objects: The Stuff You Want."

Components of UAC

UAC is primarily perceived to be the elevation prompt. However, although that part is the most visible, it is not the most important part of UAC. UAC, in fact, consists of a number of components, all of which contribute in some way to enabling more people to run as nonadministrators, which is the ultimate goal of UAC. This section discusses the various components of UAC, starting with the various types of elevation dialogs.

UAC Elevation User Experience

The most salient impact UAC has on user experience will be seen by users who are members of the local administrator group. Standard users also have the ability to perform administrative tasks without having to log off. The prompt for standard users is identical to the administrative prompt, except it requires password entry.

The Credential Prompt

On Windows Vista and Windows Server 2008, with the exception of the built-in administrators account, all users start applications without administrator-level privilege. When a given a task requires administrator privilege the interactive standard user will be presented with an elevation credential prompt, shown in Figure 4-1, requiring the entry of a valid user name and password of a user that is a member of the Local Administrators group.

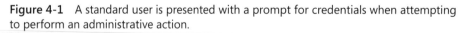

Figure 4-1   A standard user is presented with a prompt for credentials when attempting to perform an administrative action.

The Consent Prompt

By default the consent prompt, shown in Figure 4-2, is presented when a user who is a member of the local administrators group attempts to perform a task that requires administrator privilege. This consent prompt is presented only to local administrators running in Admin Approval Mode.

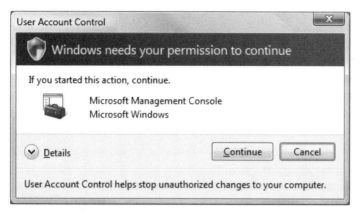

Figure 4-2   An administrator is presented with a prompt for consent when attempting to perform an administrative action.

To help users make informed decisions, the UAC elevation prompts are color-coded and use different text to indicate an application's potential security risk. For example, the color (four-color shield on blue-green bar) and text of Figure 4-2 indicate a Windows Vista or Windows 2008 application requiring administrative access, such as the Microsoft Management Console.

When an application attempts to run with an administrator's full access token, Windows Vista and Windows Server 2008 analyze the executable to determine its publisher and uses this information to determine the correct user experience.

Various alternative prompts are shown in Figures 4-3 through 4-5 and are distinguished by different colors and text. For example, in Figure 4-3 the color (yellow shield on gray bar) and text indicate that the application requiring administrative access is Authenticode signed and trusted by the local computer, such the Microsoft Firewall Client for ISA Server. In Figure 4-4 the color (yellow shield on yellow bar) and text indicate that the application requiring administrative access is unidentified and does not have a valid Authenticode signature from the publisher; therefore, take care before permitting the application to run. And in Figure 4-5 the color (red shield on red bar) and text indicate that the application requiring administrative access is from an explicitly blocked or untrusted publisher. An administrator can place the Publishers signing certificate in the local computer Untrusted certificate store to block a given publisher—this can also be set via Group Policy.

Note that UAC dialog boxes also change the displayed executable name and path details based on the trust level of the publisher's Authenticode signature. For example, in Figures 4-3 and 4-5, the user is trying to start the same application. The difference is that in Figure 4-3, the publisher is trusted, while in Figure 4-5 the publisher is explicitly blocked. When a publisher is trusted, not only does the dialog box color change, but the displayed text is also much friendlier.

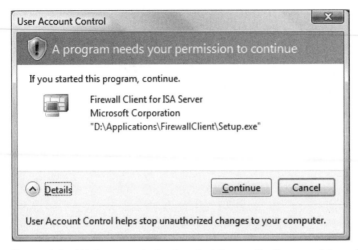

Figure 4-3   UAC prompt indicating that the application requiring administrative access is Authenticode-signed and trusted by the local computer.

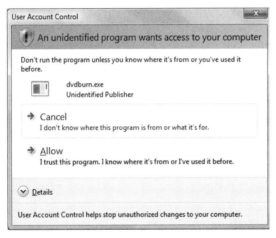

Figure 4-4   UAC prompt indicating that the application requiring administrative access is unidentified and does not have a valid Authenticode signature from the publisher.

In Windows Vista and Windows Server 2008 the shield icon shown in Figure 4-6 denotes that when a user clicks a shielded control or program, UAC will prompt for authorization before continuing.

Some Control Panel components, such as the Date and Time, contain both administrator and standard user operations. For example, standard users can view the clock and change the time zone, but a full administrator access token is required to change the local system time, as shown in Figure 4-7. One reason for this is that a user who changes the system time can reorder events in the event log or impact the ability for a computer to authenticate to a Windows domain.

Figure 4-5   UAC prompt indicating that the application requiring administrative access is from an explicitly blocked or untrusted publisher.

Figure 4-6   The shield icon denotes an administrative action in Windows Vista and Windows 2008.

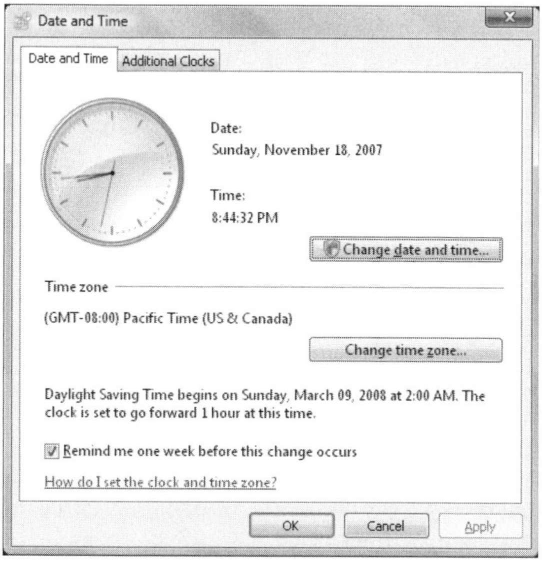

Figure 4-7   The Date And Time Control Panel utility is used to configure local computer time and time zone.

Application Information Service

The Application Information Service (AIS) is a new system service in Windows Vista and Windows Server 2008 that controls the launching of programs that require one or more elevated privileges, restricted rights, or privileged integrity levels to run. AIS is the component that actually launches these processes and attaches the right token to them. You could say that AIS is the heart of UAC. Note that AIS is disabled in Safe Mode; therefore, users who are members of the local administrator's group log on with their full administrative tokens. Windows took this approach because of the recovery and maintenance nature of Safe Mode scenarios.

File and Registry Virtualization

Windows Vista and Windows Server 2008 include file and registry virtualization, which is a new application compatibility technology to address issues encountered by applications that historically required an administrator's access token to run. Virtualization helps mitigate these applications without burdening the ISV to make changes. A large number of legacy applications that previously failed to run without the administrators access token now work on Windows Vista and Windows Server 2008, thanks to virtualization.

When a legacy application running with a filtered standard user access token attempts to write to a protected directory, such as Program Files, the application is given a virtualized view of the resource it is attempting to change. The virtualized copy is maintained under the user's profile (or registry). Each user has a completely separate copy of the virtualized file. This means that two users playing the same game on the same computer may not see the same list of high scores, because each user could have his or her own virtualized vision of the game's % PROGRAMFILES %\Game\highscores.txt file. Therefore, IT administrators must understand file and registry virtualization and may potentially need to implement custom virtualization settings within the enterprise to overcome application compatibility issues. The following section examines file and registry virtualization.

File Virtualization

File virtualization addresses the situation in which an application relies on creating or modifying files, such as a configuration file, in a protected location (%PROGRAMFILES%, %PROGRAMDATA%, or %SYSTEMROOT%) writeable only by administrators. Running such a program with a filtered standard user token may result in unexpected failures, or in some cases might be entirely blocked from running because of insufficient file or registry access.

When a program writes to a protected system location, the file virtualization filter driver (%SYSTEMROOT %\System32\Drivers\Luafv.sys) "traps" the operation and redirects it to a per-user location under the Virtual Store directory, located at %LOCALAPPDATA%\ VirtualStore. When the program later reads the file, Luafv.sys traps the operation and again redirects it to the user's Virtual Store. If the file is not found in the Virtual Store, Luafv.sys will query the nonvirtualized location. Because file virtualization happens automatically, the program believes it was successful in writing to %PROGRAMFILES%*appName*. For security reasons file virtualization by default will not allow the redirection of known executable file types such as .exe, .dll, .sys, .bat, and .cmd. If, because of application compatibility constraints, the program needs to virtualize a .bat file, you can reconfigure the file virtualization filter to support this. The following examples demonstrate how to configure file virtualization.

Configuring file virtualization to improve application compatibility   The FileList registry is not present by default and must be manually created to configure file virtualization.

Scenario: An enterprise relies on a legacy accounting application that writes a log file back to the application's restricted program folder. To enable virtualization on the accounting program's folder C:*appNameX*, create a new DWORD named **Exclude** with a value of 0 under the following registry key:

```
[HKLM\SYSTEM\CurrentControlSet\Services\luafv\Parameters\FileList\Device\
HarddiskVolume1 \appNameX]
```

Scenario: An enterprise forces all users to save their data to a specific location by locking down all user-writeable locations except the designated backup location. With virtualization enabled, a user can potentially store data in any virtualization-enabled location. To disable virtualization on a specific folder C:\Program Files*appNameY*, create a new DWORD named **Exclude** with a value of 1 under the following registry key:

```
[HKLM\SYSTEM\CurrentControlSet\Services\luafv\Parameters\FileList\Device\HarddiskVolume1
\Program Files\appNameY]
```

Scenario: An enterprise relies on a legacy accounting application that happens to write a .bat file back to the application's restricted program folder. To enable virtualization of .bat file extension types, create a new REG_MULTI_SZ named **ExcludedExtensionsRemove** with a value of bat under the following registry key:

```
[HKLM\SYSTEM\CurrentControlSet\Services\luafv\Parameters]
```

Note   To expose virtual files and folders, browse to the virtualized file location using Windows Explorer and click Compatibility Files on the Explorer toolbar.

Registry Virtualization

Registry virtualization is similar to file virtualization but applies to registry keys under HKLM\SOFTWARE. This feature permits applications that rely on the ability to store configuration information in HKLM\SOFTWARE to continue to operate when running without administrative privilege. The keys and data are redirected to HKEY_CLASSES _ROOT\

VirtualStore\SOFTWARE. Note that the VirtualStore location is created on demand by the first application utilizing virtualization. As with file virtualization, each user has a virtualized copy of values that an application has stored in HKLM. If, because of application compatibility constraints, a program needs to configure registry virtualization, this is supported. The following examples demonstrate how to configure registry virtualization.

Configuring Registry Virtualization to Improve Application Compatibility

Scenario: An enterprise wants to prevent the virtualization of registry values under the key *DontVirtMe*. To do so, run the following command from an elevated command prompt:

```
Reg.exe flags HKLM\Software\DontVirtMe SET DON'T_VIRTUALIZE
```

Scenario: An enterprise wants to prevent the virtualization of all registry values and subkey values under the parent registry key *DontVirtMe*. To do so, run the following command from an elevated command prompt:

```
Reg.exe flags HKLM\Software\appName RECURSE_FLAG DONT_VIRTUALIZE
```

Although virtualization allows the overwhelming majority of pre-Windows Vista applications to run, it is a short-term fix rather than a long-term solution. In addition, some applications cannot be fixed, including applications that contain specific checks for user privileges. For example, many process-control applications check whether the user is an administrator, and exit if the user is not. You can get those applications to run on Windows Vista by attaching an application manifest that states the application needs to be run with administrative privileges and redeploy. Developers should modify all applications to comply with the Windows Vista and Windows Server 2008 Logo Program rather than relying on file and registry virtualization.

Manifests and Requested Execution Levels

Applications running on Windows Vista and Windows Server 2008 can use application manifests to describe or declare requirements to the operating system at run time. Administrative applications can declare their privilege requirements in the application manifest and the system will prompt the user for permission accordingly. Most pre-Windows Vista administrative applications, however, can run smoothly without modification even though they lack an entry in the application manifest. This is due to the vast array of Windows Vista and Windows Server 2008 application compatibility fixes, most of which depend on UAC being enabled. Application compatibility fixes enable applications to run that would normally fail if they ran without administrative access. For example, imagine a game that checks during start-up to see whether the user is a member of the local administrators group. Running with a filtered standard user access token, this check will fail—causing the application to fail. Using the application compatibility database, the operating system can discover that the application must run with a full token and prompt the user accordingly or discover that the application runs fine without a full token and makes the application perceive it was started with a full token. These types of application compatibility fixes are called *shims*.

All Windows Vista and Windows Server 2008 logo-compliant applications must have a valid manifest with a defined requested execution level. The application uses the *requestedExecutionLevel* attribute to declare its access requirements. If the application requires administrative access, the application manifest specifies a requested execution level of *requireAdministrator*. This will ensure that the system identifies this program as an administrative application and provide the necessary elevation experience. Note that an application can also have mixed functionality—administrative and standard user—depending on the user. For example, the Microsoft Management Console (MMC) is marked *highestAvailable*. If a standard user runs the MMC, it will start with standard user privilege and will not prompt. If the user has a filtered access token, such as a local administrator or network operator, the operating system will prompt the user to launch MMC with the user's highest available privilege, allowing the administrator to have a different level of access than the network operator and the standard user.

Installer Detection Technology

Installation programs are applications designed to deploy software, and most write to system directories and machine registry keys. These protected system locations typically require administrator-level privilege, which means that standard users do not have sufficient access to install most programs. Windows Vista and Windows Server 2008 heuristically detect installation programs, updaters, and uninstall programs that require administrator access to run. Installer detection is a key component of the UAC design. It facilitates the correct elevation experience and prevents installations from being executed without the user's knowledge.

Installer detection only applies to the following:

- 32-bit executables

- Applications without a *requestedExecutionLevel*

- Interactive processes running as a standard user with UAC enabled

The operating system will heuristically determine whether an application is an installer. Heuristics are based on the following attributes:

- Keywords included in the filename, such as *install*, *setup*, *update*, and other language equivalents

- Keywords in the following Versioning Resource fields of the executable: Vendor, Company Name, Product Name, File Description, Original Filename, Internal Name, and Export Name

- Keywords in the side-by-side manifest that are embedded in the executable
- Keywords in specific *StringTable* entries that are linked in the executable
- Key attributes in the RC data that are linked in the executable

For example, if you have an application called setup.exe or install.exe, it will be detected as an installer and will automatically get a prompt. You can find general information and an overview of the Microsoft Windows Installer at MSDN: *http://go.microsoft.com/fwlink/ ?LinkId=30197.*

User Interface Privilege Isolation

User Interface Privilege Isolation (UIPI) is a new technology in Windows Vista and Windows Server 2008 to help isolate administrator-level processes from processes running with lower privileges on the same interactive desktop. UIPI prevents a lower-privilege application from using Windows messages to send input to a higher-privilege process. Sending input from one process to another allows a process to "inject" input into another process without the user providing consent.

UIPI defines a set of permitted Windows messaging interactions controlled by the highest of the different process levels. Higher privilege levels can send Windows messages to applications running at lower levels, but lower levels cannot send certain Windows messages to application windows running at higher levels. UIPI does not interfere or change the behavior of window messaging between applications at the same privilege level. UIPI comes into play for a user who is a member of the administrators group and chooses to run both administrator and standard user privileged applications on the same interactive desktop.

Secure Desktop Elevation Prompts

Credential and consent prompts are displayed on the secure desktop by default in Windows Vista and Windows Server 2008. Every application must run on a desktop, and each interactive user receives a desktop upon logon where all her applications run. The Secure Desktop is used by the operating system for services and sensitive user interfaces such as the log-on interface.

By presenting the elevation prompt on the secure desktop, the operating system guarantees that the information being presented cannot be tampered with. When an executable requests elevation, the user is switched from the user's interactive desktop to the secure desktop. The secure desktop renders a dimmed background of the user desktop and displays a highlighted elevation prompt. When the user clicks Continue or Cancel, the desktop automatically switches back to the user's interactive desktop. While malware can paint over the interactive desktop and present an imitation of the secure desktop (spoofing), authorizing consent does not allow the malware elevation. If UAC is configured to prompt for credentials, malware imitating the credential prompt may gather the user's credentials; however, the malware will be unable to use those credentials remotely to obtain administrator privilege. Somewhat bizarrely, the malware will gain absolutely nothing from spoofing the admin approval mode dialog box. Malware cannot enter the user name and password into a valid UAC dialog box presented on the Secure Desktop, nor can it use runas.exe to invoke a process with elevated privilege or automate a legitimate UAC dialog box.

Using Remote Assistance

In Windows Vista and Windows Server 2008, a domain user can run as a standard user and have a centralized IT group provide all administration tasks. Microsoft provides both Remote Desktop (RD) and Remote Assistance (RA) access to computers for different administration purposes. RD sessions are useful when an administrator does not require end-user interaction but does require full control of the remote computer. RA is useful for diagnosing and trouble-shooting problems when the end user needs to demonstrate the problem to an IT expert. RA has been impacted by UAC; it is important that you understand how.

IT experts will experience two typical problems using RA. The first is that by default, the UAC prompts use the secure desktop and consequently are not available to the remote user. The second is if the UAC enterprise policy Behavior Of The Elevation Prompt For Standard Users is configured to Automatically Deny Elevation Requests, elevation is blocked entirely.

Windows Vista SP1 has a new UAC policy to address the challenge of the secure desktop prompting: User Account Control: UIAccess Applications To Prompt For Elevation Without Using The Secure Desktop. With this policy configured, AIS dynamically disables secure desktop prompting for UIAcess accessibility applications such as Remote Assistance and re-enables it once the program exits. For more details, see "What Is New in UAC in Windows 2008 and Windows Vista SP1" later in the chapter.

If the policy Behavior Of The Elevation Prompt For Standard Users is set to Automatically Deny Elevation Requests, the IT expert who connects using RA will be unable to launch an application with administrative privilege. To work around this issue, the IT expert can use runas.exeto launch a Command Prompt window using her own user name and password and then start a process that requires elevation. UAC will use the IT expert's UAC prompt policy.

The following procedure could be used by an IT expert for running the Registry Editor with administrator privilege:

1. Open a command prompt and type **runas /user:domain\ITExpert cmd.exe.**

2. In the new Command Prompt window that opens up, type **regedit.exe.**

3. Respond to the UAC elevation prompt.

UAC Remote Administrative Restrictions

When an administrator logs on to a Windows Vista or Windows Server 2008 computer remotely, using normal Windows networking, he logs on in Admin Approval mode, just as if he were logging on locally. To augment this behavior, UAC restricts remote administration to prevent admin loopback attacks and help protect against local malicious software running remotely with administrative privilege. For example, admin loopback would occur when a user logs on with a filtered access token and then malware simply performs a **net use** \\127.0.0.1\c$ to obtain administrative access to the file system. When UAC remote restrictions are enabled, the loopback would also obtain a filtered access token and not full administrative access. This behavior works differently for different types of user accounts, as described in the following sections.

Local User Accounts

Imagine that a user who is local to the server and a member of the local Administrators group on the server establishes a remote connection by **net use** * *server\share*. In this scenario, the token used for that user on the server will not be a full administrative token as in previous versions of Windows. The user has no elevation potential on the remote computer and cannot perform administrative tasks. If the user wants to administer the workstation with a local account, she must interactively log on to the remote computer by Remote Assistance or Remote Desktop if available.

Domain User Accounts

When a user with a domain user account logs on to a computer remotely, and he is a member of the local Administrators group, the domain user will run with a full administrator access token on the remote computer and UAC will not be in effect.

Managing UAC Remote Restrictions

To disable UAC remote restrictions for local accounts and obtain Windows XP and Windows 2003 parity, create a DWORD named **LocalAccountTokenFilterPolicy** with a value of 1 under the following registry key:

```
HKLM\SOFTWARE\Microsoft\Windows\CurrentVersion\Policies\system
```

Mapping Network Drives When Running in Admin Approval Mode

When an administrator in Admin Approval mode maps a network share, that share is only associated to the current log-on session for the current process access token. This means that if a user running a command prompt (cmd.exe) with a filtered access token explicitly maps a network share, that network share would not be exposed to any elevated cmd.exe instances running with a full administrator access token. Note that only in the case of UNC paths will the sessions be automatically linked by the system.

You can configure a registry value to share network connections between processes started with the filtered access token and full access token for a member of the Administrators group only. When you enable this registry setting, if a network resource is mapped to an access token, the LSA checks whether another access token is associated with the current user session. If the LSA determines that there is a linked access token, it adds the network share to the linked location.

To enable a linked network drive, create a DWORD named **EnableLinkedConnections** with a value of 1 under the following registry key:

```
HKLM\SOFTWARE\Microsoft\Windows\CurrentVersion\Policies\System
```

Direct from the Field: Which Accounts Are Accepted for Elevation

Recently I was asked to troubleshoot some elevation problems for a friend of mine. She was unable to elevate to change some networking parameters on her laptop. The laptop was domain-joined, but the DC was unavailable at the time. After a few minutes of troubleshooting, I wrote up the following scenario, which I think helps highlight how UAC is not always intuitive, as well as how it interoperates with other features of Windows:

- The computer is called Denise-PC.

- The computer is joined to example.com.

- The DC for example.com is offline—in other words, Denise-PC is roaming.

- She has only previously logged on to Denise-PC using EXAMPLE\Denise.

- EXAMPLE\Denise is a member of BUILTIN\Users.

- BUILTIN\Administrators on Denise-PC contains BUILTIN\Administrator and DENISE-PC\Denise.

- When she attempts an administrative action she gets an elevation prompt asking for an admin account.

We have several options for how to elevate:

1. Attempt to elevate to BUILTIN\Administrator.

2. Attempt to elevate to EXAMPLE\Denise.

3. Attempt to elevate to EXAMPLE\Administrator.

4. Attempt to elevate to EXAMPLE\Foo, where Foo is a member of EXAMPLE\Domain Admins.

5. Attempt to elevate to DENISE-PC\Denise.

Option 1 will fail because BUILTIN\Administrator is disabled by default in Windows Vista as long as there is another local admin account. Because DENISE-PC\Denise is a local admin, and it is enabled, BUILTIN\Administrator is not available for use.

Option 2 will fail as well. EXAMPLE\Denise is only a member of users. It is not an admin and therefore you cannot elevate to it.

Option 3 will fail because although EXAMPLE\Administrator is a member (indirectly) of BUILTIN\Administrators, it has never logged on to Denise-PC. Because the computer is offline, authentication of domain accounts has to happen against the password verifier. (See Chapter 2, "Authenticators and Authentication Protocols," for information on cached credentials.) Cached credentials exist only for accounts that have previously logged on interactively; therefore, we have nothing to verify EXAMPLE\Administrator against. It should also be pointed out that elevating to a domain administrator on a member workstation would be an extraordinarily bad idea. For more information on why, see Chapter 13, "Securing the Network."

Option 4 fails for the same reason as Option 3.

Option 5 will succeed. DENISE-PC\Denise is a local account. Therefore, no cached credentials are necessary. It is a member of BUILTIN\Administrators, so it is legal to elevate to this account. And it is not disabled, so it can be actively used to log on with.

I have found this write-up very helpful in explaining to people which accounts can be used for UAC elevation, as well as the relationship between domain accounts, password verifiers, and UAC.

Jesper M. Johansson
Windows Security MVP

Application Elevations Blocked at Logon

Windows Vista and Windows Server 2008 block administrative applications that try to start in the user's log-on path. Many ISVs place programs in the user's log-on launch path to ensure that they run each time the user logs on. While this solution may be convenient, it often results in application compatibility problems when the user logging on is not an administrator but the application requires him to be. This behavior is also convenient for malware, which can simply place itself in the user's log-on launch location. From that point forward, every time the user logs on the malware runs silently with administrator-level access and without the user's consent. To block this behavior, Windows Vista and Windows Server 2008 create a workflow to help the user manage the blocked list of programs. An elevation balloon notifies the user, as shown in Figure 4-8, and the tray icon allows the user to run the blocked program or enter the management UI, as shown in Figure 4-9.

With UAC, applications that require administrator-level privileges to run are blocked when launched from the following locations:

- Per-User Startup Folder   %USERPROFILE%\Start Menu\Programs\Startup.

- Per-Machine Startup Folder   %ALLUSERSPROFILE%\Start Menu\Programs\Startup.

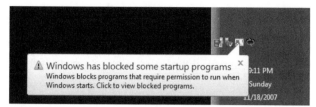

Figure 4-8   Blocked application balloon: Windows has blocked some start-up programs.

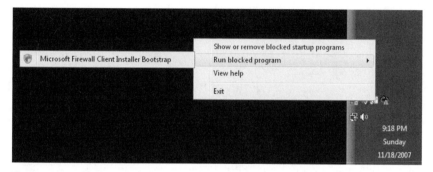

Figure 4-9   Blocked application tray icon: Run Blocked Program/Show Or Remove Blocked Start-up Programs.

■ Per-User RUN Key   HKEY_USERS*\Software\Microsoft\Windows \CurrentVersion\Run

■ Per-Machine RUN Key   HKEY_LOCAL_MACHINE\SOFTWARE\Microsoft \Windows\CurrentVersion\Run.

> **Note**   In the preceding section, the asterisk ("*") denotes all user security identifiers (SIDs) including the .Default SID.

It is important to note that enterprise Group Policy supports a user log-on script that will use the currently logged-on user's highest available access token; if the user is a member of the local administrators group, the script will elevate without prompting the Administrator in Admin Approval mode.

Configuring Pre-Windows Vista Applications for Compatibility with UAC

The final and most important step in configuring UAC is ensuring that your software is either designed to be UAC compliant by following logo requirements or has been configured to run with Windows Vista or Windows Server 2008.

For new applications that are Windows Vista and Windows Server 2008 logo-compliant, the application must either run with a standard user privilege or, in the case of an administrative application, be marked with an application manifest entry. For more information, visit the Microsoft Windows logo home page at *http://www.microsoft.com/ whdc/winlogo/hwrequirements.mspx.*

During the deployment of Windows Vista and Windows Server 2008, IT departments may discover some existing line-of-business (LOB) applications that will not function properly. In most cases, the problem is due to application incompatibility with the enhancements incorporated in the new operating systems. Microsoft provides an Application Compatibility Toolkit that assists in identifying the compatibility problems and aids in the creation of application compatibility fixes or shims. Some programs may need to perform administrative operations. For this to work correctly on Windows Vista and Windows Server 2008 under UAC, the program needs declare this to the operating system so that users will be prompted for approval before the application can run with a full administrator access token. The Application Compatibility Toolkit 5.0 with the Standard User Analyzer provides the means to test, build, and install the application compatibility database entries, which facilitate the requested execution level marking mechanism.

For information about application compatibility and the Application Compatibility Toolkit 5.0 featuring the Standard User Analyzer, visit TechNet at *http://go.microsoft.com/fwlink /?LinkId=23302.*

UAC Group Policy Settings

The following section explores each of the eleven UAC group policies supported on Windows Vista and Windows Server 2008. These settings can be applied locally using the Local Security Policy editor or across an enterprise by using Group Policy.

UAC Policy Settings Found Under Security Options

You can find the following nine UAC settings in the Group Policy Editor or the Local Security Policy editor under: Local Computer Policy\Computer Configuration\Windows Settings \Security Settings\Local Policies\Security Options.

User Account Control: Admin Approval Mode for the Built-in Administrator Account

This security setting controls the behavior of the Built-in Administrator (BA) account. If you use the BA account for daily administrative tasks, you may consider disabling this setting. However, if you do so, you also lose Internet Explorer Protected Mode. All applications will run as a full administrator. By default this policy is enabled.

User Account Control: Behavior of the Elevation Prompt for Administrators in Admin Approval Mode

If an operation requires administrator privilege to start, this policy will control the UAC prompt experience for administrators in Admin Approval Mode. Although the default consent configuration is convenient, enforcing credentials may be desirable. For example, if a parent and child share the same user account, the child will be unable to perform elevated tasks without knowledge of the password. Also, in some cases administrators may want to disable elevation prompting without disabling UAC and therefore can set the elevation prompt to Silent. This retains Internet Explorer Protected Mode, but removes the elevation prompts. By default this policy is Prompt For Consent.

User Account Control: Behavior of the Elevation Prompt for Standard Users

UAC provides an in-context elevation prompt experience, and if the user can provide a valid administrator user name and password, the elevated operation will succeed. For enterprises that do not want their users to have the opportunity to elevate, you can set this policy to automatically deny all elevation requests. By default this setting is Prompt For Credentials.

User Account Control: Detect Application Installations and Prompt for Elevation

This setting enables or disables application installer detection. It is best to leave this setting enabled, which is the default.

User Account Control: Only Elevate Executables That Are Signed and Validated

This setting will enforce Authenticode signature validation on any interactive applications requesting elevation. If an enterprise runs only Authenticode-signed programs, this setting can increase security by controlling which application publishers are allowed to run with elevated privileges. However, most users would experience significant application compatibility problems if they tried to use this setting, which is why it is disabled by default.

User Account Control: Only Elevate UIAccess Applications That Are Installed in Secure Locations

UIAccess applications are most often accessibility programs that need to interact directly with the Windows UAC elevation dialogs. Windows Vista and Windows Server 2008 UAC elevation dialogs are protected with a high integrity level. For UIAccess applications to interact they must declare this requirement in the application manifest. When the program starts, it receives a special integrity level permitting interaction. Because UIAccess applications are powerful, this setting enforces that such programs be started only from a secure directory file path. UIAccess applications must also have a valid and trusted Authenticode signature. By default this setting is enabled.

User Account Control: Run All Users, Including Administrators, as Standard Users

This is the UAC on/off switch. Don't disable UAC! If UAC is disabled, all related features also become disabled. File and registry virtualization no longer function and all virtualized data appear lost to the user. Users who were running in Admin Approval Mode now log on with full administrative rights, and all applications run with administrator privilege, silently! Application compatibility shims designed to increase compatibility with pre-Windows Vista applications are also disabled. Internet Explorer's Protected Mode is disabled, forcing Internet Explorer to run with administrative privilege. Have we convinced you to leave UAC on? By default this setting is enabled.

User Account Control: Switch to the Secure Desktop When Prompting for Elevation

This setting determines whether elevation requests are presented on the interactive user's desktop or on the secure desktop. The secure desktop prevents output spoofing, which means that whatever is presented on the secure desktop cannot be tampered with. UAC dialog boxes on the interactive user's desktop can be spoofed and therefore are less secure than those presented on the secure desktop. By default this setting is enabled.

User Account Control: Virtualize File and Registry Write Failures to Per-User Locations

This setting enables or disables the redirection of write failures for the file system and registry. Disable this feature if you use only Windows Vista or Windows Server 2008 logo-compliant software. If you require custom virtualization settings, see "Configuring Registry Virtualization to Improve Application Compatibility" earlier in the chapter. By default this setting is enabled.

Related UAC policies

Windows Vista and Windows 2008 also have two complementary policy settings: the Require Trusted Path For Credential Entry and Enumerate Local Administrator Accounts On Elevation settings. You can find both settings in the Group Policy Editor under: Local Computer Policy\Computer Configuration\Administrative Templates\Windows Components\ Credential User Interface.

Require Trusted Path for Credential Entry

This setting controls whether the user must enter Windows credentials using a trusted path. The trusted path is a secure key sequence—sometimes referred to as a Secure Attention Sequence (SAS)—which prevents malware from stealing your Windows credentials. When a standard user tries to perform a task requiring administrator privilege, the system forces the user to enter Ctrl+Alt+Delete before being redirected to the secure desktop to enter a valid administrator user name and password to complete the operation. This trusted path credential workflow prevents input spoofing and output spoofing, making this the most secure Windows credential input configuration. By default this setting is disabled.

Enumerate Administrator Accounts on Elevation

This setting enables the automatic enumeration of local administrator accounts in the UAC credential UI, as shown in Figure 4-10. Note that in some domain-joined environments that encounter networking connectivity issues, this setting can cause unexpected delays when enumerating the local administrator accounts. By default this setting is disabled.

Figure 4-10   Automatic local administrator account enumeration in the UAC credential dialog box.

What's New in UAC in Windows Server 2008 and Windows Vista SP1

UAC underwent only a few small changes in Windows Server 2008 and Windows Vista SP1 when compared to the original release in Windows Vista. The following sections summarize the UAC changes.

New Group Policy Setting: UIAccess Applications to Prompt for Elevation without Using the Secure Desktop

This setting enables UIAccess applications such as Remote Assistance to request the disabling of secure desktop prompting. When the UIAccess application is complete, the secure desktop prompting is automatically enabled, thus removing the necessity for the end user to allow the desktop admin elevation access. (See Figure 4-11.) As discussed earlier in this chapter, this is a convenient setting for those enterprises that rely on Remote Assistance to provide end user desktop help desk support. By default this setting is disabled.

Figure 4-11   Windows Remote Assistance: Allow Helpdesk To Respond To User Account Control Prompts.

UAC Prompt Reduction When Performing File Operations in Windows Explorer

When a user creates a new folder in a protected location, the user will be prompted only once to create and name the folder. This was a two-prompt scenario in Windows Vista RTM.

More Than 40 Additional UAC-Related Application Compatibility Shims

The UAC team in conjunction with the Application compatibility team produced over 40 new application shims to help increase Windows Vista and Windows 2008 compatibility.

UAC Best Practices

Managing UAC is not as hard as it seems. How you deploy in an organization depends largely on your organization's security needs and tolerance to implement the required policies to meet those needs. The following solutions are presented in reverse order of preference (good, better, best) with respect to security value.

Good Practice

Run users in Admin Approval Mode. If an administrative user requires elevated privileges, the enterprise UAC policy should enforce that the user enters a valid administrator user name and password instead of simply clicking the Consent dialog box. This configuration prevents unauthorized elevations on the off-chance that a user leaves his workstation unattended. To improve security you could also require the Ctrl+Alt+Delete key sequence for any elevation to complete. This makes entering administrative credentials far more secure.

Better Practice

Enforce that all users who require administrator privilege have two accounts: one standard user account for day-to-day activities such as reading e-mail and one for the occasional administrative operation. The standard user can log on and when needed can elevate using a UAC credential prompt. This is not the best solution because now the user is running both standard user and administrator-privileged applications in the same interactive session. To increase security an enterprise can enforce that the user must use Fast User Switching (FUS) anytime she needs to perform an elevated operation. Although FUS is more secure, it does have user experience drawbacks. To improve security you could also require the Ctrl+Alt+Delete key sequence as with the previous option.

Best Practice

Run all users as standard users. The IT department must then assume that standard users will generally not be able to install applications and therefore must deploy software on their behalf. Windows provides an installation service to do this called the Microsoft Software Installer (MSI) Service. In addition, the Group Policy Software Installation (GPSI) extension allows applications to be distributed to a user's computer without any user interaction required. See the Group Policy Software Installation Extension documentation at *http://go.microsoft.com/fwlink/?LinkId=71356* for more information.

Summary

UAC is probably the most talked-about feature in Windows Vista. It is even the subject of advertisements from rival software vendors. It is hard to say whether to be flattered or annoyed that Microsoft's competitors are now advertising their products as more desirable because Windows is too secure. Regardless, UAC is a critical step for Windows. The status quo, where users run as administrators to get normal tasks done, is unacceptable and has led to a malware pandemic. Only by helping users run as nonadministrators can we ever hope to stem the flood of malware and reduce desktop total cost of ownership (TCO).

The future is one where users only use administrative privileges where necessary. UAC is a step in that direction, but it will only work if people use it, and if they demand that their ISVs get software that works as a standard user. You can do your part in protecting the IT ecosystem by using UAC, and by buying software that works with it and rejecting software that does not.

Additional Resources

- Microsoft Corporation (2006). "The Windows Vista and Windows Server 2008 Developer Story: Windows Vista Development Requirements for User Account Control (UAC)," at *http://msdn2.microsoft.com/en-us/library/aa905330.aspx.*

- Mark Russinovich (2007). "Inside Windows Vista User Account Control," at *http://www.microsoft.com/technet/technetmag/issues/2007/06/UAC/.*

- Raymond Chen (2006). "An Administrator Is Not the Administrator," at *http://www.microsoft.com/technet/technetmag/issues/2006/03/WindowsConfidential/ ?related=/technet/technetmag/issues/2006/03/WindowsConfidential.*

- Wole Moses (2007). "Services Hardening in Windows Vista," at *http:// www.microsoft.com/technet/technetmag/issues/2007/01/SecurityWatch/?related= /technet/technetmag/issues/2007/01/SecurityWatch.*

Chapter 5

Firewall and Network Access Protection

— Kurt Dillard

If, like me, you were born back when music was recorded in an analogue format on vinyl, you might remember using computers without continuous Internet access or even no network connection at all. As today's network technologies made their way from labs to your living room, people started to see the consequences of unauthenticated access and plain-text communication protocols. It seems like we have been playing an incredibly challenging game of cat and mouse with the malintentioned ever since. Unfortunately, the good guys are the mice far too often.

The first firewalls were introduced in the late 1980s in response to security breaches such as the Morris Worm. Early firewalls were simple compared to what is deployed now: They allowed or blocked incoming traffic based on information in the packet header such as source IP address and port number. They did not track the state of a communication sequence between the trustworthy host on the internal network and the anonymous one on the outside. Firewalls continued to evolve, however. First, firewalls became *stateful*—that is, they understood the normal sequence of packets used to establish and maintain communications between two hosts. Then, firewalls emerged that understood application layer protocols: They actually examined the payload within the packet to look for malicious traffic. For example, a firewall protecting a Web server could look at an HTTP request from a remote client to determine whether it was a legitimate request for data or an attempt to compromise the server. Application-layer firewalls have since become very sophisticated; anyone who understands what Microsoft's Internet Security and Acceleration Server (ISA Server) is doing when protecting a server providing Microsoft Office Outlook Web Access will realize how powerful the capabilities of that technology are.

So far, we have been talking about what organizations do to protect their network perimeters using corporate network firewalls. However with so many mobile devices and complex network architectures, where critical business data is shared with business partners over the public Internet, most organizations also deploy host-based firewalls.

Authentication and encryption technologies have also advanced considerably since the days of Gopher and Veronica. Remote hosts can now establish secure communication channels using Transport Layer Security (TLS), Internet Key Exchange (IKE), and other protocols; they can authenticate users in many ways; and they can encrypt the network traffic using Internet Protocol Security (IPsec), Secure Hypertext Transport Protocol (HTTPS), and many other protocols. Windows Server 2008 includes support for many of these protocols. This chapter will focus specifically on Windows Firewall with Advanced Security, IPsec, Network Access Protection (NAP), and some new capabilities that have been added to Routing And Remote Access Service (RRAS).

Ancient Protocols: The Internet Before the Web

This may shock some readers, but millions of people used the Internet for communication and information retrieval long before Sir Tim Berners-Lee and Robert Cailliau developed the Hypertext Transport Protocol (HTTP) and Hypertext Markup Language (HTML). It is true—people were able to find each other and access useful information online without using browsers! Electronic mail use predates the Internet and actually helped drive its development. People also shared information online by publishing documents and other types of data on File Transfer Protocol (FTP) servers, but if you did not already know where the location of the file you wanted, finding it was very difficult. Gopher—a distributed document search and retrieval system—was a predecessor of the World Wide Web. Veronica, one of the Internet's earliest search engines, could find information based on the names of menu items on Gopher sites. Wide Area Information Servers (WAIS) was an early client-server searching system capable of doing full-text searches on Gopher servers. Yes, I used all of these technologies and more when I got bored with USENET and Bulletin Board systems, via a 2400 baud modem. I am a dinosaur.

Windows Filtering Platform

To facilitate the development of network traffic filtering products, Microsoft created the Windows Filtering Platform (WFP). It is available in both Windows Vista and Windows Server 2008. WFP is not a firewall but rather a set of system services and Application Programming Interfaces (APIs) for use by Microsoft and third-party developers. WFP enables unparalleled access to the Transmission Control Protocol/Internet Protocol (TCP/IP) stack so that inbound and outbound network packets can be examined or changed before allowing them to proceed. Developers can use WFP to build a variety of diagnostic and security tools, including firewalls and antivirus software. Figure 5-1 illustrates the WFP architecture and where third-party tools can plug into it.

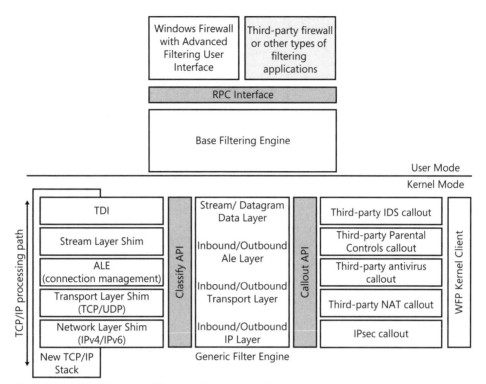

Figure 5-1   The Windows Filtering Platform architecture.

WFP includes the following architectural components:

■ The RPC Interface provides access to the WFP. Firewalls and other applications make calls to the WFP API, which are then passed to the Base Filtering Engine (BFE).

■ The Base Filtering Engine is the user-mode component that arbitrates between applications making filter request and the Generic Filter Engine, which runs inside the driver that implements the next-generation TCP/IP stack. The BFE adds and removes filters from the system, stores filter configuration, and enforces WFP configuration security.

■ The Generic Filtering Engine (GFE) is the kernel mode component that receives filter information from the Base Filtering Engine, interacts with callout drivers, and interacts with the TCP/IP stack. As packets are processed up and down the new TCP/IP stack they are evaluated by the Generic Filter Engine to see whether they should be allowed through. The Generic Filter Engine performs this evaluation by comparing each packet with the relevant filters and callout modules.

■ Callout modules are used when an application wants to perform deep packet inspection or data modification. For example, an antivirus tool may want to inspect traffic at the application layer before it is actually forwarded to the target application to ensure that no malware is present in the data.

Windows Firewall with Advanced Security

Connectivity is ubiquitous. Most computers are not only connected to an internal business network, but they are also connected to the Internet. High-speed wireless networks and mobile users are everywhere, often exposed directly to the Internet with its vast botnets hosting all sorts of viral malware and spewing measureless floods of spam. Even servers sitting on managed corporate networks face risks from returning travelers who plug in their laptops that became infected while on the road; from visiting consultants and customers who ask to share your network; and of course from malicious insiders who for whatever reason believe it is in their best interests to exploit your business systems.

For these reasons it makes sense to consider using the host firewall included with Windows Server 2008 to provide another layer of protection in your defense-in-depth architecture. Windows Firewall with Advanced Security provides bidirectional filtering to help keep unwanted traffic from getting to the services running on the system, and to prevent compromised servers from assaulting the rest of your network. Management of the Windows Firewall and Internet Protocol Security (IPsec) is integrated into a single Microsoft Management Console (MMC) console so that the firewall becomes the cornerstone of your network's isolation strategy.

Improvements in the Windows Firewall

Before we dive into the details of how to use the new Windows Firewall to protect your Windows Server 2008 hosts, let us quickly review the major enhancements over earlier versions.

Better Management Interface

The most significant improvement is a new graphical interface for managing the Windows Firewall locally and through Active Directory domain-based group policies. The old Control Panel item, Windows Firewall, still provides access to basic controls. The new user interface is a Microsoft Management Console (MMC) snap-in. For controlling local settings you can access Windows Firewall with Advanced Security console in the Administrative Tools folder. This snap-in is also part of the Group Policy editor console for managing the firewall via Active Directory domain group policies. Improvements have also been made to netsh.exe, the command-line tool for managing the firewall and IPsec. The netsh command now has a new context, advfirewall, which you can use to script configuration of the firewall or to manage it on a Server Core installation.

Windows Service Hardening

While many steps have been taken to protect the services themselves, an attacker can possibly still find a way to exploit a Windows system service. If a service is compromised, Windows Service Hardening will help to reduce the impact in several ways: The firewall will block abnormal behavior such as a service that does not need to access the network trying to send out HTTP traffic. Chapter 6, "Services," covers Windows Service Hardening in significant detail.

Outbound Filtering

After many years observing hand-wringing, hyperventilation, and multi-page walls of text from vendors, pundits, and security experts (both genuine and self-proclaimed), I concluded that in most cases, outbound filtering of network traffic on host firewalls is wasted effort. The key words in that sentence are *most cases*; I will address what I believe are legitimate uses of outbound filtering in a moment. To borrow a well-coined phrase from Bruce Schneier, whom I consider to be a true expert (even if I disagree with him frequently), outbound filtering is typically nothing more than "security theater." Inbound filtering is what will stop malicious network traffic such as Nimda, Slammer, Sasser, Blaster, or anything else that sends unwanted network traffic to your server.

A whole lot of bloviating was directed at Microsoft when it released the much-improved firewall in Service Pack 2 for Windows XP because it did not do outbound filtering. I am here to tell you that most of those complaints came from people who do not have a good grasp (to say it politely) of what is feasible in computer security or from organizations marketing their own client firewall products. If an attacker (or a piece of malware) has taken control of your computer, what will stop them from reconfiguring the firewall to allow traffic from whatever applications they want to run? The attacker probably does not even have to reconfigure the firewall—they could simply use whatever ports are already allowed, or take control of an application that can already send out traffic. Another really bad aspect of most client firewall solutions that do outbound filtering is the miserable user experience: After you install the cursed thing you are barraged by hundreds of pop-up dialog boxes asking if you really want to let Internet Explorer open a connection to *www.microsoft.com* or if you are absolutely certain it is a good idea for MSN Web Messenger to send traffic to *msn.com*. After a week of seeing several score of these dialog boxes, users—including paranoid systems administrators and security experts—tend to either disable the thing completely or become trained to click Yes or Accept immediately so they can get on with whatever it was they were hoping to accomplish on the computer!

Microsoft's newest server operating system makes intelligent use of outbound filtering by blocking system services from initiating network connections except for what they require to function properly. If a service is exploited, it is not going to be able to reconfigure the firewall without alerting the user because it is blocked from modifying the firewall settings. By default, the new firewall allows all other outbound network packets. You could change the default behavior to block all outbound traffic, but I do not recommend it because you will spend many hours, days, and perhaps even weeks trying to figure out every exception you need to make to allow your server to do everything you need it to do.

Granular Rules

In Windows Server 2008 and Windows Vista the firewall is enabled for both inbound and outbound connections. The default policies block most inbound traffic and allow most outbound traffic. The firewall supports filtering any IP protocol number, unlike the Windows XP firewall that could only filter Transmission Control Protocol (TCP), User Datagram Protocol (UDP), and Internet Control Message Protocol (ICMP) traffic, as shown in Figure 5-2. You can configure specific rules for blocking or allowing traffic by using IP addresses, IP protocol numbers, Active Directory directory service accounts and groups, system services, UDP and TCP source and destination ports, specific types of interfaces, and ICMP by type and code.

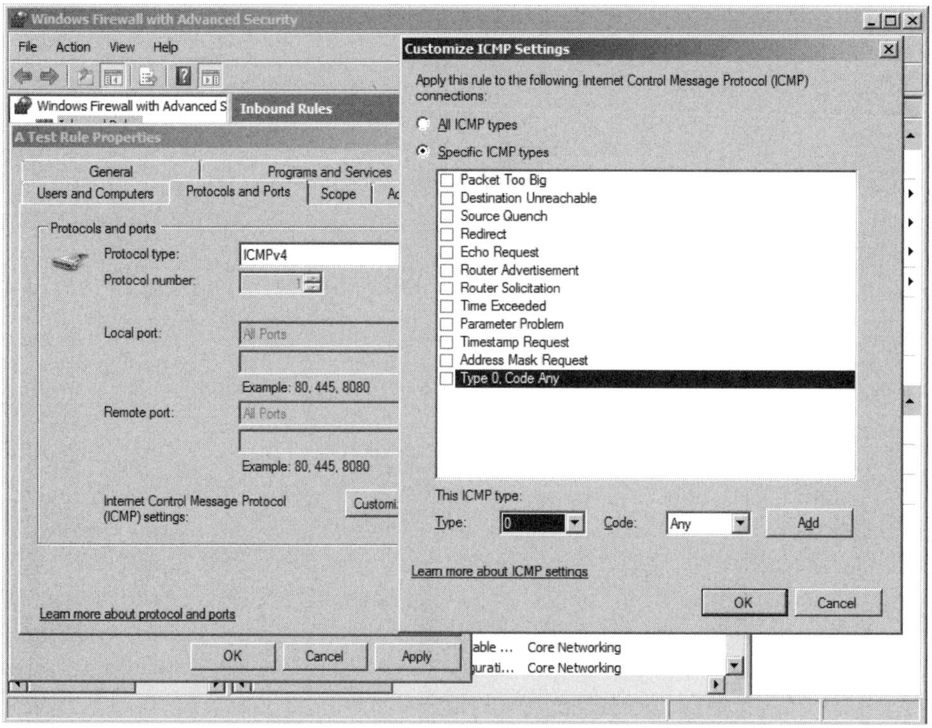

Figure 5-2   Some of the granular options for filtering in Windows Firewall with Advanced Security.

Location-Aware Profiles

Windows Firewall takes advantage of the new TCP/IP stack's ability to automatically track what network it is connected to. You can configure rules and settings for each of the three profiles: Domain, Private, and Public. The Domain profile applies when all of the computer's networks include Active Directory domain controllers for the domain that the computer belongs to. The Private profile is used when all active network connections have been designated by an administrator as a private ones protected by a firewall. The public profile is used when the computer is connected directly to the Internet, or the network has not been defined as Private or Domain.

Authenticated Bypass

You can configure rules that allow specific computers or groups of computers to bypass other firewall rules by using IPsec authentication in those rules. This means that you can block a particular type of traffic from all other hosts, but allow a select few systems to bypass that restrictions and access the blocked service. The rules can be even more specific, detailing which ports or programs can receive the traffic.

Active Directory User, Computer, and Groups Support

Rules can include users, computers, and groups defined in Active Directory, but you must secure connections affected by these types of rules with IPsec using an Active Directory account credential.

IPv6 Support

Windows Firewall with Advanced Security fully supports IPv6.

IPsec Integration

In Windows XP and Windows Server 2003, rules for the Windows Firewall and IPsec are configured separately. Because both can block or allow inbound traffic, you could accidentally create redundant or even contradictory rules. These types of configuration errors can be difficult to troubleshoot. The new Windows Firewall combines the configuration of both the firewall and IPsec into the same graphical and command-line tools, which both simplifies management and reduces the risk of misconfiguration.

Direct from the Source: Outbound Protection Is Security Theater

What is the purpose of a firewall? To block incoming traffic that you did not ask for. Does it make sense, perhaps, for a firewall to also block outgoing traffic that you did not approve? The manufacturers of many third-party firewalls believe so. They claim that the design of the Windows firewall offers insufficient functionality for a client firewall. Their argument is that a sufficient client firewall should block all traffic—inbound and outbound—unless the user has specifically granted permission.

Now, let us think this through for a moment. Two scenarios emerge. If you are running as a local administrator and you are infected by malware, the malware will simply disable the firewall. You are 0wn3d. If you are not running as a local administrator and you get infected by malware, the malware will cause a third-party firewall to raise a dialog filled with a foreign language involving ports and IP addresses and a very serious question: "Do you want to allow this?" The only answer, of course, is "Yes, you stupid computer, stop harassing me!" And once that dialog goes away, so does your security. Or, more commonly, the malware will simply hijack an existing session of a program you have already authorized, and you will not even see the dialog. Again, you are 0wn3d.

There is an important axiom of security that you must understand: Protection belongs on the asset you want to protect, not on the thing you are trying to protect against. The correct approach is to run the lean yet effective Windows Firewall on every computer in your organization, to protect each one from every other computer in the world. If you try to block outbound connections from a computer that is already compromised, how can you be sure that the computer is really doing what you ask? The answer: you cannot. Outbound protection is security theater—a gimmick that only gives the impression of improving your security without doing anything that actually does improve your security with one exception as noted earlier in this chapter: service hardening in Windows Vista and Windows Server 2008 does augment security.

Steve Riley, Security Evangelist
Microsoft Corporation

Managing the Windows Firewall

While the Windows Firewall Control Panel applet allows you to configure some basic settings, to manage the enhanced features you need to use the Windows Firewall with Advanced Security MMC console, the Group Policy Editor MMC console, or the netsh command-line tool. You can use the Windows Firewall with Advanced Security console to configure settings on remote computers as well as on the local host.

To manage the new Windows Firewall via Group Policy, navigate to Computer Configuration/ Windows Settings/Security Settings/Windows Firewall with Advanced Security in the Group Policy Editor snap-in, as shown in Figure 5-3. Group Policy settings for the new Windows Firewall are ignored by computers running Windows XP or Windows Server 2003—they continue to apply settings defined at Computer Configuration\Administrative Templates \Network\Network Connections\Windows Firewall. This may seem confusing, but because of the fundamental design changes and the IPsec integration, creating a new location in Group Policy for managing the new firewall was necessary.

Graphical Management

The Windows Firewall with Advanced Security console and the Windows Firewall with Advanced Security snap-in that appear in the Group Policy Editor console are virtually identical. The main difference is that the stand-alone console displays a Monitoring node where you can view real-time information on the status of firewall filtering rules, IPsec connection security rules, and Main Mode and Quick Mode Security Associations, as shown in Figure 5-4.

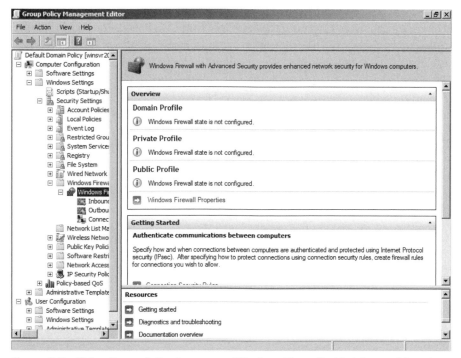

Figure 5-3   Using Group Policy to manage Windows Firewall with Advanced Security.

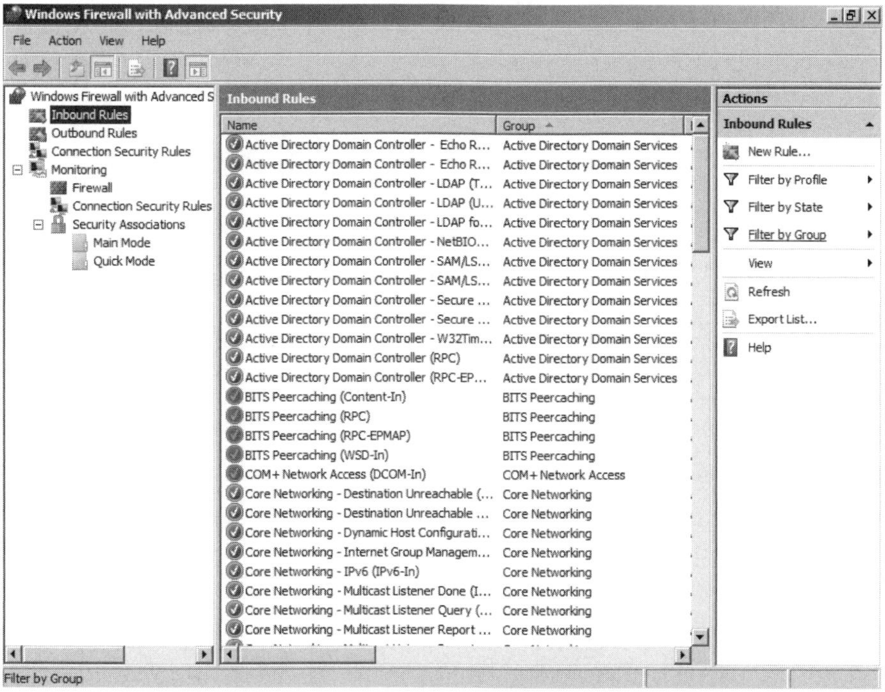

Figure 5-4   The Windows Firewall with Advanced Security Microsoft Management Console.

Many elements can be specified in a rule, including source and destination IP addresses; IP protocol numbers; source and destination TCP and UDP ports; Active Directory computer and user accounts; Active Directory groups; programs; system services; ICMP types and codes; and interface types such as wired, wires, or remote access. The process of creating inbound, outbound, and connection security rules is wizard-driven. As shown in Figure 5-5, you can choose one of four types: Program, Port, Predefined, or Custom when creating a new inbound rule. The wizard for outbound rules is virtually identical to the inbound one.

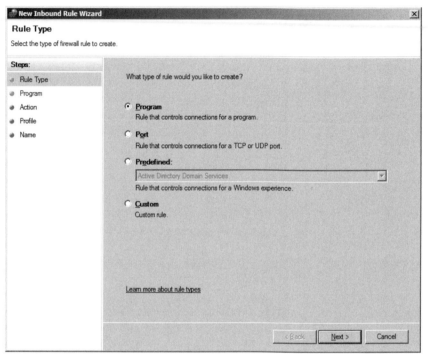

Figure 5-5   The New Inbound Rule Wizard.

On the first page of the wizard you specify what type of rule you want to create.

- **Program**   Select Program if you want to create a rule based on the name of a program. You must also specify what action to take: Allow The Connection, Allow The Connection If It Is Secure, or Block The Connection. You must choose which profile(s) the rule applies to—Domain, Private, or Public—and a name for the rule.

- **Port**   Select Port if you want to create a rule based on TCP or UDP port numbers. You must also specify what action to take: Allow The Connection, Allow The Connection If It Is Secure, or Block The Connection, You must choose which profile(s) the rule applies to—Domain, Private, or Public—and a name for the rule.

- **Predefined**   Select Program if you want to create a rule based on one of the predefined services. You must also specify what action to take: Allow The Connection, Allow The Connection If It Is Secure, or Block The Connection.

■ **Custom**   Select Custom if you want to create a rule that does not fit any of the three preceding types. You can define all combinations of characteristics, including a program name, system service, protocol type and number, local and remote ports, local IP addresses, and remote IP addresses. You must specify what action to take: Allow The Connection, Allow The Connection If It Is Secure, or Block The Connection. You must also specify which profile(s) the rule applies to—Domain, Private, or Public—and a name for the rule.

You can view and modify the properties of rules. However, many of the settings of the predefined rules cannot be altered. To configure advanced properties, right-click the name of the rule and then click Properties. A dialog box similar to that shown in Figure 5-6 will appear.

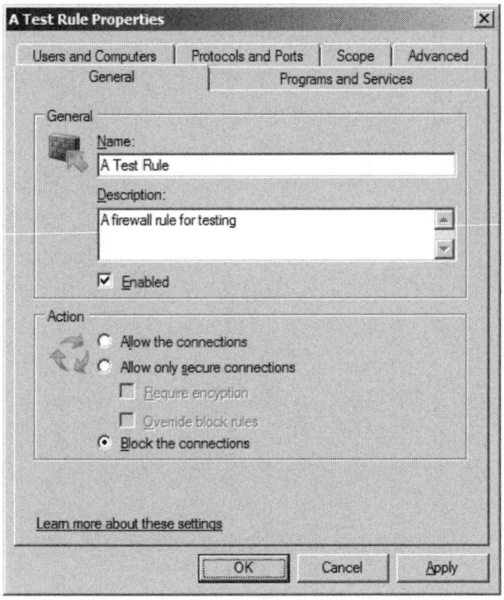

Figure 5-6   Advanced properties of a firewall rule.

Within the properties dialog box for either inbound or outbound rules, use the following tabs to configure various settings:

■ **General**   Use to define the name of the rule, its description, whether it is enabled, and what action to take (Allow, Allow If Secure, or Block).

■ **Programs and Services**   Use to specify whether the rule applies to all programs or only a specific one, and which service the rule applies to.

■ **Users And Computers**   If the rule's action is Allow If Secure, you can specify which accounts and groups are allowed to make the protected connection.

■ **Protocols And Ports**   Use to define the rule's protocol type and number, the source and destination port numbers, and the ICMP settings.

- **Scope**   Use to identify the rule's source and destination IP addresses.

- **Advanced**   Use to spell out the profiles, interface types, and whether edge traversal is allowed for the rule.

To create a new Computer Connection Security rule, right-click Connection Security Rules in the tree and then click New Rule. The New Connection Security Rule Wizard starts, as shown in Figure 5-7.

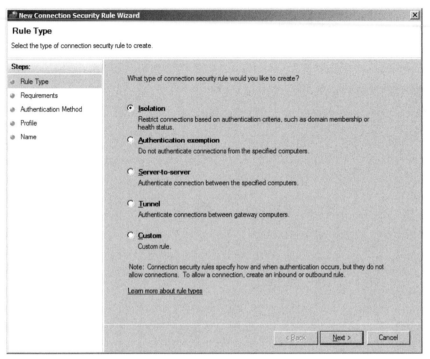

Figure 5-7   New Connection Security Rule Wizard.

On the first page of the wizard, specify what type of connection security rule you want to create.

- **Isolation**   Select Isolation to restrict connections based on the other computer's health status or domain membership. You must also specify whether you want to request or require authentication for inbound and outbound traffic, the authentication method, which profile(s) the rule applies to (Domain, Private, or Public), and a name for the rule. Isolation based on a computer's health status requires the deployment of the Network Access Protection (NAP) platform in Windows Vista and Windows Server 2008. NAP is discussed in more detail later in this chapter.

- **Authentication Exception**   Select Authentication Exception to define a list of hosts that do not have to authenticate or protect their traffic by their IP addresses. You must also specify which profile(s) the rule applies to—Domain, Private, or Public—as well as a name for the rule.

- **Server-To-Server**   Select Server-To-Server to require protection of network traffic between specific hosts. You must specify the endpoints that will exchange the protected traffic, whether you want to request or require authentication for inbound and outbound traffic, the authentication method, which profile(s) the rule applies to (Domain, Private, or Public), and a name for the rule. These rules are typically used in a Server Isolation deployment, which is discussed at length in Chapter 13, "Securing the Network."

- **Tunnel**   This rule is normally used to secure traffic across the Internet between two gateway computers. You must define the tunnel endpoints by IP address, the authentication method, which profile(s) the rule applies to (Domain, Private, or Public), and a name for the rule.

- **Custom**   Select Custom to create a rule that does not fit any of the previous types. You must specify the endpoint computers by IP address, whether you want to request or require authentication for inbound and outbound traffic, the authentication method, which profile(s) the rule applies to (Domain, Private, or Public), and a name for the rule.

You can view and modify the properties of connection security rules by right-clicking the name of the rule and clicking Properties. A dialog box similar to that shown in Figure 5-8 will appear.

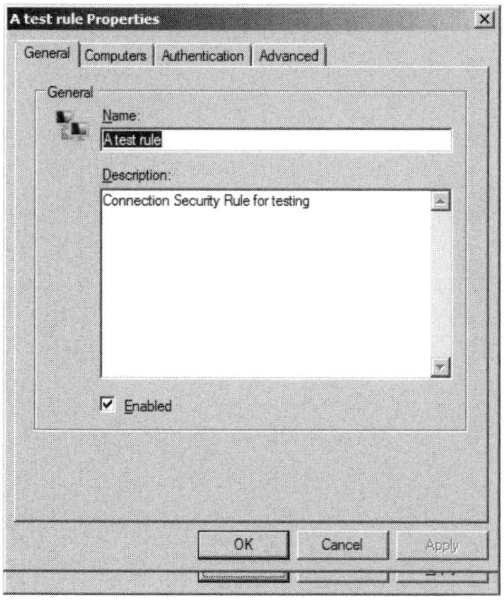

Figure 5-8   Advanced properties of a connection security rule.

Within the Properties dialog box for the rule you can use the following tabs to configure various settings.

General

Use this tab to define the name of the rule, its description, and whether it is enabled.

- **Computers**   Use this tab to specify which computers (by their IP addresses) have protected traffic.

- **Authentication**   Use this tab to identify what authentication is required for the protected traffic.

- **Advanced**   Use this tab to spell out the profiles, interface types, and whether the rule requires IPsec tunneling.

The firewall processes rules in the following order:

1. Service Restrictions

2. Connection Security Rules

3. Authenticated Bypass

4. Block Rules

5. Allow Rules

6. Default Rules

Command-Line Management

Netsh is a command-line tool that provides a text-based shell for managing network components. In Windows Server 2008 you can configure Windows Firewall with Advanced Security by utilizing commands available in the advfirewall context. With netsh you change to a specific context to modify components within that context. Many other contexts are available beyond the advfirewall context, including interface, nap, ras, and rpc. A complete discussion of all of the capabilities of netsh is beyond the scope of this chapter. We will focus on the context used for managing the firewall.

You need to use netsh in a command prompt that has administrative privileges. Although UAC is not enabled by default in Windows Server 2008, it might be enabled on your servers, and some readers are likely to be performing management tasks on Windows Vista computers, where UAC is enabled by default. To open an elevated command prompt, follow these steps:

Click Start.

Type **command prompt** in the Start Search field.

Right-click the command prompt icon and select Run As Administrator.

When the UAC prompt appears, click Continue. Depending upon how UAC is configured in your environment you may need to provide credentials for an account with administrative privileges.

Enter **netsh** at the command prompt to launch the tool. At the netsh prompt enter **advfirewall** to enter the advanced firewall context. Many commands are available. You can enter a question mark symbol (**?**) or **help** to see a list of commands available in your currently selected context. The following commands are available in the advfirewall context:

- **Dump**   Displays a configuration script.

- **Export**   Exports the current policy to a file.

- **Import**   Imports a policy file into the current policy store.

- **Reset**   Resets the policy to the default out-of-box policy.

- **Set**   Sets the per-profile or global settings.

- **Show**   Displays profile or global properties.

The following subcontexts are also available. To enter one, type the name of the subcontext at the netsh advfirewall prompt.

- **Consec**   Changes to the netsh advfirewall consec context where you configure connection security rules

- **Firewall**   Changes to the netsh advfirewall firewall context where you view and configure inbound and outbound firewall rules

- **Monitor**   Changes to the netsh advfirewall monitor context where you can view and monitor security associations.

You can use netsh to create elaborate scripts to automate configuration procedures that you need to implement on multiple computers. This can be very useful for computers that are not joined to a domain, such as computers in a test lab or a screened subnet that is accessible to visitors from the Internet.

Network Profiles

Although the ability to remember and recognize networks is more important on mobile computers, it may still be useful to have a deeper understanding of how Windows determines what kind of network it is connected to. When a domain-joined computer successfully logs onto its domain, the domain profile is automatically applied—you cannot specify this profile, as shown in Figure 5-9. When the computer is connected to a network that is protected by a perimeter firewall, you can select the private profile if you have administrative privileges. When the computer is connected directly to the Internet, you should select the public profile. You probably noticed that the dialog box presents three choices, but note that selecting either Work or Home will cause the private profile to be applied.

In the event of a network change, such as a new IP address or a new network interface, the Network Location Awareness (NLA) service notes the change. NLA creates a database of previously used networks so that it can recognize them when the computer reconnects to them. The database includes information about which interface is connected to the network, whether the computer authenticated to a domain controller, and the default gateway's MAC address. If NLA recognizes the network, the appropriate profile is automatically selected and the firewall applies the corresponding policy. NLA tries to select the most restrictive profile, so if you are simultaneously connected to the corporate network and to your cellular provider via a wireless modem, the public profile will be applied, not the domain profile. Additionally, when you make a VPN connection to your corporate network, the public or private profile will apply depending upon which profile you specified when you connected the system to your home network (or wherever you are physically located). This means that rules that may have been set up to facilitate remote management of the system will be overridden by the more restrictive profile in effect. It is important to understand that only one profile can be active at any one time. The most restrictive profile is always the one that is active if the computer is on multiple networks that use different profiles.

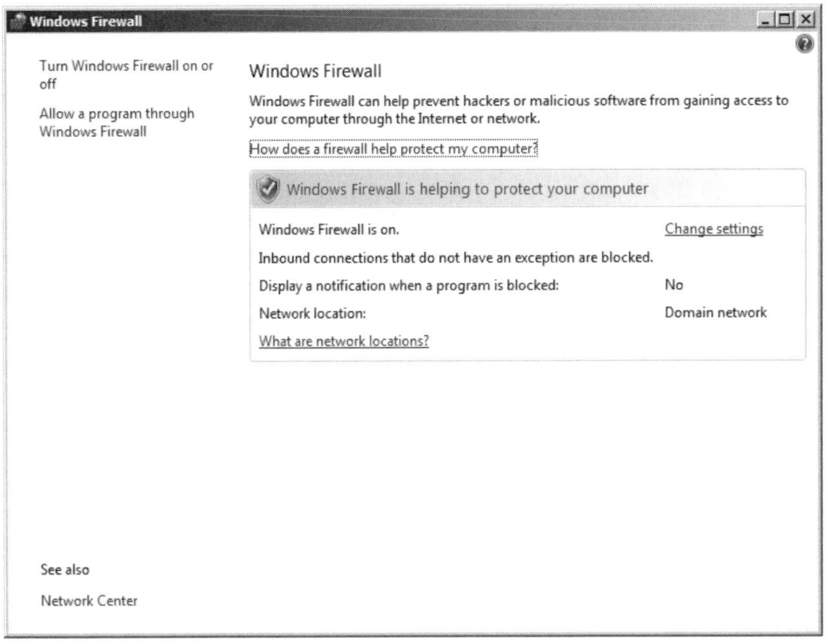

Figure 5-9   Windows Firewall configuration screen illustrating that the Domain Network profile has been automatically applied.

Caution   If you use Group Policy to block outbound connections, be sure to thoroughly test all of your applications; otherwise, they may fail. In fact, computers will be unable to update their domain-based group policies if you have misconfigured outbound rules.

Routing and Remote Access Services

This chapter assumes that you are already familiar with previous versions of Routing And Remote Access Services (RRAS) and will therefore focus on what is new and improved in

Windows Server 2008. This chapter focuses in particular on what I think is the most important addition: Secure Socket Tunneling Protocol (SSTP), which is an SSL VPN technology. Technology like this was previously available only as separate products from Microsoft and third-party vendors. If you need to establish a foundation of knowledge on RRAS, you should visit the links provided in the Additional Resources section at the end of this chapter.

Important   You might miss how to install RRAS with the Add Roles Wizard if you don't read the descriptions of each server role. RRAS is part of Network Policy and Access Services. When you select that role RRAS is one of the role services you can choose.

Improvements in RRAS

The following sections provide a brief summary of the new and improved capabilities in Windows Server 2008's RRAS.

Support for IPv6

Both the remote access client and RRAS fully support IPv6 for Point-to-Point Protocol (PPP) and Layer Two Tunneling Protocol with IPsec (L2TP/IPsec) VPN connections. Additional support for IPv6 is included in the DHCPv6 Relay Agent, RADIUS, and static packet filters.

NAP Enforcement for Remote Access VPN Connections

RRAS can now enforce NAP requirements on incoming VPN connections. For more information, see "Network Access Protection" later in this chapter.

Updated Connection Creation Wizard

Configuring dial-up, broadband Internet, and VPN connections has been simplified in the Connection Creation Wizard.

Secure Socket Tunneling Protocol

Windows Server 2008 supports a new type of VPN tunnel that is commonly referred to as an SSL VPN. The Secure Socket Tunneling Protocol (SSTP) allows traffic to pass through firewalls, proxy servers, and network address translation (NAT) devices that block PPTP and L2TP/IPsec connections. PPP traffic is encapsulated in the SSL channel of the HTTPS protocol. This means that the traffic will be blocked by fewer network security devices and will be protected by strong encryption and integrity checking. When a user running Windows Server 2008 or Windows Vista with Service Pack 1 initiates an SSTP-based VPN connection, the following process occurs:

1. The client requests an SSL session with the SSTP server.

2. The SSTP server sends its computer certificate to the client.

3. The client validates the computer certificate, determines the encryption method, generates a session key, encrypts the session key using the SSTP server's public key in the certificate, and then sends the encrypted session key to the SSTP server.

4. The SSTP server decrypts the session key using the private key that corresponds to the computer certificate. Henceforth all traffic is encrypted with the SSL session key.

5. The client negotiates an SSTP tunnel with the SSTP server.

6. The client requests a PPP connection with the SSTP server using the SSTP tunnel. During the negotiation the user provides his credentials, and IPv4 or IPv6 settings are determined.

7. The client begins sending IPv6 or IPv4 traffic over the PPP link.

Support for Multiple Locations in CMAK

The Connection Manager Administration Kit (CMAK) allows Connection Manager profiles to be created on a server of any locale and deployed on clients of any locale, which simplifies CMAK-based management.

Support for Dynamic DNS Updates in Connection Manager

Connection Manager clients now support registration of client names and addresses using Dynamic DNS.

Support for the Network Diagnostics Framework

RRAS now supports the Network Diagnostics Framework for client-based connections, which should make managing and troubleshooting RRAS easier.

Enhanced WinLogin Support

Third-party access providers can configure their connections to automatically establish remote access connections when users log on.

Additional Cryptographic Algorithms

L2TP/IPsec-based connections now support Advanced Encryption Standard (AES) with 128- and 256-bit keys. Weaker algorithms such as 40- and 56-bit Microsoft Point-to-Point (MPPE) for PPTP and DES with Message Digest 5 (MD5) for L2TP/IPsec are disabled by default. You can enable 40- and 56-bit MPPE for PPTP connections by configuring the DWORD value of HKEY_LOCAL_MACHINE\System\CurrentControlSet\Services \Rasman\Parameters\AllowPPTPWeakCrypto to 1 and rebooting the computer. To enable DES with MD5 for L2TP/IPsec connections, set the DWORD value of HKEY_LOCAL_MACHINE\System\CurrentControlSet\Services\Rasman\Parameters \AllowL2TPWeakCrypto to 1, and then reboot the computer. Of course, you have to question the sanity of enabling a switch called *weak crypto*.

Robust Certificate Checking for VPN Connections

RRAS supports more rigorous certificate checking to help block man-in-the-middle attacks. The additional analysis by the VPN client includes verifying that the Subject or Subject Alternative Name fields of the VPN server's certificate match the name or IP address of the VPN server as defined for the VPN connection. You can disable this additional certificate checking on the VPN client as follows: Open the Properties dialog box for the connection, click the Networking tab, click IPsec Settings, and then clear the Verify The Name And Usage Attributes Of The Server's Certificate check box, as shown in Figure 5-10.

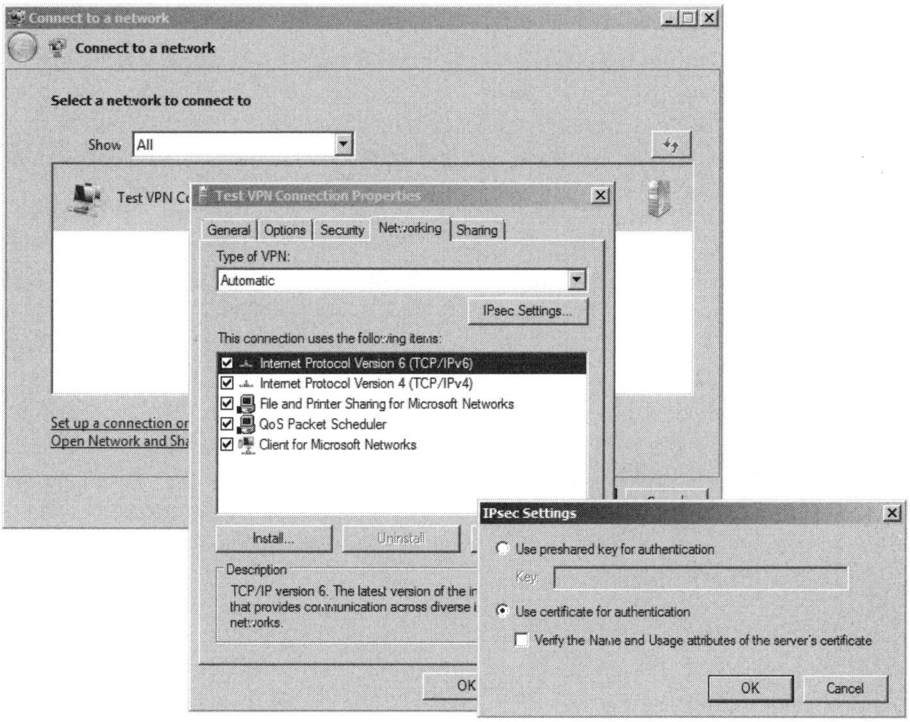

Figure 5-10   Disabling rigorous certificate checking for a VPN connection.

Internet Protocol Security

This section starts with a quick refresher on the basics of IPsec, then spends more time discussing the new capabilities relating to IPsec in Windows Server 2008, and finally shows you how to use the technology to isolate servers and domains, a foundation for your NAP architecture.

IPsec Basics

IPsec is an open standard used to protect information transiting networks from unauthorized access and modification. This is done using a combination of authentication protocols, data encryption, and digital signatures. When two hosts begin to use IPsec to communicate they initially establish two security associations. In *phase one* or *main mode*, the hosts authenticate with one another; in *phase two* or *quick mode*, the hosts negotiate what protocols they will use to digitally sign or encrypt network traffic. Each packet can be signed to let the receiving host be certain that it came from the trusted host and that it has not been altered in any way. Each packet can be encrypted to protect the data from being accessed by anything other than the receiving host. You can configure IPsec rules to implement either or both of these forms of protection.

IPsec Authentication

Security associations are negotiated using the Internet Key Exchange (IKE) protocol, which itself consists of three other protocols: ISAKMP, Oakley, and SKEME. Via IKE, the two hosts agree how authentication messages will be constructed and exchanged. (The complete details are quite complex and beyond the scope of this chapter.) The hosts can authenticate using a number of methods, including the following:

- **Kerberos version 5**   If both hosts are in the same Active Directory forest, they can use Kerberos for mutual authentication. Kerberos is ideal when you do not have a public key infrastructure (PKI) and trusts do not have to be established with hosts outside of your forest.

- **Digital certificates**   If the hosts have access to a robust PKI, digital certificates may be the ideal authentication method. Windows XP and later versions of the Microsoft operating system support automated distribution of computer certificates, which overcomes one of the biggest challenges of managing a large PKI: distributing certificates. As long as each host has a certificate signed by a Certificate Authority (CA) trusted by the other, they will authenticate to one another.

- **Preshared keys**   Support for preshared keys is only included for conformance with the IPsec standard. The only time using this method might make sense is when you are developing and testing your IPsec policies. Every host that is part of the policy will need to have the same key. Just as having multiple users share the same password is a bad idea, having multiple computers share the same key for authentication is poor practice.

New authentication capabilities in Windows Server 2008 are described later in this section.

IPsec Communication Modes

IPsec communication happens in one of two modes: Transport mode or Tunnel mode.

Transport mode is appropriate when you want to have multiple computers use IPsec with each other. In this mode the two hosts authenticate with one another in phase one, and then agree on traffic signing and encryption procedures. Although it may seem to be the opposite of what you expected, this is the mode used for L2TP VPNs between the remote client and the VPN server.

Tunnel mode is suitable for protecting site-to-site connections that traverse an untrusted network such as the Internet. In other words, each of the two hosts is the gateway that routes traffic between the sites. At the gateway the outbound traffic is encrypted and sent to the remote gateway, where it is unencrypted and routed across the internal network to its ultimate destination.

IPsec Methods

If an IPsec rule requires the hosts to negotiate security, it does so using one or both of two methods: Encapsulated Security Payload (ESP) or Authentication Header (AH).

ESP can provide both confidentiality (via encryption) and integrity (via signatures). Both the encryption and signature include the payload and TPC/UDP header of each packet, but not the IP address, which means that with supporting technologies such as NAT Traversal (NAT-T), ESP traffic can be sent across NAT devices. It is also possible to use null encryption with ESP, which means that each packet is signed but not encrypted. Similar to AH, this means that you can be confident that the traffic has not been tampered with while en route between hosts. This the default method when you select to authenticate sessions between two hosts.

AH ensures message integrity via digital signatures calculated on the entire packet, including the IP header (which includes the source and destination IP addresses). AH has two significant limitations: it provides no confidentiality because it does not support data encryption, and AH traffic cannot traverse NAT devices because these devices change the IP address of the internal host on each packet before forwarding them.

> **Important**   Authentication Headers are no longer supported in Windows Server 2008. The information provided here is for reference only.

IPsec Rules and Policies

An IPsec policy consists of one or more IPsec rules. Each host can have only a single IPsec policy. Each rule has both a filter list and a filter action. Filter lists specify the characteristics of the traffic that the rule applies to, such as addresses, ports, and protocols. Filter actions define what the rule does to the traffic: allow it, block it, or negotiate security. The first two actions are similar to what a port-filtering firewall does, and some security guidance for Windows 2000, Windows XP, and Windows Server 2003 showed how to use IPsec filtering to mimic a host-based firewall. However, IPsec filtering is not stateful, which means its value as a firewall replacement is limited. When negotiating security, the rule tells the host whether to require ESP or AH; request ESP or AH but allow unprotected traffic; and the details of which authentication, encryption, and signing protocols to use.

New Capabilities in Windows Server 2008

The improvements described in the following sections were made to IPsec in Windows Server 2008.

Integrated Firewall and IPsec Configuration

In Windows XP and Windows Server 2003, rules for Windows Firewall and IPsec are configured separately. Because both can block or allow inbound traffic, accidentally creating redundant or even contradictory rules is possible. These types of configuration errors can be difficult to troubleshoot. The new graphical and command-line management tools combine the configuration of both the firewall and IPsec, which both simplifies management and reduces the risk of misconfiguration. In the past the firewall and IPsec supported different characteristics for elements in rules. For example you could create a firewall exception based on an application name but IPsec did not support rules based on application names.

Simplified IPsec Policy Configuration

Prior to Windows Vista and Windows Server 2008, you needed to configure one set of rules to protect traffic and another set of rules to create protected traffic exemptions that were required for infrastructure servers such as DHCP, DNS, and domain controllers. During start-up, the client computer could not access these services if the server required IPsec. The new version of IPsec is able to overcome this challenge by simultaneously initiating both IPsec-protected and in-the-clear connections. If the other host does not respond to the IPsec request, the initiating host will continue to communicate in the clear. If it receives a response to the IPsec request it will continue to communicate in the clear until the negotiation is complete. When that happens all additional traffic is protected. Obviously, this only happens if IPsec is requested, not if it is required. While this behavior is optional, it is recommended because it greatly simplifies the IPsec policies for an enterprise. This new behavior also allows for quicker network connections because Windows XP and Windows Server 2003 hosts that are configured to request IPsec but allow in-the-clear communications will wait for up to 3 seconds for IPsec to fail before switching to unprotected communications.

Improved IPsec Authentication

In addition to authenticating with Kerberos, digital certificates, and preshared keys, Windows Server 2008 systems can authenticate with health certificates. Health certificates are given to clients by a Health Registration Authority (HRA) after the client has proven that its health state complies with the current policy. This is a component of NAP, which is discussed in "Network Access Protection" later in this chapter. Available authentication methods for IPsec include:

- A computer health certificate
- A user certificate

- NTLMv2 credentials of the computer

- NTLMv2 credentials of the logged on user

- Kerberos credentials of the logged on user

This means that you could require Kerberos credentials for the initial computer authentication and subsequently require a health certificate. The second authentication can be also be used without the first one.

Improved Load Balancing and Clustering Server Support

Earlier versions of IPsec typically took 3 to 6 seconds to recover from an administration change and up to 2 minutes when a cluster node failed, but in Windows Server 2008 and Windows Vista the time-out is much shorter; typically it is fast enough to allow the application to continue functioning. Rather than waiting for idle time-outs to detect a failed cluster node, IPsec actively monitors TCP connections for established security associations (SAs). If the SA begins retransmitting packets, IPsec will renegotiate SAs to try to restore the connection to another node in the cluster.

Client-to-DC IPsec Protection

Windows Server 2008 supports IPsec between domain controllers and member computers in two modes. First, you can configure policy to request but not require IPsec—domain controllers will protect most traffic with domain members but allow in-the-clear communications for domain joins and other types of traffic. Second, you can configure policy to require IPsec and allow NTLMv2 authentication, in which case all communication with domain controllers will be protected. This more restrictive configuration will work because NTLMv2 user credentials can be used for authentication. When a computer running Windows Server 2008 or Windows Vista attempts to join the domain, the user will be prompted for a user name and password for an account in the domain that is allowed to add computer accounts. This new behavior is only available with client computers running Windows Vista or Windows Server 2008 and domain controllers running Windows Server 2008.

Integrated IPv4 and IPv6 Support

Support for IPsec with IPv6 is identical to support for IPsec with IPv4, which was not the case prior to Windows Vista and Windows Server 2008. IPsec policy rules for both IPv6 and IPv4 are configured in the same way using the same tools, such as the Windows Firewall with Advanced Security console.

Integration with Network Access Protection

You can use NAP to require hosts to perform a second authentication with a health certificate, ensuring that each host meets your organization's system health requirements. For more information, see "Network Access Protection" later in this chapter.

Additional Configuration Options for Protected Communication

Connection security rules support the following additional settings:

- **Ranges of IP addresses**   You can now use numeric ranges such as 192.168.10.15 to 192.168.10.68.

- **For all wireless adapters**   Wireless adapters are another interface type that you can specify for a rule.

New Cryptographic Support

As the science of cryptography evolves, Microsoft continues to add support for newer, more robust algorithms to its operating systems. Windows Server 2008 and Windows Vista add support for the following algorithms for the master key material derived during main mode negotiation.

- **Diffie-Hellman (DH) Group 19**   This is an elliptic curve algorithm using a 256-bit random curve group (NIST identifier P-256).

- **DH Group 20**   This is an elliptic curve algorithm using a 384-bit random curve group (NIST identifier P-384).

Windows Server 2008 and Windows Vista now support these new data encryption algorithms:

- Advanced Encryption Standard (AES) with cipher block chaining (CBC) and a 128-bit key size (**AES 128**)

- AES with CBC and a 192-bit key size (**AES 192**)

- AES with CBC and a 256-bit key size (**AES 256**)

> **Caution**   Earlier versions of Windows, such as Windows 2000, Windows XP, and Windows Server 2003, include some of these algorithms for other functions; they do not support the them for use in IPsec.

Network Diagnostics Framework Support

IPsec now supports the Network Diagnostics Framework (NDF). NDF is an infrastructure and a set of built-in components that try to diagnose and fix connection issues automatically. When a problem arises NDF will offer to help the user determine what has gone wrong and repair the issue within the context that the problem arose. That means that the messages from NDF are presented to the user in the application she was using when the problem arose.

Extended Events and Performance Monitor Counters

New IPsec-specific audit events have been added, and the text of existing events has been updated to include more useful information to assist you with troubleshooting IPsec-related problems. IPsec performance counters have also been added.

Expanded Authenticated Bypass

You can configure bypass rules so that connections from certain computers can bypass the other IPsec rules. This means that you can block the traffic from all hosts, but allow the authenticated computers to bypass the block. This is useful when you want to allow vulnerability scanners or other management tools to be able to access the protected hosts.

Network Access Protection

Network Access Protection (NAP) is a platform for enforcing system health requirements on hosts before they are allowed to access network resources. NAP can ensure that the system complies with a particular update level and configuration requirements such as firewall state. NAP can also ensure that certain software, such as antimalware, is installed and up to date.

Windows Server 2008 includes the server components required for NAP. It can also be a NAP client, as can Windows Vista, Windows XP, and Windows Server 2003–although the latter two require updates from Microsoft that are due to be released in 2008. Health policies define which updates, antimalware signatures, software versions, security settings, and other settings must be present on the NAP client for it to gain access to network resources. Noncompliant systems can be granted access to a limited network where they can make whatever changes are required to become compliant. After reading about IPsec in the previous section, you may be able to start thinking about ways to incorporate NAP into your overall isolation strategy.

> **Note** Although NAP is a powerful management and policy enforcement tool, it may not be able to stop users with nefarious intent—especially malicious insiders—from doing things on your network you do not welcome.

Although Windows Server 2008 includes the foundation required for deploying and managing NAP, Microsoft also envisions that many third-party developers will want to integrate their security solutions into the architecture. NAP includes a set of APIs that you can use to incorporate other tools for health policy validation, controlling access to the network, remediation, and ongoing compliance. Microsoft is participating in several vendor consortiums and working with numerous partners to ensure operability with as wide a range of complementary technologies as is feasible.

Architecture

Current enterprise solutions for protecting networks from computers that do not meet security requirements may seem daunting. Some analysts and pundits have criticized these solutions for their complexity, management challenges, and poor interoperability. Windows Server 2008 and Windows Vista address these issues head on with easy-to-use wizards, powerful management tools, and the ability to interoperate with solutions from a wide range of partners. The NAP architecture consists of a number of server and network components that interact with NAP clients to distribute and enforce health policies and to address noncompliance. Figure 5-11 illustrates these components.

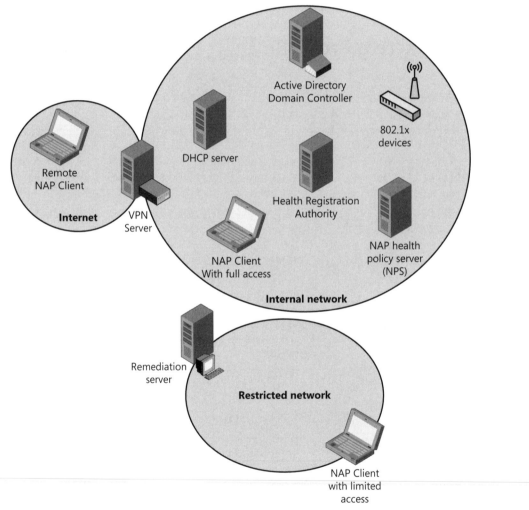

Figure 5-11   Summary view of the NAP components illustrating VPN, DHCP, and 802.1s enforcement.

Network Policy Server

Network Policy Server (NPS) is Microsoft's implementation of a Remote Authentication Dial-In User Service (RADIUS) server in Windows Server 2008. It replaces Internet Authentication Server (IAS) in Windows Server 2003. NPS performs health evaluation and determines what access to grant NAP clients. When an access request is received, NPS extracts the client's statement of health (SoH) and forwards it to the NAP Administration Server. Based on the Statement of Health Requests (SoHRs) from the System Health Validators (SHVs) and the health policies, NPS creates a System Statement of Health Response (SSoHR) that states whether the client complies.

> **Note**   Notice all the acronyms in the preceding paragraph? An unstated requirement of any new technology is to introduce new acronyms, and NAP does so with enthusiasm. You might want to keep a written list handy while you read about NAP, or refer to the IPSec, Firewall, RRAS, and NAP Acronyms section later in this chapter.

NAP Administration Server

The NAP Administration Server facilitates communication between the SHVs and the NPS server. The Administration Server receives SSoH from the NAP Enforcement Server (NAP ES) via the NPS service, distributes the SoHs in the SSoH to the SHVs, and collects SoHRs from the SHVs, which are then evaluated by the NPS service.

Health Registration Authority

The Health Registration Authority (HRA) receives SSoHRs for NAP clients when they have demonstrated compliance. The SSoHR is used to authenticate NAP clients when they connect to other NAP clients via IPsec.

Host Credential Authorization Protocol

Host Credential Authorization Protocol (HCAP) is provided for interoperability with Cisco's Network Access Control technology. NPS provides the Extended State and Policy Expiration attributes in network policy for Cisco integration.

Remediation Servers

Remediation servers are used to update clients in whatever ways are necessary to bring them into compliance when they have failed to prove that their health status meets the organization's policies. Remediation servers could host the latest antimalware signatures, updates and service packs for Windows, configuration scripts, and other resources to bring clients into compliance.

Enforcement Components

A NAP ES regulates the NAP client's network access, passes the client's SoH to the NPS for evaluation, and then provides either restricted or complete access based on the NPS server's response. Windows Server 2008 has four built-in Enforcement Servers: IPsec, VPN, Terminal Server Gateway, and DHCP.

Enforcement Methods

The following options are available for enforcing network restrictions on noncompliant hosts:

- **IPsec**   This is the preferred method because every managed host protects itself from hosts that do not meet your organization's system health requirements. Regardless of how and where the potentially dangerous computer is connected, all managed computers will ignore communications until that computer proves that it meets policy.

- **IEEE 802.1x**   This technique controls access by using restrictions that are enforced by network switches and wireless access points. Until the host has proven its health status it can be restricted by a virtual LAN identifier or a set of IP packet filters.

- **VPN**   VPN is a good way to enforce policy on remote clients. After the user has proven his identity, his access is limited until the computer he is using has demonstrated its compliance with your health policies. If you are familiar with the Network Access Quarantine feature in Windows Server 2003, NAP may sound similar, but it is built with completely new technology.

- **Terminal Server Gateway**   Terminal Server Gateway (TS Gateway) restricts access for remote terminal services clients when they access internal resources via Remote Desktop Protocol (RDP) over HTTPS.

- **DHCP**   DHCP enforcement may seem like the easiest solution to deploy, but it is also the weakest. With this approach, access is controlled via the host's IPv4 address configuration and routing tables. An ingenious user with administrative privileges can easily bypass it by manually configuring her TCP/IP settings. If you support hosts that do not understand NAP, or claim not to, on the same network, anyone can get on by simply claiming to not speak NAP.

System Health Validators

- A System Health Validator (SHV) is an element on the NAP client that can be matched to a System Health Agent (SHA). An SHA corresponds to one or more health requirement servers. Antivirus is a good example. You could have an SHA for the antivirus program and an SHV to compare the antivirus signatures on the client with the server that hosts up-to-date signature files. Windows Server 2008 includes the Windows Security Health Validator. Microsoft and other vendors can create additional SHVs to plug into the NAP platform. The Windows SHV can enforce the following scenarios for NAP clients:

❑ The client computer has firewall software installed and enabled.

❑ The client computer has antivirus software installed and running.

❑ The client computer has current antivirus updates installed.

❑ The client computer has antispyware software installed and running.

❑ The client computer has current antispyware updates installed.

❑ Microsoft Update Services is enabled on the client computer.

System Health Agents

■ SHAs monitor the client's health state so that NPS knows whether the NAP client is compliant. For example, the Windows System Health Agent (WSHA), which corresponds to the Windows SHV described previously, can watch the Windows Firewall. The WSHA can also determine the following:

❑ whether antivirus software is installed, enabled, and up to date

❑ whether antispyware software is installed, enabled, and up to date

❑ whether Microsoft Update Services is enabled

❑ whether the host has the most recent security updates installed

Other vendors can create additional SHAs for other security solutions.

NAP Agent

The NAP agent collects health information, processes SoHs from SHAs, and reports the health state to enforcement clients. It uses a system SoH to report overall health.

NAP Enforcement Clients

To use NAP, a NAP enforcement client (NAP EC) must be running on the client computers. Individual NAP ECs correspond to each of the enforcement methods discussed earlier, such as IPsec and TS Gateway. The NAP EC requests network access, communicates with the NPS server, and communicates the status of the NAP client to other components in the NAP client architecture.

NAP Implementation

NAP is flexible. You can configure it to meet the needs and capabilities of your organization; therefore, implementations will vary from network to network. This section demonstrates how NAP would work on a sample network: Hosts requesting access to network resources will be granted limited access if they are either noncompliant NAP clients or clients incapable of authenticating with the NAP infrastructure. The hosts will be granted full access if they are NAP clients configured in accordance with health policy. Read on for greater detail.

When the NAP client tries to access network resources, the NAP agent on the client gathers SoHs from each of the SHAs. The NAP agent combines these into an SSoH. It then creates a RADIUS Access Request message, which it sends to the NAP EC. The NAP EC sends the Access Request message to the NAP ES, which sends it to the NPS service on the NAP health policy server. The NPS service rejects any RADIUS messages from clients that it is not configured to manage. The NPS service checks to see whether the Access Request message corresponds to its set of connection request policies. The Access Request message should match one that requires the NPS service to authenticate and authorize locally.

The NPS service evaluates the health information in the Access Request message, which has an SSoH with one or more SoHs. The NAP Administration Server component on the NAP health policy server forwards each SoH to the corresponding SHV. Each SHV determines whether the SoH it received is compliant. The NAP Administration Server generates a set of SoHRs from the SHVs. The NPS service compares the Access Request message and the SoHRs to the network policies. The SoHRs are compared to the Health Policies within the network policies. The NPS service then applies the network policy that best matches the Access Request message. The best match is either the first match with a specific source (for requests that specify a source tag that specifies the type of RADIUS client) or the first one with an unspecified source.

The NPS service generates an SSoHR based on the best matching network policy and the NAP settings within the policy. The SSoHR includes the SoHRs from the SHVs and declares whether the client has limited or unlimited access. If access is limited, the SSoHR also states whether the client should attempt automated remediation. The NPS service sends a RADIUS Access Accept message with the SSoHR to the NAP ES. The NAP ES then forwards the SSoHR to the client. In some cases the NPS service will send the SSoHR directly to the client, and access limitation instructions to the NAP ES. If the client has limited access, this message can also include a list of addresses for the remediation servers. The NAP ES sends the SSoHR to the NAP client. This process is illustrated in Figure 5-12. The solid lines show the request for access as it originates in the client, is transmitted to the Enforcement Server, and then moves up through the server-side components. The dotted lines show the response as it is created at the Administration Server and communicate back through the Enforcement Server to the client.

Note   Hosts that are unable to use NAP will get limited access by default. For example, if IPsec is used for enforcement, hosts will be unable to connect to any other protected host on the network because those systems will ignore traffic from the foreign host. If DHCP is used for enforcement, the client will receive IP address configuration information and routes that restrict access.

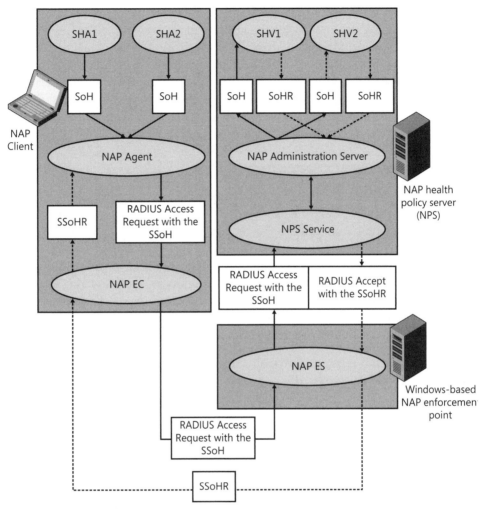

Figure 5-12   Path of messages between NAP components.

Direct from the Source: 802.1x and IPsec Enforcement in Network Access Protection

NAP includes a variety of methods for enforcing network policies for both local and remote computers. The two methods most suited for local enforcement on enterprise networks are 802.1x and IPsec. Do not think of these two methods as mutually exclusive options, but rather as complementary technologies that can be combined to provide two powerful layers of defense-in-depth for your network.

802.1x is a physical network authentication standard that originally was mostly widely adopted for securing wireless networks. However, most modern, enterprise-class wired network switches also support this technology, which can control who and what can associate with physical ports. NAP can integrate with any standards-compliant, 802.1x-based switch to assign systems to specific VLANs based on their health. For example, you can configure NAP to place all unhealthy computers into a remediation VLAN that only has access to update servers and cannot send traffic to the rest of the network. By using the open 802.1x standard, NAP can provide powerful layer 2 connectivity controls based on system health.

Although 802.1x provides valuable security benefits for enterprises, using it alone may not always provide complete, organization-wide protection. This is because 802.1x protection only occurs at the port where a device is connected. After that connection is successfully made, 802.1x provides no further restriction of the client's traffic routing abilities. Thus, if an unhealthy computer is able to connect anywhere on the network where 802.1x is not deployed—such as a network printer port exempted from 802.1x enforcement or a branch office that lacks 802.1x compatible hardware—that computer will have full connectivity to the rest of the enterprise. In other words, 802.1x is port-level rather than host-level protection.

IPsec is another open standard that NAP integrates with. IPsec can complement 802.1x or be deployed on its own. IPsec protection is host-level protection and protects systems on the network regardless of whether an unhealthy system is able to physically associate with a port. IPsec enforcement works by deploying an enterprise-wide IPsec policy to all systems (typically accomplished through Group Policy). This policy configures systems to reject traffic unless the initiator signs the traffic with a certificate issued by a NAP HRA. The HRA integrates with NAP to ensure that only systems that pass an organization's health policy are provisioned with these certificates. Thus, IPsec enforcement provides protection at the host layer and can act as a stand-alone enforcement method or an additional layer of defense-in-depth when combined with 802.1x. IPsec enforcement also has the additional value of being easier to integrate into virtualized environments where virtual machines may not be connected to 802.1x capable ports (either physical ports or those on virtual switches).

John Morello, Senior Program Manager
Windows Server Division

NAP Scenarios

The following likely NAP scenarios help to illustrate the value of this new platform:

- **Desktop Computers**   Desktop computers can pose a threat to the network if they are missing updates, are configured poorly, or have become infected by malware. Each of these situations can allow nefarious individuals to access information that should not leave the organization. Computers might be missing updates because they have been turned off for an extended period of time, or if they were unable to connect to the network for some reason. They could become misconfigured if users have more privileges on their systems than best practices prescribe. They could become infected with malicious software because the user accessed dangerous Web sites or opened files infected with a virus.

■ **Roaming Laptops** Although the mobility of laptops has tremendous value, it also increases the risk of compromise beyond that faced by the typical desktop computer. A laptop can be missing updates or the most recent antivirus signatures because the user has not connected the laptop to the corporate network for several weeks. A laptop faces potential attack when used in wireless networks, or when left unattended in a place accessible by untrustworthy individuals. With NAP, administrators can verify the health state of laptops each time they reconnect to the organization's network, whether via a VPN or when the user returns to the office.

■ **Unmanaged Home Computers** Some organizations allow their users to connect to the corporate network through a VPN using their own personal computers. These computers are not under the control of the organization. With NAP, however, network administrators can inspect the health state of these systems every time they establish a VPN connection, and limit access if the systems do not meet health requirements.

■ **Visiting Computers** Businesses allow all sorts of people to visit their premises: Consultants, partners, friends of employees, recruits, and vendors may all ask for access to your network. Their computers may not meet the organization's health policies but with NAP, administrators can evaluate those computers and isolate them on a restricted network. Presumably the restricted network would include Internet access to enable the visitors to access their own e-mail accounts and other outside resources.

IPSec, Firewall, RRAS, and NAP Acronyms

AES – Advanced Encryption Standard

AH – Authentication Headers

API – Application Programming Interface

BFE – Base Filtering Engine

CA – Certificate authority

CBC – Cipher block chaining

CMAK – Connection Manager Administration Kit

DES – Data encryption standard

DH – Diffie-Hellman

ESP – Encapsulated Security Payload

FTP – File Transfer Protocol

GFE – Generic Filtering Engine

HCAP – Host Credential Authorization Protocol

HRA – Health Registration Authority

HTML – Hypertext Markup Language

HTTP – Hypertext Transport Protocol

HTTPS – Secure Hypertext Transport Protocol

ICMP – Internet Control Message Protocol

IKE – Internet Key Exchange (IKE)

IPsec – Internet Protocol security

ISA – Internet Security and Acceleration Server

ISAKMP – Internet Security Association and Key Management Protocol

L2TP – Layer two tunneling protocol

MD5 – Message Digest 5

MMC – Microsoft Management Console

MPPE – Microsoft Point-to-Point

NAP – Network Access Protection

NAP EC – Network Access Protection Enforcement Client

NAP ES – Network Access Protection Enforcement Server

NAT – Network address translation

NAT-T – Network address translation – traversal

NDF – Network Diagnostics Framework

NLA – Network Location Awareness

NPS – Network Policy Server

NTLMv2 – New Technology LAN Manager version two

PKI – Public key infrastructure

PPP – Point-to-point protocol

PPTP – Point-to-point tunneling protocol

RADIUS – Remote Authentication Dial-In user Service

RDP – Remote Desktop Protocol

RRAS – Routing and Remote Access Service

SA – Security association

SHA – System Health Agent

SHV – System Health Validator

SKEME – Secure Key Exchange Mechanism

SoH – Statement of Health

SoHR – Statement of Health Request

SSL – Secure Sockets Layer

SSoHR – Statement of Health Response

SSTP – Secure Socket Tunneling Protocol

TCP – Transmission Control Protocol

TCP/IP – Transmission Control Protocol/Internet Protocol

TLS – Transport Layer Security

TS – Terminal Server or Terminal Service

UAC – User Account Control

UDP – User Datagram Protocol

VPN – Virtual Private Network

WAIS – Wide Area Information Servers

WFP – Windows Filtering Platform

WSHA – Windows System Health Agent

Summary

This chapter has presented a lot of information about several closely related technologies in Windows Server 2008. Windows Firewall with Advanced Security is the new host-based firewall that tightly integrates with IPsec and NAP. You can use isolation rules in conjunction with NAP and IPsec to protect servers from potentially dangerous hosts on the network. The chapter also briefly discussed improvements in the Routing And Remote Access service, especially SSTP, which can simplify the management of VPNs for remote users. You can use all of these technologies to facilitate communication between network hosts while limiting the risk of miscreants compromising them.

Additional Resources

- Microsoft Corporation. (2006, 2007). "New Networking Features in Windows Server 2008 and Windows Vista," at *http://technet.microsoft.com/en-us/library/bb726965.aspx*.

- Johansson, J. M. *Protect Your Windows Network*. (Addison-Wesley, 2005).

- Microsoft Corporation. (2004). "Windows Filtering Platform," at *http://www.microsoft.com/whdc/device/network/wfp.mspx*.

- Microsoft Corporation. (2007). "Windows Firewall with Advanced Security - Diagnostics and Troubleshooting," at *http://technet2.microsoft.com/WindowsVista/en/library/9428d113-ade8-4dbe-ac05-6ef10a6dd7a51033.mspx?mfr=true*.

- Microsoft Corporation. (2007). "Routing and Remote Access," at *http://technet.microsoft.com/en-us/network/bb545655.aspx*.

- Microsoft Corporation. (2007). "Routing and Remote Access Blog," at *http://blogs.technet.com/rrasblog/default.aspx*.

- Microsoft Corporation. (2007). "Deploying SSTP Remote Access Step-by-Step Guide," at *http://download.microsoft.com/download/b/1/0/b106fc39-936c-4857-a6ea-3fb9d1f37063/deploying%20sstp%20remote%20access%20step%20by%20step%20guide.doc*.

- Microsoft Corporation. (2007). "Server and Domain Isolation," at *http://technet.microsoft.com/en-us/network/bb545651.aspx*.

- Microsoft Corporation. (2007). "Network Access Protection," at *http://technet.microsoft.com/en-us/network/bb545879.aspx*.

- Microsoft Corporation. (2007). "NAP Blog," at *http://blogs.technet.com/nap/*.

- Riley, Steve (2007). "Exploring the Windows Firewall," at *http://www.microsoft.com/technet/technetmag/issues/2007/06/VistaFirewall/default.aspx*.

Chapter 6

Services

— Roger A. Grimes

A new default Enterprise installation of Windows Server 2008 contains more than 100 services, of which more than 40 are active and started during the Windows boot process. A full installation of all server roles, although unlikely in the real world, adds another 40 or so active, auto-start services. If you add more Windows components (such as WINS Server, Subsystem for UNIX-based Applications, Telnet Server, and so on), you can end up with another few dozen services. Even Server Core, the installation option with no graphical user interface, is not as minimalist as you might first think. It is a bit leaner at 70 services, with just over half auto-started. From a security point of view, each service is an additional attack vector—a fact that malicious hackers grasp all too well.

Understanding how services work and how to appropriately secure them is essential to minimizing the risk of malicious exploitation. This chapter will discuss Windows services in general, discuss threats, and cover ways you can minimize risk from services. After reading this chapter, you will understand the difference between an application and a service, understand the most common threats against services, and be able to use and configure the various Windows security mechanisms designed to minimize the potential of service exploitation.

Introduction to Services

Services provide client and server communication mechanisms for local and remote users, applications, and Windows itself. This functionality is encapsulated in services—processes that run even when nobody is logged on. Some services are required for Windows to function, while others are necessary only when performing particular tasks or roles.

What Is a Service?

Understanding how a service differs from a normal application is important for understanding services themselves. Most Microsoft-installed Windows services are loaded as DLLs or EXEs located under the \System32 folder, but they can also be located in any valid local drive location. Services are started in Session 0, with System integrity, Data Execution Prevention (DEP) enabled, include the SERVICE security identifier (SID), and with file and registry virtualization disabled. And unlike normal applications, services may have service-specific SIDs associated with them to allow granular access control.

> **Note**   See Chapter 1, "Subjects, Users, and Other Actors," for more information on SIDs; see Chapter 4, "Understanding UAC," for more information on virtualization.

Service Log-on Account

All services are assigned a service log-on account, which determines the primary security context that the service runs in. The built-in service log-on accounts are Local System, Local Service, and Network Service; but administrators and developers are free to create and use new custom accounts. The rights, permissions, and privileges assigned to the service log-on account is a primary (although not singular) method of determining what access a particular service has to local and network resources. Table 6-1 lists the built-in service log-on accounts with a general description of how they interact with local and remote resources.

Table 6-1   Built-in Service Log-on Accounts

Log-on Account Name	Local Resources	Network Resources
Local System (Often rendered as LocalSystem or System, and may be preceded by an NT AUTHORITY\ label.)	The highest privilege account on a computer; has full access to all resources.	Connects to network resources with the security context of the computer the account is located on.
Local Service (Often preceded by the NT AUTHORITY\ label.)	Has the access normally assigned to standard authenticated users, with slightly more privileges.	Connects to network resources as a null (anonymous credentials) session account.
Network Service (Often preceded by the NT AUTHORITY\ label.)	Similar to Local Service, it has the access normally assigned to a standard authenticated user, with slightly more privileges.	Similar to the Local System account, it connects as the computer. Remote token contains Everyone and Authenticated Users SIDs also.

Services can use the built-in service log-on accounts, or they can use any valid local or domain user account. In early versions of Windows, all Microsoft-provided services ran in the Local System context. Unfortunately, this policy did not follow the least-privilege principle. Starting with Windows XP, Microsoft created the more restricted Local Service and Network Service accounts and began to incrementally follow a least-privilege model when developing and deploying services. In Windows Server 2008, 58 percent of the installed services run in the Local System context, followed by Local Service at 26 percent, and Network Service at 16 percent.

These service log-on accounts are used to authenticate services to local and remote resources. Services wishing to use Kerberos authentication (instead of NTLM or LM) need to have one or more Service Principal Names (SPNs) assigned to the service log-on account as well. The SPN is used to specifically identify a service, allowing mutual authentication between a client application and the service.

> **Note**   See Chapter 2, "Authenticators and Authentication Protocols," for more information on NTLM and LM.

Service Control Manager

All service log-on accounts must be assigned the Log-on As A Service right, which gives the service the ability to interact with and be controlled by the Service Control Manager (SCM), which in turn allows the service to log on and access resources without another external security principal having to log on first.

The SCM is started during the Windows boot sequence as a Remote Procedure Call (RPC) server so that service management and control programs (Sc.exe, Services.msc, WMIC, and so on) can interact with local and remote services. The SCM is responsible for starting services defined to start automatically during the Windows boot process. SCM will read the service values located in the registry, log on the service account to the local computer using the found credentials, load the service account's user profile, start the service in a suspended state, associate the service with the service account's log-on token, and then finish starting the service. SCM will detect any registered service dependencies and start them first, if needed.

The SCM is tasked with many service-oriented responsibilities, including:

- Maintaining the database of installed services
- Starting services and driver services either upon system start-up or upon demand
- Enumerating installed services and driver services
- Maintaining status information for running services and driver services
- Transmitting control requests to running services
- Locking and unlocking the service database

When it needs to start a service, the SCM creates a log-on session for the service's log-on account, loads the associated log-on account's user profile, and starts the service. If the SCM is successful, it attaches the resulting process token (which holds the service's SIDs and privileges) to the service's process.

Configuration information about each service is stored under the Windows registry at HKLM\System\CurrentControlSet\Services. Figure 6-1 is an example of a registry entry detailing a service.

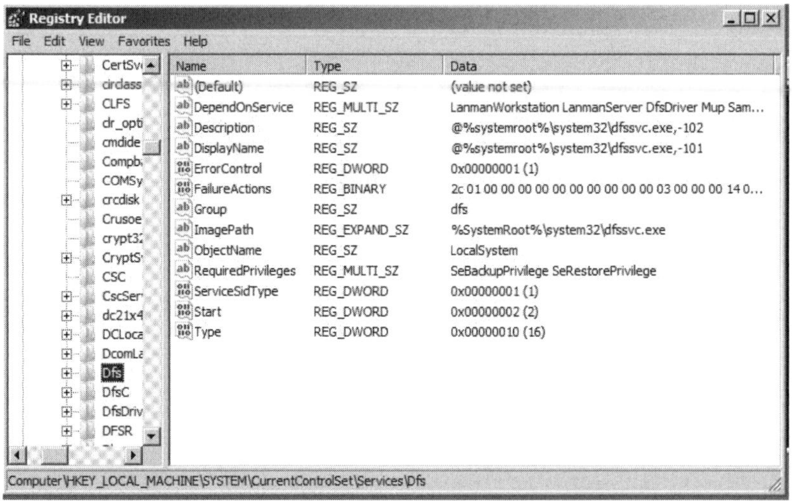

Figure 6-1   Example registry entry of a service.

Both services and drivers are located under the preceding Services registry key, but services can be identified by the *Type* value of 0x10 (a service that runs in its own process as a stand-alone program) or 0x20 (a service that runs in a shared process). A driver has type 0x1 (a kernel driver) or 0x2 (a file system driver). In addition, the service's *Start* value is always either 2 (automatic), 3 (manual), or 4 (disabled), while drivers have a *Start* value of 0 (boot) or 1 (System).

All service log-on accounts have an associated password. Built-in service accounts have long and complex passwords assigned by Windows. Administrators cannot easily enumerate those passwords and never have to change them. Custom service log-on account passwords must be set by administrators and are stored in a protected local registry area. Any service account password can be enumerated by local administrators using specialized software.

Service Listener Ports

Most services have an endpoint listening handle to receive or send service-related information. Normally the listening handle is represented by a TCP or UDP port number (such as Terminal Services at TCP port number 3389) and IP address, but services can also listen using RPC, Named Pipes or another valid listener protocol (such as Net.msmq). A service's listening TCP/IP port can be enumerating using Windows Sysinternals Process Explorer (see Figure 6-2) or at the command line using *netstat − anob*.

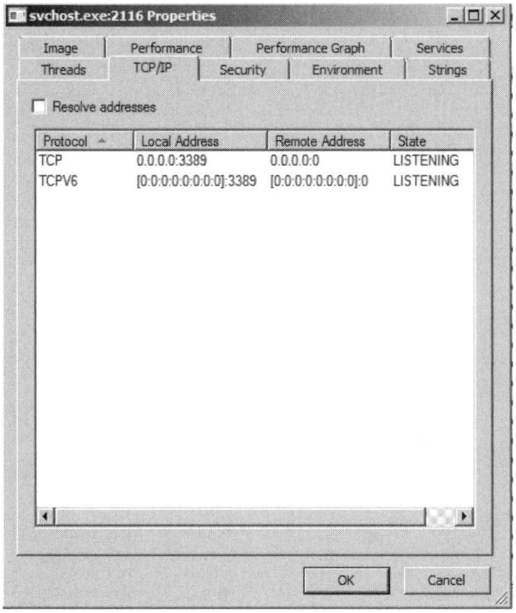

Figure 6-2   Using Process Explorer's TCP/IP tab to reveal the listener port number as 3389.

As Figure 6-2 shows, if the service uses a TCP port number, most services (on Windows Vista and later) will automatically listen on both TCP version 4 and TCP version 6 by default. If the listening port's IP address is listed as 0.0.0.0, the service will respond to connections on any interface port, including local host. If the listener port's IP address is listed as 127.0.0.1, the service will only answer connection attempts from the local host. If the service is listening on a specific IP address (such as 192.168.1.10), the service will only respond to connection attempts to that specific IP address.

> **Note**   Note: The next section, "Configuring Services," is very general in scope and readers who are already generally familiar with configuring Windows services can skip it.

Configuring Services

Services may or may not have a graphical interface that users interact with during run time, but all services have information that can be configured programmatically or by using the Services console (Services.msc), which gets stored to the registry for the SCM to read. Figure 6-3 shows the Services console.

You can double-click any service listing to reveal the underlying details, as shown in Figure 6-4. Standard users can view service information, but only members of the Account Operators, Domain Admins, or Enterprise Admins groups can modify settings.

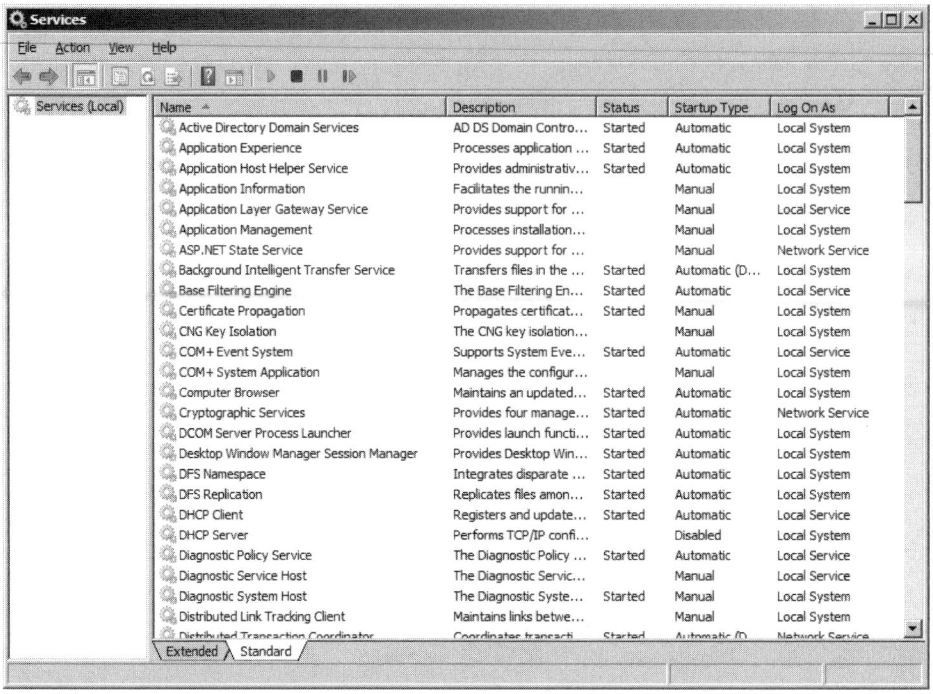

Figure 6-3   Services console showing service information.

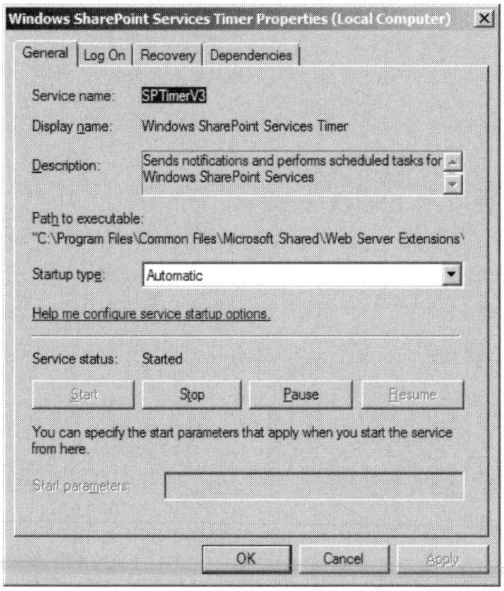

Figure 6-4   The General tab.

General Tab

The General tab contains several fields of information. Service Name, which is the internal name used in Windows to refer to the service, is also known as the short name. Service Name is often required by service management tools to manipulate the given service. The Display Name field is often known as the common name and is the label displayed most prominently in the Services console when listing all services. The Description field displays a short, developer-created message describing what the service does.

The Path To Executable field tries to display the full path to the service executable, although as Figure 6-4 shows, it is possible for the full path to be incorrectly truncated in the GUI (in other words, there is no word wrap feature). The Path To Executable field can be very useful when troubleshooting potential malware that uses names similar or identical to Microsoft service names. For example, I once found a malicious Trojan named svchost.exe, but it was located in the \Windows\Fonts folder instead of \Windows\System32 where the legitimate copy would always be located.

Startup Type is an important service field. It can be configured as one of four values:

- Automatic (Delayed Start)
- Automatic
- Manual
- Disabled

Automatic (Delayed Start) instructs SCM to start a service after all other services marked with a value of Automatic (and their dependencies). This option was first introduced in Windows Vista. Services set to Automatic start during the Windows boot process, in an order dictated by several registry keys. If any service marked as Automatic depends on other services to be started, those services will be started first (unless marked as Disabled). Services set to Manual are not automatically started during the Windows boot process unless required by other services or applications. Many services set to Manual are started when needed and stop when their required functionality is no longer needed. A service marked as Disabled will not be started by the SCM and cannot be started manually until the service is defined with a different value.

The *Service Status* field shows the service's current operational state. The operational state can be Started, Stopped, or Paused. Paused does not always mean what most users think. It does not stop the service. The service remains active in memory, and may even finish serving active requests, but stops taking additional requests. Services must be specially coded to interact with the SCM and to take the appropriate action, when asked if allowed. For security and reliability reasons, many default Windows services cannot be paused (more than 80 percent) and almost 50 percent of them have permissions that prevent them from being stopped. The *Start Parameters* field allows additional run-time switches, directives, or commands to be passed to the service during its start-up.

Log On Tab

The Log On tab (see Figure 6-5) determines which service account is associated with the service, along with determining desktop interactions and hardware profiles. In the Log On As field you can configure the service to run in the Local System context, or input another service

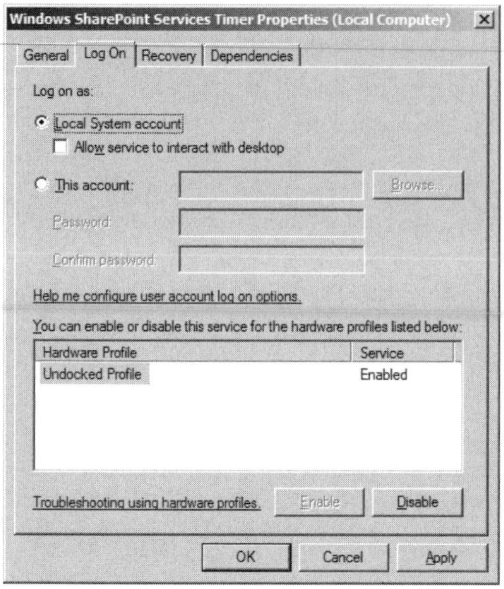

Figure 6-5   The Services Log On tab.

account name, including Local Service, Network Service, or another valid service name. The service log-on account must exist in the local SAM database or in Active Directory. If the service account has not been previously assigned the Log-on As A Service right, it will be given it when confirming the selection during configuration. The service account's valid password must be entered here, although if the account is Local System, Local Service, or Network Service it should not have a password entered. Passwords placed here are stored in the registry for future use by the SCM.

Note: There is no check here to make sure the password entered in the Log On tab is the correct password. As long as the password is typed in identically twice, the SCM will accept and store it, although the service will fail to start when requested if the password is incorrect.

You can also enable the Allow Service To Interact With Desktop option. Some services require this option to work and interact with the user. Desktop interaction is required by the Print Spooler and Interactive Services Detection services. In most cases this option should not be enabled; if enabled, it could present an additional security risk to the interactive end user, the desktop, the service, or the computer. For example, if a service is allowed to interact with the user's desktop, it is easier for the service to be maliciously manipulated by the end user or by malware acting in the end user's security context. The exploited service could more easily infect other users and desktops on the same computer. Restricting services from interacting with user desktops is a recent feature, and many older services are still not fully compliant.

You can also enable or disable a service in any existing hardware profiles. This option is most commonly used for docked versus undocked states on laptops. Services that are not needed in a particular hardware profile should be disabled to provide a reduced attack surface area for malicious hackers. (This could also improve performance and save energy, which I am sure was Microsoft's primary intent.)

Recovery Tab

The Recovery tab (shown in Figure 6-6) defines what actions should occur if a particular service fails (or hangs). You can choose from the following options:

- Take No Action
- Restart The Service
- Run A Program
- Restart The Computer

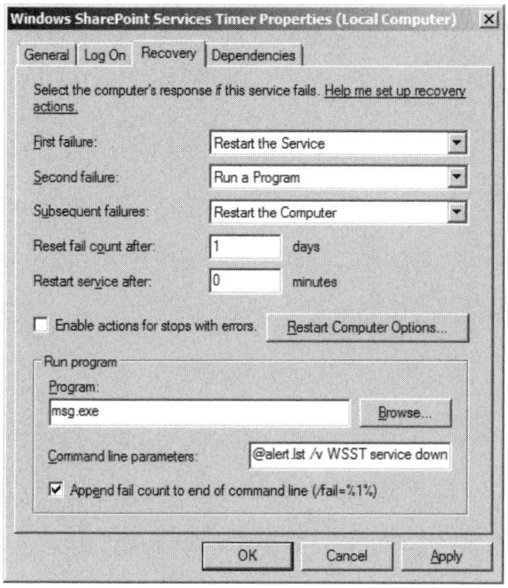

Figure 6-6   The Services Recovery tab.

You can define separate actions for first, second, and subsequent failures. You can determine, in intervals of days, how often Reset Fail Counter is reset. For example, if the reset counter is set to 1 day (a common value), after 24 hours the counter would be reset to 0, and the next additional failure reaction would be dictated by the First Failure option. If the Reset Fail count is set to 0 it means the counter is not reset until the computer is restarted. If the recovery action is set to Restart The Service, you can instruct the SCM on how long to wait, in minutes, before restarting the service. The Enable Actions For Stops With Errors option can be enabled to make recovery actions apply to error stops also, instead of complete failures only.

If the Run A Program recovery option is selected, a program or other script can be run upon failure. Figure 6-6 shows an example of the Msg.exe program being used to send a message to a predetermined list of users with the message of "WSST service down". Using this feature, a help desk ticket can be opened to investigate the failed service or another debugging program started.

Another common use for this field is to use the Network Monitor utility to capture network packets headed to and from the service after the service restart to aid in troubleshooting.

The captured information could be useful in identifying malicious connections. Use a drive letter and full path to locate the executable. UNC style paths (such as \\server\sharename) do not work here.

> **Note**   Prior to Windows XP Professional Service Pack 2, administrators could use NET SEND to send out network-based messages. However, it depended on the insecure Messenger service. Windows Vista and Windows Server 2008 administrators can use the Msg.exe program instead.

Microsoft anticipated that a common reason for sending a message might be to warn users about the computer restarting because of a service restart or failure. The Before Restart, Send This Message To Computers On The Network option can be enabled under the Restart Computer Options, as shown in Figure 6-7.

Figure 6-7   Example of the Default Restart Computer Options message.

Interestingly, recovery options that automatically restart a failed service can give malicious attackers additional opportunities to compromise a computer. For example, Address Space Layout Randomization (ASLR) randomly places core Windows APIs in 256 different memory address locations every time the computer starts. Many buffer overflows require that the attacker correctly guess the needed API address or else the buffer overflow attack fails. If a service is automatically restarted after a failure, the attacker has a better chance of guessing the right memory address with subsequent retries.

Dependencies Tab

Figure 6-8 shows the Dependencies tab. It displays all the services (and their dependencies) that this service depends on to run—or conversely, have this service as a dependency.

There are many other service values that you cannot see or configure in the Services console GUI (we will cover more of those later in the chapter), including permissions, privileges, and whether the service is stoppable or pausable. Several other methods are available for configuring services in addition to the Services console, including Group Policy, sc.exe, Windows Management Instrumentation (WMI), and other programmatic means.

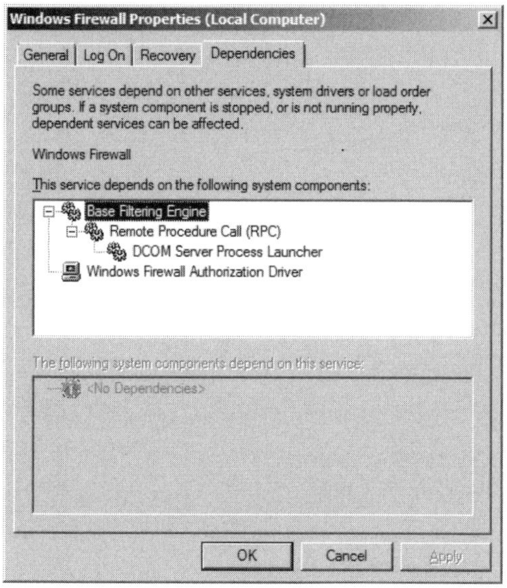

Figure 6-8   The service's Dependencies tab.

Any unexpected service failure should be investigated for operational and security issues. While service issues are often caused by nonmalicious causes, many malware incidents (MS-Blaster worm, DDoS, and so on) have been known to cause previously unexplainable service problems.

Windows Server 2008 Services by Role

As covered in the introduction to this chapter, Windows Server 2008 has more than 100 available services that can be installed, depending on which roles and features are enabled. The document "Windows Server 2008 Services by Role" found on the companion CD contains a table that shows the status of the various services under each server role. Administrators can refer to the table when attempting to minimize the number of running services to reduce attack surface area.

Attacks on Services

Because Windows comes with so many default services that are started automatically with every Windows boot, malicious hackers know they are likely to be available and often target them. This section will cover the most prolific Windows service attack to date and the most common ways a service can be attacked.

Blaster Worm

Probably the most infamous Windows service attack was the so-called Blaster worm (*http://support.microsoft.com/kb/826955*) of 2003. Blaster attacked a known buffer overflow vulnerability in the Windows DCOM RPC service on Windows 2000 and Windows XP computers. Although the vulnerability was known and a Microsoft security update was available, a large percentage of Windows computers were not updated. Adding to the lack of defense preparation was a mistaken belief that "correctly configured" perimeter firewalls would prevent the Blaster worm from infiltrating inside corporate networks.

The Blaster worm worked by connecting to the DCOM RPC service at TCP port 135 and initiating a buffer overflow attack. When the service was overflowed the Blaster worm was given Local System access to the compromised system, started a new shell on TCP port 4444, and downloaded the rest of the worm using TFTP on UDP port 67. The Trojan re-created itself in a file called msblaster.exe, which it referenced in one of the registry auto-start locations. The worm then rebooted the computer and began using the newly exploited host to infect other computers.

When Blaster was first reported, many organizations were slow to react because it was widely believed that an appropriately configured perimeter firewall (one that did not allow inbound access to TCP port 135) would prevent Blaster infections on local computers. But then infected computers joined the corporate network via VPNs and previously infected laptops were plugged into the "protected" corporate networks, unleashing Blaster on the corporate multitudes without security updates. One infected computer quickly infected every vulnerable computer on the network. Blaster was responsible for infecting hundreds of thousands of vulnerable computers in a few hours.

Complicating recovery efforts, a related worm called Nachi (*http://support.microsoft.com/kb/ 826234*) was developed a few days later in a misguided attempt to update vulnerable PCs. It would infect vulnerable computers in the same way Blaster did, but then attempt to install the security update that prevented the Blaster infection. Unfortunately, Nachi became the storybook example of why automated malware should never be used to resolve computer issues without the expressed consent of the computer's owner. Nachi essentially instructed every vulnerable computer on a network to begin downloading a security update, all at once, overwhelming network resources. And when it installed the update, it did so incorrectly, often leaving the system it was trying to protect vulnerable. In an ironic twist, Nachi was ultimately responsible for more problems and downtime than the Blaster worm it was designed to protect against.

Microsoft made significant changes to its operations following Blaster, choosing to be more aggressive in pushing out and automating security updates to computers. Although Windows users had long been using Windows Update and other updating clients (since Windows 98), Microsoft developed and pushed out even more auto-update services, including improved versions of Automatic Updates and introduced free Software Update Services/Windows Server Update Services (SUS/WSUS) for businesses that were not using other patch management solutions. Microsoft also made it easier for new operating system installations to be installed and updated with a minimum risk of exposure to the network by minimizing network access until after updates are installed.

Blaster's biggest lesson to computer security analysts was to prove that perimeter firewall security was not enough. The "crunchy outer shell with the soft, chewy center" discussed by

Bill Cheswick and Hal Burch (*http://www.cheswick.com/ches/papers/index.html*) in their seminal work on perimeter firewalls had finally come to light. Windows XP Service Pack 2 (SP2) and later Windows client computers enable the host-based Windows Firewall by default. This single measure is responsible for preventing millions of computers from becoming compromised by various remote malicious attacks. Microsoft also began implementing other strong service hardening (as discussed in "Service Hardening" later in the chapter).

Common Service Attack Vectors

Each installed and active service presents an additional attack vector to a malicious hacker. This section will summarize the most common threats.

Buffer Overflows

As covered earlier, almost all services provide an inbound listening channel for remote access. Buffer overflows are caused when a service contains an unchecked input routine that allows more information to be sent than the previously set aside buffer area. Vulnerable services can be exploited, causing service disruption or, in the worst cases, allowing the attacker to gain access to the exploited system in the security context of the service's log-on account. If this account is Local System or an administrator, attackers can then perform any programmatic action they like on the exploit system, including system control, downloading content, installing more malware, and loading remote control shells.

Denial of Service

A service with a programming bug can be prevented from performing its normal operations, temporarily or "permanently" (until the service is restarted or the computer is rebooted). Sometimes it takes a more sophisticated buffer overflow attack and sometimes a single network packet or character. For example, an old version of the Microsoft SQL Server Resolution Service was found to be vulnerable to a single unexpected ASCII character of 0x04 (*http://www.iss.net/security_center/reference/2106151.html*). A single malformed network packet was the culprit in the XP SP2 LAND attack (*http://seclists.org/bugtraq/2005/Mar/0112.html*). Denial of service attacks prevent legitimate servicing and can cause system processing interruptions, uncontrollable resource consumption, and unexpected computer reboots.

Remote Log-on Access

Many services (FTP, IIS, Remote Desktop, Terminal Services, and so on) provide additional log-on points where an intruder can attempt to guess at log-on names and passwords to gain unauthorized access. By default the Administrator account is not locked out using normal Account Lockout settings. Intruders can use an advertised log-on service to attempt to guess the Administrator password over and over, either manually or using automated password-guessing tools. Unless the Security log is being monitored for bad log-ons, password guessing using the Administrator account could go on for quite awhile without being noticed.

Eavesdropping/Sniffing

Because each listening service sends and receives data, attackers can intercept communications data to reveal unauthorized information. Many services (SNMP, Telnet, FTP, POP, and so on) use plaintext log-on names and passwords. Even other services that do not send plaintext data can be exploited. For instance, RDP was susceptible to man-in-the-middle (MitM) attacks for a while after its release. (This has been fixed.) Even though RDP used encryption, a new session could be intercepted and redirected through a remote attacker. Because RDP did not authenticate endpoint clients until version 6.0 and later, it was possible, although extremely difficult, for MitM attackers to inject themselves into the communication's stream and pull out encrypted log-on passwords one character at a time. Several hacking tools made implementing an RDP MitM attack as easy as clicking a few buttons, once the attacker got over the significant hurdle of inserting himself into the communication path. Eavesdropping can also be used to capture confidential and personal information beyond log-on credentials.

Password Compromise

Fully compromised systems can lead to additional network privilege escalation using passwords enumerated from service log-on accounts. If an attacker has privileged access (such as Administrator or Local System) to a system, he can use various methods and tools to recover custom service log-on account credentials in plaintext. If the recovered credentials are used on other computers or throughout the Windows domain, they can allow additional resources to be compromised. This is discussed in depth in Chapter 13, "Securing the Network."

Misconfiguration

A service may be well coded and not contain any known vulnerabilities and still be subject to malicious use. It is common for users and administrators to misconfigure services in a way that opens their computers to unauthorized access. For example, a user could install the IIS or FTP service, but use weak passwords. Or a user may install a peer-to-peer file-sharing program intending to share a smaller subset of folders, but instead share out her entire hard drive. This latter problem has led to many instances of confidential and top-secret documents being accidentally revealed on the Internet.

Unauthorized Information Disclosure

Many services also advertise system information that can be used by malicious attackers. Sometimes the information is related to the service itself, and is crucial to the service's normal operations; at other times unexpected information is disclosed when malicious connection data is sent to it. For example, Microsoft security bulletin MS05-007 (*http://www.microsoft.com/technet/security/Bulletin/MS05-007.mspx*) discusses how the Computer Browser service and the Named Pipes feature can be used to enumerate logged-on user account names.

Social Engineering

Services that actively interact with the end user, such as peer-to-peer file sharing, present an additional avenue for malware spreaders to trick users into running malicious programs. Peer-to-peer-aware malware can fake a chat with an end user and then send an invitation to the user to accept a new file transfer. The file transfer is advertised as having some legitimate content or use, but instead contains Trojaned malware. And many anti-malware programs do not scan content coming in on all services, allowing the infection to get by unnoticed even on a protected computer.

Services are subject to many different types of malicious attacks, and each additional running service on a computer increases the risk of malicious exploit.

Service Hardening

After the Blaster worm, Microsoft threat-modeled the default Windows services to understand and minimize their security exposure. This effort involved changing default permissions and privileges and led to the creation of many new service protective measures. Consequently, services running in Windows Vista and later have many security improvements over previous Windows client versions, including:

- Each service has a least-privilege security model.
- Services were factored so that more services run in the Local Service or Network Service log-on context.
- Each service is given a security identifier (SID) to enable per-service access control.
- Restricting SIDs are applied to some services.
- Services are allowed to be restricted by network domain.
- Session 0 Isolation is required for all Windows services.
- All services have System mandatory integrity level.
- Data execution prevention is enabled for all services.
- SCM status notification is enhanced.

Each of these improvements will be discussed in more detail in the following sections.

Least Privilege

Windows privileges determine what a security principal can do on given computer. (In other words, privileges are not tied to a particular securable object.) Windows Server 2008 has 35 different privileges (*SeImpersonatePrivilege*, *SeCreateGlobalPrivilege*, and so on) that can be assigned to a security principal. The list of possible privileges is shown in Table 6-2. You can also see the various privileges in Group Policy at \Computer Configuration\Windows Settings\Security Settings\Local Policies\User Rights Assignments. However, the latter also includes nine rights that are not considered privileges.

Table 6-2   Service Log-on Account Privileges Enabled by Default

Privilege	Local System	Local Service	Network Service	Administrators	Standard User
AssignPrimaryToken	D	D	D	-	-
SeAudit	E	D	D	-	-
SeBackup	D	-	-	D	-
SeChangeNotify	E	E	E	E	E
SeCreateGlobal	E	E	E	E	E
SeCreatePagefile	E	-	-	D	-
SeCreatePermanent	E	-	-	-	-
SeCreateSymbolicLink	E	-	-	D	-
SeCreateToken	-	-	-	-	-
SeDebug	E	-	-	D	-
SeEnableDelegation	-	-	-	D	-
SeImpersonate	E	E	E	E	E
SeIncreaseBasePriority	E	-	-	D	-
IncreaseQuotaPrivilege	D	D	D	D	-
SeIncreaseWorkingSet	E	D	D	D	D
SeLoadDriver	D	-	-	D	-
SeLockMemory	E	-	-	-	-
SeMachineAccount	-	D	D	D	D
SeManageVolume	D	-	-	D	-
SeProfileSingleProcess	E	-	-	D	-
SeRelabel	-	-	-	-	-
SeRemoteShutdown	-	-	-	D	-
SeRestore	D	-	-	D	-
SeSecurity	D	-	-	D	-
SeShutdown	D	-	-	D	-
SeSyncAgent	-	-	-	-	-
SeSystemEnvironment	D	-	-	D	-
SeSystemProfile	E	-	-	D	-
SeSystemtime	D	D	-	D	-
SeTakeOwnership	D	-	-	D	-
SeTcb	E	-	-	-	-
SeTimeZone	E	D	-	D	-
SeTrustedCredManAccess	-	-	-	-	-
SeUndock	D	-	-	D	-
SeUnsolicitedInput	-	-	-	-	-

E = enabled by default; D = disabled by default, but can be enabled; - = privilege not assigned and cannot be enabled

Direct from the Field: Rights versus Privileges

Rights give a user the right (or deny the right) to log on in some particular way. Most people mix them up with privileges, but they are quite different. For example, a user may have the right to log on locally, deny log on as a batch job, and so on. Those rights are evaluated only during a security principal's log-on. If the log-on succeeds, based on the authenticator validation and the user right verification, the principal's access token is created. The user rights are not attached to the access token. However, the privileges are, and they are evaluated on an ongoing basis throughout the log-on session.

A privilege, by contrast, permits the principal to take some action after log-on. For example, one privilege is the *SeChangeNotifyPrivilege*, known in Group Policy as Bypass Traverse Checking. *SeChangeNotifyPrivilege* is the most basic privilege in Windows and is attached to every single process. It permits the principal—or rather, a process acting on the principal's behalf—to bypass certain security checks. To understand how that works, imagine we have a folder called C:\ForYourEyesOnly008. Inside the folder is a file called For009.txt. The folder has permissions only for user 008. However, the file has read permissions for user 009. Using *SeChangeNotifyPrivilege*, user 009 can access the file directly, without having the access attempt be denied because he cannot read the folder it is in. If 009 had not had that privilege in his access token, he would have received an access denied because the directory bars him access.

Jesper M. Johansson
Microsoft Security MVP

The Local System account has the most default-enabled privileges, followed by members of the Administrators group, Local Service, Network Service, and then standard users without elevated privileges. Table 6-2 shows the various default privileges granted to each built-in service log-on account, Administrators, and standard users, if not otherwise restricted.

Interestingly, if a privilege is present in a service process's token, but disabled, it can still be considered as enabled (because the service can always enable a disabled privilege). Processes running as a standard user have only five default privileges, as do un-elevated processes running as an administrator subject to UAC. An elevated process has considerably more privileges in its token. Service log-on accounts are not subject to UAC; nor, of course, is the built-in Administrator.

Note Windows Vista and Windows Server 2008 differ slightly in privileges given to standard users. In Windows Vista, users are given *SeTimeZone* so that they can change the system's time zone without having to be an administrator. In Windows Server 2008, this privilege is replaced by *SeCreateGlobal*, which is needed for share objects, as might be needed in Terminal Services and other shared services.

Microsoft analyzed every default Windows service using extensive threat modeling. If a service does not require Local System access, the service is instead assigned Local Service or Network Service access. By using the least-privilege service log-on account, Microsoft reduced the overall threat that could be caused by malicious manipulation of the service. Unfortunately, even though just over half of the provided services are running in the Local System context, overall more services are running as Local System as compared to Windows Server 2003. This is a reflection of significant added functionality in the new operating system.

To help provide additional protection, Windows Vista and Windows Server 2008 can remove any unneeded default privileges given to any service log-on account during the service's start-up. Microsoft's developers reviewed each default Windows service and removed unneeded privileges. Accordingly, many services (such as DHCP client) run with fewer privileges than are assigned to the service log-on account they run under. Microsoft provides many helpful tools and encourages developers to analyze their own services and remove unneeded privileges. Each privilege removed potentially protects against malicious attack. During a service's installation, the service can populate a registry key called RequiredPrivileges (see the example in Figure 6-1) with the privileges absolutely required for the service to function appropriately.

When enabled, the SCM will examine the privileges requested by the service and remove any from the service's log-on accounts that are not specifically designated as required. If no privileges are listed as required, the SCM will remove any additional privileges beyond the defaults set in the service log-on account. If a service requests more privileges than are already allocated to the service log-on account, the service will not be started.

If one service process (such as Svchost.exe) hosts multiple services, the SCM will calculate the least-privilege footprint union required by all services and then strip unneeded privileges. However, if one of the services sharing a single service process requires all the privileges allocated to the service log-on account, no privileges are stripped, and the privileges are available to all the services in the shared host. In other words, sharing processes can significantly reduce the value of the privilege analysis. You can view the required privileges (not the privileges actually granted to the process) of a service by using Sc.exe with the qprivs parameter. The syntax is:

```
sc.exe <server> qprivs [servicename]
```

Figure 6-9 shows an example of the sc.exe qprivs command.

You can also use the priv command-line parameter with Sc.exe to set privileges. The syntax is:

```
sc.exe <server> privs [Privileges]
```

[Privileges] is a string that contains a list of privileges that are separated by a forward slash (/). For example, to specify backup and restore privileges, set Privileges to *SeBackupPrivilege/SeRestorePrivilege*. Service developers and system administrators can take advantage of the SCM privilege stripping to help minimize surface area available to malicious attacks. However, users and administrators are cautioned against changing a service's requested privileges without significant analysis and testing.

Figure 6-9   Using Sc.exe to display a service's required privileges.

You can also use Process Explorer (see Figure 6-10) to display a service process's privileges (and permissions and SIDs). Remember, if the privilege is listed (enabled or disabled), it is available to the service. Disabled does not mean disabled forever. If a privilege is not allowed, it will not be listed.

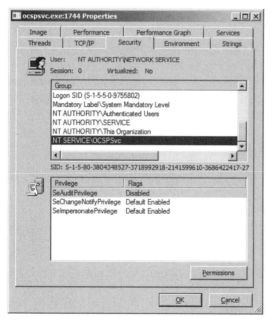

Figure 6-10   Displaying the privileges of a service process.

Service SIDs

Each service's process token includes the NT AUTHORITY\SERVICE SID (S-1-5-6). Looking for the presence of this SID on a running process is one quick way to determine whether the process is a service or just an application.

Starting with Windows Vista and Windows Server 2008, each service can also be assigned a service-specific SID based on its name. (In other words, services with the same name will have identical SIDs on different systems.) A service-specific SID allows services to be directly assigned permissions on any securable object. It can also be used to control the service in other ways, such as opening ports in the Windows Firewall and IPsec.

You can view the SID of any service, including ones you do not even have yet, by using the Sc.exe command with the showsid command-line parameter. The syntax is:

```
sc.exe showsid [servicename]
```

A service's SID is computed by taking the service's Unicode name (in all uppercase letters) and running it through a SHA-1 hash function and adding the hash result to S-1-5-80-. For example, the SID of the W32Time service is: S-1-5-80-4267341169-2882910712-659946508-2704364837-2204554466. This SID will be identical across all Windows Vista and Windows Server 2008 systems.

If you add a service-specific SID to a service, you must add it before the service is started, and you cannot change it while the service is running. When a service-specific SID is used, it is added to the service's process token along with the service's log-on account SID. If a shared service process (such as Svchost.exe) has several services with service-specific SIDs, all SIDs are added to the service's process token and can be used by all services in the shared service process. If a service-specific SID is not enabled, the service log-on account's SID will still be added to the service's process token.

Defining Access Control Entries for a Service

If a service token has a service-specific SID, you can define permissions programmatically or using icacls.exe and other tools. Figure 6-11 shows an example of how to reference a service's

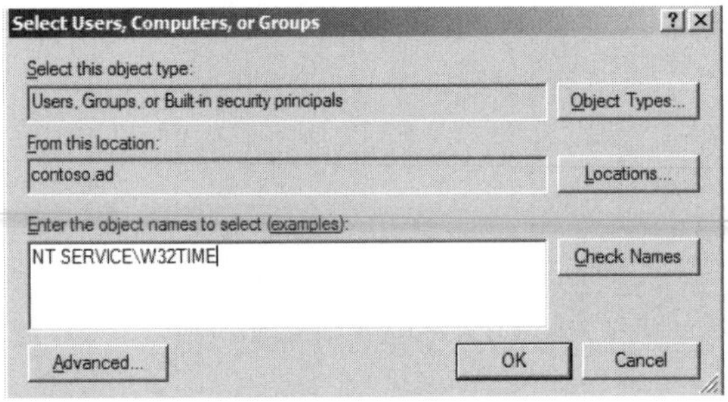

Figure 6-11   Example of assigning W32Time service permissions.

name when setting permissions in the Windows ACL editor GUI. You must include
NT SERVICE\ label before the service's short name. Figure 6-12 shows the result in the ACL
Editor. Interestingly, although you must include the NT Service label to assist Windows in
finding the correct security principal, if you use the Check Name button in the same GUI,
Windows will convert the typed-in label to the service's short name alone (such as W32Time).
But you cannot use the short name by itself when defining permissions.

Figure 6-12   Example of giving permissions to W32Time service.

You can use NT SERVICE\servicename or the service's SID when defining access control
permissions using the Icalcs.exe command (see Figure 6-13).

Figure 6-13   Using Icacls.exe to set permissions for a service.

The importance of a service-specific SID cannot be understated. Prior to Windows Vista, services were granted the permissions granted to the service log-on account. If the service log-on account (such as Local Service) had to be given additional permissions for one service to function correctly, it ended up available to all services which shared the same service log-on account. Now permissions can be allowed or denied by service. And because services have SIDs, Object Access auditing can more easily reveal service access successes and failures. In addition, this enables control of network traffic by service. For example, the Windows Firewall enables outbound filtering of traffic by default, permitting each service only to transmit traffic on its specifically granted ports.

On a related note, you can also show the permissions associated with a service (who has what access to the service) by running the Sc.exe command with the showsd command-line parameter. The syntax is:

```
Sc.exe showsid [service name] <showrights>
```

The resulting output is rendered using SDDL. Add the optional showrights parameter to assist with converting the SDDL output more easily understood access control entries. You can, of course, see the set permissions using the normal Windows GUIs and using Process Explorer, as well.

Write Restricted SIDs

A service has three valid SID types:

- None
- Unrestricted
- Restricted

A SID type of None means the service has no service-specific SID. It can be used for legacy services with application compatibility issues. A SID type of Unrestricted indicates that the service has a service-specific SID that can be used for access control and that SID is added to the service's process token. A SID type of Restricted is used to explicitly enforce additional access control on the service. For more information on Restricted tokens, please see Chapter 3, "Objects: The Stuff You Want."

When a service is marked with a SID type of Restricted, the service's own SID is added to the restricted SID list of the process token along with three additional SIDs:

- Everyone SID (S-1-1-0)
- Log-on SID (S-1-5-5-0-64163)
- Write Restricted SID (S-1-5-33)

When a service attempts to write to a resource, if it contains the Write Restricted SID in its access token, the access will be prevented unless the Everyone group, the write-restricted SID, or one of the service SIDs is explicitly granted write permissions. Most securable objects do not allow write permissions using those SIDs, so most writes are prevented by default. The idea is if a malicious attack is able to take control of a write-restricted service, the areas they can write to on the system (such as System32) are limited and complicated.

Unfortunately, only a handful of services are marked as write restricted. You can view a service's SID type by running the Sc.exe command with the qsidtype command-line parameter (see Figure 6-14) or use Process Explorer. The Sc.exe syntax is:

```
sc.exe qsidtype [service name]
```

Figure 6-14   Using Sc.exe qsidtype to reveal a service's SIDType.

A good example of how the WRITE RESTRICTED SID is used is with Windows Firewall. By its very nature, Windows Firewall is exposed to incoming malicious attacks. Windows places the four cooperative Windows Firewall services—Windows Firewall (Mpssvc), Base Filtering Engine (Bfe), Diagnostic Policy Service (Dps), and Performance Logs and Alerts (Pla)—under one Svchost.exe instance. All services are marked as write-restricted and contain the WRITE RESTRICTED SID (Figure 6-15).

Using the Icacls.exe /t /findsid "NT AUTHORITY\WRITE RESTRICTED" command you can locate what securable objects have explicit permissions for the Write Restricted SID. In my test system, the Icacls.exe query returned two files related to Windows security configuration that the services could write to.

You can set a service's SID type by using the sc sidtype command. The syntax is:

```
sc.exe sidtype [servicename] <none | restricted | unrestricted>
```

SID type changes will not take effect until the service starts or restarts. End users and administrators should be cautioned against changing SID types without testing and understanding the repercussions.

Note   There is a RESTRICTED SID that is more restrictive than the WRITE RESTRICTED SID, because it prevents reads as well as writes.

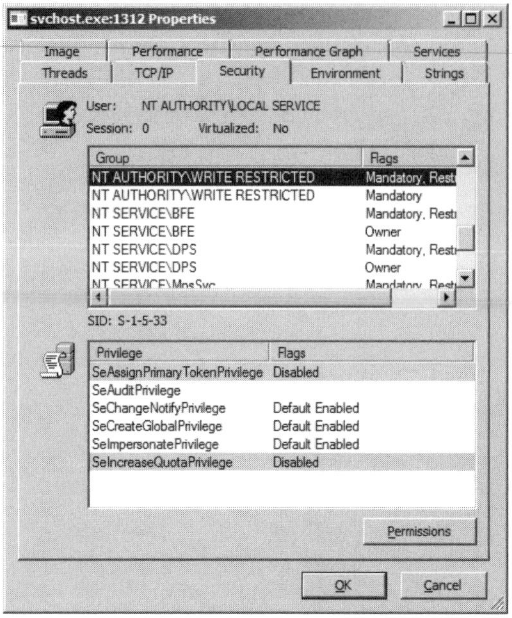

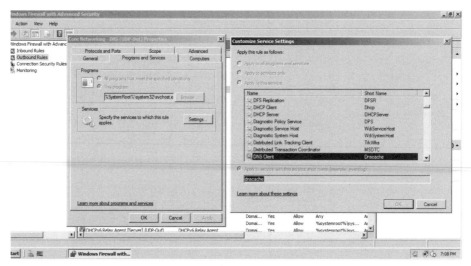

Figure 6-15   Process Explorer showing a write-restricted SID on a service.

Restricted Network Access

You can now restrict network access by service name (or SID) and limit it by port, protocol, or network. The improved Windows Firewall With Advanced Security will allow an administrator to define rules for any service over three profiles (Public, Private, and Domain). Windows Server 2008 comes with dozens of predefined rules. Many of the rules apply to services. Sometimes a rule applies to all programs and services, and sometimes they only apply to a specific service (see Figure 6-16 for an example) or set of services.

Figure 6-16   Service-based firewall rule.

Windows Server 2008 comes with the Windows Firewall enabled by default, and more than 170 inbound rules and more than 80 outbound rules enabled (see Figure 6-17).

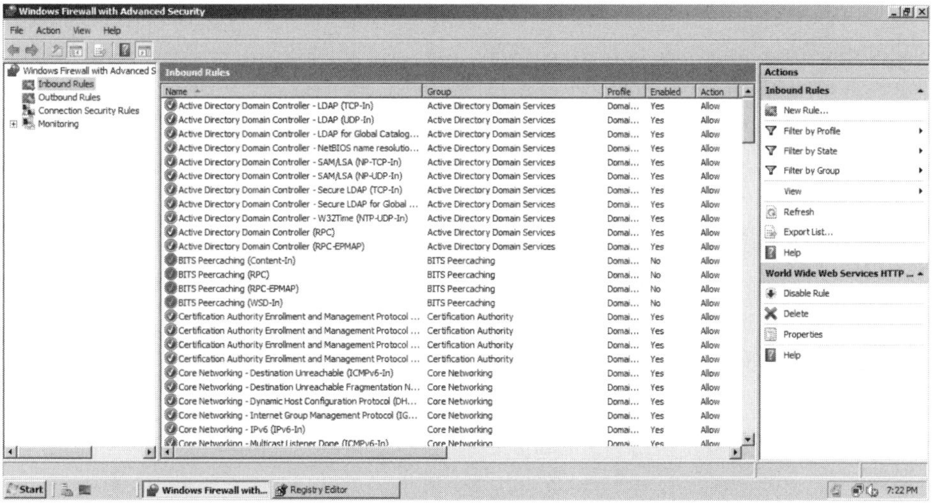

Figure 6-17 Example listing of Windows Firewall rules protecting services.

Most firewall rules deal with Windows services, restricting what connections can reach them and where on the network they can contact. Each rule can be customized or disabled, and of course, administrators can define new rules to cover new or existing services. As you can with any Windows Firewall rule, you can also require IPsec to be used with encryption and/or authentication before a connection is established. You can also establish rules by using scripting.

Windows Vista and Windows Server 2008 also include more than 80 predefined outbound rules, enabled by default. You can see a list of the rules at HKLM\System\ CurrentControlSet\Services\SharedAccess\Parameters\FirewallPolicy\ RestrictedServices\static (see Figure 6-18).

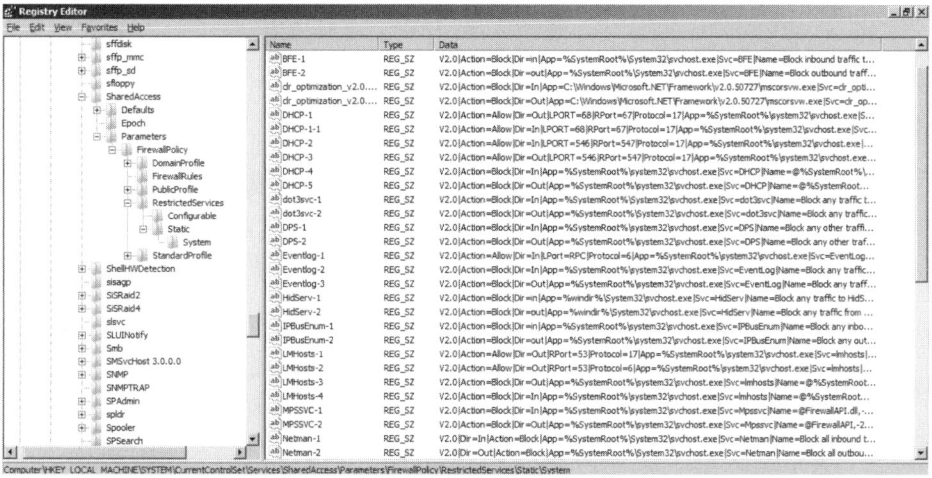

Figure 6-18 A sample of static service firewall rules.

The rules are not visible in a normal GUI because they should not be modified. If you need to add rules for custom services, the right way is using COM scripting tools. See *http://blogs.technet.com/voy/archive/2007/04/02/network-restrictions-for-service-hardening.aspx* for more details and scripting examples. The rules are considered static because they apply whether or not the firewall is enabled and over all three firewall profiles. Also, they can only be used to restrict access, not to grant it. Microsoft's new focus on extending domain isolation to services will only increase the resilience of Windows to network attacks. Several attacks, including the Blaster worm, would have been prevented or minimized had these firewall rules been in effect at the time.

Also, if someone tells you that Windows Firewall doesn't have any outbound blocking turned on by default, you can show them the dozens of rules in effect by default.

Session 0 Isolation

At the beginning of this chapter I mentioned that all services run in Session 0 on Windows. All user mode applications and programs do not. This serves to prevent users and the programs they run (which might be malware) from easily modifying core services. Since roughly 86 percent of all Windows vulnerabilities reported over the last few years require an end user to be socially engineered into executing code on the desktop (*http://www.infoworld.com/article/07/10/19/42OPsecadvise-insider-threats_1.html*), service session isolation is a very good thing.

The one potential downside to Session 0 Isolation is the fact that legacy services expecting to directly interact with the end user can no longer display messages and prompts. Without some sort of shim, a legacy service would display its service message in Session 0, where the end user cannot read it. Microsoft included the Interactive Services Detection (ui0detect) service to allow legacy services to communicate to interactive end users. When started (it is not started by default) the service will detect services trying to communicate with the user and alert the logged-on interactive user. Microsoft has publicly stated that the Ui0detect service is a temporary shim and will be going away in the future. Vendors need to recode their services to communicate to users in different sessions using RPC, COM, Named Pipes, or other communication methods. Find more details on Session 0 Isolation at *http://www.microsoft.com/whdc/system/vista/services.mspx*.

Mandatory Integrity Levels

All services by default have the System mandatory integrity level. (See Chapter 2, for more detail on integrity levels.) Figure 6-19 shows the labels on several services. Only the Trusted-Installer mandatory integrity level is higher. This allows Windows, using the TrustedInstaller service, to upgrade, install, remove, and replace services, while minimizing the chance that other processes and users can modify services.

Data Execution Prevention

As Figure 6-19 also shows, most services are protected with Data Execution Prevention (DEP) and ASLR. DEP mitigates many different types of buffer overflows by attempting to prevent

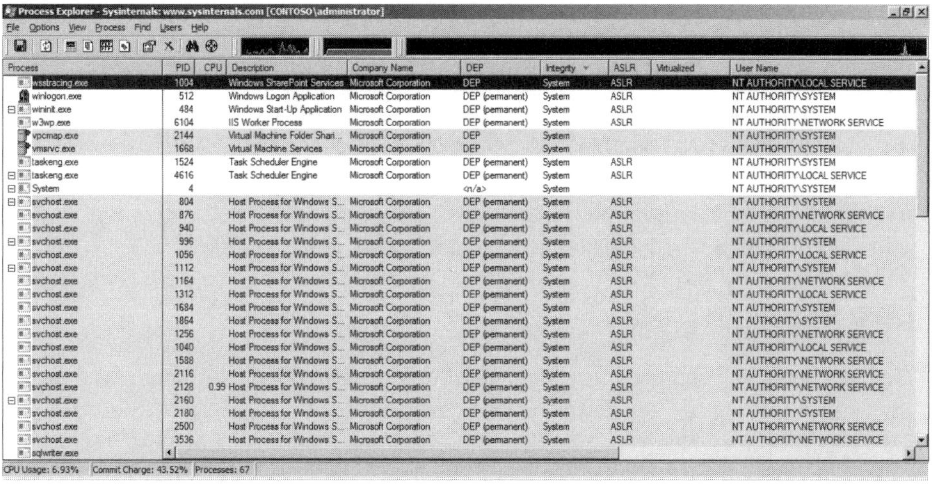

Figure 6-19   Process Explorer showing service attributes.

nonexecutable memory areas from executing program instructions.. Both DEP and ASLR make it harder for a buffer overflow to find the actual function addresses. Both security mechanisms prevent some types of malicious attacks, and have been successful in putting down other attacks that were successful on previous Windows platforms. Neither can stop all malicious attacks. Developers creating services should make sure their services utilize DEP and ASLR.

Other New SCM Features

Prior to Windows Vista and Windows Server 2008, the only way for a client to determine whether a service had changed its status, or been created or deleted, was to use the service query application programming interface (API), *QueryServiceStatusEx* function, and poll the status of the service. Having to constantly poll for changed status was not efficient. Windows Vista introduced a new API, *NotifyServiceStatusChange*, which allows the SCM to notify registered clients when a specific service changes status. This means that applications that monitor services can now receive notifications when services change status, making it far easier to write management tools.

Services can also register to get preshutdown notifications to give them a longer time to prepare for a system shutdown. And shutdown can take into account each service's dependencies and shut them down (if configured) in a more orderly manner.

SCM was also enhanced to detect and recover from nonfatal errors better. In early versions of Windows, it took a complete crash of the service to kick off a recovery event. Now, memory leaks, slow processing, and other issues can initiate a recovery event.

Microsoft has spent significant effort to make Windows services more secure. While no software as complex as Windows will ever be without security bugs, Windows Vista has already proven to be more resistant to newly announced security vulnerabilities. Check out the security blog of Microsoft's Jeff Jones (*http://blogs.technet.com/security/archive/tags/Studies/default.aspx*) to see what I mean. We should expect Windows Server 2008 to be similarly more resilient.

Securing Services

Microsoft understands the security risk with each running service. To that end, the development team has analyzed and improved the security of all included Windows services beyond the levels in previous Windows operating systems. Still, you as the administrator should do some things that can improve the situation even further. Administrators should take the following steps to minimize the risk of malicious exploitation. These steps should be implemented in security policies and guidelines.

Inventory Services

To begin to secure services, an administrator must understand and document what services should be running on each of their computers or types of computers. Without a service list and an explanation of what that service does, it is difficult to remove unneeded services. Many built-in and third-party tools can provide you with a list of services per computer. The easiest program to query a single computer is the Service Controller (Sc.exe) tool. It can be used to query local and remote services and return all sorts of individual service information, along with allowing the administrator to modify service information (privileges, status, start-up type, and so on). The Windows Management Instrumentation (WMI) and Windows Management Instrumentation Command-line (WMIC) allow service querying and scripting. For example, to retrieve services information for a server called Server1, type the following at a command prompt:

```
wmic /output:c:\services.htm /node:server1 service list full / format:htable
```

Use Microsoft Internet Explorer to examine the resulting C:\services.htm file. Other tools, such as Microsoft System Management Server (SMS) or System Center Configuration Manager (*http://www.microsoft.com/smserver/default.mspx*) are excellent choices for returning detailed and summarized list of services. Service inventories should be run on a periodic basis, according to the risk-acceptance level of the organization. If you cannot inventory all computer systems, start with the highest risk and most valuable systems first, and the systems that connect to them.

Minimize Running Services

The next step is to decide what services are really needed, and remove or disable the rest. This is the single biggest step you can take to minimize malicious risk from services. Every disabled and remove service is one less attack vector. Chapter 11, "Securing Server Roles," goes into depth on how to configure services using server roles and the Security Configuration Wizard (SCW).

In general, be cautious in disabling or modifying Windows default services outside of the Server Manager and SCW. In most instances, Microsoft has determined what services are most likely to be needed in most environments for particular roles, and configured them to start or not start accordingly. What is enabled has been relatively well protected using the mechanisms discussed here. What you should be looking for are services that are obviously not needed or used, or against company policy. A common example of the former is the DHCP

Client. It is turned on by default on many servers, even if the server has a static address. An example of the latter type of service might be an unauthorized peer-to-peer file-sharing program. It is the rare administrator who queries her environment and does not find lots of unauthorized and potentially dangerous services.

If you are still trying to determine whether a default Windows service is needed, consult one of the many Windows service guides available from Microsoft. The following links describe various Windows services and offer baseline recommendations for Windows Vista and Windows Server 2008:

- *http://www.microsoft.com/whdc/system/vista/Vista_Services.mspx*

- *http://www.microsoft.com/downloads/details.aspx?FamilyID=a3d1bbed-7f35-4e72-bfb5-b84a526c1565&displaylang=en*

- *http://www.microsoft.com/downloads/details.aspx?FamilyID=fb8b981f-227c-4af6-a44b-b115696a80ac&DisplayLang=en*

Unneeded services should be disabled or uninstalled. Uninstalled is more secure, but disabling a service allows it to be quickly re-enabled if it is needed in the future or was disabled by mistake. SCW allows you to significantly reduce the attack surface in a safe way and with the ability to roll back your changes. See Chapter 11 for more details.

Note   Before disabling or removing an active service, make sure you know what it is used for and what dependencies may break if it is removed. Always back up a system (or at least perform a Systemstate backup) before removing or disabling services.

Apply a Least-Privilege Model to Remaining Services

Microsoft already applies a least-privilege security model to all of its services. Applying a least-privilege security model applies more to third-party and custom-developed services. Unfortunately, many software vendors are still slow to come around to the idea of threat modeling and least-privileged security, especially for services.

If you install a new service and are unsure about its level of security, contact the software vendor. Using the Sc.exe command, enumerate the service's SID, SID Type, log-on account, and Required Privileges. If the privileges and permissions seem overly generous for the benefit the service is giving, consider contacting the vendor and asking for least-privilege assistance. If the vendor and/or the service does not practice least-privilege programming, consider removing the service and not using it. Nothing speaks louder to vendors than customer reaction and dollar votes.

Keep Your Updates Up to Date

Microsoft routinely updates its software, providing bug fixes, security updates, new features, and performance improvements. If a critical bug is found in a service and it threatens a large portion of customers, Microsoft works quickly to resolve the vulnerability with a security update and/or other recommendations. Keeping your system full up to date is another great way to minimize security risk. The two biggest Windows malware incidents in recent history (SQL Slammer and Blaster) only worked on computers that had not yet applied the delivered security updates.

Creating and Using Custom Service Accounts

Microsoft recommends using the built-in service accounts (Local System, Local Service, and Network Service) whenever possible. At times, however, it makes more sense to create and use a custom service log-on account.

Use Strong Passwords and Change Them at a Reasonable Interval

Custom service log-on accounts should be protected by a strong password policy (meaning strong passwords with frequent enough password changes). Custom service accounts store their passwords in two areas: Active Directory or the local SAM database and on the local system in a location where the SCM can retrieve and use. When you change your service log-on account passwords you have to do it in two places at the same time or you risk your service not starting. Do not let the hassle of changing service account passwords in two locations prevent you from changing the service log-on account on a reasonable time schedule. Several scripts are available on the Internet to make the chore easier, including this one on the Microsoft Developer Network: *http://msdn2.microsoft.com/en-us/library/ms675577.aspx*. You can also use the Passgen tool included on this book's CD to help set strong passwords for local and remote service accounts.

> **Note**   Use password-auditing tools to audit service log-on accounts for password weaknesses.

Use Group Policy Restricted Groups Feature

If highly privileged custom service log-on accounts are used, use the Restricted Groups feature of Group Policy to simplify assigning permissions and keeping other accounts from accidentally getting those permissions. When a group and its members are defined in Restricted Groups (Computer Configuration\Windows Settings\Security Settings\Restricted Groups), changes to the group's membership outside of the Restricted Groups feature will be undone by Group Policy. The permissions and privileges the custom log-on accounts need can be assigned to the group, and then the group's membership enforced using Restricted Groups.

Minimize the Use of Domain Administrator Accounts

Never use custom service log-on accounts belonging to the Domain Admins (or similarly configured privileged) groups on nondomain controllers. If a service using a service log-on account with domain admin privileges is compromised, essentially the entire forest is compromised. Use nearly any other account type, including Local System, to see whether it is acceptable by the service. Any computers running highly privileged service accounts should be considered high risk and subjected to the same security restrictions and policies as domain controllers.

Consider Using Local System Instead

Many guides recommend moving service accounts needing Local System access to lesser privileged custom service accounts, if the service can perform adequately with the new custom service account. However, many administrators have taken this to mean that services running at Local System should be avoided at all costs. These administrators think nothing of making a custom service account that is a domain or local administrator, while ignoring the base protections offered by the Local System account. For one, there is no password for a criminal to compromise. If an attacker compromises a service running in the Local System context, he may own the local computer, but at least he does not own your domain or forest automatically, as he would if he recovered a domain admin account.

Service best practices say to use the least-privileged service log-on account you can get away with. Start with Local Service or Network Service if they meet your needs. If you do not need admin or LocalSystem access, create a custom service account with only the access you need. If a software vendor says you must let their service run in a domain admin context on nondomain controllers, try using a customized service account with Full Control permissions to the resources the service needs access to. Or better yet, return the product and demand a refund. Giving any service account Full Control permissions to significant file and registry resource is even preferable over adding the service log-on account to the domain admins group. Full control permissions to most files and folders, without belonging to an admins group, does not give the service the ability to add and remove users, change user passwords, and a myriad of other common administrator asks. Giving Full Control to a system is not the same as giving administrator access. And if a service account does need administrator access to a system, try to give it Local System access instead. Local System is a local administrator, and you do not have any passwords to change periodically (or to get hacked).

Use Windows Firewall and IPsec for Network Isolation

Consider using Windows Firewall and IPsec to isolate your services to the security domains they need. Many services do not need access from the local network or need to accept inbound connections coming off the Internet, and as such should be restricted.

Auditing Service Failures

Because services now have their own SIDs, it is easier to monitor service failures and the failure of a service to get appropriate access to a needed resource. Consider implementing a common response program or script to service failures to alert IT support. Most widespread service failures are due to normal operational or service life issues, but if history is any indicator, monitoring for widespread service outage could give IT support early warning about newly arriving threats.

Develop and Use Secure Services

Lastly, if your organization develops Windows services, use the tools and mechanisms Microsoft has provided to write secure services. If you are a consumer of services, refuse to run insecure services, and hold your vendors accountable for following the basic security recommendations set forth in these pages. More secure services helps protect the computer it is installed on, and protects its neighbors.

Summary

Services running on Windows Server 2008 (and Windows Vista) have improved significantly over previous versions of Windows. Services now run in least-privilege modes, with service-specific SIDs, isolated in Session 0, with restricted network access, and with DEP and ASLR protections. Administrators can help minimize malicious risk from services by removing unneeded services from their environment, and following a least-privilege model for services they design and purchase. Although Windows will always be a target for malicious hackers, least-privileged services will make it tougher for them to succeed.

Additional Resources

■ Microsoft Corporation (2004). "Services in Windows Vista," at *http://www.microsoft.com/whdc/system/vista/Vista_Services.mspx.*

■ Microsoft Corporation (2007). "Windows Vista Security Guide," at *http://www.microsoft.com/downloads/details.aspx?FamilyID=a3d1bbed-7f35-4e72-bfb5-b84a526c1565&displaylang=en.*

■ Microsoft Corporation (2007). "Windows Server 2008 Security Guide," at *http://www.microsoft.com/downloads/details.aspx?FamilyID=fb8b981f-227c-4af6-a44b-b115696a80ac&DisplayLang=en.*

Chapter 7
Group Policy

— Darren Mar-Elia

Group Policy technology has been around since Windows 2000 shipped. It is the multi-function configuration technology within Windows Server and desktop Operating Systems. The technology is designed to let you centrally configure literally thousands of options that can apply to some or all of your Windows systems across different networks and geographies. Most important for this book, Group Policy is your key mechanism for deploying security configuration settings to all of your systems. If nothing else, you have at least used Group Policy to configure password policy within your Active Directory domains. But Group Policy can do much   more than just password policy, and in this chapter, I will show you how Group Policy works and the security-related configuration capabilities that are available in Windows Server 2008.

What Is New in Windows Server 2008

Before I introduce how Group Policy works and how you can use it to manage configurations across your environment, I want to highlight some of the key changes that have occurred in Group Policy since Windows XP and Windows Server 2003. In fact, many of the changes introduced to Group Policy showed up first in Windows Vista, and these changes have carried forward to Windows Server 2008. But Windows Server 2008 brings its own set of changes—primarily related to the Group Policy Management Console (GPMC)—that provide additional manageability for Group Policy. The following key changes were introduced in Windows Server 2008 and Windows Vista:

- Support for new policy areas, including new wired and wireless network security policies, improved Windows Firewall and IPsec policy configuration interfaces, support for power management configuration, and USB device restriction policies.

- Improved slow-link detection between client and domain controllers. This provides a more reliable mechanism for determining when the client is across a slow link, which can affect Group Policy processing behavior.

183

- Group Policy refresh based on availability of the domain controller rather than just on a fixed cycle. This means that when a client connects back to the corporate network or connects remotely via a VPN connection, Group Policy will refresh more quickly.

- Support for multiple Local Group Policy Objects (LGPOs) to allow per-user and administrative versus non-administrative filtering of local Group Policy.

- Support for the new XML-based Administrative Template file format (ADMX), which improves multi-language support for Administrative Templates.

- Support for per-GPO and per-GP setting comments

- Improvements to GPMC and Group Policy editor in Windows Server 2008 that add new capabilities such as filtering policies that appear based on keywords and the ability to create "Starter" GPOs of Administrative Template policy.

- The Group Policy Preferences feature, which incorporates new policy settings that were formerly part of the DesktopStandard PolicyMaker technology that Microsoft acquired.

But before I talk in detail concerning these new Group Policy features and capabilities, let us begin with the basics—how does Group Policy work, what does it do, and how can you use it to help secure your Windows Infrastructure?

Group Policy Basics

The first thing to know about Group Policy is that you will need to deploy an Active Directory infrastructure to take full advantage of its features. Having Active Directory in the mix allows you to use advanced features and targeting with Group Policy that are not available in workgroups. That being said, each computer running Windows Server 2008, Windows Vista, or an earlier version of Windows back to Windows 2000 comes with a local GPO that you can use to manage certain configuration settings within a workgroup environment.

The Local GPO

The local GPO or LGPO is accessed by simply clicking Start, then Run, and then typing **gpedit.msc** in the Run dialog box. This opens the Local Group Policy Editor (Figure 7-1).

> **Note**   From the Administrative Tools Start Menu program group enabled on your Windows Server 2008 system, you will see an item called Local Security Policy. If you launch this tool, you will get the Group Policy Editor MMC snap-in focused on the security section within the local GPO—namely, the security settings available under Computer Configuration\Windows Settings\Security Settings. This tool is just a convenient way to view and edit only the security options within the local GPO. But keep in mind that it is still focused on the local GPO only.

The local GPO on a Windows system applies to all users that log onto that system. Pre-Windows Vista systems had no capability to control which user logging onto the local system received policy from the local GPO. All users received all the settings equally. However, in Windows Vista and Windows Server 2008, you now have the ability to create multiple, user-specific local GPOs for those scenarios in which you do not have Active Directory but want to filter the effects of the local GPO based on who logs onto the system. I will talk about multiple local GPOs more in a bit.

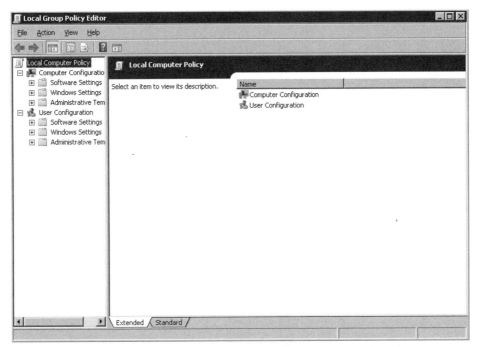

Figure 7-1   Viewing the local GPO using the Microsoft Management Console on Windows Server 2008.

Active Directory–Based GPOs

Although you are limited in terms of how much control local GPOs can give you, with Active Directory in place, you have the full capability of Group Policy at your disposal. Despite the word "Group" in Group Policy, GPOs only apply to user and computer objects within your Active Directory environment. Group Policy Objects are linked to containers within Active Directory. That linking lets you control which users and computers will process a given GPO (see Figure 7-2).

You can link GPOs to Active Directory sites (a collection of IP subnets), domains, and OUs. You can even have multiple GPOs linked at each of these container levels—resulting in possibly tens or hundreds of GPOs applying to a given user or computer. The users and computers that process the GPOs that apply to them observe the following order of precedence:

1. Local GPO(s) apply first.

2. Site-linked GPOs apply next.

3. Domain-linked GPOs apply next.

4. OU-linked GPOs apply last.

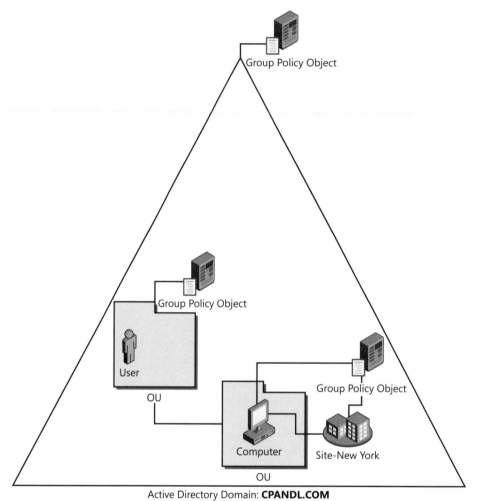

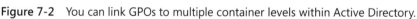

Active Directory Domain: **CPANDL.COM**

Figure 7-2   You can link GPOs to multiple container levels within Active Directory.

This order of precedence means that if there are conflicting settings within GPOs linked to (for example) a site and an OU, the settings within the OU will usually be the effective settings applied to the user or computer. This is because Group Policy processing follows a "last writer wins" order of precedence that guarantees that GPOs linked more closely to the user or computer in the Active Directory hierarchy will be the ones that win out.

Security Filtering of GPOs

To give you some more granularity in terms of targeting the effect of Group Policy, Windows lets you use security groups to filter the effect of a GPO. This provides a more fine-grained targeting system than simply applying a GPO to all domain or OU users and computers.

Security Group Filtering is fairly easy to use if you have the GPMC installed on your Windows Vista or Windows Server 2008 system.

> **Tip** The Group Policy Management Console (GPMC) is installed by default on Windows Vista, but not on Windows Vista, Service Pack 1. To install the GPMC on Windows Server 2008, start the Server Manager utility and under the Features section, add the Group Policy Management feature. To get access to the GPMC on Windows Vista, Service Pack 1, you need to install the Remote Server Administration Tools (RSAT) package on that Vista system. RSAT includes GPMC and other Active Directory management tools.

Security filters are set on the GPO object. You can use the GPMC to modify which groups will process a given GPO. By default, when you create a new GPO, its security filter contains Read and Apply Group Policy permissions for the Authenticated Users group. Despite the name, this group includes all user and computer accounts in the domain. This means that wherever the GPO is linked, all users or computers will process it by default. Note that for a group to process a GPO, it must have both of these permissions—Read and Apply Group Policy. Having one or the other is not sufficient. Luckily, you do not have to worry about granting individual permissions if you use the GPMC to manage security filtering. In the next section, I will walk you through an example of how this works.

Modifying GPO Security Filtering Using GPMC

1. Start the GPMC on Windows Server 2008 by clicking Start, then Administrative Tools, and then Group Policy Management.

2. If you have not already added your Active Directory Forest to the GPMC, do so by right-clicking the root Group Policy Management node and typing in the DNS name of your forest root domain.

3. Now expand the forest node to manage the domain of interest. If the domain you want to manage is not the forest root domain, right-click the Domains node and select Show Domains to choose additional domains.

4. Within each domain node is a Group Policy Objects node. Expand this node and high-light the GPO whose security filter you want to modify.

5. With the target GPO highlighted, ensure that the Scope tab in the right-hand result pane is selected. The Security Filtering section will appear within this pane. Within that pane, the Authenticated Users group is listed by default, as shown in Figure 7-3. (This is because, as I mentioned, all users and computers can process a GPO when its created.)

6. First, remove Authenticated Users from the security filtering list—while this permission is in place, all users and computers will process this GPO. Highlight the Authenticated Users entry and click Remove.

7. Click Add button and enter the name of a user or computer group that you want to use for security filtering. Note that computer groups are used to filter computer-specific policy (that policy which exists within the Computer Configuration section of a GPO)

and user groups are used to filter user-specific policy (that policy which exists within the User Configuration section of a GPO). Click Check Names to resolve the group name and then click OK to confirm your choice. The new group is added to the Security Filtering section of the GPO Scope tab.

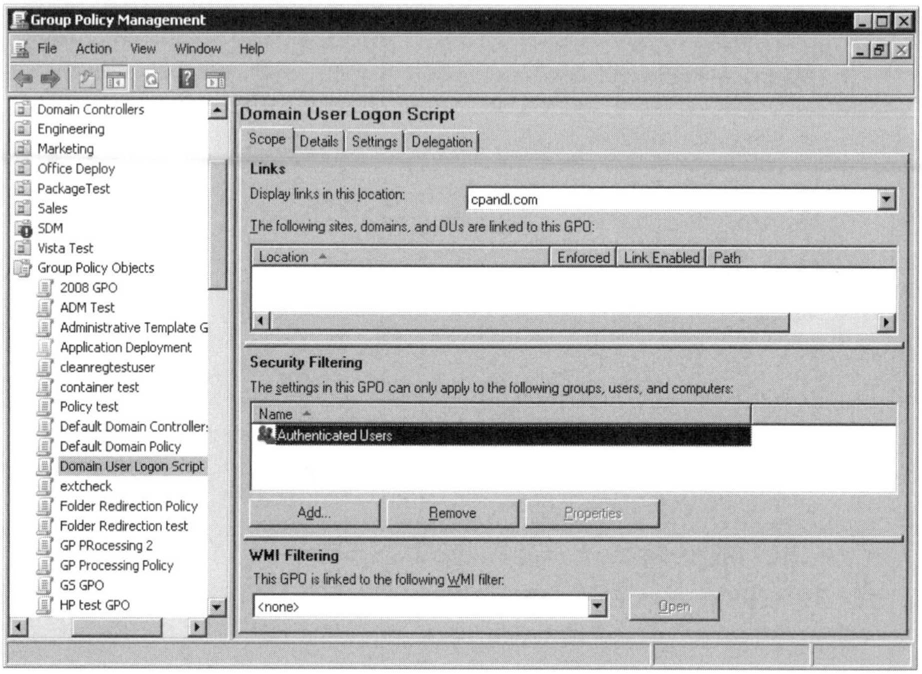

Figure 7-3   Viewing the default security filtering on a GPO.

What is happening behind the scenes is that the GPMC is really adding the Read and Apply Group Policy permissions for the group you added to this GPO. Note that you could also add an individual computer or user account to a security filter. While this is not a best practice, it may be useful for testing purposes to have a GPO only apply to a single computer or user.

A common misunderstanding occurs regarding the difference between linking a GPO and security filtering it. A GPO must be linked to a container where the computer or user account of the intended targets reside. If I am trying to deploy per-computer security policy to all of the computers in my organization's marketing division, I will link my GPO to the Marketing OU. If, within the Marketing OU, a subset of computers needs a different security policy—perhaps because they run a different operating system—I can use security group filtering on a second GPO, also linked to that Marketing OU, to segregate those computers. It does not matter if the security group I used to filter with resides in an OU outside of the Marketing OU—remember that Group Policy is only processed by user and computer accounts. Therefore, a security group can reside anywhere in Active Directory and still be used to filter Group Policy for a particular OU's computers or users. However, at this point you might realize that using security groups for certain kinds of filtering, including filtering by operating system, is a bit clunky. That is why we have WMI filtering.

WMI Filtering of GPOs

So far I have discussed linking GPOs to control which users and computers process them, and I have discussed security group filtering to more finely control targets within the bounds of linking to sites, domains, and OUs. Now let us look at the final mechanism for controlling Group Policy processing: the WMI filter.

WMI filtering was introduced first in Windows Server 2003 and Windows XP. Unlike security group filtering, which requires you to place users and computers in groups to control Group Policy application, WMI filtering relies on the inherent Windows Management Instrumentation (WMI) framework built into Windows since Windows XP to dynamically filter Group Policy application based on the hardware and software configuration of the computer and user being targeted.

WMI filtering requires knowledge of the WMI Query Language (WQL). Within Active Directory—and using the GPMC—you create WMI filters that contain a WQL statement. That statement might ask questions such as, "Is the system processing this policy running Windows XP, Service Pack 2? Is it running Windows Vista? Is it running Windows Vista Business edition?" Once you create one of these filters, you can link it to a GPO—again using the GPMC. Once you have done that, the computer or user processing that GPO will evaluate the WQL statement and, if the statement returns true, the GPO is processed. If the statement returns false, the GPO is not processed. Using WMI filters in this way, you can filter Group Policy processing based on the hardware or software installed on a computer.

WMI filter statements must always take the form of a query that evaluates to true or false when run on the computer processing that filter. Figure 7-4 shows an example of WMI filter that looks for Windows XP with Service Pack 2 running on the target system.

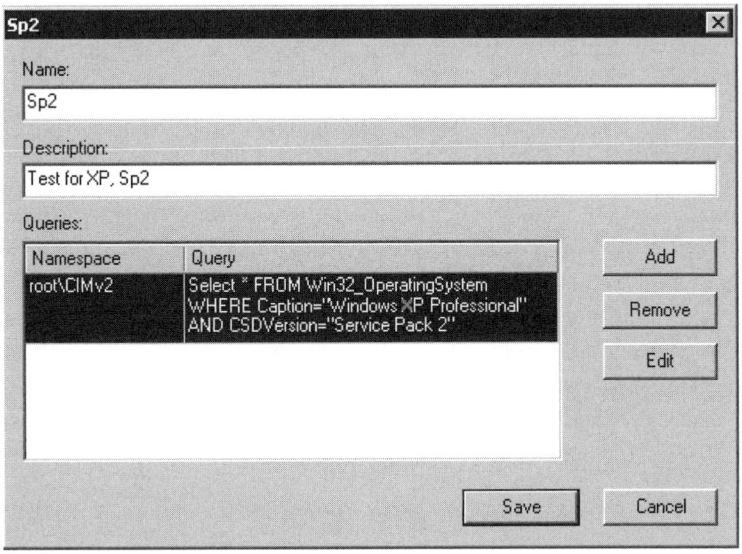

Figure 7-4   A WMI Filter query that looks for Windows XP, Service Pack2.

Note from Figure 7-4 that WQL statements take the form of a Select statement that asks for all instances of a particular WMI class (in this example, *Win32_OperatingSystem*) and then provides qualifiers for the particular property of interest (such as *Caption="Windows XP Professional"*). While a full treatment of writing WQL statements is outside the scope of this chapter, you can find more information on the Microsoft Web site at *http://msdn2.microsoft.com/en-us/library/ aa392902.aspx.*

As I mentioned, WMI filters are managed using the GPMC. You will find a WMI Filters node within each domain loaded in the GPMC. This is because WMI filters are stored per domain, just as GPOs are. If you right-click the WMI Filters node and then click New, you can create a new WMI filter. Note that when you type the WQL statement into the WMI filter editor, the GPMC immediately validates that you have a well-formed WQL statement. If it is not a valid statement, you will see a message like that shown in Figure 7-5 when you try to save the filter.

Figure 7-5 WQL query syntax validation occurs when you try to save a WMI filter.

One thing to keep in mind about WMI filters is that some queries can impose performance issues during Group Policy processing. For example, if you were to write a query that evaluates Active Directory group membership, this could take a long time to process in a large Active Directory environment and could cause Group Policy processing to slow down significantly as the query is evaluated.

Now that we have looked at Group Policy from the Active Directory perspective, let us switch gears and talk about how Group Policy works from the perspective of the system that processes policy.

Group Policy Processing

While the creation and management of GPOs themselves is an important part of the overall Group Policy story, understanding how Group Policy is processed (or why it is not being processed), is just as important to ensuring that your users and computers receive the security configuration that you expect to deliver. To that end, let us look at the client side of Group Policy. As I mentioned, user and computer objects that reside in Active Directory process Group Policy Objects. The Group Policy processing engine on Windows—whether on Windows Server 2008, Windows Vista, or an earlier version—works basically the same way. Namely, two kinds of Group Policy processing occur—foreground and background:

- *Foreground* processing occurs when a Windows computer starts up, or when a user logs on. Foreground processing is important because certain Group Policy areas—such as

Folder Redirection and Software Installation—only run during the foreground process-ing cycle. This is because they need to have exclusive access to the computer or user environment to complete their tasks. Without this exclusive access, it would be hard to know in what state the user would be getting the computer. You would not want software being installed while you are trying to run it!

■ *Background* processing occurs periodically in the background based on time. Domain controllers run background processing every five minutes by default. Workstations and member servers run background processing every 90 minutes with a 0–30–minute random offset to ensure that all systems do not process policy at once.

> **Tip**   You can modify the default refresh interval for domain controllers, workstations, and member servers by modifying the policy settings at Computer Configuration\Administrative Templates\System\Group Policy\Group Policy Refresh Interval For Domain Controllers and Computer Configuration\Administrative Templates\System\Group Policy\Group Policy Refresh Interval For Computers.

In addition to these two processing modes, foreground policy can run in one of two ways—synchronous or asynchronous. Background policy is asynchronous by definition. With syn-chronous policy processing, Group Policy processing must be completed before the user is presented with a log-on dialog (for computer policy) or before the user is presented with the desktop (for user policy). This ensures that policy processing that may affect the current session is fully processed before the user can interact with the system. This also slows down the start-up and log-on process, which is why Windows XP and Windows Vista have asyn-chronous foreground policy processing enabled by default. Asynchronous processing tells the Group Policy engine to continue running computer policy while the user is logging on, and to present the desktop to the user even though user policy might still be getting processed. Windows Server 2003 and Windows Server 2008 always have foreground processing set to synchronous. However, if you are using Terminal Server, Windows Server 2008 now lets you set foreground processing for Terminal Server users to asynchronous by enabling the policy at Computer Configuration\Administrative Templates\System\Group Policy\Allow Asynchro-nous User Group Policy Processing when logging on through Terminal Services.

Just as with foreground and background policy, certain policy areas will not run unless foreground processing is running synchronously. An example of this is Software Installation policy. If the Group Policy engine is running in the foreground and detects a Software Instal-lation policy, it will set a flag to tell Windows to run policy synchronously during the next foreground refresh. This is why it can sometimes take two reboots or logons for a software installation package to deploy.

Luckily, most other policy areas, such as Security and Administrative Templates, will run during foreground and background processing regardless of whether it is running synchro-nous or asynchronous.

Slow-Link Processing

In addition to the two different types of processing outlined previously, certain conditions can affect which Group Policy areas run. For example, Group Policy has a slow-link detection mechanism built in that is designed to detect when the computer or user has a slow network connection to the closest domain controller. By default, a slow link is defined as 500 Kilobits/second; you can modify this setting through Group Policy. The slow-link detection process itself has changed in Windows Vista and Windows Server 2008. In prior versions of Windows, this process relied on ICMP pings between client and domain controller to determine link speed. This method was not reliable and organizations often restricted or prevented ICMP traffic on their internal network for security reasons. As a result, the slow-link detection process in Windows Vista and Windows Server 2008 now uses the Network Location Awareness (NLA) service to calculate link speed between client and domain controller during Group Policy processing. In this capacity, NLA measures LDAP traffic between client and domain controller to calculate link speed.

If the slow-link detection threshold is crossed during this testing process, certain Group Policy areas will not process by default. Those areas include Software Installation, Folder Redirection, Internet Explorer Maintenance Policy, and Scripts Policy. However, you can modify the behavior of these policy areas to force them to process even if a slow link is detected. You do this by modifying the individual policy area settings under Computer Configuration\Administrative Templates\System\Group Policy. The key thing to note about Group Policy and slow-link detection is that security policy processing occurs whether a slow link is detected or not.

Policy Processing Optimizations

The Group Policy engine is responsible for processing GPOs that apply the current computer or user. And as I have already discussed, processing occurs in both the foreground and background on a periodic basis. However, if the Group Policy engine reprocessed all GPOs that applied each time a processing cycle occurred, regardless of whether any changes had been made to those applicable GPOs, that would waste network and system resources. As a result, Microsoft built some optimizations into the Group Policy engine. Chief among those optimizations is the notion that during each policy processing cycle, no policy processing will actually occur if nothing has changed within the environment. Change can be a tricky thing, however. What constitutes a change is not always clear or obvious. It is more than just a change to a GPO—primarily because several things can affect which GPOs apply to a given computer or user. In addition, if one GPO out of ten that apply to a computer is changed, all ten may need to run again to preserve the processing precedence I discussed earlier.

The following types of changes will cause Group Policy processing to reprocess GPOs during a given cycle:

- A change is made to the settings within a GPO processed by the user or computer
- The list of GPOs applied to the computer or user changes (in other words, a new GPO is added or a previously processed one is removed)

- A change is made to the user or computer's security group membership, which may effect security group filtering

- A change is made to a WMI filter (one is added to a GPO or one is removed) processed by the computer or user

---

How It Works: Group Policy Versioning

Obviously if the Group Policy engine processes policy only if there has been a change, there must be a mechanism for determining when a GPO has changed. This is accomplished through versioning. Each time you make a change to a setting within a GPO, the version number of that GPO is incremented. This version number is held in both the Active Directory and SYSVOL parts of the GPO, called the Group Policy Container (GPC) and Group Policy Template (GPT) respectively. When the Group Policy engine on a client system processes policy, it compares version numbers for each GPO to be processed with those it holds in its registry from the last time Group Policy was processed, also called the Group Policy history. If the versions between the GPO and the history are different, the engine knows it must process policy during that current cycle.

Note that because each policy area does not keep version information separately, but rather only for the whole GPO, the following scenario can occur. Let us say a client computer must process two GPOs—GPO A and GPO B. GPO A contains Administrative Template and Security policy settings. GPO B contains only security policy settings. An administrator makes a change to GPO A's Administrative Template settings only, which increment GPO A's version number. The client computer must process GPO A to pick up the new Administrative Template settings, but it must also process GPO B, because both GPO A and GPO B contain security settings, and must process the security settings of both GPOs to maintain GPO processing precedence.

Thus, the way you structure your GPOs in terms of which policy areas you implement in which policies can have an effect on how often they are processed.

I have established that Group Policy is not processed during each foreground and background cycle if nothing has changed, but there is an exception to that rule. Namely, security policy processing will refresh its settings every 16 hours by default, even if nothing has changed in the Group Policy infrastructure. The reason for this is a good one. If a user intentionally or inadvertently is able to make a change to her local system's security policy, having Group Policy automatically reapply that policy from Active Directory every 16 hours can be useful.

On the Disc   The CD of this book includes a custom ADMX file called Securityrefresh.ADMX (and the accompanying Securityrefresh.ADML) that lets you set this interval using Administrative Template policy.

> **Note**   You can modify the default 16-hour refresh value on the security Client Side Extension
> (CSE) by modifying the following registry value on client computers:
> HKEY_LOCAL_MACHINE\SOFTWARE\Microsoft\Windows NT\CurrentVersion\Winlogon\
> GPExtensions\{827D319E-6EAC-11D2-A4EA-00C04F79F83A}\MaxNoGPOListChangesInter-
> val. This value stores the number of minutes between forced refresh intervals with a default of
> decimal 960.
>
> You can also adjust each CSE's policy processing behavior to force it to process policy, even if
> there are no changes, during each foreground and background cycle. This may result in a lot of
> additional network traffic and system utilization, but will ensure that a given CSE's policies are
> always the most recent. You can do this by modifying each CSE's policy processing item under
> Computer Configuration\Administrative Templates\System\Group Policy for each computer
> you want to impact.

Now that we have laid the foundation for how Group Policy is processed, let us look in more
detail at some of the changes to Group Policy management that have been introduced
in Windows Server 2008.

What Is New in Group Policy

Windows Server 2008 and Windows Vista introduced some significant enhancements to
both the management of Group Policy and the items available for configuration using Group
Policy. Let us look at some of these management enhancements first and then dive into the
policy improvements related to security configuration management.

Group Policy Service

The first change to the Group Policy infrastructure was mostly invisible to administrators.
Prior to Windows Vista and Windows Server 2008, the Group Policy engine ran within the
trusted Winlogon process in Windows. This made a certain amount of sense at the time but
also presented some challenges. Primarily, Microsoft or third-party Client Side Extensions
(CSEs) also ran within this process, and if bugs arose in these CSEs, they could cause
Windows to stop responding. In Windows Vista and Window Server 2008, Microsoft moved
the Group Policy engine out of Winlogon and into the Group Policy Client service running
within a svchost.exe process, except that it cannot be stopped or started by an administrator—
at least not very easily. The service is hardened to improve the odds that it is always running
when Windows is running. And because the service is no longer running in Winlogon, errant
CSEs will only crash the service, rather than the entire operating system.

ADMX Templates and the Central Store

In versions of Windows prior to Windows Vista and Windows Server 2008, Administrative
Template settings were governed by language-specific ADM template files. These files were
provided by Microsoft; administrators can also create custom ones. The syntax of these files

was proprietary and the text strings that appeared in the Group Policy editor were held within the same ADM file that held the registry locations for a given binding. In addition, each GPO held a set of ADM files within the SYSVOL portion of the GPO—called the Group Policy Template (GPT). These ADM files were generally the same across all GPOs in a domain but were nonetheless replicated redundantly to all domain controllers in the domain.

Starting with Windows Vista and Windows Server 2008, Microsoft introduced the new ADMX and ADML file formats. The ADMX file is a new XML-based syntax for describing Administrative Template policies. Each ADMX file has a corresponding ADML file that contains language-specific strings for that set of policy settings. By separating the policy items from the text string representations, Microsoft can more easily allow administrators using multi-language versions of Windows Vista or Windows Server 2008 to manage Administrative Template policies in their native languages.

The new ADMX and ADML files also use a different storage model than previous versions. ADMX and ADML files ship from Microsoft by default and are found in the %windir%\policydefinitions folder in a standard Windows Vista or Windows Server 2008 installation (see Figure 7-6).

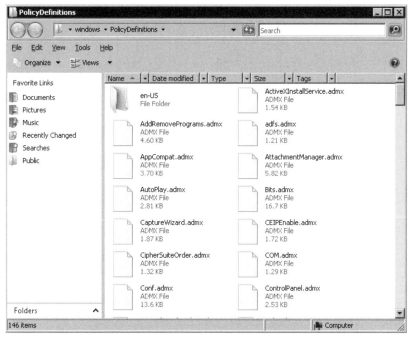

Figure 7-6   Viewing ADMX files that come with Windows Server 2008.

Note the folder called en-us within the PolicyDefinitions folder in Figure 7-6. This is the language-specific folder for U.S. English ADML files. When you start Group Policy Editor in Windows Vista or Windows Server 2008 and then expand the Administrative Templates node, the editor automatically looks in this %windir%\policydefinitions folder for ADMX and

ADML files. However, you also have the option of copying these files to a central location known as the Central Store.

The Central Store is simply a file folder within the SYSVOL share replicated to all of your domain controllers that you create manually and copy your ADMX and ADML files into. The Central Store must exist within a folder called PolicyDefinitions underneath the \\<domain>\sysvol\<domain>\policies folder. One advantage of using the Central Store is that all administrators that edit Group Polices will have access to all ADMX files in use through the Central Store. Administrators will no longer have to copy ADM files around to their local computers to see new Administrative Template settings. The Group Policy editor will look for the central store first before looking in %windir%\policydefinitions. If it finds the Central Store, it will use the ADMX and ADML files from there instead of locally.

Note that in no situation are ADMX and ADML files copied automatically into the SYSVOL portion of each GPO. That is, if you create new GPOs from Windows Vista or Windows Server 2008, they will not contain any ADMX files within that portion of the GPO. All ADMX and ADML files are referenced locally or from the Central Store when you edit a Windows Vista or Windows Server 2008 GPO. This saves storage space within your domain controller's SYSVOL shares, because these template files are no longer stored in every GPO on every domain controller.

Direct from the Field: The ADMX Central Store

One of the great features available in Windows Vista and Windows Server 2008 is the new Central Store for ADMX files. In previous versions of Windows, the ADM templates that were used to generate the Administrative Templates portion of the Group Policy Objects were copied to each Group Policy Template. This duplication of the ADM templates caused problems with replication traffic, administration of the Group Policy Objects, and version control issues. Windows Server 2008 and Windows Vista solve this by changing from a proprietary format of ADM templates to an XML format with ADMX files. This provides language compatibility and flexibility, as well as an opportunity for better management capabilities.

To solve the replication and management issues that ADM templates had, ADMX files can now be centralized into a Central Store. The solution is very simple because you only need to create a new folder named PolicyDefinitions under C:\Windows\ Sysvol\sysvol\<domain name>\Policies on each domain controller. After creating the new folder, copy all of the ADMX files to the new location. Upon subsequent edits of any GPO, the centralized ADMX files will be used simply because this folder exists. Place any custom ADMX files in this folder, too, and they will automatically be consumed by the Group Policy Management Editor.

Derek Melber, MCSE, MVP, CISM, President
BrainCore.Net AZ, Inc. (www.braincore.net)

Starter GPOs

Starter GPOs are a brand new feature in Windows Server 2008. As the name implies, Starter GPOS are essentially templates that you can use to create real GPOs. A Starter GPO only supports Administrative Template settings—no other policy area is currently supported. But because you can find many thousands of policy settings within this area of a GPO, this is not a bad limitation for the time being.

You can create and edit Starter GPOs by opening the GPMC and looking for the Starter GPOs node beneath the WMI Filters node within an Active Directory domain. (See Figure 7-7.)

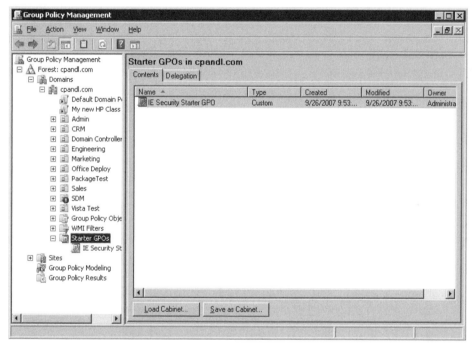

Figure 7-7   Starter GPOs in Windows Server 2008.

The way Starter GPOs work is fairly simple. Let us say I have a set of Administrative Template settings that I would like to apply to multiple GPOs across multiple domains. I can create a Starter GPO that contains those settings, and then I can right-click that Starter GPO and choose New GPO from Starter GPO. This will create a new, unlinked GPO in my domain and will copy all Administrative Template settings from the Starter GPO into the new GPO.

Keep in mind that Starter GPOs are not real Group Policy Objects. You cannot link a Starter GPO to a site, domain, or OU. They are only used as templates that can then be copied to a real GPO. In addition, you can save Starter GPOs to cabinet (.cab) files and copy them between domains. So you can create a set of Starter GPOs in the UK domain, save them as Cabinet files, and then e-mail them to your Australian colleagues to be used as Starter GPOs in their domain.

GPO Comments

Another handy feature that comes with the versions of GPMC and Group Policy editor that ship in Windows Server 2008 is support for putting in both per-GPO and per-setting comments. Comments are a way for you as the administrator to explain what a particular GPO or GPO setting might be used for. An administrator who does not know why a particular GPO exists or why a particular setting is being made can read the comments to see the purpose behind a policy. You can create both per-GPO and per-setting comments via the Group Policy editor. With the Group Policy editor open on a GPO, right-click the root node containing the GPO's name, and then choose Properties. Click the Comment tab to add comments to the GPO as a whole.

Direct from the Source: Comments

The Group Policy team has worked hard to provide some great new features to help Group Policy administrators get a better handle on their environments. One of those features is comments, an incredibly important new feature that will provide essential inline annotations so that we do not lose track of why something was done. I was recently working with some folks taking a look at their GP environment and we looked at one GPO which was created in 2000. "No way!" you say. It floored me, too. (Granted, I do not get out much.) Think about it: These GPOs provide configuration to many client systems throughout the enterprise. Why certain configuration was done, who did it, and what the expected results were are all pretty important bits of data, are they not?

Thus the need for comments. You can put comments on the top level of a GPO to document the purpose of that GPO or possibly the theme. You can also put comments down on the individual settings contained within the GPO to document why a setting is configured, provide contact information if other GP admins need more information— whatever you want. You can filter the settings to show, in the console, only the commented settings to quickly see what other admins are doing, or to see what you were doing if you cannot remember. This is a quick way to ensure that when actions are taken that affect the environment, you provide some clues. We have all looked at this stuff and said to ourselves, "Why would I have done that? It just does not make sense," Well now at least you can talk back to yourself, "Ohhhhhh, that is why I did that!"

A few caveats: Comments are only on the GPO itself or on Administrative Template Settings. Other settings in Group Policy, such as security settings, do not allow comments. The comments on settings are viewable on the settings report and the comments on the GPO show up on the Details tab in the GPMC. To comment on a GPO, open the editor for that GPO and go to the properties of the GPO (top node). You will see the Comment tab. To comment on a setting, go to the properties of that setting and you will see the Comment tab there.

> At last we have a way to document inline and justify why certain configuration settings exists. As we get older and our GPOs get older keeping track of this will be a huge help.
>
> *Kevin Sullivan*
> *Lead Program Manager – Group Policy*

Per-setting comments are only supported for Administrative Template policy items. Within a given Administrative Template policy item, you will now see a Comment tab, where you can enter your text, as shown in Figure 7-8.

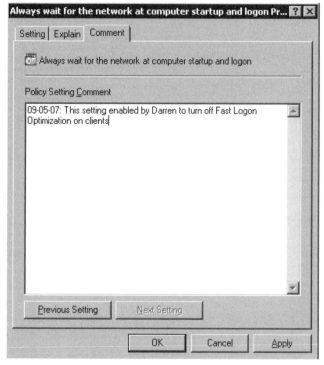

Figure 7-8   Adding per-setting comments in Group Policy.

Once you have added comments to your Group Policies, the GPMC can report on comments added to a GPO or Group Policy setting.

Filtering Improvements

The final Group Policy infrastructure improvement I will talk about is the improvements that have been made in Group Policy editor for filtering Administrative Template policy settings based on a variety of criteria. Prior to Windows Server 2008, you had no way to search or filter Administrative Template policies based on criteria such as the name of the policy item or even words contained in the Explain text. The new filtering feature essentially gives you a nice search mechanism within Administrative Templates for showing only those policy items that meet your filter criteria. To access this feature, right-click the Administrative Templates node from within the Group Policy editor and choose Filter Options. You will see the dialog shown in Figure 7-9.

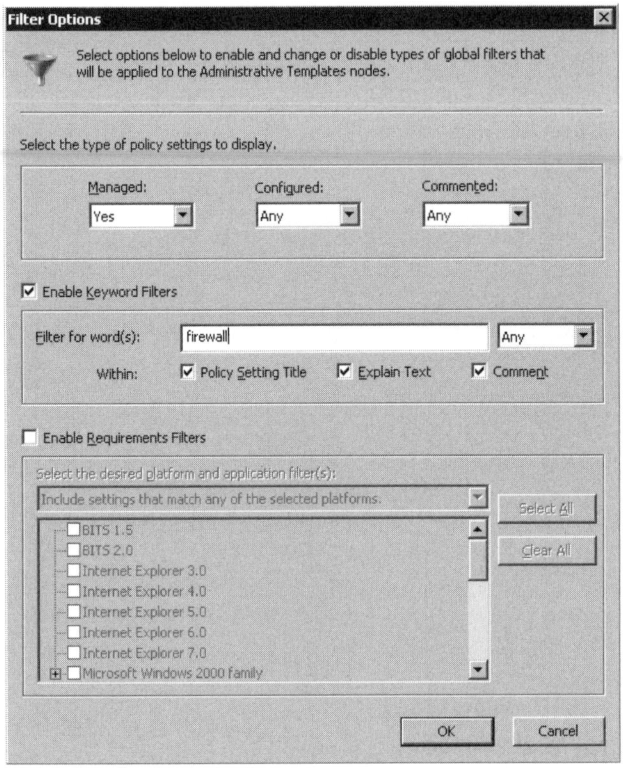

Figure 7-9 Using filtering to search for policy settings containing the word *firewall*.

In the example in Figure 7-9, I entered a filter for all policies where the title contains the word *firewall*. I could also search within the Explain text or comments for this text or enable the Requirements filters to look at only policies containing the word *firewall* that apply to Windows Vista. I also have the ability to choose whether I want to see only configured policies, only managed policies (as opposed to preferences), or only commented policies. After I define my filter, I simply right-click the Administrative Templates node again and choose Filter On. At that point, the view of policy settings under the Administrative Templates node will change to show only those policies that meet my filter criteria, as shown in Figure 7-10.

The final feature I will mention here is the new All Settings node , which you see in Figure 7-10 under the Administrative Templates node. All Settings is essentially a flat list view of all Administrative Template policies available within the GPO. It provides a different—and in some ways simpler—view of the thousands of settings found within the folder and subfolders under this section of the Group Policy editor.

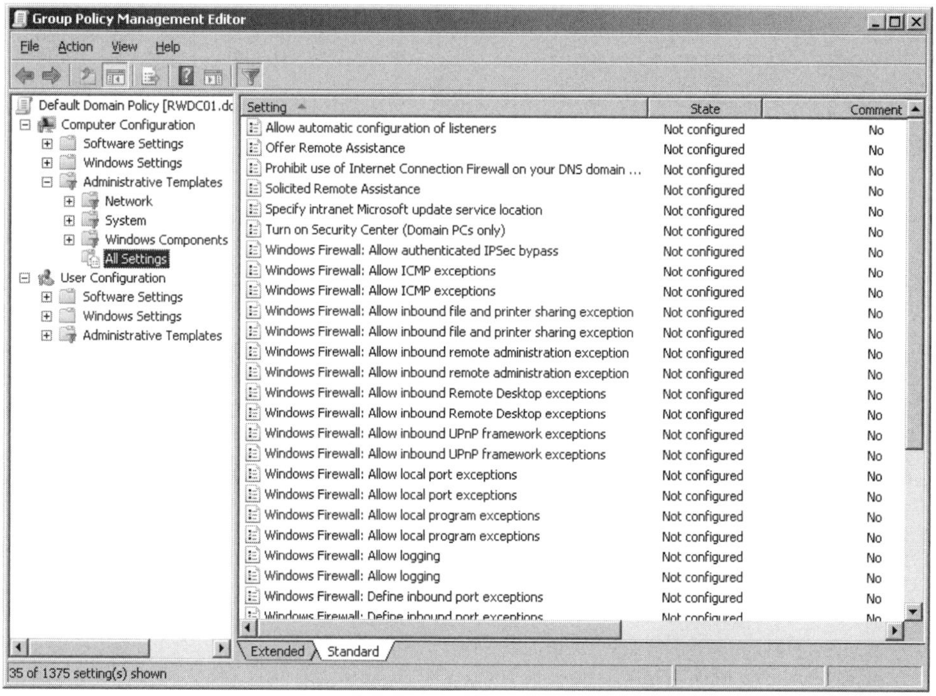

Figure 7-10   Viewing the effects of a filter within Group Policy Editor.

We have gone through the basics of Group Policy, and what is new in Windows Server 2008. Now it is time to look at some of the new areas of policy support in Windows Server 2008, especially as they relate to supporting new security features.

New Security Policy Management Support

In addition to adding quite a few new Administrative Template settings, Windows Vista and Windows Server 2008 also introduced a number of new Client Side Extensions CSEs for managing a variety of policy areas. We will focus on the security-related ones here because those are what this book is all about, but suffice to say that Group Policy has become an even more powerful tool for centrally managing configuration for most aspects of the operating system.

Device Restrictions

Device restriction is a high-demand item for most organizations. Namely, how do you keep your users from bringing their USB Flash drives and USB backup devices to work and taking away a bunch of sensitive information? Well, Group Policy in Windows Vista and Windows Server 2008 has the answer: a set of Administrative Template policies provided in Group Policy that give you two levels of control over these removable devices. The first level of control gives you the ability to prevent installation of device drivers for any class of device, specifically removable storage devices. The second class of policy lets you control access to that media, assuming installation of the driver is allowed. This second class of policy has the ability to let you control read-only or write access to a removable device that the user was allowed to install.

Let us look at the device installation restrictions first. These policies are located within the Group Policy editor under Computer Configuration\Administrative Templates\System\Device Installation\Device Restrictions. From within this per-computer policy, you can define device setup classes that can be installed or prevented from being installed or you can restrict all removable devices from being installed. Note that this policy area is designed to prevent the device driver installation in the first place. If a device driver for a particular device is already installed, this particular policy will only prevent subsequent updates to that driver.

Caution   It is important to understand that using these device restrictions does not represent a complete solution for preventing users from getting unwanted access to critical data. Users can still e-mail data around and, if they are administrators on their computers or have physical access to their workstations, they will always be able to get data you do not want them to have. The best solution is to ensure proper access controls on the data that you really want to protect!

So, what is a device setup class anyway, and how do you use it to prevent, for example, installation of a USB thumb drive? Every device that gets installed on a Windows system comes with a unique device class ID. This ID is a GUID that represents that type of device. You can find this device ID by starting the Device Manager utility (go to Control Panel and then Device Manager) and locating the device you want to restrict. Right-click that device, choose Properties, and then click the Details tab. On the Properties drop-down list, select Device Class GUID, as shown in Figure 7-11.

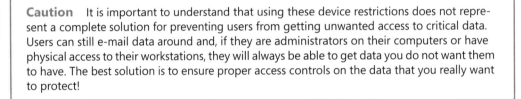

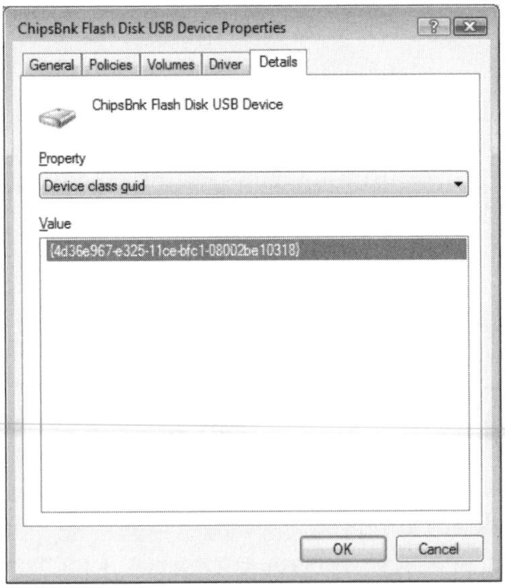

Figure 7-11   Identifying the device class for a USB Flash drive.

You can then right-click the GUID in the Value dialog box and choose Copy to copy it to the clipboard.

When you have the GUID, you can enable the policy at Computer Configuration\Administrative Templates\System\Device Installation\Device Restrictions\Prevent Installation Of Devices Using Drivers Matching These Device Setup Classes, and enter the GUID into the dialog box for that policy, as shown in Figure 7-12.

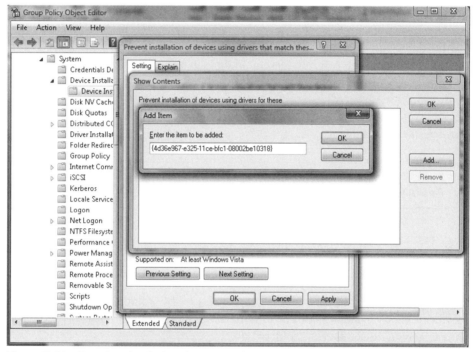

Figure 7-12   Entering the device class into a device restriction policy.

So, now you have restricted installation of any new USB Flash drives for your Windows Vista and Windows Server 2008 computers. But what if you have users that have already installed thumb drives and you want to prevent them from writing any data to those drives? You can use the policies under Computer (and User) Configuration\Administrative Templates\System\Removable Storage Access to control this behavior. Namely, by enabling the policy Removable Disks: Deny Write Access, you can prevent writing to all removable media installed on the computer. However, that may include legitimate backup or storage devices supported by the IT organization in addition to USB Flash drives, which may not be desirable for your users. In those cases, you can also use the policy Custom Classes: Deny Write Access to restrict particular device classes. Again, this policy requires the device class GUID identified previously within Device Manager.

> **Warning**   In many cases, if you apply a removable storage access policy to a computer or user and the user already has his removable device plugged in and working on his Windows Vista system, the policy will not take effect until he removes that device and reinserts it.

Windows Firewall with Advanced Security

Prior to Windows Vista and Windows Server 2008, network-based security configuration tasks such as managing Windows Firewall or IPsec policy could be accomplished using Group Policy, but with each using separate user interfaces to accomplish the tasks. Now Group Policy has been improved to provide a much better, unified UI for managing these settings, allowing you to create server and domain isolation rules with more clarity. You can find this UI under Computer Configuration\Windows Settings\Security Settings\Windows Firewall With Advanced Security. It combines management of Windows Firewall rules with creation of IPsec policy to allow for a more complete end-to-end network security management capability.

> **Note**   For more detailed coverage of Windows Firewall, refer to Chapter 5, "Windows Firewall(s)."

The first thing you will notice in this new policy area is the ability to set outbound as well as inbound rules, as shown in Figure 7-13. This is different than the old Windows Firewall configuration capabilities.

In addition, the new Windows Firewall provides a new profile categorization system from earlier versions. Windows Firewall in Windows Vista and Windows Server 2008 now includes the following three different profiles:

- **Domain Profile**   This profile applies when the computer is connected to the network where its Active Directory computer account resides.

- **Private Profile**   This profile applies when the computer is on a network that a local administrator designates as private.

- **Public Profile**   This profile applies to all networks that are not covered by the domain or private profiles, including all networks that have not yet been classified.

You can use Group Policy to configure different levels of firewall restrictions based on which profile the computer is currently working in. Note that these policies are under the Computer Configuration section within Group Policy—this means, of course, that they will apply to computer accounts only. When the policy is delivered to the computer, all profiles as defined are stored with the computer and, as network conditions change, the appropriate profile becomes active. This allows the computer to receive firewall instructions during Group Policy processing and not have to be in contact with a domain controller as the computer moves from network to network. As network state changes, the network is evaluated as being domain, private, or public and the appropriate profile is activated.

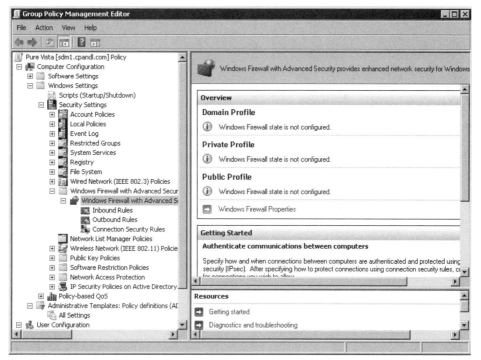

Figure 7-13   Viewing new Windows Firewall configuration rules.

> **Note**   Note that the Windows Vista and Windows Server 2008 Group Policy editor still includes Windows Firewall policies within the Administrative Template portion of Group Policy. These "older" policies are meant to be applied to Windows XP and Windows Server 2003. If you apply these older policies to Windows Vista or 2008 systems, the results may be unpredictable because there is not a one-to-one mapping between old and new Windows Firewall features.

IPsec Configuration

The Connection Security Rules section of the Windows Firewall With Advanced Security policy area lets you define IPsec policies. Unlike the old method for defining these policies, the new UI provides a more intuitive wizard that walks you through the decisions required to create an IPsec relationship between computers. Obviously, because we are using Group Policy to configure and deliver these policies, if you define an IPsec relationship between Computer A and Computer B, both of those computer accounts in Active Directory should be in line to process the GPO that delivers the IPsec instructions. Like Windows Firewall rules, IPsec rules are subject to the same three profiles—you can have an IPsec rule take effect based on which network the computer is connected to at the time.

Wired and Wireless Network Policy

Windows Vista and Windows Server 2008 introduced enhancements and new capabilities in terms of managing the protection of wireless and wired networks through Group Policy. Within the Group Policy editor, you will see a new policy node at Computer Configuration\Windows Settings\Security Settings\Wired Network (802.3) Policies, and an updated set of policy controls for wireless networks at Computer Configuration\Windows Settings\Security Settings\ Wireless Network (802.11) Policies.

Wired Network Policies

Wired Network Policies let you enforce 802.1x authentication for your computers communicating over Ethernet networks. You can force the use of 802.1x and also control the network authentication method to be used, as shown in Figure 7-14.

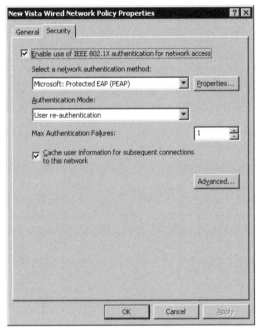

Figure 7-14 Configuring Wired Network Policy for Windows Vista.

As with IPsec policy, if you want to ensure that groups of computers all communicate on the network using 802.1x, you need to ensure that the Group Policy containing these settings is processed by all computers participating in this authentication policy.

Wireless Network Policies

Wireless network policies were first introduced in Windows Server 2003. However, they were fairly limited in terms of the amount of lockdown that could be done with respect to which wireless network a computer was connected. With the new wireless policies in Windows Vista and Windows Server 2008, you now have more options for both locking down access to wireless networks as well as controlling which encryption and authentication schemes are used for a given wireless network.

The most notable change in Wireless Network Policy is support for creation of profiles. Profiles let you configure groupings of network SSIDs that you want your computers to connect to, as shown in Figure 7-15.

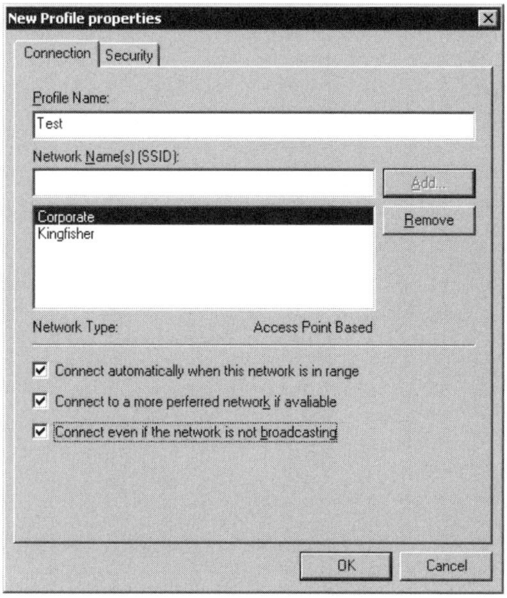

Figure 7-15   Configuring wireless profiles for connecting to well-known SSIDs.

The purpose of a profile is to group wireless networks that have similar authentication and encryption requirements. Wireless policy in Windows Vista and Windows Server 2008 supports the following authentication schemes:

- Open: Authentication with no encryption. Can optionally use Wired Equivalent Privacy (WEP) encryption

- Shared: Similar to Open but uses a shared WEP key

- WPA-Enterprise: Authentication using Wi-Fi Protected Access (WPA) encryption with 802.1x authentication

- WPA-Personal: Authentication using WPA with a pre-shared key

- WPA2-Enterprise: Authentication using Wi-Fi Protected Access version 2 (WPA-2) encryption with 802.1x authentication

- WPA2-Personal: Authentication using WPA-2 with a pre-shared key

- Open with 802.1X: Uses WEP with 802.1x authentication

You can also define something called network permissions for wireless networks that are not explicitly defined within your profiles. For example, suppose you know that there is a public wireless network SSID called Free Wireless that you do not want your users connecting to. You can define a network permission using the Network Permissions tab within the wireless policy to prevent use of this SSID, as shown in Figure 7-16.

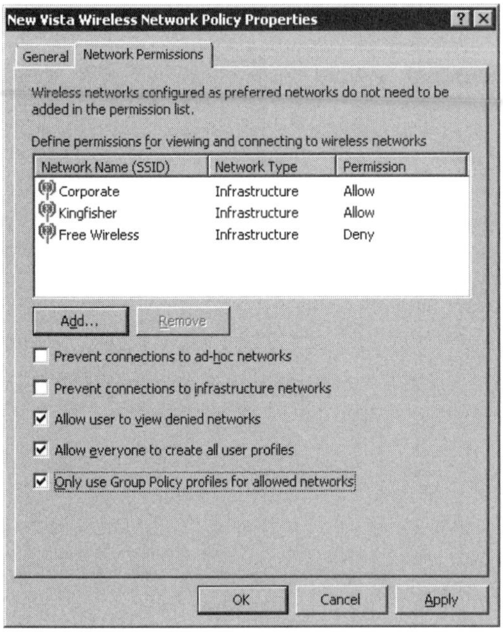

Figure 7-16   Preventing access to specific wireless access points using network permissions policy.

In addition to these new enhancements in Group Policy–based control of security settings, a number of security policy settings allow you to harden your Windows Server 2008 and Windows Vista systems. Many of these settings are very useful under many circumstances, but some come with warnings about their impact on the ability to administer your systems and the ability to coexist with earlier versions of Windows. We will examine these settings in the next section.

Managing Security Settings

If you open Group Policy editor and navigate to Computer Configuration\Windows Settings\Security Settings\Local Options, you will see a couple of policy nodes—Users Rights Assignment and Security Options—that provide a number of settings for the hardening of your Windows systems. As with any security decisions that you make, however, there are always trade-offs between the level of security you desire and the loss of functionality or manageability you can tolerate. With many of the settings within these two policy areas, you often must make the decision about that trade-off prior to implementing that policy. The good news is that since Windows Server 2003, SP1, Microsoft has provided warnings within each policy item regarding the potential impact to that particular setting. Table 7-1 lists some of the more important risks and benefits of these settings.

Table 7-1   **Risks and Benefits of Security Hardening Settings**

Policy	Benefit	Risk
Computer Configuration\Windows Settings\Security Settings\ Local Options\Users Rights Assignment\Access This Computer From The Network and Deny Access To This Computer From The Network	These rights let you control who can access a computer remotely. This includes operations such as domain controller to domain controller replication, user authentication to domain controllers, remote administration, and user access to shared resources.	If you remove the wrong groups from these rights, access to systems will break down. For example, do not remove the Enterprise Domain Controllers group from the Access right or add them to the Deny right. If you remove the Authenticated Users group from the Access right, make sure that an equivalent group has the same right. Never remove all users and groups from these rights or deny all users and groups these rights.
Computer Configuration\Windows Settings\Security Settings\ Local Options\Users Rights Assignment\Allow Logon Locally and Deny Logon Locally	Lets you control who can log on to the console of a computer that processes this policy.	Be careful when removing the Access right from a particular group or denying access to this right for a particular group. For example, do not remove administrative accounts or groups from the right unless you do not want them to have console log-on capabilities. Do not prevent service accounts from having this right because they require it to log on to a system.
Computer Configuration\Windows Settings\Security Settings\ Local Options\Users Rights Assignment\Bypass Traverse Checking	This right grants a user the ability to browse NTFS folders without checking the permissions on folders higher in the folder hierarchy to determine whether they grant Traverse Folder rights. This right is typically granted to all users and allows them to browse folders (but not the folder contents) even though they do not have access rights to parents of those folders. This is a fundamental right that all users must have to function properly and be able to perform even basic tasks.	Removing this right from the Everyone group or other non-administrative users will impact their ability to browse NTFS folder structures.

Table 7-1   Risks and Benefits of Security Hardening Settings

Policy	Benefit	Risk
Computer Configuration\ Windows Settings\Security Settings\Local Options\ Users Rights Assignment\ Enable Computer And User Accounts To Be Trusted For Delegation	Allows a user to grant a computer, any service that runs as the computer, or a user the right to impersonate a user account to access resources on another system.	Enabling this right for a given group allows that group to set computer objects in Active Directory as trusted for delegation. This can open these systems to attacks that impersonate a user via a Trojan horse.
Computer Configuration\ Windows Settings\Security Settings\Local Options\ Security Options\Domain Member: Digitally Encrypt Or Sign Secure Channel Data (Always)	Requires that all secure channel communication between workstations or member servers and their domain controllers must be able to be encrypted or signed.	If there are domain controllers in a domain that cannot encrypt or sign secure channel data, such as domain controllers running NT 4.0 prior to SP 6a, clients with this setting configured will fail to authenticate to the domain using those domain controllers.
Computer Configuration\ Windows Settings\Security Settings\Local Options\ Security Options\Microsoft Network Client: Digitally Sign Communications (Always)	Requires a client communicating with a Server Message Block (SMB) v. 1 server for file sharing to require SMB signing be used. This helps prevent session hijacking attacks.	If the client is configured to always use SMB signing and the server either does not support it or does not allow it, SMB communication between client and server will fail.
Computer Configuration\ Windows Settings\ Security Settings\Local Options\Security Options\ Microsoft Network Server: Digitally Sign Communications (Always)	This works the same way as for the client in the previous entry, except that this guarantees that SMB servers always sign communications with clients.	If an SMB server always requires signing and the client does not support it, the client will not be able to communicate. For example, older versions of Windows and non-Microsoft SMB clients will not support SMB signing. Note that enabling this setting can cause network slowness. See *http://support.microsoft.com/kb/ 823659* for more details.
Computer Configuration\ Windows Settings\Security Settings\Local Options\ Security Options\Domain member: Require strong (Windows 2000 Or Later) Session Key	Requires 128-bit encryption on security channel communications between clients receiving this policy and domain controllers.	Requires that all domain controllers be running at least Windows 2000, otherwise secure channel communications will fail.
Computer Configuration\ Windows Settings\Security Settings\Local Options\ Security Options\Domain Controller: LDAP Server Signing Requirements	When applied to a domain controller, requires that domain controller to communicate with LDAP clients using LDAP data signing to prevent man-in-the-middle attacks.	Some LDAP clients, including Windows 2000 before Service Pack 3, will not support this. Also, non-Windows LDAP clients may not support it.

Table 7-1   Risks and Benefits of Security Hardening Settings

Policy	Benefit	Risk
Computer Configuration\ Windows Settings\Security Settings\Local Options\ Security Options\Domain Controller: LDAP Client Signing Requirements	When applied to a computer, requires that the client communicate with any LDAP server using LDAP data signing to prevent man-in-the-middle attacks.	If domain controllers are not configured with the same settings, all LDAP communication between client and domain controller will fail.
Computer Configuration\ Windows Settings\Security Settings\Local Options\ Security Options\Network Access: Allows Anonymous Sid/Name Translation	This policy is disabled in the most secure configuration. Enabling it allows an anonymous user to translate a SID into a user name. (For example, if an anonymous user provides the well-known SID of the administrator account, that user could get the actual account name, even if it has been renamed.)	If this policy is enabled, some earlier Windows systems that rely on this anonymous translation capability may fail to function, including NT 4.0 Remote Access Service (RAS) and SQL Servers running in NT 3.x or 4.0 domains. Of course, if you have any of those in your environment, the best thing you can do is to ensure that they cannot talk to anyone!
Computer Configuration\ Windows Settings\Security Settings\Local Options\ Security Options\Network Access: Do Not Allow Anonymous Enumeration Of SAM Accounts And Shares	Enabling this policy prevents anonymous users from being able to get a list of user names in a domain, which can then be used for various attacks.	If you disable this policy on a domain level, you will not be able to establish a domain trust with NT 4.0 domains. (Trust me, you do not want one.)
Computer Configuration\ Windows Settings\Security Settings\Local Options\ Security Options\Network Security: LAN Manager Authentication Level	Sets the version of NTLM authentication that is required on computers processing this policy.	Certain levels of NTLM authentication (such as v2) are not supported on earlier Windows clients such as NT 4.0 prior to Service Pack 4 or Windows 95 and Windows 98 without the Directory Services client installed. Today, all computers really ought to be running with this setting set to 5 (the most secure option).
Computer Configuration\ Windows Settings\Security Settings\Local Options\ Security Options\Audit: Shut Down System Immediately If Unable To Log Security Audits	By enabling this policy, you ensure that the system shuts down if something prevents security audit from being generated (such as if the security log is full).	If you set this policy but do not allow audit logs to roll over when they fill up or their size is not sufficient, the system will shut down when the log is full! Attackers can (and have in the past) use this to shut down your network.

Summary

In this chapter, we looked at how Group Policy is used in local and Active Directory environments, how you can link GPOs at different levels in the Active Directory hierarchy, and how you can use security group and WMI filtering to further control which computers and users get which policy.

We also looked at some of the new Group Policy management features introduced in Windows Server 2008, including Starter GPOs, comments, and filtering. We looked at some of the new policy areas introduced in Windows Vista and Windows Server 2008 specifically related to security, such as device restrictions for controlling removable storage use, the unified Windows Firewall, and IPsec configuration policies and wired and wireless policies.

Finally, we looked at a number of security hardening settings provided within Group Policy and detailed those settings that can cause compatibility problems when enabled—particularly when earlier or non-Windows systems are involved.

Additional Resources

- *Windows Group Policy Resource Kit: Windows Server 2008 and Windows Vista* from Microsoft Press.

- "What Is New in Group Policy in Windows Vista," at *http://technet2.microsoft.com/ WindowsVista/en/library/a8366c42-6373-48cd-9d11-2510580e48171033.mspx?mfr=true.*

- "Virtual Lab: Managing Windows Server 2008 and Windows Vista Using Group Policy," at *http://go.microsoft.com/fwlink/?linkid=92472.*

- "Managing Group Policy ADMX Files Step-by-Step Guide," at *http:// technet2.microsoft.com/windowsvista/en/library/02633470-396c-4e34-971a-0c5b090dc4fd1033.mspx.*

- "Security Group Policy Settings in Windows Vista," at *http://technet.microsoft.com/ en-us/bb679962.aspx.*

Auditing

— Eric Fitzgerald

In computer security, the word *audit* is commonly used as a verb meaning to compare something against a standard or baseline ("to audit the effectiveness of the organization's security controls") and as a noun meaning a log of security-relevant event records ("audit trails") or a verb meaning to generate an audit trail. In this chapter we use *audit* in the log-related sense.

Since the introduction of Windows NT, the security event log has often been a source of frustration for Windows server administrators. Although the security event log contains a great deal of information about what security decisions Windows is making and about critical system and user activity that can affect system security, the lack of fine-grained controls for audit policy cause large volumes of log entries, and the specific events Microsoft chose to audit and the information presented in those event records sometimes do not provide the answers that administrators really want to know.

In Windows Server 2008, the auditing subsystem has gained a number of improvements that will make it much more useful for administrators. Audit policy is expanded so that it is much easier to select only the events you are interested in seeing. Audit event record format and content is improved to make it easier for you to understand the events in the security log. A much larger set of events cause audit event records. And finally, improvements in the event subsystem and related tools remove many of the scalability, performance and analysis problems of the past.

Why Audit?

When discussing security access control policy, there are three basic control groups: authentication, authorization and audit (sometimes called accounting). Access control, covered in

Chapter 2, "Authenticators and Authentication Protocols," and authentication, covered in Chapter 4, "Understanding UAC," are called preventative controls—the purpose of these controls is to prevent things from happening unless they are things you want to happen. Auditing is called a detective control—it does not prevent anything, but it leaves a trail that can be examined to detect whether your security policy was violated, and if so, in what manner.

Detective controls such as audit trails provide the proof that your preventative controls are working, even when you are not looking. You can examine the audit trail at any time to see that the activities of your users are consistent with your intent.

Audit trails also provide useful forensic evidence in the case such evidence ever becomes necessary. It is too late to have your system start generating logs after an incident; at that point you want to know about things that have already happened.

Understanding the security decisions that the system is making can also help troubleshoot problems. When the error message consists entirely of "access denied", it is useful to have a source of information other than the error message to draw on for diagnostic purposes.

Finally, many laws and regulatory frameworks are generally interpreted to require the generation and review of audit trails. For example, some healthcare industry regulations require that organizations that collect and store patient data ensure that the data is only accessed by authorized individuals. It would be difficult for an organization to assert the effectiveness of their access controls without an audit trail to indicate who actually accessed patient data.

How Windows Auditing Works

The Windows audit subsystem works in conjunction with components that make security decisions, and with the event log service, to generate security events in a trustworthy manner. Components that make security decisions—often called security reference monitors—are instrumented so that when a security decision is made or other security relevant activity takes place, these monitors notify the auditing subsystem and pass along the details of the activity. The auditing system formats these as event records, making sure that the data is presented in a consistent fashion, and discards any events that have been generated that are not supposed to be logged according to audit policy. The remaining events are sent to the event log service to be stored in the security log. Figure 8-1 shows a conceptual view of the audit subsystem in Windows.

> **Note**   Most audit-generating components of Windows check audit policy before they raise an event to the auditing subsystem, preventing any unnecessary performance impact.

The Windows audit subsystem is implemented in the LSA (local security authority) process, which appears in the Windows process list as lsass.exe, and in the Windows kernel. The LSA contains the user-mode components of Windows, which enforce security policy and perform other security functions such as authentication. Components such as authentication packages reside inside the LSA and deliver events directly to the audit subsystem. Components that run in user mode outside the LSA–such as Active Directory Domain Services (AD DS)–and applications that use Windows audit APIs and deliver events to the LSA via RPC. The kernel contains a generic audit interface for kernel components such as drivers to use, and also contains the Object Manager, which is responsible for the generation of most Object Access events. Events are delivered to the event log service either by means of the kernel event tracing engine (ETW) or via RPC to the event log service. Most events generated in the kernel are delivered directly to ETW, but events which require complex formatting are routed to LSA for formatting. LSA delivers most events to the event log through ETW, using the RPC channel mainly for cases where part of the audit subsystem has failed.

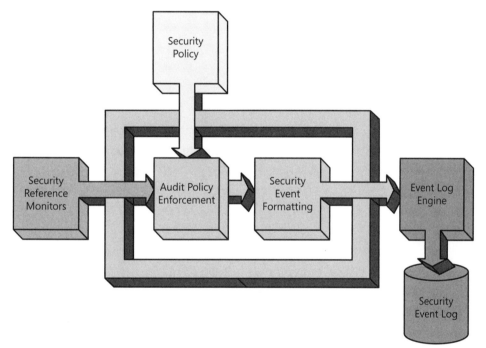

Figure 8-1 Conceptual diagram of the Windows audit subsystem.

Direct from the Source: Event Log Service Improvements

The event log engine in Windows was completely rewritten for the 6.0 release of Windows (Windows Vista and Windows Server 2008). The performance and scale issues that affected the old event log engine are no longer significant. Where the old event log service had a maximum effective log file size of 4 GB (significantly less on 32-bit computers), logs using the new service can be up to $2^{53}-1$ bytes in size–more than a petabyte. And where the old log had a maximum throughput of only a few thousand events per second when configured as circular, the new log has a throughput of tens of thousands of events per second.

The new event log engine exposes events to applications in XML format. This not only permits events to be self-descriptive, but also allows the engine to pre-filter events based

> on XPATH expressions. This allows rich filtering in applications like Event Viewer, and also allows narrowly targeted subscriptions—monitoring applications can specify very precisely which events are of interest to them.
>
> *Eric Fitzgerald, Senior Program Manager Forefront Security*

As mentioned earlier, most security events, with the exception of events related to the health of the audit subsystem, originate in components outside the audit subsystem. Each event is raised under a specific set of conditions. For most events, the conditions are:

- An auditable activity occurred.
- Audit policy indicates that specific activity should be logged.

In one case there is actually a third prerequisite. Resource managers are a specific kind of security reference monitor that arbitrate the access to a set of objects. When resource managers receive a request to access an object, they not only check the audit policy but also compare the access request with the specific audit settings on the object in question. As discussed in Chapter 2, objects in Windows have a security descriptor that describes various aspects of object-specific security policy. Part of the security descriptor data structure is the discretionary access control list (DACL). This is the list of permissions for the object that is used in access checking, and that most people refer to as the object's ACL. However, a second ACL is associated with each object, used to describe the audit policy specific to that object and to contain the integrity label (covered in Chapter 2) for that object. This ACL is officially designated the system access control list (SACL). Its construction is identical to the construction of a DACL, except that specific access control entries (ACEs) in the SACL will not grant permissions to users and groups, but rather will indicate which accesses to audit for specific users and groups.

When an access check is performed, the resource manager must decide whether to generate an audit for that particular request. First the access check routine determines whether object access audit policy is enabled for that resource manager. If so, the access check routine compares the object's SACL to the result of the access check after the DACL is evaluated. In general, SACL evaluation is very similar to DACL evaluation. If a SACL is on the object and one or more of the SIDs in the requestor's token match any of the SIDs in the ACEs in the SACL, and any of the associated accesses in the access masks of matching ACEs match the requested access mask, an event is generated. The event records the requested access mask and is logged as a handle open event. This process applies to both successful and failed access requests, with the resultant event recording the success or failure of the handle open operation. The access mask is retained by the Object Manager, and when subsequent operations are performed using that handle, the first instance of any audited access causes an event to be generated.

Setting an Audit Policy

In Windows Vista and Windows Server 2008, audit policy is organized hierarchically. This is a significant enhancement to audit policy; previous versions of Windows had a flat audit policy with a much smaller degree of control over the resultant audit volume.

Prior to Windows Vista, each security event was mapped to one of nine audit policy categories. By enabling either success or failure auditing for an audit category, you enable all the audit events for that category. Figure 8-2 shows the organization of audit policy in pre-Windows Vista systems.

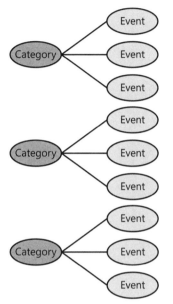

Figure 8-2   Pre-Windows Vista hierarchical audit policy organization.

In Windows Server 2008 and Windows Vista, every security event is mapped into an audit policy subcategory. When you enable audit policy for that subcategory, all the events mapped to that subcategory are enabled. Each subcategory has a setting to enable event generation for successful activities and a setting to enable event generation for failed activity attempts.

Audit policy subcategories are themselves grouped into the same audit policy categories that existed in Windows Server 2003 and earlier releases, for compatibility purposes. When an audit policy category is enabled, all the subcategories for that category, and therefore the associated events, are enabled. Likewise when an audit policy category is disabled, all the associated subcategories and their events are disabled. Figure 8-3 shows the organization of audit policy in Windows Server 2008 systems.

Audit policy can be set with two tools: a graphical user interface used by the security policy editor MMC snap-in and the Group Policy editor MMC snap-in, or the AuditPol.exe command-line tool. However, only AuditPol.exe can set audit policy at the subcategory level: Microsoft did not update the audit policy graphical user interface (UI), shown in Figure 8-4, or the Group Policy mechanism for audit policy deployment for Windows Server 2008, to include audit policy subcategories. This will be corrected in a future release but for now you will have to work around it or live with legacy audit policy.

Because of the hierarchical relationship between audit policy categories and subcategories, it is usually undesirable to use legacy audit policy on Windows Server 2008 and Windows Vista.

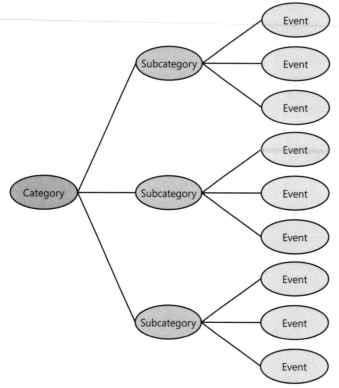

Figure 8-3   Windows Server 2008 hierarchical audit policy organization.

The point of audit policy is to control which events are generated and stored in your audit logs, and the new granular audit policy (GAP) feature gives you a much higher level of control. But most Windows systems get their audit policy from domains through group policy, which does not support GAP. This means that you could develop a great audit policy for your new Windows Server 2008, but as soon as you join the server to your domain, the new audit policy will be overwritten by legacy audit policy settings from group policy.

Figure 8-4   Audit Policy user interface in Local Security Policy MMC snap-in.

Thankfully, Microsoft provided a mechanism to prevent legacy audit policy distributed by group policy from overriding GAP. A registry value called *SCENoConfigLegacyAuditPolicy* causes the security configuration engine (the component that enforces security-related group policy settings) from applying legacy audit policy. If this registry value is present and set to a nonzero value, category-level audit policy will not be applied if it is set through the security policy snap-in or through Group Policy. This registry value is described in Microsoft Knowledge Base article 921468 (http://support.microsoft.com/kb/921468) and is linked to directly from the audit policy user interface, as shown in Figure 8-5. Better still, the registry setting itself can be deployed through Group Policy, as shown in Figure 8-6, causing all of your Windows Vista and Windows Server 2008 computers to ignore legacy audit policy and preferentially use granular audit policy. You should be aware of the fact that the audit policy UI might be confusing while using this setting—the UI might show that some categories are enabled or disabled, but those settings will not be honored.

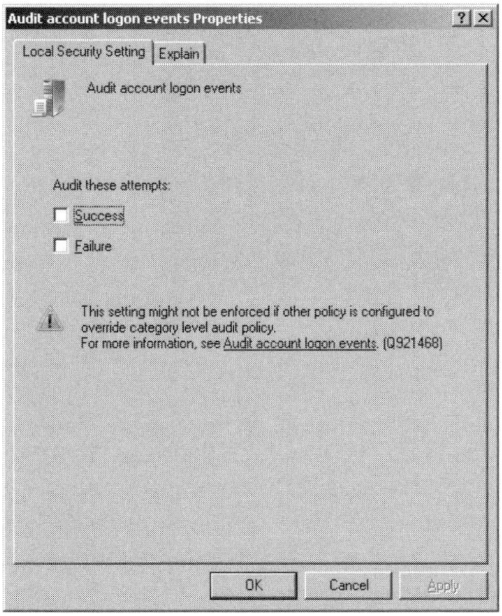

Figure 8-5   Audit Policy user interface settings for the Logon/Logoff audit policy category.

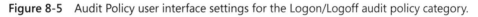

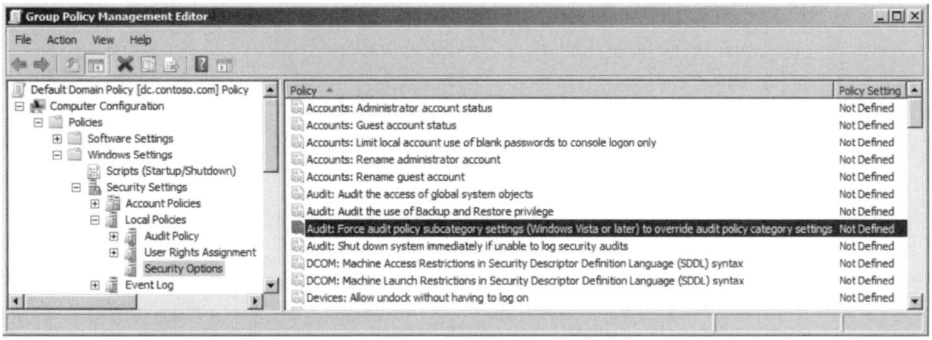

Figure 8-6   Group Policy editor showing Force Audit Policy Subcategory Settings To Override Audit PolicyCategory Settings, also called SCENoConfigLegacyAuditPolicy.

The one other limitation to the audit policy user interface is a side effect of the relationship between categories and subcategories. When you use the UI to examine audit policy category settings, the UI will show that the category is enabled if all the subcategories of that category are enabled. Likewise the UI will show that the category is disabled if all the related subcategories are disabled. But the UI has to handle one other case—the case where some of the subcategories are enabled and some are not. In this case the UI indicates that the category is disabled, but you can still see the correct effective audit policy settings by using the Audit-Pol.exe utility, as shown in Figure 8-7.

```
Administrator: Command Prompt                                          _[][X]
Microsoft Windows [Version 6.0.6001]
Copyright (c) 2006 Microsoft Corporation.  All rights reserved.

C:\Users\Administrator>auditpol -get -category:"logon/logoff"
System audit policy
Category/Subcategory                      Setting
Logon/Logoff
  Logon                                   Success and Failure
  Logoff                                  Success
  Account Lockout                         Success
  IPsec Main Mode                         No Auditing
  IPsec Quick Mode                        No Auditing
  IPsec Extended Mode                     No Auditing
  Special Logon                           Success
  Other Logon/Logoff Events               No Auditing
  Network Policy Server                   Success and Failure

C:\Users\Administrator>_
```

Figure 8-7   You can use AuditPol.exe to display the effective GAP settings.

The bottom line is this: granular audit policy goes a long way toward ending the audit volume problem of previous Windows releases, but if you choose to use it, you will need to do all of your audit policy administration using the AuditPol.exe tool. Even though Group Policy does not directly support granular audit policy, it is still possible to deploy GAP using Group Policy. This is done by deploying a script that executes AuditPol.exe to set audit policy. The script must be a startup script that runs with system privileges on the computer; audit policy cannot be set by non-privileged users and therefore cannot be deployed using logon scripts.

The full procedure for this, including sample scripts, is described in Microsoft Knowledge Base article 921469 (*http://support.microsoft.com/kb/921469*). In brief, you follow these steps:

1. Deploy *SCENoConfigLegacyAuditPolicy* to your Windows Vista and Windows Server 2008 computers using Group Policy.

2. Write a script to apply the policy settings you want using AuditPol.exe, and copy this script to a share.

3. Write a script to schedule a task to run the audit policy script regularly, and set that script as a startup script.

This mechanism has been tested and works well. You can deploy this solution in such a way that if you subsequently need to change any audit policy settings, it will not be necessary to change any Group Policy objects (GPOs) or scripts. This is accomplished by having the policy application script read the auditing settings from a text file.

Audit Policy Options

There are a few optional audit-policy related features which you can enable with AuditPol.exe or through the Security Options section of the security policy user interface in either local or Group Policy mode.

CrashOnAuditFail is a setting required for compliance with the Common Criteria protection profile for single level operating systems. The Common Criteria requirement is that a compliant system must be able to immediately halt all auditable activity whenever the auditing system is unable to generate or store security events. In Windows, this is implemented by halting the system (in the form of a blue screen) when the auditing system is unable to log security events. When CrashOnAuditFail occurs, only administrators will be able to log on after the system reboots, until the security event log is cleared and the condition that caused the failure is remediated.

Only use this setting if absolutely required. It turns a possible repudiation attack into a definite denial-of-service attack.

CrashOnAuditFail has three states:

- The feature is not enabled.
- The feature is enabled but that the system has not crashed yet.
- The feature is enabled, a crash has occurred because of audit system failure, and the system has been rebooted. Only administrators of the computer will be able to log on. Until CrashOnAuditFail is set back to enabled or disabled and the log is cleared, normal users will be unable to log on.

The FullPrivilegeAuditing setting causes privilege use events, if enabled through audit policy, to be generated for all privileges except *SeAuditPrivilege*. Under normal circumstances, privilege use events are not generated for the following privileges:

- Bypass traverse checking (*SeChangeNotifyPrivilege*)
- Debug programs (*SeDebugPrivilege*)
- Create a token object (*SeCreateTokenPrivilege*)
- Replace process level token (*SeAssignPrimaryTokenPrivilege*)
- Generate security audits (*SeAuditPrivilege*)
- Back up files and directories (*SeBackupPrivilege*)
- Restore files and directories (*SeRestorePrivilege*)

These privileges are suppressed because they are used very frequently by normal operating system functions and by applications, or because in the case of the Backup and Restore privileges, they tend to occur in very high volumes in situations where they are commonly used. Additionally, if the use of the privilege to generate audit were itself audited, the log would fill with this event, so *SeAuditPrivilege* is never audited. You could think of it this way: Every event in the Security event log is also a privilege use event for *SeAuditPrivilege*. Either way, this is another setting that you should probably not enable unless you are required to do so.

The AuditBaseObjects and AuditBaseDirectories settings cause named kernel objects (such as mutexes and semaphores) to be given SACLs when they are created. AuditBaseDirectories affects container objects; AuditBaseObjects affects objects that cannot contain other objects. Base objects are usually used to synchronize activity between two processes. Most kernel objects are not named—they are referred to only by a number called a *handle*. Handles are unique to a specific process, so processes cannot see or access unnamed kernel objects that they did not create. Named kernel objects are visible to other processes unless a process requests a private namespace. The risk of named kernel objects is that if they are not properly secured, a malicious process can manipulate them, possibly causing a malfunction in the processes that normally use the objects. This is commonly known as a *squatting attack*. AuditBaseObjects and AuditBaseDirectories exist so that you can audit the access to these objects and detect squatting attacks from the log.

The main problem with AuditBaseObjects and AuditBaseDirectories is that they can cause significant audit volume because of the large number of accesses to these objects that occurs during normal operation. The SACLs that are applied are hard-coded and cannot be adjusted by the user, but were tuned in Windows Vista and Windows Server 2008 to only audit "write" type accesses to these objects, reducing the volume significantly over previous releases. Another limitation of the SACL mechanism is that SACLs persist for the lifetime of the object—they are applied when the object is created, which is during startup for system-created objects and during the initialization procedure for processes that create their own objects. The SACLs do not change until the object is destroyed, which is usually during shutdown (for system objects) or process termination of the process that created the object. This basically means that effectively you must reboot to enable or disable AuditBaseObjects or AuditBaseDirectories.

There is no central repository of information about kernel objects. Most software development organizations would typically not publish this kind of information because it deals with internal workings of software and is not user-configurable. Therefore even if you enable AuditBaseObjects or AuditBaseDirectories you will probably find it difficult or impossible to determine what a particular object does or is used for, unless the name of the object is especially descriptive. For this reason you should not enable these settings in production environments unless you are required to do so. You can examine base objects using the Process Explorer tool from Microsoft's SysInternals Web site at *http:// www.microsoft.com/technet/sysinternals/SystemInformation/ProcessExplorer.mspx*. (See Figure 8-8.)

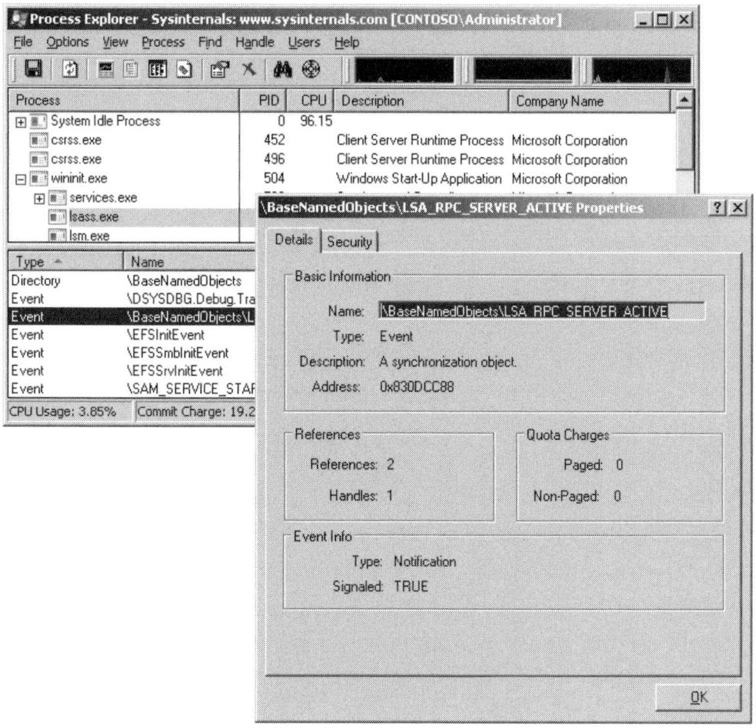

Figure 8-8 Process Explorer being used to examine a base named *object*.

Audit Policy Improvements

In addition to the Granular Audit Policy feature, there are a couple of minor enhancements to audit policy in Windows Server 2008.

Per-User Selective Audit Policy

Windows XP introduced a mechanism to set exceptions to audit policy on a per-user basis, called Per User Selective Audit, or *per-user auditing*. In Windows Vista and Windows Server 2008 that mechanism still exists and has been integrated more tightly into the audit policy mechanism: Where separate tools were once used to set per-user audit policy, now the tools (and their underlying APIs) are the same for both per-user and system audit policy.

Audit Policy Delegation

A Windows system has six audit-policy–related tasks:

- Review the security event log.
- Clear the security event log.
- Review audit policy settings.

- Set audit policy.
- Review SACLs.
- Set SACLs.

These six tasks have all been delegated as a unit using Manage Audit And Security Log Privilege, also known as *SeSecurityPrivilege*, since the introduction of Windows NT.

In Windows Server 2003 a mechanism was introduced to set the permissions on event logs using the *CustomSD* registry value. (For more information, see Microsoft Knowledge Base article 323076.) Event log permissions allow the first two tasks to be delegated separately from the others and from each other, and independently of *SeSecurityPrivilege*.

In Windows Vista and Windows Server 2008 a new audit policy delegation mechanism has been introduced to allow the right to review and/or set audit policy to be delegated separately from the rest of these tasks. This mechanism takes the form of an ACL on audit policy itself.

By default, only BUILTIN\Administrators have the right to set and view audit policy. This means that the default access to audit policy is unchanged from previous releases.

You can set and view the audit policy ACL by using the AuditPol.exe command-line tool. If the ACL is accidentally misconfigured, it can be reset by anyone possessing *SeSecurityPrivilege* using *AuditPol.exe*.

Developing a Good Audit Policy

You can only use the auditing feature effectively if you develop an audit policy that both generates the events that you are interested in seeing and generates few enough events that you can effectively manage the resultant logs.

Many administrators who have not yet used the feature start by enabling all audit policy, only to be dismayed in short order by the large volume of events that is generated.

As with any other form of security policy, the most effective results are usually achieved by analyzing the security threats that concern you the most and deploying the correct policy settings to mitigate that threat.

The temptation is strong to select audit policy settings as you might select things from a mail-order catalog or menu in a restaurant. Many of the settings look good, and nothing prevents you from choosing them all. However, as noted earlier, Windows is probably capable of generating much more audit than you are able to manage. Careful selection of just the minimum set of events that will mitigate your security risks will probably result in a much better experience.

On the companion CD to this volume you will find files containing the mapping of audit events to the category and subcategory of audit policy that causes the events to be generated. You can use this to help plan your audit policy settings.

After you have selected your audit policy, it is wise to host it on a small number of production computers and examine the resultant security log volume. If you find the volume to be higher than you are comfortable with, you should consider trying less aggressive auditing settings.

Event Viewer is a very useful tool in Windows Server 2008 for determining exactly which policy settings are causing your audit volume. The main Event Viewer window allows you to group events by Task Category (which is the same thing as subcategory), Event Source, Event ID, and other attributes, as shown in Figure 8-9, and shows you a count for each group. If you see a high volume event, look at a few instances of that event to verify that the event is telling you something that you find useful. If not, consider disabling the policy that causes that event to be generated.

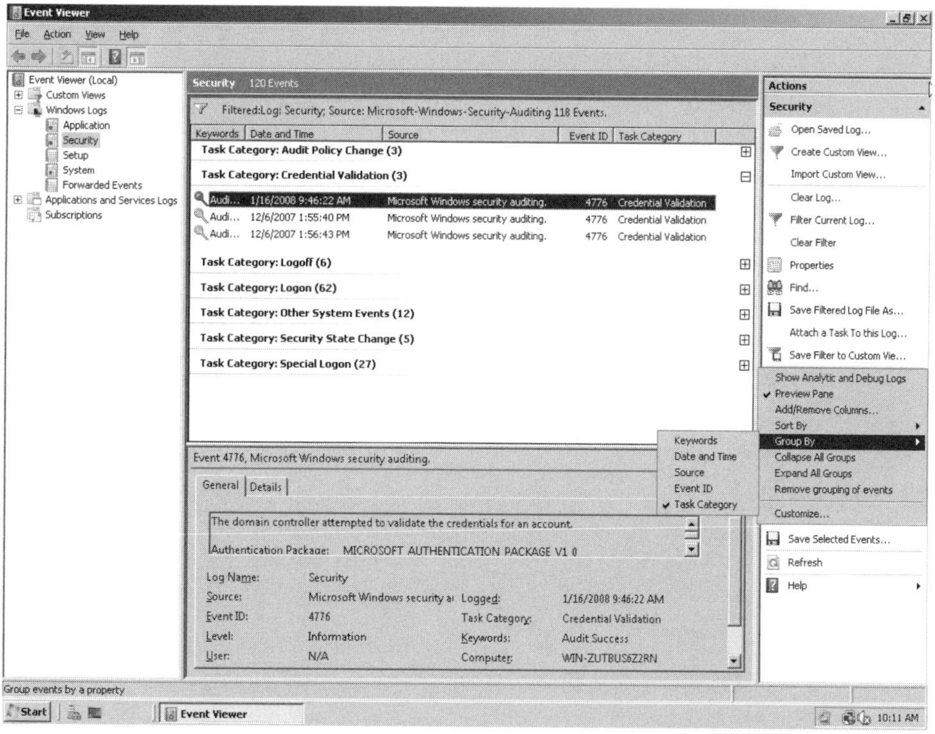

Figure 8-9   Event Viewer grouping security events by Task Category (Subcategory).

Once you have selected your audit policy, tested it and tuned it, you are ready to deploy.

If you need assistance developing an audit policy, the Windows Server 2008 Security Guide contains recommendations for audit policy and is available on the TechNet Security Web site: *http://www.microsoft.com/technet/security/guidance.*

New Events in Windows Server 2008

Windows Server 2008 has introduced significant changes to the security event log events, compared to previous versions of Windows.

The first thing you will notice looking at the Event Viewer is that none of the event ID numbers are familiar. The security events were all renumbered as well as reorganized. If you have become familiar with the security event ID numbers in Windows, that knowledge has not become useless. In general, the event ID number of a security event in Windows Server 2008 is 4096 higher than the equivalent event in Windows Server 2003. For example, the logon success event, ID 528 in Windows Server 2003, has become event 4624 in Windows Server 2008 (528+4096=4624). Similarly, the system time change event, formerly event ID 520, has become event ID 4616 in Windows Server 2008.

The next thing you will notice is that the information in the events is laid out a little differently in the Event Viewer. If you are very familiar with the events on previous versions of Windows, you will also notice that many events have additional fields. For example, let us examine the logon success event on Windows Server 2003 and the equivalent event on Windows Server 2008.

Windows Server 2003:

```
Successful Logon:
   User Name:administrator
   Domain:CONTOSO
   Logon ID:(0x0,0x13CC2)
   Logon Type:7
   Logon Process:User32
   Authentication Package:Negotiate
   Workstation Name:DC
   Logon GUID:{00000000-0000-0000-000000000000}
   Caller User Name:DC$
   Caller Domain Name:CONTOSO
   Caller Logon ID:(0x0,0x3E7)
   Caller Process ID:-
   Transited Services:-
   Source Network Address:127.0.0.1
   Source Port:0
```

Windows Server 2008:

```
An account was successfully logged on.

Subject:

    Security ID:SYSTEM
    Account Name:DC$
    Account Domain:CONTOSO
    Logon ID:0x3e7

Logon Type:7

New Logon:
```

```
      Security ID:CONTOSO\Administrator
      Account Name:Administrator
      Account Domain:CONTOSO
      Logon ID:0x16d30b
      Logon GUID:{00000000-0000-0000-0000-000000000000}

  Process Information:
     Process ID:0x20c
     Process Name:C:\Windows\System32\winlogon.exe

  Network Information:
     Workstation Name:DC
     Source Network Address:127.0.0.1
     Source Port:0

  Detailed Authentication Information:
     Logon Process:User32
     Authentication Package:Negotiate
     Transited Services:-
     Package Name (NTLM only):-
     Key Length:0
```

You can see several significant changes in this event. First, the event layout has been changed to make it easier to locate the information that you are looking for at a glance. Similar information has been grouped into sections for display purposes. A standard section, Subject, has been added to most events to disambiguate the role of the user. Subject is the account that is responsible for generation of the event; it is the account which performed the auditable activity. Note that in this case it is LocalSystem. Why? Because the activity is not "a user logged on." The activity is "a user account was logged on"–passive voice. A process running as LocalSystem (in this case WinLogon) requested the logon. A separate set of fields describes the user who was logged on.

Next, the events contain both automation-friendly correlation fields as well as human-friendly text fields. For example, the Process ID (PID) is also accompanied by the process image path.

Event Viewer appears to be displaying the user account names twice, but in actuality the first instance of each account is stored as a Security ID (SID, discussed in Chapter 1, "Subjects, Users, and Other Actors"), and the second is stored as a name. Event Viewer automatically translates the SID to an account name if possible. However, because the names are also stored textually, you will still see the names (and the untranslated SID) if you view the log on another computer where the lookup cannot be performed, or if the account has been deleted. Name lookup failures were a source of frustration for many security log analysts in previous versions.

Extra information has been added. Had this example been an NTLM logon, the particular NTLM-suite protocol would have been listed (LM, NTLM V1, or NTLM V2), and if an NTLMv2 session key had been negotiated, the key length would have been listed. This will assist those of you who are considering migration to an NTLM-less environment and wish to assess the impact beforehand.

A couple of minor but important formatting changes have occurred. For instance, the Logon ID field is no longer expressed as a high DWORD and low DWORD , such as " (0x0,0x16d30b)", as in previous releases–the comma made this field hard to parse. Instead the field is now a single value expressed in hexadecimal notation. Process IDs are also displayed in hexadecimal.

Another significant change is that old and new values have been added to the object access events for registry and Active Directory objects:

```
A registry value was modified.

Subject:
    Security ID:CONTOSO\Administrator
    Account Name:Administrator
    Account Domain:CONTOSO
    Logon ID:0x31e01

Object:
    Object Name:\REGISTRY\MACHINE\SOFTWARE\Microsoft\Windows\CurrentVersion\Run
    Object Value Name:StartupProgram
    Handle ID:0x118
    Operation Type:Existing registry value modified

Process Information:
    Process ID:0xa58
    Process Name:C:\Windows\regedit.exe

Change Information:
    Old Value Type:REG_SZ
    Old Value:C:\Windows\System32\windows_component.exe
    New Value Type:REG_SZ
    New Value:C:\Windows\System32\malware.exe
```

In this case the event tells us that Administrator modified a value named StartupProgram in the Run registry key (this key lists programs that will automatically run when a user logs on interactively). The normal value, pointing to windows_component.exe, has been replaced and now points to malware.exe.

There are many new events in Windows Server 2008. Tables 8-1 through 8-8 below illustrate some highlights.

Table 8-1   Directory Service Changes

Event ID	Description
5136	A directory service object was modified.
5137	A directory service object was created.
5138	A directory service object was undeleted.
5139	A directory service object was moved.
5141	A directory service object was deleted.

Table 8-2   Network Policy Server (These events are in support of the Internet Authentication Service [IAS], the RADIUS server in Windows Server, and the Network Access Protection feature.)

Event ID	Description
6272	Network Policy Server granted access to a user.
6273	Network Policy Server denied access to a user.
6274	Network Policy Server discarded the request for a user.
6275	Network Policy Server discarded the accounting request for a user.
6276	Network Policy Server quarantined a user.
6277	Network Policy Server granted access to a user but put it on probation because the host did not meet the defined health policy.
6278	Network Policy Server granted full access to a user because the host met the defined health policy.
6279	Network Policy Server locked the user account because of repeated failed authentication attempts.
6280	Network Policy Server unlocked the user account.

Table 8-3   Task Scheduler Events (Other Object Access Events)

Event ID	Description
4698	A scheduled task was created.
4706	A scheduled task was disabled.
4707	A scheduled task was updated.

Table 8-4   Windows Firewall Low-Level Events (Filtering Platform Connection)

Event ID	Description
5031	The Windows Firewall Service blocked an application from accepting incoming connections on the network.
5152	The Windows Filtering Platform blocked a packet.
5153	A more restrictive Windows Filtering Platform filter has blocked a packet.
5154	The Windows Filtering Platform has permitted an application or service to listen on a port for incoming connections.
5155	The Windows Filtering Platform has blocked an application or service from listening on a port for incoming connections.
5156	The Windows Filtering Platform has allowed a connection.
5157	The Windows Filtering Platform has blocked a connection.
5158	The Windows Filtering Platform has permitted a bind to a local port.
5159	The Windows Filtering Platform has blocked a bind to a local port.

Table 8-5   ACL Change Events (Audit Policy Change, Resource Manager-specific subcategory)

Event ID	Description
4715	The audit policy (SACL) on an object was changed.
4670	Permissions on an object were changed.

Table 8-6   File Share Access Events

Event ID	Description
5140	A network share object was accessed.

Table 8-7   RPC Events

Event ID	Description
5712	A Remote Procedure Call (RPC) was attempted.

Table 8-8   Computer-Use-Related Logon Events (Other Logon/Logoff Events)

Event ID	Description
4778	A session was reconnected to a Window Station.
4779	A session was disconnected from a Window Station.
4800	The workstation was locked.
4801	The workstation was unlocked.
4802	The screen saver was invoked.
4803	The screen saver was dismissed.

In addition, there are new events for the following types of events:

- Cryptography Events (System Integrity)
- IPsec Events (completely re-implemented)
- Firewall Policy Change Events (MPSSVC Rule-Level Policy Change)
- Filtering Platform Policy Change Events

The total population of unique security-related events rose from around 200 or so in Windows Server 2003 to over 350 in Windows Server 2008. Many activities are now auditable for the first time. The CD which accompanies this volume contains files with the complete list of events in Windows Server 2008. You can also create your own list using the *WEvtUtil.exe* command at the command prompt:

```
C:>wevtutil gp Microsoft-Windows-Security-Auditing/ge/gm:true
   /f:xml > %temp%\WS08_Security_Events.xml
C:>notepad %temp%\WS08_Security_Events.xml
```

Using the Built-In Tools to Analyze Events

The tools you use to analyze events in Windows have dramatically improved. The command-line tools now have about the same power as the graphical tools, and the graphical tools have become much more sophisticated. Previously you could filter on header fields and do simple searches—now you can search any field of any event. Plus, events can be exposed and analyzed as text or as XML, enabling automation scenarios that were previously much more labor-intensive.

Event Viewer

As mentioned earlier, Event Viewer—the primary tool in Windows for analyzing events—has improved dramatically in Windows Server 2008 when compared to previous releases.

As in previous releases, Event Viewer displays a list of events when a log is selected, and allows sorting on several fields by clicking the column heading. In the Windows Server 2008 Event Viewer, you can also group events in the same way.

To understand grouping, try a simple experiment. Right-click the heading of the Task Category column in the event list and choose Group Events By This Column. Event Viewer will take a moment and then will group all the events by subcategory. If you then right-click the Task Category heading again, and choose Collapse All Groups, you will see something like Figure 8-10.

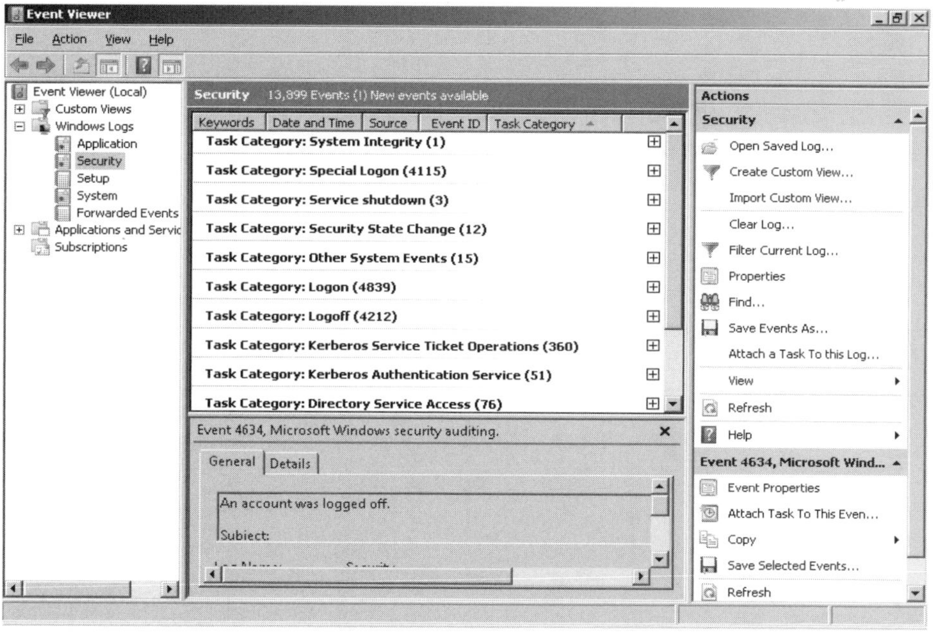

Figure 8-10   Event Viewer grouping security events by Task Category (Subcategory).

To filter the log, right-click the log name in the lefthand pane of Event Viewer, and choose Filter Current Log. The Filter Current Log dialog box will appear. First, choose just the Windows audit events. The source name for these events is Microsoft-Windows-Security-Auditing; this is displayed as Security-Auditing in Windows Vista. Display the list of event sources by expanding Event Sources. Select this event source by checking the box next to it and then click outside the list. Figure 8-11 shows an example of filtering events by event source.

Next, narrow the filter to only include Logon subcategory events. If you recall, the subcategories in audit policy correspond to Task Categories in Event Viewer. Click the expand list

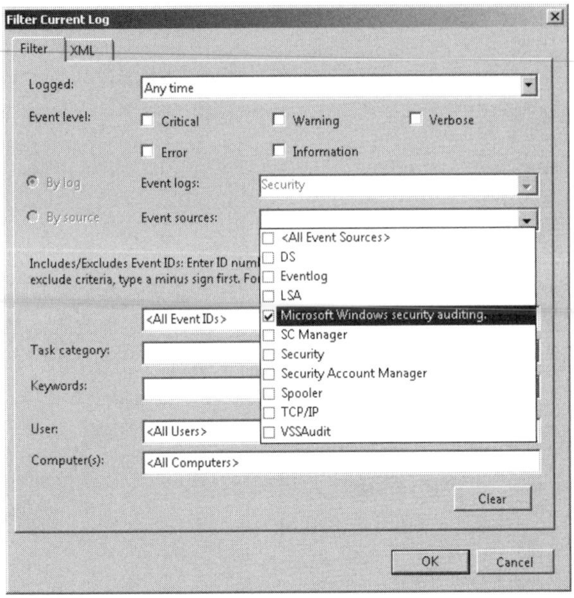

Figure 8-11   Filtering events in Event Viewer by Event Source.

(down arrow) button next to the Task Categories field and then select the check box next to the Logon task category. Click outside the list to collapse the list. Figure 8-12 shows an example of filtering events by task category.

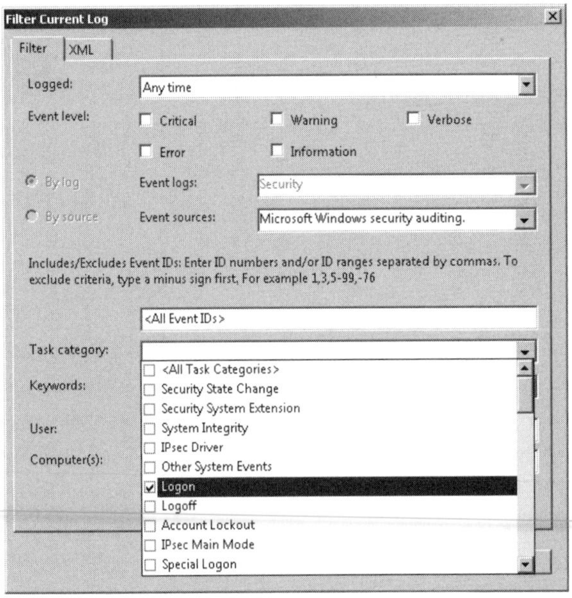

Figure 8-12   Filtering events in Event Viewer by Task Category.

If you have done everything correctly, you can click OK and you will see a filtered events list, as shown in Figure 8-13.

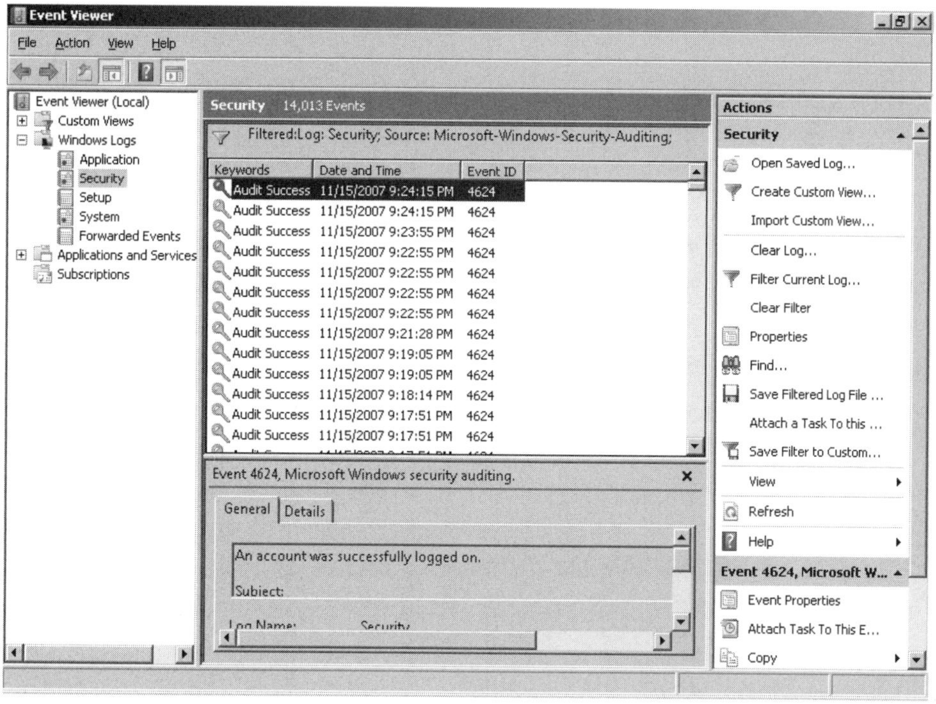

Figure 8-13   Event Viewer showing only a filtered list of logon events.

Although the Filter dialog box is quite powerful, it only exposes part of the full filtering capability of the event system. By using XPATH you can filter events more granularly.

Open the Filter dialog box again. Then click the XML tab at the top of the dialog box. The XPATH expression that is displayed corresponds to the options you selected from the Filter dialog box. Select the Edit Query Manually check box and then click OK in the confirmation dialog box. You can now edit the XPATH text. A full discussion of XPATH is beyond the scope of this book, but here is a simple change that you can make to demonstrate the capabilities. You can change the filter expression to only display interactive logon events—events with logon type 2.

The XPATH displayed in the dialog box will match the following code:

```
<QueryList>
  <Query Id="0" Path="Security">
    <Select Path="Security">*[System[Provider[@Name='Microsoft-Windows-Security-
        Auditing'] and Task = 12544]]</Select>
  </Query>
</QueryList>
```

Change it to the following code. This has been formatted for readability—XML ignores white space (outside of *string literals*, which are strings in single quotes). Note that the Filter dialog box supports copy and paste via the keyboard shortcuts (Ctrl+C and Ctrl+V) if you prefer to edit using Notepad.

```
<QueryList>
   <Query Id="0" Path="Security">
     <Select Path="Security">
       *[System[Provider[@Name='Microsoft-Windows-Security-Auditing'] and Task = 12544]
          and EventData[Data[@Name='LogonType'] = '2']]
     </Select>
   </Query>
</QueryList>
```

When you have made the change, click OK. Event Viewer will apply the filter and you will only see interactive logon events. Take a look at a couple to verify that the logon type field is 2 in each. If you have made a mistake, Event Viewer will inform you and you can choose Clear Filter from the Action menu in the lefthand pane to clear the filter and start over. Figure 8-14 shows the XML filter expression.

Figure 8-14   Editing the XPATH filter expression in Event Viewer.

XPATH 101

You do not have to be an XPATH expert to use the XML tab of the Filter dialog box in Event Viewer. Usually the easiest way to get started is to follow these steps

1. Dump the XML of an event of interest so that you can see the data field labels.

2. Build the closest filter you can using the Graphical Filter tab.

3. Edit the *Select* element in the XML tab to match the specific data elements with the specific values that you are interested in.

The XPATH expression in the *Select* element is constructed as a series of paths to XML elements. Let us take a sample XPATH expression:

```
*[System[Provider[@Name='Microsoft-Windows-Security-Auditing'] and Task
    = 12544] and EventData[Data[@Name='LogonType'] = '2']]
This expression is looking for XML that matches this:
<System>
    <Provider Name="Microsoft-Windows-Security-Auditing" />
    <Task>12544</Task>
</System>
<EventData>
    <Data Name="LogonType">2</Data>
</EventData>
```

How do we know this? First, the asterisk at the beginning tells us "every event that matches the following criteria." Next, XPATH uses square brackets rather than parentheses for grouping, so we must count them very carefully. XPATH also does not tolerate extra square brackets.

Next we see the following:

```
System[
```

This means to match any elements inside the *<Event>* named system. In the Windows event schema, there is always exactly one *<System>* element. The following means to match the *<Provider>* element in the element we just matched (*<System>*):

```
Provider[
@Name='Microsoft-Windows-Security-Auditing']
```

This means that we are only interested in *<Provider>* elements that have an attribute named *Name* with a value of *Microsoft-Windows-Security-Auditing*. This is the standard name of the auditing event provider in Windows. Pay very close attention, notice the right bracket (]) after the *@Name* clause. The next part of the query is an "and". This means that we are done with the *<Provider>* element.

The next part of the query tells us to match the *<Task>* child element of the *<System>* element. (Remember we finished with *<Provider>*.):

```
and Task=12544]
```

It only matches *Task* elements with value 12544. Also note that we are matching the element value, not an attribute. Finally the bracket tells us that we are done with the *<System>* element—we have to keep track of which bracket refers to which element.

The next clause is a little more complex, but get used to it—this is how you get to information in the Data section of events.

```
and EventData[
```

This tells us that we want to match the *<EventData>* child element of the *<Event>*.

The next bit actually does almost all the work:

```
Data[@Name='LogonType'] = '2']
```

This essentially says: Match *<Data>* elements with value 2, but only if they have an attribute called *Name* with a value of *LogonType*. This is really a complex way of describing in XML that we want events where the LogonType=2. The extra right bracket at the end of the expression ends the *<EventData>* element portion of the XPATH expression.

Finally the entire expression ends with a right bracket. Counting brackets, we have the same number of left and right brackets. Now all that is left is to try it out!

WEvtUtil.exe

The EventQuery command-line utility from Windows Server 2003 has been replaced with a new tool, WEvtUtil.exe. WEvtUtil can manage the entire event system from the command prompt.

Edit the XPATH query from the previous example (you can view the filter and press Ctrl+C to put it on the clipboard) using Notepad. WEvtUtil can take an XML file as input, but in this case you will only use the filter expression.

```
<QueryList>
  <Query Id="0" Path="Security">
    <Select Path="Security">
      *[System[Provider[@Name='Microsoft-Windows-Security-Auditing'] and Task = 12544]
          and EventData[Data[@Name='LogonType'] = '2']]
    </Select>
  </Query>
</QueryList>
```

Edit this text to remove the XML tags; the only text remaining should be the filter expression (the text between the *<Select>* tags). Remove all carriage returns from the text.

```
*[System[Provider[@Name='Microsoft-Windows-Security-Auditing'] and Task
    = 12544] and EventData[Data[@Name='LogonType'] = '2']]
```

After editing, copy the text to the clipboard and open a command prompt. At the command prompt type the following command. You can paste in the XPATH expression using the application menu (upper-left corner) of the command prompt. The full command will look like this:

```
C:\>wevtutil qe Security /q:"*[System[Provider[@Name='Microsoft-Windows- Security-Auditing']
and Task = 12544] and EventData[Data[@Name= 'LogonType'] = '2']]"
```

When you press Enter, WEvtUtil will start dumping the events, as XML, to the command prompt. You can pipe this output to a text file and view it with another program. WEvtUtil also has command-line options to output as text or as RenderedXML. RenderedXML includes the XML of the event as well as the text.

Note that the XML that WEvtUtil generates is not well formed—it does not have an XML declaration and it usually does not consist of one element. If you are using automation you might want to add an *XMLDecl* and a tag at the beginning of the WEvtUtil output, and a close tag at the end, if your automation expects well-formed XML.

Summary

Even though it is a bit of work to initially create the policies and select the settings, it is probably very worthwhile to deploy granular audit policy if you are using Windows Server 2008 or Windows Vista in your organization.

Enable the least amount of auditing that will allow you to meet your needs. Some auditing is good, but if you enable everything you will probably have problems managing the volume of your security event logs.

Enable auditing before you have a problem. Auditing occurs when something auditable happens. If something auditable happens but auditing is not enabled, that event is lost forever.

Finally, do not expect auditing to be a panacea. Auditing records what happens on the system. A lot of useful information is in the security log—you can monitor all sorts of activities if you plan in advance. But it is not a detective service: It does not place value judgments on the events and it will not tell you "this event means that your employee is stealing your data." You have to figure that out for yourself.

Part II
Implementing Identity and Access (IDA) Control Using Active Directory

Chapter 9

Designing Active Directory Domain Services for Security

— Jimmy Andersson

When I first started to look at Windows Server 2008 Active Directory Domain Services (AD DS), it was obvious that Microsoft had been focused on improving security and making it easier to deploy and manage AD DS. I will discuss multiple new features in this chapter, but let me give you a short description of my favorite one: the read-only domain controller (RODC).

You might wonder why I think this is a very important piece of technology. It's simple: Most of my customers are global organizations with multiple branch offices spread across the world. Most of them are only sales offices or production sites with very limited bandwidth to the hub site, and often very little or even no physical security of their domain controllers.

In these scenarios, it is imperative that we have the ability to serve the users' demand for fast logons and availability, but at the same time we must also control what we actually expose at the domain controller (DC). The RODC will help you secure your DCs in scenarios like these. In the next sections I will go through these new features in more depth.

The New User Interface

For a long time, Microsoft customers have asked for an easier graphical interface for installing AD DS. Now there is an updated installation wizard and new AD DS installation options. Microsoft has also made some new management options available for features such as RODC, as well as such longed-for features as a way to find all DCs in an entire enterprise. All of us administrators have spent time connecting to domain after domain, hunting for that one DC whose location we couldn't remember. Many of us gave up using the Microsoft Management Console (MMC) and instead wrote a script to search the whole domain hierachy.

Another nice feature of the new user interface is the ability to protect an object from accidental deletion directly from the object's Properties sheet. When you select the Protect Object From Accidental Deletion check box (see Figure 9-1), the security descriptor is updated to protect the object from deletion. To display the check box and the Object tab, select Advanced Features from the View menu in Active Directory Users And Computers (ADUC).

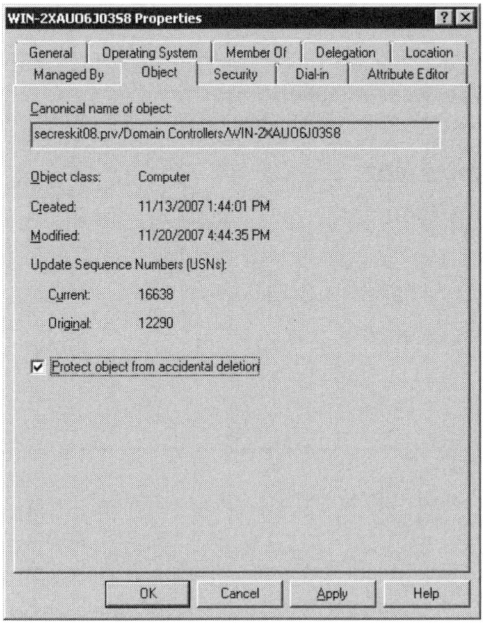

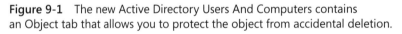

Figure 9-1   The new Active Directory Users And Computers contains an Object tab that allows you to protect the object from accidental deletion.

This new feature will help you protect important objects from accidental deletions. If you are an administrator, you can always clear the check box and delete the object. But this at least requires an extra step that will make you think twice before deleting the object. When you create a new orgazational unit (OU), this option is selected by default.

One of the biggest drawbacks with ADUC in previous versions was that you could not see all available attributes for an object. Many of my customers use more attributes than are visible from within ADUC. This gave them two choices: either write their own graphical user interface to extend ADUC, or use ADSIEdit.msc. If you are not good at writing a new or extended graphical user interface, you are pretty much stuck with ADSIEdit.msc. Do not get me wrong, I like ADSIEdit.msc. But it is not the friendliest tool I have ever seen. Especially if you think about help desk personnel who will create users and then need to fill out attributes that are not shown by default in ADUC. And think about how easy it is to make a mistake when you are in a hurry, or how long it takes to find an object if many objects are in one container. In the new ADUC, you will see an extra tab—the Attribute Editor tab—that will show you the available attributes for the object. You can edit the attributes directly from ADUC. Just enable Advanced Features in the View menu in ADUC. No more need to extend the user interface or write special tools—at least for this purpose. Figure 9-2 shows this new tab.

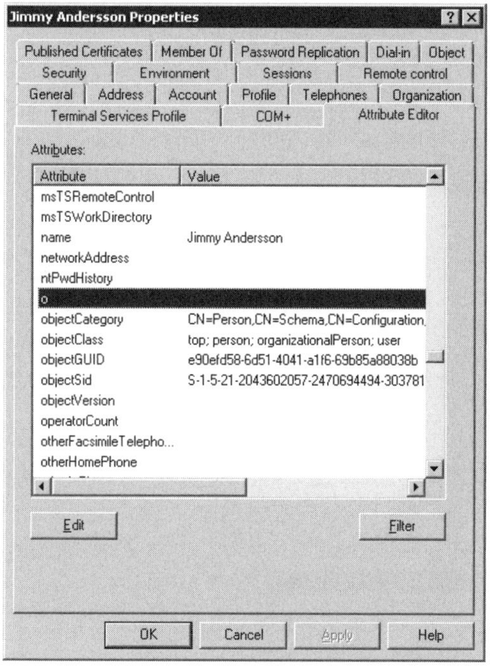

Figure 9-2   The new ADUC contains an Attribute Editor tab, which you can use to edit attributes that have no simple interface.

One thing that struck me was that I did not need to do anything special to use the new improvements—they are all available by default. Even though you must enable Advanced Features in ADUC or select a check box for some features, they are still available via the GUI. Let me give you an example. Suppose you want to see the advanced pages in the AD DS Installation Wizard. Select the Use Advanced Mode Installation check box on the Welcome page of the wizard. (See Figure 9-3.)

The New Active Directory Domain Services Installation Wizard

If you want to install AD DS, use the Add Roles wizard. For more details about server roles, please refer to Chapter 11, "Securing Server Roles." To access the Add Roles Wizard, click Add Roles in Initial Configuration Tasks window that appears when you install the operating system. You can also find the Add Roles Wizard in the Server Manager, which is available on the Administrative Tools menu, which can be found on the Start menu.

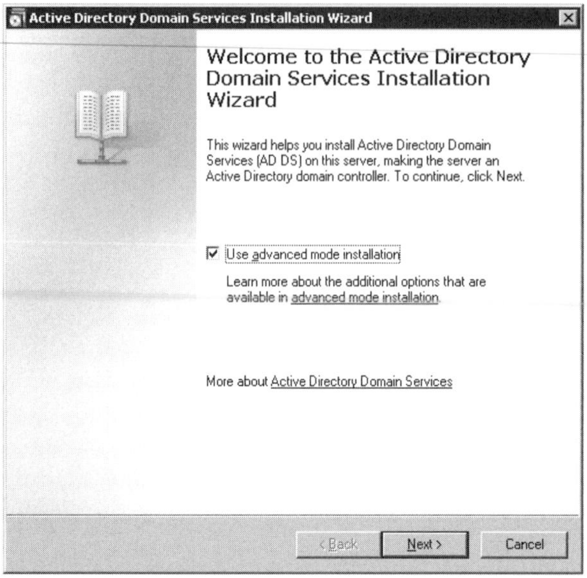

Figure 9-3   The new Welcome page of the AD DS Installation Wizard has the option to use advanced mode installation.

■ **Additional Domain Controller Options**   On this page, you can configure additional options for the DC, such as DNS, GC, or RODC. (See Figure 9-4.)

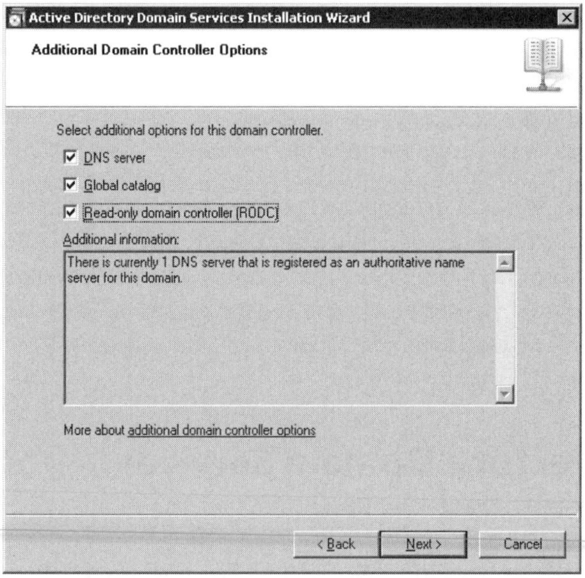

Figure 9-4   The new page of the Active Directory Installation Wizard, showing the additional options for the domain controller installation.

■ **Select A Domain**   This option lets you specify the domain in case you want to install an additional DC.

- **Select A Site**   If you want to specify which site the DC should belong to after installation, do so on this page.

- **Set Functional Levels**   When you install the first DC in a new forest or domain, this page lets you predefine the functional level.

- **Delegation Of RODC Installation And Administration**   Use this page to set the name of the group or user to which you want to delegate administration and second-step installation.

- **Password Replication Policy**   This page allows you to specify which account passwords to allow or deny from being cached on an RODC. This page appears only if you select the Use Advanced Mode Installation check box. See "Credential Caching" later in this chapter for details.

- **DNS delegation creation**   Depending on the type of DC installation you specified and your DNS environment, this page will provide a default option to create DNS delegation.

Other changes to this wizard show that Microsoft wants the promotion process to be as easy and error-free as possible. For example, you do not need to type the domain name when you install an additional DC. Instead you select the domain from a tree view. Thus, there is no chance that you will type the domain name wrong. In addition, the wizard now uses the credentials of the user who is currently logged on to complete the promotion, if the user is logged on with a domain account. Of course, you have the ability to use other credentials if you prefer. Another nice feature is that when you have finished the wizard, a Summary page appears, which you can export directly into an answer file. You can then use this file as a template for other installations and uninstallations. For security reasons, not all information will be available in the answer file. For example, the password for Directory Services Restore Mode (DSRM) will be excluded when you export it to the file. You can modify the answer file to include specific values, but be very careful with this because the file might end up in the wrong hands. For passwords, I recommend that you type **password=*** in the answer file so that the process will prompt for it.

Read-Only Domain Controllers

As I mentioned at the beginning of the chapter, with the release of Windows Server 2008, Microsoft introduces a new type of DC: the read-only domain controller (RODC). With the RODC, organizations can now deploy a DC in locations where physical security cannot be guaranteed. An RODC hosts read-only partitions of the AD DS database. One big benefit is that this will help you secure your environment. Before the RODC role, I always saw the DC in the branch office as the weakest point. (Please refer to Chapter 14, "Securing the Branch Office," for an explanation of what a branch office is and for the security implications of using an RODC.) With this new role we can actually move the writable DCs to the hub site in a proper data center and replace the writable DCs at the branch office with RODCs, which will lower the security risks.

Before the introduction of the RODC, users in a branch office had to authenticate with a DC at the hub site over a wide area network (WAN). Either that, or you needed to have a local

DC at the branch office. This was not an efficient solution because small sites often cannot provide the physical security required for a writable DC. The network bandwidth between a branch office and a hub site is often poor, however. For branch office users, this can increase the amount of time required to log on, as well as hamper access to network resources. Now, however, you can address these problems by deploying an RODC at your branch offices to provide your branch office users with the following benefits:

- Improved security
- Faster log-on times
- More efficient access to resources on the network

One of the biggest reasons I see for using an RODC is inadequate physical security, and we all know that security starts with physical security. How can an RODC help you here? It provides a way for you to deploy a DC more securely in locations where you need fast and reliable authentication services but cannot ensure physical security. To my mind, this is a requirement for a writable DC. Another favorite example of where to use an RODC is when I have special requirements, such as an application that must be installed on a DC. Or where the only server locally at the site is the DC, and I must host applications on it as well. An application owner must often log on to the DC interactively or use Terminal Services to configure and manage the application, which creates an unacceptable security risk on a writable DC. Yet another scenario would be where local storage of all domain user passwords is a threat, such as on an extranet or application-facing role. As I see it, the primary focus for the RODC is to be deployed in remote or branch office environments.

Read-Only AD DS Database

The RODC actually holds all the Active Directory objects and attributes that a writable DC holds, but you cannot make changes to its database—you have to make them on a writable DC and then replicate them back to the RODC. A local application that requests read access to the directory will get access. An application that requests write access will receive an LDAP referral response. This means that the response directs the application to a writable DC where it can get access.

RODC Filtered Attribute Set

No attributes that are defined in the RODC filtered attribute set are allowed to replicate to any RODC in the forest. This means that if you have applications that use AD DS to store credential data such as passwords, credentials, or encryption keys and you do not want that data to be stored on an RODC (in case it is compromised), you can dynamically define this set of attributes as part of the filtered attribute set in the schema for domain objects. The attribute set will not replicate to any RODC.

If a malicious user compromises an RODC and attempts to configure it to replicate attributes that are defined in the RODC filtered attribute set, the replication request will be denied the next time the RODC tries to replicate those attributes from a DC running Windows Server 2008.

But if the RODC tries to replicate those attributes from a DC running Windows Server 2003, the replication request will succeed. If you plan to use the RODC filtered attribute set that I recommend, ensure that your forest functional level is Windows Server 2008. If the forest functional level is Windows Server 2008, DCs that are running Windows Server 2003 are not allowed in the forest, so an RODC that has been compromised cannot be exploited in this manner.

To ensure that AD DS functionality does not get manually misconfigured, you are not allowed to add system-critical attributes to the RODC filtered attribute set. An attribute is system-critical if it is required for AD DS to function properly, such as Local Security Authority (LSA), Security Accounts Manager (SAM), and Microsoft-specific Security Service Provider Interfaces (SSPIs) such as Kerberos. A system-critical attribute has a *schemaFlagsEx* attribute value equal to 1 (*schemaFlagsEx* attribute value & 0x1 = TRUE).

If you want to configure the RODC filtered attribute set, you configure it on the server that holds the schema operations master role. If you try to add a system-critical attribute to the RODC filtered set and the schema master is running Windows Server 2008, the server will return the LDAP error "unwillingToPerform". If you try to add a system-critical attribute to the RODC filtered attribute set on a Windows Server 2003 schema master, the operation appears to be successful but the attribute is not actually added. Because of this—and to ensure that system-critical attributes are not included in the RODC filtered attribute set—I recommend that the schema master role should be on a Windows Server 2008 DC when you add attributes to an RODC filtered set. On the companion CD you will find a Microsoft Office Excel file that documents the default Schema for Windows Server 2008.

Unidirectional Replication

Because we do not write directly to the RODC, no changes will originate at the RODC. In turn this means that the writable DCs that are replication partners to the RODC do not have to pull changes from the RODC. This also reduces the workload of bridgehead servers in the hub and the effort required to monitor replication. Any changes or corruption that a malicious user might make on an RODC cannot replicate from the RODC to the rest of the forest.

RODC unidirectional replication applies to both AD DS and Distributed File System (DFS) Replication. The RODC performs normal inbound replication for AD DS and DFS Replication changes.

Credential Caching

The default setting for an RODC is to not store user or computer credentials with the exceptions of the computer account of the RODC itself and a special krbtgt account for the RODC. You must explicitly configure any other credential caching on an RODC. Please see Chapter 14 for more information.

In branch offices that have an RODC, the RODC will advertise itself as the Key Distribution Center (KDC), but when it signs or encrypts ticket-granting ticket (TGT) requests, the RODC uses a different krbtgt account and password than the KDC on a writable DC.

After successful authentication of an account the RODC attempts to contact a writable DC at the hub site and requests a copy of the appropriate credentials. The writable DC will recognize that the request is coming from an RODC and will check the Password Replication Policy that is in effect for that RODC (Figure 9-5).

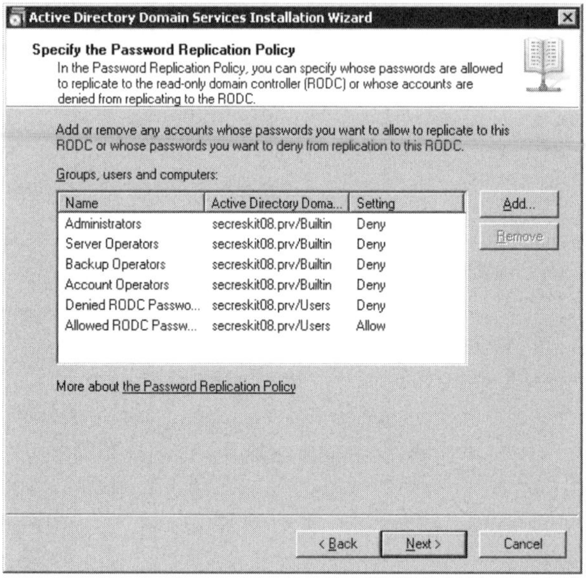

Figure 9-5   The default replication password policy during a new RODC installation.

The Password Replication Policy will then determine whether a user's credentials or a computer's credentials can be replicated from the writable DC to the RODC. If the Password Replication Policy allows it, the writable DC replicates the credentials to the RODC, and the RODC caches them for future use. After the credentials are cached on the RODC, the RODC can directly service that user's log-on requests until the credentials change, which means that it does not have to cross the WAN for each log-on request. When a TGT is signed with the krbtgt account of the RODC, the RODC recognizes that it has a cached copy of the credentials; if another DC signs the TGT, however, the RODC forwards requests to a writable DC.

You should limit credential caching only to users who actually need to be authenticated by the RODC, thereby limiting the potential exposure of credentials by a compromise of the RODC. I recommend that you allow only a small subset of domain users to have credentials cached on any given RODC. In the event that the RODC is stolen, only those credentials that are cached can potentially be cracked, and in most cases these are only domain users and do not have privileged rights. An administrator can modify the default Password Replication Policy to allow users' credentials to be cached at the RODC. You manage this via the new Password Replication Policy tab on the DC Properties sheet (Figure 9-6).

If you click the Advanced button on this tab, you will see what passwords have been sent to the RODC, what passwords are currently stored on the RODC, and what accounts have authenticated to the RODC, including accounts that are not currently defined in the security groups that are allowed or denied replication. This means that you have the ability to easily see who is using the RODC and determine whether to allow or deny password replication. You can also export this list to a CSV file by clicking the Export button so that you can keep a record of which users are actually using the RODC as well as prepopulate the RODC with passwords for the accounts you select.

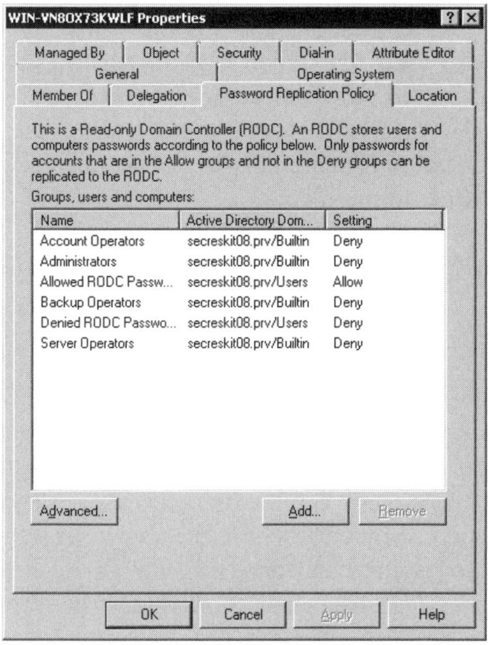

Figure 9-6   The new Password Replication tab.

To support the RODC Password Replication Policy, Windows Server 2008 AD DS had to include the following new attributes. (For a complete list of all attributes and classes, see the Schema documentation on the book companion CD.)

- **msDS-NeverRevealGroup**   Identifies the security group with users that will never have their secrets disclosed to a particular instance.

- **msDS-Reveal-OnDemandGroup**   Identifies the security group that has users that may disclose their secrets to a particular instance.

- **msDS-AuthenticatedToAccountList**   Is actually a backlink for *ms-DS-AuthenticatedAtDC* that identifies which users that have authenticated to this computer.

- **msDS-RevealedList**   A list of users whose secrets that have been disclosed.

Read-Only DNS

If I need an RODC, I certainly need a DNS server in the branch office as well since I do not want to perform name resolution over the WAN as that would contradict the idea of placing RODCs at branch offices for authenticating users locally. To provide for name resolution at branch offices, you can run the DNS Server service on an RODC to replicate all application directory partitions that DNS uses, including ForestDNSZones and DomainDNSZones. If you install the DNS server on an RODC, your clients can query it for name resolution just like they query any other DNS server, but it will not support client updates directly. This means that the RODC does not register name server (NS) resource records for any Active Directory–integrated zone that it hosts. When a client attempts to update its DNS records against an RODC, the server returns a referral to another writable DNS server so that the client can attempt to update against the writable DNS server instead. What really happens in the background is that the DNS server on the RODC will attempt to replicate the updated record from the DNS server that made the update. This replication request is only for a single object (the DNS record)–the entire list of changed zone or domain data does not get replicated during this special replicate-single-object request.

Staged Installation for Read-Only Domain Controllers

Sometimes it is very beneficial to be able to run the installation in two steps. When you create the RODC you will be able to delegate installation and administration of the RODC to either a security group or a user. The first step must be done by someone that is a member of the Domain Admins group, but the second step can be run by anybody that you delegate this task to while you use the wizard. From a security perspective it means that you can do all the configuration that require admininstrator privileges before you send the physical server, without having to preload it with sensitive data or send the sensitive data via courier service. You can do this by right-clicking the DC's OU, clicking Action, and choosing Pre-create Read-only Domain Controller. I recommend that you delegate the second step of the installation to a group, which will ease the management overhead in the long term.

When you run the AD DS Installation Wizard you will see a new option on the Welcome page that enables advanced mode directly from the wizard. The old way of running the command dcpromo/adv is still available. In advanced mode you have additional configuration options available, such as staged installation of an RODC. You can complete each step with the Active Directory Domain Services Installation Wizard.

In the first stage of the installation, you create an account for the RODC in AD DS. The second stage of the installation attaches the server that will be the RODC to the account that was previously created for it. During the first stage the wizard records all data about the RODC that will be stored in the Active Directory database, such as the DC account name and the site where it will be placed. When you create the RODC account you can also specify which users or groups that can complete the next stage of the installation. This next stage can be performed at another site, such as the branch office, by any user or group to which you have delegated the right to complete the installation. That user or group will finish the installation by running the command **dcpromo.exe /UseExistingAccount:Attach**, which will attach the server to the precreated RODC account. If you have not specified an account to complete the installation and administer the RODC, the second step can only be done by a user who is a member of the Domain Admins or Enterprise Admins groups. The second stage of the installation installs AD DS on the new RODC server; all AD DS data that resides locally, such as log files and the database, will be created on the RODC itself. For the installation source files, you have two options: either replicate it to the RODC from another DC or the Install From Media (IFM) feature.

> **Note**   You must use Ntdsutil.exe to create the installation media to use IFM.

During the installation, the wizard automatically detects whether the name of the server matches the names of any RODC accounts that have been created in advance. When the wizard finds a matching account name, it prompts the user to use that account to complete the RODC installation. Therefore it is important that the server is not joined to the domain before you try to attach it to the RODC account.

What Are the Prerequisites?

Before you can deploy an RODC, the following criteria must be met:

- An existing writable DC running Windows Server 2008 must exist in the domain. The RODC must forward authentication requests to this DC because the Password Replication Policy is set on it.

- The domain functional level must be Windows Server 2003 or higher so that Kerberos constrained delegation is available. Constrained delegation is used for security calls that must be impersonated under the context of the caller.

- The forest functional level must be Windows Server 2003 or higher so that linked-value replication is available. This provides a higher level of replication consistency.

- You must run adprep/rodcprep once in the forest to update the permissions on all the DNS application directory partitions in the forest. This will make it possible for all RODCs that are also DNS servers to replicate the permissions successfully.

- The PDC emulator role holder must be running Windows Server 2008; otherwise, the RODC will not advertise itself as a time source for its clients. See details at *http:// technet2.microsoft.com/windowsserver2008/en/library/49eaca29-3399-4dd6-adcc-87a574e5d7921033.mspx?mfr=true.*

> **Note**   If you want to use RODC filtered attribute set, I recommend that you have the forest functional level set to Windows Server 2008. For details, see "RODC Filtered Attribute Set" earlier in this chapter.

Restartable Active Directory Domain Services

Why would you want to use such a feature as Restartable AD DS? The first time I heard about it I was not convinced, but the more I thought about it the more I liked the idea. The benefit is that you will be able to perform some of the operations that usually required a restart of the DC, such as applying security updates without having to reboot your server! It will also let you stop AD DS to perform tasks such as offline defragmentation of the Active Directory database. The real benefit is that other services that are running on the server and do not depend on AD DS to function, such as Dynamic Host Configuration Protocol (DHCP), remain available for client requests while you are doing a security update or an offline defragmentation!

> **Note**   If you stop AD DS, the DNS, KDC, and Intersite Messaging services will stop as well.

Restartable AD DS is available by default on all DCs that run Windows Server 2008. There are no functional-level requirements or any other prerequisites for using this feature, and you can use the Services Microsoft Management Console (MMC) snap-in or the command line to stop and start AD DS, just as you would with a normal service.

Stopping AD DS is very similar to logging on in Directory Services Restore Mode. But restartable AD DS provides a new state for DCs running Windows Server 2008: AD DS Stopped. A DC that is in the AD DS Stopped state has the characteristics of both a DC in Directory Services Restore Mode and a domain member server. The Active Directory database (Ntds.dit) on the DC is offline, as it is with DSRM. First, while in this mode, another DC can be contacted for logon if one is available. If no other DC can be contacted, you can use the DSRM password to log on. And second, as a normal member server, a DC that is in AD DS Stopped state is still part of the domain, which means that Group Policy and other settings are still applied to the computer. But it cannot service log-on requests or replicate with other DCs while it is in this state.

Active Directory Database Mounting Tool

Microsoft has improved the Active Directory recovery process by providing a way to compare data as it exists in snapshots or backups that are taken at different times. You might wonder why I think this is important in a security perspective. The reason is quite simple. It gives you the means to follow the changes that happened before a security breach—simply a way of doing forensics by comparing data. For this you use the new Active Directory database mounting tool (Dsamain.exe), which will help you decide which data to restore after data loss. For me, this feature has eliminated the need to restore multiple backups to compare the Active Directory data that they contain.

> **Note**   This feature had the code names "Snapshot Viewer" and "Active Directory Data Mining Tool" during product development. You may still see those names in some documentation.

First you need to understand that the Active Directory database mounting tool does not recover deleted objects by itself, but helps you streamline the process for recovering objects that have been accidentally deleted. In previous versions of Active Directory, when objects or

OUs were accidentally deleted, the only way to determine exactly which objects were deleted was to restore data from backups. This approach had two major drawbacks:

- You needed to restart the DC in DSRM to perform an authoritative restore.

- Unless you restored the backups to different DCs, you had no way to compare the data in the backups from different points in time. This made for a tedious task.

The Active Directory database mounting tool allows you to view AD DS data that is stored in snapshots or backups online. You can then compare data in snapshots or backups from different points in time, which will help you to make a better decision about what data to restore. The Active Directory database mounting tool makes it possible for you to save deleted AD DS or Active Directory Lightweight Directory Services (AD LDS) in the form of snapshots taken by the Volume Shadow Copy Service (VSS). The tool does not actually recover the deleted objects and containers—you must perform data recovery as a separate step.

Because backups contain sensitive data, the backups are stored as read-only and only members of the Domain Admins and Enterprise Admins groups are allowed to view the snapshot with a Lightweight Directory Access Protocol (LDAP) tool such as Ldp.exe. I recommend that you use encryption or other data security precautions with AD DS snapshots to help mitigate the chance of unauthorized access to AD DS snapshots.

To use the Active Directory database mounting tool, follow these steps:

1. Schedule a task that regularly runs Ntdsutil.exe to take snapshots of the volume that contains the AD DS database. This is optional. You can do it manually if you want, but I recommend scheduling it.

2. Run Ntdsutil.exe to list the available snapshots and mount the snapshot that you want to view.

3. Run Dsamain.exe to see the snapshot volume as an LDAP server. For example, if I want to see my latest snapshot in the default path, the command will be: **dsamain–dbpath c:\\$snap_200711201220_volumec$\\windows\\ntds\\ntds.dit – ldapport 41389**. This will make the snapshot available for Ldp.exe on port 41389. Dsamain.exe will take the following arguments:

   - ❏ AD DS database (Ntds.dit) path. This path must be ASCII and by default it is opened as read-only.

   - ❏ Log path. You must have write access to the path.

   - ❏ Four port numbers for LDAP, LDAP-SSL, Global Catalog, and Global Catalog–SSL. The only port that is required is the LDAP port. If you do not specify the other ports, they use LDAP+1, LDAP+2, and LDAP+3. This means that if you specify LDAP port 41389 without specifying other port values, the LDAP-SSL port will be 41390, Global Catalog will be 41391, and Global Catalog-SSL will be 41392. Even though this might look strange for people that know the default ports, it actually works this way.

4. Use Ldp.exe to connect to the snapshot's LDAP port that you specified when you exposed the snapshot as an LDAP server in the previous step.

5. Browse the snapshot just as you would with any live DC. When you want to stop Dsamain, press Ctrl+C in the Command Prompt window. Or, if you are running the command remotely, you need to set the *stopservice* attribute on the *rootDSE* object.

If you know which OU or objects were deleted, you can look up the deleted objects in the snapshots and record the attributes and backlinks that belonged to the deleted objects. Then you reanimate these objects by using the tombstone reanimation feature. For details about tombstone reanimation, please see the Microsoft TechNet article "Reanimating Active Directory Tombstone Objects" at *http://www.microsoft.com/technet/technetmag/issues/2007 /09/Tombstones/default.aspx.*

After that, you have to manually repopulate these objects with the stripped attributes and backlinks as it was in the snapshots. Even though you must manually re-create the stripped attributes and backlinks, the Active Directory database mounting tool makes it possible for you to re-create deleted objects and their backlinks without restarting the DC in Directory Services Restore Mode—this will save you time, I promise! You can also use the tool to look up aspects of previous configurations of AD DS, such as permissions that were in effect, which will be of great help if you need to do a restore. This feature is also tremendously helpful if AD DS stops and you want to know how it was configured when it last worked.

AD DS Auditing

This section will only cover AD DS auditing. For more information about auditing Windows, see Chapter 8, "Auditing."

One thing that my customers have asked for is the ability to log old and new values when a change occurs. Now you can set up AD DS auditing with a new audit policy subcategory called Directory Service Changes. This will log both old and new changes when they are made to AD DS objects and their attributes. This will help you to do forensics and follow the preceding events before a security breach or issue.

 Note   This new auditing feature also applies to AD LDS.

By modifying the system access control list (SACL) on an object, you can control which operations to audit. This gives you the detail you always wanted. If you decide to define this policy setting, which you do by modifying the default Domain Controllers Policy, you can specify whether to audit successes, audit failures, or not audit at all. Success audits generate an audit entry when a user successfully accesses an object that has a SACL specified; failure audits generate an audit entry when a user unsuccessfully attempts to access an object that has a SACL specified.

Previously, AD DS auditing only logged the name of the attribute that was changed—it did not log the previous and current values of the attribute as it does with Windows Server 2008 AD DS. This will help you identify changes and previous values, which makes the event logs more useful as a tracking mechanism for changes that occur over the lifetime of an object.

Auditing AD DS Access

You may recall that Windows 2000 Server and Windows Server 2003 had only one audit policy, the Audit directory Service Access, which controlled whether auditing for directory service events was enabled or disabled. In Windows Server 2008, this policy is divided into four subcategories:

- Directory Service Access
- Directory Service Changes
- Directory Service Replication
- Detailed Directory Service Replication

If you want the ability to audit changes to objects, you enable the subcategory Directory Service Changes. Table 9-1 lists the auditable operations.

Table 9-1 AD DS Operations

Type	Event ID	Description
Modify	5136	Logged after successful modification of an attribute.
Create	5137	Logged when a new object is created.
Undelete	5138	Logged when an object is undeleted.
Move	5139	Logged when an object is moved within the domain.

Note   The delete operation is actually a modify operation. The attribute *isDeleted* is set to True when an object is deleted.

These operations are changes that are performed on an object. The corresponding events will appear in the Security log.

As an example I will modify the *Office* attribute in ADUC for a user called Jimmy Andersson and the following two events will appear in the Security log:

1. The first event tells me that I deleted the value for attribute *physicalDeliveryOfficeName*. This is the actual attribute name where the Office field in ADUC stores its values.

```
A directory service object was modified.

Subject:
    Security ID:SECRESKIT08\Administrator
    Account Name:Administrator
```

```
        Account Domain:SECRESKIT08
        Logon ID:0x438594

    Directory Service:
        Name:secreskit08.prv
        Type:Active Directory Domain Services

    Object:
        DN:CN=Jimmy Andersson,OU=AuditPolicy,DC=secreskit08,DC=prv
        GUID:CN=Jim Andersson,OU=AuditPolicy,DC=secreskit08,DC=prv
        Class:user

    Attribute:
        LDAP Display Name:physicalDeliveryOfficeName
        Syntax (OID):2.5.5.12
        Value:Uppsala HQ

    Operation:
        Type:Value Deleted
        Correlation ID:{31e232b9-35df-4b26-8bd0-e5797f5172b4}
        Application Correlation ID:-
```

2. The second event tells me again that a modification occurred to the same attribute and the new value.

```
    A directory service object was modified.

    Subject:
        Security ID:SECRESKIT08\Administrator
        Account Name:Administrator
        Account Domain:SECRESKIT08
        Logon ID:0x438594

    Directory Service:
        Name:secreskit08.prv
        Type:Active Directory Domain Services

    Object:
        DN:CN=Jimmy Andersson,OU=AuditPolicy,DC=secreskit08,DC=prv
        GUID:CN=Jim Andersson,OU=AuditPolicy,DC=secreskit08,DC=prv
        Class:user

    Attribute:
        LDAP Display Name:physicalDeliveryOfficeName
        Syntax (OID):2.5.5.12
        Value:HQ

    Operation:
        Type:Value Added
        Correlation ID:{31e232b9-35df-4b26-8bd0-e5797f5172b4}
        Application Correlation ID:-
```

You will see all the modifications that occur within the database as separate events as they are written to the database. As my modification actually was seen as a two-step modification it will first show the attribute as deleted and the next event shows the operation as adding a value.

But, for example, if you move a user from one OU to another, the event will show both the old and new value, as seen here:

```
A directory service object was moved.

Subject:
    Security ID:SECRESKIT08\Administrator
    Account Name:Administrator
    Account Domain:SECRESKIT08
    Logon ID:0x438594

Directory Service:
    Name:secreskit08.prv
    Type:Active Directory Domain Services

Object:
    Old DN:CN=Jimmy Andersson,OU=AuditPolicyExample,DC=secreskit08,DC=prv
    New DN:CN=Jimmy Andersson,OU=Test,DC=secreskit08,DC=prv
    GUID:CN=Jim Andersson,OU=AuditPolicy,DC=secreskit08,DC=prv
    Class:user

Operation:
    Correlation ID:{d8ed2341-aaa1-4d3c-9485-67a69de53622}
    Application Correlation ID:-
```

This was the behavior in Windows 2008 RC1. I do not know if this will be the behavior in the final release or if Microsoft will add the old and new attributes on all types of changes as it did when I moved the user in the above example.

If you want to implement the new auditing feature, use the controls that I will describe in the next sections. I recommend that you keep close auditing on all objects that you decide are critical for your AD DS implementation. This way you can trace all changes to find the root cause of both security and other issues because of changes such as modifications and deletions. You should also closely monitor modifications to privilege accounts and groups.

Global Audit Policy

If you want to enable all the directory service policy subcategories, you simply enable the global audit policy Audit Directory Service Access. You set this global audit policy in the Default Domain Controllers Policy under Security Settings\Local Policies\Audit Policy.

The two audit subcategories are independent of each other, so you can disable Directory Service Access and still see change events that are generated if the subcategory Directory Service Changes is enabled. The same thing applies if you disable Directory Service Changes and enable Directory Service Access.

Unfortunately there is no GUI tool to view or set audit policy subcategories; you have to use the command-line tool Auditpol.exe to view or set audit policy subcategories. The following auditpol.exe command enables the audit subcategory Directory Service Changes:

auditpol /set /subcategory:"directory service changes" /success:enable

> **Note**   To see a list of all categories and current settings, type **auditpol /get /category:***

SACL

SACL is the part of an object's security descriptor that specifies which operations will be audited. To enable auditing of Directory Services events you must enable auditing for the appropriate subcategory of events as well as configure a proper SACL. For instance, if you want to log change auditing events, an access control list entry (ACE) in the SACL must be present and auditing for the Directory Service Changes subcategory must be enabled. This ACE will require attribute modifications to be logged even if the Directory Service Changes subcategory is enabled. To see what this means, I will use the mobile attribute as an example.

If there is no ACE in a SACL that requires Write Property access on the mobile attribute, then no auditing events will be generated when the mobile attribute is modified—even if the subcategory Directory Service Changes is enabled.

For more information on SACLs and auditing, please see Chapter 8.

Schema

If you audit all events, an excessive number of events will be generated, which is not recommended. To avoid this, an additional control in the schema allows you to create exceptions to what is audited. For example, if you want to see changes for all attribute modifications on a user object, but you want to exclude one or two attributes, you can use the *searchFlag* property of the attribute to define whether it should be audited. This is a flag you can set in the schema for the attribute. The *searchFlags* property of each attribute defines a number of behaviors for the particular attribute. If bit 9 (value 256) is set for an attribute, AD DS will not log change events when a modification is made to this attribute. Please refer to Microsoft online documentation at *http://msdn2.microsoft.com/en-us/library/ms679765.aspx* before changing the *searchFlags* value, because it can have a big impact on your AD DS implementation.

Active Directory Lightweight Directory Services Overview

Active Directory Lightweight Directory Services (AD LDS) was formerly known as Active Directory Application Mode (ADAM). I use it to provide a directory service that can be used for directory-enabled applications without having the overhead of forests and domains. AD LDS is an LDAP directory service without the dependencies that are required for AD DS. This gives you flexible support for directory-enabled applications without requiring a domain with DCs, even though you have much the same functionality as with AD DS. One of the things I like most about AD LDS is the ability to run multiple instances concurrently on a single computer with independent schemas. This way I can separate each AD LDS to be used only for one application. In a security context this means that I can have multiple instances on one physical server even though they are not connected to each other and thus do not share anything.

As you know, AD DS provides directory services for both directory-enabled applications and Microsoft Windows Server operating systems. AD DS stores critical information about the network infrastructure, users, groups, network services, and so on. To do that, AD DS must have a single schema throughout an entire forest. This gives you less flexibility. But if you use the AD LDS server role, you can provide directory-enabled applications with directory services without having to rely on (and require) an Active Directory forest. However—and this is a nice feature—if you already have AD DS, you can use it for authentication of Windows security principals—for example, if you have an application that needs to extend the schema but for some reason you are not allowed to do so or simply do not want to. You can extend the AD LDS schema and store the information there. You then let the users authenticate with AD DS, connect to the application, and let AD LDS store the application-specific values.

Directory Store

All directory-enabled applications can use AD LDS as their directory store because AD LDS is an LDAP directory solution built for enterprises. AD LDS is often used to store private directory data in a local directory service. The benefit is that you do not need to replicate data that is only relevant to the actual application, and in some scenarios you can have the data on the same server as the application. By using AD LDS, you can reduce replication traffic on the network between DCs (which I believe should be dedicated to serve the domain infrastructure). But in some cases you might have to replicate data between multiple AD LDS instances.

Enterprise applications must often store personalization data associated with authenticated users in AD DS. If you store this personalization data in AD DS, you are often required to change the AD DS schema. Remember that an AD DS schema change is forest-wide, even if you only have one application connected to a specific DC. What I usually do instead is use AD LDS to store application-specific data, such as policy and management information. Then I use the user principals in AD DS for authentication and for controlling access to objects in AD LDS. This solution makes it unnecessary for each AD LDS directory to have its own user database, thereby preventing a proliferation of user IDs and passwords for end users every time a new directory-enabled application is introduced to the network. Both the end users and the administrator benefit.

Extranet Authentication Store

AD LDS can be helpful in many scenarios, such as in a Web portal scenario where the AD LDS will store personalization data for users who have been authenticated by AD DS. In this scenario you will store user IDs in AD DS and personal data in AD LDS. By separating this information, you do not need to extend the schema in the global AD DS, nor do you need to store personal data that is only relevant to that specific portal application. This will reduce network traffic for AD DS (especially if the data changes frequently). If you want to store the personal data on multiple servers for redundancy, you can set up another instance of AD LDS and configure replication between them.

You can also deploy AD LDS as an extranet authentication store along with Active Directory Federation Services (AD FS), which will enable Web single-sign-on (SSO) to authenticate users to multiple Web applications with a single user account. See "Active Directory Federation Services Overview" later in the chapter for more information.

Consolidating Identity Systems

My last couple of projects have been about consolidating different identity systems, so let me give you an example. One project was for a global organization with multiple forests with multiple domains in each forest throughout the world. Each domain had multiple identity systems such as Active Directory, SAP databases, phone systems, special applications with their own identity systems, and so on. To consolidate all these systems into one common system with all the information, my colleagues and I used AD LDS along with a metadirectory. Microsoft offers two versions of metadirectories: Microsoft Identity Integration Server (MIIS) and Microsoft Identity Integration Feature Pack (IIFP). IIFP is a free version of MIIS but with many fewer features. The metadirectory allowed us to provide directory-enabled applications with a unified view of all known identity information about enterprise users, applications, and network resources by integrating identity, synchronizing passwords, and directories and account provisioning/deprovisioning between AD DS and AD LDS.

Development Environment for AD DS and AD LDS

AD LDS is a very good choice for developers who are staging and testing various Active Directory–integrated applications because AD LDS uses the same programming model and provides almost the same administration experience as AD DS. Often when an application is under development it requires a different schema from the current server operating system AD DS. The application developer can use AD LDS to provide the application with a tailored schema without altering the configuration of the production Active Directory deployment. Developers can work with a local instance of AD LDS on a developer workstation and then move the application to AD DS at a later time when it is fully tested and approved.

AD LDS also saves time for developers because it is a simple directory that they can easily write to without needing extensive setup or hardware support during the development process. AD LDS can be easily installed or uninstalled on a developer's workstation, allowing for rapid restoration to a clean state during the application prototyping and development process.

Configuration Store for Distributed Applications

If you have a distributed application that requires a configuration store with multimaster update and replication capabilities to service its multiple components (such as a workflow application that accesses enterprise data), you might want to consider using AD LDS as a lightweight configuration store. In a scenario like that, you can include AD LDS as part of the application's installation process to ensure that the application has access to a directory immediately after installation. The application then configures and manages AD LDS entirely on its own, or it can be partially managed—that depends on how the application is written.

How Do I Create an AD LDS Instance?

The AD LDS role includes features that will make it easy for you to set up and manage your AD LDS instances. You have a wizard to guide you through the creation process. You also have command-line tools so that you can create unattended installations and removal of instances, as well as managing, synchronizing, and populating instances. You even have an MMC snap-in for configuration and management of your instances as well as the schema. But do not forget that you can also use many of the AD DS tools to administrate AD LDS instances!

New Features in Windows Server 2008 for AD LDS

The new features include:

- Audit AD LDS changes works the same way as it does in AD DS.

- The Data Mining Tool works the same way as it does in AD DS.

- Support for Active Directory Sites and Services. To use this tool you must first extend the schema with the classes that can be found in MS-ADLDS-DisplaySpecifiers.ldf. Then you can use Active Directory Sites And Services to manage replication among AD LDS instances.

- Install from Media (IFM) Generation. This feature lets you use a one-step Ntdsutil.exe or Dsdbutil.exe process to create installation media for the next installations.

- A dynamic list of LDAP Data Interchange Format (LDIF) files during instance setup enables you to make custom LDIF files available during AD LDS setup. You just need to add them to %systemroot%\adam directory and they will run in addition to the default LDIF files.

- Recursive linked-attribute queries can be used to determine group membership and ancestry with a single LDAP query.

Active Directory Federation Services Overview

I am asked more and more often about how to create a solution for identities that can operate across multiple platforms, even non-Windows environments. Customers want a solution that is Internet-scalable, highly extensible, and has an identity access solution that is as secure as possible. In those cases I always consider the Active Directory Federation Services (AD FS) server role, which comes with the Microsoft Windows Server 2008 operating system. In the following sections I will give an overview of AD FS. The idea behind AD FS is to take advantage of single-sign-on (SSO) to authenticate a user to multiple Web applications over the entire life of a particular session. AD FS can accomplish this by securely sharing a digital identity across security boundaries. To my knowledge this is the most secure solution.

What Is AD FS?

It is not unusual to have to remember multiple digital identities. This often happens to me when I try to use an application that is not in the same network I am normally on. What happens is that your credentials—which you already used to log on to your network—are not in the same realm as the application. So you often encounter a secondary log-on dialog box that asks for secondary credentials when you attempt to access the application. These secondary credentials represent the identity of your user in the realm where the application resides. The Web server that hosts the application usually requires these credentials so that it can make the authorization decision to allow or deny you access.

AD FS makes secondary accounts and their credentials unnecessary because it provides a trust relationship that you can use to protect a user's digital identity and access rights to your trusted partners. In a so-called federated environment, each organization manages its own identities (users), but also allows each organization to securely project and accept identities from other organizations, which makes it seamless for end users. Another common scenario is to deploy federation servers in multiple organizations to facilitate business-to-business (B2B) transactions between your trusted partners. Federated B2B partnerships let you identify business partners as one of the following types of organization:

- **Resource organization**   This is an organization that owns and manages the resources that are accessible from the Internet. A resource organization can deploy AD FS federation servers and AD FS–enabled Web servers that will manage access to protected resources for trusted partners.

- **Account organization**   This is an organization that owns and manages user accounts. An account organization can deploy AD FS federation servers that authenticate local users and create security tokens that the federation servers in the resource organization use to make authorization decisions.

The process name of authenticating to one network but accessing resources in another network without having to do multiple logons are called single-sign-on (SSO). AD FS provides a Web-based SSO solution that authenticates users to multiple Web applications, but only during a single browser session. This will make it easier for end users—they only need to remember one password.

What Is New in Windows Server 2008?

With Windows Server 2008 AD FS, Microsoft designed the new functionality to ease administrative overhead and extend support for applications. The following features are the most important parts:

- Installation. AD FS is now included as a server role.

- Application support. This is now more integrated with Microsoft Office SharePoint Server 2007 and Active Directory Rights Management Services (AD RMS).

- User experience when establishing federated trusts. Microsoft has improved the trust policy import and export functionality that will help you to minimize partner-based configuration issues.

AD FS Role Services

When we talk about the AD FS server role, we often forget that it actually includes multiple services such as federation services, proxy services, and Web agent services. You must configure these services to enable Web SSO, federate Web-based resources, customize access, and manage how existing users are authorized to access applications. Depending on your requirements, you can deploy servers running any one of the following services:

- **Federation Service**   One or more federation servers that share a common trust policy. You use federation servers to route authentication requests from user accounts in other organizations.

- **Claims-aware agent**   This is used on a Web server that hosts a claims-aware application to allow the querying of AD FS security token claims. To be called a claims-aware application, the application must use claims that are present in an AD FS security token to make authorization decisions and personalize applications.

- **Federation Service Proxy**   This is a proxy to the Federation Service in the perimeter network. The Federation Service Proxy uses WS-Federation Passive Requestor Profile (WS-F PRP) protocols to collect user credential information from browser clients; it then sends the user credential information to the Federation Service on their behalf.

- **Windows token–based agent**   This is used on a Web server that hosts a Windows NT token–based application to support conversion from an AD FS security token to an impersonation-level Windows NT access token. A Windows NT token–based application is an application that uses Windows-based authorization mechanisms.

You use the MMC snap-in to manage server roles, and after you install AD FS you can use the AD FS snap-in to manage both the Federation Service and Federation Service Proxy role services. To manage the Windows token–based agent, you use Internet Information Services (IIS) Manager.

Summary

All these new features in Active Directory will help you in the daily task of securing your environment. The key to making your environment as secure as you can is to understand the technologies we use. But never forget that "secure" is only a word in the dictionary. Nothing is secure forever—only when you first implement it and just before the technology is widely known—because people will try to hack it as soon as it becomes available. We never know what will happen tomorrow—that is why it is so important that we understand the underlying technology and the biggest threat of all: users.

Additional Resources

- Microsoft Corporation (2007). Windows Server 2008 home page, *http://www.microsoft.com/windowsserver2008/default.mspx*.

- Microsoft Corporation (2006, 2007). "New Networking Features in Windows Server 2008 and Windows Vista," at *http://technet.microsoft.com/en-us/library/bb726965.aspx*.

- Microsoft Corporation (2007). "Windows Firewall with Advanced Security - Diagnostics and Troubleshooting," at *http://technet2.microsoft.com/WindowsVista/en/library/9428d113-ade8-4dbe-ac05-6ef10a6dd7a51033.mspx?mfr=true*.

- Microsoft Corporation (2007). Server and Domain Isolation home page, *http://technet.microsoft.com/en-us/network/bb545651.aspx*.

- Microsoft Corporation (2007). Network Access Protection home page, *http://technet.microsoft.com/en-us/network/bb545879.aspx*.

Chapter 10
Implementing Active Directory Certificate Services

— Brian Komar

The goals of this chapter are to enable you to identify new features added to Windows Server 2008 Active Directory, identify threats to Active Directory Certificate Services and the mitigation options to reduce the threats, identify physical security measures for protecting certification authorities, and review best practices for Active Directory Certificate Services deployments.

The installation of Active Directory Certificate Services enables you to configure a Certification Authority (CA) in a Microsoft network that issues digital certificates to users and computers. Active Directory Certificate Services is the core component of the Microsoft Windows 2008 Public Key Infrastructure (PKI).

Active Directory Certificate Services allows for the installation of two types of CAs: *stand-alone CAs* and *enterprise CAs*. A stand-alone CA is typically used for off-line CAs (CAs that are removed from the network to increase security). An enterprise CA is typically used to issue certificates to users, computers, and network devices.

More Info   **Learning More About Certificate Services**

This chapter focuses on securing your Certificate Services deployment. For details on designing your PKI, implementing Certificate Services, designing certificate templates, and deploying certificates for common applications, see *Microsoft Windows Server 2008 PKI and Certificate Security* (Microsoft Press, 2008).

What Is New in Windows Server 2008 PKI

Windows Server 2008 introduces some new features for public key infrastructure, including:

- **Cryptography Next Generation (CNG)**   Cryptography Next Generation is a replacement cryptography API for the original Windows CryptoAPI. The new APIs will allow the use of newer, stronger encryption and signing algorithms when implementing cryptography. The most recognized feature of CNG will be the implementation of Suite B algorithms. Suite B algorithms were announced by the United States National Security Agency (NSA) in 2005 and provide enhanced standards for symmetric encryption, key exchange, digital signatures, and hash algorithms. The algorithms, although publicly known, are considered very secure. These include elliptical curve Diffie-Hellman (ECDH) for key exchange, elliptical curve digital signing (ECDS) for signing information, increased length Shivest Hash Algorithm (SHA) support, and Advanced Encryption Standard (AES) for symmetric encryption.

- **Online Certificate Status Protocol (OCSP)**   Online Certificate Status Protocol allows clients to receive immediate revocation status for a specific certificate. The OCSP client sends the request to an OCSP responder. The OCSP responder, using revocation information retrieved directly from the certification authority (CA), responds with the status of the requested certificate. OCSP provides more up-to-date revocation information than the standard practice of certificate revocation lists (CRLs) and also results in known data traffic patterns because the request and response are known sizes. The Windows Server 2008 OCSP responder works with both Windows CAs and non-Windows CAs.

- **Network Device Enrollment Services (NDES)**   Windows Server 2008 implements Cisco System's Simple Certificate Enrollment Protocol (SCEP) as a standard component of the operating system. Where Windows Server 2003 required add-on software from the Windows Server 2003 Resource Kit, NDES is now available through the Add Roles Wizard. NDES allows network devices that support SCEP to request certificates automatically from a Windows Server 2008 CA without having a computer account in Active Directory.

- **Version 3 Certificate Templates**   Windows Server 2008 takes provides further customization options for certificate templates by introducing version 3 certificate templates. Version 3 certificate templates allow you to implement CNG algorithms within certificates based on the version 3 certificate template. Because of the requirement of CNG algorithms, version 3 certificate templates can only be published at Windows Server 2008 enterprise CAs.

Threats to Certificate Services and Mitigation Options

When you deploy Certificate Services, you need to consider a number of new threats that come along with them, including the following:

- Compromise of a CA's key pair
- Preventing revocation checking
- Attempts to modify the CA configuration
- Attempts to modify a certificate template
- Addition of nontrusted CAs to the trusted root CA store
- Enrollment Agents issuing unauthorized certificates
- Compromise of a CA by a single administrator
- Unauthorized recovery of a user's private key from the CA database

We will start this chapter by discussing each threat in detail and providing you with methods to mitigate these threats.

Compromise of a CA's Key Pair

Each CA in a CA hierarchy has a digital certificate that represents the CA. The certificate has an associated public key and private key. If attackers can gain access to a CA's private key and export the certificate and associated keys, they can build a replica of the CA and issue network-valid certificates. You must protect all the CA's private and public key pairs so that attackers cannot gain access to them.

If you use a software-based cryptographic service provider (CSP), any member of the local Administrators group can export the CA's private key and certificates to a portable file format. This exported private key can then be imported to *any* computer, which can then issue certificates that are trusted on your organization's network. In addition, because the rogue certificates are not known by the *true* CA, they cannot be easily revoked. The only way to recover from such an attack is to invalidate the CA certificate, implement a replacement CA, and reissue all certificates issued by the attacked CA.

You can take the following measures to protect the CAs in your CA hierarchy from these types of attacks:

- Monitor and control the membership of the local Administrators group. By controlling membership in the local Administrators group, you can limit which user accounts can access the CA's private key. In addition, you should monitor the membership to detect whether an unauthorized user has been added.
- Implement Federal Information Processing Standards (FIPS) 140-2 level 2 or level 3 hardware protection of the CA's private keys. A hardware security module (HSM) protects the CA's private key in a dedicated hardware device. The private key material is protected with security tokens that require multiple people to be involved to access the CA's private key.

Preventing Revocation Checking

Certificate-based applications typically validate certificates before using the certificates for authentication, signing, or encryption purposes. One of the validation checks done is determining whether the presented certificate was revoked before its normal expiration date. When a certificate is revoked, the certificate's serial number, the revocation date and time, and a revocation reason are recorded into a certificate revocation list (CRL).

An attacker can prevent such revocation checking from occurring in three ways:

- The attacker can prevent the application from checking for certificate revocation. In this attack, the attacker prevents the application from checking the revocation status of a certificate. For example, Internet Explorer 7.0 has increased security defaults to automatically check the revocation status of an application publisher's certificates and Secure Sockets Layer (SSL)–protected Web sites. As shown in Figure 10-1, you can check for revocation for downloaded applications (check for server certificate revocation) and for revocation of the Web site's certificate (check for server certificate revocation).

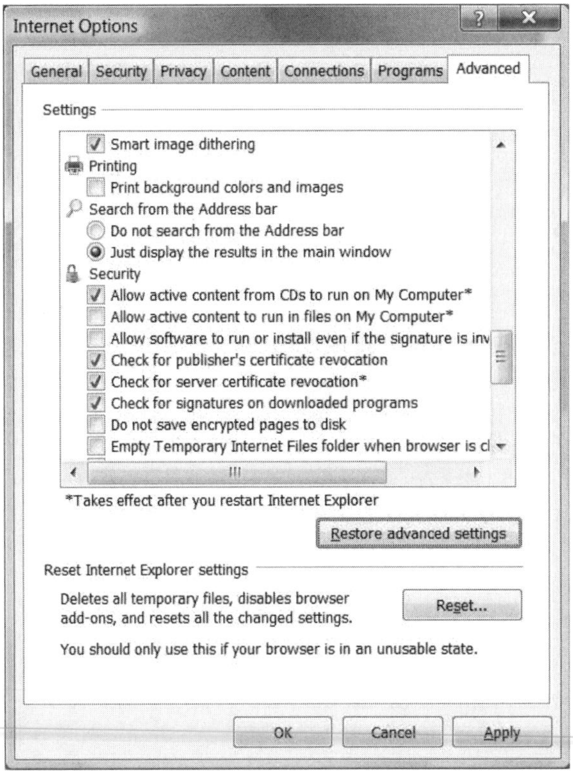

Figure 10-1   Enabling revocation checking in Internet Explorer.

You can prevent this attack by locking down the applications to ensure that they enforce revocation checking. For example, Internet Explorer allows you to enable revocation checking through Group Policy.

You can define a Group Policy object that enables the User Configuration\
Administrative Templates\Windows Components\Internet Explorer\Internet Control
Panel\Advanced Page\Check For Server Certificate Revocation setting to enforce revocation
checking of all Web server certificates. Likewise, you can enable the User Configuration\
Administrative Templates\Windows Components\Internet Explorer\Internet Control
Panel\Advanced Page\Allow Software To Run Or Install Even If The Signature Is Invalid
setting to enforce revocation checking for applications.

- An attacker can prevent access to the servers hosting the CRLs or CA certificates. If an
  application does not have cached, time-valid versions of the CRL or CA certificates, the
  application will attempt to download an updated version based on the following:

  - Authority Information Access (AIA) URLs, which allow the download of an updated
    CA certificate if a CA certificate is renewed or has not been downloaded to the client.

  - Certificate Revocation Lists (CRLs), which allow the download of updated base
    CRLs or delta CRLs (a truncated list that only includes certificates revoked since
    the last base CRL was published).

Note   Revocation checking involves checking the client or server certificate and every CA
certificate in the certificate chain. If any certificate in the chain fails the revocation check, the
client or server certificate is considered revoked. If any CRL is unavailable, the certificate is considered untrustworthy. The application will typically respond with a message that the revocation status cannot be determined.

- An attacker can prevent access to the server cluster acting as an Online Certificate Status
  Protocol (OCSP) responder. OCSP is a protocol used to query an OCSP responder
  regarding the certificate status of a single certificate represented by the certificate's serial
  number. The OCSP responder responds with one of three messages: OK, Revoked, or
  Cannot Determine Revocation Status. If the OCSP client cannot communicate with the
  OCSP responder, the application will consider the certificate revoked, with the revocation reason of Cannot Determine Certificate Revocation Status.

Direct from the Source: Watch Out for HTTP URLs on Multiple Servers

Be careful when you host CA certificates or CRLs on multiple servers. The batch file that
pushes the CA certificate and CRLs to the host Web server must ensure that the CA certificate or CRL is copied to *all* servers in the cluster or server group. If the CA certificate
or CRL is only available on some of the nodes in the cluster, a subset of the clients will
receive revocation-checking errors. The clients that are connecting to the node with
either an expired or nonexistent CA certificate or CRL will fail any revocation checks,
perhaps preventing execution of the application.

> Around 80 percent of PSS support calls regarding certificate usage are due to incorrectly published CA certificate and CRL information.
>
> *Seth Scruggs, PSS Support Engineer*

The best way to prevent revocation checking attacks is to ensure that revocation checking publication points are accessible by all users at all times. The certificate-chaining engine must have access to the CRL and CA certificate for each CA in the certificate chain or to the OCSP responder for each CA in the chain if using OCSP for revocation checking. If any CA in the certificate chain's CRL, CA certificate, or OCSP responder is not available, the chaining engine will prevent that certificate from being used if certificate revocation is enabled. You can ensure that the clients can contact the CRL distribution point or OCSP responder by hosting the URLs on clustered servers or load-balancing clusters with very high availability.

When you define the CDP and AIA URLs, ensure that you order the URLs so that the majority of applications performing revocation checking can access the primary URL. In Figure 10-2, the URLs are ordered so that an HTTP URL is the primary URL and LDAP is the secondary URL. This ordering allows non-Windows computers to access the CRL or CA certificate from the primary URL without having to resort to the secondary URL.

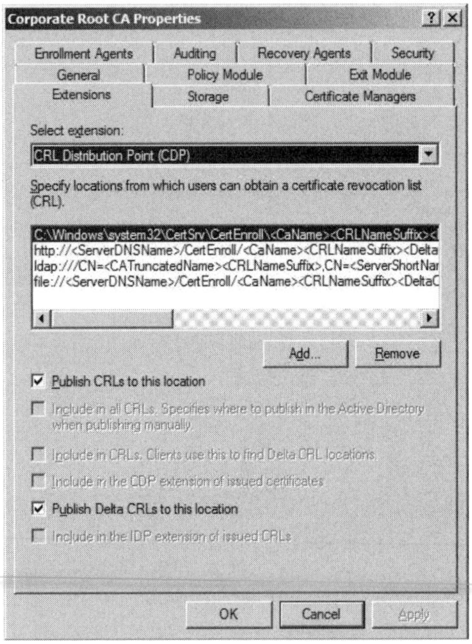

Figure 10-2   URL ordering is very important for the CDP and AIA extensions.

If you implement OCSP for revocation checking, you must ensure that the OCSP responder is available for all revocation checking. You can implement Network Load Balancing to ensure that the OCSP responder is highly available.

Attempts to Modify the CA Configuration

If an attacker can gain local administrator access to the computer running Active Directory Certificate Services, the attacker can modify the CA configuration. This modification can include altering URLs for CRL publication, revoking legitimate certificates, and issuing certificates to nonvalid computers or users.

You can protect against change to the CA configuration by restricting membership in CA management groups. The configuration changes are stored as registry entries. Only members of the local Administrators group and groups assigned the Manage CA permission at the CA can make CA configuration changes. The catch is that a member of the Administrators group *can* make changes to the CA configuration. To detect *who* made an authorized or unauthorized change to the CA configuration, ensure that you enable auditing at the CA. Windows Server 2008 allows you to define which management actions are included in the CA's Security log. To ensure that all events related to Active Directory Certificate Services auditing are logged to the Security log, enable both success and failure events for Object Access at the CA. The settings can be applied directly in the Local Security Policy console or by applying a Group Policy Object (GPO) with the required auditing settings.

Once you have enabled object access auditing, you can enable specific audit settings in the Certification Authority console. As shown in Figure 10-3, you can enable the following auditing options on the Auditing tab of the CA Properties dialog box.

- **Back Up And Restore The CA Database** Logs any attempts to back up or restore the CA database to the Windows Security log.

- **Change CA Configuration** Logs any attempts to modify CA configuration, including defining Authority Information Access (AIA) and CRL distribution point (CDP) URLs or a Key Recovery Agent.

- **Change CA Security Settings** Logs any attempts to modify CA permissions, including adding CA administrators or certificate managers.

- **Issue And Manage Certificate Requests** Logs any attempts by a certificate manager to approve or deny certificate requests that are pending subject approval.

- **Revoke Certificates And Publish CRLs** Logs any attempts by a certificate manager to revoke an issued certificate or by a CA administrator to publish an updated CRL.

- **Store And Retrieve Archived Keys** Logs any attempts during the enrollment process to archive private keys in the CA database or attempts by certificate managers to extract archived private keys from the CA database.

■ **Start And Stop Active Directory Certificate Services**   Logs any attempts by the CA administrator to start or stop Certificate Services.

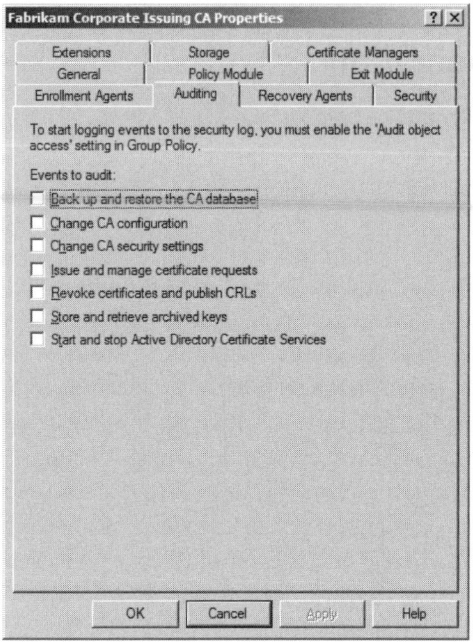

Figure 10-3   Available CA Audit Options for a Windows Server 2008 CA.

Attempts to Modify Certificate Templates

Certificate templates are best described as blueprints for the certificates issued by a Windows Server 2008 enterprise CA. If attackers gain Enterprise Admin-level access—or forest root Domain Admin-level access—they can modify certificate template properties in the CN=Certificate Templates,CN=Public Key Services,CN=Services,CN=Configuration, *ForestName* container, where *ForestName* is the Lightweight Directory Access Protocol (LDAP) distinguished name of the forest root domain. The extent of the changes that an attacker can perform is subject to the type of certificate template they modify:

■ For version 1 certificate templates, the only change an attacker can make is to modify permissions for the individual certificate templates. Modifying permissions enables the attacker to enroll a certificate that provides excess permissions (such as an Enrollment Agent certificate), thereby permitting the attacker to request additional certificates on behalf of other users.

■ Version 2 or version 3 certificate templates published on enterprise CAs running on Windows Server 2008, Enterprise Edition, or Datacenter Edition, provide an attacker with many more misconfiguration opportunities. Modifications can include changing the entire purpose of the certificate, application policies, key archival requirements, validity periods, and subject name format. For example, an attacker can change the purpose of the certificate template to enable key archival if the certificate template is an encryption-enabled certificate template.

> **Note** For more information on the role of certificate templates in a Microsoft Windows network, please see the white paper "Implementing and Administering Certificate Templates in Windows Server 2008," available at *http://go.microsoft.com/fwlink/?LinkID=92522*.

Periodically, you should review the certificate template definitions for the certificate templates you deploy in your forest. Ensure that the settings match your design. Pay special attention to permission assignments to ensure that unauthorized users are not assigned Read and Enroll permissions to a certificate template. For example, an attacker may try to gain access to a certificate with special privileges, such as an Enrollment Agent certificate. The Enrollment Agent certificate allows the holder to request the certificate on behalf of another user. When an attacker has an Enrollment Agent certificate, he could request a certificate for *any* user in the forest without needing to know the user's account or password.

Addition of Nontrusted CAs to the Trusted Root CA Store

If attackers can add a nontrusted CA certificate to the trusted root store, all certificates that chain to that trusted root CA certificate are considered trusted. A certificate that chains to a trusted root CA certificate is trusted for any and all purposes. A trusting partner would trust such a certificate the same way that partner would trust one issued by a legitimate CA in the same hierarchy.

Alternatively, an attacker might try to create a certificate trust list (CTL)—a list of CA certificates that are not issued by your company's CA hierarchy but are trusted for specific purposes and periods of time—so that she can use a certificate issued by a foreign, nontrusted CA on your network. When an unsuspecting client loads the Certificate Trust List, he will trust the attacker's certificate.

By default, Windows Vista and Windows Server 2008 provide the following mechanisms to protect against the installation of rogue root CA certificates:

- **User Account Control (UAC)** Only members of the local Administrators group can add root CA certificate to the computer's trusted root store. If the attacker places a link to his rogue root certificate, UAC would warn the client that administrative privilege is required to install the root certificate.

- **Trusted Root Group Policy** Group Policy allows you to define rules for the addition of root CA certificates. As shown in Figure 10-4, you can define whether a user-added root certificate can be used to validate certificates. You can also define whether the client can trust peer trust certificates (CTLs), and whether the client computers will trust both commercial and enterprise root CAs or enterprise root CAs only.

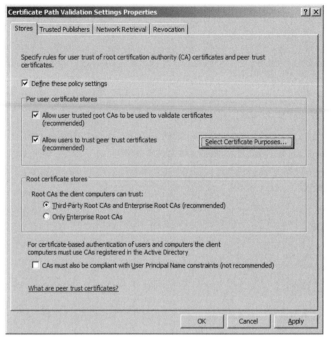

Figure 10-4   Defining root trust GPO settings.

Enrollment Agents Issuing Unauthorized Certificates

In previous versions of Windows, the enrollment agent role was able to issue smart card certificates for *any* user in Active Directory. Many organizations considered this a security issue because an enrollment agent could issue a smart card for a privileged account, such as a member of Enterprise Admins, and then act in that role. In essence, a user who was an enrollment agent was as trusted and sensitive as any other user in the domain.

In Windows Server 2008, an enterprise CA running on Windows Server 2008, Enterprise Edition, or Windows Server 2008, Datacenter Edition, allows you to enforce restrictions on enrollment agents. Restrictions prevent an enrollment agent from issuing smart cards to unauthorized users.

As shown in Figure 10-5, you can now restrict enrollment agents in two ways:

■ You can first limit enrollment agents to requesting certificates based on a predefined list of certificate templates. Event if the enrollment agent has been mistakenly assigned Read and Enroll permissions for additional certificate templates, the enrollment agent is restricted to the list on the Enrollment Agents tab. In both screenshots shown in Figure 10-5, the West RAs group is restricted to only enrolling smart card certificates based on the Federal Bridge Signing and the Corporate Smart Card Logon certificate templates.

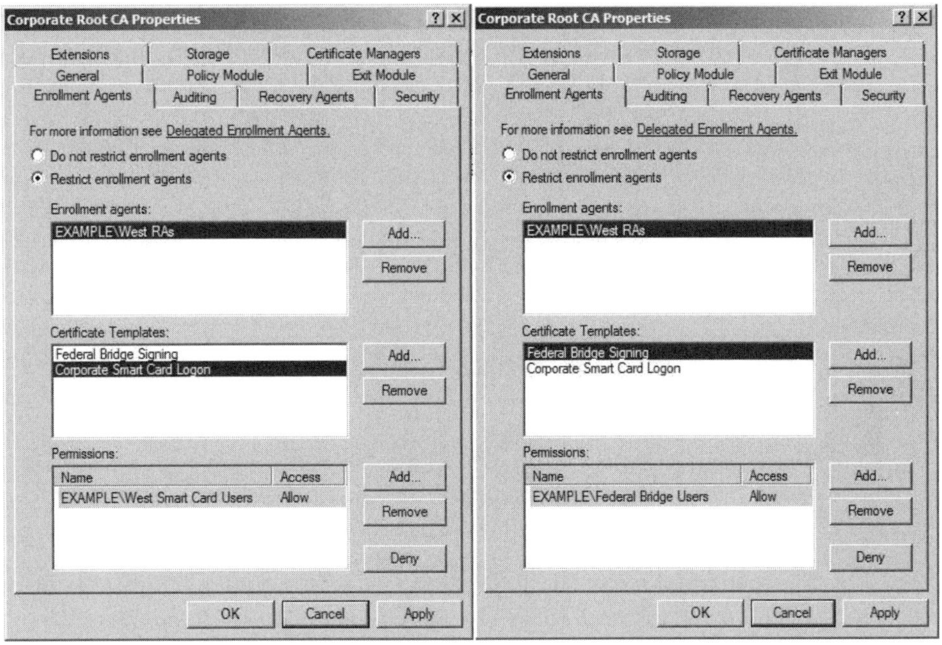

Figure 10-5   Restricting enrollment agents.

- You can further limit *which* groups can be the targets for smart card enrollment by certificate template. In Figure 10-5, the left-hand version of the dialog box shows that the West RAs group can only request certificates based on the Corporate Smart Card Logon certificate template for members of the West Smart Card Users group. Likewise, the right-hand version of the dialog box shows that the West RAs group can only request certificates based on the Federal Bridge Signing certificate template for members of the Federal Bridge Users group.

> **Tip**   You don't have to list all certificate templates to allow a specific enrollment agent group to request certificates for all certificate template or for all users. You can choose <All> certificate templates and Everyone for the target users. In addition, you can add explicit Deny permissions to prevent issuance to a specific group or specific certificate template.

Compromise of a CA by a Single Administrator

By default, Windows Server 2008 grants the built-in Administrators group permissions and user rights to perform all administrative tasks. If the computer hosting Certificate Services is a stand-alone computer, the permissions are assigned to the local Administrators group. If the computer is a member of a domain, the permissions are also assigned to the Enterprise Admins and forest root domain's Domain Admins groups.

Assigning all management permissions to a single account or group enables any member of the administrative groups to perform *any* management function, without oversight by other administrators. It's possible that a rogue administrator could make changes to the CA configuration, revoke a mass quantity of certificates, delete the Audit log to cover up her tracks, or perform a backup of the CA's private key and database to build a duplicate of the CA.

You can reduce your exposure to the thread of a single rogue administrator by following the recommendations in "*Certificate Issuing and Management Components (CIMC) Family of Protection Profiles,*" a standards document by the National Institute of Standards and Technology (NIST). The document defines requirements for the issuance, revocation, and management of X.509 certificates.

> **Note**   The CIMC protection profiles are often referred to as Common Criteria guidelines.

The Windows Server 2008 PKI follows the recommendations in the standards document, allowing an organization to deploy a PKI that meets the Security Level 4 protection profile. The Security Level 4 profile defines four PKI management roles:

- **CA Administrator**   This role is responsible for account administration and key generation of the CA certificate's key pair. A member of this role can modify the configuration of the CA. To assign this role, assign the user or group the Manage CA permissions in the Certification Authority console.

- **Certificate Manager**   This role is responsible for certificate management. Management functions include issuing and revoking certificates and extracting private key blobs from the CA database during key recovery operations. To assign this role, assign the user or group the Issue and Manage Certificates permission in the Certification Authority console.

- **Auditor**   This role is responsible for maintaining and configuring CA audit logs. To assign this role, assign the user or group the Manage auditing and security log user right in either the Local Security Policy or in a GPO linked to the OU where the CA computer account exists.

- **Backup operator**   This role is responsible for performing backups of PKI information. To assign this role, assign the user or group the Backup files and directories user right in either the Local Security Policy or in a GPO linked to the OU where the CA computer account exists.

Windows Server 2008, Enterprise Edition, and Windows Server 2008, Datacenter Edition, enable you to enforce Common Criteria role separation so that a single person cannot hold multiple Common Criteria roles. A user can hold only one of the CA administrator, certificate manager, auditor, or backup operator roles. Assignment of two or more of these roles results in the user being blocked from *all* certificate management actions.

By default, members of the Enterprise Admins, forest root Domain Admins, and local Administrators group on the CA are blocked from PKI management if you enable role

separation. The block occurs because these groups hold both the Auditor and Backup operator roles through default permission assignments.

> **Note**   Common Criteria role separation enforcement is enabled by a local Administrator run-
> ning **certutil –setreg CA\RoleSeparationEnabled 1** at the command prompt and then
> restarting Certificate Services. Remember that any user who is assigned two or more certificate
> administrative roles will be blocked from all CA management activities from that point
> forward, unless you disable the enforcement of Common Criteria role separation by running
> **certutil –delreg CA\RoleSeparationEnabled** and then restarting Certificate Services.

Unauthorized Recovery of a User's Private Key from the CA Database

Windows Server 2008 provides the ability to archive, or escrow, the private key associated
with a user's encryption certificates if the CA is running on Windows Server 2008, Enterprise
Edition, or Windows Server 2008, Datacenter Edition. An attacker could acquire any user's
certificate and private key from the CA database if the attacker is both a local administrator
and an existing Key Recovery Agent at the CA computer where the user's private key
is archived.

If the attacker gains access to the user's private key, the attacker can decrypt any information
protected with the recovered certificate. In addition, if the certificate enables signing, the
attacker can impersonate the user the user for digital signing operations.

You can prevent this attack by separating certificate managers from key recovery agents.
Doing this has the following result:

- The Certificate Manager role holder determines who the Key Recovery Agent is for the
  archived private key and extracts an encrypted PKCS#7 blob file from the CA database.
  Only the certificate manager role holder can perform this extraction of the blob file.

- The Key Recovery Agent role holder can decrypt the encrypted blob file with the Key
  Recovery Agent certificate's private key. Only the Key Recovery Agent has access to the
  private key that can decrypt the encrypted blob file.

An administrator cannot make herself a Key Recovery Agent for existing escrowed certificates.
The Key Recovery Agent is designated at the time the private key is archived. As long as the
private key is protected (such as by storing the private key on a smart card), an administrator
cannot gain access to the private key.

Securing Certificate Services

To further prevent the likelihood of the different types of threats described previously, you can
take the following measures:

- Implement physical security measures.
- Implement logical security measures.

Implementing Physical Security Measures

Physical security measures prevent attackers from gaining physical access to the computer running Active Directory Certificate Services. When an attacker gains physical access to a computer, any number of attacks can take place. Physical security measures can include the following:

- Use off-line CAs. By creating a three-tier hierarchy, the root CA and second-level CAs (also referred to as *policy CAs*) can be off-line CAs that are not accessible remotely or even turned on. With a two-tier hierarchy, only the root CA can be an off-line CA. An off-line CA is removed from the network and is turned on only to issue new subordinate CA certificates, renew subordinate CA certificates, and to publish updated CRLs. Even during these operations, it is not connected to the network and does not need to leave its secure storage location. The certificates and CRLs can be hand-carried to the place where they will be deployed.

- Store off-line CAs in physically secure locations, such as vaults, safes, or secured server rooms, based on your company's security policy.

- Deploy hardware-based key modules, such as hardware security modules (HSMs), for the generation and protection of the CA key pair and for the signing of all issued certificates and CRLs. HSMs enable you to implement split key management, where a quorum of key holders must be present to activate and use an off-line CA's private key. For example, you can designate that any attempts to access a root CA's private key require the presentation of 4 tokens from a total pool of 11 tokens, each held by a separate physical person.

- Implement BitLocker Drive Encryption (BDE) to protect the root CA's hard drive in the event that the hard drive is removed from the CA computer for an attempted off-line attack. BitLocker also prevents access to the local computer if the person at the console cannot provide the Trusted Platform Module (TPM) password or BDE recovery key on a USB token.

> **Warning**   When you implement BDE on an off-line CA, you cannot store the recovery key in Active Directory because the computer account is not a member of a domain. Be sure to store multiple copies of the recovery key to multiple USB tokens and to store the recovery keys in a safe location.

- Disable hardware in the CA computer's BIOS. If you want to prevent the attachment of the CA computer to the network, you can disable the network cards in the server's BIOS and implement BDE with a TPM password to prevent unauthorized console access to the CA. In addition, you can consider disabling USB ports and other devices to prevent data from being copied from the CA computer's hard disk.

Warning   It really is not advisable to consider BIOS startup passwords as a method of securing the off-line CA. BIOS start-up passwords can be reset to a blank password in some systems by shorting out the battery on the motherboard of the computer. A better option is to implement BDE to protect unauthorized console access.

- Implement Syskey level 2 or level 3 security to restrict the booting of an offline CA. Syskey level 2 requires that a password be entered before the local accounts database is accessed, allowing the offline CA computer to start. The Syskey level 3 setting increases security by requiring that a floppy disk containing the Syskey password be inserted to boot the computer.

Warning   If you implement Syskey level 2 or level 3 security and either forget the password or lose access to the password on the Syskey disk, you lose all access to the off-line CA computer. Ensure that the password is recorded in a secure location or that copies of the Syskey disk are maintained to protect against this type of failure.

Best Practices

The following best practices should be followed when security Active Directory Certificate Services:

- **Increase the security of root CA computers**   You can do this by deploying off-line CAs and, if possible, by deploying off-line policy CAs, depending on your company's security policy.

- **Implement a hardware security module**   You should do this only if your company's security policy or organizations that you want to exchange certificates with require strong protection of CA key pairs.

- **Ensure that CRLs and CA certificates are published to accessible locations**   The certificate-chaining engine must have access to all CRLs and CA certificates in the certificate chain to validate a presented certificate. If any certificate or CRL is unavailable, its status cannot be determined.

- **Ensure that OCSP Responders are highly available**   If you implement OCSP, you must ensure that the OCSP responder is not just available to both internal and external users, but *highly* available. You can implement Windows Load Balancing Services to ensure that the OCSP responder can still respond to OCSP requests in the event that a single node in the cluster fails.

- **Enable CRL checking in all applications**   CRL checking ensures that a presented certificate passes validation tests for approval. If the certificate fails any tests, it is considered invalid.

- **Apply the latest service packs and security updates to CAs**   This way, you ensure that the CA is protected against known vulnerabilities.

- **Separate the certificate manager and Key Recovery Agent roles**   If a person holds both roles, it is possible for that single user to extract an encrypted private key from a Windows Server 2003 CA and decrypt the private key for his own use. Separating the roles ensures that two people must be involved in the recovery process.

- **Implement role separation**   By following Common Criteria guidelines, your organization can ensure that one person does not hold all PKI management roles. Implementing role separation enables oversight of the PKI management process to ensure that one person cannot perform all management functions. If your security policy requires it, enforce role separation to block any person from PKI management tasks if they hold two or more Common Criteria roles.

- **Enable all audit options in a Windows Server 2008 CA**   Enabling all auditing options ensures that all modifications to the PKI are captured in each CA's Security Event log.

- **Enable enrollment agent restrictions**   Ensure that an enrollment agent only requests certificates for authorized users by enabling enrollment agent restrictions. You can limit the enrollment agent to a specific certificate template and to request certificates for specific security groups.

Summary

When designing your security strategy for Active Directory Certificate Services, ensure that you identify all threats that are relevant to your deployment. For each threat, ensure that you take measures to mitigate the threats, yet deliver the functionality that you need from Certificate Services.

In addition to mitigating threats, ensure that you provide good physical security for your CAs:

- Off-line CAs should be removed from the network at all times and stored in physically secured locations.

- Online CAs should be provided the same physical security as domain controllers.

Finally, ensure that you follow best practices for CA deployment.

Additional Resources

- *Microsoft Windows Server 2008 PKI and Certificate Security* by Brian Komar (Microsoft Press, 2008) (*http://www.microsoft.com/MSPress/books/9549.aspx*).

- Microsoft Official Curriculum course 2821: Designing and Managing a Windows Public Key Infrastructure (*http://www.microsoft.com/learning/syllabi/en-us/2821Afinal.mspx*).

- *Microsoft Windows Server 2003 PKI and Certificate Security* by Brian Komar with the Microsoft PKI Team (Microsoft Press, 2004) (*http://www.microsoft.com/MSPress/books/6745.aspx*).

- Windows Server 2008 Security Guide at *https://www.microsoft.com/downloads/details.aspx?familyid=FB8B981F-227C-4AF6-A44B-B115696A80AC&displaylang=en*.

- *Security Watch–PKI Enhancements in Windows* by John Morello at *http://www.microsoft.com/technet/technetmag/issues/2007/08/SecurityWatch/*.

- The white paper "Best Practices for Implementing a Microsoft Windows Server 2003 Public Key Infrastructure," at *http://www.microsoft.com/technet/prodtechnol/windowsserver2003/technologies/security/ws3pkibp.mspx*.

- The white paper "Windows Server Active Directory Certificate Services Step-by-Step Guide," at *http://go.microsoft.com/fwlink/?LinkID=85472*.

- The white paper "Key Archival and Recovery in Windows Server 2008," at *http://go.microsoft.com/fwlink/?LinkID=92523*.

- The white paper "Troubleshooting Certificate Status and Revocation," at *http://technet.microsoft.com/en-us/library/bb457027.aspx*.

- "Certificate Issuing and Management Components Family of Protection Profiles," at *http://www.commoncriteriaportal.org/public/files/ppfiles/PP_CIMCPP_SL1-4_V1.0.pdf*.

- "Installing, Configuring, and Troubleshooting Microsoft Online Responder," at *http://technet2.microsoft.com/windowsserver2008/en/servermanager/activedirectorycertificateservices.mspx*.

- nCipher HSMs (*http://www.ncipher.com/cryptographic_hardware/hardware_security_modules/*).

- SafeNet HSMs (*http://www.safenet-inc.com/products/pki/index.asp*).

- Knowledge Base article 281271, "Windows 2000 Certification Authority Configuration to Publish Certificates in Active Directory of Trusted Domain," at *http://support.microsoft.com/kb/281271*.

- "Certificate-Related Changes for Vista," at *http://technet2.microsoft.com/WindowsVista/en/library/73bdca07-a9f0-40d7-a26e-6f4f11759e4c1033.mspx?mfr=true*.

Part III
Common Security Scenarios

Chapter 11
Securing Server Roles

– Jesper M. Johansson

It should be relatively obvious that every server fulfills some kind of role. Some are Web servers. Some are file servers. Others are domain controllers (DCs) or infrastructure servers, such as Domain Name System (DNS) and the Dynamic Host Configuration Protocol (DHCP). Then, of course, there is the DC/File Server/Web Server/Application Server/Firewall/DHCP/ DNS server, also known as "the server" in a small business. (For more on that, see Chapter 15, "Small Business Considerations.") But, none of them are anything until you deploy one or more roles to them.

Because every server is not made equal, it stands to reason that the same configuration is not optimal for every server. This seems rather obvious if one considers the fact that to meet the needs of each role, the server must have certain software installed and settings made. As soon as you install new software on a server you modify how that server operates, and that means you need to reanalyze how that server is secured. This is discussed at length in Chapter 13, "Securing the Network."

In spite of the logic in the argument that servers must be secured in accordance with their roles, the appearance of tools and documentation that really support doing so is relatively recent. The first tool dedicated to this was the Security Configuration Wizard (SCW), which first shipped in Windows Server 2003 Service Pack 1 in 2005. In this chapter we will discuss the concept of role-based security, the tools you use to manage server roles in Windows Server 2008, and the ultimate roles-based server: Server Core. Before we do that, however, we will start with some crucial terminology.

Roles vs. Features

Windows Server 2008 is entirely roles-based in how you manage it. There is no longer a concept of installing many separate and unrelated components the way there was in older server operating systems. In Windows Server 2008 you decide what role you wish your server to play and the Server Manager tool provisions it with the necessary software to do that.

Microsoft distinguishes between roles and features. A *role* is a collection of software that collectively enables the server to provide some service to the network. Generally, a role is what you bought the server for. An example of a role is "Domain Controller" or "Application Server" (such as a Web server with application frameworks). Often a role can be installed in one step, but may require significant configuration to function the way you want it to. For instance, you can easily promote a server to become a Domain Controller but unless you add user and computer accounts to it, having a DC does not do much good.

Features, on the other hand, are simpler. They are things that many servers need, and that there is a good reason to have, but that you may not consider as the primary reason you bought the server. They do not *describe* the server in the way roles do. In some cases, features involve no services at all, as is the case with the Recovery Disk feature, which is just a tool. Other features do have services associated with them. In many cases, a feature is simply a way to surface the installation of a service to an administrator. Many of the things you saw under the Programs And Features Control Panel in Windows Vista are listed as features in Windows Server 2008. In some cases, the distinction between roles and features is quite unclear. For example, Dynamic Host Configuration Protocol (DHCP) and Domain Name Service (DNS) are both roles, but Windows Internet Name Service (WINS) is a feature. WINS keeps track of DHCP-assigned Internet Protocol (IP) addresses and provides the same services for legacy Windows networks that DNS provides for up-level ones. As you go through the features, you will find that some optional components slated for deprecation are listed as features. This is now the only way to install them.

Some roles require certain features to work. For instance, the Active Directory Rights Management Services (AD RMS) role requires the Windows Internal Database feature (Microsoft SQL Server 2005 Embedded Edition). Likewise, some features may require other features, as is the case with Windows System Resource Manager (WSRM), which also requires the Windows Internal Database.

In many cases, the links between features and roles are quite intricate. For example, consider the case of an Application Server. If you attempt to install that role on a freshly laid down server you are asked to install two features—.NET Framework 3.0 Features and Windows Process Activation—as shown in Figure 11-1.

Unless you specifically modify the default selections you will get all the roles and features installed that are needed for the essential services of the particular role, along with the basic feature support. You can uncheck things you do not want, but if you uncheck something that you must have, the system will inform you that you cannot install the role in that case.

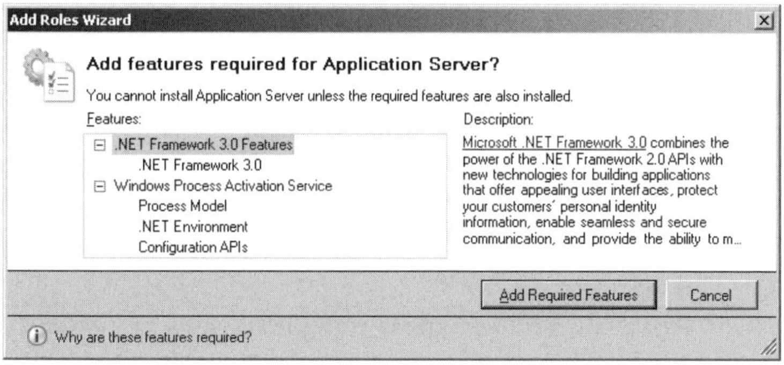

Figure 11-1   When you install a role or a feature, the Add Roles Wizard also prompts you to install all the roles and features it depends on.

Default Roles and Features

A clean installed server has no roles or features installed by default. There are a total of 16 roles in the Standard, Enterprise, and Datacenter editions; 34 features in the Standard edition; and 35 features in the Enterprise and Datacenter Editions. Table 11-1 shows all of the roles; Table 11-2 shows all of the features.

Table 11-1   Roles Included in Windows Server 2008

Role Name	Description	Role Dependencies
Active Directory Certificate Services (AD CS)	Used to create certificate authorities. This used to be called Microsoft Certificate Services. It is discussed in depth in Chapter 10, "Implementing Active Directory Certificate Services."	None.
Active Directory Domain Services (AD DS)	This role promotes the server to a DC. In addition to running dcpromo.exe manually, as in prior versions, you install this role. This role is discussed in depth in Chapter 9, "Designing Active Directory Domain Services for Security."	None, but a DNS server somewhere in the network is required.
Active Directory Federation Services (AD FS)	A federation service to provide single-sign-on to multiple Web applications for the life of a single session.	None, but certain components of AD FS must run on separate computers. In addition, AD DS and AD LDS are required in the network.
Active Directory Lightweight Directory Services (AD LDS)	An LDAP provider for organizations that want to use Microsoft's LDAP services without Active Directory.	None.

Table 11-1 Roles Included in Windows Server 2008

Role Name	Description	Role Dependencies
Active Directory Rights Management Services (AD RMS)	A service that permits users to incorporate usage policy statements into data they share with other users to restrict what users can do with the data. For instance, a user may create a Microsoft Office Word document and apply a policy onto it that permits others only read permission, but denies them edit, save, and print abilities. AD RMS handles the authentication portion of the policy enforcement.	Computer must be domain-joined.
Application Server	Provides access to programs written using an application framework. It is typically not used by itself but rather in conjunction with the Web Server role.	.NET Framework 3.0 Feature and Windows Process Activation Service feature.
	Note that although the Application Server role requires the Windows Process Activation Service feature, that feature is essentially disabled within the Web server unless you chose to enable it.	The Web Server role is required if you install the Web Server (IIS) support. The Web Server, .NET Framework 3.0 Features, and Message Queuing features are required for Windows Process Activation Service support.
DHCP Server	Provides DHCP (dynamic IP address assignment) to computers throughout a network.	None.
DNS Server	Provides host name-to-IP address name resolution services throughout a network.	None.
Fax Server	Provides centralized fax services to a network.	Print Services.
File Services	Adds additional file server services such as the Distributed File System (DFS), the shared folder management tools, and Network File System (NFS) for Unix-based clients. Note that basic Windows file sharing services are provided by default and do not require installation of this role. In other words, if you do not install this role but manually create a share, your computer will automatically consider this role to be installed and will open the firewall to permit Server Message Block (SMB) protocol traffic.	None.

Table 11-1   Roles Included in Windows Server 2008

Role Name	Description	Role Dependencies
Network Policy and Access Services	This role provides the collection of services related to remote network access. It includes Microsoft's VPN server as well as Microsoft's Network Access Protection (NAP) service, which provides policy enforcement on network connections.	Requires the Web Server role if the Health Registration Authority or Host Credential Authorization Protocol role services are installed.
Print Services	Provides advanced printer management services. By default, this role includes only the Print Management snap-in. It can also be used to provide additional print services to Unix-based computers and to clients on the Internet. Note that this role is not required to print from this computer, nor is it required to share printers on the network or access shared printers. Those functions are supported by default.	Requires the Web Server role if the Internet Printing role service is installed.
Terminal Services	Creates a terminal services application server that users can use to run programs on. Note that with Windows Server 2008 you must enable this role, even for administrative terminal services.	Requires the Web Server role if the TS Gateway or TS Web Access role services are installed. The TS Gateway role service also requires the Network Policy and Access Services role and the RPC over HTTP Proxy feature.
UDDI Services	Universal Description, Discovery, and Integration (UDDI) services is a technology for discovering and accessing information about Web services.	Requires Windows Internal Database if the UDDI Services Database is installed on this computer. Also requires the Web Server role if the UDDI Web Services Application is installed.
Web Server (IIS)	By default, if no configuration options are made during installation of the role, IIS 7.0 provides only static HTML support. See Chapter 16, "Securing Server Applications," for details on IIS.	None.
Windows Deployment Services (WDS)	WDS is Microsoft's latest technology to remotely deploy the operating system to computers over the network.	None.

Table 11-2   Features Included in Windows Server 2008

Feature Name	Description	Role Dependencies
.NET Framework 3.0 Features	A collection of subfeatures that collectively support the .NET Framework 3.0 application framework.	Web Server and Windows Process Activation Service are required only if the WCF Activation Feature Service is selected.
BitLocker Drive Encryption	BitLocker provides full hard disk encryption. It is discussed in depth in Chapter 14, "Securing the Branch Office."	None.
BITS Server Extensions	BITS Server Extensions allows a server to receive files via the Background Intelligent Transfer Service (BITS), an asynchronous file transfer service designed to efficiently transfer files without interfering with normal network traffic.	Web Server and Windows Process Activation Service.
Connection Manager Administration Kit (CMAK)	The CMAK allows an administrator to build automated connection profiles for connection to a Microsoft VPN server.	None.
Desktop Experience	Makes Windows Server 2008 look and feel like Windows Vista. It includes the themes, Windows Media Player, and Windows Photo Gallery. This feature should not be installed on any production server.	None.
Failover Clustering (Enterprise and Datacenter editions only)	Provides clustering services to cluster-aware applications.	None.
Group Policy Management	Installs the Group Policy Management Console (GPMC).	None.
Internet Printing Client	Installs a print client to enable the server to print to print servers using the Internet Printing Protocol (IPP).	None.
Internet Storage Name Server	Provides discovery services for iSCSI storage area network (SAN).	None.
LPR Port Monitor	Printer client for Unix-style Line Printer Daemon (LPD) print servers.	None.
Message Queuing	Provides message delivery services with secure, prioritized, and guaranteed delivery even if the recipient service is offline at the time.	Requires Web Server and Windows Process Activation Service if HTTP support is installed. Some services are only supported in domain environments or on a DC, such as the Routing Service and Windows 2000 Client Support.

Table 11-2   **Features Included in Windows Server 2008**

Feature Name	Description	Role Dependencies
Multipath I/O	Provides support for multiple input/output (I/O) channels to the same device. This is used primarily on high-throughput storage servers.	None.
Network Load Balancing	Provides load-balancing services for Windows. Used in front of server clusters.	None.
Peer Name Resolution Protocol	Allows peer-to-peer applications to register and resolve names for easier discovery of applications.	None.
Quality Windows Audio Video Experience	Provides Quality of Service (QoS) services for streaming audio and video over IP networks. Primarily used for home networks; on Server platforms qWAVE provides only rate-of-flow and prioritization services.	None.
Remote Assistance	Remote Assistance is used to provide interactive technical support. The Remote Assistance feature provides functionality for both the user requesting support and the person providing it.	None.
Remote Differential Compression	Used to transfer only deltas of files across a network.	None.
Remote Server Administration Tools	A collection of tools for managing other servers remotely. Remote Server Administration Tools include support for managing most roles and six features without installing the related role or feature. These tools are also available for download on download.microsoft.com so that you can install them on Windows Vista.	Dependencies differ depending on which roles and features you want to support. The Web Server (IIS) Tools require the Windows Process Activation Service feature. The BITS Server Extension Tools require the Web Server role and Windows Process Activation Service feature. The SMTP Server Tools require the Web Server role.
Removable Storage Manager	Manages and catalogs removable media and operates automated removable media devices.	None.
RPC over HTTP proxy	Supports the ability to tunnel Remote Procedure Call (RPC) connections through Hypertext Transport Protocol (HTTP) and HTTPS connections. This feature is used, for example, to provide Outlook Anywhere access, enabling users of Microsoft Office Outlook to work against a Microsoft Exchange Server from anywhere on the Internet. Although this may sound like a security problem, done properly it can significantly enhance network security.	Web Server role and Windows Process Activation Service feature.

Table 11-2   Features Included in Windows Server 2008

Feature Name	Description	Role Dependencies
	The vast majority of VPN connections are used almost exclusively for e-mail access, yet they provide the user with complete access to the corporate network. By exposing only RPC over HTTP and enabling users to connect using Microsoft Outlook, the organization eliminates the need for many of these VPN connections, significantly reducing the risk that malware will enter the organizational network over a VPN connection.	
Simple TCP/IP services	Originally designed to troubleshoot TCP/IP connections in the days when those were very unreliable, today the Simple TCP/IP services have no place in a network. The services include a character generator, daytime, discard (a service that takes any input and simply ignores it), echo, and quote of the day. If these services are installed, an attacker can very simply disable all network operations on a host by piping output from the character generator into the echo service.	None.
SMTP Server	Provides mail transport services and relays.	Web Server role and Remote Server Administration Tools.
SNMP Services	Simple Network Management Protocol (SNMP) is a very commonly used protocol to monitor and aggregate monitoring information from network devices.	None.
Storage Manager for SANs	Management tool for SANs.	None.
Subsystem for Unix-based Applications (SUA)	Includes a POSIX subsystem. A set of Unix tools, including a bash shell, are available for download from Microsoft.	None.
Telnet Client	A Telnet client for remote command-line access to Telnet servers.	None.
Telnet Server	A Telnet server. It is highly recommended that you do not install and use this. Telnet is a clear-text protocol and is deemed highly insecure unless the channel is encrypted. Use Terminal Services instead.	None.

Table 11-2   Features Included in Windows Server 2008

Feature Name	Description	Role Dependencies
TFTP Client	A client for the Trivial File Transfer Protocol (TFTP). TFTP is a lightweight, completely unauthenticated file transfer protocol that is primarily used by attackers to transfer files to a compromised server. It should not be installed on any server.	None.
Windows Internal Database	A version of Microsoft SQL Server Embedded edition. It is designed to provide database services to other services, not to be used by itself as a stand-alone database.	None.
Windows PowerShell	A very powerful command shell.	None.
Windows Process Activation Service	Provides remote process services to applications using the Windows Communications Framework (WCF). Previously this was available only to HTTP-based applications via IIS. By factoring these services into a separate feature, the dependency on IIS has been removed.	None.
Windows Server Backup Features	Unlike Windows Server 2003 and earlier versions, the backup tools are not installed by default. This feature installs them.	The command-line tools require Windows PowerShell.
Windows System Resource Manager (WSRM)	Allows you to manage resource allocation within the system.	Windows Internal Database.
WINS Server	WINS is used to provide host name resolution for older Windows networks. Since Windows 2000 WINS is not necessary and its functionality is supported by DNS instead. This service should be avoided unless absolutely necessary.	None.
Wireless LAN Service	Provides configuration support for wireless network adapters. This service is not needed if the server has no wireless network adapters.	None.

On the CD   On the CD you will find a document mapping services to roles and features, showing you exactly which services are used by every role and feature. Look for it in under Chapter 6 in the Chapter-Related Materials section of the CD.

Please note that although the dependencies column lists an entire role, in many cases only a small portion of that role is needed for any given role or feature dependency. For example, the SMTP Server requires only the IIS 6 Management tools from the Web Server role and the SMTP Server remote administration tools from the Remote Server Administration Tools feature. Only by trying to uncheck the various features will you discover the relationships.

Your Server Before the Roles

It is interesting to note that when you install additional features you can do so without inserting the installation disk. That is because all the bits needed to support every role and feature are copied to the hard disk during the initial installation. This means that the files are actually already there. They are not, however, present in their normal locations in the file system in their final form. Rather, they are stored in the %systemroot%\winsxs directory. This is important to features such as Telnet Client and TFTP Client. Those features are nothing more than the executables being present in the file system. To be able to execute these programs, the associated catalog and manifest files must also be installed, and those are not installed until the feature itself is installed. Of course, a criminal with administrative access can still quite easily install the feature, so the security benefit from not having it installed by default is minimal.

This tactic of laying down all the files that could ever be needed at initial installation has also been practiced by Microsoft Office since Office 2003. It actually takes less disk space than one might think, although it still has a significant footprint. The disk footprint for the 32-bit editions of Windows Server 2008 was roughly 5.3 GB in one of the later prerelease versions. Compare that to 1.72 GB used by Windows Server 2003 R2 with Service Pack 2.

Default Service Footprint

Before you configure a server by adding various roles and features, it still has a relatively significant footprint of services. By default there are 105 services, of which 42 are set to auto start, 55 are set to manual, and 8 are disabled. Contrast that with a clean installation of Windows Server 2003 R2 with Service Pack 2, which has 86 services installed by default, with 34 set to start automatically, 32 set to demand start, and 20 disabled. Clearly, even with the roles metaphor and the reduction in default roles supported, Windows Server 2008 has a larger footprint and requires that you take additional care when hardening it. For more details on hardening services, please refer to Chapter 6, "Services."

Server Core

We have mentioned Server Core a few times so far. It is a stripped-down version of Windows Server 2008 that has no graphical user interface and supports only a subset of roles and features. The user interface on Server Core is simply a command line, as shown in Figure 11-2.

Server Core is not a separate version in and of itself, but rather an installation option during setup. After you type your product key you get to choose whether you want to install the full version or the Server Core version of the edition you purchased. The selection dialog box is shown in Figure 11-3.

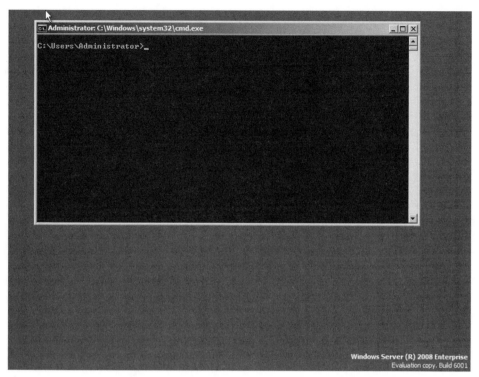

Figure 11-2   Server Core is a stripped-down version of Windows Server that supports only a subset of the roles.

Server Core is an excellent choice for many infrastructure servers because it affords you the ability to run them with a minimal feature set.

> **Note**   Server Core by default has a blank administrator password. The password for the local administrator is set during the first logon as that user. Because you normally log on to the computer to join it to a domain, you would be asked to set this at that time, but it is still worth knowing.
>
> It is not necessarily a bad idea to leave the built-in administrator password blank. If the computer is physically secure, doing so would present no significant attack surface because blank passwords cannot be used remotely. On the other hand, leaving the password blank makes managing the local administrator passwords on hundreds or thousands of servers in a data center drastically easier. Evaluate your situation: If you are comfortable with the physical security of your servers, you may decide that leaving the password blank is the best option. It is likely to be more secure by far than using the same password on thousands of servers. If any one of those thousands of servers gets compromised, all of them should be considered compromised. This is a type of security dependency discussed in Chapter 13.

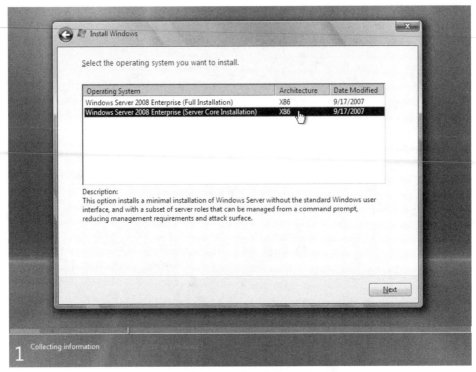

Figure 11-3   Server Core is an installation option during initial setup.

Roles Supported by Server Core

Server Core supports only a subset of the roles available on a full installation. It is designed primarily to act as an infrastructure server. The roles supported by Server Core are:

- Active Directory Domain Services
- Active Directory Lightweight Directory Services (Just LDAP, formerly ADAM)
- DHCP Server
- DNS Server
- File Services
- IIS
- Print Services

Most of the roles are installed using the OCSetup.exe command, which wraps the Package Manager (pkgmgr.exe). You may see references to either being used to install roles. Note that the ServerManagerCmd.exe command line utility that is present on a full installation is not present on Server Core.

To see which roles are available, run OCList.exe, which is a tool unique to Server Core. For example, to install the DNS Server role, you would run the following command:

```
start /w ocsetup DNS-Server-Core-Role
```

The reason you use the start command to run *ocsetup* is that *ocsetup* otherwise returns immediately, and you get no indication that the installation succeeds. By wrapping it in *start /w* you ensure that the command line does not return until the installation is complete.

The one exception to this installation procedure is the Active Directory Domain Services role. Installing the role does not actually promote a computer to a domain controller. It merely enables that to happen later, when you run the DCPromo tool as in prior versions of Windows. The catch in Server Core is that you must use an unattend file to install Active Directory Domain Services because there is no GUI wizard. For more information on how to promote a Server Core installation to Active Directory, and how to manage Server Core in general, refer to the article "Server Core Installation Option of Windows Server 2008 Step-by-Step Guide" on Microsoft TechNet at *http://technet2.microsoft.com/windowsserver2008/en/library/ 47a23a74-e13c-46de-8d30-ad0afb1eaffc1033.mspx?mfr=true.*

Features Supported by Server Core

Server Core also only supports a subset of the features of the regular editions of Windows Server. The following features are included:

- Backup
- BitLocker Drive Encryption
- Failover Clustering (Enterprise and Datacenter Editions only)
- Multipath IO
- Network Load Balancing
- Removable Storage Management
- QWAVE
- Simple Network Management Protocol (SNMP)
- Subsystem for UNIX-based Applications
- Telnet client
- Windows Internet Name Service (WINS)

What Is Not Included in Server Core

A lot of things are not included in Server Core. The most obvious are Windows Explorer and Internet Explorer. Server Core is the first version of Windows in many years to ship without a Web browser. Server Core also does not ship with any version of Windows Media Player, or most any other strictly consumer-oriented tool. More to the point, however, Server Core comes with a smaller service and disk footprint. Compared to the full installation, with a disk footprint of 5.3 GB, Server Core has a disk footprint of just over 1 GB. In addition, Server Core has only 38 services auto-started by default, with another 30 set to demand start and one (Browser) disabled. The 37 services shown in Table 11-3 are missing on a Server Core installation, compared to a full installation of the same product.

Table 11-3   Services Removed from Full Installation in Server Core

Application Layer Gateway (alg)	Application Information (appinfo)
Windows Audio Endpoint Builder (AudioEndpointBuilder)	Windows Audio (Audiosrv)
Microsoft .NET Framework (clr_optimization_<version>)	Offline files (CscService)
Wired AutoConfig (dot3svc)	Extensible Authentication Protocol (EapHost)
Function Discovery Provider Host (fdPHost)	Function Discovery Resource Publication (FDResPub)
PNP-X IP Bus Enumerator (IPBusEnum)	Multimedia Class Scheduler (MMCSS)
Network Connections (Netman)	Remote Access Auto Connection Manager (RasAuto)
Remote Access Connection Manager (RasMan)	Routing and Remote Access (RemoteAccess)
Remote Procedure Call (RPC) Locator (RpcLocator)	Internet Connection Sharing (ICS) (SharedAccess)
Shell Hardware Detection (ShellHWDetection)	SL UI Notification Service (SLUINotify)
Print Spooler (Spooler)	SSDP Discovery (SSDPSRV)
Secure Socket Tunneling Protocol Service (SstpSvc)	Superfetch (SysMain)
Telephony (TapiSrv)	Themes (Themes)
Thread Ordering Server (THREADORDER)	Distributed Link Tracking Client (TrkWks)
Interactive Services Detection (UI0Detect)	UPnP Device Host (upnphost)
Desktop Window Manager Session Manager (UxSms)	Problem Reports and Solutions Control Panel Support (wercplsupport)
Windows Error Reporting Service (WerSvc)	Portable Device Enumerator Service (WPDBusEnum)
Windows Driver Foundation – User-mode Driver Framework (wudfsvc)	

Clearly, for the minimalist or anyone who wants a single-purpose computer, Server Core is the way to go.

Tools to Manage Server Roles

Windows Server 2003 R2 first shipped with the new Manage Your Server Wizard. This was the first tool that enabled administrators to easily configure their servers to support whatever roles were appropriate. The toolset in Windows Server 2008 got a bit richer and more full-featured. In this section we will cover the three main tools used to manage server roles on full installations of Windows Server 2008, paying particular attention to the security implications of each.

Initial Configuration Tasks

The first tool you are likely to notice is the tool called Manage Your Server in Windows Server 2003. It is called Initial Configuration Tasks (ICT) in Windows Server 2008, and shows up as soon as you log on for the first time. As shown in Figure 11-4, this tool gives you basic configuration information on your server, and also lets you launch the Add Roles and Add Features wizards.

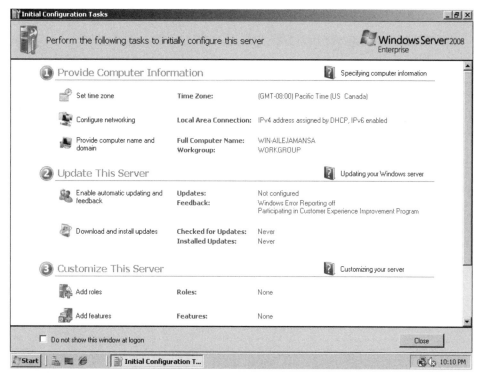

Figure 11-4   The new ICT tool shows some useful information about your server and also lets you easily launch the configuration tools.

The ICT tool is quite useful to get you started, and also gives you some useful at-a-glance information even on a stable, configured server. Server Manager does duplicate the same information, but the page there is far bigger. You may find yourself actually leaving ICT turned on.

Add Roles and Add Features Wizards

If you click Add Roles or Add Features in the Initial Configuration Tasks tool, you are taken to the respective wizards. These wizards walk you through enabling a particular role or feature on the server.

You can also add roles and features on the command line using ServerManagerCmd.exe. On a Server Core installation you obviously must use the command line because it has no graphical user interface (GUI). However, you would use pkgmgr.exe or ocsetup.exe to manage roles on Server Core. Most administrators will probably use one of the two wizards, however. The two are very similar, and can be launched either from the Initial Configuration Tasks tool or from Server Manager.

Server Manager

Server Manager, shown in Figure 11-5, combines the features of Add/Remove Programs in the Control Panel, Windows Security Center, the Computer Management console, and assorted MMC snap-ins—all in a single tool.

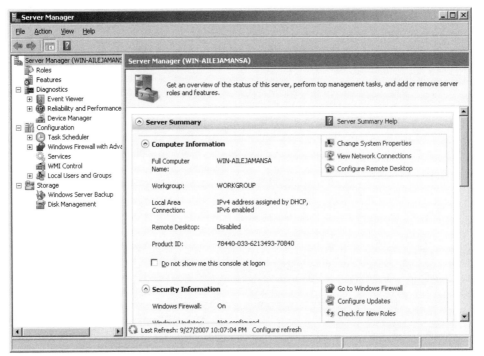

Figure 11-5   The Server Manager puts most of the tools you need to manage a server in one console.

To install a role using either Server Manager or the Initial Configuration Tasks tool, click Add Roles. A page pops up with some basic background information. Click Next. You will see the page shown in Figure 11-6.

The page shown in Figure 11-6 is where the main work is being done. However, do not ignore the rest of the pages. For example, if you select the Application Server role you see the page shown earlier in Figure 11-1. You cannot modify anything there, but click Next a few times and you see the page in Figure 11-7.

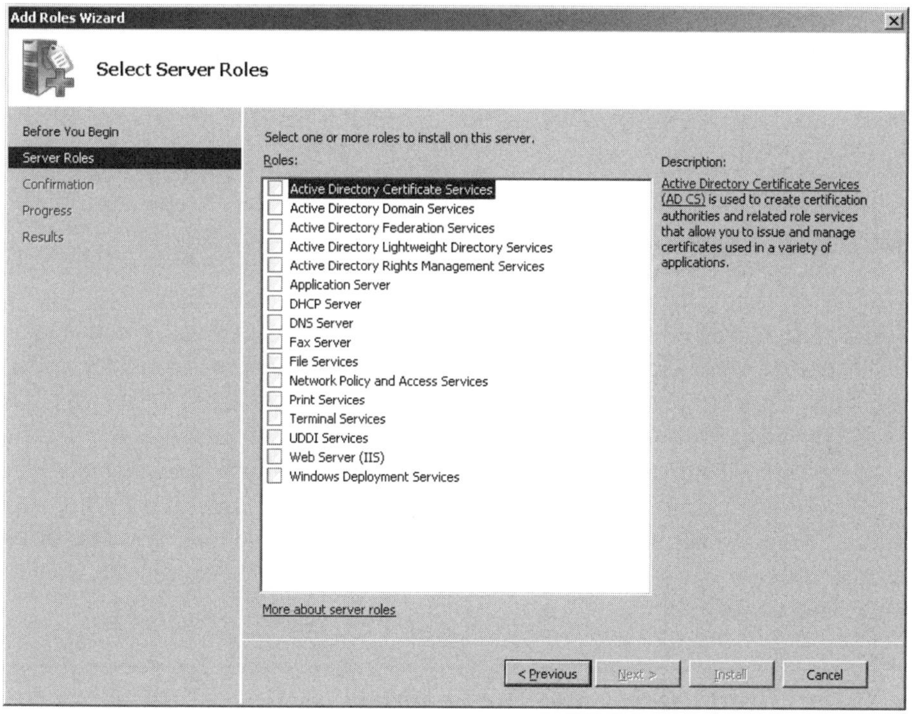

Figure 11-6   You select roles on the Add Roles Wizard's main page.

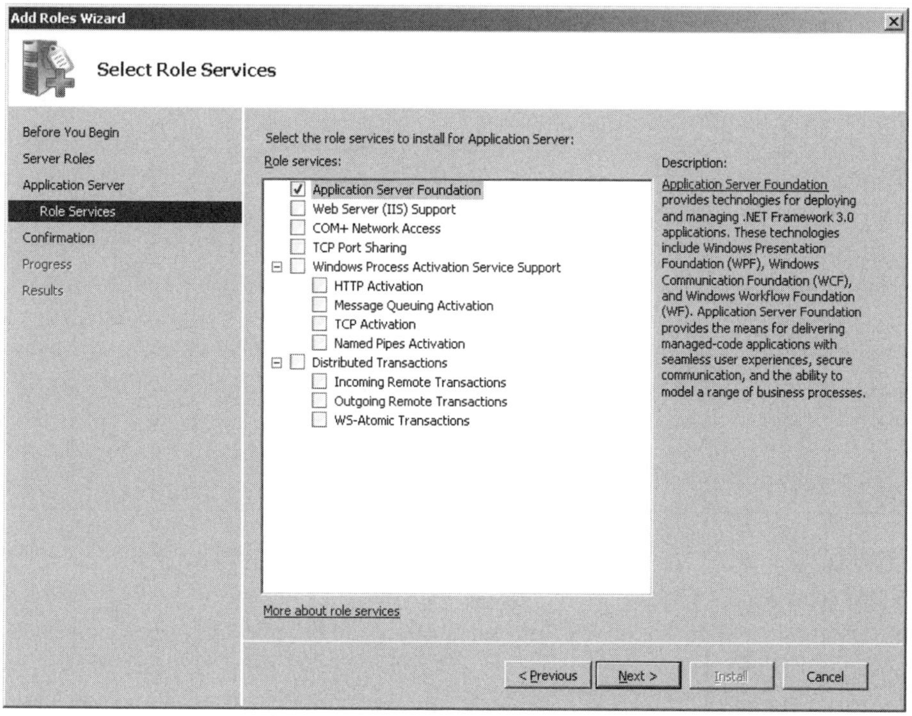

Figure 11-7   At some stage during role installation you can choose which role services to configure.

In Figure 11-7 you notice several things that you may not need on your Application Server. Depending on the role, you may or may not be able to remove some of these. For example, you can opt not to install COM+ Network Access, but in some cases, the dependency is hard-coded. Consequently, you must select Application Server Foundation. The nature of the dependency will vary with the role you elected to install.

The Security Configuration Wizard

The new role and feature metaphors for server management are quite helpful and go a long way toward helping us configure a server with the smallest attack surface possible. However, while the Add Roles and Add Features wizards open ports in the firewall, they do not permit you to restrict them to only certain hosts. Nor do they close the ports again when you remove a role. They merely install the roles/features, configure the services and other settings they need, and open the necessary ports to everyone on the network. To maximize security you also need to configure the firewall to minimize access to the server. This used to be extremely difficult, requiring sophisticated analysis of what ports needed to be exposed, to which computers, for which services. Then, in Windows Server 2003 Service Pack 1, we got the Security Configuration Wizard (SCW).

Direct from the Source: The Security Configuration Wizard

The Security Configuration Wizard is an attack-surface reduction tool originally produced for the Windows Server 2003 family. It determines the minimum functionality required for a server's role or roles, and disables functionality that is not required. Prior to the release of SCW, the majority of server configuration guidance for our customers came from multiple sources in the form of lengthy documents, and it was not an easy task for administrators to know how best to lock down their servers based on each computer's role and environment. We created SCW as the de facto security policy authoring tool for Windows servers, which not only allows system administrators to define the policy for each computer role, but also supports enterprise deployment of those policies through Group Policy or direct client-server communication. All the computer roles that ship with SCW have been tested by our product groups and are also extensible, so that administrators can define their own unique computer policies based on the default templates. It's a great tool for our customers!

Lara Sosnosky, Senior Program Manager
Windows Experience

SCW takes a completely different approach to server hardening than existing tools. SCW also works with a roles metaphor to configure the system to support those roles and little if anything else. In addition to helping you configure the firewall, as mentioned earlier, SCW also disables unnecessary services and configures some security settings. Finally, while the Add Roles and Add Features wizards are only able to install and configure roles built into

Windows, SCW is completely extensible. A developer or an administrator can write a custom role and/or feature configuration file and use SCW to configure any product.

In a sense, you can think of the Add Roles and Add Features wizards as the tools that take a default server and configure it to securely support the roles and features you want. In the same way, you can think of SCW as the tool that configures your server to support *only* the roles and features you want. SCW also has a pedagogical effect in that it helps you understand more about how the server is configured. Therefore, the author highly recommends that you run SCW after the server has been configured with its complement of roles and features.

Using SCW to Audit and Enhance the Security of Each Server Role

SCW is designed to be run after you have installed all the roles and features the server is supposed to have. To show how it works I configured a server with the following roles and features:

Roles

- Application Server
- DNS Server
- Web Services (IIS)

Features

- .NET Framework 3.0 Features
- Windows Process Activation Service

Obviously this is not a particularly logical set of roles and features, but rather is meant just to demonstrate how the tools work. To start SCW, just run it from the Administrative Tools menu. You will see the page shown in Figure 11-8.

The first step is to choose whether you want to create a new security policy, edit or apply an existing policy, or roll back a policy so the system returns to the original settings. The choices are relatively self-explanatory. When you choose Create A New Security Policy, SCW will create a new policy using some computer as the template for what the policy must support. It will analyze the computer, determine what features and roles it supports, and ensure that those work but that many unnecessary features are not supported. Always remember the prototype nature of SCW. This means that you should configure the computer to do what you want it to do before you run SCW. SCW is there to configure your computer securely for the roles you selected. It does not install any of the roles for you.

Notice that you can create a policy on one system and then apply it to many systems. If you are building out a network with many systems, you would do very well to define host classes that are all configured separately. Then you can create a policy using one of them as a prototype and apply the policy to all the others with little to no modifications.

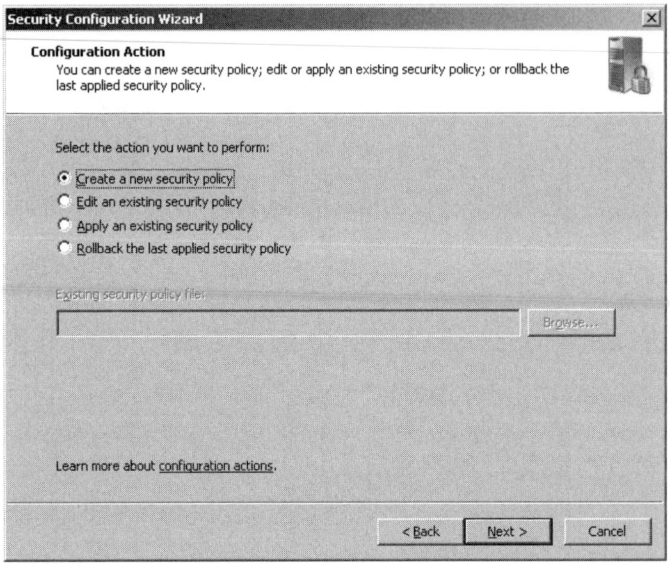

Figure 11-8   SCW begins by asking you what you want to do.

When you click Next, SCW asks which computer you want to use as the baseline, or proto-type, for this new policy. Normally, you would choose the local computer, but you can also use a remote computer. During the analysis phase SCW enumerates which roles and features are installed and matches those up against a database of roles and features. The database contains information regarding which services are used by each role and feature, what network ports they need, and other configuration information. After the analysis is complete you can click View Configuration Database, shown in Figure 11-9, and see what SCW found. This is a read-only view that you cannot change, but shows you a plethora of information about the configuration of the computer.

When you click Next, you will enter the first of four sections in SCW–Role-Based Service Configuration. (See Figure 11-10.) This is where you decide or confirm which roles your server should support. The answers you give in this section are very important because they drive what you will see in the network section later. The detection logic, however, is quite good and typically the correct set of roles is usually selected for you. Note also that by default you see Installed Roles, which are the roles that the server is capable of supporting with the bits laid down on the disk. To see all the roles, select All Roles from the drop-down list.

In Figure 11-11, you may note that the roles you find in SCW are not the same set that you find in the remainder of the roles tools. The roles you can install using the Roles Wizard are mostly there, but there are others as well, and some are missing. For example, the Application Server role that we selected is not present. This is because SCW uses a slightly different metaphor for roles than the Roles Wizard uses. The mixing of metaphors is quite confusing, however, and will take some getting used to. In addition, other programs that you install may add roles and features to SCW. If you want to write your own role and feature definition, see the document entitled "Extending the Security Configuration Wizard," available at *http://www.microsoft.com/downloads/details.aspx?FamilyID=903fd496-9eb9-4a45-aa00-3f2f20fd6171&DisplayLang=en.*

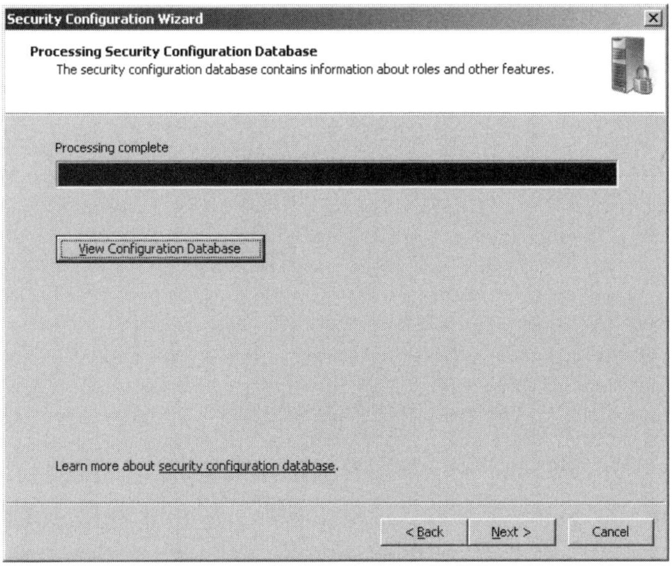

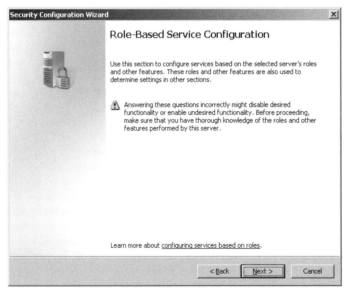

Figure 11-9   After SCW has analyzed your computer you can view the configuration database to see what it found.

Figure 11-10   Each section of SCW is preceded by a page explaining what you do in that section.

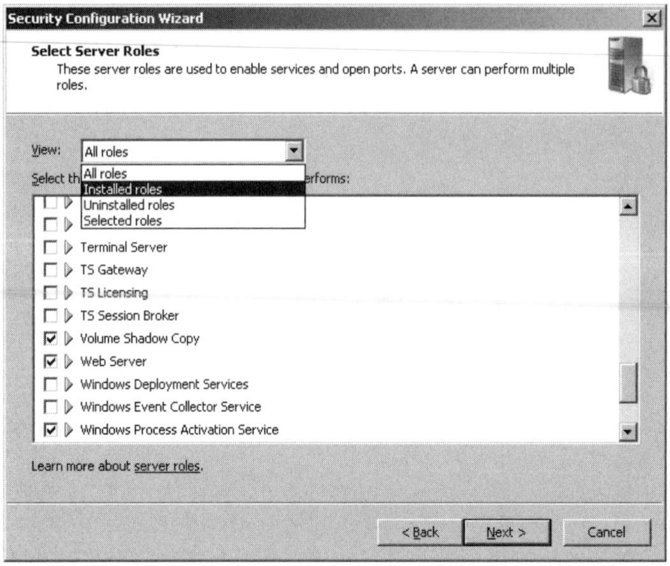

Figure 11-11 In SCW you select the roles you want your server to support.

After roles configuration, you get to select the client features you want to support. The feature set is similar but not identical to that in the Add Features wizard we saw before, and there are fewer features in the set. Again, the metaphors do not transfer cleanly, and SCW can be extended. As we can see in Figure 11-12, a "feature" in SCW is something the computer does to act as a client, while a "role" is something it does to act as a server.

This is different from the metaphor used in the other tools where a role is a collection of services and features that can be thought of as a unit and a feature is something that supports roles. The two metaphors and the two different uses of the same terms are bound to confuse people.

Normally, you will have the right set of roles selected already in Figure 11-11. Verify that the analysis found what you think it should find. If it did not, check whether the role has been installed, and install it if it is missing before you rerun SCW. If you make a mistake it is not the end of the world. SCWs rollback feature will bring you back to where you started by undoing the changes the policy made.

When you click Next on the Client Features page in SCW, you get to pick Administration And Other Options, as shown in Figure 11-13.

An option in SCW is something that does not neatly fit into either a role or a feature. It may provide administrative support, or it may just be a single service, such as the Interactive Services Detection. Again, most of the default options should be correct here. It is worth pointing out the drop-down menu, too. It will be populated with options relevant to the roles and features you selected earlier and will be different on different computers.

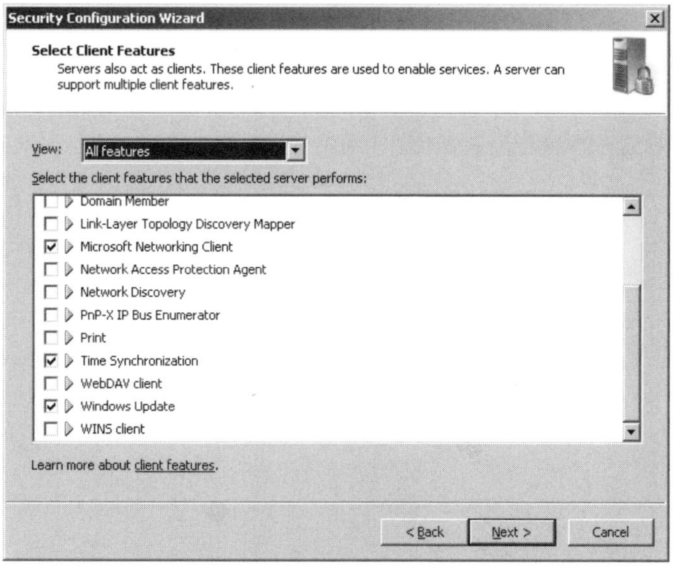

Figure 11-12   In SCW, a "feature" is a client feature.

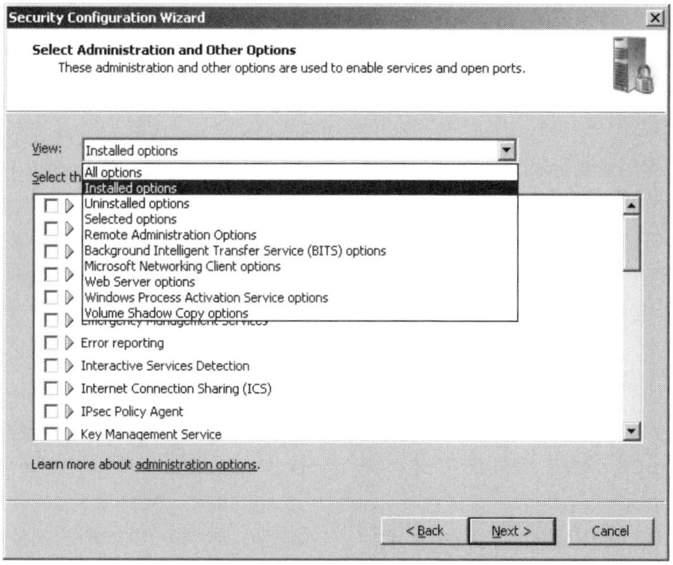

Figure 11-13   Other services and features are in the Administration and Other Options page in SCW.

Finally, you get the Additional Services page, shown in Figure 11-14.

Although SCW ships with a very large database of services, not everything is described in that database. Those services that SCW finds on a computer and that are not described in the database are shown on the Additional Services page. As shown in Figure 11-14, you see three built-in services. This screenshot was taken on a beta version of Windows Server 2008. By the time the product ships, all built-in services should be described and, unless you have some third-party service installed, you should not see this page at all.

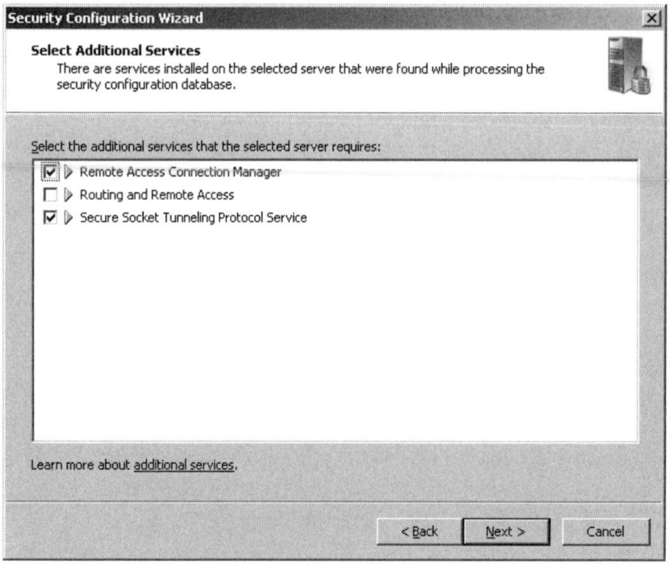

Figure 11-14   The Additional Services page shows services that are not described in the SCW database.

On the next page you get to select what you do with services that you are not configuring. This option is only interesting if you take the policy you are creating and apply it to a different computer. If that computer has different services than the one you created the policy on, SCW needs to know what to do with them. One option is to leave them alone, which is the default. The other option is to disable them, which is more secure, but may break things. If you follow the advice of only applying policies to servers that are identical to the one you created them on, your choice on this page will be irrelevant.

Finally, you are finished with the Roles Configuration portion of SCW and the wizard tells you what you did. As you can see from Figure 11-15, even if you just click right through you will significantly affect the attack surface of the computer. For instance, because this computer is not a Print Server, and it has no printers installed, you have no reason to install the Print Spooler service. SCW disables all services that are not necessary. On our test server SCW disables 17 services that were set to automatic start and sets 42 manual start services to disabled. Your results will obviously vary depending on how your server is configured but, clearly, SCW enables you to relatively easily tailor a policy to your specific and unique servers.

You will now move on to, arguably, the most important section of SCW: Networking. After the initial welcome page, you see Figure 11-16, which contains a list of all the firewall rules SCW proposes. The rules proposed are based on the role support you selected in the prior pages. If no further configuration is made in the Network section, SCW will build firewall rules that lock down the network interfaces so that only these roles and features are supported but all clients can access them. In Chapter 13 we will discuss how to minimize this attack surface using threat modeling. SCW is a valuable tool in this process.

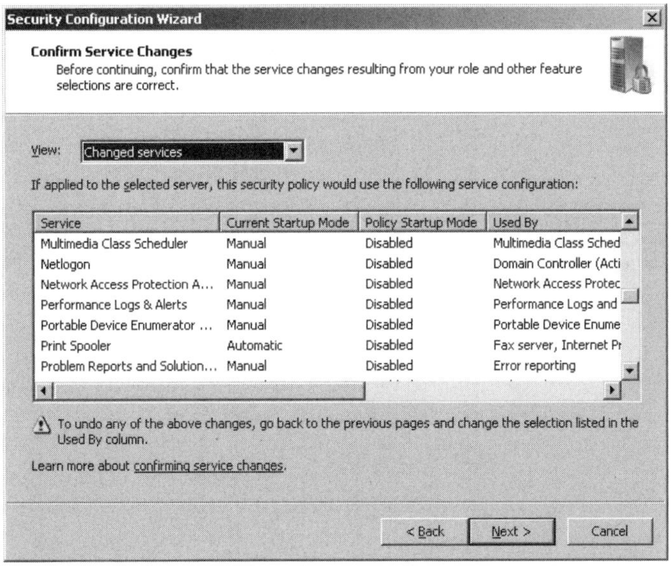

Figure 11-15   At the end of each section SCW tells you what you changed in this section.

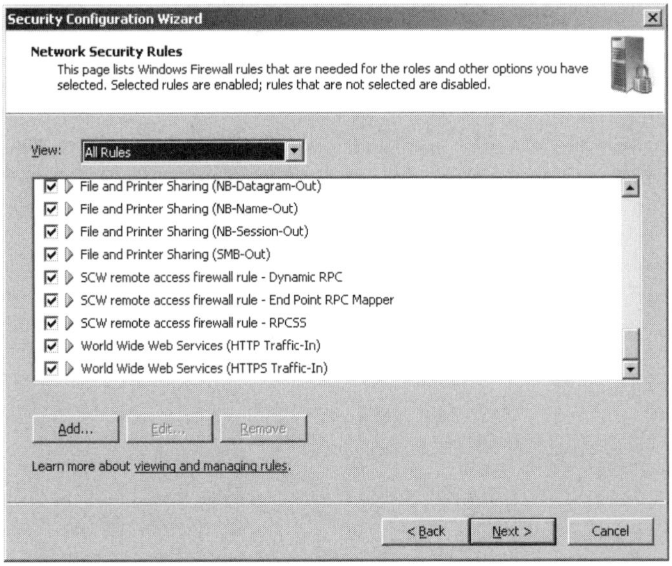

Figure 11-16   The Network Security Section contains a list of all the rules SCW determines that you need.

You can configure restrictions on the proposed rules by selecting the rule and clicking Edit. This takes you to the page shown in Figure 11-17. This is one page of four that all let you put further restrictions on the networking rules. For instance, you can require IPsec authentication, as is done in Figure 11-17. If you do so, you can also tie the port to only certain endpoints. For example, if you wanted to permit remote administration only from certain hosts, you can use SCW to configure that.

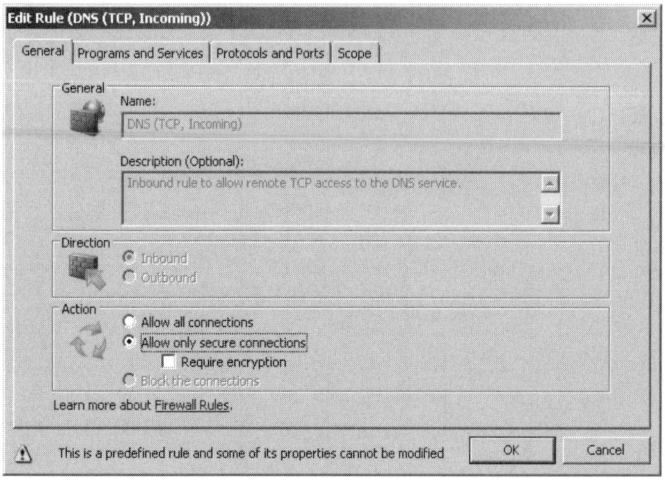

Figure 11-17   SCW allows you to build firewall and IPsec rules without leaving the wizard.

This ability to build rules based on the roles you selected serves two important purposes. First, it is a golden learning opportunity to understand what your servers are doing. You do not even need to build out a server. Just run the wizard, make different selections, and see how they affect the options on later pages. Second, it allows you to tie the very abstract concept of a port to a much more realistic concept of a service and configure network restrictions based on exactly what the system is actually doing. Done right, this permits you to develop a very tight configuration for your servers. The networking section of SCW is undoubtedly the section where you should be spending the majority of your time while you are building the security policy of your servers.

The remainder of SCW allows you to configure auditing and a few registry settings. Generally, the default settings of these parameters are adequate for most organizations, and unless you have special needs, you should not need to do much there. The roles and firewall settings are the most valuable by far.

After you create your policy you can save it and apply it to this computer or one or more other computers. You can also transform your policy to a Group Policy Object (GPO) using the **scwcmd.exe /transform** command. However, if you have computer-specific settings in the policy, this may not succeed—and it may give very strange results if it does. For example, if you create endpoint restrictions that include local adapters in the networking section, the policy is deemed computer-specific and will not successfully transform. SCW is far better used on a server-by-server basis and as a learning tool. For large server farms, use SCW as a way to learn about the computers and develop a basic policy. Then take that policy and re-create it to be rolled out using whatever tool you use to configure the servers, such as Group Policy or an Enterprise Management System (EMS) such as Microsoft Systems Center.

Direct from the Source: Skeletons from the SCW Closet

Every product has a few anecdotes from its development. SCW is no different. Here are a few:

- The original code name for SCW was Secure Server Roles. That name still survives. If you run dcomcnfg.exe and expand the DCOM Config tree, you see a class called SSR DCOM Back-end classes.

- If you look at the TCP/IP properties for this class, you'll notice that when the SSR DCOM component is activated, it listens on a hard-coded port: 64129. That port number comes from my birthday, 10/29/64. I told the developers to pick any port number they wanted as long as it was ephemeral and not already used by something that showed up in a Web search. That's what they came up with!

- SCW was almost called SPW, for "Security Policy Wizard," to emphasize its nature as a policy authoring tool. Another proposed name was FSW–"Firewall and Service Wizard."

- Originally, we had no user interface program manager for SCW. It was not until I showed my first attempt at UI design that they found one for me.

- The UI PM invented a custom control for the wizard UI. The concept came from the Web. You don't see that right arrow (>) in other Windows applications.

Kirk Soluk, original SCW Program Manager. Currently Senior University Security Analyst, University of Michigan

---

Multi-Role Servers

Before we finish, a few words about multi-role servers is in order. Multi-role servers are servers that support more than one role. For example, a DNS server that is also an Active Directory Domain Controller is a multi-role server. In some cases, as in that one, multi-role servers are acceptable, and even encouraged. However, in general, multi-role servers degrade the security you can achieve and are not recommended. With a multi-role server, management becomes more complex because you have to account for how each role will behave in the presence of other roles, and you potentially have to work harder to keep the server updated. You may find that certain highly recommended security settings for one role do not work in the presence of another role. This is why you should avoid multi-role servers if at all possible. Compared to the clean-up costs after a breach, and the simplified configuration and management costs, a few additional servers, or virtualized servers, are relatively inexpensive.

There are two very notable exceptions to this policy: Windows Server Code Name "Cougar" (the next update to Windows Small Business Server 2003) and Windows Essential Business Server, the mid-market edition of Windows Server 2008. Both of these are multi-role servers, and as such they make significant trade-offs in security. However, one needs to account for those trade-offs in the context of their deployment scenarios. They are designed for organizations without large IT departments and personnel with expertise in server management and security. While it certainly would be possible to build a network consisting of several servers that perform the same functions as "Cougar," doing so is far beyond the skill levels of the IT people in the typical small business, not to mention beyond their allotted budgets. At the same time, if these products did not exist, these organizations would attempt to put together the same services themselves on a single or a few servers, and would almost invariably achieve a result that was far less secure than the out-of-the-box configuration of "Cougar" and Windows Essential Business Server. In one case, it took a consultant three days to configure Microsoft Exchange Server to run on a single computer, and that was only after using "Cougar" to compare with. For the markets they are targeted at, multi-role servers fit an important niche. Taking all these trade-offs into account, "Cougar" and Windows Essential Business Server clearly fill an important market niche, all the while making significant security trade-offs.

Summary

The roles-based metaphor for server management is one of the most important concepts in the field of security today. Servers today are far too complex for the average administrator, and the interactions and dependencies between the various services and features is so difficult to grasp and model that a simpler abstraction is necessary. Roles-based management provides exactly that. It permits us to think of a relatively small number of roles, instead of more than 100 services, and to make decisions and trade-offs at that level of abstraction. If we choose to, we may then dive deeper and manage services individually.

The roles-based metaphor is also an overloaded term, as is evidenced by the fact that the Add Roles and Add Features wizards and SCW present different roles and features. The metaphor can mean different things to different people. This makes management a little harder, but still far easier than it would be without roles.

Chapter 12
Patch Management

— Brian M. Lich

Patch management is the process by which software updates are deployed to computers on your network. Software updates come in all forms, including performance, reliability, and security-related. It is important to establish a patch management strategy to ensure that updates are deployed in a reasonable amount of time with little or no impact on your business.

In this chapter, we will look at the four phases to consider when building your patch management strategy. After we offer an overview of patch management, we will look at some of the services and products offered by Microsoft to help you identify the computers that do not have the required updates installed. These include the Microsoft Download Center, Microsoft Update Catalog, Windows Update (WU), Automatic Updates (AU), Microsoft Security Baseline Analyzer (MBSA), Windows Server Update Services (WSUS), and System Center Essentials 2007.

The Four Phases of Patch Management

Patch management has four phases, as shown in Figure 12-1.

Analyzing each phase separately can help you develop your patch management strategy. The following list gives an overview of each phase. Detailed explanations of these phases are given in the sections that follow.

■ **Phase 1: Assess**   The assessment phase is used to gather information about the computers on your network, review (or create, if necessary) policies and procedures for establishing the security standards in your organization, and decide on the infrastructure by which updates will be managed and deployed.

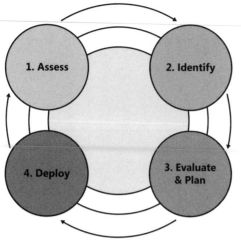

Figure 12-1   The four phases of patch management.

- **Phase 2: Identify**   The identify phase is the process by which you are notified of new updates as soon as they are released. After this notification, you assess whether the update is relevant to the types of computers on your network and you choose the priority—as it falls within your change management process—with which the update should be deployed to computers belonging to your production network.

- **Phase 3: Evaluate and Plan**   In the evaluate and plan phase, you make the final decision as to how and when to deploy the update. This phase also includes enough testing in a sandbox environment to ensure that the update will not adversely affect any applications critical to your organization.

- **Phase 4: Deploy**   The deploy phase is the final phase, in which the update is installed on computers within your organization's network. This phase determines the success of the deployment, including a check to ensure that the update installed successfully.

Phase 1: Assess

The goal of this phase is to assess the current state of your organization and identify gaps that must be addressed in your patch management strategy.

First, you must collect detailed information about the computers on your network. The inventory should include information about the hardware configuration, operating system version, and all applications installed on the computer. When a new update is released, this information will help you quickly determine whether an update is relevant to your organization. In large organizations, keeping an up-to-date inventory of all computers may be difficult because that list is constantly changing. Instead, you could logically group computers together into classes and deploy updates according to class. For example, an Internet

Information Services (IIS) Web server class would include all IIS Web servers within your organization. When an IIS update is released, you could concentrate your patch management efforts on this class of computers. You could also do this for Apache Web servers, file and print servers, domain controllers, and so on.

> **Note**   You can use System Center Essentials 2007 to gather inventory information. For more information about the System Center family of products, see *http://www.microsoft.com/systemcenter*.

Next, review your organization's security standards and determine whether they are current. If they are not current—or do not exist—this is the phase in which to formalize these policies and procedures and distribute them to all users within your organization. Include items such as strong password standards, application security settings, operating system security settings, and so on. Once the policies and procedures are in place, they should be enforced with automated tools that detect when a computer is no longer in compliance. When that happens, the owner should be contacted and asked to resolve the issue.

The last step in the assess phase is to look at your current infrastructure and determine the appropriate products or set of products that will be most beneficial for your organization. Several products are tailored to different organizational needs. In "Tools for Your Patch Management Arsenal" later in this chapter, I will review the offerings from Microsoft.

Phase 2: Identify

You can choose from among several notification methods to find out when a new security update has been released. To be notified of security updates from Microsoft, sign up for the Microsoft Technical Security Notifications. You can sign up for e-mail or RSS feed notification. The Microsoft Technical Security Notifications give you early information about the security updates that will be released in the next security update cycle, detailed technical information about the security updates as soon as they are released, and any advisories released by the Microsoft Security Response Center (MSRC). You can sign up for Microsoft Technical Security Notifications here: *http://www.microsoft.com/technet/security/bulletin/notify.mspx*.

The following vendors also have Web sites that will notify you when new updates are available:

- Adobe (*http://www.adobe.com/support/security/*)
- Apple (*http://docs.info.apple.com/article.html?artnum=61798*)
- Sun Microsystems (*http://sunsolve.sun.com/show.do?target=patches/patch-access*)
- Oracle (*http://www.oracle.com/technology/deploy/security/alerts.htm*)
- Mozilla Firefox (*http://www.mozilla.org/security/*)
- Apache (*http://httpd.apache.org/security_report.html*)

The Web sites below can help you stay informed as new security advisories are released. In fact, some of these sites may give you more warning because you are seeing the vulnerabilities as they are being exposed publicly for the first time:

- **MSRC blog**   The MSRC blog is updated whenever a security advisory is released. A blog posting can be written and released much faster than other methods of communication. You should monitor this blog regularly at *http://blogs.technet.com/msrc*.

- **Microsoft TechNet Security Center**   The TechNet Security Center is a collection of links focused on helping keep Microsoft software secure. From here, you can go to the Security Bulletins and Advisories page or check out the latest update tools offered by Microsoft, as well as many other areas of interest to IT professionals. You can find the Microsoft TechNet Security Center at *http://www.microsoft.com/technet/security/default.mspx*.

- **The United States Computer Emergency Readiness Team (US-CERT)**   The US-CERT team publishes security advisories for a wide range of products, both Microsoft and non-Microsoft. You can visit their Web site at *http://www.us-cert.gov*.

- **Full Disclosure mailing list**   Although vendors prefer security researchers to work with them to responsibly disclose vulnerabilities that they discover, at times this does not happen. Instead, the vulnerability details (and sometimes the exploit code) are published on the Internet. This dramatically increases the threat to your organization because the bad guys are hearing about it at the same time as the vendor, so a security update does not exist yet. However, it is important to stay informed and know what is out there at the same time the bad guys do. Full Disclosure is a mailing list that discusses security vulnerabilities for a wide range of products and can be found at *http://archives.neohapsis.com/archives/fulldisclosure/*.

 Note   Full Disclosure gives you a good idea of what the bad guys are doing. However, keep in mind that the mailing list is full of chatter and not everything posted to the list is accurate.

- **SANS Internet Storm Center Diary**   The SANS Internet Storm Center diary is a place where different handlers write entries on the day's events. It is a good way to stay informed on any new trends as well as the occasional tip on how to help secure your network. The SANS Internet Storm Center is located at *http://isc.sans.org*.

Determining Whether the Security Update Pertains to You

Not every security update will pertain to every organization. Some security updates only affect certain components and only if these components are installed. Therefore, you must be able to determine whether the security update is relevant. You can do this by reading the security bulletin associated with the security update and comparing that to your inventory.

Every security update is accompanied by a security bulletin. The bulletin provides detailed information about the security update, organized in different sections, as shown in Table 12-1.

Table 12-1   Sections of a Security Bulletin

Section	Description
General Information	The General Information section includes an executive summary of the vulnerability, a recommendation on when this update should be applied, any known issues, and a table listing the versions of the products that are both affected and not affected by this vulnerability.
Vulnerability Information	The Vulnerability Information section includes all of the technical details Microsoft releases surrounding this vulnerability, including frequently asked questions, mitigating factors that may help you reduce the attack surface, and any workarounds that can be applied to your computers until the security update has been successfully deployed.
Update Information	The Update Information section lists the different detection and deployment tools provided by Microsoft, and whether they can be used to detect or deploy this security update. Additionally, this section will give you the supported command-line switches, specific files (and files versions) that are being replaced with this update, and the registry entries that are used to track whether installation was successful.
Other Information	The Other Information section acknowledges security researcher(s) who responsibly disclose vulnerabilities as well as a change log for any revisions to the security bulletin itself.

You should use the information in the security bulletin and compare this with your inventory list to determine whether this security update pertains to your organization. If you find that the security update is applicable within your environment, you should determine the priority of its installation.

Determine the Installation Priority

Determining the priority of when to install the security update depends on your organization's infrastructure. When determining the priority, you should consider all of the workarounds published in the security bulletin to see whether you could use any temporarily while the proper change management policies are followed. If no workarounds will work for your organization and the security bulletin's severity rating is critical, you should have a process in place by which you can "fast track" an installation of a security update to your production environment.

Caution   If you decide to fast track a security update, you must do enough testing on how the security update works with your critical business applications. Failure to thoroughly test the security update may result in data compromise and lost productivity. The rate at which you deploy an update is a risk management decision. You should determine whether the update is important enough to risk valuable computers not functioning correctly if the update is not successful.

Phase 3: Evaluate and Plan

This phase can be divided into three parts: determining the appropriate change that best suits your organization's needs, planning the release by identifying any potential deployment blockers, and then determining how to release the software update within your production environment.

The Best Approach to Mitigating the Vulnerability

You have a couple of different options when evaluating the most effective way to mitigate a vulnerability. For example, you can deploy the security update, or you can mitigate the vulnerability by applying countermeasures to reduce the attack surface.

If the binaries affected by the vulnerability are installed on the computer, deploying the security update is the best approach whenever possible. By deploying the security update, you are fixing the binaries associated with the vulnerability itself. However, if the binaries are related to a service that you do not use, a better solution might be to simply remove that service. For example, if IIS is installed on a computer, but you are not using it as a Web server, you could uninstall IIS and not have to deploy the security update because the binaries are no longer present on the computer. Applying countermeasures should only serve as a temporary workaround until you can install the security update. Two examples of countermeasures are disabling services and setting Internet Explorer kill bits. More information about setting Internet Explorer kill bits can be found here: *http://support.microsoft.com/kb/240797*. Any workaround that has been tested and signed off by Microsoft for a particular security update will be shown in the Workarounds area of the Vulnerability Information section of the security bulletin.

> **Note**   Often, your analysis of the priority of the security update may help you select your mitigation strategy. For example, if you decide that a certain security update is critical to your organization, you may not have enough time to properly test it. After looking at the available workarounds, you may decide to deploy the workaround while the full test cycle is completed on the security update itself. Just make sure that the analysis is done by class of computer. For example, a QuickTime remote code execution exploit is critical for a workstation, but if people are surfing YouTube on your domain controllers, you have a whole different set of problems you need to address.

Planning for the Release

After determining which step you will take, the next step is change management planning. First, you have to find out how many computers are affected by this vulnerability. This is where the inventory comes in handy. After that, you should identify any potential deployment blockers. Some of these deployment blockers could be insufficient disk space on the computers that need this security update, any Group Policy objects that are blocking software installation, or change management maintenance windows on servers that have a high availability requirement.

> **Important**   Make sure to include all change management maintenance windows when you are planning for the release of the security update.

Determining the Release Mechanism

Fortunately, most security updates from Microsoft have standardized command-line parameters and delivery method. This is helpful if you need to deploy these security updates through an Active Directory Domain Services start-up script. The command-line parameters are shown later in this chapter.

WSUS will automatically download Microsoft security updates to an internal update server, enabling you to control deployment more granularly. However, WSUS only applies to security updates supplied by Microsoft.

> **Note**   WSUS only supports Microsoft products. For non-Microsoft applications, you should look at System Center Essentials 2007, which will allow you to create custom deployment packages.

Phase 4: Deploy

In the deploy phase, you communicate the change with specific deployment times, test the security update on a small group of computers, and then roll it out to all computers within your organization. The deploy phase can make or break a successful security update release.

Communicating the Change

Communicating change is an important aspect of update management. You must ensure that everyone who will be potentially affected is clear on when the security update will be deployed, and you must devise a rollback plan in case things do not go as expected. You should get approval from the relevant stakeholders regarding specifics, such as when this security update will be deployed and when computers will be rebooted. Failure to get approval or inadequately communicating this change can lead to frustration and may delay future deployments.

In large environments, communicating the change within a reasonable amount of time may not be possible. If this is the case, you can implement a Service Desk solution that tracks changes and notifies the appropriate people when a change is requested. System Center Service Manager is a Microsoft product that will provide this functionality. Although as of this writing this product is still in beta, you can read about it on the Microsoft Web site (*http://www.microsoft.com/systemcenter/svcmgr/default.mspx*).

Testing the Security Update on a Small Group of Computers

Forecasting any issues that may arise between business critical applications and the security update is one of the most important things in your entire patch management strategy. The only way to proactively find and address any application compatibility issues is to test the security update alongside your applications.

One way to approach this is to have a few computers on hand with the applications installed. Install the security update on these computers and test as many scenarios as possible. However, using this method can lead to unexpected issues if the person testing the application does not test everything. A better approach is to install the security update on a group of computers that are being used throughout the business day. Make sure to inform users that this security update is being installed on their computers and have them report back any issues that they encounter. If you pick several users with different roles within your organization, you have a better chance of wide coverage of all scenarios, as opposed to having a group of IT personnel manually running through use cases. However, even this approach is unlikely to cover all scenarios that should be tested.

 Note   If you are using WSUS to deploy your security updates, you can create a test computer group, add your test client computers to this group, and then deploy the updates to this group only.

Deploying the Security Update to the Masses

All security updates that are deployed should be done so within a scheduled change maintenance window. The change maintenance should be communicated to all affected users and should tell them that the update is coming. Once this is completed, you should test the security update until you are confident that no unexpected issues will arise and then request signoff from the relevant stakeholders. After that, it is time to press the big, green GO button.

After a deployment, you should revisit the process with the relevant stakeholders and IT management to determine whether any improvements or refinements are needed to your update management strategy. Update management is a constantly evolving process that should be constantly reviewed.

The Anatomy of a Security Update

With Windows Vista and Windows Server 2008, the security update is packaged within an MSU file. The package is installed using the Windows Update Stand-Alone Installer process (wusa.exe) and contains a cabinet (CAB) file for the update, an XML file that describes the update, and a properties file that includes the strings used by the installer. (If more than one update is included in the package, a separate CAB file is included for each one.)

Supported Command-Line Parameters

Unlike previous versions of security update packages, the **/X** command-line switch no longer works. You can use the expanded command-line utility provided with the Windows operating system, or a non-Microsoft file-archiving application that is aware of MSU files, such as 7-Zip (*http://www.7-zip.org/*). Table 12-2 describes all of the available command-line parameters supported by the Windows Update Stand-Alone Installer process.

Table 12-2   **Command-line parameters of wusa.exe**

Parameter	Description
/?, /help, or /h	Displays the command-line help associated with the Windows Update Stand-Alone Installer
/quiet	Quiet mode. Does not display a user interface during the installation.
/norestart	Suppresses a reboot of the computer, if needed.

A nifty addition to the new MSU package is the fact that you can install the security update by using Package Manager (pkgmgr.exe). The following example shows you how to do this:

```
Expand -F:* "%TEMP%\x86-all-windows6.0-kb941651-x86_cf2d8dd55a356b9d27b75ead67ff45c
f3d2d9a14.msu" %TEMP%
Pkgmgr /n:%TEMP%\Windows6.0-KB941651-x86.xml
```

Integrating MSU Files into a Windows Image File

You can integrate the security updates into an offline image so that any new computer that has this image applied will already have the security update installed. To integrate the security updates into a Windows Image file (WIM), follow these steps:

> **Important**   Before you proceed with these steps, be sure to download and install the Windows Automated Installation Toolkit available at *http://www.microsoft.com/downloads/details.aspx?familyid=C7D4BC6D-15F3-4284-9123-679830D629F2&displaylang=en*.

1. Download the MSU files that you want to integrate into the WIM. For this procedure, we will save all updates to the %TEMP% folder.

2. Expand the MSU files. Repeat this step for each downloaded security update file.

    ```
    Expand -F:* "%TEMP%\x86-all-windows6.0-kb941651-x86_cf2d8dd55a356b9d27b75ead67ff45c
    f3d2d9a14.msu" %TEMP%
    ```

3. Mount the image file that you will be integrating into these updates.

    ```
    Imagex /mountrw d:\imaging\vista.wim c:\mounted_images
    ```

4. Add the MSU files to the mounted image file.

    ```
    Peimg /import=%TEMP%\Windows6.0-KB941651-x86.cab c:\mounted_images\mount\windows
    ```

5. Install the packages to the WIM file.

```
Peimg /install=*Package* c:\mounted_images\mount\windows
```

6. Commit your changes and unmount the WIM file.

```
Imagex /unmount /commit c:\mounted_images
```

Tools for Your Patch Management Arsenal

Microsoft offers a wide range of products that can assist you in deploying security updates to your organization.

Microsoft Download Center

The Microsoft Download Center (*http://www.microsoft.com/downloads/*) is a Web site dedicated to offering a wide range of updates, tools, trial software, documents—just about everything. In a security update context, the Microsoft Download Center is important because it allows you to search for a particular security update and download it. Once the update is downloaded, you can install the security updates manually, incorporate them into custom-built scripts, or package them for deployment through a patch management system. For examples of scripts that were written in VBScript or PowerShell that may help you deploy updates, see the Microsoft Script Repository at *http://www.microsoft.com/technet/scriptcenter/scripts/default.mspx?mfr=true*.

Microsoft Update Catalog

The Microsoft Update Catalog (*http://catalog.update.microsoft.com/*) is a Web site that allows you to find anything offered by the Microsoft Update Service. The types of downloads include security updates, device driver updates, other Microsoft product updates, and hotfixes that were traditionally only available by calling Microsoft Customer Service and Support (CSS). The following keys features are included in the Microsoft Update Catalog:

- **Shopping Basket**   With the Microsoft Update Catalog, you can add several downloads to a shopping basket and download them all at once.

- **Full-text Search**   You can search by keyword, product, Knowledge Base article number, MSRC bulletin number, device driver manufacturer, device driver model, and device driver version.

- **RSS feeds**   The Microsoft Update Catalog supports Really Simple Syndication Feeds so that you can save your search to an RSS feed. You will be notified when new downloads matching your criteria are released.

- **BITS support**   Background Intelligent Transfer Service (BITS) is a service that monitors the bandwidth that you are using and adjusts the download rate accordingly. Additionally, BITS has support for resume, so if you lose your Internet connection halfway through a download, the download will resume where you left off when the connection is available again.

The home page of the Microsoft Update Catalog Web site is shown in Figure 12-2.

Figure 12-2   You can search the Microsoft Update Catalog to download all security updates offered by the Microsoft Update service.

Windows Update and Microsoft Update

Windows Update is an application that allows you to check for and install updates that are missing from your computer. Optionally, you can elect to use Microsoft Update to get updates for the 2007 Office system, device driver updates, and other Microsoft products.

> **Security Alert**   You must be a member of the local Administrators group to run Windows Update.

The Windows Update user interface is shown in Figure 12-3.

Windows Update offers you several options when you open the Windows Update control panel item.

- **Get Updates For More Products**   When you click this button, it will open to the Microsoft Update Web site so that you can install the Microsoft Update Service.

- **Check For Updates**   This allows you to query the Windows Update or Microsoft Update service for new updates that may be available for your computer.

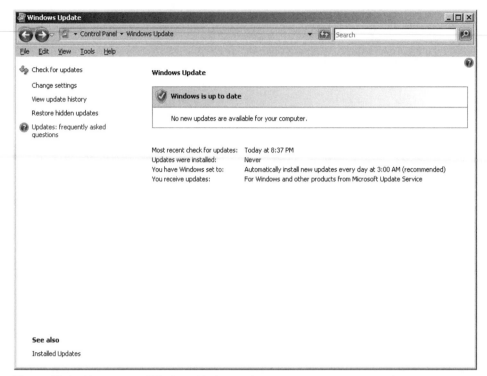

Figure 12-3   You can use Windows Update to keep your computer up to date.

- **Change Settings**   Allows you to change the Windows automatic update settings. (These are covered in the next section.)

- **View Update History**   Shows you all of the updates that are installed on this computer, as well as the status of the update (whether it was successful), the type of update, and the date the update was installed.

- **Restore Hidden Updates**   You can ask Windows Update to stop informing you of certain updates. The Restore Hidden Updates option allows you to restore the update so that it will be offered again.

- **Updates: Frequently Asked Questions**   Opens the Help And Support topic that explains that changes to Windows Update in Windows Vista and Windows Server 2008.

Windows Automatic Updating

As mentioned earlier, the Automatic Updates feature, now known as Windows automatic updating, has been integrated into the Windows Update control panel utility, where you can configure automatic updating by clicking Change Settings. The Windows automatic updating window is shown in Figure 12-4.

The default settings are shown in Figure 12-4. However, at times the defaults will not work within your organization. For example, servers require high availability and tighter control over when updates are installed and the server is rebooted. In this case, you could turn off automatic updating manually by using the settings in Figure 12-4 or by using Group Policy to disable automatic updating on more than one computer.

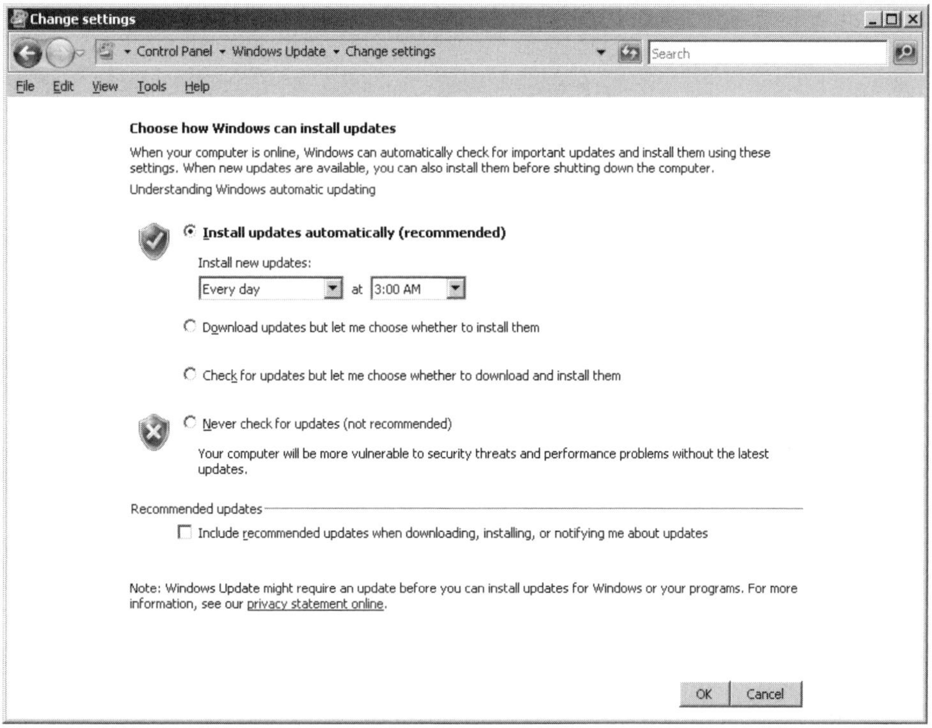

Figure 12-4   You can configure Windows automatic updating to download and install all security updates at a specific time.

There are four options to configure regarding how updates are downloaded and installed on your computer:

- **Install Updates Automatically**   This option will download and install the updates using the day and time specified in the Install New Updates box.

- **Download Updates But Let Me Choose Whether To Install Them**   This option will download the updates and notify you when they are ready for download. You can choose to install them or not.

- **Check For Updates But Let Me Choose Whether To Download And Install Them**   This option will notify you when new updates are ready for download. After you download them, you can install them.

- **Never Check For Updates**   This turns off Windows automatic updating. This option is not recommended on client computers. You may want to do this on servers where you need to strictly control which updates are downloaded and installed.

By default, Windows automatic updating will only notify you when new security updates are available. You can select the Include Recommended Updates When Downloading, Installing, Or Notifying Me About Updates check box to include recommended updates. Recommended updates are updates that are not related to a security vulnerability but could provide value to your computer. Some examples are new versions of the .NET Framework, Windows Media Player, or DirectX.

When the updates are installed, Windows automatic updating will ask you if you want to reboot now or postpone for a certain period of time. You will only be asked to reboot if necessary.

Microsoft Baseline Security Analyzer

The Microsoft Baseline Security Analyzer (MBSA) is a tool that scans your network and notifies you of computers with security settings that are not configured correctly or missing security updates. MBSA 2.1 was the first version that included support for Windows Vista and Windows Server 2008.

> **Note**   MBSA 2.1 was still in its beta stages when this book was written. Some changes might occur in this product before it is released.

MBSA 2.1 is a free download available from the MBSA Web site at *http://www.microsoft.com /mbsa*.

The initial MBSA window is shown in Figure 12-5.

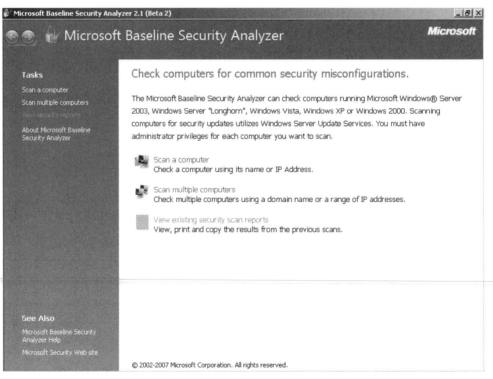

Figure 12-5   MBSA allows you to scan one computer or many computers at one time.

MBSA Scanning in Interactive Mode

When you scan in interactive mode, several options are available, as shown in Figure 12-6.

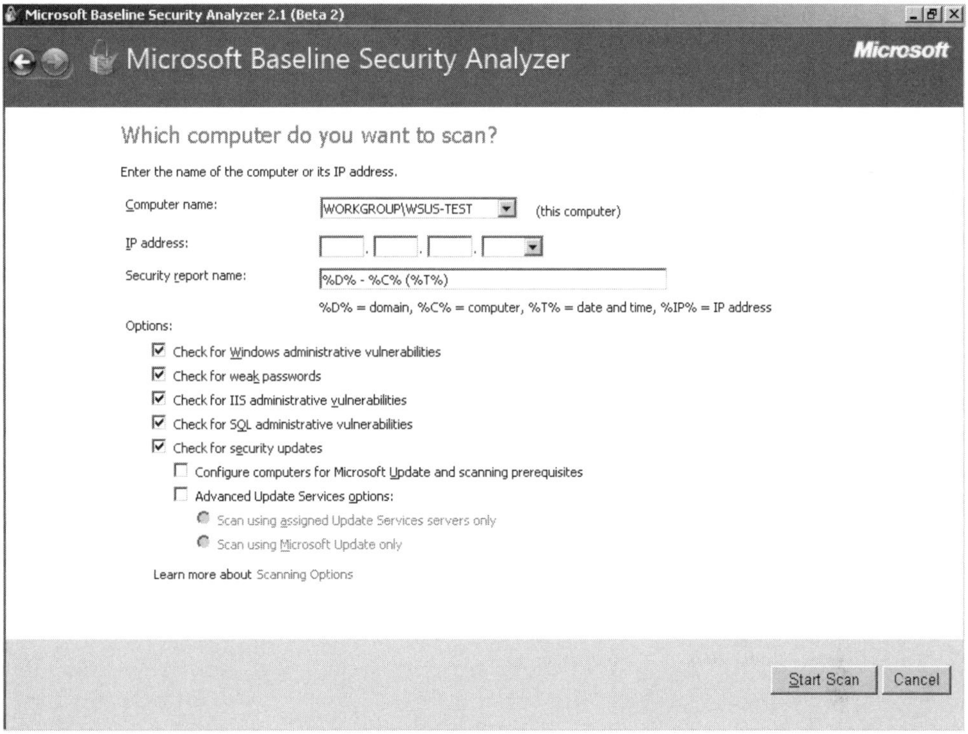

Figure 12-6   Scanning in interactive mode will show you its progress during the scan.

> **Caution**   Your user account must be a member of the local Administrators group on every computer that you scan.

To start a scan for only missing security updates in interactive mode, follow these steps:

1. Open Microsoft Baseline Security Analyzer. Click Start, point to All Programs, and then click Microsoft Security Baseline Analyzer 2.1.

2. Click Scan A Computer. If you want to scan multiple computers at once by either Domain name or IP address range, click Scan Multiple Computers.

3. In the Computer Name box, type or select the computer that you want to scan. The Computer Name box will default to the local computer. If you would rather scan by the computer's IP address, type or select the address in the IP Address box.

4. Clear the following check boxes:

    1. Check For Windows Administrative Vulnerabilities

    2. Check For Weak Passwords

3. Check For IIS Administrative Vulnerabilities

4. Check For SQL Administrative Vulnerabilities

> **Note**   MBSA can scan for much more than just missing security updates. When
> performing security assessment scans, you should select the boxes that you cleared in step 4.

5. Click Start Scan.

When the scan is complete, a report is displayed summarizing the scan results, as shown in
Figure 12-7.

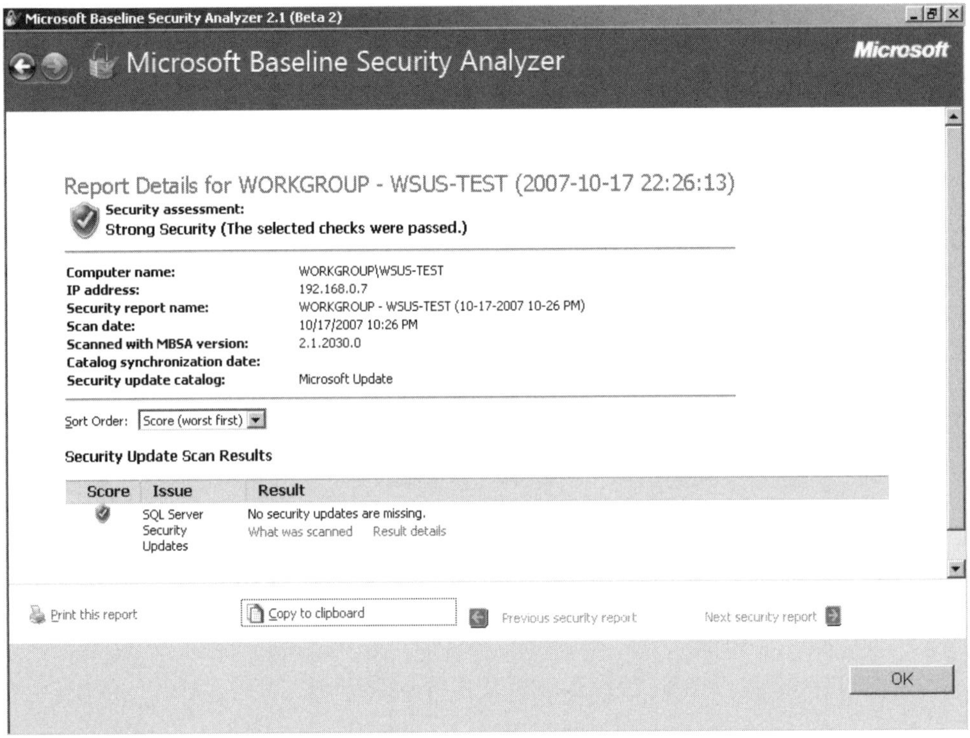

Figure 12-7   MBSA provides you a summary report after the scan is complete.

> **Tip**   The MBSA scan reports are stored in your user profile in the SecurityScans folder.
> The reports are in XML format with a file extension of .mbsa.

MBSA Scanning with the Command Prompt

The MBSA also includes an option to scan from a command prompt by using mbsacli.exe.
This may be useful if you wanted to conduct scans in a Group Policy Object's start-up script

and save the report to a share on the network. When you use mbsacli.exe, you have the same functionality as when scanning in interactive mode.

The parameters accepted by mbsacli.exe are as follows:

- **/target** *domain\computer* Scans the computer by using the computer name.
- **/target** *IP* Scans the computer by using its IP address.
- **/r** *IP_range* Scans multiple computers by using an IP address range in the form of 10.0.0.1–10.0.0.100.
- **/listfile** *file* Scans computers by reading the computer names or IP addresses from a text file.
- **/d** *domain* Scans all computers in a specified domain. The domain parameter should be in the form of the NETBIOS name and not the FQDN name.
- **/n** *option* Specifies which checks are not performed during this scan. The option parameter can accept the following values and can be concatenated together with a plus sign (+) without spaces between the values:
  - ❑ **OS** Does not check for Windows administrative vulnerabilities.
  - ❑ **Password** Does not check for weak passwords.
  - ❑ **IIS** Does not check for IIS administrative vulnerabilities.
  - ❑ **SQL** Does not check for SQL Server administrative vulnerabilities.
  - ❑ **Updates** Does not check for missing security updates.
- **/wa** If the computer is configured to install updates from a WSUS server, MBSA will only scan for updates that are WSUS-approved.
- **/wi** If the computer is configured to install updates from a WSUS server, MBSA will scan for updates that are approved and not approved.
- **/nvc** Will not check for a new version of MBSA.
- **/o** *filename* Specifies the path to the output XML file template. By default, MBSACLI.exe uses %D - %C – (%T).
- **/qp** Does not show display progress.
- **/qt** Does not display the report after the scan is complete.
- **/qe** Does not display the error list.
- **/qr** Does not display the report list.
- **/q** Does not display progress, the report after the scan is complete, the error list, and the report list.
- **/Unicode** Output file will be in Unicode text.
- **/u** *username* The scan will run under the specified user name.
- **/p** *password* The scan will run under the specified password.

- **/catalog** *filename* Specifies the data source that contains the security update information.

- **/ia** Updates the Windows Update Agent, if necessary, on the computer being scanned before starting the scan.

- **/mu** Configures the computer being scanned to use Microsoft Update instead of Windows Update.

- **/nd** Does not download any files from the Microsoft Web site when scanning.

- **/xmlout** Scan will run with only updates check enabled.

- **/l** Lists all reports available.

- **/ls** Lists reports from the latest scan.

- **/lr** Displays the overview report.

- **/ld** Displays the detailed report.

- **/?** Displays the mbsacli.exe command-line help.

Windows Server Update Services

WSUS uses a server to host updates that are deployed to computers running Microsoft Windows Server 2003, Windows Server 2008, Windows Vista, Microsoft Windows XP, and Windows 2000 with Service Pack 4.

The WSUS server deploys updates to the WSUS clients by using a Web service. The clients can be configured to connect to the WSUS server in a Group Policy Object (GPO) or by editing the client computer's registry manually. This chapter will use the GPO deployment method. For more information about using the registry to manually configure WSUS on a client, see *http://technet2.microsoft.com/windowsserver/en/library/1776f85d-a326-4f1d-a2ed-2fdd21d590d71033.mspx*.

An administrator must approve all updates before the WSUS clients can install them. When a WSUS client contacts the WSUS server it receives a list of updates that have been approved for its version of the operating system and any Microsoft products installed on the computer. When the WSUS client successfully installs an update, it notifies the WSUS server and the event is recorded in the WSUS database. This allows an administrator to run reports on the current update status of all computers managed by the WSUS server.

What's New in WSUS 3.0

WSUS 3.0 has incorporated many new features designed to help administrators better manage updates on their WSUS clients, including the following:

- The new Microsoft Management Console (MMC) Administration console

- The ability to install the WSUS Administration Console on computers other than the WSUS server

- Improved reporting, including update compliance reports on WSUS clients

Microsoft Products Supported by WSUS

As each new release of WSUS becomes available, support for more Microsoft products is introduced. WSUS 3.0 supports the following products, shown in Table 12-3:

Table 12-3   Supported Products for WSUS 3.0

Windows 2000 with Service Pack 4	Office XP
Windows XP (32-bit, IA-64, and x64 Editions)	Office 2003
Windows Vista	The 2007 Office System
Windows Server 2003	Office Communications Server 2007
Windows Server 2008	Microsoft Internet Security and Acceleration Server 2004
Windows Small Business Server 2003	Microsoft Internet Security and Acceleration Server 2006
Exchange Server 2000	Microsoft Data Protection Manager 2006
Exchange Server 2003	System Center Virtual Machine Manager 2007
Exchange Server 2007	Microsoft ForeFront
Computer Cluster	Network Monitor 3
CAPICOM SDK Components	Systems Management Server 2003
Microsoft Core XML Service	Virtual PC 2007
Visual Studio 2005	Virtual Server 2005
Windows Defender	SQL Server 2005
Windows Live	Microsoft Core XML Service

Configuring Prerequisites for WSUS 3.0

To install WSUS 3.0 on a computer running Windows Server 2008, you must configure the following installation prerequisites:

- If you do not have a server that is running SQL Server to use with WSUS, you can use the Windows Internal Database.

> **Caution**   The Windows Internal Database does not support remote connections, so you will not be able to install the WSUS Administration Console on another computer if you are using the Windows Internal Database.

- Because WSUS runs on top of a Web service, you must configure the Web Server role before installation can begin.

- If you are not using WSUS 3.0 with Service Pack 1 or later, the Web server configuration file must be modified to remove the custom error module.

> **Note**   To access some WSUS reports, you must install Microsoft Report Viewer Redistributable 2005, available at *http://go.microsoft.com/fwlink/?LinkId=70410*.

Install the Windows Internal Database

WSUS can use the Windows Internal Database to store all of its data. You can install the Windows Internal Database on Windows Server 2008 by using Server Manager:

1. Click Start, point to Administrative Tools, and then click Server Manager.

2. Click Features, and then click Add Features.

3. On the Select Features page, select the Windows Internal Database check box.

4. Click Yes, and then click Next.

5. Click Install.

6. When the installation is complete, click Close.

Install Web Server (IIS) Role

You install the Web Server (IIS) role on Windows Server 2008 by using Server Manager. Not all components of the Web Server role are required for WSUS to work correctly. You should leave the default role services enabled and also select ASP.NET, Windows Authentication, and IIS 6 Management Compatibility.

For more information about installing using Server Manager to install the Web Server (IIS) server role, see Chapter 11, "Securing Server Roles."

Configuring WSUS Prerequisites by Using ServerManagerCmd.exe

Windows Server 2008 introduces a new feature called Server Manager. Server Manager is your one-stop shop for managing server roles and features installed on your server. A command-line version of Server Manager, named ServerManagerCmd.exe, is also included. You can use ServerManagerCmd.exe to install single roles at a time, or you can provide an answer file (in XML format) to install specific roles, role services, and features. The following command passes an answer file into ServerManagerCmd.exe:

servermanagercmd -inputpath *answer_file*.xml

The following code is the XML answer file that you can use to install the role services and features required by WSUS:

```
<ServerManagerConfiguration
Action="Install" xmlns="http://schemas.microsoft.com/sdm/Windows/ServerManager
/Configuration/2007/1">
<RoleService Id="Web-Static-Content"/>
<RoleService Id="Web-Default-Doc"/>
<RoleService Id="Web-Dir-Browsing"/>
<RoleService Id="Web-Http-Errors"/>
<RoleService Id="Web-ASP-NET"/>
<RoleService Id="Web-Net-Ext"/>
<RoleService Id="Web-ISAPI-Ext"/>
<RoleService Id="Web-ISAPI-Filter"/>
<RoleService Id="Web-Http-Logging"/>
```

```
<RoleService Id="Web-Request-Monitor"/>
<RoleService Id="Web-Windows-Auth"/>
<RoleService Id="Web-Filtering"/>
<RoleService Id="Web-Stat-Compression"/>
<RoleService Id="Web-Mgmt-Console"/>
<RoleService Id="Web-Metabase"/>
<RoleService Id="Web-WMI"/>
<RoleService Id="Web-Lgcy-Scripting"/>
<RoleService Id="Web-Lgcy-Mgmt-Console"/>
<Feature Id="windows-internal-db"/>
<Feature Id="WAS"/>
</ServerManagerConfiguration>
```

Modify the Web Server Configuration File

If you are not using WSUS 3.0 with Service Pack 1 or later, you must remove the custom error module within the Web server configuration file before you install WSUS. Removing the custom error module is done by using a text editor and adding an extra line to the <System.WebServer><modules> tag. You can do so by following these steps:

1. Navigate to %WINDIR%\System32\inetsrv\config.

2. In Notepad, open the file named applicationHost.config.

3. Within the <System.WebServer><modules> tag, remove the line that reads <add name="CustomErrorModule" lockItem="true" />, if present.

4. Within the <System.WebServer><modules> tag, add **<remove name="CustomErrorModule" />**, and then save and close the file.

5. From a command prompt, type **iisreset**, and then press Enter.

Requirements for WSUS 3.0 Server

The hardware and software minimum requirements for WSUS 3.0 are shown in Table 12-4.

Table 12-4   Minimum Requirements for WSUS 3.0 Server

Requirement	Details
Operating System	Windows Server 2003 SP1 or later
	Windows Server 2008
Preinstalled software components	Internet Information Services
	Windows Internal Database or Microsoft SQL Server 2005 with Service Pack 1 (SP1)
	.NET Framework 2.0
	Microsoft Management Console 3.0
	Microsoft Report Viewer
Storage	1 GB on the system partition
	2 GB on the database volume
	20 GB on the volume where the updates are stored

Install and Configure WSUS 3.0

You can install WSUS using either the Windows Internal Database or a dedicated database server. In a production environment, a dedicated database server is strongly recommended. To install WSUS, follow these steps:

1. Download WSUS 3.0 from *http://www.microsoft.com/downloads/details.aspx? FamilyID=e4a868d7-a820-46a0-b4db-ed6aa4a336d9&DisplayLang=en.*

2. Start the installation by double-clicking WSUS3Setup.exe.

3. On the Welcome To The Windows Software Update Services 3.0 Setup Wizard page, click Next.

4. Select the Full Server Installation Including Administration Console option, and then click Next.

5. Select the I Accept The Terms Of The License Agreement option, and then click Next.

6. Choose the location where you want to WSUS to stores updates, and then click Next.

7. Select the Use An Existing Database Server On A Remote Computer option, specify the computer name of the database server, and then click Next. This step is shown in Figure 12-8.

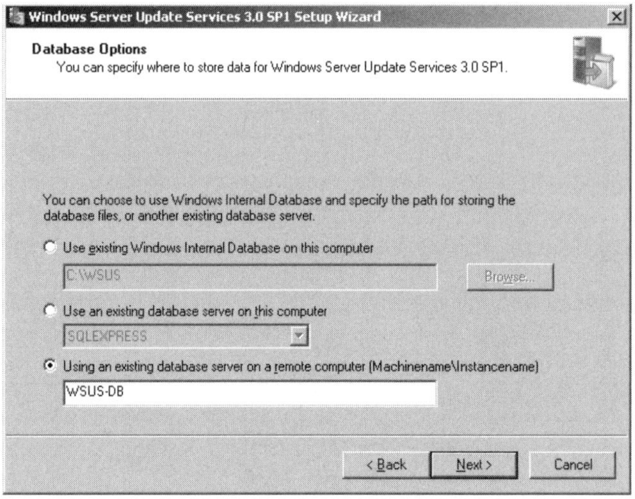

Figure 12-8   WSUS can use an existing SQL Server database or the Windows Internal Database.

8. On the Connecting to SQL Server Instance page, click Next.

9. Select the Use the existing IIS Default Web site option, and then click Next.

10. Click Next to begin the installation.

11. When the installation is compete, click Finish.

12. The WSUS Configuration Wizard is displayed automatically after the installation is finished. On the Before You Begin page, click Next.

13. If you would like to join the Microsoft Update Improvement Program, select the Yes, I would like to join the Microsoft update Improvement Program option, and then click Next.

14. Select the Synchronize from Microsoft Update option, and then click Next, as shown in Figure 12-9. If you have another WSUS server within your organization, you can synchronize from this server instead.

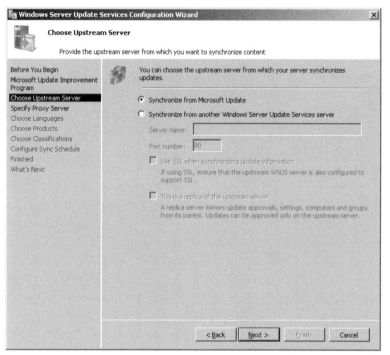

Figure 12-9 You can choose to get your updates from the Microsoft Update Service or from another WSUS server deployed within your organization.

15. If your organization requires a proxy server to connect to the Internet, enter the proxy information here. Otherwise, just click Next.

16. Click Start Connecting. When it has finished, click Next.

17. Choose the languages of the updates that should be stored locally on your WSUS computer, and then click Next.

18. Specify the products for which you want updates, and then click Next.

19. Specify the classification of updates that you want to synchronize. By default, the only classifications that are selected are Critical Updates, Definition Updates, and Security Updates.

20. Set the synchronization schedule, and then click Next. By default, it is set to synchronize manually, but you can decide whether you want your WSUS server to synchronize daily with the Microsoft Update Service.

21. If you want to synchronize now, select the Begin Initial Synchronization check box, and then click Next. The time that it takes to synchronize your local WSUS server with either the Microsoft Update Service or another WSUS server within your organization depends on the amount of available bandwidth. On average, this will take several minutes.

22. Click Finish.

Figure 12-10 shows the WSUS Administration Console after successful installation.

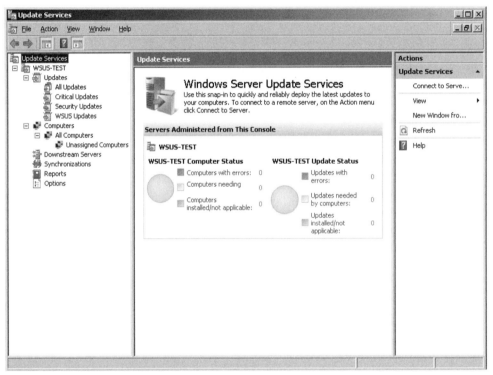

Figure 12-10   The WSUS Administration Console allows you to approve security updates, manage client computers, and run reports.

Configuring WSUS Clients

A WSUS client—a client computer on your network whose updates are managed by a WSUS server—uses Automatic Updates to receive updates from the WSUS server. You use a Group Policy Object (GPO) to configure WSUS clients. The GPO settings for WSUS are found in under the following node: Computer Configuration\Administrative Templates\Windows Components\Windows Update.

Several policy settings are available to configure Windows automatic updating. The two settings required by WSUS are Configure Automatic Updates and Specify Intranet Microsoft Update Service Location.

Figure 12-11 shows the Configure Updates policy setting.

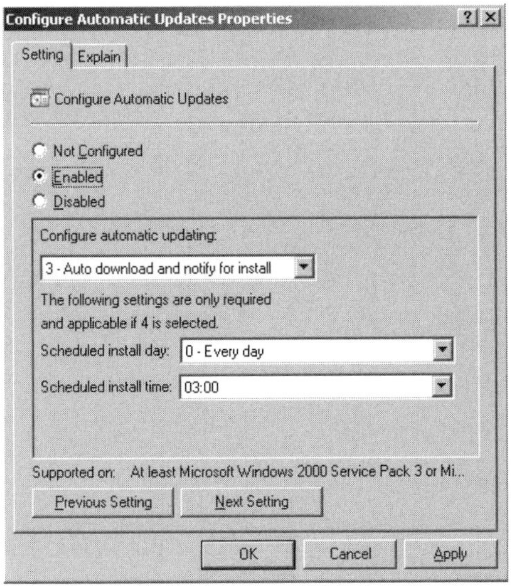

Figure 12-11   The Configure Automatic Updates policy setting allows you to use Group Policy to configure Windows automatic updating for all client computers on your network.

You can configure the Automatic Updates policy setting in the following ways:

■ **Notify For Download And Notify For Install**   Updates are not automatically downloaded or installed. If a user who is a member of the local Administrators group is logged on to the client computer, she will be notified that updates are ready to be downloaded and installed.

■ **Auto Download And Notify For Install**   Updates are automatically downloaded but not installed. If a user who is a member of the local Administrators group is logged on to the client computer, he will be notified that updates have downloaded and are ready to be installed.

■ **Auto Download And Schedule The Install**   Updates are automatically downloaded and installed according to the way that the Scheduled Install Day and Scheduled Install Time boxes were configured in the Configure Automatic Updates policy setting.

■ **Allow Local Admin To Choose Setting**   Users who are members of the local Administrators group can configure how updates are handled on the client computer. They are not allowed to disable Automatic Updates.

The Specify Intranet Microsoft Update Service Location policy setting is where you redirect the client computer to use your WSUS server, as opposed to connecting to Windows Update. You must configure both the intranet update service and intranet statistics server, but these values can point to the same server. The Specify Intranet Microsoft Update Service Location policy setting is shown in Figure 12-12.

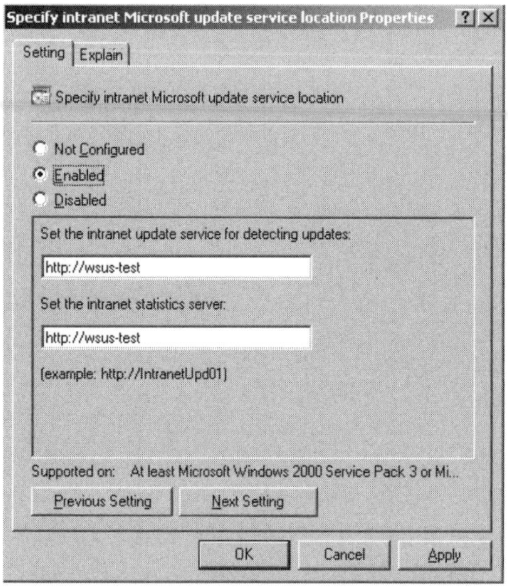

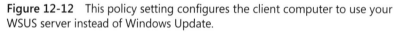

Figure 12-12   This policy setting configures the client computer to use your WSUS server instead of Windows Update.

After you configure settings in Group Policy, you can wait for the client computer to refresh them automatically or you can force the client by running **gpupdate** **/force** from a command prompt on the client computer. After the Group Policy settings are configured, you can wait approximately 20 minutes for the client computer to automatically contact the WSUS server or you can run **wuauclt.exe** **/detectnow** to force the client to contact the WSUS server immediately.

System Center Essentials 2007

The majority of this chapter focuses on free products released by Microsoft to help you in your patch management efforts. Microsoft also offers a product that can do everything within one application. Microsoft System Center Essentials 2007 is a management product aimed at midsize businesses that was developed to ease the burden of managing computers on your network. System Center Essentials 2007 offers a unified experience, proactive management, and increased efficiency in your daily activities. In this section we will look at how System Center Essentials 2007 is used in conjunction with your patch management strategy. Large organizations should use Microsoft System Center Configuration Manager 2007. For more information about the System Center family of products, see *http://www.microsoft.com/systemcenter*.

We have not yet addressed the issue of how to get an accurate inventory of all the computers on your network. System Center Essentials 2007 enables you to create and maintain a hardware and software inventory. System Center Essentials 2007 includes the following inventory features:

- **Automatic discovery** System Center Essentials 2007 can query Active Directory and determine whether any new computers have joined your domain and have not been inventoried yet. When new computers are found, System Center Essentials 2007 can inventory them the next time they are connected to the network.

- **Extensive reporting** The reporting engine allows you to distribute detailed data regarding the computers on your network. Additionally, the reports are customizable so that you can create dashboard reports to represent a quick snapshot of your network.

Now that you have an accurate computer inventory, you can use this information to deploy updates to the computers on your network by using the Update Configuration Wizard included with System Center Essentials 2007. The following features are not available in the products discussed earlier in this section:

- **Support for non-Microsoft updates** You can deploy updates that were released from any software manufacturer. This helps ensure that you have total coverage for all software that may be installed on computers within your network.

- **Update deployment deadlines** With each update, you can specify a deadline by which the update has to be installed. If the update has not been installed and the deadline has passed, System Center Essentials 2007 will not give the user an option to install. It will install and reboot if necessary.

- **Install on demand** System Center Essentials 2007 allows you to install the security update immediately without having to wait for the scheduled installation time. This can be handy if a security update has been released that fixes a serious security vulnerability.

- **Shared update schema** System Center Essentials 2007 supports use of a shared update schema that allows you to import catalogs from non-Microsoft update providers.

For additional information on System Center Essentials 2007, visit the Microsoft System Center Essentials 2007 home page at *http://www.microsoft.com/sce*.

Summary

Developing a patch management strategy is about having the right policies and procedures in place and the right tools for the job. It is something that requires extensive planning, but will pay off in the end in the form of less interruption to the productivity of your business.

This chapter talked about the four phases of developing a patch management strategy: assess, identify, evaluate and plan, and deploy. Each step is critical to the success of developing a patch management strategy that works for everybody in your organization. Additionally, this chapter talked about some of the Microsoft products and tools that have been developed to help you ensure that the computers on your network stay up to date when something new is released.

One last product not covered in this chapter is Network Access Protection (NAP). You can use NAP to ensure that all home computers that connect to your network via a VPN connection have a set level of updates installed before they are allowed on the network. For more information on using NAP to control the update level of home computers connecting to your network, see Chapter 5, "Windows Firewall(s)."

Additional Resources

- Microsoft Corporation (2008). "Security Guidance for Patch Management," at *http://www.microsoft.com/technet/security/guidance/patchmanagement.mspx.*

- Microsoft Corporation (2007). "Patch Management Process," at *http://www.microsoft.com/technet/security/guidance/patchmanagement/ secmod193.mspx.*

- Microsoft Corporation (2008). "Microsoft Update Catalog," at *http://catalog.update.microsoft.com/v7/site/Home.aspx.*

- Microsoft Corporation (2008). "Microsoft Download Center," at *http://download.microsoft.com.*

- Microsoft Corporation (2008). "Microsoft Baseline Security Analyzer," at *http://www.microsoft.com/mbsa.*

- Microsoft Corporation (2008). "Update Management Center," at *http://technet.microsoft.com/en-us/library/bb466251.aspx.*

- Microsoft Corporation (2008). "Microsoft Update," at *http://update.microsoft.com.*

- Microsoft Corporation (2008). "Windows Server Software Update Services," at *http://technet.microsoft.com/en-us/wsus/default.aspx.*

- Microsoft Corporation (2008). "System Center Essentials 2007," at *http://www.microsoft.com/sce.*

- Microsoft Corporation (2008). "Microsoft Security Tools," at *http://www.microsoft.com/ technet/security/tools/default.mspx.*

Chapter 13

Securing the Network

— Jesper M. Johansson

I am often asked how to protect workstations on a network. More specifically, the question is framed against the latest attack-du-jour that was demonstrated at some conference. For example, many people are currently extremely concerned about USB Flash Memory—those incredibly handy little finger-sized, solid-state memory devices that are now available in capacities bordering the ludicrous. People are worried about an attack that starts with the attacker inserting a USB Flash Drive into a computer, or causing the user to do so. The USB Flash Drive is laden with malware that either automatically—or with minimal user interaction—executes on the computer.

The problem with this preoccupation with USB Flash Drives is that it is an extremely narrow view of a much larger removable-device problem that also includes CDs, DVDs, FireWire drives, parallel port devices (does anyone still have these?), and just about any other port on the computer that can be used to access external content. Too often, people are only worried about workstations and not the rest of the network. I believe that the question is not how you keep workstations from getting hacked, but how you keep the rest of the network from falling like dominos once they do. Let's look at the math. If you have 10,000 end users in a network, what are the chances that you can keep all the workstations secure? Let's assume that each of those workstations is up to date with security updates, fully managed, and operated by users who are savvy enough about security to not run malicious content 99.99 percent of the time. Ignore the complete unrealism of these numbers for a moment and focus on the math. With 10,000 workstations, these numbers mean you have a 37 percent chance of having a secure network at any given time. With 20,000 workstations, your chances are about 13 percent. Add in a more realistic probability of each of your workstations being secure, and you will find that the probability of keeping all of them simultaneously secure asymptotically approaches zero as your network grows in size.

Clearly, it is absolutely critical to protect the network as a whole from the compromise of a single workstation. In fact, as an IT manager, I argue that no single thing you can to do improve the security of your operational environment is more crucial than managing dependencies in your network to isolate exposures. One part of this is to restrict communications within your network; Microsoft calls this Server and Domain Isolation. However, that puzzle has some more pieces.

Direct from the Source: Server and Domain Isolation

Server and Domain Isolation is one of the hidden security gems in Windows Server 2008 that's worth taking a closer look at. Although you had the ability to create virtual networks through end-point authentication in previous releases, the work we've done in Windows Vista and Windows Server 2008 makes this even easier to deploy. By combining IPsec connection security rules with Windows Firewall filters we have given Windows Server 2008 administrators a powerful tool to increase the security on their networks and better safeguard their important data—and all of this can be done without installing new software.

Chris Black, Program Manager
Windows Networking

Many organizations are still overconfident that their perimeter firewall solves most of the puzzle for them. However, perimeter firewalls are virtually meaningless in today's environment. To understand why, take a moment to try to enumerate the entry points into your network. If you have a medium-sized or larger network I am willing to bet a very good dinner that the last audit you had found a few egress points you were never aware of. Every computer on a virtual private network (VPN) is a potential ingress point. Every system that you have not updated is a potential ingress point. Every insecure, custom-written piece of software is a potential ingress point. Every misconfigured router, firewall, VPN device, and wireless access point is a potential ingress or egress point.

 Important   The principle of Defense in Depth simply requires that you put significant effort into reducing the impact of a compromise on your network.

One obvious method for addressing the problem of malicious removable devices is to ban everything with the potential to be malicious. This includes more than just USB Flash Drives. We would need to ban all removable devices, including anything that plugs into any device bus in the computer. I've said before that the best way to handle that problem is to use a giant tube of epoxy to plug up every opening you find on the back, front, sides, top, and bottom of the computer.

This approach has a couple of problems. First, your users might ambush you on the way to your car and perform a ritual sacrifice on you if you do. Second, they would be right to do so. Many of the aforementioned devices serve legitimate business needs. For instance, it is pretty much universally accepted that the most secure configuration of the BitLocker full hard-disk encryption technology in Windows Vista is to use an external key on a USB Flash Drive. Doing so would be rather difficult if you filled the USB ports with epoxy. I suppose you could glue the USB Flash Drive into the port, but that would sort of defeat the whole purpose of using it for encryption key storage. The same argument can be said for most ports on a computer these days.

The better option, in all but the most sensitive environments, is probably to attempt to manage the risk and contain the exposure. We need to accept a fundamental truth here. The general statement in Law 3 of the "10 Immutable Laws of Security" (see *http:// www.microsoft.com/technet/archive/community/columns/security/essays/ 10imlaws.mspx?mfr=true*) still holds:

> **Important**   If a bad guy has unrestricted physical access to your computer, it's not your computer anymore.

If an attacker has—or has ever had—access to your computer, that computer must be considered compromised. This kind of attack can even be perpetrated remotely, if the attacker can get you to run malicious code on your computer. Law 1 from the Immutable Laws states that:

> **Important**   If a bad guy can persuade you to run his program on your computer, it's not your computer anymore.

If we take it as a fact that the immutable laws still hold—and we probably can because they have proven to be remarkably resilient, and it is unlikely they will be proven invalid in any significant way until we fundamentally change how computers work—we cannot rest with a few registry tweaks to defang removable drives. Clearly, we must use additional layers of protection. In fact, if we simply make the quite reasonable assumption that many of our client computers are either already compromised, or operated by people who do not always have our best security interests front most in mind (or both), we arrive at the conclusion that we need to mitigate their effects on the remainder of the network. This leads us naturally to understand, analyze, and mitigate security dependencies.

Security Alert: On the Efficacy of Security Guides

For the past 15 years or so an unbelievable amount of effort has been devoted to building security guides. I have taken part in building about half a dozen of these over the years. These guides include a list of various security tweaks that— according to the authors—you must make to a standard installation of some software to meet some security requirement. The requirement itself is far too often unstated, and many of the guides are merely listings of every possible tweak that the authors thought might have even the most marginal impact on security; most of the time without considering the functionality your computers need to provide or threat environment your computers face. Often the settings recommended by the guides do not actually work on the software the guide is intended for.

The best of these guides make it very clear what the settings do, what application compatibility impact you can expect from them, and what specific threats they mitigate. Yet even the best of these guides spend scant space on the problem of network security at large. The guides are almost invariably focused on hardening a single computer against attacks, not fully accounting for the environment that computer is deployed in. The fact of the matter is that once the attacker has a foothold in the network, not a single setting in the security guides matters. The fact that account lockout is set to infinite lockout after three bad guesses—aggravating every user in the process—makes no difference to the attacker that has administrative privileges.

Rather than focus your efforts on which tweaks you need to make to your computers, you will get a lot more mileage out of simply accepting that some portion of your network is, and always will be, untrustworthy. The reality is that Enterprise networks today are semi-hostile at best. Let's accept that sad state as fact and move on. We deal with that problem by protecting the network as a whole from the few bad elements. You cannot secure a society by setting down rules and a sturdy wall around the society. You also need police officers. Police officers are basically a function of society's acceptance that some portion of its members refuse to live within the boundaries that have been set for them. Your network is no different.

Introduction to Security Dependencies

A **security dependency** occurs when the security of one computer is dependent on the security of another. This is quite common, and in many cases desirable. For instance, you might have heard that if your domain controller (DC) has been hacked, your entire network has been hacked. This is a simplistic way of stating that all domain members are dependent on the DCs for their security. If the domain controller is not kept secure, the member computers cannot possibly be kept secure. An attacker who can change the security configuration of the domain can take over any computer in the domain—for example, by adding new accounts to the Administrators group on a member computer. This explains why any so-called vulnerability that allows a system or network to be compromised by an administrator is not really a legitimate security vulnerability. That is because an administrator, by definition, is supposed to have complete access to the system or network he or she is administering.

Dependencies in computer systems are clearly unavoidable. However, that does not mean that they are all acceptable: Some are acceptable and even desirable, while others are unacceptable.

Before we analyze the different types of dependencies and how to mitigate them, we need to understand which types of dependencies are acceptable and which are not.

Acceptable Dependencies

Acceptable dependencies can be summed up by the following statement, from *Protect Your Windows Network*:

A less sensitive system may depend on a more sensitive system for its security.

Computers—and systems in general—can be divided into classes based on their security sensitivity. A system that is more sensitive has higher security requirements, while one that is less sensitive needs less security. The specific set of classes in any particular environment is irrelevant to the general discussion; only the fact that there are inherent classifications is important. For the sake of argument, let us assume that we have two classes of systems: workstations and DCs. The DCs, obviously, are far more sensitive than the workstations. If you control a workstation, theoretically you should have access to only the data used on that workstation. However, if you control a DC, you have the keys to the kingdom—you have complete access to everything in the forest. In that case, it is acceptable for the workstations to depend on the DCs for their security. The DCs class is far more sensitive than the workstations, and must be correspondingly better protected. This is a form of an acceptable dependency.

The same argument can be made for user accounts. It is acceptable for an administrator to compromise data owned by a user. This is what it means to be an administrator in the first place. Administrators have unfettered (although not always direct and obvious) access to the computer and everything on it. If we understand that and manage the computers appropriately, this is not a problem.

Software can be analyzed the same way. A less sensitive piece of software, such as a Web browser, may use and depend on a more sensitive piece of software for its security, such as the operating system itself. That is acceptable. If the operating system has a bug, the fact that the Web browser is now vulnerable to some new problem is really not surprising and is probably rather low on the list of worries. This also helps us understand where bug fixes go. The bug should be fixed as close to the problem as possible, to have the maximum protective impact. Rather than work around the problem in the Web browser, fix it in the operating system. Alternatively, rewrite the Web browser to reduce its dependencies on functionality in the operating system. This latter approach is appropriate if the functionality in the operating system was never intended to be used in the way it is being used, or if the functionality is not designed to protect against the particular attack the Web browser is suffering from.

Unacceptable Dependencies

Unacceptable dependencies should by now be obvious. Again, quoting from *Protect Your Windows Network*:

A more sensitive system must never depend on a less sensitive system for its security.

If we again think in terms of classes of sensitivity, this statement is easily understood. If a compromise of a workstation means that the domain controller's security has been breached, we have a serious security problem on our hands. As mentioned earlier, it is impossible to protect a network if its aggregate security is dependent on the security of every single computer in that network. The likelihood that the network is secure is inversely exponentially related to the size of the network. A network of any reasonable size is, for all practical purposes, never entirely secure. This makes it paramount that more sensitive systems are protected from less sensitive ones.

This argument can easily be extended to user accounts and software. For example, the new Terminal Services client for Windows permits storage of user names and passwords for virtually transparent Terminal Services logon. Those credentials are stored using the Credential Manager API, protected by the credentials used for the primary log-on session.

To see how this can create a security dependency, let us analyze the case of a network administrator logging on to his personal workstation. He uses this workstation for e-mail, Web browsing, and other typical information worker tasks. Naturally, he uses a low-privileged domain account for this purpose. At some point during the day he connects to one of the domain controllers to perform some form of management. He uses the Terminal Services client to do this, and elects to store his password to make future connections easier. This results in at least one, possibly two, unacceptable security dependencies. The first is that his domain administrative account credentials are now protected by his low-privileged information worker credentials. If his low-privileged user account is compromised, his domain administrative user account is also compromised, and thus the entire domain is compromised.

The second dependency results from the fact that he typed a domain administrative credential on a non-domain controller. Unless his personal workstation is protected at least as well as the domain controllers—and that is hard to believe—we have a dependency situation in which the security of the domain controllers depends on the security of this user's personal workstation. If, for example, a disgruntled employee in the same office has installed a hardware keystroke logger on the network administrator's workstation, the domain administrative credentials are now stored on that keystroke logger. Anytime you type a domain administrative credential on a non-domain controller you have exposed to entire domain to any security flaws on the non-domain controller. For instance, if an attacker inserts a removable drive into a computer where a Domain Administrator is currently logged on, or has ever logged on, or will ever log on, that Domain Administrator is compromised, and by extension the entire domain is compromised. It is absolutely imperative that you understand how these dependencies work so that you can avoid letting them compromise your network. It means, for example, that you should be very careful which computers you use to administer sensitive computers in the network.

The foregoing analysis leads us to two very concrete pieces of advice. First, never use a computer to enter, retrieve, process, or store data that is more sensitive than the computer itself. Remember, every piece of data handled by a computer should be considered accessible to everyone who has ever used that computer, or who will ever use that computer. Saving credentials on a computer whose every user you trust is safe. Saving them on a computer that may be used by untrusted users, or that may have malware installed at some point, is not safe.

Second, never administer a sensitive computer from a computer that is less sensitive. Practically speaking, this means that you should have dedicated management stations used to administer ultra-sensitive computers, such as domain controllers. Simply using runas or User Account Control (UAC) does not introduce a sufficient security boundary.

Obviously the same situation can happen with software. For instance, let us say we want to write a very secure Web browser. We want this browser to be far more secure than the built-in browser. In this case we cannot rely on any functionality provided by the built-in browser. In the case of Windows, where the browser implements much of the client-side, Internet-related functionality in the operating system, we cannot use any built-in Uniform Resource Locator (URL) validation functions or any Hypertext Markup Language (HTML) display functionality provided by the operating system, because those are really components of Internet Explorer. If we rely on functionality provided by the built-in browser, we have a security dependency on the built-in browser. Based on our stated objective of being more secure than the built-in browser, this dependency is unacceptable.

Dependency Analysis of an Attack

At this stage, it might be useful to take a quick detour and analyze an attack from a dependency perspective. Earlier we saw what can happen if a malicious removable drive is inserted into a computer. However, it may not be obvious what would happen to the network where that computer lives. Let's assume that the computer in question is domain-joined, as shown in Figure 13-1.

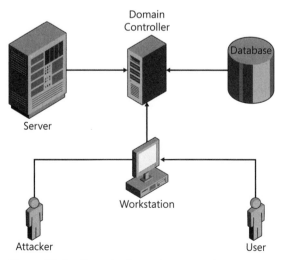

Figure 13-1 Domain dependency graph.

Figure 13-1 shows an ideal dependency graph. The arrows are directional and point in the dependency order: The security of the workstation is dependent on the security of the DC, and the security of the user is dependent on the security of the workstation. The attacker might be able to compromise the workstation, which would compromise any information the user has placed on that workstation, but the compromise would be isolated there.

Let us change the picture a little. Suppose the user logging on to the workstation is a member of the local administrators group on the Server. And suppose that a domain administrator frequently logs on to the server. We now have the dependencies shown with bold arrows in Figure 13-2.

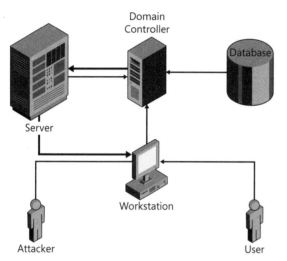

Figure 13-2   Domain dependency graph showing unacceptable dependencies.

As you can tell from Figure 13-2, we can completely violate the security of the entire network by simply changing the assumption of who logs on to which computer. Because a domain administrator logs on to the server, the security of the DC—and hence the domain—is dependent upon the security of the server. This would be acceptable if the server were managed as securely as the DC. However, a user that logs on to the workstation is a member of the Administrators group on the server, making the server dependent on the workstation for its security. Dependencies are *transitive*, which means that the security of the entire domain is now dependent on the security of the workstation, where the user, unfortunately, just ran the attacker's malicious tools. This is why it is so important to manage your dependencies appropriately.

Types of Dependencies

You need to manage many different kinds of dependencies. Some are beyond the scope of this book, such as dependencies inherent in software development. For instance, the security of code on a Web site is dependent upon proper isolation being enforced in the Web browsers that all the visitors use.

However, several different kinds of dependencies are relevant to a network, and in this section I will introduce them and discuss how to mitigate them using standard analysis techniques and actual implementation of these techniques in Windows Server 2008.

Usage Dependencies

The first and simplest kind of dependency is a **usage dependency**. A usage dependency results from usage of computing resources and data in a manner inconsistent with the trust levels of those resources. The first scenario in this chapter—the removable device—is an example of a usage dependency. A user that uses a removable device creates a usage dependency on that device. Whenever a user at one trust level uses a resource at a different trust level there are potential usage dependencies.

There are other kinds of usage dependencies as well. One great example is usage of a single credential in multiple places. For instance, suppose your network is divided into a data-center forest and a corporate forest. All the users in the datacenter forest also have accounts in the corporate forest. The likelihood that at least one user will have the same user name and password on both of these accounts is extremely high. Yet this violates the entire purpose of having the two forests, which is to ensure that a compromise in one forest does not result in a compromise of another. By using the same password in both places, this particular user has opened a potential pathway between the two. An attacker that breaches a computer in one forest that this user is using can extract the password hash and use it to authenticate to resources in the other forest.

How It Works: Password Hashes Are Plaintext Equivalent

Virtually every computer system in existence today accepts password authentication in at least some situations. On Windows Server 2008—as well as previous server versions of Windows—you can configure a domain to require smart cards for authentication from one or more users. However, as you saw in Chapter 2, "Authenticators and Authentication Protocols," even when you do so, there will still be a password hash for the user. This hash is transmitted to the client each time the user authenticates to enable automatic access to NTLM-protected resources. This means that an attacker that has access to this hash can access network resources as this user. For more information on this, see Chapter 2.

Access-Based Dependencies

An **access-based dependency** occurs when a user at one trust level accesses a resource in a way that makes the user dependent on the security of that resource. Access-based dependencies result from the access itself, not from usage of a resource or computing construct. Many times they rely on one user or entity trusting another entity that has a security problem.

For example, suppose user Alice accesses a network resource. The network resource is on the server LOKE, which, unknown to Alice, was hacked by Bob earlier that same day. Bob has installed a rootkit on the server that causes authentication to be downgraded to an insecure form of authentication. Alice's computer is running Windows XP, which by default is configured to negotiate authentication to whatever the server and client can agree upon. In doing so, Alice sends a challenge-response sequence that the attacker can replay against Alice's computer, thereby gaining access to her computer with the same privileges she has. To understand this flow, look at Figure 13-3, which shows a normal authentication flow from a client to a server.

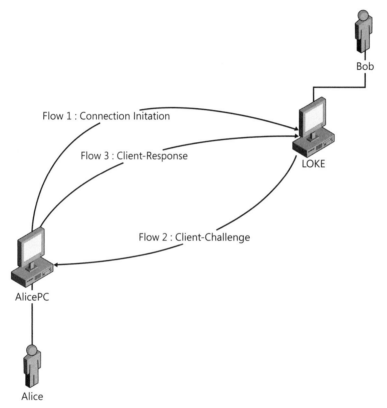

Figure 13-3 A normal challenge response flow from a client to a server.

In the normal flow a client initiates a connection to the server. The server responds with a challenge. The client creates a response to the challenge by performing a cryptographic operation with the authenticator (typically a password hash) and the challenge and returns this as the response. The server performs the same computation and compares the results. If they match, the authentication succeeds.

Now consider Figure 13-4. In this case the client does not respond as it should.

In Figure 13-4 the client attempts to connect as before. At this point, the server is supposed to send a challenge back. However, the server instead responds with its own connection attempt in flow 2. The client responds to this connection attempt with a challenge (flow 3), which the server subsequently reflects back to the client as the challenge for the connection the client initiated (flow 4). The client now has the same challenge it originally sent back. Unaware that something is amiss, the client computes a valid response to this challenge, which it originally sent, and returns it to the server for the connection the client initiated (flow 5). The server takes this response and returns it as a response to the challenge the client issued for the inbound connection (flow 6). The net result is that we now have two successful connections—one from the client to the server and one from the server to the client. This is known as the **reflection attack**. In Windows Vista and Windows Server 2008 this attack is broken using stateful challenge management. This means that the computer will no longer accept an inbound challenge that matches an outstanding challenge that it sent. In earlier versions the attack can be broken using various security settings.

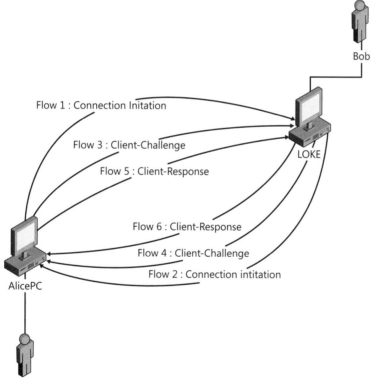

Figure 13-4   Using a reflection attack, the client can "reflect" the server's challenge back to the client to get a valid response.

This attack works because of an access-based dependency. There are other forms of such dependencies. A user might use a public kiosk to access e-mail by using Microsoft Office Outlook Web Access. Public kiosks are among the most malware-infested, untrustworthy, dangerous computers in the world today. Any resource you use on a public kiosk should be considered accessible to any user that has ever accessed that computer in the past or will ever access it the future. There is an access-based dependency between the security of the public kiosk—which you do not control—and any resource you have access to with credentials you use on a public kiosk.

Administrative Dependencies

One of the most common types of dependencies is an **administrative dependency**, which occurs when the same account is used to administer two different resources. For example, when you use a domain administrative account to administer member servers, as shown previously in Figure 13-2, you create an administrative dependency. This may sound a lot like a usage dependency, and it is. However, there is one important difference: administrative dependencies need not be usage-based. Let's say that the Administrators group on Server A includes Teddy, Maggie, and Alex, and the Administrators group on Server B includes Maggie, Jesper, and Jennifer. Maggie might never have logged on to Server A. However, Server B is compromised. When Maggie logs on to Server B, the attacker that compromised Server B has access to Maggie's credentials and can now use them to access Server A.

Service Account Dependencies

Service account dependencies occur when the same identity is used to run a service in multiple places. Suppose you use a network-wide Enterprise Management Solution (EMS). The EMS package includes an agent that runs on all computers to enable remote deployment of software, remote management, and all kinds of other goodness. The agent runs as the _DomainTools account. The _DomainTools account obviously needs to have elevated privileges on all the members to enable this type of remote management. This creates a service account dependency between all the computers where the _DomainTools account has high privileges. If any one of those computers is compromised, all of them are potentially compromised because the attacker now has access to a highly privileged account.

Operational Dependencies

Finally, we have **operational dependencies**. Operational dependencies result from the way a network is operated. For instance, Active Directory creates an ipso facto operational dependency. Any asset within a forest is dependent on the forest for its security. If the forest is compromised, so are all assets within the forest. The forest, in turn, is dependent on all domains in the forest. If a domain is compromised, so is the forest.

> **Security Alert**   The forest, not the domain, is and has always been the security boundary in Active Directory.

Another very common dependency in a network is based on the software distribution system. Very often a single server or a set of Distributed File System (DFS) shares are used to distribute software to computers within the network. If an attacker compromises the server(s) that host the software, all computers that receive software from it are potentially compromised.

The operational dependency has created an access-based dependency on the software distribution servers.

Categorizing Dependencies

As you may have noticed by now, the boundaries between the different kinds of dependencies are not always clear, and a single dependency can belong to several categories. For example, a service account used on multiple computers is both a service account dependency and an administrative dependency. The idea behind classifying the dependencies is simply to facilitate thinking about them. One type of dependency is not inherently far worse than another. Individual instances of dependencies might be more or less severe, but that is because of the facts of that instance, not the category of dependency it belongs to. Use the categories as a guideline to help you think about your network, not as a forced framework to plug things into. If you find a different taxonomy to be more useful, use that instead.

The only rule here is that everything you do should improve the security of your network.

Mitigating Dependencies

Finally, many pages into the chapter, we get to the part about how to solve the problem. It has taken this long because the concepts we have discussed so far are barely touched on in the vast majority of security literature, which often does not even mention these issues.

One of the most important techniques for mitigating security dependencies today involves isolating computers that do not need to communicate so that they cannot do so. Microsoft calls this Server and Domain Isolation. To build a strategy to do so is best done in a step-wise process:

1.   Define a classification scheme.

2.   Model your network.

3.   Analyze your network model relative to the classification scheme.

4.   Revise the classification scheme as needed and reanalyze.

5.   Define an isolation strategy consistent with your risk management strategy.

6.   Derive an operational strategy from your isolation strategy.

7.   Build a server implementation based on your isolation strategy.

These seven steps are quite a bit more complicated than they might seem. The key is to realize that this is not a single-afternoon project. You really need a far better handle on the structure and usage patterns in your network than what most organizations have. In fact, if you get no further than simply understanding your network better, you have created significant value. The remainder of this chapter discusses how to use these concepts to design and implement a Server Isolation strategy.

> **Important**   Before we go any further, it is important to better define the term *Server Isolation*. When Microsoft first coined the term, it was in conjunction with the term *Domain Isolation*. **Domain Isolation** simply meant that to communicate with any domain member (with some exceptions) you had to be a domain member. This type of isolation is quite simple and, while valuable, leaves rather large holes by assuming that all domain members are good and nice.
>
> **Server Isolation** is the next step. In Server Isolation each server has its inbound traffic restricted, usually using IPsec, so that only the traffic necessary for the server to fulfill its business purpose is permitted. This provides very good isolation indeed.
>
> When Microsoft and other customers started implementing these isolation mechanisms they discovered that while Domain Isolation was simple in concept, implementing Server Isolation was far easier because IPsec was very difficult to work with in a large network. Therefore, they generally started with Server Isolation.
>
> However, what most observers fail to recognize about Server Isolation is that every Windows-based computer is a server. Every workstation also runs the Server service by default, and if you do not restrict inbound traffic—or even if you use Domain Isolation—you will have a network where every client can attack—I mean communicate—with every other client. Therefore, do not forget to include clients in your Server Isolation strategy.

Step 1: Create a Classification Scheme

The first step in building a server isolation strategy is to classify systems. You can think of network protection mechanisms as residing on a spectrum. Take, for instance, administrative accounts. One extreme of the spectrum is using one account for all purposes, on all computers, by all administrators. On the other extreme you have one account per administrator per task, with the least possible privileges necessary to complete that task per computer. While the former example might be practically possible, it would violate more security principles than we can list. The latter example, while highly secure, is intractable to manage and so cumbersome to use that it will likely be ignored by everyone involved. A similar spectrum exists for all other techniques. For instance, in terms of restricting communications, you can certainly analyze every single computer and restrict access to each one based on exactly what you need to use it for. However, in a network with many thousands of computers, this is virtually impossible. You would be hacked long before you completed the analysis.

A far better option is to create a classification scheme. This scheme can be as simple or as complex as you need it to be. The idea is to divide your computers into categories that make sense to your business. Classifications can take many forms. In a military establishment it is common to have a two-dimensional classification scheme, such as that shown in Table 13-1.

The military-style classification can be converted to classifying computers quite easily. One variant is shown in Table 13-2.

Table 13-2 shows a subset of a computer classification based on the role the systems are fulfilling. No matter how you create your classifications, you almost certainly want to base them on the *role* the computer is fulfilling. The more granular you make the classification scheme—that is, the closer to a single role you can get—the more secure the resulting implementation will be. However, don't go overboard with this classification. First, you will probably need to revise it once you start analyzing your network and realize that you missed something and that some roles that do not clearly make sense. Second, treat this as a risk management effort. If you are designing a classification scheme for an extreme risk environment, you want more granularity. If you are in a low-risk environment, you may be fine with a coarser system.

Table 13-1   Military Classification Scheme

	Class		
	Unclassified	**Secret**	**Top Secret**
Compartment			Compartment 1
			Compartment 2
			Compartment 3

Table 13-2   System Classification by Role

	Class		
	Public	**Workstations**	**Server**
Compartment	Kiosks	Information Worker Workstations	Domain Controllers
	Infrastructure Servers	Developer Workstations	File Servers

You may have noticed that one potential problem with using the two-dimensional classification system based on the military scheme is that you cannot neatly take into account the data that a particular computer of a given type is processing as well as the server type. For instance, not all database servers are alike. Some process highly sensitive personal information such as national ID numbers. Others hold public information, such as Web pages, that can be read by all users but written only by a few. Yet others servers may be entirely public and used simply as centralized temp folders. You can add rows to the classification for each computer type, but because many of the parameters you need to apply to computers are similar within a major type, this is not the cleanest method.

One way to accommodate sub-typing of computers a bit more neatly is to use a different modeling method. I like the organizational chart metaphor. It is infinitely extensible and permits easy sub-typing. You can, of course, use a more complicated modeling scheme, but because I find parsimony in your metaphor to be far more valuable than having hundreds of modeling constructs available, I tend to use simple modeling schemes. Using an org chart metaphor, we might come up with a picture such as the one in Figure 13-5.

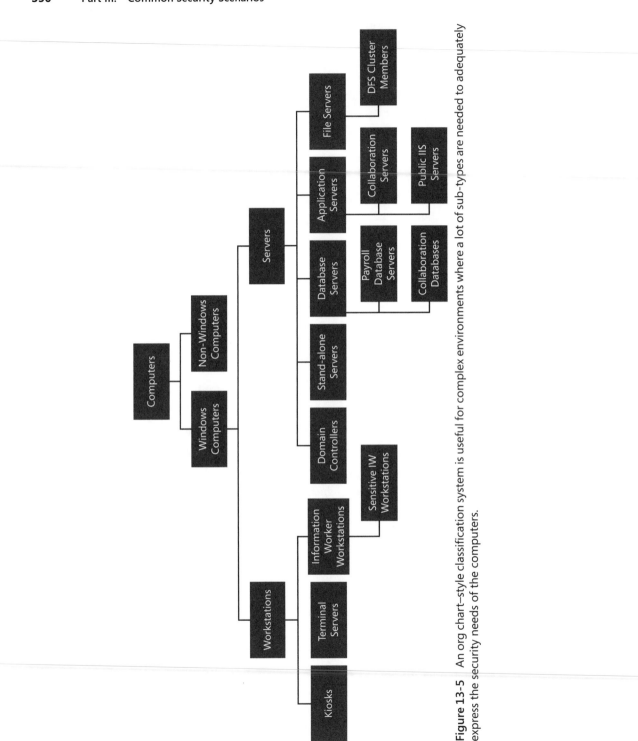

Figure 13-5   An org chart–style classification system is useful for complex environments where a lot of sub-types are needed to adequately express the security needs of the computers.

As Figure 13-5 shows, an org chart–style classification model can get rather large very quickly. Therefore, it might not be right for all environments. Note also that many of the categories are unlikely to have any computers in them. For instance, while Servers is a useful abstract super class, no computers should be assigned to it. All of them should be part of some specialization. However, when discussing server roles, as we did in Chapter 11, "Securing Server Roles," this type of hierarchical designation can be extremely valuable.

Once you have a preliminary classification model to start evaluating for fitness, you can begin your analysis. A useful technique for the analysis portion of the task is Network Threat Modeling, first described in *Protect Your Windows Network*.

Steps 2 and 3: Network Threat Modeling

The next step is to see how well your classification model maps to the actual computers in your network. If you do not already have a map of your network, build one. It should detail everything important on your network, although you may group identical things together. The objective is to have something that lets you understand what your network looks like. Figure 13-6 provides an example.

The next step is to start applying the classification scheme to the network map. As you have already noticed, Figure 13-6 is based on the physical design of the network, with each site shown separately, and with the same type of server in multiple sites. In Network Threat Modeling we are really not interested in the individual servers. Our objective is to understand the *types* of computers, not the individual computers. To that end, we take our classification scheme and overlay it on our network map. This will probably cause us to lose the distinction between sites. However, if the security needs of similar computer types are the same across sites, we have achieved exactly what we want to achieve. At this stage in the process we are trying to create a higher level of abstraction in our understanding of the network. This should result in a picture similar to Figure 13-7.

Figure 13-7 classifies computers into types based on our classification. Note that we have a new type of computer that did not appear before: the Human Resources (HR) Personnel Workstation. In this enterprise, we decided that because HR personnel have access to sensitive data on every employee, we needed to apply special security to their computers. Only some members of the client operations team that administers clients will have access to these computers. This prevents all client operations employees from having indirect access to personnel Personally Identifiable Information (PII).

When you have a classification scheme you have achieved a large portion of the objective of Network Threat Modeling. You should now be able to assign sensitivity labels to the various computer types. These labels are based on the types of data stored on that computer and the type of access to other computers you have if you successfully attack that computer. I have used numeric labels here, although you can use whatever makes sense.

DCs, obviously, are the most sensitive computers of all. Therefore, they have a sensitivity label of 10. By itself the number means nothing. It is just a way to relate one computer type to another. Workstations, because they are used by the largest proportion of users and at the highest risk, *should* be the least sensitive computers in the network. That does not mean that they are the least likely to be attacked. On the contrary, they are probably the *most* likely to be attacked. Therefore, they should be the least sensitive—in other words, the ones that give you access to the least amount of information in the network.

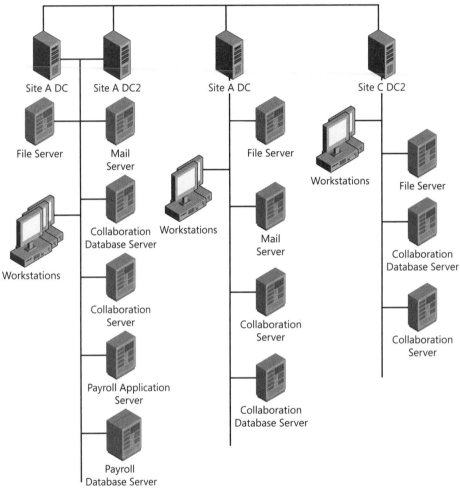

Figure 13-6 Locate or build a map of your network.

After you assign labels to all the computers, you should have a good idea of the patterns of operation in the network. This will drive your isolation strategy later. For now, we need to proceed to analyzing the communication patterns in the environment. To do that, we construct a picture similar to Figure 13-8.

Figure 13-8 is a basic Data Flow Diagram (DFD) of the network. The graph shown in Figure 13-7 does not easily lend itself to documenting communication patterns. However, a DFD is tailor-made for that purpose.

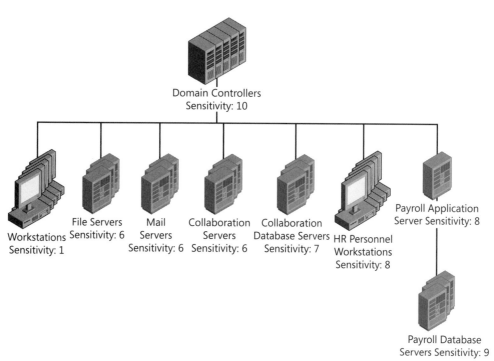

Figure 13-7 Start threat modeling by flattening the network and grouping computers into the classification scheme.

We start converting a network diagram to a DFD by simply turning the computer types into processes (the circles you see in Figure 13-8). Even databases are processes because the database server is actually what performs the processing on all database requests. Figure 13-8 also shows a little trick to make the picture far easier to read. Note the process named All Domain Members. It is marked as a duplicate entity with a slash through the corner. It represents all the non-DC computers in the domain. It serves as a very simple placeholder to clean up the diagram, letting us capture any communication pattern that is common to every computer in the entire domain. For example, all computers in the domain need to access the DCs. Instead of drawing separate lines from each computer type to the DCs, we draw just one from All Domain Members. In addition, rather than enumerating all the different types of traffic that domain members need to send to DCs, we use just one vector labeled DC Traffic. With this shortcut technique, what could easily have been 30 separate lines becomes just one.

> **Tip** To learn more about the types of traffic used to access each type of server, see Knowledge Base article KB 832017, "Service Overview and Network Port Requirements for the Windows Server System," found at *http://support.microsoft.com/kb/832017*.

Note also that all the communication vectors are directed. The fact that domain members need to access DCs does not mean that DCs need to access domain members. In fact, they rarely do. If you are diligent about not using your DCs as workstations or management stations, you might not have to access any other computer from them.

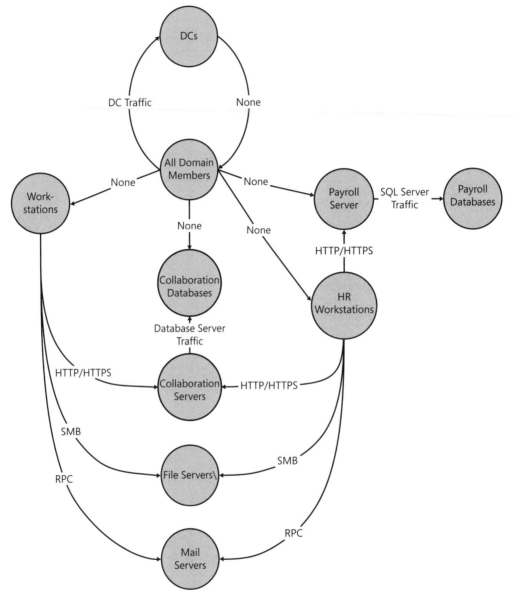

Figure 13-8   After you have grouped the systems, analyze their communication patterns.

Step 4: Analyze, Rinse, and Repeat as Needed

While going through the Network Threat Modeling exercise, you might realize that your classification scheme is deficient. You will probably have computer types that are not used, and you will almost certainly realize as you go through the exercise that you are missing some types. If you are not, you probably have not adequately considered the security needs of your systems. Keep in mind that two things drive the classification scheme: First, you need to consider communication patterns. A computer that does not need to communicate in a particular way with another computer should not be permitted to do so. Second, computers that have different sensitivities should be managed differently to ensure that if one is compromised, the others do not fall.

One common mistake is failing to consider database servers separately from application servers. With properly written database middleware, which only calls exposed store procedures on the databases—and uses least privilege to do so—application servers are typically less sensitive than database servers. Unrestricted access to a database server means that you have complete access to all the data on it. Unrestricted access to an application server means that you should have access only to what the database will give you.

> **Note**   You might have noticed that we have made an unstated assumption that there is no difference in the level of access to a particular computer, or rather, that this difference is not relevant to the Network Threat Modeling process. Windows does, in fact, have a reasonable level of isolation mechanisms to prevent someone with mere user access to a computer from taking complete control of that computer. However, Network Threat Modeling is complicated enough as it is. Mixing that in makes the model that much more complex. Instead, we are taking a worst-case scenario approach; we are basing our isolation techniques on what an attacker with complete control over a computer can do with that computer. For example, if an attacker has complete control over a collaboration server, what access would that give her on the database servers? The answer depends on how we manage the network (which users log on to the collaboration servers) and on what traffic is allowed between the two.

If the classification scheme seems inadequate to the task of adequately capturing what your network looks like—or ought to look like—the solution is simple: either modify the classification scheme or change your assumptions. The classification scheme may just not be correct for your risk management strategy. In this case, you may change the classification scheme to better match the risk management strategy. Or, you might decide that although your risk management strategy is sound on paper, it is impossible or undesirable in practice. Many organizations have developed a risk management strategy that looks great on a slide in the boardroom, but is impossible to implement in the real world. This is your opportunity to verify how well your strategy really can be implemented. If you do not have a risk management strategy, you probably ought to take this opportunity to think up one.

Step 5: Design the Isolation Strategy

Once you have a network threat model that makes sense, you can start deriving the isolation strategy. The isolation strategy is largely based on the communication patterns identified in Figure 13-8. It should be as restrictive as possible, within reason. You can document the outcome in a table that outlines the server types and the communications patterns.

The table includes the source and destination hosts and ports, the protocols, whether the traffic must be authenticated and/or encrypted, and whether the connection can also happen in reverse (mirrored). This is where you really need to get specific. Rather than simply saying "DC traffic," you need to enumerate the ports and protocols. An extraordinarily useful reference at this stage is Microsoft Knowledge Base Article 832017, "Service Overview and Network Port Requirements for the Windows Server System."

The end result of this step in the process should be a table that lists all necessary communications patterns in your network. Your table might look similar to Table 13-3, but will likely be far longer.

Table 13-3   Network Communications Patterns

Description	Source	Destination	Source Port	Destination Port	Protocol	Require Authentication	Require Encryption	Mirrored
DC SMB traffic	All Domain Members	All DCs	Any	445	TCP	No	No	No
DC RPC EP Mapper	All Domain Members	All DCs	Any	135	TCP	No	No	No
. . .								
Appserver DB Access	SharePoint Servers	SharePoint DB Servers	Any	1433	TCP	Yes	No	No
File Server Access	Workstations	File Servers	Any	(139), 445	TCP	Yes	No	No
HR Payroll Access	HR Workstations	Payroll Servers	Any	80	TCP	Yes	Yes	No
. . .								

As you can tell, the data captured in Table 13-3 can get quite extensive. However, if you have done the job of segmenting the network appropriately, the data should be mostly just tedious to gather. Once you have done so, you have almost completed the IPsec implementation of Server Isolation in your network. Notice that the headings in Table 13-3 actually capture the exact information you need for your IPsec rules. If you want to be really enterprising, you can enter Table 13-3 in a spreadsheet and then use a macro to convert it into a series of IPsec commands to generate the required IPsec policy. You can configure IPsec on the command line using the **netsh advfirewall consec add rule** command. For more information on IPsec, see the Microsoft IPsec site at *http://technet.microsoft.com/en-us/network/bb531150.aspx.*

Note that this kind of analysis will take some time. It is not unusual for a computer to have 50 or so ports open. The more standardized your OS images are, the easier it will be to track down the information you need. Furthermore, once you start doing this kind of analysis you will most definitely realize how valuable it is when the software vendor documents in a conspicuous manner what ports are used for what features.

Step 6: Derive Operational Strategy

The operational strategy is designed around how you are going to manage the various computers in your network. The strategy needs to capture the administrative needs of the computers as well as any services and other steps you take. For example, you probably want some backup strategy for your network. However, if you use a single, centralized backup system for all computers, you have probably defeated a large part of the isolation because you now have a backup server that has access to everything in the network, and it is potentially subject to attacks by every computer in the network. Therefore, you may want to analyze the risk involved in doing so. That analysis might lead you to conclude that the correct way to perform backups is to group computers by sensitivity and then handle backups uniformly within each sensitivity level. You might, by way of example, decide to use a single backup solution for all computers of sensitivity level 6.

You need to do the same analysis for administration. It would defeat the entire purpose of the exercise if you were to use a single, domain administrative account to access every computer in the domain. By doing that you expose the single administrative account to attacks on every computer. The appropriate decision is to use different administrator accounts for different purposes. You might decide that you have one account per sensitivity level. Or you might assign your sysadmins to different sensitivity levels. Doing so permits you to assign different sysadmins to different computers, rather than allowing all of them to administer every computer. You might even have separate administration stations for each sensitivity level. You have to decide how much pain you are willing to go through to manage your network. That decision will guide the rest of your decision making. With regard to security there is, as always, a trade-off between how much security you want to have, and how much inconvenience and work you are willing to put up with to get it, all while taking into account the resultant functionality you want. The key point of this part of the process is to ensure that you implement the isolation in such a way that you do not expose computers of one sensitivity level to unnecessary attacks by computers at a different sensitivity level.

Step 7: Implement Restrictions

Finally, it is time to implement your strategy. By this stage in the process you should have a complete design for how you want to manage your network as well as for what communication patterns you want to permit within it. The implementation should be relatively straightforward at this point. However, you do want to ensure that several things get done.

Before we go further, if you are like most network managers, you get cold chills thinking about rolling out changes that could disrupt communication. After all, as the old saying goes, nobody ever calls the helpdesk to inform them that everything is working today (and if they do, you have a whole different set of problems to address).

Fortunately, there is a trick. Obviously, you want to eventually require authentication of all or most network connections. However, you may want to start out by *requesting* authentication instead. That way you can test the policies, monitor where IPsec negotiation fails, and adjust as necessary, all while maintaining full connectivity. This permits you to do a safer rollout that is far less likely to result in events that have an adverse impact on your opportunities from promotion out of network management.

That being said, there are a number of other restrictions that you need to include in your plan.

Minimize Account Scope

First, reduce the scope of your accounts, particularly the highly privileged accounts. Every-one that accesses computers at different sensitivities should, at least if they have high-level permissions on those computers, have different accounts. For example, a highly trusted server administrator might need a domain administrative account for managing the DCs, a level 7 administrative account for managing servers at sensitivity level 7, and an information worker account for e-mail and surfing the Web. An HR employee might need one account for performing HR-related tasks and a different account for reading e-mail and working on presentations. Alternatively, you might decide that based on your risk management philos-ophy and the fact that both uses are at very low privilege levels, the same account might suffice. However, you should never permit an account that has administrative privileges at one level to access resources at a different level. Administrative accounts at any level must only be used to administer computers at that level.

Organizational Security Policy Changes

Much of the isolation must be done by organizational security policies, not necessarily techni-cal policies. You simply cannot technically enforce many of the isolation decisions. For instance, your domain administrators are omnipotent within the scope of your network. You cannot restrict them from seeing or doing anything within the network. However, you can set rules and guidelines for them to follow, and track those guidelines. You must also have penalties for violating those guidelines. An administrator who refuses to take necessary steps to keep your network protected should be turned into an ex-employee.

Separate Service Accounts

Service accounts are a common problem in Windows. It is a well-known fact that any administrator on any computer has access to the clear-text password of all services—and of all interactive users—on that computer. There is no standard log file where these nuggets are stored, but with commonly available hacking tools it is a simple matter to get them.

For that reason, managing service accounts is crucial. It is still quite common to see services running on many computers in a network under a domain admin account. This exposes a domain admin account on every computer in the network. For this reason, the scope of service accounts must be limited. A logical way to do this is to only use service accounts within a sensitivity level. For example, as mentioned earlier, the backup service might run in one service account on computers at level 7 and a different account on computers at level 9.

Do You Want to Back Up Workstations?

Do you really want to back up workstations? Many organizations are struggling with that question these days. Users, obviously, are storing data on their workstations, but is that what you really want? Ideally, very little data that does not exist elsewhere in the network should be on workstations. Using techniques such as roaming profiles and folder redirection, the default storage locations for users can be moved to the network. With the Offline Files feature, these files are automatically backed up to the network, and also available offline for roaming users. By using a combination of these strategies you can ensure that the only data available only on workstations is that data which users create while roaming, and that data which they choose to store locally—in possible violation of standard operating procedures. Combine that with a solid imaging strategy using (for example), the Windows Deployment Services, and you might achieve a state where you do not need to back up data on workstations. You might not even need to troubleshoot them. If anything ever goes wrong with a workstation, you could troubleshoot it by using same approach you use for servers, following this simple process:

1. Restart the service, if applicable.

2. If that does not solve the problem, restart the computer.

3. If that does not solve the problem, reimage the computer.

4. If that does not solve the problem, send the computer back to the manufacturer and deploy new hardware.

If you do not need to worry about data being stored on workstations, you can make them disposable.

Note that getting to this stage will take discipline, along with hardware that permits you to implement a strategy like this. However, this is a business decision you need to make. Do you want to greatly simplify your desktop operating procedures, buy hardware and software that lends itself to that, and buy some really big storage servers, or do you want to have complicated and costly desktop operating procedures and spend less up front?

Manage Privileges

You must not forget to manage your privileges properly when you are implementing your isolation strategy. Users with certain privileges can be just as powerful as administrators. For example, a user that has the privilege Impersonate A Client After Authentication is as powerful as any user that connects remotely to the computer. A user that has the Restore Files And Directories privilege can replace any file on the computer. Because this permits that user to control code that is executed by administrators, such a user implicitly has all the rights that administrators do. This is why it makes great sense to separate backup operators from restore operators. They are two different tasks, at very different sensitivity levels. Privileges are discussed in Chapter 3, "Objects: The Stuff You Want."

Restrict Communications

It should be obvious, after our discussion on Network Threat Modeling, that we want to restrict communications. In this step we use IPsec and Windows Firewall to restrict inbound traffic to a computer. This will greatly reduce the risk to systems from other systems. Take, for example, a database server accessed by a middleware server. Say there is a SQL Injection flaw in the middleware that permits an attacker to run arbitrary code on the database server. Once the database server has been compromised, what access does the attacker have to the middleware server? If you have set up Windows Firewall on the middleware server to reject all unsolicited inbound traffic (or, rather, to only accept exactly what it must accept) the answer is "none." You can contain the attack right there. Use the table you created listing your communication patterns and design a set of IPsec policies based on it. Deploy these policies using Group Policy or any other means that makes sense in your environment. To learn more about Windows Firewall and IPsec and how to deploy the policies, see Chapter 5, "Windows Firewall(s)."

Restrict Access to Resources

Finally, use the detailed knowledge you have gained, and the isolation strategy you have designed up to this point, to build a data and resource access strategy that enforces the principle of least privilege. You should, at this point, have a fairly detailed user account strategy. You can take advantage of that to prevent access, as well as to enforce the isolation strategy. For example, before you embarked on this project, your HR personnel might have had access to the Exchange servers, all the file servers, the internal SharePoint servers, and the payroll applications—all using the one account you gave them. After you define the isolation strategy, you have the ability to restrict their access to payroll applications to when they are using their HR_Personnel accounts, and possibly even when they are working on a specific HR workstation.

Summary

Few steps that you can take today will have as great an impact on the security of your network and its data as a proper network segmentation and Server Isolation strategy. By going through the process defined in this chapter, you can create a network that does exactly what you want it to do, and nothing else. If you do it right, the network will still be flexible enough to support new applications, with a minimal amount of modifications.

Will this strategy result in additional considerations for your end users and administrators alike? Certainly it will. However, in the world we operate in today, that might be the only way to secure your network. The conventional approach of a completely flat network, where everyone has one account that has access to everything they need, and much more, is simply unsafe in virtually all environments today. How far away from that model you are able to move depends on your risk tolerance, and the security needs you have in your environment.

Additional Resources

- Johansson, J. M. *Protect Your Windows Network*. (Addison-Wesley, 2005).

- Knowledge Base article 832017, "Service Overview and Network Port Requirements for the Windows Server System," at *http://support.microsoft.com/kb/832017*.

- "The Immutable Laws of Security," at *http://www.microsoft.com/technet/archive/community/columns/security/essays/10imlaws.mspx?mfr=true*.

Chapter 14
Securing the Branch Office

— Byron Hynes

In this chapter, we will examine the challenges of a branch office, and some solutions, techniques, and tools to address them. We will start by discussing the characteristics of a branch office, and why they present unique challenges, and then we will look at some of the common infrastructure optimization scenarios that can apply to branch offices. We will go through the features of Windows Server 2008 that support branch offices, and identify those that can particularly help secure branches, focusing on the role of Read Only Domain Controllers (RODCs) and BitLocker Drive Encryption.

An Introduction to Branch Office Issues

IT security often invokes the image of a well-maintained data center, where IT professionals are constantly striving to improve policies, procedures, settings, and software to protect the physical and knowledge assets in their control. Only a few people can enter the inner sanctum—by "carding in"—to find orderly arrangements of neatly placed computers, efficiently humming along while being securely watched.

Many of our readers—you—strive to build this sort of environment. But, did you realize that about one-third of IT budgets are spent on branch offices, or remote locations? Between one-quarter and one-third of servers running Windows Server software are installed in what we call a branch office.

Branch offices are found in many diverse environments. I worked with a customer in the fast-food industry who had a Windows server in every one of thousands of restaurants, nationwide. A colleague of mine did an early Active Directory design and deployment project with domain controllers in each one of 800 branches of a major European bank. Branch offices can include retail stores, medical facilities, hotels—perhaps even the check-in counter where you drop off your child for daycare, or the elementary school office where the secretary enters daily attendance information.

Why Do Branch Offices Matter?

Branch offices are not going away anytime soon. Quite the opposite, actually. Branches are where the vast majority of business is won or lost for a corporation; branches are where services are delivered for nonprofits and government agencies. In addition to online services, branches are where source data is collected and interpreted, and where more savvy consumers are demanding that decisions can be made by local representatives.

Unfortunately, a number of characteristics can be limiting or even negative for the branch office.

What Is Different in a Branch Office?

Branch offices come in many different configurations, but most share the following traits:

- **Remotely connected over a WAN**   While network speeds continue to increase, most branch offices depend on an externally controlled network, such as a leased line, frame relay connection, or shared fiber circuit. Some branch offices are connected only over the public Internet, using a virtual private network (VPN). Remember that when you depend on a third party, such as a telephone or network company, you have no control over what happens to your data on that network.

- **Reduced physical security**   Servers in branch offices are rarely accompanied by the same level of physical security found in a corporate data center. I hope that your server is not stuck under a receptionist's desk in a public area, or sitting on a shelf in a restroom, but I have seen both.

- **Lack of local skilled IT personnel**   In a branch office, particularly a small one, you often find that an employee with little or no formal IT skill "inherits" the care and feeding of your server in the branch. This might be the business manager (or highest-ranking employee on site), the local tech enthusiast, or even just the staff member who is "always there" and never in a meeting.

- **Distance**   As well as not being staffed with IT professionals, a branch office is more often than not geographically far from IT support. It may be impossible to get one of your own analysts or technicians on-site in less than a day or two.

- **Reduced infrastructure**   Unlike the data center, with its precise climate control, redundant power supplies, and multiple communication paths, branch offices may not be engineered to the same level of fault tolerance—both in terms of IT systems and in terms of civil infrastructure, such as power and communications.

Branch offices face growing pressures, including cost and performance pressures, pressure to remain secure and in compliance with growing laws and regulations, and the pressure to be agile and responsive to business needs. For example, branch offices face the high costs of maintaining complex, disparate, and often nonintegrated hardware sets, coupled with the high cost of bringing in IT support when needed, either from the data center or perhaps by subcontracting expensive local support agencies. Of course, branch office managers—and certainly the home office management team—are aware of the threats posed by data breaches, attacks against the system, and the difficulty of recovering from a disaster and protecting that locally collected data. (After all, why go after Jesper's well-hardened servers—you know, the ones he keeps in his data center and has guarded by men with guns, 24 hours a day—if a much less secure server is sitting in the local branch.)

But even with all of that, branch offices are expected to have and use more and more information as a "point of service," where data is collected, analyzed, and used to deliver immediate results, all while being integrated across the company. I remember opening a bank account as a teenager where the ledger was still kept by hand—and of course, that account could only be accessed at that particular branch. I do not expect that many banks would be able to compete using that kind of operation today! (And, just so you do not think I am too old, I should add that I walked down the street to a competitor with computers and multi-branch services.)

On the whole, a branch office represents a simple challenge for the consummate IT professional. All you have to do is secure remote data and access; protect systems; provide secure connectivity with reduced on-site support, simple backups, and efficient use of hardware and bandwidth—while also improving your infrastructure, delivering new capabilities quickly, and establishing a platform for the future and maintaining compliance. (Whew!)

IDC describes it this way:

> Branch locations often are looking for high levels of flexibility and autonomy in implementing IT solutions. However, expanding corporate requirements call for centralized management, enhanced security, and regulatory compliance.

Source: **IDC White Paper, Addressing Operational Efficiencies in Branch Office, May 2006,** located at *http://download.microsoft.com/download/6/d/0/6d032455-bf07-42ac-b006-ee0e4c8ab606/idc_branch_whitepaper.pdf*

Building Branch Offices

A number of design scenarios can address the branch office situation. Basically, they range on a continuum from one or more gargantuan servers in the branch office to "no servers in the branch office, do it all remotely." As you can imagine, each of these possible solutions has strengths and weaknesses.

To leave myself some room in this chapter to talk about securing Windows Server 2008 in the branch office, I am only going to present a brief overview of design approaches. Some of these approaches are very common; others are only occasionally used. Some are becoming more popular as lower costs and new technologies become more commonplace. And many branch offices have a combination of elements from more than one of the following options.

- **Virtualized server in the branch office**   A server capable of running a virtual server image for each workload provides maximum flexibility and configurability—and agility—with a solution that allows all workloads and services to be run off of a single, physical server computer. This option is best where there are numerous stand-alone servers that could be consolidated into a single unit. Services are run in-house in order to allow 100 percent uptime and functionality even when the wide area network (WAN) or VPN is offline. By managing only one server, you can gain some centralized management and data backup.

- **Single server**   Using one server offers the benefits of a server in the branch office, but without the cost and complexity of supporting virtualization and server consolidation. In this case, services that must be constantly available or that require the lowest possible latency can be run from within the remote office, while others are centralized to the data center. You must strike a balance between reliance on WAN uptime, remote management, centralized backup, and local responsiveness.

- **Branch office appliances**   Branch office appliances strive to provide a complete solution that is easy to deploy and configure out-of-the-box. These appliances typically provide WAN acceleration and HTTP compression, making it easier to centralize workloads such as storage and databases. The branch office appliance may come preloaded with some line-of-business (LOB) applications or other services to allow the branch to continue to operate during a WAN outage. Appliances can be designed to connect to a WAN or to use the Internet as VPN appliances.

- **Secure centralization**   In this sort of design, the server is removed from the branch location and all workloads are centralized. Application virtualization (such as the sort provided by Microsoft SoftGrid Application Virtualization) is used to allow LOB applications to be run from the data center but executed on the local desktop, reducing the burden of deploying and managing updates to those applications that are virtualized. A security appliance, intelligent firewall, or gateway enables secure connectivity (including packet filtering and VPN access) to the data center.

- **No infrastructure**   In this case, the branch office simply has no servers or significant networking hardware. Everyone relies on network connectivity to the data center to enable all remote office functionality. Essentially, everyone is a network client. Remote office employees either exist on the same corporate network as the head office using a WAN, or they connect via VPN to the data center to access applications, or all branch office users are treated as Internet users and applications are delivered via secured Internet protocols. This reduces remote infrastructure deployment to a bare minimum and eliminates remote server management.

Microsoft offers a number of products and solutions for the branch office, as well as extensive infrastructure optimization (IO) guidance to help you select and build an effective and secure remote or branch office infrastructure. For the rest of this chapter, we will focus on branch office features and enhancements in Windows Server 2008, primarily those that are directly related to securing the branch office. For more information about branch offices in general (or using Windows Server products in branch offices), visit *http://technet.microsoft.com/en-us/branchoffice/default.aspx*.

Windows Server 2008 in the Branch Office

Improving the situation in branch offices was one of the main goals during the development of Windows Server 2008. Features in Windows Server 2008 address the concerns of a branch office in three areas: cost control, security, and business agility. Table 14-1 summarizes the features designed in Windows Server 2008 to overcome branch office challenges.

Table 14-1   Windows Server 2008 Branch Office Challenges and Solutions

Challenge	Requirement	Windows Server 2008 Features
Cost control	Reduce the cost of managing and supporting remote offices (including making most efficient use of network links).	Server Core installation option Read-Only Domain Controller (RODC) Server Message Block (SMB) 2.0 Data Protection (Backup) Windows Server Virtualization
Security	Improve security of data and access.	BitLocker Drive Encryption Read-Only Domain Controller (RODC) Server Message Block (SMB) 2.0
Agility	Provide a flexible infrastructure that maximizes IT investment.	Server Message Block (SMB) 2.0 TCP/IP redesign

Nonsecurity Features

I want to spend most of this discussion covering security features, but other features deserve a mention too, because it is often difficult—and usually counterproductive—to look at security in complete isolation. By understanding how all of the pieces fit together, you can be more effective—and that leads to being more secure.

In a very pragmatic sense, it is also a really good idea to strive to keep your network solutions cost-effective, agile, reliable, and available. When your solutions fail to meet end users' needs (or perceived needs), your end users (and especially management) will seek workarounds or shortcuts. These shortcuts are *rarely* secure. This is not to say that these users are being malicious. They will, however, go around you or your security when what you have put in place does not do what they need, or what they think they need.

Server Core Installation Option

Server Core is a minimal server installation option for Windows Server 2008 that contains a subset of executable files and makes available only a few server roles. Server Core runs on either 32-bit or 64-bit architectures.

I consider Server Core to be a security feature because it reduces the attack surface in the server. Only the binaries need to support the role and the base operating systems. This means that generally fewer processes are running. But Server Core is also a cost-control feature because it reduces maintenance and management requirements.

The Server Core installation option installs only a subset of the executable files and supporting dynamic-link libraries (DLLs). Specifically, only those features that are required by nine specific server roles are installed. Components not installed include Graphical User Interface (GUI), the .NET Framework Common Language Runtime (CLR), the Windows Explorer user interface, and Internet Explorer. Because there is no GUI interface, administrators must access all of these services through a local command shell, either remotely from a management server or workstation (with a remote command shell or with a remote tool, such as an MMC snap-in), or by using the new remote management feature called WS-Management, or by using the Windows Management Interface (WMI).

One of the biggest single benefits of a Server Core installation is a much reduced need for updating. While updates are the bane of an IT professional's existence in the data center, updating remote and branch offices has its own special kind of pain. Based on comparisons with Windows Server 2003, Microsoft estimates that less than 60 percent of updates would have applied to a Server Core installation than would be needed for a full installation of Windows Server, if that kind of installation existed for Windows Server 2003. Server Core is described in more detail in Chapter 12, "Securing Server Roles."

Hyper-V (Windows Server Virtualization)

Windows Server 2008 Hyper-V, formerly called Windows Server Virtualization, is a virtualization platform designed to provide the flexibility through a dynamic, reliable, and scalable platform capabilities. You can also use a single set of integrated management tools to manage both physical and virtual server resources. Hyper-V is included in most Windows Server 2008 licenses, but you may need to download it from Microsoft separately.

A full discussion of virtualization is outside the scope of this chapter. But because many branch office situations will benefit from Server Virtualization, you should read more about it on the Web at *http://www.microsoft.com/windowsserver2008/virtualization/default.mspx*.

Complete Redesign of TCP/IP Stack

Sometimes called the Next Generation TCP/IP stack, the improved networking stack in Windows Server 2008 and Windows Vista has some direct benefits to the branch office. By improving network communication between servers in the data center and the branch office, and between remote clients and centralized services, you can maximize the use of WAN links.

From a security point of view, you should be aware of the following aspects of the new TCP/IP functionality:

- Expanded IPsec integration and easier IPsec management tools.

- TCP/IP includes an integrated filtering platform. Windows uses this platform for Windows Firewall and IPsec, but other applications and vendors can also make use of the Windows Filtering Platform (WFP).

Both of these issues are discussed in Chapter 5, "Windows Firewall(s)," and Chapter 13, "Managing Security Dependencies to Secure Your Network." As well, the redesign of TCP/IP is discussed extensively in TechNet online (*http://technet.microsoft.com/en-us/network/ bb545475.aspx*) and *Windows Server 2008 TCP/IP Protocols and Services* by Joseph Davies (Microsoft Press, 2008).

Server Message Block

Continuing with the theme of connectivity and protocols, Windows Server 2008 includes a new remote file sharing protocol, Server Message Block 2.0 (SMB 2.0). SMB is the protocol generally used between Windows computers, such as Windows XP, Windows Vista, Windows Server 2003, and Windows Server 2008.

SMB 2.0 greatly improves the scalability of SMB 1.0, increasing the number of open files and allowed shares. The protocols have been enhanced to reduce the "chattiness" that makes file sharing on a WAN sometimes painful. Real-world testing has shown improvements with SMB 2.0 copying large files up to 35 times faster than with SMB 1.0. However, SMB 2.0 benefits only really appear when communicating between Windows Server 2008 computers or between Windows Server 2008 and Windows Vista clients. SMB 2.0 is not available separately for older Windows operating systems.

To learn more about the WAN performance improvements in SMB 2.0, watch the TechNet webcast "Wide Area Network Performance Improvements in Windows Server 2008" at *http://msevents.microsoft.com/CUI/WebCastEventDetails.aspx?culture=en-US& EventID=1032348651&CountryCode=US.*

Data Protection—Windows Server 2008 Server Backup

Remember that security includes keeping data available and being able to recover from disasters. Windows Server Backup uses the Volume Shadow Copy Service (VSS) and block-level backup technology to back up your servers, locally or remotely, with less downtime. Support has also been added for backing up to optical media (DVD) and to another file server.

Security Features for the Branch Office

Two more major components of Windows Server 2008 have a direct impact on securing your branch offices: Read-Only Domain Controller (RODC) and BitLocker Drive Encryption.

RODC

RODC is a new feature in Active Directory Domain Services (AD DS) in Windows Server 2008. Please refer to Chapter 9, "Designing Active Directory Domain Services for Security," for an overview of AD DS features and information about using and installing RODCs. In this chapter, I want to focus on the security implications of an RODC in a branch office.

RODC Read-Only Database, Replication, and Group Memberships   As the name suggests, RODCs are read-only copies of the AD DS database. This means that they require only unidirectional replication for Active Directory, as well for the File Replication Service (FRS) and Distributed File System Replication (DFSR).

One-way replication imparts a security benefit. Any compromise or other issue that introduces poisoned data into the RODC's local copy of the AD DS database cannot be replicated back to the rest of the organization from the affected RODC. This is certainly a mitigation that can help stop a local problem from becoming a global problem! On the other hand, be aware that if malware, attacks, or other issues cause you to have a corrupt, or "owned" local domain controller—even a read-only one—you still have a big problem to deal with!

Additional steps have also been taken to minimize the problems that could potentially be caused by a rogue RODC. Each RODC has its own, unique KrbTGT account for the Key Distribution Center (KDC), allowing the system to know when a ticket has been issued by an RODC (and which one) and when it has been issued by a normal, writable DC. This is a form of *cryptographic isolation*, a phrase you will sometimes hear used in conjunction with RODC discussions.

One-way replication brings benefits in terms of designing your replication topology and controlling replication traffic, as well. Bridgeheads and hubs do not have to poll the RODC for changes. The RODC performs normal inbound replication for AD DS and FRS and any DFSR changes.

Because the RODC is a member of the domain, sometimes it has a legitimate need to write to Active Directory. However, it does not write to the local database copy, but will instead connect to a writable DC, just like a workstation. The RODC computer account is a workstation account, so it has very limited rights to write to AD DS—again to minimize any damage to the enterprise AD DS if the RODC is compromised. Because they are "workstations" in this sense, RODC computer accounts are not members of the Enterprise Domain Controllers (EDC) or Domain Domain Controllers groups.

Database Contents and Credential Caching   With the exception of account passwords and attributes specifically added to the filtered attribute set, an RODC holds all the AD DS objects and attributes that a writable domain controller holds.

Local applications that request read access to the domain directory information can obtain access directly from the RODC, while Lightweight Directory Access Protocol (LDAP) applications that request write access receive an LDAP referral response. This referral response directs them to a writable domain controller, normally in a hub site.

In the domain database, each security principal—user, computer, or iNetOrgPerson—has a set of up to 10 passwords or secrets, collectively called credentials. An RODC does not store these credentials, except for its own computer account and the special krbtgt account for each RODC. The RODC is advertised as the Key Distribution Center (KDC) for its site, which should normally be the branch office in which it is located. When the RODC issues and signs a ticket-granting ticket (TGT), it uses its own krbtgt account and keys, which are different from the krbtgt account shared by the KDCs on all writable domain controllers in the domain.

The first time a user attempts to authenticate to an RODC, the RODC sends the request to a writable domain controller at the hub site. If the authentication is successful, the RODC also requests a copy of the appropriate credentials. The writable domain controller recognizes that the request is coming from an RODC and consults the Password Replication Policy that is in effect for that RODC.

The Password Replication Policy determines whether the credentials are allowed to be replicated and stored on the RODC. If so, a writable domain controller sends the credentials to the RODC, and the RODC caches them for future use. After the credentials are cached on the RODC, the next time that user attempts to log on, the request can be directly serviced by the RODC until the credentials change.

Obviously, for this to work the RODC has to know whether it is likely to have a copy of the credentials. To avoid needless lookups, the RODC checks the signature on various requests. If a TGT has been signed with its own krbtgt account, the RODC immediately recognizes that it has a cached copy of the credentials. Conversely, if another DC has signed the TGT, the RODC will always forward requests.

The key to limiting risk by installing RODCs in branch offices is correctly using the Password Replication Policy to control which credentials are cached. By default, no user credentials will be cached on an RODC, but that is an inefficient design. If you think about most domains with a branch office, you realize that even in a large branch (say 100 users), those users are a tiny percentage of users in the domain. If you have 20,000 users in the domain, that is one half of one percent.

Because only a few domain users need to have credentials cached on any given RODC, use the Password Replication Policy to specify which groups of users can even be considered for caching. By limiting RODC caching to only users who are frequently at that branch office, you can reduce the potential exposure. You can—and should—also explicitly block the caching of credentials for high-value accounts. By denying the caching of accounts for Domain Admins, for example, you guarantee that Domain Admin credentials will never be stored on the RODC in that branch office. This is where the real security benefit comes in over Windows Server 2003, where you had no option but to have a local copy of every account in every branch office. This is a huge security improvement.

You access the Password Replication Policy by selecting the Properties of the RODC computer object. In Figure 14-1, you can see that only accounts in a group representing that Branch Office are allowed to be cached, and high-value credentials are explicitly denied.

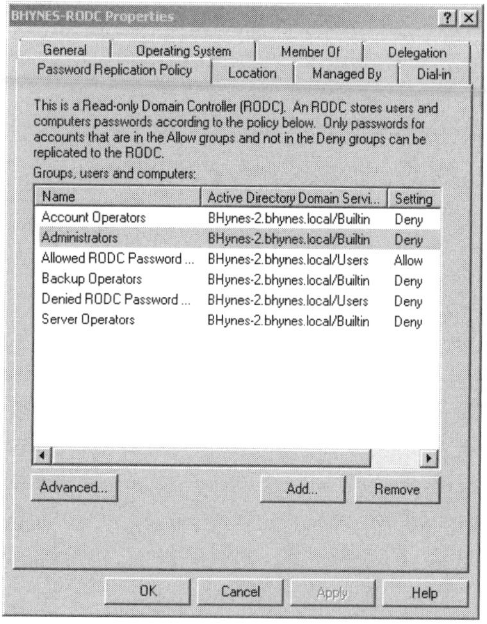

Figure 14-1   An RODC's property sheet showing its Password Replication Policy.

Let us consider for a moment that the unthinkable has happened and your RODC is stolen. The evildoer mounts the AD DS database and attempts to retrieve passwords using a commonly available, umm, "security research" tool. However, instead of seeing more and more passwords appear as the password cracking progresses, the tool only shows empty or blank passwords for almost all accounts.

In the past, if your DC was stolen, you would really have no choice but to reset all of the passwords in the domain—a formidable task if you have thousands of users. However, in this case, you only need to deal with the specific accounts that have already been cached on that RODC. To be clear: With an RODC, you know exactly which passwords have been cached. You can check which ones have been replicated to the RODC by looking at the Password Replication Policy dialog box. Initially, only the computer itself and the special KRBTG account have passwords stored locally, as you can see in Figure 14-2. After clients begin to authenticate to the RODC, additional passwords may also be stored, as shown in Figure 14-3.

You can also determine which users have attempted to authenticate to the RODC, but whose passwords have not been allowed to be cached. For example, notice in Figures 14-2 and 14-3 that no password has been cached for the Administrator account. However, as shown in Figure 14-4, the administrator has logged on in the site served by the RODC.

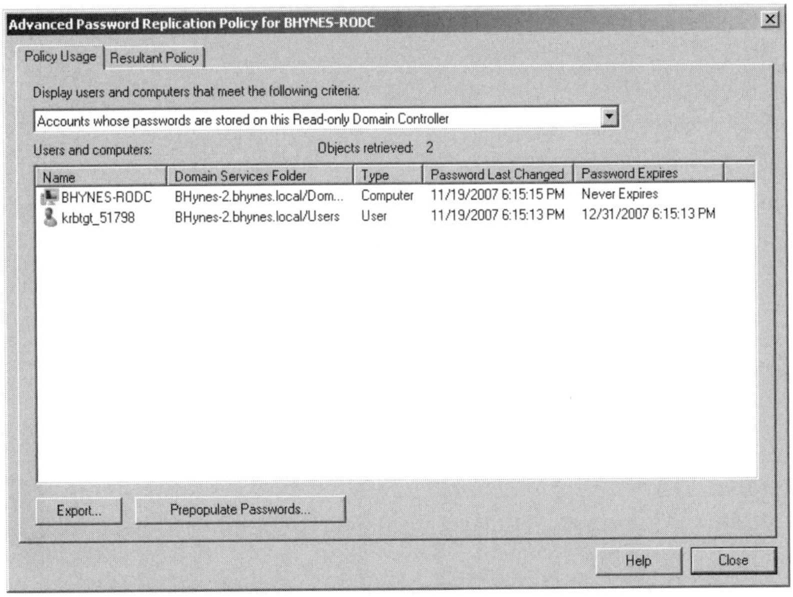

Figure 14-2   Initially, only two accounts have passwords stored on the RODC.

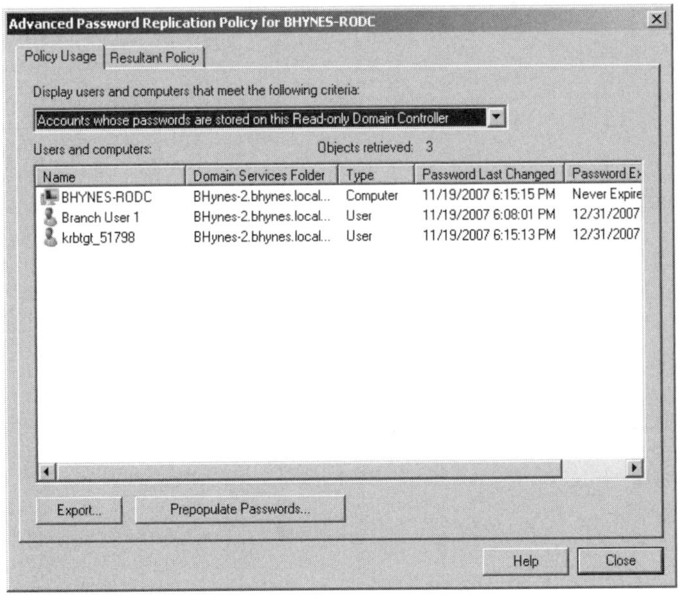

Figure 14-3   You can store additional passwords on the RODC.

Finally, as shown in Figure 14-5, you can model which accounts will be allowed or not allowed to have passwords cached on the RODC.

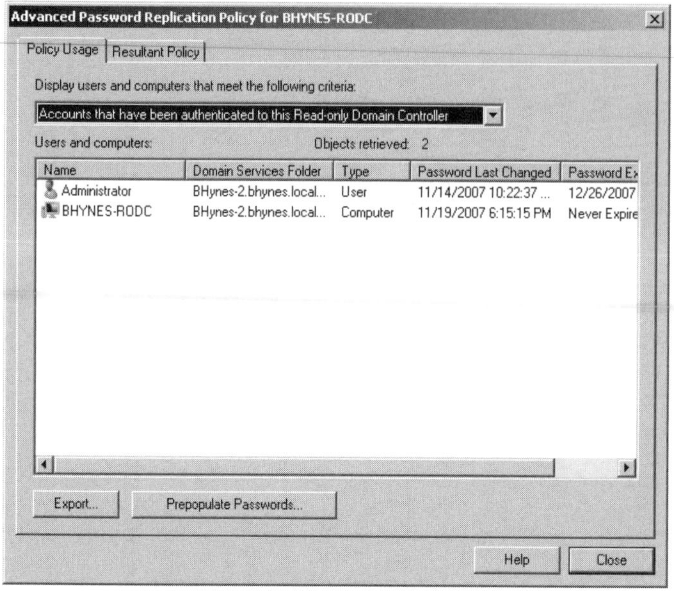

Figure 14-4   Users who have authenticated to the RODC, but have not had passwords cached.

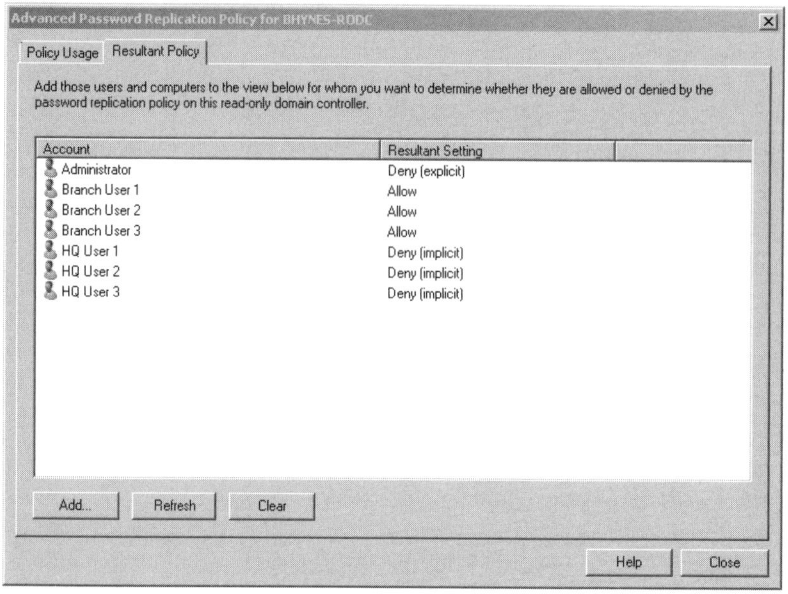

Figure 14-5   Using the Resultant Policy page to model password caching.

We have made it much easier to delete missing domain controllers, including RODCs, with a simple interface that can remove the departed RODC from the domain (no more metadata cleanup needed!) and also automatically reset the potentially compromised passwords. When you start to delete the computer object representing an RODC, you see the dialog pictured in Figure 14-6.

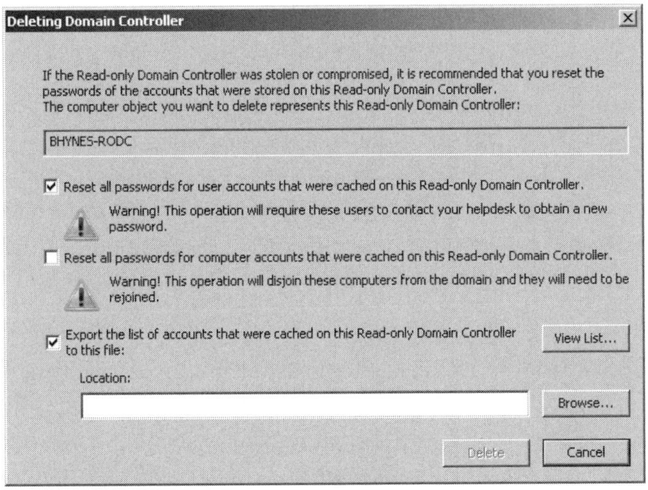

Figure 14-6   Removing an RODC that cannot be brought online from AD DS.

You should also read ahead to the section on BitLocker Drive Encryption. By using BitLocker on the Windows operating system volume of the RODC, you can prevent the thief from even being able to access the local copy of the AD DS database—which, at a minimum, buys you time to reset passwords in an orderly fashion.

Administrative Role Separation   With Role Separation you can delegate the local administrator role of an RODC computer to any domain user without granting that user any rights to the domain itself or to other domain controllers. In Windows Server 2003, DCs didn't have a local administrator; if you could administer a DC, you could administer the whole domain.

Administrative Role Separation can allow a local branch user to log on to an RODC and perform maintenance work on the server, such as upgrading a driver, without allowing that user to log on to any other domain controller or manage the domain.

RODC Benefits   RODCs provide a way to deploy domain controllers more securely in a branch office location because they are designed to be placed in locations that require rapid, reliable, and robust authentication services but that might also have a security limitation that limits or prevents deployment of a writable domain controller. With an RODC, organizations can mitigate risks with deploying a domain controller in locations where physical security cannot be guaranteed.

The RODC feature is clearly designed for branch offices, but it is an integral part of AD DS as well. Please review Chapter 9 for information about installing an RODC, using the RODC filtered attribute set, and configuring read-only DNS.

BitLocker Drive Encryption

BitLocker Drive Encryption is a component of the operating system in Windows Vista Enterprise Edition and Windows Vista Ultimate Edition, and it is also included as a feature in all editions of Windows Server 2008. You may already be familiar with the need to protect data on client hard drives, but that need can be just as important on servers, particularly in a branch office.

According to Forrester, data breaches are expensive: "The cost of a single, significant security breach may run into millions or even billions of dollars." ("Calculating the Cost of a Security Breach," Khalid Kark, April 10, 2007: *http://www.forrester.com/Research/Document/Excerpt/ 0,7211,42082,00.html*) and, unfortunately, they are also common: "34% of respondents experienced at least one personal data breach." ("Aligning Data Protection Priorities with Risk," Jonathan Penn, April 13, 2006: *http://www.forrester.com/Research/Document/Excerpt/ 0,7211,39257,00.html*)

Most IT professionals are well aware of the risk of a user's laptop being left in a taxi or stolen. Hopefully, you are not likely to leave a production server in a taxi, but have you considered what would happen if your servers were stolen? I worked with a military customer once who told me that his organization had equipped domain controllers with C4 explosive charges because they were deployed "in theater" and would be destroyed rather than risk authentication data falling into enemy hands. Now, your risk is probably not the same as those on the battlefield, but there is always some risk, and it is not just hypothetical. A colleague of mine (okay, it was Jesper), was involved with a customer's organization that did have a thief back a truck into and through the wall of their building to steal their servers.

BitLocker gives you another tool to help mitigate the risk at the level you need. I hope, however, that you are thinking beyond the data center. Here are some contrasting examples from my work experience:

- I visited one particular customer whose data center happened to be in a 100-year-old former sanatorium. The servers were all behind two-foot-thick stone walls, and staffed 24 hours a day. It would be hard to steal those servers.

- I volunteered at a large youth event, where the "data center" was in a tent. Servers strung around several hundred acres lost connectivity whenever someone plugged a kettle into the same electrical outlet as the fiber-optic repeater.

Lest anyone dismiss my second example, let me point out that both servers held confidential personal information including health information about clients or participants—and both were where they *needed to be to meet the particular business demand.*

So what is BitLocker Drive Encryption and how can it help secure the data on your servers? BitLocker performs two functions:

- BitLocker encrypts all data stored on the Windows operating system volume (and configured data volumes). This includes the Windows operating system, hibernation and paging files, applications, and data used by applications.

- BitLocker is configured by default to use a Trusted Platform Module (TPM) microchip to help ensure the integrity of early start-up components (components used in the earlier stages of the start-up process), and locks any BitLocker-protected volumes so that they remain protected even if the computer is tampered with when the operating system is not running.

BitLocker Configuration in Windows Server 2008   In Windows Server 2008, BitLocker is an optional component that must be installed before it can be used. (In Server Manager, optional components are called *features*.) To install BitLocker, select it in Server Manager or type the following at a command prompt: **ServerManagerCmd -install BitLocker–restart**.

Installing BitLocker on a production server means giving consideration to a few points. BitLocker has two optional components (OCs) included with Windows Server 2008. The BitLocker OC is used to protect volumes on that particular server. There is also a remote administration OC called RSAT-BitLocker that installs the binary files and command-line scripts required to manage BitLocker on remote servers. (RSAT stands for Remote Server Administration Tool.) If you install or remove the BitLocker feature using Server Manager, both OCs are installed or removed. If you only want to install the remote tool, you must use either the **pkgmgr** command or the **ocsetup** command. Because Server Manager is not supported with the Server Core installation option, you must use **pkgmgr** or **ocsetup** to install BitLocker on Server Core.

Because BitLocker uses a filter driver for encryption and decryption, installing or removing BitLocker requires a restart of the computer. Installing the RSAT-BitLocker component alone does not. After the component is installed, you can use the command-line tool, manage-bde.wsf, or Control Panel to enable BitLocker on particular volumes.

BitLocker is different from existing technologies like EFS because once you turn BitLocker on, it is automatic, transparent, and includes the entire volume. (Note that BitLocker is fully compatible with EFS, and you can use them both together to mitigate different risks. Active Directory Rights Management Service, or AD RMS, adds the third part of Microsoft's data encryption strategy. EFS and RMS are outside the scope of this chapter.)

BitLocker does require that a computer be configured with multiple volumes (partitions). A computer will start from the active partition, sometimes called the system partition or system volume. The operating system is installed on a second volume, which Windows Server 2008 documentation usually calls the Windows OS volume, but older documentation refers to as the boot partition. (Yes, for those keeping score: You never did boot from the boot partition and no Windows system files are on the system partition.)

The active partition is not encrypted, but the Windows OS volume is. In other words, BitLocker encrypts everything written to a protected volume: code, data, and temporary files.

BitLocker's full-volume encryption protects against offline attacks–the kind of attacks that are mounted by trying to bypass the operating system. It is absolutely essential to understand that BitLocker does not protect a *running* operating system. Once the Windows OS Volume has been unlocked at start-up, BitLocker continues to encrypt and decrypt sectors on the fly–whenever an application or the operating system itself reads or writes data on a protected volume–but it has no more protection function to perform. Instead, BitLocker helps protect you against offline attacks such as having the disk (or entire server) stolen.

Without BitLocker, it is a trivial exercise to take the disk out of a server and put it in another computer to bypass NTFS permissions and similar defenses. With BitLocker, though, nothing on that disk can be read in another computer, unless you have the required recovery password to unlock the volume. It is also true that files protected by RMS and EFS will also not be easily read, but BitLocker extends protection to the entire volume, including files that cannot be protected by RMS or EFS (such as the Active Directory database or the registry).

Direct from the Source: Automatically Unlock Data Volumes

In Windows Server 2008, Microsoft added support for fixed data volumes to BitLocker. Along with that comes the ability to automatically unlock (auto-unlock) any encrypted data volumes. To do this, BitLocker stores keys for encrypted data volumes (the "auto-unlock keys") in the system registry, where they are retrieved by BitLocker to unlock the volume.

It is very important to protect the auto-unlock keys, since they can be used to decrypt the volume. Therefore, these keys are always themselves encrypted before being stored in the registry. They are encrypted by using a new key called the Auto-Unlock Master Key (AMK). The AMK is very similar to the FVEK. The FVEK is used to encrypt the data on the volume, while the AMK is used to encrypt the data in the registry. Like the FVEK, the AMK is encrypted by the OS Volume's VMK, which explains the necessity of enabling BitLocker first on the OS Volume before it can be enabled on any data volume.

With this design, you can safely enable BitLocker on a data volume and set it to auto-unlock (which is the by default) without waiting for the OS Volume to be fully encrypted.

Also, since decrypting the OS Volume causes the AMK to be deleted and, therefore, the auto-unlock keys in the registry to become unusable, if you decrypt the OS volume, we also force decryption of all mounted data volumes that are set to auto-unlock.

Narendra S. Acharya
Software Design Engineer in Test (SDET)
System Integrity, Core OS Division

BitLocker Encryption Algorithms and Keys   BitLocker uses the Advanced Encryption Standard (AES) algorithm with a 256-bit key space. However, with the default setting only 128 bits of the key are used. For stronger encryption, the key length can be increased to 256-bit keys using Group Policy or the BitLocker Windows Management Instrumentation (WMI) provider. As with all encryption, stronger encryption and longer keys result in more processing power being used. (To take effect, any changes to the encryption settings need to be made before BitLocker is turned on for a volume.)

Before data is passed to the AES algorithm, it is run through two separate diffuser steps. A *diffuser* is a complex cryptographic algorithm with a simple purpose. The diffusers ensure that any change (even only one bit) made to the plaintext will result in the entire block being changed in the encrypted ciphertext. This makes it harder, if not impossible, to guess keys by making changes in the plaintext to see predictable output in the ciphertext.

With BitLocker, each sector in the volume is encrypted individually. Part of the encryption key is calculated from the sector number itself. This means that two sectors with the same unencrypted data will also result in two totally different encrypted blocks being written to the disk. This also makes it harder to discover the keys by encrypting known pieces of information.

One of the developers of the algorithm, and a respected cryptographer who worked on BitLocker, Niels Ferguson, presented and published a paper on the details of the BitLocker encryption algorithm. It is available on the book's companion CD-ROM and online at *http://www.microsoft.com/downloads/details.aspx?familyid=131dae03-39ae-48be-a8d6-8b0034c92555&displaylang=en*: *"AES-CBC + Elephant Diffuser: A Disk Encryption Algorithm for Windows Vista."* A simplified overview is shown in Figure 14-7.

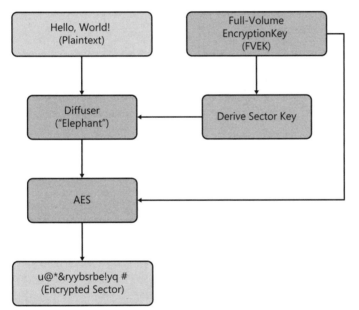

Figure 14-7 Simplified overview of BitLocker encryption algorithm.

As I mentioned, each sector is encrypted uniquely, with part of the key being derived from the sector number. The symmetric encryption key that is used for the bulk of the encryption is called the Full-Volume Encryption Key (FVEK). The FVEK is never revealed to a user or to an administrator. If the FVEK were compromised, security best practices would dictate that everything it encrypted would need to be decrypted and re-encrypted with a new key. Because we could be dealing with very large quantities of data, that would be a time-consuming process (during which noticeable performance degradation could occur). Instead, the FVEK is kept as a very closely guarded secret, and the system works with another key called the Volume Master Key (VMK). The VMK is used to encrypt the FVEK. The encrypted copy of the FVEK is written to the volume metadata. (It can also be backed up as part of a binary key package to AD DS.) This is not like leaving the key under the mat—it is more like leaving the key in a safe bolted to two tons of concrete, and then hidden under the mat. In addition, if the VMK is somehow compromised, you can re-encrypt the FVEK with a new VMK very quickly.

To decrypt sectors, the system needs to get the FVEK. To get the FVEK, the system needs to get the VMK. The VMK is also stored in the volume metadata, and it is also never written to disk without being strongly encrypted itself.

The VMK can be encrypted by any number of key protectors or authenticators. The default key protector is the computer's Trusted Platform Module (TPM), as discussed in the following sections. You can combine the TPM with a numeric PIN or a partial key stored on a USB key or both. By adding a PIN or USB requirement, you are introducing a form of two-factor authentication.

If the computer does not have a compatible TPM, you can configure BitLocker to store a key protector completely on a USB Flash Drive (although this does not provide any boot integrity checking, as discussed later). The VMK is also encrypted with a 48-digit recovery password that can be backed up to AD DS, stored in a database, or printed to be used for emergency recovery.

Finally, in a case where you want to disable BitLocker but not fully decrypt the drive, BitLocker uses a *clear key* key protector. The clear key is very much like putting the key to the door under the mat. The VMK is encrypted with a new key, but that key is stored in plaintext on the volume. This is effective for operations that require BitLocker to be deactivated, such as some kinds of upgrades, but avoids the time required to decrypt and re-encrypt the volume. However, because the VMK could be somewhat easily discovered in this state, you should not leave BitLocker in this disabled state for any longer than necessary.

BitLocker Start-up   At start-up, all BitLocker-protected volumes are locked and cannot be used, even to start the operating system. Early start-up code in the Boot Manager and Windows Loader looks for an appropriate key protector by querying the TPM, checking the USB ports, or, if necessary, prompting the user for a PIN or a recovery password. Finding a key protector lets Windows decrypt the VMK, which decrypts the FVEK. At this point, the disk is unlocked and the BitLocker filter driver decrypts the data stored on disk as each sector is read.

BitLocker Integrity Checking   When a server starts, the components used early in the process need to be unencrypted so that they can be used in start-up. If an attacker could change the code in the earliest start-up components, compromising a system is much, much easier. This is the basis of many rootkits. Once a system is compromised this way, secrets such as passwords can be much more easily obtained.

In the case of a system protected by BitLocker, a compromise of the earliest components could lead to the disclosure of the VMK or FVEK and render the protection of BitLocker useless, even though data on the disk is encrypted.

If the computer has a compatible TPM, BitLocker can use integrity checking functionality to help prevent this sort of attack. With a TPM, each time the computer starts, each of the early start-up components—such as the BIOS, the master boot record (MBR), the boot sector, and the boot manager code—examines the code about to be run, calculates a hash value, and stores the value in specific registers called platform configuration registers (PCRs) in the TPM. Once a value is stored in a PCR, the value cannot be replaced or erased unless the system is restarted.

A TPM can encrypt data (in this case, the VMK) and tie that encryption to specific PCR values, which is called *sealing* a key to the TPM. Once sealed, only that specific TPM can decrypt that key, and the TPM will decrypt the key only if the current PCR values match the values specified when the key was sealed.

By default, BitLocker seals keys to the PCRs that record the Core Root of Trust Measurement (CRTM), the BIOS and any platform extensions, option ROM code, MBR code, the NTFS boot sector, and the boot manager. If any of these items change unexpectedly, the TPM will not decrypt its key protector, and BitLocker will not be able to unlock the volume. This prevents the volume from being accessed or decrypted.

By default, BitLocker is configured to look for and use a TPM. You can use Group Policy or a local policy setting to allow BitLocker to work without a TPM and store keys on an external USB Flash Drive, but without a TPM, BitLocker cannot verify system integrity.

BitLocker in the Branch Office   "That's all well and good," you might be thinking, "and sure, it helps with laptops. But what does it have to do with my server in a branch office?" I'm glad you asked.

In several specific scenarios BitLocker can help immensely with servers, particularly those not housed in the central data center. These include:

- **Reducing exposure to malware, especially rootkits.** Most rootkits and other malware that can do serious damage on your servers require a restart to install. By using a TPM module and BitLocker's integrity checking, the server will not start if the early start-up components have been manipulated. (Windows Code Integrity features take over protecting the operating system against unauthorized changes after BitLocker unlocks the volume.) It is true that this could result in a denial of service because the server will not restart, but it is generally better to be stopped than to be running with active malware on a production server.

- **Theft of a server.** Thieves target laptops and mobile devices because they are often convenient targets. While some thieves steal them because they may contain some interesting bits of information, most laptop theft is for the hardware, not the infinitely more valuable data that is on them—information. But a server or its disks can the mother lode to a serious thief. A domain controller could contain secrets for thousands of users (see the section on RODCs!); a file server could be filled with your company's intellectual property; a database server could have reams and reams of personally identifiable information—handy for identity theft and fraud, to name but two. Note that to effectively mitigate against the risk of the entire server being stolen, using the default of TPM protection only will not be enough.

- **Theft of a disk**. It is often much easier to remove a single disk than to steal the entire server. Most server disks are swappable, so it only takes a moment for someone to remove one. Like a server, a disk contains valuable information and should be protected.

- **Shipping a server (or disk) to a remote location.** In many cases, servers are first provisioned centrally or large amounts of data need to be shipped to a remote server. In either case, you can enable BitLocker on the volume at the data center, and then ship the volume to the remote location. In the case of an entire server, it can be configured to require a start-up PIN. For a single volume, all key protectors except the recovery password can be removed. Then, after authorized personnel have possession of the server or disk at the destination, the PIN or recovery password can be provided by telephone, fax, or e-mail. Once the server is in production, if desired, you can remove the PIN requirement or even decrypt the volume. If the disk or server is lost or stolen in transit, the data cannot be accessed.

- **Secure decommissioning.** At some point, a server or disk needs to be removed from service. It is absolutely essential that no server disk with company data leave your possession with that data still readable. Most processes that remove confidential data from disk drives are time consuming, costly, or result in the permanent destruction of the hardware. Instead of removing the data after the fact, BitLocker helps ensure that confidential data is not stored on disk in a risky way in the first place. Because everything written to the disk is encrypted, you can permanently render the data completely inaccessible by destroying all copies of the encryption keys. The hard disk itself is completely unharmed and can be reused. Removal and destruction of the keys contained in the volume metadata is instantaneous and can be performed locally or remotely by an administrator. The format utility in Windows Vista and Windows Server 2008 deletes the volume metadata and overwrites those sectors to securely delete any BitLocker keys. (Note that you cannot use the format utility from Windows versions earlier than Windows Vista to achieve the same result.)

BitLocker Caveats and Trade-offs   As you consider using BitLocker on your servers, bear a few things in mind.

Remember that BitLocker protects against certain specific threats—from offline attacks. It is imperative that other security controls, such as strong passwords, remain in place. Likewise, BitLocker does not prevent the destruction of data or the denial of service. Backups are still essential. In fact, if you do not take care to ensure the accessibility of the recovery passwords, BitLocker could prevent you from accessing your data! We recommend using BitLocker's built-in ability to back up recovery information to AD DS. For more information about backing up recovery information, see "Configuring Active Directory to Back Up Windows BitLocker Drive Encryption and Trusted Platform Module Recovery Information" at *http://technet2.microsoft.com/WindowsVista/en/library/3dbad515-5a32-4330-ad6f-d1fb6dfcdd411033.mspx?mfr=true.*

In Windows Server 2008 and Windows Vista SP1, BitLocker uses a cryptographic signature to check for certain types of deliberate attacks. If one of these attacks occurs, the cryptographic signature is invalid, and BitLocker will lock out the recovery password as well as routine key protectors. This scenario will only occur if the attacker has physical possession of the volume or computer. If you regain possession of the volume, you will need to use the BitLocker Repair Tool and a backup copy of the FVEK, as well as the recovery password. Therefore, you should ensure that these items are backed up using the AD DS system or the WMI provider.

Also keep in mind that BitLocker is an optional feature on Windows Server 2008. Because the encryption and decryption operations are implemented in a filter driver, you cannot use BitLocker until you install the feature, as described earlier in this chapter. Note, however, that installing or removing BitLocker requires restarting the server.

BitLocker does not support clusters. If you configure servers in failover clusters, you cannot use BitLocker to protect shared volumes.

BitLocker—like all encryption products and technologies—incurs a performance hit. In most user scenarios, this performance is not noticeable, and can be measured at well less than 5 percent. However, if your server is performing intensive disk operations or is very heavily loaded, you may need to take this into consideration in capacity planning.

Security is often a matter of trade-offs. One significant trade-off to make with regards to BitLocker is whether to require user intervention at start-up. By default, BitLocker operates using the TPM as a key protector and, providing that the integrity validation completes successfully, BitLocker will unlock the Windows operating system volume without user intervention. However, this means that a thief who takes the entire server can also turn it on without any interference from BitLocker.

To mitigate this risk, use the TPM with a PIN, with a USB Flash Drive (called a *startup key*), or both. This increases security tremendously, but it also means that a server cannot automatically restart. (Leaving a start-up key in the server all the time would be a foolish idea.) Because servers are normally running this may not be a problem—until a power failure results in the branch being down because the one manager who had the PIN is on vacation.

My recommendation, in most cases, is to use a TPM plus PIN, but to ensure that there is an operational procedure that describes who knows the PIN, how to use it, and how to obtain the PIN from central support if needed. This also requires that any planned restarts (such as for an operating system upgrade or update) are scheduled when someone with the PIN is on-site. Only your organization can make the call about which is the more important risk: potential additional downtime or potential theft of the server.

Other Security Steps

I believe you need to invest in two other areas to protect your branch office servers: physical security and user education.

While features such as RODC and BitLocker help mitigate risk, a bad guy having physical possession of your server is still a big deal. Even if he cannot gain access to the data, he can still prevent your users from gaining access to it. Reasonable investments in physical security also increase the availability of services.

I continue to hear stories of cleaning staff unplugging servers, unnecessary water damage, and accidental shutdowns. Use locked closets or cabinets. Plan for UPS protection. Ensure proper ventilation. For large enterprises, this may be obvious—but then again, in a big firm, do you know the condition of every server in the truck shop or out on the plant floor?

Also invest in user education. Explain the importance of security and how to treat both the physical and data assets in their care. This may be more important than ever in small branch offices with no dedicated IT staff, let alone compliance and security officers.

Summary

Windows Server 2008 has been designed from the ground up to support branch offices, and introduces tools to make securing them easier than ever. The RODC and BitLocker features are key weapons in your arsenal of protection.

Additional Resources

- Windows BitLocker Drive Encryption Frequently Asked Questions
- BitLocker Drive Encryption Technical Overview
- *Data Encryption Toolkit for Mobile PCs*
- BitLocker Drive Encryption Glossary
- BitLocker Drive Encryption (from Changes in Functionality from Windows Server 2003 with SP1 to Windows Server 2008)
- BitLocker Drive Encryption Step-by-Step Guide for Windows Server 2008
- Windows BitLocker Drive Encryption Step-by-Step Guide (for Windows Vista)
- Windows BitLocker Drive Encryption Design and Deployment Guides
- *Configuring Active Directory to Back Up Windows BitLocker Drive Encryption and Trusted Platform Module Recovery Information*
- BitLocker Drive Encryption Events and Errors
- AD DS: Read-Only Domain Controllers (*http://technet2.microsoft.com/ windowsserver2008/en/library/ce82863f-9303-444f-9bb3- ecaf649bd3dd1033.mspx?mfr=true*)
- Step-by-Step Guide for Read-Only Domain Controllers (*http://technet2.microsoft.com/ windowsserver2008/en/library/ea8d253e-0646-490c-93d3- b78c5e1d9db71033.mspx?mfr=true*)
- Branch Office Infrastructure Solution for Microsoft Windows Server 2003 Release 2 (*http://www.microsoft.com/technet/solutionaccelerators/branch/default.mspx*)

Chapter 15

Small Business Considerations

— Susan E. Bradley

What drives the need for server security in a small to medium-sized organization? Do people make better business decisions because an organization has secure servers? The reality for many organizations is that budgets for security decisions are typically driven by regulation and compliance and not because securing computer systems is the right thing to do. Payment Card Industry Data Security Standards (PCI/DSS), Health Insurance Portability and Accountability Act (HIPAA), and other industry security standards have an impact even in the small business sector. The issue of limited budgets for security does not affect only small organizations, but it is typically more intense in this space.

Can you set up a small organization's network with Server Isolation (see Chapter 13, "Securing the Network"), Internet Protocol Security (IPsec) deployment (see Chapter 13), Rights Management, Secure wireless network access using digital certificate–based authentication (see Chapter 10, "Implementing AD Certificate Services"), BitLocker (see Chapter 14, "Securing the Branch Office"), and deployment of Read Only Domain Controllers (also see Chapter 14) for maximum protection? Sure you can. Does it mean that this is the best way to spend that small organization's technology budget? Or should the budget be devoted to protecting their security posture from being placed in jeopardy because the on-site junior administrator sets up the domain controller to be his music sharing, BitTorrent, or Quake gaming server during lunchtime? Perhaps some of that budget would be better spent on educating users about how their actions introduce risk to a small organization—or on the legal costs associated with the termination and/or rehabilitation of said junior administrator.

This chapter will not give you all the answers you need to provide secure server solutions. What it will do is guide you through the process of understanding the risks to the small business and taking the needed actions to reduce these risks to an acceptable level. Security of a small network is about the process of understanding the needs of the firm so that you can determine an acceptable secure solution built on the Windows Server 2008 family of products.

Running Servers on a Shoestring

The first issue you need to tackle in deploying a secure Windows Server 2008 solution in a small organization is the issue of cost and budgets. Approach the issue of budgets and price tags from the concept of current and future costs, including implementation, monitoring, and maintenance, combined with acceptable downtime and acceptable risks. If a small organization suffers a security breach and is required by regulation to inform their clientele, will the organization lose revenue as a result? In the reality of the security marketplace, customers of firms that have suffered losses are amazingly quite understanding of potential identity theft resulting from the loss of backup tapes, laptops, and the like. External breaches in some instances have not affected organizations' bottom lines as much as you might expect, considering the magnitude of the security incident. (See, for example, "The TJX Effect" Larry Greenemeier, *Information Week*.) Security breaches have actually hurt the reputations of the consultants deploying the networks more than they have hurt the companies themselves. (See, for example "Medical IT Contractor Folds After Breaches," Tim Wilson, *Dark Reading*.)

However, if the organization is affected by a virus infection that causes widespread network disruption, the impact is easier to calculate. In this example you can calculate the loss of revenue for each hour of impact. Multiply that number by the number of hours that the organization is affected by the security incident and ask the client if that is an acceptable cost. The traditional risk calculation of ALE=SLE*ARO—where SLE is the Single Loss Expectancy and ARO is the Annualized Rate of Occurrence—misses that the value of mitigation is not taken into account, nor does it factor in the issue of how hard it is to predict the "what if." The concept of this revised risk view is discussed in a May 2006 blog posting by Dr. Jesper Johansson.

Trying to impress the importance of security upon a client before an incident occurs is no easy task. It reminds me of the statement given in a radio interview by Bruce Turbeyville of the California Fire Safe Council after the massive fire that destroyed hundreds of homes in the Lake Tahoe area in late 2007. He lamented: "Why is there always enough money to fight the fire? Because we always fight them and they always go out. But there is never enough money to prevent the fire." The same lament has been made by many a small organization's network administrator. The arguable advantage of the small business technology implementer is that unlike their large network administrator counterparts, when small business technology implementers have buy-in from management on the proposed security solution, they control the network from end to end and do not need to interact with other divisions or organizations or other specific server role administrators.

Direct from the Field: The Reality of Risk

When performing risk assessments for our small and medium-sized business clients I typically find that the biggest weakness in their organization is that they do not know what information assets really exist in their business, and what value those assets play in the business workflow.

The discussion of technical safeguards to protect a business's information assets is fairly unproductive until we first know what threats the company is susceptible to. And we cannot explore the dynamics of those threats until we actually know what harm a business may suffer if an asset is accidentally or intentionally destroyed or otherwise made unavailable. We also must explore what assets an adversary may want access to, and consider how much effort we can expect that they would use to gain access. Only then can we start determining what real value can be assessed to the information, and how much expense should be spent on safeguards to mitigate these risks to acceptable levels for the business.

Dana Epp, Microsoft Security MVP
Scorpion Software

Choosing the Right Platforms and Roles

Windows Server 2008 has brought to the marketplace a huge number of choices from the Windows Server Core installation option, which is arguably perfect for many domain controllers and servers in security-adverse positions, to the different editions such as Standard, Enterprise and Datacenter, to Windows Web Server 2008. Often the most confusing part of setting up a secure network is choosing the right operating system. However, many small businesses are in a position to benefit from the cheaper offerings that are available in the marketplace. There are also varieties of licensing bundles geared toward different organizations, ranging from ISVs to not-for-profit organizations to pricing models designed for emerging marketplaces. However, be aware that if the price of the product sounds too good to be true, it probably is—and places the server at risk of piracy. Using a bootleg copy with Windows Server 2008 may cause the server to be placed in reduced functionality mode.

Typically, the worst enemy of a small network is the line-of-business (LOB) application vendor that inadvertently sets incorrect permissions and destabilizes the network. Virtualization technologies allows a small firm to limit the risks of this while not having to overspend on hardware.

When deploying a server, only choose the minimal roles needed for that server to function appropriately. The Add Server Role Wizard in Windows Server 2008 makes it easy to go back and add a role.

32- vs. 64-bit Versions of Windows Server 2008

While the desktop marketplace is still struggling to move to 64-bit platforms, the server marketplace is ripe for the move. Although Windows Server 2008 ships with both a 32-bit and a 64-bit platform version, the recommendation for even small businesses is to make the move now to 64 bits. While security is one facet of this decision, the large memory support for 64-bit

Windows is more likely to be your motivating factor. RAM is cheap. Databases demand memory. In addition, the standard Windows Server 2008 will no longer be limited to 4 gigabytes (GBs) of RAM. The advantages of 64-bit also include the fact that there is no in-place upgrade from any prior 32-bit platform. Thus, any prior network set up using 32-bit Windows servers cannot be upgraded in place to 64 bits. While this might seem like a disadvantage, it actually provides a key security advantage: *permissions*. When a system has been upgraded in place from any prior version of an operating system, what has historically been left behind has been a mixture of the new operating system's permissions and the old operating system's permissions. Even if the server is preinstalled from an OEM vendor, consider rebuilding it from scratch to practice key disaster recovery techniques. In a small organization, this may be the time to practice and document the disaster recovery planning on that server that least affects the organization.

> **Note**   The selection of 64-bit does bring additional considerations with regard to signed drivers and network attached devices, printers, or any other peripherals attached directly to the server. Microsoft Knowledge Base article KB 895612 found at *http://support.microsoft.com/ kb/895612* discusses the issues faced with using 64-bit versions of Windows. As you can see in Figure 15-1, although in the 32-bit version of Windows you can "install this driver anyway," in the 64-bit version such drivers will not install properly.

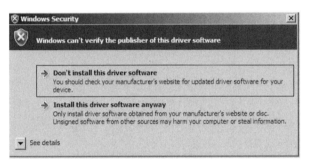

Figure 15-1   Unsigned drivers have an impact in this era of 64-bit platforms.

Check your network-attached printers, USB devices, and other items you plan to install on the server and ensure that they have digitally signed drivers. Unsigned drivers will not be installable. You can find more information in the *Windows Server 2008 Application Compatibility Cookbook* found at *http://msdn2.microsoft.com/en-us/library/Aa480152.aspx*. In the past, unsigned drivers in multi-use servers have included older print and fax drivers but, as you can see in Figure 15-1, even the installation of a new USB external hard disk that prompted the warning impacted the installation.

For many organizations the driving reason for a server is an LOB database application and a messaging platform, including shared calendar. Because Microsoft Exchange Server 2007 is 64-bit only, you will, by definition, have a 64-bit server as the base operating system. Exchange 2007 SP1 is fully supported on Windows Server 2008 64-bit.

> ## The SMB Server Lineup
>
> The following Windows Server 2008 versions are best suited for small organizations:
>
> - Windows Web Server 2008 is suitable for hosting public Web sites.
>
> - Windows Server 2008 Standard is suitable as a general, all-purpose server platform.
>
> - Windows Server Code Name "Cougar" is the follow-on product to Microsoft's Small Business Server 2003 and is a multi-role server built specifically for small organizations.
>
> - Windows Essential Business Server is a new three-server bundle specifically intended for medium-sized organizations.

Servers Designed for Small Firms

Your first goal in setting up a secure solution is to pick the proper foundation from which to design your solution. Consider the firm's plans to grow and expand and choose a platform accordingly.

Windows Server 2008 Web Edition

When you set up a publicly exposed Web site, pick the right tool for the job. While Internet Information Services 6 is a rock-solid Web platform with a stellar security track record, and Internet Information Services 7 is anticipated to be the same, it is just common sense to not place a publicly accessible Web site on your critical business server. Either externally host it through one of the many hosted or Windows Live offerings, or purchase the Web edition and set up a separate server. While small organizations may have Web services on domain controllers for purposes of remote access and e-mail, you should separate Web sites that allow anonymous connections from authenticated ones to minimize risks.

Windows Server Code Name "Cougar"

For many years, Microsoft has put together a server platform that combines server management and information worker technologies in a bundle for up to 75 users or devices. In the Windows Server 2008 era, the "Cougar" platform is only offered on the 64-bit platform and includes a bundling of Microsoft SQL Server, Windows SharePoint Services, Windows Software Update Services and parts of Forefront, Microsoft's security suite for Exchange, Windows SharePoint Services, and Windows clients.

As in the Windows Server 2003 era, the Windows Server 2008 Standard version of "Cougar" will not be able to form trusts relationships with other domains, and the products included will not be able to be split to other servers (nor will this be allowed in its end-user licensing).

In the standard installation of the product, everything must be placed on the one server. Remote access to workstations, e-mail, and Windows SharePoint Services is provided by a Secure Sockets Layer (SSL)–secured Web portal called Remote Web Workplace.

Also included in the product are the renowned administration wizards. Loved by most, hated by some, the wizards are scripted routines for installing; setting up; and deploying Domain Name Services (DNS), Active Directory (AD), Internet connections, and other networking and deployment needs—and ensuring that the deployment is easily reproduced in a consistent and secure manner. Basic tasks of the server, as shown in Figure 15-2, are clearly defined for the onsite administrator or remote consultant.

Figure 15-2   Getting Started tasks.

The biggest change in the "Cougar" platform in the 2008 era is that it will be deployed with one network interface card and will need an external firewall. ISA Server, Microsoft's firewall software, can no longer be placed on top of the single "Cougar" server, nor can the server be set up with the Routing and Remote Access Service (RRAS)–based firewall that was used in the Standard version in the past to provide alternate firewall functionality. Since the Windows Firewall is enabled, the RRAS–based IP packet filtering firewall is no longer supported, nor recommended.

As shown in Figure 15-3, this separate firewall must now be placed outside the domain controller, bringing "Cougar" in line with the best practices of separating the firewall from the domain controller and thus removing one server role from the system.

Customers with Software Assurance will have the ISA Server that they are licensed for shipped to them separately.

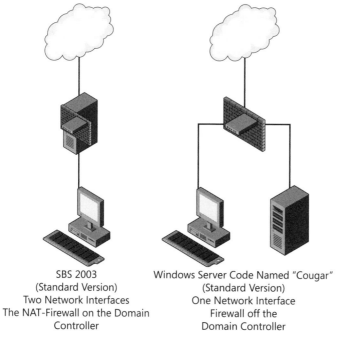

SBS 2003
(Standard Version)
Two Network Interfaces
The NAT-Firewall on the Domain
Controller

Windows Server Code Named "Cougar"
(Standard Version)
One Network Interface
Firewall off the
Domain Controller

Figure 15-3   Networking gets a major change in Windows Server Code Name "Cougar."

Choosing a Firewall

New to Windows Server Code Name "Cougar" is the ability to choose a hardened external firewall to complement the server's duties. Discuss with the business owner what his or her tolerance is for Internet use. Interview the organization about past security incidents and how virus, malware, and other issues occurred. Recommending to the business owner that the network budget may be better spent on a higher-priced, business-class firewall in the U.S. $300 to $1,000 range that provides the firm with the ability to more granularly filter inbound and outbound connections rather than the $50 consumer models that allow no such ability. This may be the best investment the organization makes. This ability to be flexible and choose the appropriate firewall for the needs of the organization opens up a great deal of flexibility and opportunity for the small-organization marketplace to choose appropriate and tailored protection that was not present in earlier versions of this product line.

Just as in prior versions, you can add an additional server for additional domain controllers, application servers, file and print servers, or whatever your needs may be. For more information on the Windows Server Code Name "Cougar" platform, please see the Microsoft Small Business Server Web site at *http://www.microsoft.com/sbs*.

Direct from the Source: Secure by Default

When building the Windows Server Code Name "Cougar" version of Small Business Server, security was a center point of the design from setup through to end of life of the product. Many security enhancements come as defaults in this new server SKU. Some of these items include:

- Strong password policies.
- Creating a new Administrator account so that the Administrator account is not well known.
- A local host firewall solution using the latest versions of Windows Firewall and enabling core functionality.
- SSL-based Web security using either a free (self-issued certificate solution) or paid trusted certificate solution to secure Web traffic.
- Anti-spam features provided by Exchange Server 2007.
- Built-in WSUS 3.0 with auto-approval policies for critical, security and definition, updates for the entire network.
- A single point of reference on the server to monitor and manage security services.

Windows Server Code Name "Cougar" can be deployed as an internal server only, using a single-NIC configuration. Deploying "Cougar" as an internal server allows for flexibility of choice in the firewall solution the company wants to use. Depending on the sensitivity of the data, and the necessity of the Internet, the company can choose to deploy a single hardware firewall solution to protect the network, or deploy Microsoft's Internet Security and Acceleration (ISA) Server on a separate box to provide authenticated access to the Internet and packet filtered traffic in from the Internet. This flexibility allows the company to choose where to spend valuable resources to provide the secure solution that is right for company.

In "Cougar," the primary means of remote access to the company is provided through HTTPS Web traffic using Remote Web Workplace. Users can securely access Web-based e-mail, internal Web sites, and the files and folders associated with their user account that live on the server. Furthermore, they have secure, encrypted access to their desktop through the Remote Desktop Protocol, and if they are a domain administrator, the server.

Windows Server Code Name "Cougar" is the most secure version of Small Business Server to be released in the market.

Sean Daniel, Program Manager
Microsoft Corporation

Windows Essential Business Server

The next server Windows Server 2008 SKU to enter the lineup is Microsoft's Windows Essential Business Server. The server setup is actually three servers: one with the management role, providing the primary active directory services, a second one called the messaging server that provides Exchange 2007 and additional domain controller duties, and a third server—the security server—where both ISA Server and certain edge messaging components needed for Exchange are deployed. The ISA Server on the edge box is deployed with two network interface cards in a domain configuration that are acceptable for smaller organizations for role- and risk-balancing, as shown in Figure 15-4.

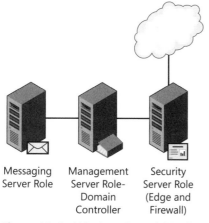

Messaging   Management   Security
Server Role   Server Role-   Server Role
        Domain   (Edge and
      Controller   Firewall)

Figure 15-4   Windows Essential Business Server.

Like its smaller sibling, Windows Server Code Name "Cougar," Windows Essential Business Server also demands 64-bit–only support for its three servers. The three servers set up a secure network that is designed to make it easy for an onsite administrator to deploy and secure the network with a minimum of deployment issues. Tools such as System Center Essentials 2007 are built in to ensure secure needs of the midsized organization as well as follow all of the best practices of splitting services and roles among servers.

This platform is not "Cougar" on steroids, but rather Microsoft's recognition that the mid-market space, pushed both by needs and by regulation, requires management it has not previously had. Tasks are designed to help administrators deploy software, secure desktops, and track compliance with network policies. Network management and control is a primary goal of this server product. It also provides a remote access portal to services and workstations that has gone through the standard Microsoft Secure Development Lifecycle review process. Combined with the fact that the Messaging Hygiene Technologies included in the Exchange Edge server is deployed from the outset to meet the needs of such an organization, Windows Essential Business Server looks to be a very interesting addition to the secure server solution lineup in the Windows Server 2008 era.

Hosted Servers

The concept of hosted servers is relatively new to the small business marketplace. With a hosted server, a server running some version of Windows Server 2008 is deployed in a data center. Consider using a hosted server when a client's needs can be met by only using applications that can be shared through a virtual private network connection, Outlook Anywhere (formerly known as RPC Over HTTP) and Windows SharePoint Services—and where connectivity and high speed from the connected workstations is optimal. Hosted servers bring their own unique security considerations. Because the servers are physically located in a data center, the security policies of the data center are key. Many U.S. data centers provide audit verification of their security processes through external verification such as a Report on the Processing of Transactions by Service Organizations, commonly referred to as an SAS 70 audit. Ask your hosting company for a copy of such a report.

Virtualization

Finally, when determining the server platform on which you want to begin building your security solution, do not overlook the issues and advantages of virtualization. Typically, in a small environment, the resources for clustering are non-existent and restoring data to a bare server takes both time and introduces risks of restoring to different hardware. Placing the entire server platform inside a virtual server means that if the hardware has issues, it no longer becomes an impediment to a fast restoration. However, as with any virtualization project, there are risks—including physical security issues, proper network configurations, and last but certainly not least, supportability. In the small business space, virtualization on a non-Microsoft platform is not supported unless you have a premier support contract.

More Virtualization Guidance

Virtualization of production servers is beyond the scope of this book. However, the interested reader is referred to the following additional resources:

- Review the guidance in "Microsoft Virtual Server Support Policy" at *http://support.microsoft.com/kb/897613* and "Windows Server System Software Not Supported within a Microsoft Virtual Server Environment" at *http://support.microsoft.com/kb/897614/* for platforms supported in a virtual environment.

- For details on the support policy for Virtualization on non-Microsoft platforms review "Support Policy for Microsoft Software Running in Non-Microsoft Hardware Virtualization Software" at *http://support.microsoft.com/kb/897615* and "Support Policy for Microsoft Programs That Are Running in a Third-party Application or Software Redirection Program or in a Third-party Application or Software Virtualization Environment" at *http://support.microsoft.com/kb/924287*.

Violating All the Principles with Multi-Role Servers

If anything puts fear into a security expert, it is looking at the number of services running on a typical small business server. Most security experts (especially experts who are not well-versed in the needs and risks of small businesses) are very concerned about the attack surface exposed by all these services, and the cumulative effect of the lack of isolation. I once counted the number of servers one would need if one followed best practices as 12 servers in total. Obviously, this number of servers is not feasible for typical small organizations. Figure 15-5 shows eight sample roles that many multi-role servers perform. These include file, e-mail, database, Web, Active Directory, print, mobility, and of course the most famous role of that of "everything else"—better known as the "kitchen sink" server.

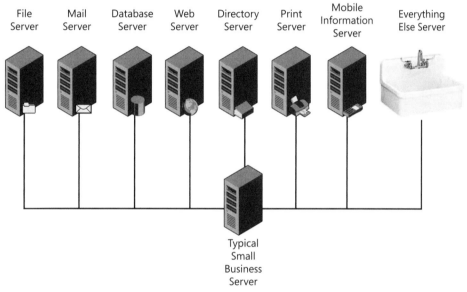

Figure 15-5   The typical multi-role server: Everything including the kitchen sink.

However, there is typically more risk to a small organization from misconfigurations—for instance, someone setting up remote access incorrectly—than there is from exposing more than one role on a given server. As a package deal, a correctly configured multi-role server with easy step-by-step build instructions is far more likely to be secure than a build-it-yourself, manually installed server in a small organization without dedicated and highly trained Information Technology (IT) personnel.

For someone maintaining the system, that very same view is a concern about the correlation to updating duties and necessary reboots. While the typical Windows Server 2008 as examined by Microsoft's Jose Barreto on his blog at *http://blogs.technet.com/josebda* has fewer than 50 services running, the average Windows Server Code Name "Cougar" server counts more than 100 services running even before any LOB applications are placed on the computer, up from SBS 2003's 67 normally running services. While each running service has had additional time and effort devoted to appropriate permissions and rights (see Chapter 6, "Services" for more details on individual services), you must accept one fundamental fact when setting up a multi-role server: you need maintenance windows for these types of servers. If the organization mandates zero downtime, a multi-role server is not acceptable.

Acceptable Roles

Your job as an implementer of an acceptable secure solution is to determine which roles and duties are acceptable on that server and which ones are not. Review the applications that you intend to deploy for that network. For many organizations, the recommendation for any key LOB application based on a database platform is to not place it on the domain controller in Windows Server Code Name "Cougar" or the file server in the Windows Essential Business Server platform, but instead to have a dedicated server for that application. Typically it is easier to secure and to set proper NTFS file system permissions, and also easier to keep the memory use of the application in check. With virtualization, you should not think in terms of real hardware for these multi-server deployments. Placing many of these LOB applications on virtual servers is quite acceptable. Furthermore, many a network has been destabilized when a vendor installed a SQL Server database on a running server and innocently paved over whatever applications were already using the default SQL instance.

Server Components

The server role that will drive many server deployment decisions is the role of messaging. The big change in the 2008 era versus 2003 is the server role–based model that Microsoft Exchange Server 2007 has taken. The roles include Mailbox Server, Client Access Server, Hub Transport Server, Unified Messaging Server, and Edge Transport Server. The Edge Transport Server's role handling all Internet mail flow for an organization demands that it be placed on a separate, stand-alone server to reduce the attack surface of the Exchange server. You can split all five roles over five different servers if you like, or combine four of them, but the Edge Transport Server role, as shown in Figure 15-6, is recommended to stay on a separate server. The exception to this rule is the Windows Server Code Name "Cougar" platform that because of special configuration is able to provide appropriate functionality on the same server.

As you peruse the many articles about the deployment of this edge role, you will find many of them are absolute in their recommendations that the edge role not be on a domain as the most secure deployment configuration. Microsoft's own server role deployment documents wisely point out that not all businesses need this "most secure" configuration to still have an acceptably secured network.

For a much more detailed overview of the needs for deploying Exchange Server 2007 in your organization, we recommend the following Microsoft Press companion books: *Microsoft Exchange Server 2007 Administrator's Companion* by Walter Glenn (2007) and *Microsoft Exchange Server 2007, Administrator's Pocket Consultant* by William Stanek (2007).

Roles allowed:
Edge Transport Server Role

Roles allowed:
Hub Transport Server Role
Mailbox Server Role
Client Access Server Role
Unified Messaging Server Role

Figure 15-6   The roles of Microsoft Exchange Server 2007.

Risk Considerations

Earlier in this chapter you read that all Windows Server Code Name "Cougar" applications and roles had to be on the same server, yet here we are discussing acceptable roles indicating that Microsoft has split off the Edge Server role onto a separate server to reduce the attack surface of Exchange Server. Obviously, the two positions are in direct opposition. So how can you balance the fact that all of the Microsoft guidance indicates that Exchange Server needs an edge role, and that domain controllers should not be file servers, and all of the other best-practice tenets that security guidelines and doctrine present to the small business consultant and still justify your multi-role solution? The key is to determining the right balance of risk.

Mitigation via Hosted Messaging

The first recommended mitigation is to maintain the file, printing, and database-style roles on the server, but outsource the entire messaging component to a hosted Exchange solution. Note, however, that this means that someone outside your organization will have access to all e-mail conversations and all meeting requests in your organization. This may be highly unde-sirable for many organizations. Outlook 2007 (and even 2003) RPC Over HTTPS (now called Outlook Anywhere) is a near-seamless means to a full, rich messaging client in a hosted manner. Outlook Web Access 2007 has transformed OWA from a clunky Outlook wannabe to a full, rich, browser-based Web mail solution that even offers search capabilities rivaling its desktop counterpart.

The Plumbing Problem

Microsoft's Senior Security Strategist Steve Riley has a blog post at *http://blogs.tech-net.com/steriley/archive/2007/07/02/protect-your-data-everything-else-is-just-plumbing.aspx* that makes the point that the energy we spend worrying about the technology plumbing just might be better served in other ways. When you look at the historical ways that small organizations tend to have security incidents, the bulk of the security issues are introduced by poor controls at the workstation level, not remote attacks at the server. A small organization is more at risk from drive-by malware introduced by drive-by browsing, clicking postcard links in e-mails, and phishing attacks than from a direct-targeted attack. Historical malware cocktails included various vulnerabilities targeting Apple QuickTime and Flash, and embedded these malware cocktails in Web banner ads and other locations. (For details, see *http://blog.washingtonpost.com/securityfix/2007/06/the_mother_of_all_exploits_1.html*.) Figure 15-7 highlights the real threat to a small organization.

Risk of Remote Attacks   Risk of Phishing E-mails
to Server

Figure 15-7   The workstation risk.

Your most at-risk asset is often not the server, but rather the workstation where the boss reads his or her personal e-mail on Webmail, visits Social Networking sites on a regular basis, downloads all those "Naked Dancing Pigs" screensavers, and opens up every "Warning! Your Woodgrove Bank account has been closed due to unusual activity!" e-mail that she receives. Do not get caught up in throwing technology at a problem before you take the time to understand the underlying cause of the security incident in the first place. Too many times I have seen people ask how to harden the "Cougar" server when it is appropriately hardened already. Rather it is the workstations that need the most attention in most small to medium-size organizations because they expose the network to the greatest risk.

Mitigation via the SDL Process

The second mitigation technique to consider if you want to offer a server with multiple roles that includes a messaging component is to choose Windows Server Code Name "Cougar." No, this is not a marketing push to get you to buy Windows Server Code Name "Cougar"; it is an acknowledgement of the fact that the product goes through the same threat modeling and secure coding process called the Security Development Lifecycle (SDL) process that all other

Microsoft applications and platforms must go through to ensure that it is built with security in mind. Thus, when that platform ships, it has already gone through an acceptable risk assessment. It was designed to build and implement a multi-role server for a small organization that will provide the proper balance of being secure while catering to small business needs, and is the only server solution able to mitigate the risk of the edge role placed on the same server. The argument could be made that Windows Essential Business Server, Microsoft's mid-market platform, does the same for a three-server deployment. Both products give you a base secure server to then build secure network solutions on.

Edge Server Issues

The key element in all of these multi-role—but not multi-server—deployments is to review what you need or want to put on the edge. Review the needs of the organization to protect that edge and deploy a solution accordingly. That solution could be an ISA firewall able to review the packets entering the network, a cheap third-party firewall appliance, or an inexpensive ISA-based hardware firewall. Regardless of the device on the edge of your network, it is strongly recommended that you review the manner in which it logs traffic across that connection. If you read Chapter 8, "Auditing," and did not get the idea that auditing is important, go back and read that chapter again. When—and please note the use of the word *when* and not *if*—a security incident happens to an organization, you will not have a complete picture of how things entered and left your organization without that edge device logging the activity. It does not matter whether that organization is a large corporation with an on-site forensic team or a small organization who will be calling Microsoft's Customer Support Services security division and asking them to perform a Windows Online Forensic analysis. Furthermore, the solution you place at the edge can assist in your attack-mitigation posture by having such policies as only allowing e-mail from the mail server and blocking all e-mail from any internal workstations (to prevent workstation zombies).

Proactive Internet and Access Policies

While you are setting up policies to limit Internet access, consider also proactively limiting what workstations can do on the network that they should not be able to do. For example, in a typical network, a workstation should not be sending out traffic on port 25. If it is, it has probably been turned into a spam zombie. But you can take proactive steps to prevent this traffic. Figure 15-8 shows a sample restriction rule done on ISA Server.

Firewall Policy Rules

1	Array	Exchange Server Publishing:...	Allow	HTTPS	External Wel
2	Array	Exchange Server Publishing:...	Allow	HTTPS	External Wel
3	Array	Terminal Services Gateway ...	Allow	HTTPS	External Wel
4	Array	Allow DNS Traffic from inter...	Allow	DNS	DNS Servers
5	Array	Internal spam bot rule	Deny	SMTP	The LAN

Figure 15-8   Using ISA Server to assist in setting edge policies.

> The sample policy looks like this:
>
> ```
> Action: Deny, log request
> Protocols: Selected: SMTP
> From: The LAN (a defined IP address range of the workstations, but excluding
>     the Server, Printer, and scanner IPs, which are specifically defined and
>     excluded in the DHCP server range)
> To: Anywhere
> Users: All
> Schedule: Always
> ```

Be Proactive Not Reactive

Small businesses tend to initially not care much about restrictions on Internet use and thus the usual design of network access is to let all authenticated workstations have full Web access. Later on, the business owner begins to realize that employees are spending too much time on social networking Web sites or spending too much time instant messaging their friends. Thus, typically you are later asked to limit Internet access—not proactively, but reactively because of this non-business use. Your best security solution will always be proactive and not reactive. Try to anticipate the threats accordingly.

If you have ever scanned comments in an online security community, you have probably noticed that one recommendation is to move services to alternative ports as a best practice. For large organizations, this step has little or no value because the attackers will be looking for unusual traffic no matter what port it is on. In a small organization, it can add some benefit, but in general, minimize as best as you can the ports that respond externally.

Supportability and Updating

Chapter 12, "Update Management," details what you need to know about security updating, but multi-role servers do have support and update management considerations unique to the platform. Because of the number of services running on the same system, it is a fact that debugging issues may be more challenging. This does not mean they are impossible to deal with, but when an issue arises, ensure that the vendors you work with understand that they are working on a multi-role server. For example, certain third-party applications may need different versions of .NET installed, and vendors need to understand their shared place on this server and not unduly change permissions, install their products on top of existing Web sites, or perform any other actions by which vendors have historically have nearly destroyed a multi-role server in the past.

LOB Application Virtualization Tip   When installing an LOB application, consider using Virtual Server. This places the application away from your other server roles, and will ensure that the vendor will have no ability to restrict the supportability on the multi-role server you are running the application.

Billing for Update Management

If you sell consultative services to the small business marketplace, one issue you will face is convincing your client of the necessity of update management. Determining the value of a service pack to a small organization can be very difficult. It can be disruptive. It costs the client. In addition, a service pack may not have advantages that a small business owner sees value in. Consultants can usually "sell" security update management to a small organization, but it is harder to "sell" the larger, more disruptive service pack. The best way to approach this conundrum is from a support standpoint. While it is highly recommended that you not install Server service packs in the middle of the lunch hour on the day the service pack is released, it is wise to deploy it within a minimal period of time after release. A new service pack released for a server product is typically a sign that some prior version is going off support. Your goal here is to never get into a state in which you have to deploy a service pack as a mandatory step before you can get help from Microsoft's Customer Support Services. Understand the Product Lifecycle, Service Pack roadmap (*http://www.microsoft.com/windows/lifecycle/servicepacks.mspx*) and stay within the support time frame.

Update Management Testing Tip   Use the power of virtualization to build replicas of your network. You can use disk-imaging programs to take physical to virtual copies of just about everything but your end users themselves to aid in security update testing.

When updating a small business network, the key is to have a good rollback plan. Server operating system updates can be uninstalled. Application updates for Windows SharePoint Services and Exchange Server can typically not be uninstalled. Updates that go on workstations have less impact on the network as a rule. If there is a security update that has a severe impact to the server, uninstall it. If the update was the culprit, typically the network functions will be restored to full functionality. If it is not, the updates may be the cause.

Remote Update Management   You can install most security updates successfully with little to no risk to the network. Service packs or any update that impacts an "edge" device (such as for ISA Server) have a higher risk of impacting remote access during the updating process. Always log on to the terminal server console session for best results in remote update management.

Server Recoverability

A redesigned backup software is new to Windows Server 2008. NTbackup is defunct and only installed in a read-only manner to allow for restorations from old media. And new to the server backup is a block-level backup. If you have done a backup in Windows Vista, you have seen this in action. The native Windows 2008 backup does not provide encryption and thus the long-term and off-site storage needs of media need to be reviewed and addressed.

Always have a restore methodology in place (and preferably tested and documented) when recovering a multi-role server. For Windows Server Code Name "Cougar" and Windows Essential Business Server, external USB and FireWire devices will be supported and a backup Setup Wizard is included. As shown in Figure 15-9, you will need to install this backup feature for Windows Server 2008. The middle of a disaster is not the time for you to be determining the disaster recovery and business continuity process for the organization.

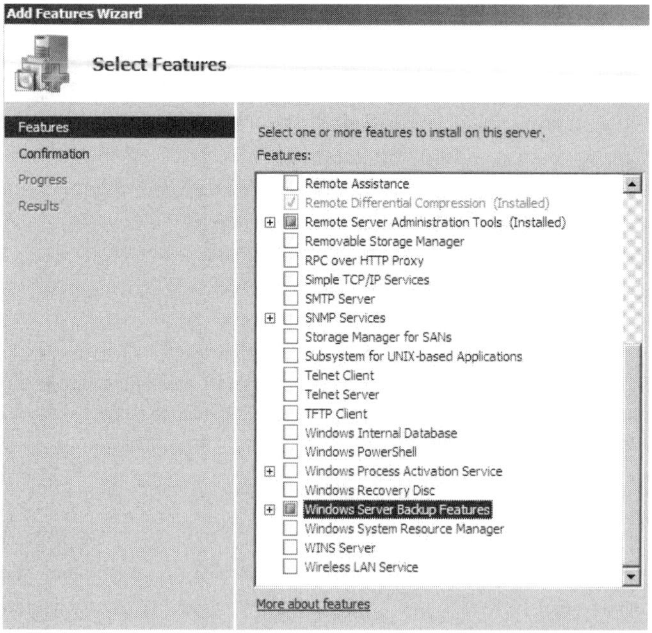

Figure 15-9   Adding the backup feature to Windows Server 2008.

System State Backup

If you are wondering where the System State Backup went in Windows Server 2008, it is still there in the command line:

wbadmin start systemstatebackup
wbadmin start systemstaterecovery
wbadmin delete systemstatebackup

Example of Use: **wbadmin start systemstaterecovery −backupTarget:f:**

Before any major change to the server, a recommended best practice for a small to medium-sized organization is to take a quick system state backup, as shown in Figure 15-10.

Given that you probably do not want to wait for a full volume backup before updating, include this little command as a best practice in change management for a multi-role server. Planned change management is key to a multi-role server stability and security.

Figure 15-10   System State Backup command line.

Best Practices for Small Businesses

When designing best practices for small businesses, be wary of the best practice trap: A security checklist created by a large agency that has not reviewed your small organization for its needs and risks may not be the wisest security checklist to follow. It is too easy to get lost in the minutiae of detail and not step back to look at the larger picture.

Best Practices Warning   While this section is called "best practices," always decide on which "practices" are actually "best" for the organization currently under review, and not just because some checklist or document says so.

While this book is clearly titled and focused on the Windows Server 2008, you need to be cautious of being too concerned about hardening the server and totally missing the rest of the insecurity of the network. A consultant also has to walk the sometimes-hazardous road of dealing with customers. The customer (or your boss) is not always right, but the customer does pay your salary. If you are asked to deploy something you are uncomfortable about, it is up to you to decide whether you can use the opportunity to educate, or if it is better to walk away and find new employment somewhere else. Conversely, be prepared to back up your solution documented with your mitigation if external auditors question your deployed solution.

Following Hardening Guidance

Once upon a time, I joined a group of industry experts looking for a master list of things I could tweak on my Small Business Server 2003. Like many, I was enticed by the promise that tweaks meant I was secure and the thrill of entering that uncharted land of the registry where in the Tweakomatic tool documentation, the Scripting Guys threaten that horrible things will happen if you go astray was just too tempting.

I found upon investigation, however, that no one really knew what would happen to my server and the LOB applications running on it after I made most of these tweaks. Generally, the folks who designed the tweaks know the details of what they do, but not how they affect an application. Conversely, an application developer is rarely aware of what tweaks the code is dependent on. Would my server survive? Or would it accidentally create

Microsoft Bob as a result of changing the registry as the Scripting Guys predict might happen? (See *http://www.microsoft.com/technet/scriptcenter/tools/twkmatic.mspx*.) Many of the settings—though able to tell me whether the server would continue to function as a domain controller—could not tell me whether the key piece of software that I depended on would stop functioning if I messed with any settings that sounded mildly interesting. And in fact, during the weeks of conference calls where the experts discussed the impact of each setting, it became clear that, when using the most secure hardening settings (now called "Specialized Security – Limited Functionality"), all of the security experts could just about guarantee that something *was* going to break. In the end, you must make a decision: your business needs or your paranoia.

The Risk of Security Guidance   You can take any number of third-party guidance and checklists and apply them to any size of server, but if you do not understand that you have now ensured that you and *only you* can support that server, you are unduly risking the supportability of that server, and ultimately the organization's business.

If you are tempted to make random changes based on security guides, I challenge you to do the same thing on a test network (with a good backup) first. Read this book. Read the Windows Server 2008 Security Guide, Windows Vista Security Guide, and the Windows XP Security Guide, all of which can be obtained from the Microsoft Download Center at *http://www.microsoft.com/downloads/*. If a setting sounds interesting, try it, but know that you have to test everything again after you do. You just built your own version of the operating system. Moreover, know that you now must test any future update or installation on your specially tweaked server. Ask yourself if the tweak you made really made that network any safer. You have now introduced the risk of possible unsupportability and have not gained much in real security.

Anyone who changed the assignment of the Bypass Traverse Checking privilege and then applied Microsoft's Security Bulletin 05-051 learned this lesson in a big way in KB 909444 "Systems that have changed the default Access Control List permissions on the %windir%\ registration directory may experience various problems after you install the Microsoft Security Bulletin MS05-051 for COM+ and MS DTC" (see *http://support.microsoft.com/kb/909444/*). Especially on a multi-role server, the developers already balanced the needs for hardening with functionality of the server and determined an appropriate balance. You need to merely determine appropriate policies that impact the end user. As long as you have followed the install and deployment wizards, the server itself is in a secure condition.

Reading the guidance geared toward larger firms can also be confusing because it assumes that you have a single role server. If you read the Windows Security guides and then read the Exchange guide and then read the SQL Server guide it will be hard to determine which guide to follow. You may need to review and understand that these are guidelines and should not be considered mandatory.

Specific Hardening for Small Networks

So you have come to this chapter for a checklist. Well, here it is. Yes, it is a small one, because when you use the wizards in both Windows Server Code Name "Cougar" and Windows Essential Business Server to set up your server solutions, the bulk of your time is then freed up to fix where the real insecurity lies: On the desktops of the end users still using their systems with administrator rights. And then you need to sit down with the owner of the firm and determine his pain points without blindly following a checklist built for larger firms. So what specific guidance is recommended for small networks? Here are some specific "best practices" to keep in mind that do make sense for small firms. Some of these suggestions are common sense. Some are recommendations for changes to the server that are good practices as well as being suggested for PCI/DSS guidelines:

1. Set passphrase policies appropriately for the firm. Remember that if they are set to be longer and more complex, you can increase the time between mandatory password changes.

2. Limit external access to the server and desktops through the use of both an external firewall and internal host–based firewalls.

3. Consider an external mail hygiene service to limit the external access to port 25 and your mail server.

4. Only open those ports external on the firewall as needed. Use a port scanner to ensure that the ports you opened are what you intended to do.

5. Restrict terminal server access to the server either in the form of ensuring that a VPN connection is required first, or that the access is limited to certain static IP ports. Ensure that the external firewall you choose has the ability to restrict access to certain ports.

6. Ensuring that the workstations are on Windows XP or Windows Vista operating systems means that you can ensure that you can enforce stronger authentication.

7. Limit Internet access to Web sites that are appropriate for the needs of the business. Discuss with the business owner his or her tolerance for personal use of business assets and limit accordingly.

8. Review all third-party software installed on the server and on workstations. Determine whether the software increases the security risk of the network and whether there is a means for updating it when needed.

9. Ensure that the server is only used for server duties. Do not surf or use the server as a workstation.

10. Educate end users in security awareness. Teach them to be suspicious of e-mail attachments, links, and other enticements. An educated end user may be your best security tweak in a small network.

11. Have a disaster recovery plan and test it. *Really* test it.

12. Install a third-party trusted certificate for use in remote access to the server. Both Windows Server Code Name "Cougar" and Windows Essential Business Server feature a remote access portal that offers up secure access over a SSL connection. Although the server(s) can be deployed with built-in self-signed certificates, purchase and install a external certificate from an SSL certificate vendor. Specific guidance on how to do this has been included in the material on the accompanying CD with step-by-step instructions.

13. Adjust the Schannel protocol to only support SSL3. PCI/DSS documents recommend this and modern browsers support this setting. Review the guidance in Microsoft Knowledge Base article 187498 and on the guidance on the accompanying CD.

14. Disable MS-CHAPv1 support on the VPN server and only allow the stronger CHAP or MS-CHAPv2 protocols instead. You will find additional information on how to do this on the accompanying CD.

On the Disc   Included on the book's accompanying CD is information about performing specific tweaks to the server for small firms, including:

- Installing a Certificate on IIS7 for remote access to Remote Web Workplace with a public certificate.
- Disabling SSLv2 to comply with PCI/DSS standards.
- Adjusting VPN to support more secure protocols.
- Changing remote desktop to support Network Level Authentication.
- Recommended firewall settings.
- WMI query tips.

Changing Settings

Before you make drastic changes to a server, you should understand which settings were made by Microsoft and why. Typically, a multi-role server has special settings, and even special hotfixes to ensure that all of the roles that were designed for separate servers can coexist on the one server.

Figures 15-11 shows a classic example of a default setting that was set by Microsoft in Windows Server Code Name "Cougar" to ensure the proper functions of the server. The setting for

Network Access: Allow Anonymous SID/Name Translation is not a default setting in a plain Windows Server 2008, but is needed on a multi-role domain controller. If you are unsure whether a setting is a default of the system, or you changed something and forgot to document it in your change management documentation, having a virtualized test bed with a default install of the typical server installs that you perform will help you identify default values.

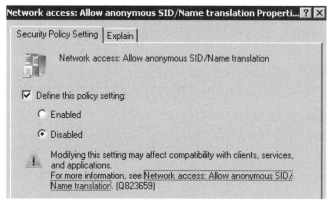

Figure 15-11   Preset server policy for anonymous SID.

You many even consider using the Windows System State Analyzer tool (see *http://microsoft.mrmpslc.com/InnovateOnWindowsServer/redirect.aspx?d=Download/WindowsSystemStateAnalyzer_x86.msi*) before and after installing the software to see what the vendor applications change on a server.

Policies

The most important security hardening one can do in a small network is to set policies. From password policies to an organization's acceptable-use policies, policies are a key element in a secure network for a small organization.

Password Policies

Passwords are mandatory. There are no exceptions to this in a secure network. Be prepared to explain to the organization why using "Password" as a password is probably not a good thing, and that the annoyance of requiring the use of Ctrl+Alt+Delete is meant to give individual accountability to the specific users that log into the network. Explain that there is really no need to have a master list of all passwords—in fact this is a serious violation of personal privacy. If an employee is not on-site to authorize Remote Assistance to work on his or her exact profile on his or her workstation, and the work must be done during off hours via Remote Desktop, reset the password to a temporary password and ensure that the end user is forced to change the password at the next logon. In small organizations, you cannot overlook or take for granted even the basics of end-user education. It may not be a bad idea to mandate a basic security-training course with an annual refresher.

Security Policy Best Practice

Never implement password policies without a corresponding Organization Security policy. A policy defines the company's risk management position and provides both a framework for action and job saving guidance for IT personnel. A subset of this policy is an Acceptable Use Policy that defines the acceptable use of an organization's business assets. Writing such policies are outside of the scope of this book, but for more guidance visit the SANS security policy project at *http://www.sans.org/resources/policies/* and refer to the book *Information Security Policies Made Easy* by Charles Cresson Wood (Information Shield, 2005).

Fine-Grained Password Policy

The good news in the Windows Server 2008 era is that you can set password policies per group of users, as documented in the Step-by-Step Guide for Fine-Grained Password and Account Lockout Policy Configuration found at *http://technet2.microsoft.com/ windowsserver2008/en/library/2199dcf7-68fd-4315-87cc-ade35f8978ea1033.mspx?mfr=true.* Chapter 2, "Authenticators and Authentication Protocols," goes into detail about this process, but rest assured that GUI-based, third-party tools are out there to make this process painless. Figure 15-12 shows one such tool from SpecCops. (See *http://www.specopssoft.com/wiki/ index.php/SpecopsPasswordPolicybasic/SpecopsPasswordPolicybasic/.*)

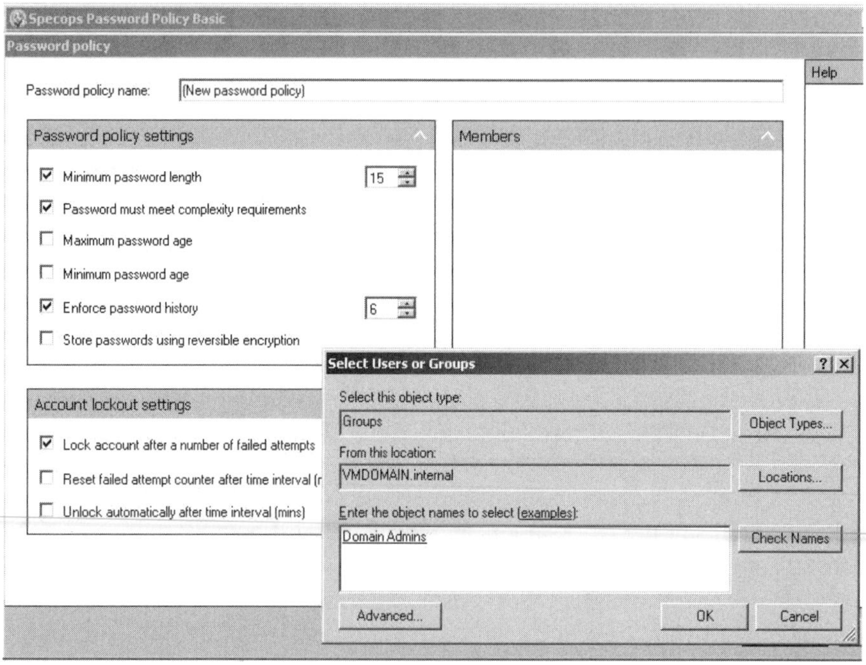

Figure 15-12   Fine-grained password policy.

The default policy on Windows Server 2008 requires that passwords be changed every 42 days. Consider the organization's business cycle and urge the organization to increase the length of the password, thereby ensuring that passphrases are better, stronger, and able to withstand not being changed as often—42 days is an interval that is unlikely to endear you to the business. A quick change to the password policy shown in Figure 15-13 means greater acceptance of passwords in general.

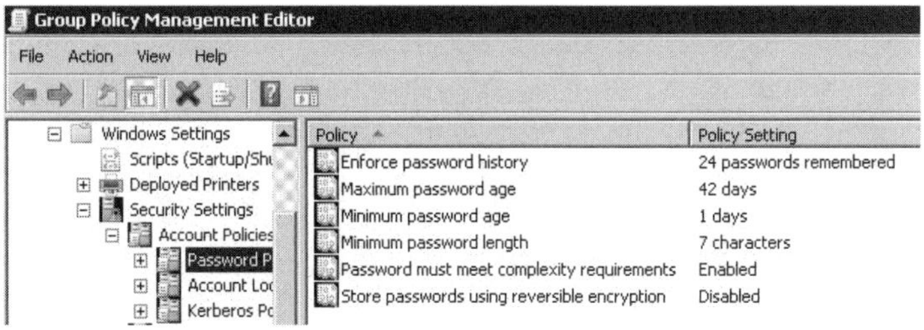

Figure 15-13   Password policy on the domain controller.

Use the opportunity of setting up a new server in a small organization as a means to train and educate users about the fundamental need to choose and protect appropriate passwords or passphrases.

Administrator Account Handling

The Administrator account is without a doubt the most important asset in any server. Thus, the protection of the password for this account is of vital importance and you must have a policy in place regarding its use. Furthermore, because of the potential for consultant turnover and vendor access, the true built-in Administrator account in a small organization should be used the way it is used in larger deployments: so sparingly you would think it has the plague. Set a very strong password, disable it, and only use a different administrator account when remotely accessing the computer, which in fact Windows Server Code Name "Cougar" by default does for you. Better yet, consider technologies to add additional two-factor means of authentication to any account with server administrative access. Consider technologies such as RSA Secure ID, and Scorpion Software's AuthAnvil token key technology to add additional protection. Each person needing domain administrator rights should have his own administrator account, to ensure that there is an auditable means of tracking access. ·

Vendor Best Practices

In a small organization, information technology needs are typically met by external vendors. Utilizing these vendors brings a new set of risks and considerations to a network.

Vendor Admin Access

Never give external vendors access to an existing administrator account. Instead always set up a separate, dedicated account for vendors needing remote access. Furthermore, if external printer or scanner vendors ask for a listing of all user names, passwords, and IP addresses on the network to be faxed to their network engineers to set up the device ahead of time, kindly say no and send a request for proposals to a different vendor.

Vendor Remote Access

If you are a vendor to businesses, and you provide consulting services, you need to be acutely aware of the security and hygiene of the computing assets you use to perform remote access to your clients. Any credential you type on a compromised computer is compromised. Laptops and wireless cards are reasonably priced and provide the ability to maintain secure remote connections.

> **Remote Access Best Practice**   Set the firewall so that Terminal Server access only responds to certain static IP addresses from the network of the remote consultant or vendor.

Outsourcing Issues

If you think that small organizations are not impacted by outsourcing because they only get IT support from on-site administrators or local consultants, you are wrong. External consultants who provide managed services plans are beginning to rely more on outsourced providers. Certain industries (like American accounting organizations) demand that if you use one of these outsourced managed services, you must inform the clients of the organization that their sensitive data is being accessed by such outsourced organizations. Consider the risks accordingly.

> **You Cannot Outsource Accountability**   "The bottom line is this: Although an organization may outsource some of its business processes, and with it part of its responsibility for privacy, the organization cannot outsource its accountability for privacy." (Marilyn Prosch, *Outsourcing and Private: 10 Critical Questions Top Management Should Ask*)

Separation of Duties

In a small organization, the need for separation of administrative duties among Exchange administrators, Windows Firewall administrators, and Live Communication Server (or Unified Communication Server) duties is not as acute as it is in larger organizations, largely because there is generally only one IT administrator. It is still a best practice to use multiple accounts with least privilege, but this is generally more difficult to implement than is worthwhile.

Vendor Changes to Your Network

If a vendor recommends that you disable either the Windows XP or Windows Vista firewall inside the network, urging you that the external firewall is enough protection for a small organization, politely request that she document the exceptions that need to be open in the firewall for the software to work properly. Some antivirus vendors may need program and port exceptions as well. Just remember that application software can and does work well inside a network with the proper exceptions in place. When a vendor requests an action that you are not comfortable with, review your options with the owner of the business. I have personally asked to speak to the management of support queues of my LOB applications when requests were outrageous and too invasive. The need for proper change management increases when you have multiple vendors providing various duties.

Remote Access Issues

A small firm needs to balance the needs of remote access with the requirements of security. What issues are involved? And what steps can they take to achieve this?

Remote Connectivity and Security Considerations

The riskiest thing to a small business network is when that network's users are not well enough informed to make the appropriate decision. If you put in draconian policies, and those policies interfere with getting that organization's work done, you will lose the argument every time. This includes policies regarding remote use. In a small organization that depends on several key employees, ensure that you have built in ways to take the computer with them in a palatable manner with appropriate policies and access. This is key to ensuring that the employees are not tempted to use something like a kiosk computer.

Dangers of Kiosks

When Windows Small Business Server 2003 first came out with the remote access portal called Remote Web Workplace back in 2003, the marketing brochures touted using "any" computer to access the network. They failed to point out that earlier that same year, the real-life stories of similar "any computer" access ended in owners' passwords, bank accounts, and credit card numbers being stolen through the use of keyloggers installed on kiosk computers in Kinko's (Robert Vamosi, in *http://reviews.cnet.com/4520-3513_7-5053016-1.html*). The use of two-factor authentication such as RSA's Secure ID and Scorpion Software's AuthAnvil can mitigate this risk, but the more sensitive that the data inside the organization is, the more rigid the policy must be. Remote access policies should be very clear regarding which computers are allowed remote access to a network. Never use a computer that you do not personally own or know the security health of when accessing network resources remotely. Period.

Mobility Choices Decrease Risk

Smart phones are a great and secure way to keep key employees connected remotely without introducing undue risk of remote access to that server environment. An organization is safer in deploying such remote technologies as Outlook over https (now called Outlook Anywhere) versus Outlook over a Virtual Private Network Connection. All too often, in a small organization we do not take the time to adjust VPN connections to limit the connection, so the workstations are making a full Network (Layer 3) connection back to the server. The choices of remote technology are key in setting up secure and affordable remote access for organizations. Technologies such as Remote Web Workplace that use more secure protocols and send more screen shots ensure that the overall network is more secure. With Remote Web Workplace—and now in Windows Server 2008—Terminal Server Gateway connections from trusted systems are a key way to allow maintainable secure access.

Account Lockout

In large firms, the policy of setting a policy on the number of times a user can incorrectly enter a password can cost a firm a great deal of help desk time and may not be an effective policy. In the small-business marketplace, setting an account lockout policy may provide value that outweighs its disadvantages. Typically, account lockout in a small organization is caused by a saved password, not by malicious use. But, accounts being locked out could also alert you to a router misconfiguration, or perhaps a disgruntled ex-employee, trying to break into the organization. Account lockout can also be used to assure the business owner that the system can mitigate something that I call "drive-by port rattling." This is sometimes seen in small networks. If you have a port that must remain open to the Internet, regular port scans will hit it. In reality, passwords should be strong enough to withstand these random attacks, but invariably the business owner sleeps a bit better knowing that the folks running the automated scans only get a set number of tries. Thus, while your best mitigation is better passwords, invariably the business owner wants to hunt these drive-by port scanners down and run them out of business. Explaining to a business owner that it is probably his own grandmother's computer that has been turned into a zombie computer normally does not gain you much in the way of trust, so this setting is one of those "comfort" settings that make business owners feel better.

Monitoring and Management Add-ons

In a small network deployment, a consultant's most important tools are the ones he deploys to assist in monitoring servers. The industry calls this packaging of remote monitoring "Managed Services." The goal is that should a server need attention, the consultant is alerted immediately. For those of you who have been taking care of networks in the Enterprise space, Windows Management Instrumentation (WMI) has been the go-to tool to allow someone to merely code up a little query to determine what was going on in a network. Because many small business administrators, including myself, consider scripting a difficult task, Microsoft first brought Microsoft Operations Management (MOM) to provide a GUI tool for managing a network.

SCE and SCE Managed Services

Microsoft has released System Center Essentials (SCE) and System Center Remote Operations Manager 2007. These two tools help manage these smaller deployments. If you are a consultant, you can install SCE on a system and then use System Center Remote Operations Manager 2007 to roll up the reports of all of the servers in your control. Depending on how you structure your services, you can provide monitoring only as a service. Or you can expand your services to provide a service level agreement (SLA) to your clients, assuring them of a certain uptime of servers, workstations, and so on. Alternatively, you can just use these tools on demand for your break/fix client base to alert you to issues. An administrator can move on to other duties when all he or she has to do is a quick check of the SCE dashboard, shown in Figure 15-14, to determine that everything is running normally.

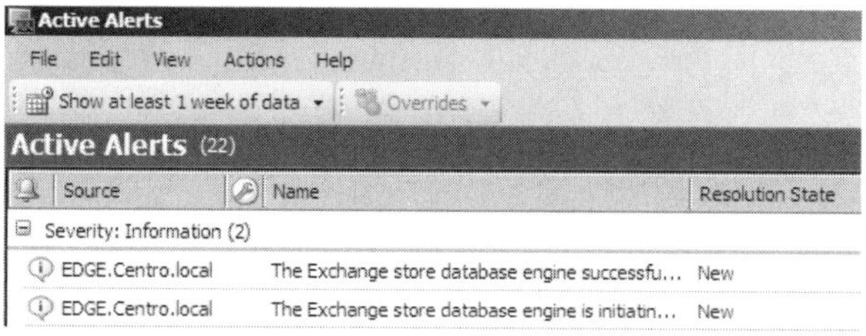

Figure 15-14   SCE's monitoring of network services.

Third-party Solutions for Managed Services

The marketplace of managed services seemingly changes on a daily basis. What was a best practice yesterday will change tomorrow. While you can do many of these remote tasks with mere scripts from the Microsoft Scripting Guys, it may make more sense to ensure that you have a supportable and repeatable framework that above all provides a reporting tool that ensures that your clients understand the role you are filling. The worst thing you can do in supporting a network is supporting it so well and so silently that your boss (or client) does not believe that you are doing anything for them. Ensure that at a minimum, you give clients a quarterly report that covers such mundane security elements as number of spam e-mail messages detected, viruses blocked at the gateway, number of times users were kept from downloading "Naked Dancing Pigs Screensaver 2.0" from the Web, and so on. Whatever tool you use to assist in remotely keeping track of that server, ensure that you communicate to the business owner a summary of what you did to make that network work. Use this time with the client as an educational process to reinforce the consequences of risky behavior. For more information on Managed Services as a service offering, see the *http://tech.groups.yahoo.com/ group/SMBManagedServices/* listserv.

Remote Management Considerations

When you chose a remote management tool, be aware that the tools may also affect the security of your network. Windows Vista does not ship with the Remote Registry service enabled, but some management solutions need to have it enabled to remotely view event logs and perform other management tasks for remote users. Turning on the Remote Registry service will affect the security posture of your network. Review guidance such as the Microsoft Threats and Countermeasures guide when vendors recommend changing default services and registry settings. The document is located at *http://www.microsoft.com/technet/security/ guidance/serversecurity/tcg/tcgch00.mspx*.

The Server's Role in Desktop Control and Management

The best way to keep a server safe and secure in a small business environment is to keep the desktops under control proactively. One of the most important steps you can take in desktop control is to stop granting end users administrative privileges on their workstations.

Windows Vista Resources   If you have not already purchased a Windows Vista Security book, I would recommend both the *Windows Vista Resource Kit* from Microsoft Press and *Windows Vista Security: Securing Vista against Malicious Attacks* by Roger Grimes and Jesper Johansson (Wiley, 2007) as two great resources for understanding Windows Vista security better.

Chapter 13 presented the argument that a network should be designed to not be dependent on backing up the workstations. Even in a small organization, you should try to build a management process that does not use customized configurations or data stored on workstations. An organization's key LOB application should be on the server, where it is better protected and backed up, rather than exposed on a workstation. Review such applications for the need for deployment of organization-wide encryption or other security solutions if they must be placed on workstations. Consider deploying BitLocker on the server if it is in a physically insecure location.

Recommended Small Business Group Policy Settings

Before you start this section, you should have already read Chapter 7, "Group Policy." In addition, you should have a copy of the group policy settings spreadsheet handy for reference. You can download this from *http://download.microsoft.com/download/c/3/8/ c3815ed7-aee7-4435-802b-8e855d549154/GroupPolicySettingsforWindowsVista.xls*.

Many new settings impact security and can be useful in a small organization. Want the ability to control every USB port connector in the network? You need Windows Vista for that. Want to improve password storage and authentication protocols inside the network? That you can do with Window Server 2008, Windows Server 2003, and Windows XP or Windows Vista workstations. You do not know why it is a good idea to do this? Review Chapter 2 for the answers to why Figure 15-15 shows one of the best settings you should leave in place on a small network. (Here is a hint: it means you finally kill off any remaining Windows 98 computers that might be lying around the network.)

Group Policy Best Practice   To set the policy (or any group policy on any server for that matter), it is recommended that you build a new policy so that you can know what unique settings you make. Then, when you open up the Group Policy Console, you will know exactly what policies you have added to that network. This is an easy way to keep track of which policies you have created and which policies came with the default install of the various small-to-medium server deployments.

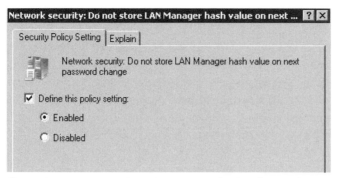

Figure 15-15   Not storing LAN manager hash value can be one of best settings you can leave enabled on a small network.

Some of the most important group policy settings in a small network are discussed in the following sections.

Interactive Logon: Message Text For Users Attempting To Log On

Arguably, one of the most overlooked Group Policy settings for small organizations is a minor setting that has major human impact. Typically, in a small organization, the attitude is one of camaraderie and collaboration. Therefore, this idea is overlooked: the organization administrator has the right and the authority to review all access, all e-mails, all Web sites, all documents, all downloads—basically anything on an employee's computer, because the hardware and software are owned by the business. Sometimes simply reminding employees in an Acceptable Use Policy that all of their actions can be monitored and reviewed is an effective blocking tool to ensure that employees do not abuse the network. If reminding them in writing is not enough, you can even gently remind them as they log on to their systems in the morning with the setting Interactive Logon: Message Text For Users Attempting To Log On. Do not overlook the human factor when securing a network.

Windows XP and Windows Vista Firewall Group Policy Settings

When deploying the Windows XP and Windows Vista firewall settings inside of an organization, the key item to remember is that the external firewall you have is just that—an external firewall on the outside. It is not going to help you one bit should something horrifically nasty wiggle its way into the network. I know you are going to argue that the latest attacks have been less extreme, but silent killers are trying to turn your network into a zombie attack force; internal firewalls can do their part for the health of the network. For more information on why internal firewalls are so important, see Chapter 13.

The typical Windows Vista firewall settings for small organization networks typically only need four categories of settings: Core Networking, File And Printer Sharing, Remote Assistance, and Remote Desktop. In many cases, you can also restrict those further and only expose those services to certain hosts. The more carefully you analyze who needs access to what, the more you can customize these firewall restrictions and limit what the workstations can and cannot do. This in turn will help you with the timing of updating and mitigating security issues. Having those workstations be a part of the security fabric of the network helps a great deal. The Windows Firewall with Advanced Security is located under Computer Configuration, Windows Settings, Security Settings, and under a special category titled Windows Firewall With Advanced Security. In Windows Server Code Name "Cougar," the hard work of setting up these policies is done for you. As you can see in Figure 15-16, the "Cougar" server has pre-enabled inbound rules, and outbound rules are staged so that if you do enable outbound filtering, the core organization needs of networking, printing, remote assistance, and remote desktop will be served.

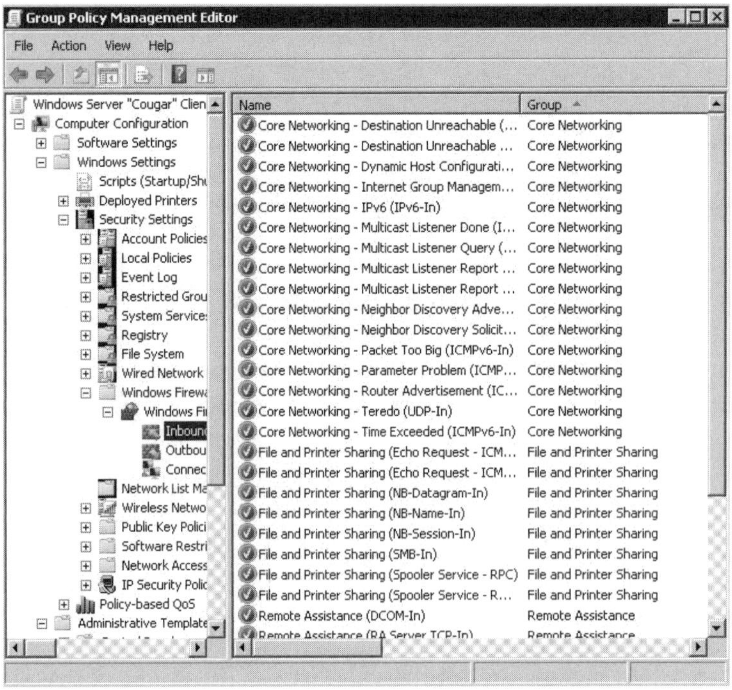

Figure 15-16   Group policy settings for Windows Vista Advanced Firewall set by the server.

Windows XP workstations can also participate in this mitigation and restrictions. The worst thing you can do in a small organization is to consider the external firewall "good enough" and believe that there is no need to enable these internal firewalls. Take the time to understand how internal firewalls can add needed limitations.

Located under Computer Configuration, Administrative Templates, Network, Network Connections, Domain profile, review the "Small Business Tweaks" document on the book's companion CD for details on the recommended policies for a small network shown in Figure 15-17. For more information on the power of group policy, also review Chapter 7.

Authentication and Clients

One of the best ways to secure a small network (and arguably any network) is to practice a procedure of standardization This is one of the most difficult security settings to enable.

In fact, it can be nearly impossible. It may break older LOB applications. It is merely a goal to get every workstation on the same platform (arguably the latest desktop operating system the vendor has), the same service pack, to ensure that each application is also updated and has also gone through the same level of security code review that is the norm for the Windows Secure Development Lifecycle. If you are lucky enough to achieve this goal, you can make additional settings such as ensuring that all Terminal Services/Remote Desktop sessions only are set to support Network Level Authentication, and setting the authentication levels to the highest such as Send Ntlmv2 Response Only\Refuse LM & NTLM.

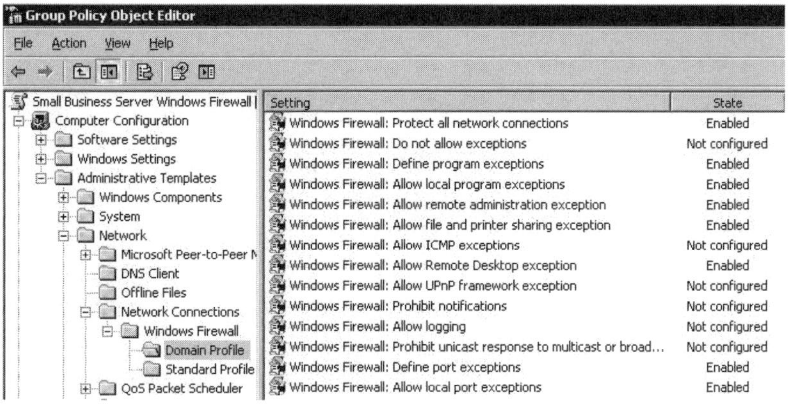

Figure 15-17   Group policy settings for Windows XP as set by the server.

Recommendations for Additional Server Settings and Configurations

Blindly following security hardening guidance is not recommended. But that does not mean that some settings on the server should not be reviewed for your specific needs. The following sections offer a few recommendations for a small firm network.

DsrmAdminLogonBehavior

In a single domain controller setup, consider modifying a new registry value in Windows Server 2008 called DsrmAdminLogonBehavior. It is located under HKLM\system\currentcontrolset\Control\Lsa and will allow you to log onto the domain controller if Active Directory Domain Services is stopped. The DSRM administrator password that is set up separately when you promote a server to be a domain controller using dcpromo.exe does not get password policies applied to it. Thus as a mitigation, the default for Windows Server 2008 is to allow the DSRM administrator to log on only when Active Directory services are running. In a typical multi-domain controller network, the loss of one server would not be an issue because any of the other domain controllers can authenticate. Therefore, DSRMAdminLogon-Behavior is configured to prevent logon when the Active Directory services are stopped. Obviously, in a single domain controller network this could prevent you from logging on to the server and recovering it. Thus, in a single domain controller environment, this is a recommended setting.

Figure 15-18 highlights this new registry setting, which has the following values:

0 – DSRM admin can only log on in DSRM mode when Active Directory Domain service is running. (This is the default.)

1 – DSRM admin can log on in DSRM and when Active Directory Domain Services service is stopped.

2 – DSRM admin can log on at any time.

This one quick setting solves the issue of not being forced to hard-reboot a domain controller, which is probably a good thing.

| DsrmAdminLogonBehavior | REG_DWORD | 0x00000001 (1) |

Figure 15-18   DsrmAdminLogonBehavior registry key.

Legacy Apps Limit Server Tweaking

In my quest for absolute security, I did an experiment and tried to limit all of my file server traffic to port 445. I found that my tax preparation software complained bitterly about the lack of port 135–139 communication and demanded that I not attempt to limit SMB communication in such a manner. Thus, you have to remember that setting up a multi-role server is exactly that—a multi-role server—and especially with LOB applications that have not been recoded in many years. Those applications very often cannot handle newer security recommendations.

Turning Off Auditing

Arguably, turning off auditing is a setting adjustment that will cause issues later down the road. When looking at the audit logs of a server, and now in the Windows Vista era, the workstations, your first request is to get them to be less overwhelming. Their "chattiness," especially on a domain controller, means that you should expect an event every second if not more often. You would be better served by increasing the storage size and leaving the audit logs for the one time you will need those logs around to investigate.

Turning On Auditing

Wait—did I not just say that turning off auditing was bad? Now I am arguing that turning it on is also bad? Yes. Beware of certain audit settings such as object access that will fill up an audit log quickly. If you want to audit a specific access event, ensure that you are precise in your auditing and do not enable this on an entire domain controller.

Turning Off UAC

Turning off User Account Control (UAC) is one of the worst things you can do in a small organization, and not just for security reasons. If a piece of software assumes it will be on and it is not, it may not install properly. If you do any adjusting to UAC for your workstations on a group policy level, only do this one setting, shown in Figure 15-19. Adjust the UAC in group policy in User Account Control: Behavior of the elevation prompt for administrators in Admin Approval Mode and set it to Elevate Without Prompting. This should be the only setting that you consider; it will keep Internet Explorer with Protected mode enabled. Leaving Internet Explorer protected as it can is one of the best things you can do for a small business. However, try leaving UAC on and enabled. You will find that once you have software installed, you will rarely see UAC again.

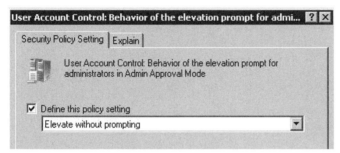

Figure 15-19   UAC group policy adjustment.

UAC on the Server

There is no good reason for a domain administrator to be surfing at the server. Not a single one. It places your entire infrastructure at risk. Therefore, it is no wonder that the "Cougar" team looked at the threats and risks to that server, disabled the Built-In Administrator account, and enabled User Account Control on the server, in contrast to Windows Server 2008. UAC is there to remind you that a server is exactly that, a server, and is not to be used as a workstation. Follow the best practice of not using the Built-In Administrator account for even the most mundane of daily administrator tasks. As shown in Figure 15-20, leave the setting in place as a reminder of how important that domain controller is.

Figure 15-20   The risk of administrative surfing on a server as mitigated by UAC.

Antivirus and Anti-Spyware

The only Web sites any server should visit are the various locations for the Microsoft Update service. Thus, because you should never be surfing at the server, there is no need for anti-spyware software on it. Is there no need for antivirus software either? On a domain controller in particular, you need to ensure that you follow the guidance of Knowledge Base articles that give a shopping list of key files, folders, and log locations so that the system will not have any issues introduced by the very software that is supposed to be protecting it. In general you need to exclude locations on the server where Active Directory, Exchange, or other key databases place their log files.

> **Note**   As an historical basis for exclusions, review the Microsoft Knowledge Base articles numbered KB822158, 815263, 817442, 821749, 309422, 328841, 823166, and 245822 for examples of the types and locations of exclusions. More information is in the resource section at the end of this chapter.

While the PCI/DSS guidelines state that one should deploy antivirus to all commonly impacted systems, which include workstations and servers. You have to balance the best practices doctrines of placing anti-malware software on such critical servers with the constant risk of such software marking a key file or dll accidentally as malicious, as in the historical case of KB924995 – "When you restart Windows Server 2003 the computer may display a gray screen or may appear to stop responding," where an antivirus vendor marked lsass.exe as a virus and brought down servers in the process. A better practice is to scan the points where potentially malicious software can enter the system. Use data hygiene services such as Microsoft's Forefront Services for SharePoint, Exchange. And, of course, have anti-malware technology on all workstations and terminal servers. If those technologies are in place, most servers (yes, even multi-role ones) do not need anti-malware software because the existing protections should already stop problems.

NAP for SMBs

Network access protection (NAP) is a new technology that holds a great deal of promise. While NAP is not set up on either Windows Server Code Name "Cougar" or Windows Essential Business Server by default, you should still consider it in your network strategy. Be aware, however, that you may not want to enable NAP in enforcement mode without ensuring that any device that you personally use to connect to the network has a MAC exclusion from the enforcement policy. You cannot use the same antivirus as your clients, so it would be wise to set up NAP in reporting mode first, to see what exclusions are necessary before you enable full enforcement. If you follow the wizard shown in Figure 15-21, you might find that you lock yourself out as being non-compliant in the policy you just set up for your clients' networks.

The issue that small organizations face with NAP is choosing enforcement policies. You can bypass DHCP by using a fixed IP. 802.1x has security issues when used in a wired network setting. VPN is difficult to enforce on an internal network. That leaves IPSec as the only defensible enforcement mechanism for NAP. This means a more complex setup. In a small firm, DHCP probably is appropriate for the firm's needs. For Windows Server Code Name "Cougar" it is recommended to place NAP on a separate server.

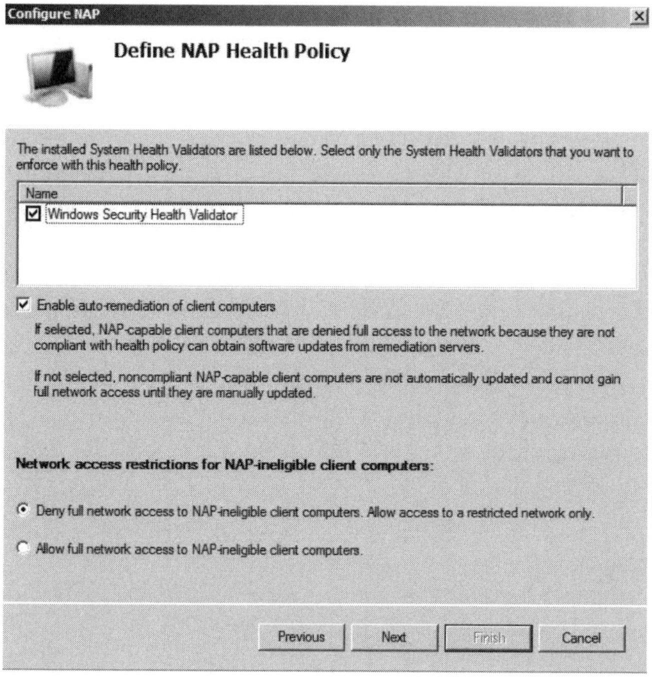

Figure 15-21   Network Access Policy can even be deployed in small organizations.

Any setup should also include a quarantining solution so that you can isolate non-compliant computers and allow them access to become compliant. Others argue that malware authors will simply find ways to trick the servers into thinking that the workstations are compliant with the policy. This is likely to happen at some point, as any network access enforcement mechanism has to trust the client. However, this argument misses the point of NAP. The idea is not primarily to keep out malicious clients, but rather to ensure that those clients that are not yet malicious stay that way. NAP provides mechanisms for ensuring that healthy clients stay healthy.

The Need for NAP

Network Access Protection has gotten quite a bit of buzz in the computing world, but I question the need in a small organization that does not use Virtual Private Networking in their remote access setup. In my own organization, I am the only one allowed to use VPN for update management purposes. All other remote access is done via Remote Web Workplace, a remote access Web portal that uses Remote Desktop and thus introduces fewer security risks. Review your needs for access and determine whether setting up NAP introduces more risk from potential misconfiguration than the security benefit it promises.

More information on Network Access Protection can be found in Chapter 13, as well as on the NAP blog at *http://blogs.technet.com/nap/archive/2007/07/28/network-access-protection-deployment-planning.aspx*. You can also refer to *Windows Server 2008 Networking and Network Access Protection (NAP)* by Joseph Davies and Tony Northrup (Microsoft Press, 2008).

Summary

A multi-role server is a balancing act of needs, budgets, business goals, and security. Some small businesses need more security, some will need less. However, all of them will need a certain level of basics that you can help guide to the right level. From urging end users to choose better passwords, to understanding the risks that older platforms bring to a network, small businesses are no different from their larger counterparts in their need for a network that will allow them to do their work in a secure and safe fashion without unreasonable risk. The hard part for any size organization or network to understand is that there is no perfect solution, and maintaining that balance is an ongoing battle. Security is a process that has to be constantly reevaluated for changing risks and threats to any size of network. What may be secure enough as a solution today may not be the right solution for that organization tomorrow. The security laws are purposely vague and vendor-neutral because they, too, understand that security is a moving target.

Additional Resources

- "The TJX Effect," at *http://www.infosecnews.org/hypermail/0708/13565.html*.

- "Medical IT Contractor Folds After Breaches," at *http://www.infosecnews.org/hypermail/0708/13587.html*.

- "Fine Grain Password Policy Tool Beta 1 Is Ready!," at *http://itbloggen.se/cs/blogs/chrisse/archive/2007/08/05/585.aspx*.

- Blackhat conference presentation on "Bypassing NAC 2.0," at *http://www.blackhat.com/presentations/bh-dc-07/Arkin/Presentation/bh-dc-07-Arkin-ppt-up.pdf*.

- "Comparing Default Services on Windows Server 2003 R2 and Windows Server 2008 (Core and Full)," at *http://blogs.technet.com/josebda/archive/2007/08/08/comparing-default-services-on-windows-server-2003-r2-and-windows-server-2008-core-and-full.aspx*.

- "Are We Too Simplistic in How We Think about Risk?," at *http://blogs.technet.com/jesper_johansson/archive/2006/05/09/427845.aspx*.

- *Windows Server 2008 Networking and Network Access Protection (NAP)*. (Microsoft Press, 2008).

- "Outsourcing and Privacy: 10 Critical Questions Top Management Should Ask," at *http://infotech.aicpa.org/Resources/Privacy/Privacy+Hot+Topics/Privacy+Outsourcing/Outsourcing+and+Privacy+10+Critical+Questions+Top+Management+Should+Ask.htm*.

- Knowledge Base article 821749 "Antivirus Software May Cause IIS to Stop Unexpectedly," at *http://support.microsoft.com/kb/821749.*

- Knowledge Base article 815263 "Antivirus, Backup, and Disk Optimization Programs That Are Compatible with the File Replication Service," at *http://support.microsoft.com /kb/815263.*

- "Deploying Server Roles," at *http://technet.microsoft.com/en-us/library/aa997610.aspx.*

- Knowledge Base article 328841 "Exchange and Antivirus Software," at *http://support.microsoft.com/kb/328841.*

- Knowledge Base article 309422 "Guidelines for Choosing Antivirus Software to Run on the Computers That Are Running SQL Server," at *http://support.microsoft.com/kb/309422.*

- Knowledge Base article 895612 "How to Find a Compatible Printer Driver for a Computer That Is Running a 64-bit Version of Windows," at *http://support.microsoft.com/kb/895612.*

- Knowledge Base article 817442 "IIS 6.0: Antivirus Scanning of IIS Compression Directory May Result in 0-Byte File," at *http://support.microsoft.com/kb/817442.*

- "New Features in Exchange 2007 SP1," at *http://blogs.technet.com/asiasupp/archive/ 2007/06/26/new-features-in-exchange-2007-sp1.aspx.*

- Knowledge Base article 823166 "Overview of Exchange Server 2003 and Antivirus Software," at *http://support.microsoft.com/kb/823166.*

- Knowledge Base article 245822 "Recommendations for Troubleshooting an Exchange Server Computer with Antivirus Software Installed," at *http://support.microsoft.com /kb/245822.*

- "Setting the LAN Manager Authentication Level on a Network That Includes RIS," at *http://technet2.microsoft.com/windowsserver/en/library/22d98712-9349-44fb-8e69- 1190ea0d039a1033.mspx?mfr=true.*

- "Step-by-Step Guide for Fine-Grained Password and Account Lockout Policy Configuration," at *http://technet2.microsoft.com/windowsserver2008/en/library/2199dcf7-68fd- 4315-87cc-ade35f8978ea1033.mspx?mfr=true.*

- Knowledge Base article 909444 "Systems That Have Changed the Default Access Control List Permissions on the %windir%\registration Directory May Experience Various Problems After You Install the Microsoft Security Bulletin MS05-051 for COM+ and MS DTC," at *http://support.microsoft.com/kb/909444.*

- "The Windows Vista and Windows Server 2008 Developer Story: Application Compatibility Cookbook," at *http://msdn2.microsoft.com/en-us/library/aa480152.aspx.*

- "Tweakomatic, by the Scripting Guys," at *http://www.microsoft.com/technet/scriptcenter/ tools/twkmatic.mspx#EFE.*

- Knowledge Base article 822158 "Virus Scanning Recommendations for Computers That Are Running Windows Server 2003, Windows 2000, or Windows XP," at *http://support.microsoft.com/kb/822158.*

- "What Type of Remote Access Should I Allow?," at *http://windowshelp.microsoft.com/ Windows/en-US/Help/ea4680d1-6962-463b-b29b-351efa676f9e1033.mspx.*

- Knowledge Base article 924995 "When You Restart Windows Server 2003, the Computer May Display a Gray Screen or May Appear to Stop Responding," at *http://support.microsoft.com/kb/924995.*

- "Windows Service Pack Road Map," at *http://www.microsoft.com/windows/lifecycle/ servicepacks.mspx.*

- "Windows System State Analyzer Tool," at *http://www.innovateonwindowsserver.com/ learnbuild.aspx.*

- "Windows Vista Group Policy Settings," at *http://download.microsoft.com/download/c /3/8/c3815ed7-aee7-4435-802b-8e855d549154/GroupPolicySettingsforWindowsVista.xls.*

- "Windows Vista Security Guide," at *http://www.microsoft.com/technet/windowsvista/ security/guide.mspx.*

- "Windows XP Security Guide," at *http://www.microsoft.com/technet/security/prodtech/ windowsxp/secwinxp/default.mspx.*

- "Threats and Countermeasures Guide," at *http://www.microsoft.com/technet/security/ guidance/serversecurity/tcg/tcgch00.mspx.*

- *Microsoft Windows Vista Resource Kit* (Microsoft Press, 2008).

- "PCI Industry Security Standards," at *https://www.pcisecuritystandards.org/pdfs/ pci_dss_v1-1.pdf.*

- "The Dangers of Remote PC Access," at *http://reviews.cnet.com/4520-3513_7-5053016-1.html.*

- *Windows Vista Security: Securing Vista Against Malicious Attacks* (Wiley, 2007).

- *Exchange Server 2007, Administrator's Pocket Consultant* (Microsoft Press, 2007).

- *Exchange Server 2007 Administrator's Companion* (Microsoft Press, 2007).

- *Information Security Policies Made Easy* (Information Shield, 2007).

Chapter 16

Securing Server Applications

— Alun Jones

Introduction

What is a server? It is a computer system whose purpose it is to expose some portion of itself to clients—whether that portion is data, applications, or a mixture of the two. A data server is naturally more at risk from other networked systems than a client because it must have some of its defenses opened to allow access. An application server is even more at risk: Not only have its defenses been opened to allow access, but it must also execute tasks on request from other systems.

Securing an application server requires paying attention to the "three As": authentication, authorization, and auditing. Only by monitoring all three can you restrict who gets in and what she can do, and trace what she did to ensure that your restrictions have been faithfully obeyed.

Windows Server 2008 has several methods of serving applications to your users. In this chapter, I will focus on using Internet Information Server 7 (IIS 7) for this purpose.

In each case, you need to decide how much you will open your server's defenses to serve applications to your users. Much of that decision involves knowing what your applications are and where they come from—as well as who your users are and where *they* come from.

Direct from the Field: Some Cool Features of IIS 7

One of the best security changes in IIS 7.0 is the new built-in anonymous account IUSR and the IIS_IUSRS user group. In the past, XCOPY deployment worked but was not completely transparent—you still needed to take care of the access control lists (ACLs) on content being copied to the IIS server. In IIS 7.0, the product team took a step forward by making the anonymous account built into the operating system; this decoupled the dependency between user account and resource content, providing a full XCOPY experience in terms of content access permissions. You also get fewer accounts to manage because the same anonymous user SID exists on all IIS 7.0 computers. And you have fewer password-expiration headaches to deal with than with the old *IUSR_computername* anonymous account. In addition, the new IIS_IUSRS user group replaces the old IIS_WPG user group that was predefined with certain privileges and rights for starting worker processes in IIS 6.0. This means that in IIS 7.0 you no longer need to make the customer application pool identity a member of the IIS_IUSRS user group. During run time, the IIS_IUSRS group SID is injected into the worker process token, implicitly making the account a member of the new built-in user group. This membership is done dynamically and enabled by default in IIS 7.0.

Bernard Cheah, Microsoft MVP
Windows Server – IIS

Security Alert: Security Came Late to the Internet

As they originated, the Internet and the World Wide Web were designed to share information freely so that everyone would get complete access to everyone else's data. Because of this, you will find that your easiest and most secure configuration is to configure your server to work in an open fashion, freely providing information to all who connect.

Do not get me wrong. I am not about to suggest that you make your company's secrets open to the world. I am simply expressing that the most easily secured Internet server is one that serves public information or provides services to the public without having to distinguish between clients, or authorize activity based on authenticating the client user in any way.

Much of the Internet still runs with static content updated at regular intervals by humans uploading new content to the server from inside the firewall. As long as users are prevented from uploading—and are restricted to seeing files only from the published data source—they will never see anything that you do not want them to.

Your site may treat client users as anonymous and undistinguished from one another, and your data as unchanging pages that contain nothing more complex than pictures or links to other pages. However, it is in the dynamic Internet—where the server executes

> code based on choices made by the client user, or accepts data from the client user, or authenticates and authorizes access between different client users—that we find the greatest security challenge, as malicious client users attempt to subvert your systems by uploading poorly formatted data and by trying to access areas of the Web site to which they have no rights.

IIS 7: A Security Pedigree

Internet Information Server (IIS) has been very much the poster child for Microsoft's Trustworthy Computing (TwC) initiative, and secure development practices in general. It takes a special focus and an attention to detail to engage in secure development practices that create truly secure software. In creating IIS version 6.0 for Windows Server 2003, Microsoft put that focus and attention to detail to work in the design, development, and testing phases.

As a result, in almost every Microsoft document on Secure Coding and TwC, IIS 6 is referred to as the example of the benefits achieved by following secure coding practices. As a testament to the work that went into IIS 6, there have been only two security updates for IIS 6 since it was released in 2003. Both were in add-on components, and one was in a core component to Windows and only exposed through IIS. (Some third-party security assessments may list more vulnerabilities in IIS 6 if they have a broader definition of what components are a part of IIS 6.)

IIS 7 builds on this legacy: threat modeling, rigorous standards of coding practices, wholesale removal and replacement of unsafe library function calls, regular and frequent code reviews, fuzz testing, and other methods too numerous to describe have all led to IIS 7 being a worthy successor to the impressive security record of IIS 6.

Configuring IIS 7

IIS 7 uses an entirely different configuration architecture from that used by IIS 6. In IIS 6, all configuration data was stored in a proprietary format database known as the metabase. IIS 7 uses an XML format for its configuration data store. In addition, where IIS 6 stored all data in one metabase file, IIS 7 distributes data storage among the layers where configuration may apply—whether global to the Web server, local to a Web site, or specific to a virtual directory or application.

We refer you to the *Internet Information Services (IIS) 7.0 Resource Kit* for a discussion of the location of these XML format configuration data files, how they are edited, and the relationship between these configuration files and the IIS Manager interface. Note, however, that if you are trying to determine the correct location for a set of attributes, you should always treat the IIS_Schema.xml in %SystemRoot%\system32\inetsrv\config\schema as authoritative.

IIS 7 also uses a completely updated (but still MMC-based) configuration interface—the Internet Information Services (IIS) Manager. As you can see from Figure 16-1, this has been advanced somewhat from the IIS Manager that was released with IIS 7 in Windows Vista, and it is a huge improvement over the interface in IIS 6 in Windows Server 2003.

Figure 16-1   The new IIS 7 Manager interface.

Feature Delegation

From the perspective of the security administrator for an IIS Web server, the most interesting aspect of this new configuration layout is the ability to delegate feature configuration—to allow configuration decisions to be made at the Web site or virtual directory level by those with access to modify content at the Web site or its virtual directories.

By delegating configuration access to content owners and site owners, the day-to-day configuration of an IIS Web site now rests where it belongs, with the owner of the Web site.

This would be a bad thing if it were completely unrestricted, but the designers of IIS were aware of this. Therefore, they ensured first that lower-level configurations could inherit from a higher-level configuration. For example, a virtual directory inherits its Default Documents list from the Web site it is a part of, and the Web site inherits its Default Documents list from the Web server on which it runs. And second, the designers allowed administrators at any level to choose whether to prevent settings made at a lower level from overwriting any particular inherited setting from a higher level. For example, a Web site manager can prevent an application's settings from overriding configuration placed at the Web site level.

You can see the order of inheritance between configuration files in Figure 16-2. Settings for the lower-level components come from web.config files at that level, and inherit from levels above. Controlling delegation prevents lower-level config files from overwriting settings made in config files at a higher level.

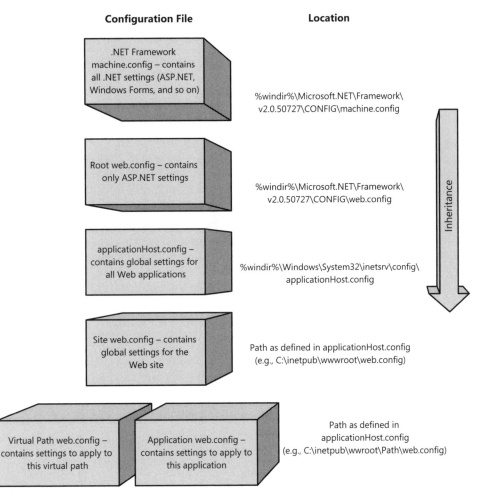

Configuration File

Location

.NET Framework machine.config – contains all .NET settings (ASP.NET, Windows Forms, and so on)

%windir%\Microsoft.NET\Framework\ v2.0.50727\CONFIG\machine.config

Root web.config – contains only ASP.NET settings

%windir%\Microsoft.NET\Framework\ v2.0.50727\CONFIG\web.config

applicationHost.config – contains global settings for all Web applications

%windir%\Windows\System32\inetsrv\config\ applicationHost.config

Site web.config – contains global settings for the Web site

Path as defined in applicationHost.config (e.g., C:\inetpub\wwwroot\web.config)

Virtual Path web.config – contains settings to apply to this virtual path

Application web.config – contains settings to apply to this application

Path as defined in applicationHost.config (e.g., C:\inetpub\wwroot\Path\web.config)

Inheritance

Figure 16-2 Order of inheritance of configuration settings.

This delegation, with its inheritance and security, is of particular interest to hosting providers and their customers, who will want to delineate which configuration is open to the customers for their convenience and control, and which configuration is reserved to the hosting providers to ensure security and standards of service.

While the distributed configuration in IIS 7 may make it harder to grasp the entire configuration of your Web server from a single location, improper configuration of the Web server can be prevented by enforcing inheritance of those settings that you do not wish to be altered.

TCP/IP-Based Security

The base protocol over which Web traffic is carried is the Hypertext Transfer Protocol (HTTP). HTTP is generally carried over TCP/IP, the standard Internet Protocol, in most environments. IIS 7 supports HTTP over TCP/IP version 4 (IPv4), the more common protocol of today's Internet and the same network-level protocol as every version of IIS to date has supported. IIS 7 also adds support for HTTP over TCP/IP version 6 (IPv6), the protocol version for the next generation of Internet support.

IP Address Security

The first consideration regarding blocking or allowing access is whether your target users can get traffic routed to and from your servers. Using an internally routed IP address will help prevent outside parties from accessing an intranet site. If your organization's routers are correctly configured, an internally routed IP address can be relied on as proof that the client requesting a connection is within your organization. Use external IP addresses with care to identify connecting clients, because they can incorrectly describe the location of the client in many ways. An external IP address may have belonged to one user yesterday, and a different user today. External IP addresses are shared between multiple users, as in the case of an *anonymizing proxy*, which is designed to hide the identity of a client.

Whitelisting by source IP address—rejecting all connections other than those from addresses of known partners—is mostly reliable, because it is very difficult to forge a TCP connection for any purpose more complex than a simple denial of service attack. *Blacklisting* by source IP address—accepting all connections, and rejecting connections from hosts known to be bad—is generally not successful, because attackers are generally able to move to a new host that is not known to be bad.

Restricting which IP addresses are allowed to connect to your Web server is possible from the IPv4 Address And Domain Restrictions feature, or by changing IP Security settings in the XML configuration file applicationHost.config under the following section:

```
<configuration>
  <system.webServer>
    <security>
      <ipSecurity>
```

The *ipSecurity* element has two attributes:

- *allowUnlisted*, which affects whether the list of child elements of *ipSecurity* is checked for known bad or known good source IP addresses. When you set *allowUnlisted* to false, only the child elements marked with *allow* can access this Web server, and all others will be denied. When you set *allowUnlisted* to true, all IP addresses will be allowed to connect except those specifically marked as *deny*.

■ *enableReverseDns*, which you must set to true if you are going to filter by domain name. Because the reverse DNS lookup can take some time that would delay connections, leave this attribute at its default value of false if you are not interested in filtering by domain name. Remember that many DNS zones do not feature reverse lookups, and Windows does not create reverse lookup zones by default. As a result, reverse DNS lookup will very often fail.

Child elements are added to the *ipSecurity* collection by the usual add, clear, or remove directives, with the following attributes:

■ *ipAddress* is the numerical IP address of the host or network being allowed or denied access. For instance, 127.0.0.1 would represent the localhost. If you are denying access by default (setting *allowUnlisted* to false), you will generally want to enable access by 127.0.0.1 and other locally bound IP addresses for testing.

■ *subnetMask* is the numerical subnet mask that defines which network is being referenced by IP address. For instance, to cut off the entire 10.*.*.* network, you would use an ipAddress of 10.0.0.0 and a *subnetMask* of 255.0.0.0. The default value is 255.255.255.255, which masks to a single IP address.

■ *domainName* is a fully qualified domain name of a host that this rule should apply to.

■ *allowed* will—when set to true—allow all clients that match the rule given, and when set to false will deny all clients that match the rule. The rules are processed in order from first to last, and the first match dictates what is done with the incoming connection.

The user interface for this setting is simple, and distinguishes between setting an Allow entry and setting a Deny entry. In Figure 16-3, I have chosen to add an Allow entry for the network 169.254.*.* (which you may see expressed elsewhere as 169.254.0.0/16).

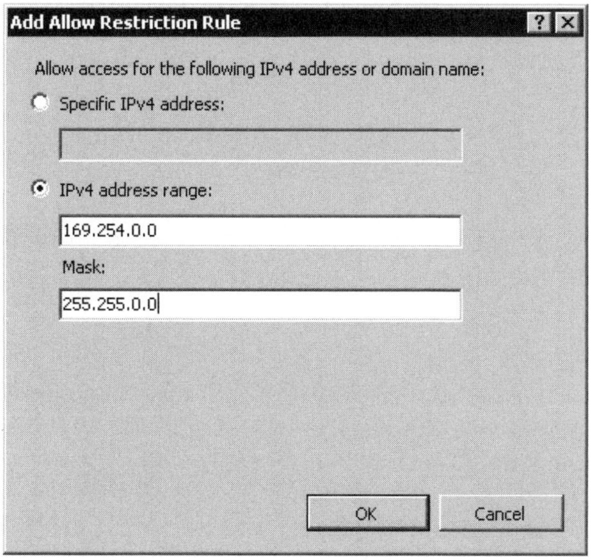

Figure 16-3   The Add Allow Restriction Rule dialog box to allow 169.254.*.*.

As you can see in Figure 16-4, this is now listed as an allow entry. There is no way, other than removing and re-adding, to turn an Allow entry into a Deny entry.

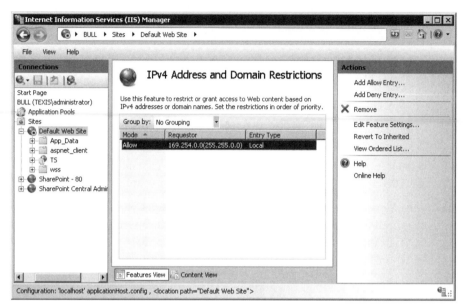

Figure 16-4   The newly added Allow Rule Entry is displayed.

The corresponding XML code in the applicationHost.config file looks like this:

```
<configuration>
  ...
    <location path="Default Web Site">
      <system.webServer>
        <security>
          <ipSecurity enableReverseDns="false">
            <add ipAddress="169.254.0.0"
              subnetMask="255.255.0.0"
              allowed="true"/>
          </ipSecurity>
        </security>
      </system.webServer>
    </location>
</configuration>
```

Port Security

By default, HTTP runs over port 80, but because URLs can embed the port number, it is common to find that a Web server is working on ports other than port 80. The HTTPS protocol, HTTP over SSL/TLS, is bound to port 443 by default.

From a security perspective, this use of ports can be useful to restrict access at the firewall. If a server has been configured to listen for incoming requests at port 8080, and is hosting intranet content only, it is an obvious security measure to set a firewall (either on the host, between the host and the Internet, or both) to only allow access to that port from IP addresses known to be internal to the intranet.

Host-Header Security

More than one Web site can exist behind the same IP address/port combination. This is achieved by recognizing the Host header sent in the client's HTTP or HTTPS request, and directing the request to the Web site listed in that Host header.

This is not truly a security method. Like moving your Web site to a different IP port, it is an obscurity measure, and while it will reduce the simpler, casual, or accidental attacks on your sites, it should really be treated as a convenience factor that allows you to host several Web sites on the same IP address with the standard port assignment.

Changing the IP and port bindings or Host header binding can only be done at the Web site level, and the bindings are stored in the applicationHost.config XML file as shown in the following example:

```xml
<configuration>
  <system.applicationHost>
    <sites>
      <site name="site-name" ... >
        <bindings>
          <binding protocol="http" bindingInformation="*:80:"/>
          <binding protocol="https" bindingInformation="*:443:"/>
        </bindings>
```

Attributes for the *binding* element include:

- *protocol*, which is normally "http" or "https", and may also contain other protocol definitions. (For instance, the protocol "ftp" if the downloadable IIS 7 FTP Server has been installed.)

- *bindingInformation* is a triplet of the IP address, port, and host header, separated with colons. You can use an asterisk (*) to represent "all IP addresses." For instance, if a binding is created for the HTTP protocol to operate on all IP addresses at port 80, under the host header *"marketing"*, the *bindingInformation* string would be "*:80:marketing".

Simple Path-Based Security

In IIS Web sites, files as well as applications are hosted and offered to the user. After you have allowed a client to make a TCP/IP connection to your server, the next step is to limit access to the files and applications relating to the requested Web site. Segregating access to files by their physical path on the server is a simple way to ensure that different Web sites are not accidentally intermingled.

Defining and Restricting the Physical Path

The very first security requirement specific to a Web server running on IIS 7—even a Web site that only serves static content to anonymous client users—is to ensure that visiting clients can only retrieve files that have been specifically published to that Web site.

Fortunately, this is the first setting you need to configure (after the name of the Web site) when you create a new site, as you can see in Figure 16-5.

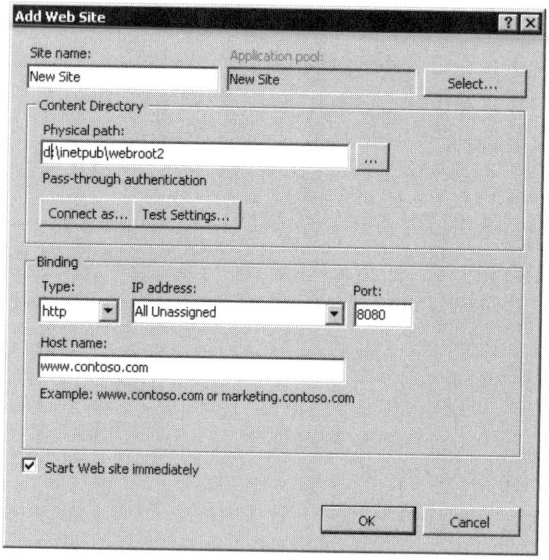

Figure 16-5   The Add Web Site dialog box showing the physical path.

The default Web site that is created when you add the Web Server role to Windows is automatically established with a physical path of %SystemDrive%\inetpub\wwwroot. You can check this—as well as change it for any Web site—from either Basic Settings or Advanced Settings on the site. You can access Basic Settings in the IIS Manager by selecting the Web site and then clicking Basic Settings in the Actions pane. Access Advanced Settings by right-clicking the Web site's name, selecting Manage Web Site and then selecting Advanced Settings, or by clicking Advanced Settings in the Actions pane.

The Basic Settings dialog box, shown in Figure 16-6, has only a few settings.

The Advanced Settings dialog box, shown Figure 16-7, contains the same settings as the Basic Settings dialog box plus a number of other settings.

In the default configuration, the physical path is on the boot volume of the Web server computer. To provide defense-in-depth against potential directory traversal attacks—using a slash (/) or a backslash (\) or the ".." sequence to navigate out of the physical path—it is a good idea to create a drive partition that is reserved solely for Web content. Although directory traversal attacks are designed to navigate up the directory structure, they do not offer the opportunity to navigate across drives. Of course, IIS 7 has the same strong restriction to application directories that IIS 6 has used for years to prevent directory navigation attacks from working at all. With all Web content on a separate partition, any successful attack that allows data to be uploaded will not cause the system or boot volumes to be filled.

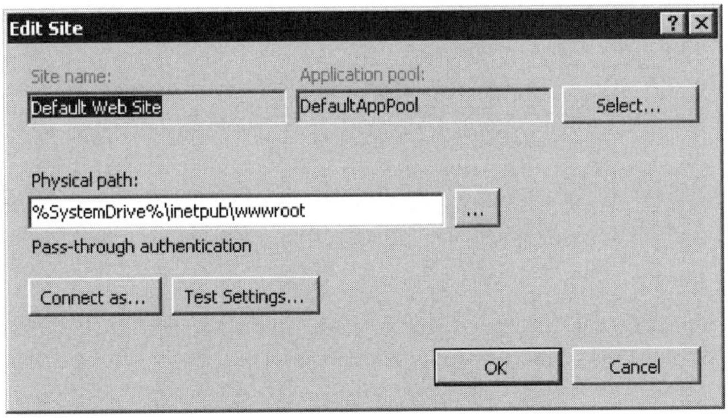

Figure 16-6   The Basic Settings dialog box showing the default configuration.

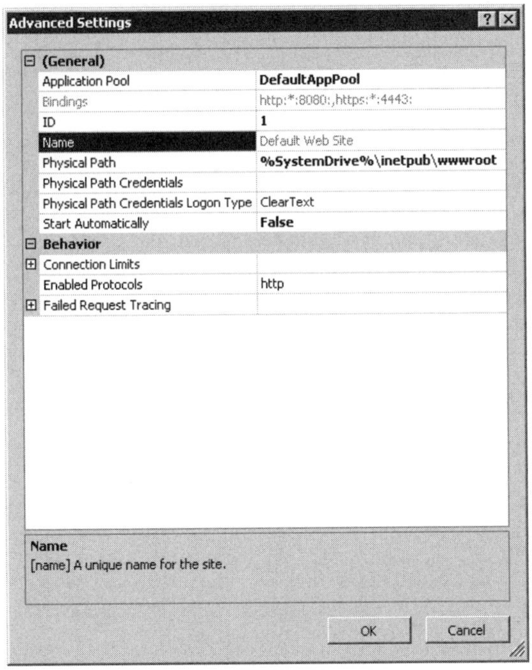

Figure 16-7   Advanced Settings configuration allows you to edit many more settings.

It is also possible to make the physical path point to a network share on a different server using a UNC path such as *server**share-name*. You can use the Advanced or Basic Settings dialog boxes to change the user credentials to access files in the Web site's physical path.

This allows you to ensure that the users of this Web site are subject to appropriate NTFS and share-level permissions when accessing files.

> **Caution** Take care with any option that stores a user's credentials for later impersonation, because even when those credentials are encrypted, there is a risk that someone getting read access to this server's configuration might also be able to authenticate as this user.
>
> For this reason, the credentials you supply should be for an account that does not represent a real person, and whose rights and privileges are limited only to accessing the Web site's folders and files.
>
> The password for this account should not be shared with any other account, and should be randomly generated, perhaps using the command:
>
> ```
> net user <accountname> /add /domain /random
> ```
>
> The passwords generated by the "net user /random" command are limited to eight characters in length. If you need to generate longer random passwords, I recommend the passgen tool, written by Jesper Johansson and found on the companion CD-ROM for this book.

The Physical Path settings of the Web site and its virtual directories, along with the user account used to access the physical path, can be found in the applicationHost.config XML file at the following location:

```
<configuration>
  <system.applicationHost>
    <sites>
      <site name="site-name"...>
        <application path="application-path"...>
          <virtualDirectory...>
```

This is set in the system-wide applicationHost.config, not under the site's individual web.config file. The physical path, user account, and password are not properties of the Web site; they will change if the Web site moves to another hosting service, and they should generally not be shared with the Web site owner.

Attributes of the *virtualDirectory* element include:

- *path* is a string that describes the virtual path from the Web site's root to this path's location.

- *physicalPath* is the physical path to the content stored in this virtual directory. For local content, the path can be of the format "X:\Path1\Path2"; for networked content, the path should be in UNC format, as "\\Server\Share\Path1\Path2".

- *username* is a string giving the name of the user whose credentials will be used to access the physical path. If this attribute is absent, pass-through authentication will be used.

- *password* is an AES-encrypted string containing the password to be used for access to the physical path. Editing this manually is not advised. Use *appcmd* for scripted alterations to the config file, or use the IIS Manager interface.

- *logonMethod* is one of *Interactive*, *Batch*, *Network*, or *ClearText*, to indicate the log-on type that should be used when authorizing access to files in this application's path. *ClearText* is the default, and is appropriate for most uses. You can use *Network*for access to network resources, and you should rarely use *Batch* and *Interactive* because they do not adequately represent the fact that files are being requested noninteractively by a remote user. Note that some resources may be only accessible to interactive users, network users, and so on. You may find that the NTFS permissions on content should be changed to match the default *logonMethod* of *ClearText*. You generally should not change the *logonMethod*.

The credentials and *logonMethod* setting described in the preceding section may be overridden by applications that use impersonation, in which case the credentials being impersonated will be the credentials used to access the Web site's content.

Default Document or Directory Browsing?

Suppose a user visits your Web site, and notices the following URL in the Address box:

```
http://www.contoso.com/public/index.html
```

A natural curiosity kicks in: "What do I get if I access any similar URLs?"

```
http://www.contoso.com/public/
http://www.contoso.com/
```

When the Web was being built, it seemed natural to emulate some of the protocols around at the time: FTP, Gopher, and so on. In clients for these protocols, if you were not looking at a file, you were looking at a directory listing. As a result, the Web servers of old would generate a page that listed the contents of a directory. In general, it is more advisable these days to reduce the temptation for browsers to go outside of the URLs displayed on hosted pages, and as a result, the directory browsing feature is disabled. When a client visits a URL that represents a directory, the Web server returns a page with a fixed name that exists in that directory.

IIS 7 is no different in this respect. Visiting a directory with directory browsing disabled (the default) results in the display of whichever of the following files it finds in the target directory first:

```
Default.htm
Default.asp
index.htm
index.html
iisstart.htm
default.aspx
```

You can add or remove these elements in the IIS Manager at the server, site, or virtual directory level by opening the feature Default Document. You can also set this in the XML configuration (in the Web server's applicationHost.config, or in the Web site, application, or virtual directory's web.config file) in the following section:

```
<configuration>
  <system.webServer>
    <defaultDocument enabled="true/false">
      <files>
        <add value="file1"/>
        <add value="file2"/>
      </files>
    </defaultDocument>
```

The *defaultDocument* element has one attribute only—*enabled*—which can be true or false, and the *defaultDocument/files* element can contain elements with the usual names (add, remove, and clear) to control the list of files in the collection, as shown in the preceding example.

You are advised to keep to a server-wide list of default documents, because this is the list of documents that will be tried and displayed if the requested URL is to a directory. Relying on the presence of a default document higher in the list to mask the presence of one lower in the list is likely to fail in the event that someone moves or renames one of the default files.

If you prefer the behavior of displaying a list of the files in a directory when a directory is requested and no default document is found, you can open and enable the Directory Browsing feature from the IIS Manager, or enable it in the web.config file at the following path:

```
<configuration>
  <system.webServer>
    <directoryBrowse enabled="true/false"/>
```

Authentication and Authorization

When creating a Web server, the first consideration, after "What content shall we host?" is generally "To whom shall we provide that content?" The concept of choosing which users are allowed access to which content rests on the foundation of a good authentication mechanism.

As befits an Internet standard, HTTP has many client authentication mechanisms to choose from, with varying benefits and drawbacks. The authentication methods available with IIS 7 as shipped are Anonymous, Basic, Client Certificate Mapping, Digest, Forms, and Windows Integrated. (See Chapter 4, "Authenticators and Authentication Protocols," for additional descriptions of some of these methods.) Of these methods, Anonymous, Basic, Client Certificate Mapping, Digest, and Forms authentication are all based on Internet standard documents and will work with multiple browsers. Some browsers other than Internet Explorer may not support Windows Integrated Authentication. Only Anonymous Authentication is enabled by default.

All access by IIS to resources served by the Web server is governed by Windows NTFS permissions. This means that all access is through a local user ID, with associated groups. It is important to distinguish between the security context that the user believes he has, and the security context that the server is using to serve that user's access. A good example is Anonymous Authentication, which by default is associated with the IUSR account for the purpose of controlling what files and resources are accessible.

Although authentication settings are enabled, disabled, and defined at the server, Web site, or virtual directory level, most of their configuration settings are stored in the server-wide applicationHost.config file, under the following section:

```
<configuration>
  <location path="...">
    <system.webServer>
      <security>
        <authentication ...>
```

This is because the settings refer to elements that are server-specific, rather than site-specific, such as physical paths, user names, and domains.

Anonymous Authentication

Anonymous authentication is the only authentication mechanism in IIS 7 that is enabled by default on installation. In many ways, this is the most secure configuration because your Web server is then serving pages to anyone who can make a connection. You, as the webmaster, will ensure that only public pages are available to be served.

The one configuration item for Anonymous authentication, when you select the Edit option, is to choose a user whose account will be used to access resources, as you can see in Figure 16-8.

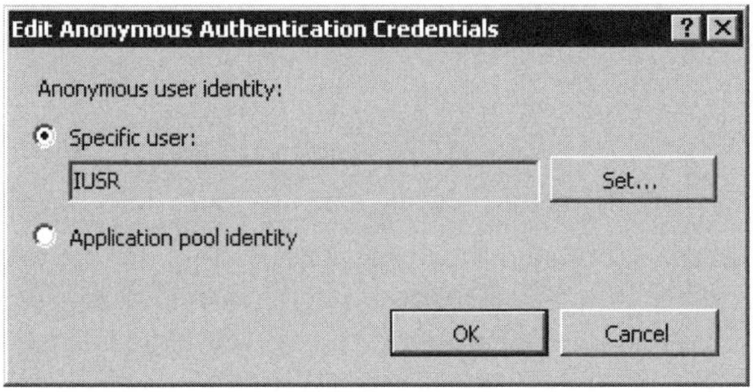

Figure 16-8   Edit Anonymous Authentication Credentials to declare which identity is used for anonymous access to Web resources.

By default, the Anonymous User Identity is the built-in IUSR account, well-known SID S-1-5-17 that is new to IIS 7. (See Chapter 1, "Subjects, Users, and Other Actors," for a description of SIDs.) In IIS 6 and prior versions, a new account with the name IUSR_<machinename> was created for each computer, with an essentially random choice of SID. You can select a different account, or choose to use the Application Pool Identity, which is the account under which the Web site application's pool is configured to run.

> **Note**   It is important to understand the difference between the Anonymous Authentication identity and the Application Pool Identity. Although you can set the two to be the same, the Application Pool Identity is the user account context within which the application's worker process(es) will run, while the Anonymous Authentication Identity is the user account context within which anonymous requests will access Web site resources.

Using an account other than IUSR or the Application Pool Identity may be useful to ensure that one site cannot make reference to another site's resources, but because these resources are public to anyone that can reach the site, this is probably only useful if the server is hosting both intranet and Internet content and the content creator for the Internet site(s) cannot be trusted to avoid making reference to intranet site content. In such a situation, it would be more appropriate to have different servers to host the different content, keeping the intranet content server behind a firewall that prevents Internet traffic—or traffic from the Internet-facing server—from accessing intranet content.

The anonymousAuthentication section in the applicationHost.config file contains the following attributes:

- *enabled,* is true to enable Anonymous Authentication, or false to disable Anonymous Authentication.

- *userName* is the user name under which access will be made using anonymous authentication.

- *password* is the password for the user name specified and is encrypted using AES.

- *logonMethod* is the method (*ClearText, Network, Interactive,* or *Batch*) by which the impersonated user will be logged on. (See the description of the *virtualDirectory* element in the Defining and Restricting the Physical Path section of this chapter for an explanation of *logonMethod*.)

Setting the *userName* and *password* values to empty strings ("") results in the anonymous user accessing resources by using the user context of the Application Pool. As discussed earlier, the choice of whether to use the Application Pool Identity, the default IUSR account, or a specific user account will depend on what permissions are present on the files that you wish to access and whether you need to separate anonymous accesses between sites.

Basic Authentication

Basic Authentication requires the client to send its user name and password in the HTTP request to the server. Although the password is encoded using Base64 encoding, this is only to allow exotic characters to be successfully passed in the password. Base64 is an easily recognized encoding, so Basic Authentication is equivalent to passing your credentials across the Internet in plain text.

You should not use Basic Authentication for Web sites that are bound to the HTTP protocol because this will cause domain-level credentials to be sent in clear text between browser and server. Use HTTPS for all pages that are to use Basic Authentication. On clients within a domain, you can prevent Basic Authentication from being used by Internet Explorer at non-HTTPS sites by using Group Policy to set the following registry value as a DWORD with the value of 1 on the client computers:

```
HKEY_CURRENT_USER\SOFTWARE\Microsoft\Windows\CurrentVersion\Internet
Settings\DisableBasicOverClearChannel
```

The following settings are available for Basic Authentication under the basicAuthentication section in applicationHost.config:

- *enabled*, which is either "true" or "false," dictates whether Basic Authentication is enabled.

- *realm* will usually be the name of the domain to which you are inviting users to access. This does not have to be a real domain name; it is merely the text placed in the dialog box prompting users to log on.

- *defaultLogonDomain* is the domain against which authentication will take place if no domain name is passed by the browser in the user name.

- *logonMethod* takes any of these four values (like the other *logonMethod* elements): *ClearText*, *Network*, *Batch*, or *Interactive*.

Client Certificate Mapping

Client Certificate Mapping is only available on HTTPS connections because it relies on the client exchanging certificate information with the server when initially establishing the SSL/TLS connection.

There are three types of Client Certificate Mapping: One-to-One, Many-to-One, and Active Directory. Each type of Client Certificate Mapping requires the module CertificateMapping-AuthenticationModule.

One-to-One Client Certificate Mapping

For one-to-one mapping, as the name implies, each client certificate recognized at the server as being valid is mapped to an individual user account. (The certificate chains up to a trusted root, and the certificate matches one identified in the site's configuration.)

Because the certificate acts as a unique key to the list of mappings, more than one certificate can map to the same user account and password. One-to-one client certificate mapping is controlled by the following configuration settings in the applicationHost.config XML file:

```
<configuration>
 <system.webServer>
  <security>
   <authentication>
    <iisClientCertificateMappingAuthentication ...>
```

- *enabled* is set to "true" to enable Client Certificate Mapping.

- *oneToOneCertificateMappingsEnabled* is set to "true" to enable One-to-One Client Certificate Mapping.

- *defaultLogonDomain* is the domain to which users will be authenticated if the domain is not provided in the *userName* element.

- *logonMethod* is the log-on method that will be used.

- *oneToOneCertificateMappings* is a collection that can be cleared with a *clear* element or added to with an *add* element, whose elements are:

  ❑ *enabled* is set to "true" to enable this certificate for use.

  ❑ *userName* is the user name to which this certificate maps. To authenticate to a domain other than that specified in the *defaultLogonDomain* attribute, specify the *userName* value as *domain\username*.

  ❑ *password* is the password for the user in *userName* (encrypted with AES).

  ❑ *certificate* is the certificate (in Base64 encoded form, as you would find in a CER file, but with line breaks removed).

Many-to-One Client Certificate Mapping

Use many-to-one Client Certificate Mapping when you want to map a certificate to a user based on matching defined criteria, such as "The certificate was issued by the Contoso CA." Because you can apply multiple rules to determine whether a client certificate matches to allow a logon to a user account, this can be a very flexible technique.

Many-to-one Client Certificate Mapping is controlled by the following configuration settings under the applicationHost.config in the following section:

```
<configuration>
 <system.webServer>
  <security>
   <authentication>
    <iisClientCertificateMappingAuthentication ...>
```

- *enabled* is set to "true" to enable Client Certificate Mapping.

- *manyToOneCertificateMappingsEnabled* is set to "true" to enable many-to-one Client Certificate Mapping.

- *defaultLogonDomain* is the domain to which users will be authenticated, if the domain is not provided in the *userName* element.

- *logonMethod* is the log-on method that will be used.

- *manyToOneCertificateMappings* is a collection that can be cleared with a *clear* element or added to with an *add* element, whose elements are:

  - ❑ *name* is a short name by which you will be able to recognize this rule-set.

  - ❑ *description* is a description of this rule-set.

  - ❑ *enabled* is set to "true" to enable this rule-set for use.

  - ❑ *permissionMode* is set to "Allow" or "Deny" to determine whether certificates matching this rule-set will be allowed or denied access.

  - ❑ *userName* is the user name that will be impersonated for access if this rule-set is matched and the permissionMode is "Allow".

  - ❑ *password* is the password for the user to be impersonated.

  - ❑ *rules* is a collection that may be cleared with the *clear* element, or added to with an *add* element, which may contain the following elements:

- *certificateField* is set to either "Subject" or "Issuer" to determine which certificate field is being examined.

- *certificateSubField* is set to the subfield of the selected certificate field—for example "CN" for Common-Name or "O" for Organization.

- *matchCriteria* is a wildcard to be matched against the contents of the specified certificate subfield. "*" matches anything.

- *compareCaseSensitive* is set to "true" to check case when comparing against *matchCriteria*, so that "Contoso" does not match "contoso"; is set to "false" to ignore case in the comparison.

Active Directory Client Certificate Mapping

If the users in your organization already have client certificates associated with their user accounts in Active Directory, you may want to use Active Directory Client Certificate Mapping to authenticate them as they log on. Rather simply, the configuration setting for Active Directory Client Certificate Mapping is in the applicationHost.config file in the following section:

```
<configuration>
  <system.webServer>
    <security>
      <authentication>
        <clientCertificateMappingAuthentication
          enabled="true/false"/>
```

It consists of the single element, *enabled*, whose value may be "true" or "false".

> **Note**   Please note carefully that while the other models of Client Certificate Mapping are under an XML Path ending in *iisClientCertificateMapping,* the Active Directory Client Certificate Mapping XML Path ends in *clientCertificateMapping.*

When Active Directory Client Certificate Mapping is enabled, the incoming client's certificate information is looked up in Active Directory, and the user who is identified by that certificate is the user under which access will be granted. Access will be denied if the client's certificate is not found.

Digest Authentication

In Digest Authentication, a user name is provided by the client, along with a hash generated from the user's password and some random data. Like Basic Authentication, Digest Authentication is supported by many browsers, and is an Internet standard defined in Request for Comment (RFC) 2617. It specifies how the hash is to be generated from the password and random information (known as a *nonce* value) specified in the server's challenge to the client's initial anonymous request.

Because the password is not sent in this authentication method, and the nonce provides for protection against a replay attack, the Digest Authentication method is preferable over the Basic Authentication method described earlier.

You can easily enable Digest Authentication through the user interface, if you have enabled the module DigestAuthenticationModule. The one configuration parameter for Digest Authentication is the *realm* parameter, which is given as a prompt to the client when asking for user name and password. Note that the realm should match the domain name where users' passwords are to be verified.

Configuration for Digest Authentication is under the following section of the application-Host.config XML file:

```
<configuration>
  <system.webServer>
    <security>
      <authentication>
        <digestAuthentication ...>
```

There are two elements under this section:

- *enabled* is set to "true" to enable Digest Authentication; is set to "false" otherwise.

- *realm* is the name of the realm prompted in the challenge to the client. This must be the same as the domain name to generate the digest that will match the hash stored at the domain controller.

For more information about Digest Authentication, see Chapter 4, "Understanding UAC."

ASP.Net Impersonation

ASP.Net Impersonation is a means of using the authentication that is present on a connection to an ASP.Net application. With ASP.Net Impersonation disabled, an ASP.Net application will run in the same user context as its Application Pool. When you enable ASP.Net Impersonation, you can set it to either always impersonate a fixed user context, or to impersonate whatever Windows user has been authenticated (whether through Basic, Digest, Client Certificate, or even Anonymous Authentication).

ASP.Net Impersonation is enabled and configured by editing the element at the following section in the application or Web site's web.config file:

```
<configuration>
  <system.web>
    <identity...>
```

This element has one required attribute, *impersonate*. Set this attribute to "true" to enable ASP.Net impersonation or "false" (the default) to disable it.

Use the following optional attributes when you want the application to always impersonate one fixed user:

- *userName* is the name of the user to impersonate.
- *password* is the encrypted password.

Forms Authentication

Forms Authentication allows the Web site to control the interface presented for entering credentials, rather than relying (as Basic and Digest Authentication both do) on the browser to display the log-on dialog box. An access to a page that requires Forms Authentication is initially redirected to a log-on page, generally a Web form, where the credentials can be entered. If the server accepts the credentials, a cookie is set at the browser, and the browser is redirected back to the page that it originally requested. With the cookie correctly set, the page protected by Forms Authentication will display.

You can fetch a copy of an example log-on page—and the code to make it work—from many sources, such as *http://support.microsoft.com/kb/301240*.

The configuration for Forms Authentication is stored in the Web site's or virtual directory's web.config file, under the following section:

```
<configuration>
  <system.web>
    <authentication mode="Forms">
      <forms...>
```

The authentication element should have a value *mode* whose value should be "Forms". If you are not using the default values, you will need to set a *forms* attribute under the authentication element, with the following values:

- *cookieless*, which defaults to "UseDeviceProfile" (to store authentication information in cookies where the browser is known to support them, and in URIs where the browser is not known to support cookies). Other possible values are "UseCookies" (to always store authentication information in cookies), "UseUri" (always store authentication information in the URI), and "AutoDetect", which probes the browser to determine which can be used.

- *loginUrl*, which defaults to "login.aspx". This is a URL, relative to the level at which you are setting authentication configuration, to which the browser will be redirected to get credentials.

- *name*, which defaults to ".ASPXAUTH". This is the name of the cookie (or URI component) that will be tested for authentication information.

- *protection*, which defaults to "All", and can be set to "None", "Encryption", or "Validation". "Encryption" causes the cookie to be encrypted using the Web server's machine key; "Validation" adds a validation code to the cookie to ensure that it is not tampered with by the client. "All" causes encryption and validation to occur.

- *requireSSL*, which defaults to "false". If set to "true", the authentication cookie is marked as *secure*, which a properly compliant browser will only send over an HTTPS connection. Setting this value to "true" does not force the browser to use SSL for the form submission containing the user name and password—this must be done as part of your log-on page.

- *slidingExpiration*, which defaults to "true". When you set this value to "true", the expiration time on the cookie is reset to the initial time-out after every use of the cookie. When you set it to "false", the initial time-out is how long the browser can maintain the authenticated connection without having to re-authenticate.

- *timeout*, which defaults to "30"—the number of minutes before the cookie expires and authentication has to begin again for further access to the resource.

Windows Authentication

Windows Authentication is a convenient and secure method of authenticating users in a domain-based environment. When a client uses Windows Authentication, it authenticates to the Web server using the same protocols (NTLM and Kerberos) as when a Windows logon occurs. (See Chapter 4 for more information on these protocols.) This may not be supported by all browsers in a heterogeneous environment, but its convenience, simplicity, and security make it a worthwhile choice for authentication where possible.

The configuration for Windows Authentication is stored in the Web site's or virtual directory's web.config file, under the following section:

```
<configuration>
  <system.web>
    <authentication mode="Windows">
```

The authentication element should have a value *mode*, whose value should be "Windows". This setting has several configuration attributes under the following section:

```
<configuration>
  <system.webServer>
    <security>
      <authentication>
        <windowsAuthentication>
```

The attributes are:

- *enabled*, which you set to "false" to disable Windows Authentication and "true" to enable it.

- *authPersistSingleRequest*, which you set to "false" (the default) to persist the authentication across multiple requests in a single session and "true" to require re-authentication for every request, even in the same browser session. Setting this attribute to anything but the default, "false", will generally be more of an irritation than a good security measure.

- *authPersistNonNTLM*, which you set to "false" (the default) to persist non-NTLM (such as Kerberos) tokens across subsequent requests in the same session and "true" to require re-authentication for each request.

- *useKernelMode,* which you set to "true" (the default) if the authentication is to be carried out in Kernel Mode and "false" otherwise.

- *providers,* which is a collection that can be added to, removed from, or cleared. Each element in the collection has an attribute called *value* that can be the string "Kerberos" or "NTLM". This is the list of providers that will be used when negotiating protocols with the client.

Trusting the Server

Now that we have discussed various ways by which the server can identify—and thus choose to trust—the client browser and the user presumed to be operating it, it is only fair that we discuss how the user at the other end of the client browser will determine that your server is worthy of his trust.

For instance, who hasn't been called, at one time or another, by their bank? "Mr Smith, this is Contoso bank calling to ask about a recent charge that was made on your credit card." Do you really know that the person calling you is from your bank? When you call the bank, how do you know that you reached the right number? What if you misdialed, or your phone was redirected?

In the physical world, we have few, if any, solutions in place to address this problem of identifying the organization to which you are connected. Fortunately, this is covered in the Web world by using Secure Sockets Layer (SSL) and Transport Layer Security (TLS).

SSL has a couple of basic requirements that can be relied on in all but the most pathological of environments:

- SSL traffic is encrypted, and has integrity checking.
- An SSL connection uses certificates (see Chapter 10, "Implementing Active Directory Certificate Services") to positively identify the server to the client.

As we shall see later in this chapter, you can apply other options to SSL traffic for authenticating the client.

The first requirement—that SSL traffic is encrypted and has integrity checking—ensures that if the communication between client and server completes from start to finish, the communication has not been read or altered by any third party between the client and server.

The second requirement—that the SSL connection positively identifies the server to the client—is an important part of the client's trusting the communication to the server.

Configuring SSL

Once you have a server certificate for SSL in the local computer certificate store, adding SSL support for IIS is a simple matter of adding a binding for *https* and choosing the server certificate. Start by selecting the Web site that you want to configure, and choose Edit Bindings—either from the Web site's context menu, by right-clicking the Web site, or from the Actions pane. This will display the Site Bindings dialog box. Because you want to add HTTPS support for this site, click the Add button, and in the Add Site Binding dialog box that displays, select HTTPS from the Type drop-down list. This will enable the SSL certificate drop-down list, as shown in Figure 16-9. This list contains all server certificates that have been installed to the local machine store.

Adding a binding for an SSL connection without using the interface is a little harder, but not much—the configuration has been made easier, and less error-prone, than in previous versions of IIS. First, you will need to add a binding to the XML configuration for the site, as described in "Host Header Security" earlier in the chapter. As a reminder, the binding setting for a default HTTPS binding on port 443 (the default HTTPS port), for all IP addresses, is as follows:

```
<binding protocol="https" bindingInformation="*:443:"/>
```

When you have the binding in place, you will need to add the certificate to the HTTP.SYS driver's configuration by using the following netsh command:

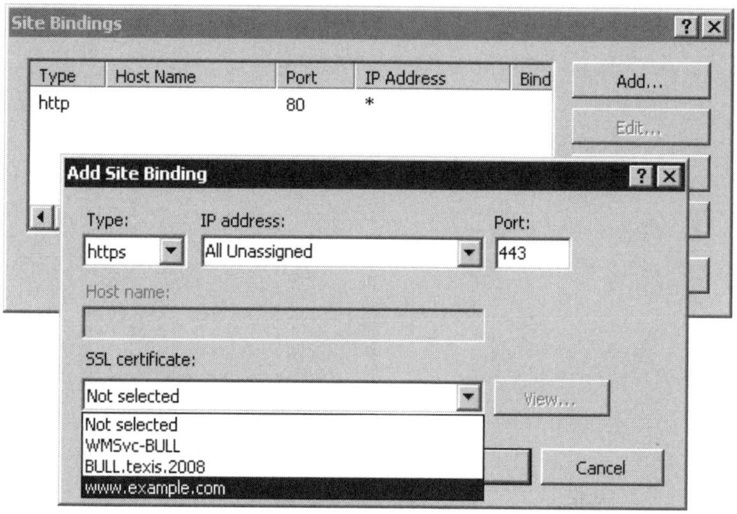

Figure 16-9   The Add Site Binding dialog box showing certificate selection.

```
netsh http add sslcert ipport=0.0.0.0:443 certhash=thumbprint appid={4dc3e181-e14b-4a21-
b022-59fc669b0914}
```

The *ipport* value of 0.0.0.0:443 corresponds to the binding of —*:443:;

thumbprint should contain the hex value of the certificate's thumbprint, which you can see from the certificate's properties in the Certificates snap-in of the Microsoft Management Console.

The HTTP.SYS driver will only access certificates from the local machine certificate store—when you import your certificate, you should do so using a Certificates MMC snap-in created with the Computer Account option specified.

When requesting your certificate—as well as when testing the connection to the HTTPS server—remember that Web browsers are configured to check that the name provided in the URL matches the common name in the certificate. Request a certificate from your certificate provider by using a name that matches the fully qualified domain name to which you will eventually deploy the certificate.

This effectively means that you cannot use one certificate for both the Internet and intranet sides of a Web server, and also means that when you test by using *localhost* or an IP address to connect to your Web server, you will face a certificate error indicating that the certificate's name does not match the name of the site to which you are connecting.

Further Security Considerations for IIS

Authentication and authorization are the major parts of securing a Web site, but they are not by any means the end of your work. You still need to ensure that there is no inadvertent means of breaking out of the security that you have applied.

Application Development

When developing applications for IIS, whether you are developing ISAPI modules or ASP.NET applications, always remember that you are only developing about half of the software. The other half is that portion which runs at the client, and it may be written by someone whose only intent is to cause harm to your server.

Developers should be aware of and follow secure development practices, such as those described in *Writing Secure Code, 2nd Edition*, by Michael Howard and David LeBlanc (Microsoft Press, 2004).

Request Filtering

In IIS 5.0, much use was made of the URLScan tool to ensure that URLs passed to the Web server conformed to a number of rules that kept out bad content. In IIS 7, the same functionality is available through the *requestFiltering* configuration setting. Currently these settings have no graphical user interface, but you can find them under the following section of the applicationHost.config XML file:

```
<configuration>
  <system.webServer>
    <security>
      <requestFiltering>
```

The settings in this configuration path apply to HTTP and HTTPS requests, and can also be configured to apply to WebDAV requests. These settings include:

- *allowDoubleEscaping*, which, when set to the default "false", decodes requested URLs once, and then again. If the first decoding differs from the second encoding, the request is rejected. Set to "true" if you need this feature disabled.

- *allowHighBitCharacters*, which you set to "true" (the default) if your URLs use characters in the ASCII range 127-255 and "false" to deny requests featuring characters in that range. Most of these characters are graphics characters or accented characters from character sets outside of English. In an English-only environment, bona fide requests to your site are not likely to use characters in this range, and denying them may prevent possible abuse of your site. Even in a non-English or mixed environment, you may find characters in URLs that are in the range of 32-127, and disallowing high-bit characters may be a worthwhile setting to make.

- *fileExtensions* is a collection that a server manager may add to, remove from, or clear. The *fileExtensions* collection has two attributes:
    - *allowUnlisted*, which you can set to "true" (the default) to use the file extension list as a set of "dangerous" file extensions that you do not want users to request, or to "false" to deny everything but known good file extensions. It is generally good security practice to do the latter, so we recommend setting this to "false" and building a list of extensions that match files that your server will legitimately offer to users.

❑   *applyToWebDAV*, which you can set to "true" (the default) to make this list apply to WebDAV requests coming in to this server and "false" to make this list apply only to Web requests.

■ Elements added in this collection have two attributes:

❑   *fileExtension*, which is the key attribute for elements in this collection, and is the file extension that you want to allow or deny.

❑   *allowed*, which you set to "true" (default) to allow requests for files with this extension and "false" to deny such requests.

■ *requestLimits* is an element describing various limits on a client's requests. It has the following attributes:

❑   *maxAllowedContentLength* is the maximum content length, in bytes, that can be requested. This prevents the possibility that a request could produce so much output that it overwhelms either your server or a client's computer. Defaults to 30000000.

❑   *maxURL* is the maximum size URL in bytes that will be passed to the application. This prevents buffer overruns in IIS or its hosted applications by a client that sends a maliciously long URL. Defaults to 4096.

❑   *maxQueryString* is the maximum size in bytes of a query string, the portion of a URL beyond the "?" character. Defaults to 2048.

❑   *headerLimits* is a collection whose elements have two attributes: *header* and *sizeLimit.header* is the name of the HTTP request header being limited, and *sizeLimit* is the maximum number of bytes that can be supplied as the value for that header.

■ *verbs* is a collection of HTTP request verbs that are allowed or denied. The attributes for the *verbs* element are:

❑   *allowUnlisted*, which you set to "true" (the default) to allow HTTP command verbs other than those listed as denied and "false" to allow only those HTTP command verbs specifically listed.

❑   *applyToWebDAV*, which you set to "true" (the default) to apply the restriction in verbs to WebDAV.

■ Verbs can be added, removed, or cleared from this collection. Each element in the verb collection has two elements:

❑   *verb*, which is the name of the verb being described. The most used verb is *GET*, which you will almost certainly want to allow. For forms to operate, you will generally also need to allow *POST*. A list of common applications and the required verbs for them is available at *http://support.microsoft.com/kb/823175*.

❑   *allowed* is set to "true" (the default) if you want to allow this verb; "false" if you want to reject it.

- *hiddenSegments* is a collection of elements that will be rejected if they match a path segment of a requested URL. Each element in this collection contains one attribute only, *segment*, whose value should be a string representing the segment to be blocked. For instance, if a segment is *bin*, this will block requests for *http://example.com/bin/scanme.pl*, but will not block requests for *http://example.com/rubbish-bin/image.jpg*. You can also apply the *hiddenSegments* collection to WebDAV by setting its *applytoWebDAV* attribute.

- *denyUrlSequences* is a collection of sequences of characters that will be rejected if a request URL contains them. It is very common to include ".." as a member of this collection, to prevent directory navigation upward. Elements to be added to this collection have one attribute, *sequence*, which is a string of characters that will cause the URL to be rejected if they are found anywhere in the URL.

A rather simple example is the following XML, which prohibits double escaping and high-bit characters; only allows the file extensions .html, .htm, .aspx, and .mspx; sets far shorter maximum length limits on content, URL, and query string; prohibits the server from using verbs other than *GET* and *POST*; and blocks any URL containing "/../" or "...".

```
<configuration>
  ...
    <system.webServer>
      <security>
        <requestFiltering
          allowDoubleEscaping="false"
          allowHighBitCharacters="false">
          <fileExtensions
              allowUnlisted="false"
              applytoWebDAV="false">
              <clear>
              <add fileExtension="html" allowed="true"/>
              <add fileExtension="htm" allowed="true"/>
              <add fileExtension="aspx" allowed="true"/>
              <add fileExtension="mspx" allowed="true"/>
          </fileExtensions>
          <requestLimits
              maxAllowedContentLength="1000000"
              maxURL="2048"
              maxQueryString=256/>
          <verbs
              allowUnlisted="false"
              applyToWebDAV="false"/>
              <clear/>
              <add verb="GET" allowed="true"/>
              <add verb="POST" allowed="true"/>
          </verbs>
          <denyUrlSequences>
              <add sequence="/../"/>
              <add sequence="..."/>
          </denyUrlSequences>
        </requestFiltering>
      </security>
    </system.webServer>
</configuration>
```

ASP.NET Server Farms: Machine Keys

When you operate applications in server farms, you should configure a number of modifications. Because HTTP is a stateless protocol, it is necessary to carry session state information either in the URL or in a cookie. (Recall the earlier discussion of how to configure Forms Authentication to store its authentication state in either a cookie or the query string portion of the URL.)

Much of the information in this state, however, needs to be encrypted and/or validated, which requires keys to be used by the Web server. If an encrypted or validated cookie or URL is set at one server, and then fed back as session state to another server, the request will be incomprehensible or invalid if the two servers do not share the same encryption key. By default, ASP.NET machine keys are automatically generated when the application starts, and each application gets its own machine key (so that in a shared hosting environment, one application cannot accidentally access another application's session state).

In a Server Farm environment, then, the machine key needs to be shared. This is accomplished by using the ASP.NET Machine Keys feature, and clearing the Automatically Generate At Run Time boxes. At one computer in your server farm, you will then click Generate Keys to put a new, random machine key into the encryption and validation boxes. You can then copy and paste these key settings into the other computers in your server farms.

If you are managing a large server farm, or if you will be frequently cycling your Machine Key, you should automate this feature, which you can do through WMI or by directly modifying the Web site's web.config file, as shown in the following example. Note that the validation key should be a randomly generated, 40-128 character hexadecimal string, representing a 20-64 byte random sequence and the decryption key should be a hexadecimal string 16 characters in length when using DES encryption and 48 characters in length when using Triple-DES encryption.

```
<configuration>
  <system.web>
    <machineKey
      decryptionKey="E91D...7DB3,IsolateApps"
      validationKey="215C...528E,IsolateApps"/>
```

If session state seems to be lost intermittently by users, you should check whether the machine keys at all of your servers are set to the same value for the failing application. If one server has a different machine key from another, a user's session state from the first server cannot be read by the second server (and vice versa). All servers must share the same machine key value to be able to use session state from other servers in the farm.

Custom Errors

Custom Error Pages are a double-edged sword. To begin with, they are a valuable debugging tool to cope with errors because they provide more information to the client browser regarding the problems in the application. Some custom error pages may give sensitive information out, and this is where the security consideration lies. Review the custom error pages in use. By default, they are in %SystemDrive%\inetpub\custerr\<Language-tag>\<Error-code>.htm.

For instance, in the U.S. English environment, in a default installation to the C: drive, the error page for a custom 401 error would be in C:\inetpub\custerr\en-US\401.htm. These default custom error pages are relatively minimal, and give only the error code, its short description, and a generic explanation of possible causes of the error. We recommend using the standard custom error pages, which do not divulge any significant information. For secured environments, we recommend replacing the standard error messages with a generic "An error has occurred" page. If code reaches production that generates these errors it can be tested on a computer without custom error messages. The adventurous can modify the pages to use ASP, ASP.NET, or some other server-side coding to only produce error details if the client IP matches a selected set of IPs.

FTP Server

The FTP Server that ships with Windows Server 2008 is essentially the same FTP Server as in IIS 6. The new FTP Server for IIS 7 did not quite make it for release time. However, it features several security features that have been absent for some time, so if you use FTP servers in your company and are deploying IIS7, you should seriously consider downloading the FTP Server add-on (see *http://www.iis.net/articles/view.aspx/IIS7/Managing-IIS7/Using-FTP-Server-in-IIS7/Installing-and-Troubleshooting-FTP7* for details). If you use FTP to publish to your Web site, you will no doubt appreciate the way in which the FTP site can be tied easily to the Web site as just another binding to add.

Other new FTP features include:

■   UTF-8 support, for character sets outside of those expressed in ASCII.

■   FTP over SSL/TLS (generally abbreviated to FTPS–not be confused with SFTP, which is not an FTP-based protocol) for enhanced security including encryption and server authentication.

■   Virtual hosting support, using the nonstandard HOST command or a format of "example.com|user" in the user name. This allows users to specify which Web site they are attempting to log on to, which will lead them to different folders and content being served by the FTP server.

■   Custom authentication, using ASP.NET Membership providers.

■   Support for IPv6, the next-generation Internet Protocol.

■   Configuration in the new, XML-based configuration format, rather than the older metabase. Also added is a new configuration user interface.

Summary

In this chapter we have seen how access to Internet Information Services Web Sites can be secured in normal operation. From anonymous authentication, where the information provided is publicly readable, to use of advanced techniques such as client certificates and federated identity services, many methods to secure authentication are available, each with advantages and disadvantages.

Additional Resources

- Howard, M., and LeBlanc, D. *Writing Secure Code for Windows Vista*. Redmond, WA: Microsoft Press, 2007.

- Howard, M., and LeBlanc, D. *Writing Secure Code, 2nd Ed*. Redmond, WA: Microsoft Press, 2007.

- Microsoft Corporation 2007. "Fine-Tuning and Known Issues When You Use the Urlscan Utility in an Exchange 2003 Environment," at *http://support.microsoft.com/kb/823175*.

- Microsoft Corporation 2007. "How to Implement Forms-Based Authentication in Your ASP.NET Application by Using C#.NET," at *http://support.microsoft.com/kb/301240*.

Index

About the Authors

This book was written a bit differently from previous resource kits. Rather than have one person chiefly responsible for the writing, most of the chapters were written by world-class experts in each area. Servers are complicated things, and Windows Server is no exception. By using top talent in each area we were able to produce a Security Resource Kit that truly contains real expertise. Therefore, no fewer than 12 authors created this book.

Jesper M. Johansson

Jesper M. Johansson served as the lead author, designed the contents, and put together the author team. While the coauthors are the ones who should be credited with the great content they produced, Jesper is the one to blame if significant pieces are missing.

Jesper M. Johansson is a well-known authority on information security in general and on Windows security in particular. He is currently a principal software security architect, designing software infrastructure. Prior to his current role, Jesper worked on security issues at Microsoft, ranging from hacking its networks to designing security software. Jesper has delivered presentations on information security on five continents; spoken at most major security events; written many articles on security; and is a Microsoft Security Most Valuable Professional (MVP). He has a Ph.D. in Management Information Systems and is a Certified Information Systems Security Professional (CISSP) and a certified Information Systems Security Architecture Professional (ISSAP). When he is not working on information security, Jesper teaches scuba diving.

Jimmy Andersson

Jimmy Andersson is a consultant and principal advisor at Q Advice AB in Sweden with a focus on directory services. He is also a trainer and speaker and has developed his own Active Directory (AD) course entitled "AD troubleshooting and Advanced Theory." He has been awarded an MVP title by Microsoft each year for the last nine years. He is usually contracted as project lead for directory services in global enterprise projects.

Susan Bradley

Susan has been using computers since her firm first bought an IBM 8088 computer. As the one in the office known as "into that technology," she's gone from sneaker networks to floppy disks, to Novell, and now to Microsoft networks. As well as being involved in maintaining and planning the technology for her firm, she's used her roles in various industry associations to push for better and more secure software for small businesses. When not blogging at *sbsdiva.com*, she writes on software patching issues for *WindowsSecrets.com*. She also pushes vendors to code more securely from her Web site *threatcode.com*. She likes Windows Vista, and while writing the chapter and materials for this book she never got a UAC prompt. Susan is a Windows Small Business Server MVP.

Darren Canavor

Darren Canavor is an architect with Microsoft. He joined Microsoft in 1999 and has made significant security engineering and testing contributions to the Windows core operating system, including PKI in Windows 2000, Certificate Services in Windows Server 2003, and most recently, User Account Control in Windows Vista and Windows Server 2008. Darren has been a contributing author on a number of white papers and Microsoft Press books about Microsoft Security and PKI, such as *Windows Vista Security Guide and Planning* and "Implementing Cross-Certification and Qualified Subordination Using Windows Server 2003."

Kurt Dillard

Based in Buenos Aires, the alluring capital of Argentina, Kurt writes books, articles, and other documents that suggest ways to overcome the challenges of protecting digital information and the computers that store it. He has collaborated on many of the solutions published by Microsoft, such as the "Windows Server 2003 Security Guide," "Security Risk Management Guide," and "Threats and Countermeasures: Security Settings in Windows Server 2003 and Windows XP." Kurt has presented at numerous conferences including RSA, TechEd, and Microsoft Federal Security Summits. His current industry certifications include CISSP, ISSAP, CISM, and MCSE + Security.

Eric Fitzgerald

Eric (CISSP, MCSE) works in Microsoft's Forefront Security products division, specializing in analysis of data from security sensors. He spent six years in the Windows Core OS Security team working on audit and authorization technologies in Windows, and several years providing support for Microsoft's enterprise customers for security, networking, and directory service problems. Outside of information security Eric enjoys competitive sailboat racing.

Roger Grimes

Roger A. Grimes (CPA, CISSP, CISA, MCSE: Security) is a 22-year security veteran specializing in host security, PKI, identity management, and preventing hackers and malware from being successful. Roger works for Microsoft's ACE Team as a Senior Security consultant. He is the security columnist for *InfoWorld* magazine and has authored or contributed to 8 books on computer security and written more than 200 national magazine articles. Roger runs 8 honeypots capturing malicious hacker activity and travels the world speaking at conferences and helping customers be as secure as possible.

Byron Hynes

Byron Hynes is an Enterprise Technology Strategist at Microsoft. Since joining Microsoft in 2005 he has focused on security technologies including BitLocker Drive Encryption, User Account Control, and many others. Byron works directly with customers and has also contributed content for help files, Web sites, magazine articles, books, and presentations. He enjoys leaving the safety of the office for conferences, events and meeting customers as often as the boss will let him. Byron was born in Canada and spent most of his time in the arctic winter of the far North. He still can't believe he ended up living in the suburbia of Redmond, Washington. Byron is married with two young and very active boys.

Alun Jones

Alun Jones (MVP, MCP) is president of Texas Imperial Software, which develops secure networking software and provides security engineering consulting services. Texas Imperial Software's flagship product is WFTPD Pro, a secure FTP server for Windows, written entirely by Alun.

Alun entered the security field when more and more of WFTPD's support needs indicated that few companies could meet their needs for security on the Internet without help. His current day job is security architect for an online travel booking company. Alun attended university at Corpus Christi College, Cambridge, and Bath University, and now lives near Seattle, Washington, with his wife, Debbie, and son, Colin. Alun thanks his wife and son for their suffering his absence for such a long time while he worked on this book. He is a Microsoft Security MVP.

Brian Komar

Brian Komar is the president of IdentIT Inc., a consulting firm specializing in Public Key Infrastructure design and implementation and identity integration solutions. Brian partners with Microsoft on several ventures, writing PKI and ILM 2007 training materials and white papers, and working as a principal consultant for the enterprise PKI and ILM 2007 deployment engagements. Brian is a frequent speaker at IT industry conferences such as Microsoft TechEd, Microsoft IT Forum, and Windows IT Pro Magazine Connections. Brian is a Microsoft Security MVP.

Brian Lich

Brian Lich is a core security technical writer in the Windows Server User Assistance group writing on Active Directory Rights Management Services. Before joining Microsoft, he worked in the Information Technology industry for 11 years as a system administrator and security analyst. Brian has a degree in Electrical Engineering Technology from Purdue University.

Darren Mar-Elia

Darren Mar-Elia, is founder and CTO of SDM Software and has more than 20 years experience in information technology and software development. He was Sr. Director of Product Engineering at DesktopStandard (acquired by Microsoft) and prior to that, served as CTO for Windows management solutions at Quest Software. He was also a director of distributed systems at Charles Schwab & Co. and directed that company's use of Windows technologies. Darren has written or contributed to 12 books on Windows management topics and is a Microsoft MVP for Group Policy. He created the popular *gpoguy.com* Web site for information and utilities related to Group Policy.

System Requirements

To use this book's companion CD-ROM, you need a computer equipped with the following minimum configuration:

- Microsoft Windows Server 2008, Windows Vista, Windows Server 2003, or Windows XP

- 1 GHz 32-bit (x86) or 64-bit (x64) processor (depending on the minimum requirements of the operating system)

- 1 GB of system memory (depending on the minimum requirements of the operating system)

- A hard disk partition with at least 1 GB of available space

- Appropriate video output device

- Keyboard

- Mouse or other pointing device

- Optical drive capable of reading CD-ROMs

In addition, many of the tools have separate system requirements and may require one or more of the following:

- Microsoft Windows Server 2008 or Windows Vista

- Windows PowerShell 1.x

- A network connection

Please refer to the documentation for each tool to determine its system requirements.

What do you think of this book?

We want to hear from you!

Do you have a few minutes to participate in a brief online survey?

Microsoft is interested in hearing your feedback so we can continually improve our books and learning resources for you.

To participate in our survey, please visit:

www.microsoft.com/learning/booksurvey/

...and enter this book's ISBN-10 or ISBN-13 number (located above barcode on back cover*). As a thank-you to survey participants in the United States and Canada, each month we'll randomly select five respondents to win one of five $100 gift certificates from a leading online merchant. At the conclusion of the survey, you can enter the drawing by providing your e-mail address, which will be used for prize notification only.

Thanks in advance for your input. Your opinion counts!

* Where to find the ISBN on back cover

ISBN-13: 000-0-0000-0000-0
ISBN-10: 0-0000-0000-0

Example only. Each book has unique ISBN.